CRIC

WHO S WHO 2009

Foreword by

ANDREW STRAUSS

Edited by

MICHAEL HEATLEY

Statistics by

RICHARD LOCKWOOD

Photographs by

GETTY IMAGES

This edition first published in the UK in 2009 by Green Umbrella Publishing

www.gupublishing.co.uk

Publishers: Jules Gammond and Vanessa Gardner

ISBN: 978-1-906635-664

Editor (for Green Umbrella Publishing): Kirsty Ennever
Design: Alan Kinsman
Assistant editor: Peter Gamble
Picture research: Ellie Charleston
Quiz compiled by Chris Mason
Cover design by Kevin Gardner
Printed and bound in the UK by
J F Print Ltd., Sparkford, Somerset
Produced by Unique Productions

ACKNOWLEDGEMENTS

Cover photographs by Getty Images, 101 Bayham Street, London, NW1 0AG

The publishers would also like to thank the county clubs, the players
and their families for their assistance in helping to assemble
the information and photographs in this book.

Extra information has also been gathered from
cricinfo.com and cricketarchive.com

Thanks also to the following for providing additional photographs:
Neville Chadwick Photography, Kent Messenger Group, Pete Norton
Oxford Mail, Archant, Peter Power, Derbyshire CCC, Durham CCC, Essex CCC,
Hampshire CCC, Kent CCC, Lancashire CCC, Leicestershire CCC, Middlesex CCC,
Northamptonshire CCC, Somerset CCC, Surrey CCC, SWpix, Worcestershire CCC,
www.philbrittphotography.co.uk, Yorkshire CCC

CONTENTS

Foreword
by Andrew Strauss

Welcome to the 30th anniversary edition of *The Cricketers' Who's Who*. I had the privilege of writing the foreword for the 2006 edition and I could not have imagined then, as I looked forward to a new season in the flush of the 2005 Ashes victory, that the landscape of cricket would have altered so radically in the short time since.

In 2006 I said 'Twenty20 is the most exciting new competition since Kerry Packer got involved in cricket…' which seems like such an understatement now. We have an ICC Twenty20 World Championship in England this summer, the second season of the $2bn Indian Premier League starts in April and our domestic T20 winners will head for the Champions League to compete for over $1m in prize money and all of that without mentioning the Stanford T20 for 20 or the quadrangular T20 later this year… so much so fast is unprecedented in sport and, whilst we welcome it, we must be careful to deal with its challenges responsibly and professionally.

Cricket is in exciting times. I am writing this as I leave with England for the West Indies, proud to be the captain and optimistic of exciting and victorious cricket. On our return, we have an amazing domestic season to look forward to – the West Indians return and the Australians arrive – there is nothing like an Ashes summer. At the same time, the County Championship, already in the best shape it has been in for decades, will be played for three times the prize money we played for just last year. This is part of the ECB's strategy to encourage competitiveness and interest in the Championship because it is the most important domestic trophy and the best producer of England Test cricketers.

The challenges cricket faces in 2009 should not be underestimated. T20 threatens to dominate other formats of the game and the administrators and marketers need to turn into reality the oft-repeated mantra about the primacy of Test cricket. As our Test match venues overflow this coming summer, we should not lose sight of the fact that it is not so in most other Test nations and I look forward to the ICC finally providing the structure for a meaningful Test championship for international cricket. Then every Test match will take on added significance and we can all find out, every four or five years, who the best Test team in the world really is – I aim to do my utmost to ensure that it is England.

Enjoy the summer and enjoy searching through this invaluable book for those titbits of information about me and my colleagues that you just can't get anywhere else.

Andrew Strauss
England and Middlesex
February 2009

International Fixtures 2009

ENGLAND v WEST INDIES

Test Matches:

May 6-10	1st Test	Lord's
May 14-18	2nd Test	Chester-le-Street

NatWest Series one-day internationals:

May 21	Headingley
May 24	Bristol
May 26	Edgbaston

ENGLAND v AUSTRALIA

Test Matches:

July 8-12	1st npower Test	Cardiff
July 16-20	2nd npower Test	Lord's
July 30 - Aug 3	3rd npower Test	Edgbaston
August 7-11	4th npower Test	Headingley
August 20 - 24	5th npower Test	The Oval

Twenty20 Internationals:

August 30	Old Trafford
September 1	Old Trafford [f]

NatWest Series one-day internationals:

September 4	The Oval [f]
September 6	Lord's
September 9	Southampton [f]
September 12	Lord's
September 15	Trent Bridge [f]
September 17	Trent Bridge [f]
September 20	Chester-le-Street

[f] = Floodlighting involved

Twenty20 Vision

When the International Cavaliers started playing one-day cricket in the early Sixties, few would have predicted the rise of the one-day game which was to come. Yet the popularity of limited overs competitions was soon to lead to the founding of the Gillette Cup in 1963 followed, in 1969, by the 40-over John Player League - better, and more simply, known at the time as the Sunday League. One-day competitions in general soon took hold and, while there were various experiments with the number of overs to be bowled (it was 65 per side in the first season of the Gillette Cup) nobody considered a reduction to 20 overs a side for a very long time.

The one-day game was largely promoted in order to boost the flagging attendances at county grounds, and it certainly worked. Of course, there were those who predicted the end of cricket, not to say civilisation, as we know it. One-day cricket most certainly did change the face of the game - even though it had been played by village teams for centuries and continued to be played by most amateur cricketers up and down the country, so there was really nothing new about it.

As its popularity grew, one-day cricket became recognised internationally as an intriguing, exciting and, of course, lucrative form of the game. It did much to stimulate a revival of interest in cricket in general and, amongst other things, it helped to create a new and more aggressive style of batting. Then along came Twenty20.

Many considered that the 40-over version of one-day cricket was too short, so when Stuart Robinson, marketing manager of the ECB, proposed the launch of a series of matches of half that length, many felt that such games would prove farcical. There would however clearly be financial incentives and marketing opportunities and so, after no little discussion, the first-class counties voted 11-7 in favour of a Twenty20 tournament.

The tournament, which came into being in 2003 and was known as the Twenty20 Cup, was a success more or less from the outset, and Twenty20 cricket began to attract increasing numbers of young spectators. Traditionalists were unhappy with the associated razzmatazz, but the income generated was welcomed and Twenty20 soon went global. In February 2005 Australia beat New Zealand in the first full international Twenty20 match which was not taken too seriously, but again the potential was to be soon realized. So much so that in 2007 the ICC launched the first World Twenty-20 Competition in South Africa, with India beating Pakistan in the final.

Since then the situation has become somewhat less clear-cut. In 2008, the Board of Control for Indian Cricket created the Indian Premier League for franchised teams made up of Indian and foreign players. Auctions were held, with the eight team owners bidding for star performers, and the first season's competition commenced on 18 April

2008, running until 1 June. The winners were Rajasthan Royals who, interestingly, were the least expensive team at $67m. The most expensive, Mumbai Indians ($111.9m) finished fifth. Broadcasting rights brought in millions of dollars, but most of the team owners made a loss.

A few months later the Stanford Super Series took place in Antigua – still being talked about for all the wrong reasons. Hopefully Twenty20 cricket will eventually be recognised for what it is: a fun game, very different from other forms of cricket, which can bring additional revenue to the game.

The ICC tournament of 2007 was considered by many to be a great success. It is to be repeated in England during June of this year, and the schedule of fixtures is below.

2009 WORLD TWENTY20 COMPETITION

GROUP STAGE

June 5	Eng v Ned (B)	Lord's		
June 6	Ind v Ban (A)	Trent Bdge	Aus v WI (C)	The Oval
	NZ v Sco (D)	The Oval		
June 7	Eng v Pak (B)	The Oval	SA v Sco (D)	The Oval
June 8	Ire v Ban (A)	Trent Bdge	Aus v SL (C)	Trent Bdge
June 9	Pak v Ned (B)	Lord's	NZ v SA (D)	Lord's
June 10	Ind v Ire (A)	Trent Bdge	SL v WI (C)	Trent Bdge

SUPER EIGHTS

June 11	B2 v D2	Trent Bdge	D1 v A2	Trent Bdge
June 12	A1 v C1	Lord's	B1 v C2	Lord's
June 13	C1 v D2	The Oval	D1 v B1	The Oval
June 14	A1 v B2	Lord's	A2 v C2	Lord's
June 15	B2 v C1	The Oval	B1 v A2	The Oval
June 16	D2 v A1	Trent Bdge [f]	D1 v C2	Trent Bdge

SEMI-FINALS

June 18	Semi-final 1	Trent Bridge
June 19	Semi-final 2	The Oval

FINAL

June 21	Final	Lord's

Editor's Notes

The cricketers listed in this volume include all those who played 1st XI cricket for a first-class county at least once last season, in first-class or one-day (including Twenty20) cricket, and all those registered (at the time of going to press at the beginning of February) to play for the 18 first-class counties in 2009. The umpires' section contains the officials making up the first-class list for 2009, plus Mark Benson, who is on the ICC Elite Panel.

All players' statistics are complete to the end of the last English season (the Stop Press section for individual players notes subsequent highlights) and cover first-class, List A and Twenty20 fixtures played that season. Such matches that took place elsewhere in the cricket-playing world during the period do not feature in the players' season statistics but are recorded in their career tables. Test, ODI and Twenty20 International tallies for umpires are up to and including 30 January 2009.

Within the season statistics tables, List A refers to the English domestic one-day competitions and limited-over games such as those between the counties and sides touring England. In addition, just as a player's first-class figures include Test matches, which are also extracted and listed separately, so his List A figures include One-Day Internationals, which are pulled out and appear separately in the same way. Furthermore, in the career tables the List A category contains figures of all the official 'full-length' one-day games in which a player has taken part worldwide. The categories 20/20 Int (Twenty20 Internationals) and 20/20 (all Twenty20 matches) operate in similar fashion to the corresponding first-class and one-day categories.

Numbers of hundreds given in the statistics tables include all multiples (200s, 300s etc.). Tallies of multiple hundreds for players and also of one-day hundreds and one-day five-wicket innings for umpires who are former players are shown in the body of the entry, since these cannot be found in the statistics tables. Statistics for 2008 are not given for players whose appearances that season were only for teams other than a county – e.g. universities (excluding international cricketers on tours to England). These appearances are, however, reflected in their career statistics and reference is made in the Extras section to the team for which they played.

Figures about 1000 runs, 50 wickets and 50 dismissals in a season refer to matches in England only. The figures for batting and bowling averages refer to the full first-class English list for 2008, followed in brackets by the 2007 figures. Inclusion in the batting averages depends on a minimum of six completed innings and an average of at least 10.00; a bowler has to have taken at least ten wickets for inclusion in the averages.

In the Overseas tours section, the layout 'England to Pakistan 2005-06 (one-day series)', for example, indicates that a player was selected for only the one-day portion of the tour; the layout 'England to Zimbabwe (one-day series) 2004-05', on the other hand, indicates that the tour consisted of a one-day series only.

The following abbreviations apply in the text: ODI means One-Day International; Twenty20 Int means Twenty20 International; * means not out. In statistics tables FC means all first-class matches, including figures for Test matches; List A – 'full-length' one-day matches classified as such by the ICC (e.g. Friends Provident Trophy, NatWest Pro40 and limited-overs matches against touring sides), including figures for One-Day Internationals; 20/20 Int – Twenty20 Internationals; 20/20 – all 'official' Twenty20 matches, including figures for Twenty20 Internationals and Twenty20 matches between counties and touring sides. Some further abbreviations appear in the Best batting and Best bowling sections. These identify particular grounds in cities and towns that boast more than one. A list of the abbreviations featured and the grounds to which they refer is set out overleaf.

Please note that Worcestershire ceased awarding caps in 2001 and now present 'colours' to each player who appears for the county in the Championship; that beginning in 2004 Gloucestershire have awarded caps to players on making their first first-class appearance for the county; that Durham ceased awarding caps after the 2005 season, replacing the cap system with grades of player seniority.

A book of this complexity and detail has to be prepared some months in advance of the new cricket season, and occasionally there are recent changes in a player's circumstances or the structure of the game which cannot be included in time. Many examples of facts, statistics and even opinions which can quickly become outdated in the period between the compilation of the book and its publication, months later, will spring to the reader's mind, and I ask him or her to make the necessary commonsense allowance and adjustments.

Michael Heatley, February 2009

GROUND ABBREVIATIONS

Abu Dhabi (SZ) – Sheikh Zayed Stadium
Brisbane (AB) – Allan Border Field
Bulawayo (AC) – Bulawayo Athletic Club
Chittagong (B) – Bir Shrestha Shahid Ruhul Amin Stadium (Chittagong Divisional Stadium)
Christchurch (VG) – Village Green
Colombo (Bur) – Burgher Recreation Club Ground
Colombo (CCC) – Colts Cricket Club Ground
Colombo (PP) – Police Park Ground
Colombo (PSS) – P Saravanamuttu Stadium
Colombo (RPS) – R Premadasa Stadium
Colombo (SSC) – Sinhalese Sports Club Ground
Delhi (KS) – Karnail Singh Stadium
Harare (A) – Alexandra Sports Club
Harare (T) – Takashinga Sports Club
Johannesburg (WM) – Walter Milton Oval, University of Witwatersrand
Karachi (UBL) – United Bank Limited Sports Complex
Lahore (C) – Lahore City Cricket Association Ground
Melbourne (SK) – St Kilda Cricket Club Ground (Junction Oval)
Paarl (PCC) – Paarl Cricket Club Ground
Portsmouth (BP) – Benjamin's Park
Pretoria (LCD) – LC de Villiers Oval
Pretoria (SCC) – Sinovich Park
Rajkot (MS) – Madhavrao Scindia Cricket Ground
Rawalpindi (KRL) – Khan Research Laboratory Ground
Stellenbosch (US) – Stellenbosch University Ground
Toronto (MSE) – Maple Leaf South-East Ground, King City

THE PLAYERS

KOLPAK

If a cricketer is a national of a country that has an Association Agreement with the EU (such as South Africa or Zimbabwe) and also has a valid UK work permit, he enjoys the same right to work within the EU as an EU citizen and may be eligible to play county cricket as a domestic (that is, non-overseas) player. Cricketers playing in England under this system are commonly referred to as Kolpak players, after the Kolpak ruling, a judgement in the European Court of Justice that found in favour of Maros Kolpak, a Slovakian handball goalkeeper who challenged his status as a non-EU player in Germany.

ASHES QUIZ

Throughout the book there are 100 quiz questions relating to Test encounters over the years between England and Australia. Answers can be found on page 755.

ABDUL RAZZAQ Surrey

Name: Abdul Razzaq
Role: Right-hand bat, right-arm fast-medium bowler
Born: 2 December 1979, Lahore, Pakistan
Height: 5ft 11in
County debut: 2002 (Middlesex), 2007 (Worcestershire), 2008 (Surrey)
County cap: 2002 (Middlesex), 2007 (Worcestershire colours)
Test debut: 1999-2000
ODI debut: 1996-97
Twenty20 Int debut: 2006
1st-Class 200s: 1
Education: Furqan Model Secondary School, Lahore
Overseas tours: Pakistan U19 to West Indies 1996-97, to South Africa 1996-97, to Australia 1997-98, to South Africa (U19 World Cup) 1997-98; Pakistan A to England 1997, to New Zealand 1998-99; Pakistan to Sri Lanka 1996-97, to UK, Ireland and Netherlands (World Cup) 1999, to Australia 1999-2000, to West Indies 1999-2000, to Sri Lanka 2000, to Kenya (ICC Knockout Trophy) 2000-01, to England 2001, to Bangladesh 2001-02, to Sharjah (v West Indies) 2001-02, to Sri Lanka (ICC Champions Trophy) 2002-03, to Sri Lanka and Sharjah (v Australia) 2002-03, to South Africa 2002-03, to Africa (World Cup) 2002-03, to New Zealand 2003-04, to England (ICC Champions Trophy) 2004, to Australia 2004-05, to India 2004-05, to West Indies 2004-05, to Sri Lanka 2005-06, to Scotland and England 2006, to India (ICC Champions Trophy) 2006-07, plus other one-day series and tournaments in India, South Africa, Toronto, Sharjah, Bangladesh, Singapore, New Zealand, Morocco, Kenya, Sri Lanka, England, Netherlands and Abu Dhabi; Asian Cricket Council XI to Australia (Tsunami Relief Fund) 2004-05, to South Africa (Afro-Asia Cup) 2005-06
Overseas teams played for: Several in Pakistan, including Lahore City 1996-97 – 1998-99, Zarai Taraqiati Bank 2003-04 – 2007-08; Hyderabad Heroes (ICL) 2007-08 –
Extras: Formerly known as Abdur Razzaq. Returned figures of 2-68/7-51 on first-class debut for Lahore City v Karachi Whites in the final of the Quaid-e-Azam Trophy at Thatta 1996-97. Took hat-trick (Kaluwitharana, Herath, Pushpakumara) in the second Test v Sri Lanka at Galle 2000, becoming only the second Pakistan bowler, after Wasim Akram (twice), to take a hat-trick in Tests. FICA Young Player of the Year 2001. His series and match awards include Man of the [Test and ODI] Series v West Indies 2001-02, Man of the [ODI] Series v Sri Lanka 2005-06; Man of the Match v Sri

Lanka at Jaipur in the ICC Champions Trophy 2006-07 (4-50/24-ball 38*). Was an overseas player with Middlesex in 2002 and 2003; was a temporary overseas player with Worcestershire during the 2007 season as a replacement for Phil Jaques and Doug Bollinger. He joined Surrey in June 2008 on a short-term contract
Best batting: 203* Middlesex v Glamorgan, Cardiff 2002
Best bowling: 7-51 Lahore City v Karachi Whites, Thatta 1996-97

2008 Season

	M	Inn	NO	Runs	HS	Avg	100	50	Ct	St	Balls	Runs	Wkts	Avg	BB	5I	10M
Test																	
FC	1	2	0	4	4	2.00	-	-	-	-	145	77	3	25.66	3-46	-	-
ODI																	
List A																	
20/20 Int																	
20/20	9	9	1	185	65	23.12	-	1	-	-	192	232	15	15.46	4-17	-	

Career Performances

	M	Inn	NO	Runs	HS	Avg	100	50	Ct	St	Balls	Runs	Wkts	Avg	BB	5I	10M
Test	46	77	9	1946	134	28.61	3	7	15	-	7008	3694	100	36.94	5-35	1	-
FC	111	174	27	4965	203 *	33.77	8	25	30	-	17656	10316	316	32.64	7-51	10	2
ODI	231	198	49	4465	112	29.96	2	22	31	-	9797	7658	246	31.13	6-35	3	
List A	285	244	58	5626	112	30.24	2	30	42	-	12437	9929	330	30.08	6-35	3	
20/20 Int	2	2	1	27	17 *	27.00	-	-	-	-	36	58	3	19.33	3-30	-	
20/20	21	20	3	512	65	30.11	-	3	3	-	450	561	30	18.70	4-17	-	

ACKERMAN, H. D. — Leicestershire

Name: Hylton Deon (HD) Ackerman
Role: Right-hand bat, right-arm medium bowler
Born: 14 February 1973, Cape Town, South Africa
Height: 5ft 11in **Weight:** 13st
County debut: 2005
County cap: 2005
Test debut: 1997-98
1000 runs in a season: 2
1st-Class 200s: 2
1st-Class 300s: 1
Place in batting averages: 13th av. 56.60 (2007 159th av 27.80)
Parents: Hylton and Dawn
Wife and date of marriage: Kerryn, 22 March 2008
Family links with cricket: Father (H. M. Ackerman) played first-class cricket in

South Africa and also for Northamptonshire
Education: Rondebosch Boys' High School, Capre Town, South Africa
Career outside cricket: Family business
Off-season: In South Africa, playing for the Dolphins
Overseas tours: South Africa U24 to Sri Lanka 1995; Western Province to Australia 1995-96, to Zimbabwe 1996-97; South Africa A to England 1996, to Sri Lanka 1998, to Zimbabwe 2004; South Africa to Zimbabwe 2001-02; Leicestershire to Pakistan and India 2005
Overseas teams played for: Western Province 1993-94 – 2002-03; Gauteng 2003-04; Lions 2004-05; Cape Cobras 2005-06; Warriors 2006-07; Dolphins 2008-09 
Career highlights to date: 'Being picked for South Africa in 1998'
Cricket moments to forget: 'Being dropped from South African team'
Cricket superstitions: None
Cricketers particularly admired: Steve Waugh
Young players to look out for: JP Duminy
Other sports followed: Football (Manchester United), golf (Ernie Els)
Favourite band: Snow Patrol
Relaxations: 'Golf, movies, reading, spending time with friends and family'
Extras: Scored maiden first-class double century (202*) v Northerns at Centurion in the SuperSport Series 1997-98, in the process breaking Barry Richards's record for the most first-class runs by a South African in a domestic season (ended 1997-98 with 1373 at 50.85). Scored century (145) for South Africa A v Sri Lanka A at Matara 1998, winning Man of the Match award. Man of the SuperSport Series 2000-01. His other domestic awards include Man of the Match v Griqualand West at Kimberley (81) and v KwaZulu-Natal at Durban (86*), both in the Standard Bank Cup 2003-04. Captain of Leicestershire 2005. Scored 309* v Glamorgan at Cardiff 2006, setting a new record for the highest individual first-class score by a Leicestershire player; also scored 62 in second innings to set a new record individual match aggregate for the county (371). Leicestershire Cricketer of the Year 2006. In 2008, he scored runs at will in all competitions scoring close to 2000 runs which included 8 centuries and 7 fifties. Is not considered an overseas player
Opinions on cricket: 'If a player has an opinion he is considered controversial, so no, no opinions.'
Best batting: 309* Leicestershire v Glamorgan, Cardiff 2006

2008 Season

	M	Inn	NO	Runs	HS	Avg	100	50	Ct	St	Balls	Runs	Wkts	Avg	BB	5I	10M
Test																	
FC	16	26	3	1302	199	56.60	6	3	12	-	0	0	0		-	-	-
ODI																	
List A	11	11	0	424	139	38.54	2	1	4	-	0	0	0		-	-	
20/20 Int																	
20/20	8	8	2	239	63	39.83	-	3	2	-	0	0	0		-	-	

Career Performances

	M	Inn	NO	Runs	HS	Avg	100	50	Ct	St	Balls	Runs	Wkts	Avg	BB	5I	10M
Test	4	8	0	161	57	20.12	-	1	1	-	0	0	0		-	-	-
FC	204	342	32	13563	309 *	43.75	38	69	170	-	102	57	0		-	-	-
ODI																	
List A	210	203	23	5916	139	32.86	3	40	78	-	48	52	0		-	-	
20/20 Int																	
20/20	43	43	6	1463	87	39.54	-	14	12	-	0	0	0		-	-	

ADAMS, A. R. — Nottinghamshire

Name: André Ryan Adams
Role: Right-hand bat, right-arm fast-medium bowler
Born: 17 July 1975, Auckland, New Zealand
Height: 5ft 11in **Weight:** 14st 7lbs
Nickname: Dre, Doctor
County debut: 2004 (Essex), 2007 (Nottinghamshire)
County cap: 2004 (Essex)
Test debut: 2001-02
ODI debut: 2000-01
Twenty20 Int debut: 2004-05
Place in batting averages: 240th av. 13.30
Place in bowling averages: 7th av. 19.16 (2007 101st av 35.78)
Parents: Felise du Chateau and Keith Adams
Wife and date of marriage: Ardene, 5 April 2003
Children: Danté, 24 February 2004, and Balian
Family links with cricket: 'Parents West Indian!'
Education: West Lake Boys, Auckland

Off-season: Coaching
Overseas tours: New Zealand to Sharjah (ARY Gold Cup) 2000-01, to Australia 2001-02 (VB Series), to Sharjah (Sharjah Cup) 2001-02, to Pakistan 2002, to Africa (World Cup) 2002-03, to Sri Lanka 2003 (Bank Alfalah Cup), to England 2004 (NatWest Series), to Bangladesh 2004-05 (one-day series), to Zimbabwe 2005-06 (Videocon Tri-Series), to South Africa (one-day series) 2005-06
Overseas teams played for: Takapuna, Auckland; Auckland 1997 – 2008; Kolkata Tigers/Royal Bengal Tigers (ICL) 2007-08 –
Career highlights to date: 'Test victory against England in final game (Auckland) in 2002, my Test debut'
Cricket moments to forget: 'Losing to India in 2003 World Cup'
Cricket superstitions: None
Cricketers particularly admired: Viv Richards, Richard Hadlee, Garfield Sobers
Young players to look out for: Samit Patel, Ravinder Bopara
Other sports followed: Rugby (Auckland Blues, All Blacks)
Favourite band: Dr Comfort and the Lurid Revelations
Relaxations: Xbox 360
Extras: Member of New Zealand team to 1998 Indoor Cricket World Cup. Leading wicket-taker in 1999-2000 Shell Cup one-day competition (28; av. 13.50). His ODI match awards include Man of the Match v India at Queenstown 2002-03 (5-22) and v West Indies at Port Elizabeth in the 2002-03 World Cup (35*/4-44). An overseas player with Essex July to September 2004 and in 2005 and 2006. Scored maiden first-class century (91-ball 124) v Leicestershire at Leicester 2004 in his first Championship innings and batting at No. 9. Took Championship hat-trick (Burns, Jayasuriya, Hildreth) v Somerset at Taunton 2005. Was a temporary overseas player with Nottinghamshire during the 2007 season as a replacement for David Hussey; came back in 2008. . Signed a two-year contract with the ICL in 2008
Opinions on cricket: 'Let it be played'
Best batting: 124 Essex v Leicestershire, Leicester 2004
Best bowling: 6-25 Auckland v Wellington, Auckland 2004-05

2008 Season

	M	Inn	NO	Runs	HS	Avg	100	50	Ct	St	Balls	Runs	Wkts	Avg	BB	5I	10M
Test																	
FC	8	11	1	133	58	13.30	-	1	4	-	1384	594	31	19.16	4-39	-	-
ODI																	
List A	8	6	3	57	30	19.00	-	-	2	-	324	264	7	37.71	2-25	-	
20/20 Int																	
20/20	9	7	0	47	17	6.71	-	-	5	-	198	257	9	28.55	2-23	-	

Career Performances

	M	Inn	NO	Runs	HS	Avg	100	50	Ct	St	Balls	Runs	Wkts	Avg	BB	5I	10M
Test	1	2	0	18	11	9.00	-	-	1	-	190	105	6	17.50	3-44	-	-
FC	90	120	10	2618	124	23.80	3	11	55	-	17603	8358	352	23.74	6-25	13	2
ODI	42	34	10	419	45	17.45	-	-	8	-	1885	1643	53	31.00	5-22	1	
List A	136	100	26	1343	90 *	18.14	-	1	36	-	6329	4983	173	28.80	5-7	3	
20/20 Int	4	2	1	13	7	13.00	-	-	1	-	77	105	3	35.00	2-20	-	
20/20	31	24	6	257	54 *	14.27	-	1	10	-	648	851	38	22.39	3-35	-	

ADAMS, C. J. — Sussex

Name: Christopher (Chris) John Adams
Role: Right-hand bat, right-arm medium bowler, slip fielder
Born: 6 May 1970, Whitwell, Derbyshire
Height: 6ft **Weight:** 13st 7lbs
Nickname: Grizzly, Grizwold
County debut: 1988 (Derbyshire), 1998 (Sussex)
County cap: 1992 (Derbyshire), 1998 (Sussex)
Benefit: 2003 (Sussex)
Test debut: 1999-2000
ODI debut: 1998
1000 runs in a season: 9
1st-Class 200s: 4
Place in batting averages: 170th av 23.70 (2007 44th av. 46.81)
Parents: John and Eluned (Lyn)
Wife and date of marriage: Samantha Claire, 26 September 1992
Children: Georgia Louise, 4 October 1993; Sophie Victoria, 13 October 1998
Family links with cricket: Brother David played 2nd XI cricket for Derbyshire and Gloucestershire. Father played for Yorkshire Schools and uncle played for Essex 2nd XI
Education: Chesterfield Boys Grammar School; Repton School
Qualifications: 6 O-levels, NCA coaching awards, Executive Development Certificate in Coaching and Management Skills
Overseas tours: Repton School to Barbados 1987; England NCA North to Northern Ireland 1987; England XI to New Zealand (Cricket Max) 1997; England to South Africa and Zimbabwe 1999-2000; Sussex to Grenada 2001, 2002; Blade to Barbados 2001
Overseas teams played for: Takapuna, New Zealand 1987-88; Te Puke, New Zealand 1989-90; Primrose, Cape Town, South Africa 1991-92; Canberra Comets, Australia 1998-99; University of NSW, Australia 2000-01

Cricket moments to forget: 'The death of Umer Rashid in Grenada [2002]'
Cricketers particularly admired: Ian Botham
Other sports played: Golf, football, 'dabbled a bit with ice hockey'
Other sports followed: Football ('Arsenal!')
Relaxations: 'Family time'
Extras: Represented English Schools U15 and U19, MCC Schools U19 and, in 1989, England YC. Took two catches as 12th man for England v India at Old Trafford in 1990. Set Derbyshire record for the highest score in the Sunday League (141*) v Kent at Chesterfield 1992. Sussex Player of the Year 1998 and 1999. Set individual one-day record score for Sussex of 163 (off 107 balls) v Middlesex in the National League at Arundel 1999. Sussex 1st XI Fielder of the Season 2000. BBC South Cricketer of the Year 2001. One of *Wisden*'s Five Cricketers of the Year 2004. Scored 200 against Northamptonshire at Hove 2004, in the process becoming the third batsman (after Mark Ramprakash and Carl Hooper) to score a century against all 18 counties. Captain of Sussex since 1998, he stood down in September 2008, and three months later took the post of cricket manager at Surrey. During his captaincy, Sussex won eight trophies.
Best batting: 239 Derbyshire v Hampshire, Southampton 1996
Best bowling: 4-28 Sussex v Durham, Riverside 2001

2008 Season

	M	Inn	NO	Runs	HS	Avg	100	50	Ct	St	Balls	Runs	Wkts	Avg	BB	5I	10M
Test																	
FC	15	23	3	474	61	23.70	-	2	13	-	12	13	0		-	-	-
ODI																	
List A	12	11	2	305	109*	33.88	1	-	-	-	0	0	0		-	-	
20/20 Int																	
20/20	8	8	2	142	57	23.66	-	1	1	-	0	0	0		-	-	

Career Performances

	M	Inn	NO	Runs	HS	Avg	100	50	Ct	St	Balls	Runs	Wkts	Avg	BB	5I	10M
Test	5	8	0	104	31	13.00	-	-	6	-	120	59	1	59.00	1-42	-	-
FC	336	546	41	19535	239	38.68	48	93	404	-	3288	1935	41	47.19	4-28	-	-
ODI	5	4	0	71	42	17.75	-	-	3	-	0	0	0		-	-	
List A	369	347	58	11481	163	39.72	21	69	165	-	1391	1217	32	38.03	5-16	1	
20/20 Int																	
20/20	42	38	8	880	63	29.33	-	3	10	-	0	0	0		-	-	

1. In which year was English cricket said to have died at the Oval?

ADAMS, J. H. K. Hampshire

Name: James (Jimmy) Henry Kenneth Adams
Role: Left-hand opening bat, left-arm medium bowler
Born: 23 September 1980, Winchester
Height: 6ft 1in **Weight:** 14st 7lbs
Nickname: Bison, Nugget, Hippy, HC
County debut: 2002
County cap: 2006
1000 runs in a season: 1
1st-Class 200s: 1
Place in batting averages: 220th av. 17.16 (2007 68th av. 40.68)
Parents: Jenny and Mike
Marital status: Engaged
Family links with cricket: 'Dad played a bit for Kent Schoolboys. Brothers Ben and Tom, Hampshire age groups'
Education: Sherborne School; Loughborough University
Qualifications: BSc Human Biology, ECB Levels I and II coaching
Career outside cricket: 'A bit of coaching, and other bits and bobs'
Off-season: 'Coaching and wedding planning'
Overseas tours: West of England to West Indies 1995; England U19 to Sri Lanka (U19 World Cup) 1999-2000; Sherborne School to Pakistan
Overseas teams played for: Woodville, Adelaide 1999-2000; Melville, Perth 2000-01; Bayswater-Morley, Perth 2004-05
Career highlights to date: 'Maiden hundred and county cap'
Cricket moments to forget: 'Kidderminster, June 2000'
Cricket superstitions: 'Routines more than anything – I like a long breakfast, though'
Cricketers particularly admired: M. Parker, R. Smith, B. Lara
Young players to look out for: James Vince, Chris Wood, Danny Briggs
Other sports played: 'Bit of five-a-side, but not as much in terms of other sport as I'd like'; hockey (Dorset age group when 14)
Other sports followed: 'Most sports' – football (Aston Villa), NFL
Favourite band: 'Been listening to Pearl Jam, Rose Hill Drive and Howlin Rain recently...'
Relaxations: 'Music, reading and food'
Extras: Played in U15 World Cup 1996. Hampshire Young Player of the Year 1998. Represented England U19 2000. Played for Loughborough UCCE 2002-04 (captain 2003), scoring a century in each innings (103/113) v Kent at Canterbury 2002. Represented British Universities 2002-04 (captain 2003). Scored maiden

Championship century (168*) as Hampshire scored 404-5 to beat Yorkshire at Headingley 2006
Opinions on cricket: 'Twenty20 pulls the crowds and draws a younger audience which is great, but I think the powers that be may bleed it dry in an attempt to maximise profits. All pretty good in general.'
Best batting: 262* Hampshire v Nottinghamshire, Trent Bridge 2006
Best bowling: 2-16 Hampshire v Durham, Riverside 2004

2008 Season

	M	Inn	NO	Runs	HS	Avg	100	50	Ct	St	Balls	Runs	Wkts	Avg	BB	5I	10M
Test																	
FC	7	12	0	206	50	17.16	-	1	10	-	72	42	0		-	-	-
ODI																	
List A	9	7	0	266	90	38.00	-	2	4	-	18	27	0		-	-	
20/20 Int																	
20/20	1	1	1	3	3 *		-	-	1	-	0	0	0		-	-	

Career Performances

	M	Inn	NO	Runs	HS	Avg	100	50	Ct	St	Balls	Runs	Wkts	Avg	BB	5I	10M
Test																	
FC	71	127	11	3722	262 *	32.08	4	18	57	-	841	569	10	56.90	2-16	-	-
ODI																	
List A	23	20	1	483	90	25.42	-	2	10	-	73	88	1	88.00	1-34	-	
20/20 Int																	
20/20	13	6	3	48	17 *	16.00	-	-	4	-	36	60	0		-	-	

2. Which England batsman scored 158 in the 2nd Test of the 2006-07 Ashes series?

ADSHEAD, S. J. — Gloucestershire

Name: Stephen John Adshead
Role: Right-hand bat, wicket-keeper
Born: 29 January 1980, Worcester
Height: 5ft 8in **Weight:** 13st
Nickname: Adders, Top Shelf
County debut: 2000 (Leicestershire), 2003 (Worcestershire), 2004 (Gloucestershire)
County cap: 2003 (Worcestershire colours), 2004 (Gloucestershire)
Parents: David and Julie
Wife: Becky
Family links with cricket: Father and brother club cricketers in Worcester; mother keen spectator
Education: Brideley Moor HS, Redditch
Qualifications: 9 GCSEs, 3 A-levels, ECB Level 2 coaching
Career outside cricket: Coaching
Overseas tours: Leicestershire to Potchefstroom, South Africa 2001
Overseas teams played for: Fish Hoek, Cape Town 1998-99; Witwatersrand Technical, Johannesburg 1999-2000; Central Hawke's Bay, New Zealand 2000-01
Career highlights to date: 'Winning C&G final at Lord's 2004'
Cricket moments to forget: 'The whole 2002 season was a fairly miserable one'
Cricket superstitions: None
Cricketers particularly admired: Alec Stewart, Steve Waugh
Young players to look out for: Steve Davies
Favourite band: U2
Relaxations: 'Spending as much time as possible with my wife Becky; gym, eating'
Extras: Scored 187-minute 57* to help save match v Lancashire at Cheltenham 2004. Played in only one first-class match in 2008 but took nine catches in two innings. Appeared regularly in one day and Twenty20 fixtures.
Best batting: 148* Gloucestershire v Surrey, The Oval 2005

2008 Season

	M	Inn	NO	Runs	HS	Avg	100	50	Ct	St	Balls	Runs	Wkts	Avg	BB	5I	10M
Test																	
FC	1	1	0	47	47	47.00	-	-	9	-	0	0	0		-	-	-
ODI																	
List A	12	7	2	171	71	34.20	-	1	8	1	0	0	0		-	-	
20/20 Int																	
20/20	7	5	1	37	16	9.25	-	-	4	1	0	0	0		-	-	

Career Performances

	M	Inn	NO	Runs	HS	Avg	100	50	Ct	St	Balls	Runs	Wkts	Avg	BB	5I	10M
Test																	
FC	66	108	17	2812	148 *	30.90	1	17	170	14	0	0	0		-	-	-
ODI																	
List A	81	70	16	1199	77 *	22.20	-	5	87	27	0	0	0		-	-	
20/20 Int																	
20/20	40	26	8	347	81	19.27	-	1	16	15	0	0	0		-	-	

AFZAAL, U. Surrey

Name: Usman Afzaal
Role: Left-hand bat, slow left-arm bowler
Born: 9 June 1977, Rawalpindi, Pakistan
Height: 6ft **Weight:** 12st 7lbs
Nickname: Saeed, Gulfraz, Usy Bhai, Trevor
County debut: 1995 (Nottinghamshire), 2004 (Northamptonshire), 2008 (Surrey)
County cap: 2000 (Nottinghamshire), 2005 (Northamptonshire)
Test debut: 2001
1000 runs in a season: 6
Place in batting averages: 41st av. 46.42 (2007 99th av. 35.62)
Parents: Firdous and Shafi Mahmood
Marital status: Single
Family links with cricket: Older brother Kamran played for NAYC and for Nottinghamshire U15-U19 ('top player'); younger brother Aqib played for Notts and England U15; 'Uncle Mac and Uncle Raja great players'
Education: Manvers Pierrepont School; South Notts College
Qualifications: Coaching certificates
Overseas tours: Nottinghamshire to South Africa; England U19 to West Indies 1994-95, to Zimbabwe 1995-96; 'the great ZRK tour to Lahore, Pakistan' 2000; England A to West Indies 2000-01; England to India and New Zealand 2001-02
Overseas teams played for: Victoria Park, Perth
Career highlights to date: 'Playing for England in the Ashes [2001]'
Cricket moments to forget: 'Every time I get out'
Cricketers particularly admired: David Gower, Saeed Anwar, Ian Botham, Clive Rice, Uncle Raja and Uncle Mac
Other sports played: Indoor football

Other sports followed: Football ('a bit of Man Utd')
Relaxations: 'Praying; spending time with friends and family; listening to Indian music'
Extras: Played for England U15 and U17. Won Denis Compton Award 1996. Took wicket (Adam Gilchrist) with third ball in Test cricket v Australia at The Oval 2001. C&G Man of the Match award for his 3-8 (from four overs) and 64* v Ireland at Clontarf 2002. Left Northamptonshire at the end of the 2007 season and joined Surrey for 2008, where he had an excellent season with the bat. Only Ramprakash and Newman scored more first-class runs during the 2008 season
Best batting: 168* Northamptonshire v Essex, Northampton 2005
Best bowling: 4-101 Nottinghamshire v Gloucestershire, Trent Bridge 1998

2008 Season

	M	Inn	NO	Runs	HS	Avg	100	50	Ct	St	Balls	Runs	Wkts	Avg	BB	5I	10M
Test																	
FC	16	26	5	975	134 *	46.42	2	7	7	-	624	395	4	98.75	2-62	-	-
ODI																	
List A	16	16	2	485	126 *	34.64	1	2	6	-	384	421	14	30.07	4-49	-	
20/20 Int																	
20/20	10	10	1	187	38	20.77	-	-	1	-	87	100	3	33.33	1-15	-	

Career Performances

	M	Inn	NO	Runs	HS	Avg	100	50	Ct	St	Balls	Runs	Wkts	Avg	BB	5I	10M
Test	3	6	1	83	54	16.60	-	1	-	-	54	49	1	49.00	1-49	-	-
FC	206	356	39	12104	168 *	38.18	28	63	97	-	8109	4513	83	54.37	4-101	-	-
ODI																	
List A	171	160	23	5026	132	36.68	6	32	45	-	1449	1429	53	26.96	4-49	-	
20/20 Int																	
20/20	41	38	6	677	64 *	21.15	-	2	6	-	135	166	5	33.20	2-15	-	

3. Which England batsman scored a double century in the 2nd Test of the 2006-07 Ashes series?

AGA, R. G. Sussex

Name: Ragheb Gul Aga
Role: Right-hand bat, right-arm medium-fast bowler; all-rounder
Born: 10 July 1984, Nairobi, Kenya
Height: 6ft 3in **Weight:** 13st 3lbs
Nickname: Rags
County debut: 2007 (one-day), 2008 (first-class)
ODI debut: 2004
Twenty20 Int debut: 2008
Parents: Munawar and Zeenat
Marital status: Single
Education: Hillcrest Secondary School, Kenya; Brighton University (Eastbourne Campus)
Qualifications: 'Sport and exercise scientist – specialist area environmental physiology'
Career outside cricket: 'BDM MKK Sports. Eastbourne College hockey coach'

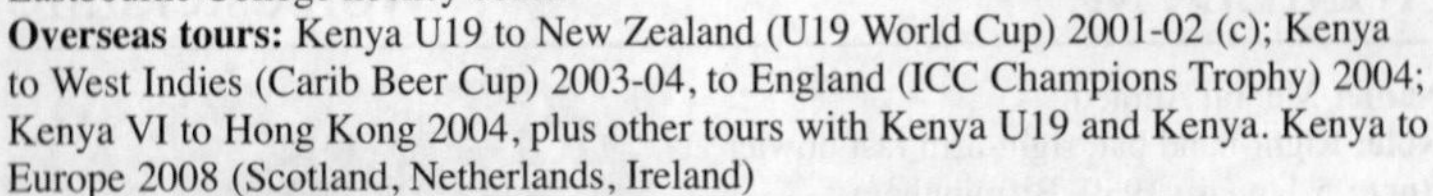

Overseas tours: Kenya U19 to New Zealand (U19 World Cup) 2001-02 (c); Kenya to West Indies (Carib Beer Cup) 2003-04, to England (ICC Champions Trophy) 2004; Kenya VI to Hong Kong 2004, plus other tours with Kenya U19 and Kenya. Kenya to Europe 2008 (Scotland, Netherlands, Ireland)
Career highlights to date: 'Man of the Match v India A in Nairobi [2004] – 4-18 to win match'
Cricket moments to forget: 'First club game, aged 16 – ran out club captain'
Cricketers particularly admired: Jacques Kallis, Chris Cairns, Wasim Akram
Young players to look out for: Andy Hodd
Other sports played: Hockey (Eastbourne 1st XI – Player of the Season 2006-07; Eastbourne U21 captain – Sussex Cup winners 2005)
Other sports followed: Football (Spurs), rugby (Leicester Tigers)
Relaxations: 'Cooking (and eating), reading'
Extras: Made first-class debut for Kenya v Jamaica in Grenada in the Carib Beer Cup 2003-04. Man of the Match v India A in the Kenya Triangular Tournament in Nairobi 2004 (17-ball 16 followed by 4-18). Appointed stand-in captain of Kenya for the semi-final of the ICC Inter-Continental Cup v Scotland in Abu Dhabi 2004. Brighton University Sporting Hall of Fame: Achievement in Cricket (with Kenya) 2006. Eastbourne CC 1st XI Player of the Season 2007. Signed a new two-year contract with Sussex in October 2008
Best batting: 43 Kenya v Namibia, Nairobi (AK) 2004
Best bowling: 4-63 Sussex v Kent, Canterbury, June 2008

2008 Season

	M	Inn	NO	Runs	HS	Avg	100	50	Ct	St	Balls	Runs	Wkts	Avg	BB	5I	10M
Test																	
FC	5	6	1	71	26	14.20	-	-	-	-	371	232	9	25.77	4-63	-	-
ODI																	
List A	2	1	0	4	4	4.00	-	-	-	-	54	84	3	28.00	3-53	-	
20/20 Int																	
20/20																	

Career Performances

	M	Inn	NO	Runs	HS	Avg	100	50	Ct	St	Balls	Runs	Wkts	Avg	BB	5I	10M
Test																	
FC	13	22	3	209	43	11.00	-	-	6	-	1170	668	22	30.36	4-63	-	-
ODI	2	2	0	1	1	.50	-	-	-	-	78	87	2	43.50	2-17	-	
List A	12	10	0	72	16	7.20	-	-	3	-	396	420	14	30.00	4-14	-	
20/20 Int	4	4	1	51	28	17.00	-	-	1	-	83	83	3	27.66	2-12	-	
20/20	4	4	1	51	28	17.00	-	-	1	-	83	83	3	27.66	2-12	-	

AHMED, M. Worcestershire

Name: Mehraj Ahmed
Role: Right-hand bat, right-arm fast bowler
Born: 5 January 1989, Birmingham
Weight: 13st 3lbs
Nickname: Maz
County debut: 2008
Parents: Altaf and Nassim
Marital status: Single
Education: Kingsbury School; Josiah Mason College
Qualifications: Level 1 Maths, Level 2 English
Cricket moments to forget: 'None'
Cricket superstitions: 'I wear my silver chain round my neck'
Cricketers particularly admired: Waqar Younis
Young players to look out for: Aneesh Kapil
Other sports played: Football, rugby ('just for college')
Other sports followed: Football (Manchester United)
Favourite band: G-Unit

Relaxations: 'Listening to music'
Extras: Bowling has been clocked at 87mph. Player of the year three times for club
Opinions on cricket: 'I love the game and it can't get any better at the moment.'
Best bowling: 1-28 Worcestershire v Loughborough UCCE, Kidderminster, 2008

2008 Season

	M	Inn	NO	Runs	HS	Avg	100	50	Ct	St	Balls	Runs	Wkts	Avg	BB	5I	10M
Test																	
FC	1	0	0	0	0		-	-	2	-	96	70	2	35.00	1-28	-	-
ODI																	
List A	1	0	0	0	0		-	-	-	-	18	34	1	34.00	1-34	-	
20/20 Int																	
20/20																	

Career Performances

	M	Inn	NO	Runs	HS	Avg	100	50	Ct	St	Balls	Runs	Wkts	Avg	BB	5I	10M
Test																	
FC	1	0	0	0	0		-	-	2	-	96	70	2	35.00	1-28	-	-
ODI																	
List A	1	0	0	0	0		-	-	-	-	18	34	1	34.00	1-34	-	
20/20 Int																	
20/20																	

ALI, K. Worcestershire

Name: Kabir Ali
Role: Right-hand bat, right-arm medium-fast bowler
Born: 24 November 1980, Birmingham
Height: 6ft **Weight:** 12st 7lbs
Nickname: Kabby, Taxi
County debut: 1999
County colours: 2002
Test debut: 2003
ODI debut: 2003
50 wickets in a season: 5
Place in batting averages: 212th av. 18.15 (2007 273rd av. 11.10)
Place in bowling averages: 6th av. 18.74 (2007 27th av. 24.44)
Parents: Shabir Ali and M. Begum
Marital status: Single
Family links with cricket: Father played club cricket. Cousins Moeen and Omar also play for Worcestershire. Cousin Kadeer plays for Gloucestershire
Education: Moseley School; Wolverhampton University
Qualifications: GNVQ Leisure and Tourism, coaching
Overseas tours: Warwickshire U19 to Cape Town 1998; ECB National Academy to Australia and Sri Lanka 2002-03; England to Australia 2002-03 (VB Series), to South Africa 2004-05 (one-day series), to Pakistan 2005-06 (one-day series), to India 2005-06 (one-day series); England VI to Hong Kong 2003, 2004, 2005, 2006; England A to West Indies 2005-06; England Lions to India 2007-08
Overseas teams played for: Midland-Guildford, Perth; Rajasthan, India 2006-07
Career highlights to date: 'Playing for England'
Cricketers particularly admired: Wasim Akram, Glenn McGrath
Young players to look out for: Moeen Ali, Omar Ali, Atif Ali
Other sports played: Football, snooker
Other sports followed: Football, snooker
Relaxations: 'Playing snooker and spending time with family and friends'
Extras: Warwickshire Youth Young Player of the Year award. Represented England U19. NBC Denis Compton Award for the most promising young Worcestershire player 2000. Junior Royals Player of the Year 2001. Worcestershire Player of the Year 2002. PCA Young Player of the Year 2002, 2003. Made Test debut in the fourth Test v South Africa at Headingley 2003, taking a wicket (Neil McKenzie) with his fifth ball. Worcestershire Young Player of the Year 2003. Don Kenyon Award 2003. Player of the Final in the Hong Kong Sixes 2004. Had an excellent 2008 season with the ball, taking 59 wickets at an average of less than twenty

Best batting: 84* Worcestershire v Durham, Stockton 2003
Best bowling: 8-50 Worcestershire v Lancashire, Old Trafford 2007

2008 Season

	M	Inn	NO	Runs	HS	Avg	100	50	Ct	St	Balls	Runs	Wkts	Avg	BB	5I	10M
Test																	
FC	11	15	2	236	46	18.15	-	-	3	-	1869	1106	59	18.74	6-58	4	-
ODI																	
List A	9	8	1	105	43	15.00	-	-	-	-	369	318	10	31.80	2-14	-	-
20/20 Int																	
20/20	8	7	1	109	28	18.16	-	-	2	-	186	238	13	18.30	4-44	-	

Career Performances

	M	Inn	NO	Runs	HS	Avg	100	50	Ct	St	Balls	Runs	Wkts	Avg	BB	5I	10M
Test	1	2	0	10	9	5.00	-	-	-	-	216	136	5	27.20	3-80	-	-
FC	108	148	21	2238	84 *	17.62	-	7	27	-	18526	11035	418	26.39	8-50	20	4
ODI	14	9	3	93	39 *	15.50	-	-	1	-	673	682	20	34.10	4-45	-	
List A	155	96	25	1080	92	15.21	-	3	25	-	6628	5689	226	25.17	5-36	2	
20/20 Int																	
20/20	24	19	4	261	49	17.40	-	-	7	-	513	669	32	20.90	4-44	-	

ALI, K. Gloucestershire

Name: Kadeer Ali
Role: Right-hand opening bat, right-arm medium bowler
Born: 7 March 1983, Birmingham
Height: 6ft 2in **Weight:** 12st
Nickname: Kads, Kaddy, Rat
County debut: 2000 (Worcestershire), 2005 (Gloucestershire)
County cap: 2002 (Worcestershire colours), 2005 (Gloucestershire)
Place in batting averages: 88th av. 35.95 (2007 115th av. 33.44)
Parents: Munir Ali and Maqsood Begum
Marital status: Single
Family links with cricket: 'Father has cricket academy – "Streets to Arena". Cousin Kabir Ali plays for Worcestershire. Brothers Moeen and Omar Ali also play for Worcestershire'

Education: Handsworth Grammar; Moseley Sixth Form College
Qualifications: 5 GCSEs, Level 1 coach
Overseas tours: England U19 to India 2000-01, to Australia and (U19 World Cup) New Zealand 2001-02; England A to Malaysia and India 2003-04
Overseas teams played for: WA University, Perth 2002-03; Lahore Model Town CC, Pakistan 2005; PTCL, Pakistan 2005-06
Career highlights to date: 'Playing in Twenty20 finals day; playing in the final against Kent (2007). Playing against Australia'
Cricket moments to forget: 'My debut against Glamorgan – got a pair'
Cricketers particularly admired: Graeme Hick, Younus Khan
Young players to look out for: Moeen Ali, Omar Ali, Aatif Ali
Other sports played: Football, snooker
Other sports followed: Football (Birmingham City FC)
Favourite band: Yusuf Islam (formerly Cat Stevens)
Relaxations: 'Cinema; relaxing with friends and family'
Extras: Young Player awards at Warwickshire CCC. Represented England U19 2000-02; England U19 Player of Series v India U19 2002. NBC Denis Compton Award for the most promising young Worcestershire player 2001, 2002. ECB National Academy 2003-04. Became first player to hit a ball over the Basil D'Oliveira Stand at Worcester, v New Zealanders 2004. Gloucestershire Young Player of the Year and Players' Player of the Year 2007. Scored over 1000 runs for the county in first-class and one-day games in 2008. In January 2009 he committed himself to the county until 2011
Opinions on cricket: 'Twenty20 is definitely the way forward'
Best batting: 161 Gloucestershire v Northamptonshire, Bristol 2008
Best bowling: 1-4 Gloucestershire v Glamorgan, Bristol 2005

2008 Season

	M	Inn	NO	Runs	HS	Avg	100	50	Ct	St	Balls	Runs	Wkts	Avg	BB	5I	10M
Test																	
FC	12	22	0	791	161	35.95	3	2	7	-	0	0	0		-	-	-
ODI																	
List A	7	7	0	278	73	39.71	-	2	2	-	0	0	0		-	-	
20/20 Int																	
20/20																	

Career Performances

	M	Inn	NO	Runs	HS	Avg	100	50	Ct	St	Balls	Runs	Wkts	Avg	BB	5I	10M
Test																	
FC	77	140	5	3832	161	28.38	6	20	39	-	456	289	3	96.33	1-4	-	-
ODI																	
List A	48	48	1	1509	114	32.10	2	10	8	-	63	59	1	59.00	1-4	-	
20/20 Int																	
20/20	12	12	2	289	53	28.90	-	1	3	-	0	0	0		-	-	

ALI, M. M. Worcestershire

Name: Moeen Munir Ali
Role: Left-hand bat, right-arm off-spin bowler; batting all-rounder
Born: 18 June 1987, Birmingham
Height: 6ft **Weight:** 11st
Nickname: Brother Mo
County debut: 2005 (Warwickshire), 2007 (Worcestershire)
County colours: 2007 (Worcestershire)
Place in batting averages: 126th av. 30.00
Parents: Munir Ali and Maqsood Begum
Wife and date of marriage: Firuza Parveen Hussain, 11 October 2008
Family links with cricket: Brother Kadeer plays for Gloucestershire; younger brother Omar and cousin Kabir are also at Worcestershire. Father has 'Streets to Arena' cricket academy
Education: Moseley School
Qualifications: GCSEs and Leisure and Tourism
Off-season: 'Here in England'
Overseas tours: 'Streets to Arena' to Pakistan 2002; England U19 to India 2004-05, to Bangladesh 2005-06, to Sri Lanka (U19 World Cup) 2005-06 (c); England Performance Programme to India 2007-08
Overseas teams played for: Claremont-Nedlands, Perth 2003-04, St Augustine's, South Africa, 2008
Career highlights to date: 'Winning Pro40 in 2007. Scoring a hundred off 46 balls [v Northamptonshire at Kidderminster in the Pro40 2007]'
Cricket moments to forget: 'Don't have any'
Cricket superstitions: None
Cricketers particularly admired: Saeed Anwar, Graeme Hick, Nick Knight
Young players to look out for: Steve Davies, Joe Denly
Other sports played: Football ('Worcester YC's - always score a goal!')
Other sports followed: Football (Liverpool)
Favourite band: No Beats Necessary
Relaxations: 'Islam and praying'
Extras: Represented England U15 2002. Won five Warwickshire youth awards from age of 11. Represented England U19 2004, 2005, 2006. NBC Denis Compton Award for most promising young Warwickshire player 2004, 2005. Scored a 56-ball century against Sri Lanka in 2005 U19 Test
Opinions on cricket: 'Too many days of cricket in the season'

Best batting: 92 Worcestershire v Loughborough UCCE, Kidderminster, 2008
Best bowling: 2-50 Warwickshire v Lancashire, Edgbaston 2006

2008 Season

	M	Inn	NO	Runs	HS	Avg	100	50	Ct	St	Balls	Runs	Wkts	Avg	BB	5I	10M
Test																	
FC	6	9	2	210	92	30.00	-	1	1	-	222	133	0		-	-	-
ODI																	
List A	15	15	1	198	51	14.14	-	1	3	-	90	98	2	49.00	1-6	-	
20/20 Int																	
20/20	7	7	2	95	26*	19.00	-	-	-	-	6	11	0		-	-	

Career Performances

	M	Inn	NO	Runs	HS	Avg	100	50	Ct	St	Balls	Runs	Wkts	Avg	BB	5I	10M
Test																	
FC	16	24	2	624	92	28.36	-	6	5	-	806	572	3	190.66	2-50	-	-
ODI																	
List A	35	34	2	730	100	22.81	1	5	6	-	334	320	7	45.71	2-45	-	
20/20 Int																	
20/20	11	10	2	128	26*	16.00	-	-	-	-	6	11	0		-	-	

ALLENBY, J. — Leicestershire

Name: James (Jim) Allenby
Role: Right-hand bat, right-arm medium bowler, county vice-captain
Born: 12 September 1982, Perth, Australia
Height: 6ft **Weight:** 13st 8lbs
Nickname: Jimmy, Jay, Jay Bay, Ducktails
County debut: 2005 (one-day), 2006 (first-class)
Place in batting averages: 131st av. 29.30 (2007 108th av. 34.31)
Place in bowling averages: 62nd av. 28.30 (2007 128th av. 44.13)
Parents: Michael and Julie
Marital status: 'Unmarried'
Family links with cricket: 'Great-grandfather played at Yorkshire/Hampshire'
Education: Christ Church Grammar School, Perth
Qualifications: Level 1 coach

Career outside cricket: 'Working in ANZ bank'
Off-season: 'Playing and coaching in Perth; working in the bank; going to the beach!'
Overseas teams played for: Claremont-Nedlands CC, Perth 1993 –. Western Australia 2006-07
Career highlights to date: 'Playing in and winning Twenty20 [2006]. Hundred (103*) and 68* on Championship debut [v Essex at Leicester 2006]'
Cricket moments to forget: 'Pro40 match against Glamorgan, Colwyn Bay [2008]'
Cricket superstitions: 'Put gear on same way each time I bat'
Cricketers particularly admired: Steve Waugh, Dean Jones, Paul Nixon
Young players to look out for: David Brown, Stewart Walters
Other sports followed: Football (Leeds United)
Favourite band: Powderfinger
Relaxations: 'Playing golf, swimming/surfing at beach'
Extras: Set record individual score for Western Australia in U19 cricket (180) v Northern Territory 2000-01. Played for Durham Board XI in the 2003 C&G. Scored 103* and 68* on Championship debut v Essex at Leicester 2006. Appointed vice-captain of Leicestershire at the end of August 2007. Became first player ever to take 4 wickets in 4 balls in Twenty20 for Leicestershire v Lancashire in June 2008. Is not considered an overseas player. In 2008, he scored over 1000 runs in all competitions
Opinions on cricket: 'The use of technology for umpires would be good to help them make decisions. "Young players" should include those in their early-mid 20s, not just those who are 17 or 18'
Best batting: 138* Leicestershire v Bangladesh A, Grace Road, 2008
Best bowling: 5-125 Leicestershire v Gloucestershire, Bristol 2007

2008 Season

	M	Inn	NO	Runs	HS	Avg	100	50	Ct	St	Balls	Runs	Wkts	Avg	BB	5I	10M
Test																	
FC	17	23	3	586	138 *	29.30	1	3	17	-	1624	736	26	28.30	4-40	-	-
ODI																	
List A	14	13	0	301	62	23.15	-	1	3	-	563	519	19	27.31	4-27	-	
20/20 Int																	
20/20	9	9	1	190	57	23.75	-	2	1	-	129	148	14	10.57	5-21	2	

Career Performances

	M	Inn	NO	Runs	HS	Avg	100	50	Ct	St	Balls	Runs	Wkts	Avg	BB	5I	10M
Test																	
FC	35	53	9	1580	138 *	35.90	2	9	34	-	2934	1421	41	34.65	5-125	1	
ODI																	
List A	42	38	6	831	91 *	25.96	-	4	16	-	1274	1070	40	26.75	5-43	1	
20/20 Int																	
20/20	30	26	7	397	64	20.89	-	3	12	-	309	410	24	17.08	5-21	2	

AMBROSE, T. R. Warwickshire

Name: Timothy (Tim) Raymond Ambrose
Role: Right-hand bat, wicket-keeper
Born: 1 December 1982, Newcastle, New South Wales, Australia
Height: 5ft 7in
Nickname: Shambrose, Freak, Mole
County debut: 2001 (Sussex), 2006 (Warwickshire)
County cap: 2003 (Sussex), 2007 (Warwickshire)
Test debut: 2007-08
ODI debut: 2008
Twenty20 Int debut: 2008
1st-Class 200s: 1
Place in batting averages: 116th av. 31.25 (2007 58th av. 43.10)
Parents: Raymond and Sally
Marital status: Single
Family links with cricket: Cousin played Sydney first grade; father captain of local grade D4 team
Education: Merewether Selective High, NSW
Career outside cricket: Greenkeeping
Overseas tours: Sussex to Grenada 2001, 2002; England Performance Programme to India 2007-08; England to New Zealand 2007-08, to India 2008, to West Indies 2009; England Lions to New Zealand 2009
Overseas teams played for: Wallsend, NSW 2000; Nelson Bay, NSW 2001; Newcastle, NSW 2002
Career highlights to date: 'Winning the Championship 2003. Maiden first-class century, 149 v Yorkshire [2002]. Making my England Test debut.'
Cricketers particularly admired: Alec Stewart, Ian Healy, Steve Waugh, Mushtaq Ahmed
Other sports played: Football, squash, golf, rugby league, rugby union, AFL, 'I'll have a go at anything'
Other sports followed: Rugby league (Newcastle Knights), Australian Rules (Sydney Swans), football (Tottenham Hotspur)
Favourite band: Jeff Buckley, Ben Harper, Jack Johnson
Relaxations: 'Guitar, music'
Extras: Captained Newcastle (NSW) U16 1999 Bradman Cup winning side. Played for New South Wales U17. Won NSW Junior Cricketer of the Year three years running. C&G Man of the Match award for his 95 v Buckinghamshire at Beaconsfield 2002. Scored maiden first-class double century (251*) v Worcestershire at Worcester

2007, in the process sharing with Heath Streak (66) in a new Warwickshire record partnership for the sixth wicket (226). Represented England Lions 2007
Best batting: 251* Warwickshire v Worcestershire, Worcester 2007

2008 Season

	M	Inn	NO	Runs	HS	Avg	100	50	Ct	St	Balls	Runs	Wkts	Avg	BB	5I	10M
Test	7	9	0	167	67	18.55	-	1	19	-	0	0	0		-	-	-
FC	14	19	3	500	156 *	31.25	1	2	42	-	0	0	0		-	-	-
ODI	5	5	1	10	6	2.50	-	-	3	-	0	0	0		-	-	
List A	11	10	2	169	111 *	21.12	1	-	5	1	0	0	0		-	-	
20/20 Int	1	0	0	0	0		-	-	1	1	0	0	0		-	-	
20/20	2	1	0	18	18	18.00	-	-	1	1	0	0	0		-	-	

Career Performances

	M	Inn	NO	Runs	HS	Avg	100	50	Ct	St	Balls	Runs	Wkts	Avg	BB	5I	10M
Test	10	15	0	371	102	24.73	1	2	30	-	0	0	0		-	-	-
FC	90	140	12	4376	251 *	34.18	6	25	202	14	6	1	0		-	-	-
ODI	5	5	1	10	6	2.50	-	-	3	-	0	0	0		-	-	
List A	88	81	12	2041	135	29.57	3	8	93	12	0	0	0		-	-	
20/20 Int	1	0	0	0	0		-	-	1	1	0	0	0		-	-	
20/20	22	18	4	453	77	32.35	-	2	12	8	0	0	0		-	-	

ANDERSON, J. M. — Lancashire

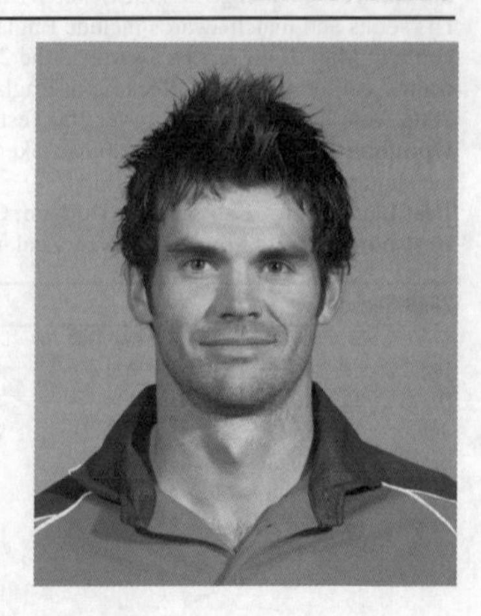

Name: James Michael Anderson
Role: Left-hand bat, right-arm fast-medium bowler
Born: 30 July 1982, Burnley
Height: 6ft 2in **Weight:** 13st
Nickname: Jimmy
County debut: 2001 (one-day), 2002 (first-class)
County cap: 2003
Test debut: 2003
ODI debut: 2002-03
Twenty20 Int debut: 2006-07
50 wickets in a season: 2
Place in bowling averages: 17th av. 21.04 (2007 81st av. 33.34)
Parents: Michael and Catherine
Wife and date of marriage: Daniella (Lloyd), February 2006

Family links with cricket: Father and uncle played for Burnley
Education: St Theodore's RC High School and Sixth Form – both Burnley
Qualifications: 10 GCSEs, 3 A-Levels, Level 2 coaching award
Overseas tours: Lancashire to Cape Town 2002; ECB National Academy to Australia 2002-03; England to Australia 2002-03 (VB Series), to Africa (World Cup) 2002-03, to Bangladesh and Sri Lanka 2003-04, to West Indies 2003-04, to Zimbabwe (one-day series) 2004-05, to South Africa 2004-05, to Pakistan 2005-06, to India 2005-06, to India (ICC Champions Trophy) 2006-07, to Australia 2006-07, to West Indies (World Cup) 2006-07, to South Africa (World 20/20) 2007-08, to Sri Lanka 2007-08, to New Zealand 2007-08, to India 2008, to West Indies 2009; England A to West Indies 2005-06
Career highlights to date: 'ODI hat-trick. Two five-fors at Lord's'
Cricket moments to forget: 'Ashes 2006-07'
Cricketers particularly admired: Allan Donald, Darren Gough, Peter Martin
Young players to look out for: Jonathan Clare
Other sports played: Golf (12 handicap), football, tennis
Other sports followed: Football (Burnley, Arsenal), 'interested in all sports'
Favourite band: Oasis, U2
Relaxations: 'Reading, music'
Extras: Represented England U19 2001. Took 50 first-class wickets in his first full season 2002. NBC Denis Compton Award for the most promising young Lancashire player 2002. Took Championship hat-trick (Robinson, Hussain, Jefferson) v Essex at Old Trafford 2003. Recorded a five-wicket innings return (5-73) on Test debut in the first Test v Zimbabwe at Lord's 2003. Became the first England bowler to take an ODI hat-trick (Abdul Razzaq, Shoaib Akhtar, Mohammad Sami) v Pakistan at The Oval in the NatWest Challenge 2003. Cricket Writers' Club Young Player of the Year 2003. His series and match awards include England's Man of the [Test] Series v India 2007 and two Man of the Match awards in the 2002-03 World Cup. England 12-month central contract 2007-08. Because of England duty his appearances for the county in 2008 were limited. Now has over 100 Test wickets to his name.
Opinions on cricket: 'Twenty20 has taken all forms of the game to a new level, but we should be very wary of overkill.'
Best batting: 37* Lancashire v Durham, Old Trafford 2005
Best bowling: 7-43 England v New Zealand, Trent Bridge June 2008

2008 Season

	M	Inn	NO	Runs	HS	Avg	100	50	Ct	St	Balls	Runs	Wkts	Avg	BB	5I	10M
Test	7	8	3	91	34	18.20	-	-	6	-	1661	876	34	25.76	7-43	1	-
FC	10	11	4	92	34	13.14	-	-	9	-	2086	1031	49	21.04	7-43	2	-
ODI	10	4	2	13	11	6.50	-	-	3	-	366	297	6	49.50	3-61	-	
List A	13	5	3	16	11	8.00	-	-	4	-	492	389	10	38.90	3-61	-	
20/20 Int	1	0	0	0	0		-	-	-	-	24	25	2	12.50	2-25	-	
20/20	2	0	0	0	0		-	-	-	-	42	49	3	16.33	2-25	-	

Career Performances

	M	Inn	NO	Runs	HS	Avg	100	50	Ct	St	Balls	Runs	Wkts	Avg	BB	5I	10M
Test	29	41	23	246	34	13.66	-	-	13	-	5906	3590	104	34.51	7-43	5	-
FC	81	95	43	491	37 *	9.44	-	-	35	-	14498	8376	291	28.78	7-43	13	1
ODI	97	39	19	124	15	6.20	-	-	26	-	4725	3859	127	30.38	4-23	-	
List A	145	59	35	215	15	8.95	-	-	34	-	6925	5493	196	28.02	4-23	-	
20/20 Int	10	2	2	1	1 *		-	-	2	-	234	322	11	29.27	2-24	-	
20/20	27	5	4	22	16	22.00	-	-	4	-	577	809	25	32.36	2-24	-	

ANDREW, G. M. — Worcestershire

Name: Gareth Mark Andrew
Role: Left-hand bat, right-arm fast-medium bowler
Born: 27 December 1983, Yeovil
Height: 6ft **Weight:** 14st
Nickname: G-Train, Brad, Sobers
County debut: 2003 (Somerset); 2008 (Worcestershire)
County colours: 2008
Place in batting averages: 224th av. 16.58
Place in bowling averages: 116th av. 37.70
Parents: Peter and Susan
Marital status: Single
Family links with cricket: Father and younger brother club cricketers
Education: Ansford Community School; Richard Huish College, Taunton
Qualifications: 10 GCSEs, 3 A-levels, Level 1 coach
Overseas tours: West of England U15 to West Indies 1999; England U17 to Australia 2001; Somerset Academy to Western Australia 2002; 'Aus Academy' to Perth 2003
Overseas teams played for: Swanbourne CC, Perth 2002-03; Glenelg CC, Adelaide 2005-06, 2006-07
Career highlights to date: 'Twenty20 champions 2005, division two winners 2007, Pro40 promotion 2007 – all with Somerset'
Cricket moments to forget: 'Whenever bowling in the Twenty20'
Cricket superstitions: 'Always put my boots on the right feet'
Cricketers particularly admired: Ian Botham, Andrew Flintoff, Chris Cairns
Young players to look out for: Joss Buttler, Rob Travers
Other sports played: Football (Bruton Town FC, Yeovil District U11-U16, Castle Cary AFC)

Other sports followed: Football (Yeovil Town, Manchester Utd)
Favourite band: Red Hot Chili Peppers
Extras: Represented England U19 v South Africa U19 2003. Signed a new two-year contract in September 2008
Best batting: 44 Somerset v Sri Lanka A, Taunton 2004
Best bowling: 5-58 Worcester v Middlesex, Kidderminster 2008

2008 Season

	M	Inn	NO	Runs	HS	Avg	100	50	Ct	St	Balls	Runs	Wkts	Avg	BB	5I	10M
Test																	
FC	12	15	3	199	38 *	16.58	-	-	5	-	1433	1018	27	37.70	5-58	1	-
ODI																	
List A	16	10	3	137	30 *	19.57	-	-	6	-	522	534	18	29.66	3-12	-	
20/20 Int																	
20/20	9	5	2	22	14	7.33	-	-	2	-	180	252	8	31.50	2-20	-	

Career Performances

	M	Inn	NO	Runs	HS	Avg	100	50	Ct	St	Balls	Runs	Wkts	Avg	BB	5I	10M
Test																	
FC	23	29	4	362	44	14.48	-	-	10	-	2770	2007	55	36.49	5-58	1	-
ODI																	
List A	59	35	9	317	33	12.19	-	-	19	-	1933	2011	60	33.51	4-48	-	
20/20 Int																	
20/20	39	19	6	93	14	7.15	-	-	11	-	715	1032	36	28.66	4-22	-	

4. In 1879 which Australian bowler achieved the first hat-trick against England, some years before the Ashes themselves were to be fought for?

ANYON, J. E. Warwickshire

Name: James Edward Anyon
Role: Left-hand bat, right-arm fast-medium bowler
Born: 5 May 1983, Lancaster
Height: 6ft 2in **Weight:** 13st
Nickname: Jimmy, Cheese'n'
County debut: 2005
Place in batting averages: (2007 228th av. 18.09)
Place in bowling averages: 89th av. 32.46 (2007 131st av. 44.50)
Parents: Peter and Christine
Marital status: Single
Family links with cricket: 'Dad used to play village cricket for Calder Vale CC'
Education: Garstang High School; Preston College; Loughborough University
Qualifications: GCSEs, 3 A-levels, BSc Sports Science with Management, Level 1 coaching
Off-season: 'Resting, getting fit again, maybe some cricket overseas before Christmas'
Overseas teams played for: Claremont-Nedlands, Perth 2004-05
Career highlights to date: 'Bowling at Brian Lara, Twenty20 hat-trick in 2005'
Cricket moments to forget: 'A few run-outs, getting relegated'
Cricketers particularly admired: Glenn McGrath, Michael Atherton
Other sports played: Football, darts
Other sports followed: Football (Preston North End, AC Roma), Moto GP
Favourite band: Muse
Relaxations: 'Music, films'
Extras: Young Player of the Year awards at Preston CC. Bowler of the Year award at Farsley CC (Bradford League) 2004. Played for Loughborough UCCE 2003, 2004. Took Twenty20 hat-trick (Durston, Andrew, Caddick) v Somerset at Edgbaston 2005, Played half as many first-class games in 2008 as in 2007, but had a better return for his efforts
Opinions on cricket: 'Mainly good; not sure about the EPL and how it will work - too many teams in it.'
Best batting: 37* Warwickshire v Durham, Riverside 2007
Best bowling: 6-82 Warwickshire v Glamorgan, Swalec Stadium (Cardiff), 2008

2008 Season

	M	Inn	NO	Runs	HS	Avg	100	50	Ct	St	Balls	Runs	Wkts	Avg	BB	5I	10M
Test																	
FC	7	6	2	14	6	3.50	-	-	4	-	1370	844	26	32.46	6-82	1	-
ODI																	
List A	5	2	2	6	5 *		-	-	1	-	159	131	7	18.71	3-6	-	
20/20 Int																	
20/20	1	0	0	0	0		-	-	-	-	0	0	0		-	-	

Career Performances

	M	Inn	NO	Runs	HS	Avg	100	50	Ct	St	Balls	Runs	Wkts	Avg	BB	5I	10M
Test																	
FC	43	54	21	325	37 *	9.84	-	-	15	-	6929	4198	108	38.87	6-82	2	-
ODI																	
List A	36	10	5	22	12	4.40	-	-	8	-	1303	1197	38	31.50	3-6	-	
20/20 Int																	
20/20	19	3	3	16	8 *		-	-	3	-	309	433	24	18.04	3-6	-	

ASHLING, C. P. — Glamorgan

Name: Christopher (Chris) Paul Ashling
Role: Right-arm fast-medium opening bowler, lower-order right-hand bat
Born: 26 November 1988, Manchester
Nickname: Bruce
County debut: No first-team appearance
Marital status: Single
Education: Millfield School, UWIC
Overseas tours: England U16 to South Africa 2005
Cricket moments to forget: 'Being on a hat-trick twice when younger, and bowling a wide on each occasion!'
Cricketers particularly admired: Brett Lee, Darren Gough
Young players to look out for: All the Cardiff UCCE team
Other sports followed: Football (Manchester City)
Extras: Played for England U15, U16, U17 and Select XI. Played for Lancashire 2nd XI 2004-07. Signed a development contract with Glamorgan for 2008

AZEEM RAFIQ Yorkshire

Name: Azeem Rafiq
Role: Right-arm off-spin bowler, right-hand bat
Born: 27 February 1991, Pakistan
County debut: 2008 (Twenty20)
Education: Holgate School, Barnsley
Overseas tours: England U19 to South Africa 2009
Extras: Captained England U15's, North U15's and Yorkshire U15's in 2006. BBC Young Sports Personality of the Year for Yorkshire 2006. Yorkshire CC Academy Junior Performer of the Year 2007. Captained England U17's 2007. Yorkshire CC Academy Player of the Year 2008. After making his first-team debut in the Twenty20 Cup, it was found that he was ineligible to play for the county. The situation was resolved in August 2008, and in October he signed a three-year contract

2008 Season

	M	Inn	NO	Runs	HS	Avg	100	50	Ct	St	Balls	Runs	Wkts	Avg	BB	5I	10M
Test																	
FC																	
ODI																	
List A																	
20/20 Int																	
20/20	1	0	0	0	0		-	-	-	-	12	18	0		-	-	

Career Performances

	M	Inn	NO	Runs	HS	Avg	100	50	Ct	St	Balls	Runs	Wkts	Avg	BB	5I	10M
Test																	
FC																	
ODI																	
List A																	
20/20 Int																	
20/20	1	0	0	0	0		-	-	-	-	12	18	0		-	-	

AZHAR MAHMOOD Kent

Name: Azhar Mahmood Sagar
Role: Right-hand bat, right-arm fast-medium bowler; all-rounder
Born: 28 February 1975, Rawalpindi, Pakistan
Height: 6ft **Weight:** 13st 5lbs
Nickname: Aju
County debut: 2002 (Surrey), 2008 (Kent)
County cap: 2004 (Surrey), 2008 (Kent)
Test debut: 1997-98
ODI debut: 1996
1st-Class 200s: 1
Place in batting averages: 22nd av. 51.00 (2007 154th av. 28.00)
Place in bowling averages: 9th av. 19.23
Parents: Mohammed Aslam Sagar and Nusrat Perveen
Wife and date of marriage: Ebba Azhar, 13 April 2003
Education: FG No. 1 High School, Islamabad
Qualifications: 'A-level equivalent'

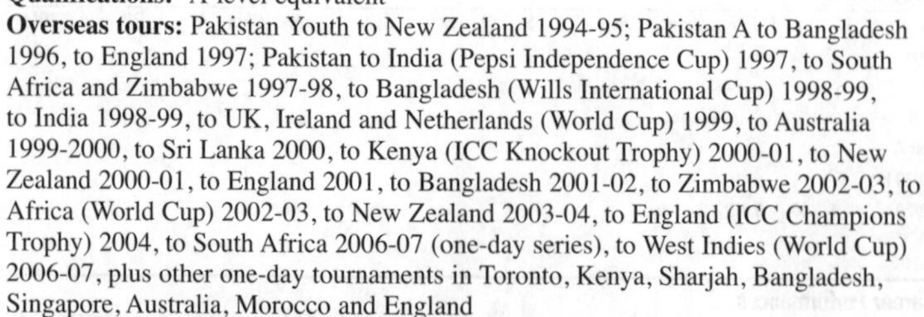

Overseas tours: Pakistan Youth to New Zealand 1994-95; Pakistan A to Bangladesh 1996, to England 1997; Pakistan to India (Pepsi Independence Cup) 1997, to South Africa and Zimbabwe 1997-98, to Bangladesh (Wills International Cup) 1998-99, to India 1998-99, to UK, Ireland and Netherlands (World Cup) 1999, to Australia 1999-2000, to Sri Lanka 2000, to Kenya (ICC Knockout Trophy) 2000-01, to New Zealand 2000-01, to England 2001, to Bangladesh 2001-02, to Zimbabwe 2002-03, to Africa (World Cup) 2002-03, to New Zealand 2003-04, to England (ICC Champions Trophy) 2004, to South Africa 2006-07 (one-day series), to West Indies (World Cup) 2006-07, plus other one-day tournaments in Toronto, Kenya, Sharjah, Bangladesh, Singapore, Australia, Morocco and England
Overseas teams played for: Islamabad; United Bank; Rawalpindi; Pakistan International Airlines; Habib Bank. Played for Hyderabad Heroes and Lahore Badshahs in ICL
Career highlights to date: 'First Test match (debut) against South Africa in 1997 in Pakistan (Rawalpindi). I scored 128* in the first innings and 50* in the second, plus two wickets – Man of the Match'
Cricket moments to forget: 'World Cup 1999 – final against Australia (which we lost)'
Cricket superstitions: None
Other sports played: Snooker, basketball, kite-flying

Other sports followed: Football (Man U)
Relaxations: 'Listening to music, training, spending time with my family'
Extras: Scored 128* and 50* on Test debut in the first Test v South Africa at Rawalpindi 1997-98; during first innings shared with Mushtaq Ahmed (59) in a stand of 151, equalling the world tenth-wicket record in Tests. Scored century (136) in the first Test v South Africa at Johannesburg 1997-98, becoming the first Pakistan player to score a Test century in South Africa and achieving feat of scoring a century on Test debuts home and away. Took 6-18 v West Indies in the Coca-Cola Champions Trophy in Sharjah 1999-2000 and 5-28 v Sri Lanka in the final of the same competition, winning the Man of the Match award on both occasions. An overseas player with Surrey at the start of the 2002 season and 2003-07. Signed a two-year deal with Kent (as a non-overseas player) in late 2007 having moved from Surrey.
Best batting: 204* Surrey v Middlesex, The Oval 2005
Best bowling: 8-61 Surrey v Lancashire, The Oval 2002

2008 Season

	M	Inn	NO	Runs	HS	Avg	100	50	Ct	St	Balls	Runs	Wkts	Avg	BB	5I	10M
Test																	
FC	6	8	2	306	116	51.00	1	1	4	-	882	404	21	19.23	6-55	2	-
ODI																	
List A	14	12	0	258	68	21.50	-	2	2	-	637	459	20	22.95	4-29	-	
20/20 Int																	
20/20	13	13	6	294	55	42.00	-	1	-	-	287	368	15	24.53	3-27	-	

Career Performances

	M	Inn	NO	Runs	HS	Avg	100	50	Ct	St	Balls	Runs	Wkts	Avg	BB	5I	10M
Test	21	34	4	900	136	30.00	3	1	14	-	3015	1402	39	35.94	4-50	-	-
FC	151	234	29	6557	204 *	31.98	9	33	126	-	25099	13048	515	25.33	8-61	21	3
ODI	143	110	26	1521	67	18.10	-	3	37	-	6242	4813	123	39.13	6-18	3	
List A	268	214	44	3599	101 *	21.17	2	14	80	-	11888	9065	289	31.36	6-18	5	
20/20 Int																	
20/20	48	47	16	978	65 *	31.54	-	3	8	-	937	1169	52	22.48	4-20	-	

5. Which Australian spinner conceded 298 runs when England made 903-7 in 1938?

BAILEY, S.P. Northamptonshire

Name: Shaun Peter Bailey
Role: Right-hand bat, right-arm fast-medium bowler
Born: 19 February 1990, Norwich, Norfolk
Nickname: Bud
County debut: 2008
Education: Hockham School; Wayland Community High School
Career highlights to date: "When I got a hat-trick'
Extras: Made his cricketing debut for East Anglian Premier League side Swardeston at the age of 13. Played for Norfolk U15's and U17's 2005; for Norfolk 2006; for Northamptonshire U17's 2007; for Northamptonshire 2nd XI 2005-08
Best batting: 15 Northamptonshire v Essex, Chelmsford, 2008
Best bowling: 2-119 Northamptonshire v Essex, Chelmsford, 2008

2008 Season

	M	Inn	NO	Runs	HS	Avg	100	50	Ct	St	Balls	Runs	Wkts	Avg	BB	5I	10M
Test																	
FC	1	2	0	18	15	9.00	-	-	1	-	156	127	3	42.33	2-119	-	-
ODI																	
List A																	
20/20 Int																	
20/20																	

Career Performances

	M	Inn	NO	Runs	HS	Avg	100	50	Ct	St	Balls	Runs	Wkts	Avg	BB	5I	10M
Test																	
FC	1	2	0	18	15	9.00	-	-	1	-	156	127	3	42.33	2-119	-	-
ODI																	
List A																	
20/20 Int																	
20/20																	

BAIRSTOW, J.M. Yorkshire

Name: Jonathan Mark Bairstow
Role: Right-hand bat, right-arm bowler, wicket-keeper
Born: 26 September 1989, Bradford, Yorkshire
County debut: No first-team appearance
Parents: David (deceased) and Janet
Family links with cricket: Father, David Bairstow, who kept wicket for Yorkshire and England
Education: St Peter's School, York
Other sports played: Rugby (Yorkshire Schools U16s), Football (Leeds Utd U15s)
Extras: Represented Yorkshire Schools from U11 through to U15. Member of Yorkshire's ECB U15 Championship and Cup double side 2005. Selected for North of England at various levels. Selected for England U17s. Young Wisden Schools Cricketer of the Year 2008. Signed a two-year contract in September 2008 after averaging over 60 in the season's 2nd XI championship

6. How many double centuries did Don Bradman score in the 1930 Ashes series?

BALAC, M. Warwickshire

Name: Michael Balac
Role: Right-hand batsman, wicket-keeper,
Born: 3 August 1988, Nuneaton, Warwickshire
County debut: 2008
Extras: Played for Leamington CC 2005-07; for Warwickshire 2nd XI 2008. Secured six catches on his first-class debut v Bangladesh A, his only first-class game in 2008
Best batting: 11 Warwickshire v Bangladesh A, Edgbaston, 2008

2008 Season

	M	Inn	NO	Runs	HS	Avg	100	50	Ct	St	Balls	Runs	Wkts	Avg	BB	5I	10M
Test																	
FC	1	1	0	11	11	11.00	-	-	6	-	0	0	0		-	-	-
ODI																	
List A																	
20/20 Int																	
20/20																	

Career Performances

	M	Inn	NO	Runs	HS	Avg	100	50	Ct	St	Balls	Runs	Wkts	Avg	BB	5I	10M
Test																	
FC	1	1	0	11	11	11.00	-	-	6	-	0	0	0		-	-	-
ODI																	
List A																	
20/20 Int																	
20/20																	

BALCOMBE, D. J. Hampshire

Name: David John Balcombe
Role: Right-hand bat, right-arm fast-medium bowler
Born: 24 December 1984, City of London
Height: 6ft 4in
Nickname: Balcs, Spalko
County debut: 2006 (one-day), 2007 (first-class)
Place in batting averages: 248th av. 12.14 (2007 185th av. 24.00)
Place in bowling averages: (2007 135th av. 47.90)
Parents: Peter and Elizabeth
Marital status: Single
Education: St John's School, Leatherhead; Durham University
Qualifications: 9 GCSEs, 3 A-levels, BA (Hons) 2.1, Level 1 coaching award
Overseas tours: Surrey Academy to Perth 2004; MCC A to Canada 2005; Hampshire to Cape Town 2007
Overseas teams played for: Midland-Guildford CC, Western Australia 2003-04; Mount Lawley CC, Western Australia 2005-06
Career highlights to date: 'Taking maiden first-class five-wicket return against Durham CCC. Making my Championship and Pro40 debuts for Hampshire'
Cricket moments to forget: 'Bowling two overs for 35 in a one-day game'
Cricket superstitions: 'Left equipment on first – i.e. left shoe, left pad'
Cricketers particularly admired: Shane Warne
Young players to look out for: Robbie Williams, Richard Morris, Chris Benham, Liam Dawson
Other sports followed: Rugby (London Wasps), football (Arsenal)
Favourite band: Five for Fighting, Kings of Leon
Relaxations: 'Sleeping, films'
Extras: Played for Durham UCCE 2005-07 (awarded cap for performances in 2005). Represented British Universities 2006. Recorded best match figures by a Hampshire bowler in a 2nd XI game – 14-88 (8-40/6-48) v Gloucestershire 2nd XI at The Rose Bowl 2007
Opinions on cricket: 'It is continuously moving forward and developing. It is an exciting time to be involved in the game – with new regulations allowing only one overseas player and fewer non-qualified players, younger players will inevitably be given more opportunities.'
Best batting: 73 DUCCE v Leicestershire, Leicester 2005
Best bowling: 5-112 DUCCE v Durham, Durham 2005

2008 Season

	M	Inn	NO	Runs	HS	Avg	100	50	Ct	St	Balls	Runs	Wkts	Avg	BB	5I	10M
Test																	
FC	6	10	3	85	20 *	12.14	-	-	1	-	679	412	9	45.77	2-1	-	-
ODI																	
List A	4	1	0	0	0	0.00	-	-	2	-	138	110	4	27.50	2-39	-	
20/20 Int																	
20/20																	

Career Performances

	M	Inn	NO	Runs	HS	Avg	100	50	Ct	St	Balls	Runs	Wkts	Avg	BB	5I	10M
Test																	
FC	18	27	6	356	73	16.95	-	1	6	-	2613	1732	36	48.11	5-112	1	-
ODI																	
List A	5	2	0	2	2	1.00	-	-	2	-	168	129	4	32.25	2-39	-	
20/20 Int																	
20/20	1	1	0	3	3	3.00	-	-	-	-	12	15	0		-	-	

BALLANCE, G. S. Yorkshire

Name: Gary Simon Ballance
Role: Left-hand top-order bat, occasional right-arm leg-spin bowler
Born: 22 November 1989, Harare, Zimbabwe
Nickname: Gazza
County debut: 2006 (one-day, Derbyshire) 2008 (Yorkshire)
Parents: Simon and Gail
Marital status: Single
Family links with cricket: 'Father – Zimbabwe Country Districts.' Is nephew of David Houghton, former captain of Zimbabwe
Education: Peterhouse, Zimbabwe; Harrow School
Overseas tours: Zimbabwe U19 to Sri Lanka (U19 World Cup) 2005-06
Career highlights to date: 'Making 73 for Derbyshire first team against Hampshire [2006]'
Cricket superstitions: None
Cricketers particularly admired: Andy Flower, Shane Warne

Other sports played: Golf, tennis, rugby
Other sports followed: Football (Liverpool)
Favourite band: Blink-182, The Killers
Relaxations: 'Watching TV'
Extras: Man of the Match v England U19 at Colombo in the U19 World Cup 2005-06 (3-21/47). Made Derbyshire one-day debut aged 16 v West Indies A in a 50-over match at Derby 2006, scoring 48; made Pro40 debut v Hampshire at The Rose Bowl 2006, scoring 73. Left Derbyshire at the end of the 2007 season and joined Yorkshire for 2008
Best batting: 5 Yorkshire v Kent, Canterbury, July 2008

2008 Season

	M	Inn	NO	Runs	HS	Avg	100	50	Ct	St	Balls	Runs	Wkts	Avg	BB	5I	10M
Test																	
FC	1	2	0	6	5	3.00	-	-	-	-	0	0	0		-	-	-
ODI																	
List A																	
20/20 Int																	
20/20																	

Career Performances

	M	Inn	NO	Runs	HS	Avg	100	50	Ct	St	Balls	Runs	Wkts	Avg	BB	5I	10M
Test																	
FC	1	2	0	6	5	3.00	-	-	-	-	0	0	0		-	-	-
ODI																	
List A	4	4	0	129	73	32.25	-	1	1	-	0	0	0		-	-	
20/20 Int																	
20/20																	

BANERJEE, V. Gloucestershire

Name: Vikram Banerjee
Role: Left-hand bat, left-arm orthodox spin bowler
Born: 20 March 1984, Bradford
Height: 6ft **Weight:** 11st
Nickname: Banners
County debut: 2006
County cap: 2006
Place in bowling averages: (2007 133rd av. 45.30)
Parents: Biren and Shyamli
Marital status: Single
Education: King Edward's School, Birmingham; Cambridge University
Qualifications: 12 GCSEs, 4 A-levels, BA (Econ), coaching Level 2
Overseas tours: ECB Emerging Players to Mumbai (World Cricket Academy) 2006-07
Overseas teams played for: Shivaji Park Gymkhana, Mumbai 2003
Career highlights to date: 'Winning at Lord's in 2005 Varsity Match. First wicket for Gloucestershire (Mark Butcher)'
Cricket moments to forget: 'Innings defeat to Somerset on debut'
Cricket superstitions: 'Right pad on first'
Cricketers particularly admired: Viv Richards, Sachin Tendulkar, Bishan Bedi
Other sports followed: Football (Aston Villa)
Favourite band: U2, Status Quo, Sting, Jack Johnson, Coldplay
Relaxations: 'Movies, reading, spending time with mates'
Extras: Cambridge Blue 2004-06. Played for Cambridge UCCE 2006. ECB National Skills Set. NBC Denis Compton Award for the most promising young Gloucestershire player 2006
Best batting: 29 Cambridge University v Oxford University, Fenner's 2005
Best bowling: 4-38 Gloucestershire v Northamptonshire, Gloucester 2007

2008 Season

	M	Inn	NO	Runs	HS	Avg	100	50	Ct	St	Balls	Runs	Wkts	Avg	BB	5I	10M
Test																	
FC	6	6	1	22	15	4.40	-	-	1	-	814	457	7	65.28	3-31	-	-
ODI																	
List A																	
20/20 Int																	
20/20																	

Career Performances

	M	Inn	NO	Runs	HS	Avg	100	50	Ct	St	Balls	Runs	Wkts	Avg	BB	5I	10M
Test																	
FC	26	36	14	207	29	9.40	-	-	6	-	4776	2724	49	55.59	4-38	-	-
ODI																	
List A																	
20/20 Int																	
20/20																	

BANKS, O. A. C. — Somerset

Name: Omari Ahmed Clemente Banks
Role: Right-hand bat, right-arm off-spin bowler; all-rounder
Born: 17 July 1982, Anguilla, Leeward Islands
County debut: 2001 (Leicestershire), 2008 (one-day, Somerset)
Test debut: 2002-03
ODI debut: 2002-03
Overseas tours: West Indies U19 to England 2001; West Indies A to England 2006; West Indies to Zimbabwe and South Africa 2003-04, to England 2004, to Sri Lanka 2005, to Pakistan 2006-07
Overseas teams played for: Leeward Islands 2000-01 – ; played for Anguilla in Stanford Twenty20 in 2007-08
Extras: Played for Leicestershire 2nd XI in 2000 and 2001, making one first-class appearance for the county against the Pakistani tourists at Leicester. First cricketer from the island of Anguilla to play Test cricket for West Indies. In only his second Test, scored 47* as West Indies chased down a Test record fourth innings target of 418 in the fourth Test v Australia in St John's 2002-03. His awards include Man of the Match v Jamaica in the Busta Cup 2000-01 (7-70/3-78 plus 43) and v Jamaica in the Carib Beer Cup 2006-07 (100 plus 2-88/1-3), both at grounds on St Kitts. Man of the Match v Jamaica (62/2-46) and v West Indies U19 (2-18/55*), both in Guyana in the KFC Cup 2007-08. Is not considered an overseas player
Best batting: 100 Leeward Islands v Jamaica, Cayon 2006-07
Best bowling: 7-70 Leeward Islands v Jamaica, Molyneaux 2000-01

2008 Season	M	Inn	NO	Runs	HS	Avg	100	50	Ct	St	Balls	Runs	Wkts	Avg	BB	5I	10M
Test																	
FC																	
ODI																	
List A	7	6	3	59	28	19.66	-	-	-	-	216	208	5	41.60	2-43	-	
20/20 Int																	
20/20	4	4	2	91	50 *	45.50	-	1	-	-	66	92	2	46.00	1-30	-	

Career Performances	M	Inn	NO	Runs	HS	Avg	100	50	Ct	St	Balls	Runs	Wkts	Avg	BB	5I	10M
Test	10	16	4	318	50 *	26.50	-	1	6	-	2401	1367	28	48.82	4-87	-	-
FC	59	91	14	1832	100	23.79	1	10	33	-	11995	6072	165	36.80	7-70	6	1
ODI	5	5	0	83	33	16.60	-	-	-	-	270	189	7	27.00	2-24	-	
List A	55	48	15	1009	77 *	30.57	-	7	12	-	2479	1773	66	26.86	4-23	-	
20/20 Int																	
20/20	5	5	2	135	50 *	45.00	-	1	-	-	84	130	3	43.33	1-30	-	

BARKER, K. Warwickshire

Name: Keith Hubert Douglas Barker
Role: Left-hand bat, left-arm medium-pace bowler
Born: 21 October 1986, Manchester
County debut: No first-team appearances
Family links with cricket: Son of Keith Henderson Barker (British Guiana and Natal); half-brother of Andrew Barker (Enfield and Accrington) and Gary Barker (Enfield and Lancashire 2nd XI)
Other sports played: Football (with Blackburn Rovers, Rochdale and Northwich Victoria)
Extras: Clive Lloyd is his godfather; Former England U20 footballer. Turned down a contract with Lancashire aged 16 because Blackburn Rovers had offered terms the previous week. Released by Blackburn Rovers in 2008; made debut for Warwickshire 2nd XI v Hampshire, Sutton Coldfield, June 2008 and scored 118 in the team's second innings. Signed a two-year contract with Warwickshire in August 2008

BATTY, G. J. — Worcestershire

Name: Gareth Jon Batty
Role: Right-hand bat, off-spin bowler, county vice-captain; all-rounder
Born: 13 October 1977, Bradford, Yorkshire
Height: 5ft 11in **Weight:** 12st 7lbs
Nickname: Batts, Boris, Red, Terry, Stuta
County debut: 1997 (Yorkshire), 1998 (one-day, Surrey), 1999 (first-class, Surrey), 2002 (Worcestershire)
County colours: 2002 (Worcestershire)
Test debut: 2003-04
ODI debut: 2002-03
50 wickets in a season: 2
Place in batting averages: 124th av. 30.14 (2007 172nd av. 25.63)
Place in bowling averages: 76th av. 30.64 (2007 12th av. 40.07)
Parents: David and Rosemary
Marital status: Single
Family links with cricket: Father was Yorkshire Academy coach; brother played for Yorkshire and Somerset
Education: Bingley Grammar; Worcester College
Qualifications: 9 GCSEs, BTEC Art and Design, coaching certificate
Career outside cricket: Property development and coaching
Overseas tours: England U15 to South Africa 1993; England U19 to Zimbabwe 1995-96, to Pakistan 1996-97; ECB National Academy to Australia and Sri Lanka 2002-03; England to Bangladesh and Sri Lanka 2003-04, to West Indies 2003-04, to Zimbabwe (one-day series) 2004-05, to South Africa 2004-05, to India 2005-06 (one-day series); England A to West Indies 2005-06; England Lions to New Zealand 2009
Overseas teams played for: Marist Newman, Australia 1999
Career highlights to date: 'Making England debut'
Cricket moments to forget: 'Whenever we lose'
Cricket superstitions: None
Cricketers particularly admired: Adam Hollioake, Alec Stewart 'to name but two'
Young players to look out for: Daryl Mitchell, Steve Davies
Other sports played: Golf, rugby
Other sports followed: Rugby league (Leeds Rhinos), 'all sports'
Favourite band: Rick Astley
Relaxations: 'Property and spending time with family and friends'
Extras: *Daily Telegraph* Young Player of the Year 1993. Surrey Supporters' Club Most Improved Player Award 2001. Surrey CCC Young Player of the Year Award

2001. ECB 2nd XI Player of the Year 2001. Leading all-rounder in the inaugural Twenty20 Cup 2003. Made Test debut in the first Test v Bangladesh at Dhaka 2003-04, taking a wicket (Alok Kapali) with his third ball. Vice-captain of Worcestershire since 2005. ECB National Academy 2005-06. Selected for England Lions in 2009

Opinions on cricket: 'Wickets in general are batter-friendly. Would be good to see it evened out. Keep the kids interested at all costs.'

Best batting: 133 Worcestershire v Surrey, The Oval 2004

Best bowling: 7-52 Worcestershire v Northamptonshire, Northampton 2004

2008 Season

	M	Inn	NO	Runs	HS	Avg	100	50	Ct	St	Balls	Runs	Wkts	Avg	BB	5I	10M
Test																	
FC	15	20	6	422	66	30.14	-	3	6	-	2325	1042	34	30.64	5-33	2	-
ODI																	
List A	16	13	5	219	52	27.37	-	1	5	-	576	476	14	34.00	4-14	-	
20/20 Int																	
20/20	6	6	2	55	29 *	13.75	-	-	3	-	132	143	5	28.60	1-11	-	

Career Performances

	M	Inn	NO	Runs	HS	Avg	100	50	Ct	St	Balls	Runs	Wkts	Avg	BB	5I	10M
Test	7	8	1	144	38	20.57	-	-	3	-	1394	733	11	66.63	3-55	-	-
FC	122	186	36	4061	133	27.07	2	21	81	-	23750	11452	352	32.53	7-52	15	1
ODI	7	5	1	6	3	1.50	-	-	4	-	362	294	4	73.50	2-40	-	
List A	166	133	30	1818	83 *	17.65	-	5	60	-	6443	4858	143	33.97	4-14	-	
20/20 Int																	
20/20	39	36	8	416	87	14.85	-	1	12	-	678	922	30	30.73	3-38	-	

7. Which England and Australian captains opposed each other on either side of World War Two?

BATTY, J. N. Surrey

Name: Jonathan Neil Batty
Role: Right-hand bat, wicket-keeper
Born: 18 April 1974, Chesterfield
Height: 5ft 10in **Weight:** 11st 6lbs
Nickname: JB
County debut: 1997
County cap: 2001
1000 runs in a season: 1
50 dismissals in a season: 4
Place in batting averages: 130th av. 29.33 (2007 51st av. 43.86)
Parents: Roger and Jill
Marital status: Single
Family links with cricket: Father played club cricket to a high standard
Education: Wheatley Park; Repton; Durham University (St Chad's); Keble College, Oxford
Qualifications: 10 GCSEs, 4 A-levels, BSc (Hons) in Natural Sciences, Diploma in Social Studies (Oxon)
Overseas tours: Repton School to Netherlands 1991; MCC to Bangladesh 1996; Surrey to South Africa 1997, 2001
Overseas teams played for: Mount Lawley CC, Perth 1997-2002
Career highlights to date: 'Winning three County Championships'
Cricket moments to forget: 'None!'
Cricketers particularly admired: David Gower, Alec Stewart, Jack Russell
Other sports played: Golf, squash
Other sports followed: Football (Nottingham Forest)
Relaxations: Reading, listening to music, movies
Extras: Represented Combined Universities 1994, 1995. Oxford Blue 1996. Surrey Supporters' Club Most Improved Player 2002, 2003. BBC Radio London Listeners' Cricketer of the Year 2003. Became second wicket-keeper (after Kent's Steve Marsh in 1991) to take eight catches in an innings (a new Surrey record) and score a century (129) in the same match, v Kent at The Oval 2004. Achieved double of 1000 (1025) runs and 50 (53) dismissals in first-class cricket 2006. Captain of Surrey 2004
Best batting: 168* Surrey v Essex, Chelmsford 2003
Best bowling: 1-21 Surrey v Lancashire, Old Trafford 2000

2008 Season

	M	Inn	NO	Runs	HS	Avg	100	50	Ct	St	Balls	Runs	Wkts	Avg	BB	5I	10M
Test																	
FC	16	25	4	616	136 *	29.33	2	3	34	4	0	0	0		-	-	-
ODI																	
List A	15	14	2	341	63	28.41	-	1	19	6	0	0	0		-	-	
20/20 Int																	
20/20	8	8	1	122	42 *	17.42	-	-	1	2	0	0	0		-	-	

Career Performances

	M	Inn	NO	Runs	HS	Avg	100	50	Ct	St	Balls	Runs	Wkts	Avg	BB	5I	10M
Test																	
FC	175	268	34	7851	168 *	33.55	18	37	454	60	78	61	1	61.00	1-21	-	-
ODI																	
List A	178	145	26	2726	158 *	22.90	1	13	185	33	0	0	0		-	-	
20/20 Int																	
20/20	50	43	14	589	59	20.31	-	2	31	18	0	0	0		-	-	

BEER, W. A. T. Sussex

Name: William (Will) Andrew Thomas Beer
Role: Right-hand bat, leg-spin bowler
Born: 8 October 1988, Crawley
Height: 5ft 9in **Weight:** 12st
Nickname: Ferret, Beero
County debut: 2008
Parents: Andrew and Sarah
Marital status: Single
Family links with cricket: 'Dad and Uncle Robin both played for Horsham 1st XI for many years'
Education: Reigate Grammar School
Qualifications: 3 A-levels
Off-season: 'Playing abroad, in Hobart'
Overseas teams played for: Western Province CC, Cape Town 2007-08, Lindisfarne Cricket Club, Hobart 2008-09
Career highlights to date: 'Five wickets v Hants in 2nd XI Championship 2007. Playing for England U17. 6-53 for England U19 v New Zealand 2008.'

Cricket moments to forget: 'Getting out first ball in first ever county game, for Sussex U10'
Cricket superstitions: None
Cricketers particularly admired: Shane Warne
Young players to look out for: Ben Brown, Matt Machan, Michael Thornely
Other sports played: Golf, squash (Sussex U15)
Other sports followed: Football (Manchester United), rugby, golf
Favourite band: Maroon 5
Relaxations: 'Listening to music'
Extras: Sussex Academy Player of the Year 2006
Best batting: 6* Sussex v MCC, Lord's, 2008
Best bowling: 1-18 Sussex v MCC, Lord's, 2008

2008 Season

	M	Inn	NO	Runs	HS	Avg	100	50	Ct	St	Balls	Runs	Wkts	Avg	BB	5I	10M
Test																	
FC	2	2	1	6	6 *	6.00	-	-	-	-	96	81	1	81.00	1-18	-	
ODI																	
List A																	
20/20 Int																	
20/20	4	4	2	22	17 *	11.00	-	-	-	-	84	105	3	35.00	2-32	-	

Career Performances

	M	Inn	NO	Runs	HS	Avg	100	50	Ct	St	Balls	Runs	Wkts	Avg	BB	5I	10M
Test																	
FC	2	2	1	6	6 *	6.00	-	-	-	-	96	81	1	81.00	1-18	-	-
ODI																	
List A																	
20/20 Int																	
20/20	4	4	2	22	17 *	11.00	-	-	-	-	84	105	3	35.00	2-32	-	

8. Who captained Australia in six Test series against England?

BELL, I. R. Warwickshire

Name: Ian Ronald Bell
Role: Right-hand bat, right-arm medium bowler
Born: 11 April 1982, Coventry
Height: 5ft 10in **Weight:** 11st
Nickname: Belly
County debut: 1999
County cap: 2001
Test debut: 2004
ODI debut: 2004-05
Twenty20 Int debut: 2006
1000 runs in a season: 2
1st-Class 200s: 3
Place in batting averages: 23rd av. 50.81 (2007 87th av. 37.76)
Parents: Terry and Barbara
Marital status: Single
Family links with cricket: Brother Keith played for England U18, Staffordshire and Warwickshire 2nd XI
Education: Princethorpe College, Rugby
Career highlights to date: 'The Ashes 2005'
Overseas tours: Warwickshire U19 to Cape Town 1998-99; England U19 to New Zealand 1998-99, to Malaysia and (U19 World Cup) Sri Lanka 1999-2000, to India 2000-01 (c); England A to West Indies 2000-01, to Sri Lanka 2004-05 (c); ECB National Academy to Australia 2001-02, to Sri Lanka 2002-03; England to Zimbabwe (one-day series) 2004-05, to South Africa 2004-05, to Pakistan 2005-06, to India 2005-06, to India (ICC Champions Trophy) 2006-07, to Australia 2006-07, to West Indies (World Cup) 2006-07, to Sri Lanka 2007-08, to New Zealand 2007-08, to India 2008-09, to West Indies 2008-09
Overseas teams played for: University of Western Australia, Perth 2003-04
Cricketers particularly admired: Dominic Ostler, Alec Stewart, Robin Smith
Young players to look out for: Chris Woakes
Other sports played: Football (was at Coventry City School of Excellence), rugby, golf
Other sports followed: Football (Aston Villa), rugby union (Northampton Saints)
Relaxations: Golf, listening to music
Extras: Played for England U14, U15, U16, U17; captained England U19. NBC Denis Compton Award for the most promising young Warwickshire player 1999, 2000, 2001. Gray-Nicolls Trophy for Best Young Schools Cricketer 2000. Cricket Society's Most Promising Young Cricketer of the Year Award 2001. Recorded maiden one-day century (125) and maiden one-day five-wicket return (5-41) v Essex at Chelmsford in the NCL

2003. Scored maiden first-class double century (262*) v Sussex at Horsham 2004, in the process setting with Tony Frost (135*) a new Warwickshire record partnership for the seventh wicket (289*). Cricket Writers' Club Young Cricketer of the Year 2004. PCA Young Player of the Year award 2004. ECB National Academy 2004-05. Made ODI debut in the first ODI v Zimbabwe at Harare 2004-05, scoring 75 and winning Man of the Match award. His other match and series awards include Man of the Match in the fourth ODI v Pakistan at Trent Bridge 2006 (86*) and Player of the [ODI] Series v India 2007. Appointed MBE in 2006 New Year Honours as part of 2005 Ashes-winning England team. Recalled to the Test side for series v Pakistan 2006, scoring three hundreds (100*, 106*, 119) in successive Tests. ICC Emerging Player of the Year award 2006. Named as one of *Wisden*'s Five Cricketers of the Year 2008

Best batting: 262* Warwickshire v Sussex, Horsham 2004

Best bowling: 4-4 Warwickshire v Middlesex, Lord's 2004

2008 Season

	M	Inn	NO	Runs	HS	Avg	100	50	Ct	St	Balls	Runs	Wkts	Avg	BB	5I	10M
Test	7	11	1	377	199	37.70	1	1	5	-	0	0	0		-	-	-
FC	11	17	1	813	215	50.81	2	2	11	-	0	0	0		-	-	-
ODI	10	9	1	288	73	36.00	-	1	5	-	0	0	0		-	-	
List A	11	10	1	291	73	32.33	-	1	5	-	0	0	0		-	-	
20/20 Int	1	1	1	60	60 *		-	1	1	-	0	0	0		-	-	
20/20	2	2	1	102	60 *	102.00	-	1	1	-	0	0	0		-	-	

Career Performances

	M	Inn	NO	Runs	HS	Avg	100	50	Ct	St	Balls	Runs	Wkts	Avg	BB	5I	10M
Test	43	77	8	2923	199	42.36	8	19	41	-	108	76	1	76.00	1-33	-	-
FC	134	230	21	9157	262 *	43.81	23	49	92	-	2719	1490	47	31.70	4-4	-	-
ODI	75	72	6	2399	126 *	36.34	1	15	21	-	88	88	6	14.66	3-9	-	
List A	168	160	14	5154	137	35.30	3	38	54	-	1290	1138	33	34.48	5-41	1	
20/20 Int	5	5	1	109	60 *	27.25	-	1	4	-	0	0	0		-	-	
20/20	24	23	5	397	66 *	22.05	-	2	11	-	132	186	3	62.00	1-12	-	

BENHAM, C. C. Hampshire

Name: Christopher (Chris) Charles Benham
Role: Right-hand bat, right-arm off-spin bowler
Born: 24 March 1983, Frimley, Surrey
Height: 6ft 2in **Weight:** 'It varies'
Nickname: Cut-snake, Togo, Benoit, Benny
County debut: 2004
Place in batting averages: 135th av. 28.76 (2007 201st av. 22.28)
Parents: Frank and Sandie
Marital status: Single
Family links with cricket: 'Both older brothers, Nick and Andy, played local club cricket'
Education: Yateley Comprehensive School; Yateley Sixth Form College; Loughborough University
Qualifications: 10 GCSEs, 3 A-levels, BSc (Hons) 2.1 Sport and Exercise Science
Overseas tours: West of England U15 to West Indies 1998
Overseas teams played for: Perth CC 2004-05; Casey-South Melbourne 2007-08
Career highlights to date: '158 (off 130 balls) in Pro40 play-off match v Glamorgan at The Rose Bowl, September 2006, which we won to gain promotion to first division'
Cricket moments to forget: 'Getting a king pair in a pre-season friendly match against Essex in 2005'
Cricket superstitions: 'There's a few!'
Cricketers particularly admired: Ricky Ponting, Sachin Tendulkar, Shane Warne, John Crawley, Darren Lehmann, Mark Ramprakash
Young players to look out for: Benny Howell, Liam Dawson
Other sports played: Football (school, district and county sides; trials with Swindon and Crystal Palace), tennis, golf
Other sports followed: Football (Reading FC), 'follow all sports'
Favourite band: Newton Faulkner
Relaxations: 'Reading, music, PlayStation, "Champ Man"'
Extras: Played for ESCA U15 and England U16. Played for Loughborough UCCE 2002, 2004. Represented British Universities 2004. Scored 74 on Championship debut v Derbyshire at Derby 2004. NBC Denis Compton Award for the most promising young Hampshire player 2006. Scored 130-ball 158 v Glamorgan at The Rose Bowl in Pro40 play-off 2006, winning Man of the Match award.
Best batting: 95 Hampshire v Warwickshire, Rose Bowl 2006

2008 Season

	M	Inn	NO	Runs	HS	Avg	100	50	Ct	St	Balls	Runs	Wkts	Avg	BB	5I	10M
Test																	
FC	8	13	0	374	89	28.76	-	3	9	-	0	0	0	-	-	-	-
ODI																	
List A	13	12	2	338	68	33.80	-	2	7	-	0	0	0	-	-	-	-
20/20 Int																	
20/20	8	8	0	40	19	5.00	-	-	7	-	0	0	0	-	-	-	-

Career Performances

	M	Inn	NO	Runs	HS	Avg	100	50	Ct	St	Balls	Runs	Wkts	Avg	BB	5I	10M
Test																	
FC	35	58	1	1509	95	26.47	-	9	33	-	30	37	0	-	-	-	-
ODI																	
List A	37	35	3	1144	158	35.75	3	6	14	-	0	0	0	-	-	-	-
20/20 Int																	
20/20	23	21	2	292	59	15.36	-	1	11	-	0	0	0	-	-	-	-

BENKENSTEIN, D. M. — Durham

Name: Dale Martin Benkenstein
Role: Right-hand bat, right-arm off-break or medium bowler
Born: 9 June 1974, Harare, Zimbabwe
County debut: 2005
ODI debut: 1998-99
1000 runs in a season: 3
1st-Class 200s: 2
Place in batting averages: 49th av. 43.00 (2007 21st av. 55.56)
Family links with cricket: Father, Martin, and two brothers, Brett and Boyd, played first-class cricket
Education: Michaelhouse, KwaZulu-Natal
Overseas tours: KwaZulu-Natal to Australia (Champions Cup) 2000-01; South Africa U24 to Sri Lanka 1995; South Africa A to Sri Lanka 1998, to West Indies 2000; South Africa to Malaysia (Commonwealth Games) 1998-99, to Bangladesh (Wills International Cup) 1998-99, to New Zealand 1998-99, to Sri Lanka (ICC Champions Trophy) 2002-03, plus one-day series and tournaments in Kenya, India and Sharjah

Overseas teams played for: Natal/KwaZulu-Natal 1992-93 – 2003-04; Dolphins 2003-04 – 2006-07; Delhi Giants (ICL) 2007-08 –
Extras: Captained Natal Schools and South Africa Schools and has played ODI cricket for South Africa. One of *South African Cricket Annual*'s Five Cricketers of the Year 1997. Was captain of KwaZulu-Natal, leading the side to the double (SuperSport Series and Standard Bank Cup) in 1996-97 and 2001-02. Has won numerous domestic awards, including Man of the Match in the final of the Standard Bank Cup 2001-02 at Durban (77*) and in the final of the SuperSport Series 2005-06 at Durban (151). Scored century (125) v Middlesex at Lord's 2006, in the process sharing with Gareth Breese (110) in a new record fifth-wicket partnership for Durham (222). Scored century (151) v Yorkshire at Headingley 2006, in the process sharing with Ottis Gibson (155) in a new record seventh-wicket partnership for Durham (315). Captain of Durham since 2006. Stood down as captain at the end of 2008 season in favour of Will Smith. Contracted to Durham until 2011. Is not considered an overseas player
Best batting: 259 KwaZulu-Natal v Northerns, Durban 2001-02
Best bowling: 4-16 Dolphins v Warriors, Durban 2005-06

2008 Season

	M	Inn	NO	Runs	HS	Avg	100	50	Ct	St	Balls	Runs	Wkts	Avg	BB	5I	10M
Test																	
FC	15	23	4	817	110	43.00	1	7	5	-	150	60	1	60.00	1-13	-	-
ODI																	
List A	16	14	1	399	80 *	30.69	-	3	8	-	300	268	7	38.28	2-50	-	
20/20 Int																	
20/20	11	10	4	239	48 *	39.83	-	-	2	-	12	13	0		-	-	

Career Performances

	M	Inn	NO	Runs	HS	Avg	100	50	Ct	St	Balls	Runs	Wkts	Avg	BB	5I	10M
Test																	
FC	191	291	37	11733	259	46.19	28	63	129	-	6251	3059	85	35.98	4-16	-	-
ODI	23	20	3	305	69	17.94	-	1	3	-	65	44	4	11.00	3-5	-	
List A	256	229	55	6141	107 *	35.29	1	36	94	-	2963	2465	83	29.69	4-16	-	
20/20 Int																	
20/20	44	42	9	860	56 *	26.06	-	2	15	-	264	339	14	24.21	3-10	-	

9. Which England batsman scored seven centuries against Australia between 1964 and 1981?

BENNING, J. G. E. Surrey

Name: James Graham Edward Benning
Role: Right-hand bat, right-arm medium bowler; batting all-rounder
Born: 4 May 1983, Mill Hill, London
Height: 5ft 11in **Weight:** 13st
Nickname: Benno
County debut: 2002 (one-day), 2003 (first-class)
Place in batting averages: 205th av. 19.87 (2007 160th av. 27.70)
Parents: Sandy and David
Marital status: Single
Family links with cricket: 'Dad played for Middlesex'
Education: Caterham School
Qualifications: 12 GCSEs, 3 AS-levels
Overseas tours: Surrey YC to Barbados 1999-2000, to Sri Lanka 2002
Overseas teams played for: North Dandenong, Australia 2001-02
Cricket moments to forget: 'Dropping two catches in front of a lively crowd at Canterbury, live on Sky'
Cricket superstitions: 'Order in which I put my kit on'
Cricketers particularly admired: Alec Stewart, Adam Hollioake
Other sports played: Rugby, football
Other sports followed: Football (Watford)
Favourite band: 'Listen to almost all music apart from thrash metal'
Relaxations: 'Going to the gym, music, spending time around friends'
Extras: Played for England U15-U19. First recipient of Ben Hollioake Scholarship. NBC Denis Compton Award for the most promising young Surrey player 2003. Scored maiden Championship century from 100 balls (finishing with 112) v Gloucestershire at The Oval 2006 on his 23rd birthday. Carried bat for 146-ball 189* as Surrey fell two short of Gloucestershire's 339-8 at Bristol in the C&G 2006. Scored 134-ball 152 v Gloucestershire at The Oval in the Friends Provident 2007, in the process sharing with Alistair Brown (176) in a Surrey record one-day partnership (294) as the county posted a world record List A total of 496-4
Best batting: 128 Surrey v OUCCE, The Parks 2004
Best bowling: 3-57 Surrey v Kent, Tunbridge Wells 2005

2008 Season

	M	Inn	NO	Runs	HS	Avg	100	50	Ct	St	Balls	Runs	Wkts	Avg	BB	5I	10M
Test																	
FC	6	8	0	159	69	19.87	-	1	1	-	264	144	1	144.00	1-41	-	
ODI																	
List A	15	15	0	498	106	33.20	1	3	7	-	114	136	3	45.33	2-35	-	
20/20 Int																	
20/20	4	4	1	75	50 *	25.00	-	1	-	-	0	0	0			-	

Career Performances

	M	Inn	NO	Runs	HS	Avg	100	50	Ct	St	Balls	Runs	Wkts	Avg	BB	5I	10M
Test																	
FC	34	53	4	1601	128	32.67	4	7	14	-	1197	938	12	78.16	3-57	-	
ODI																	
List A	76	75	3	2458	189 *	34.13	3	15	27	-	968	1087	31	35.06	4-43	-	
20/20 Int																	
20/20	42	42	2	953	88	23.82	-	7	11	-	30	43	2	21.50	1-7	-	

BERG, G. K. Middlesex

Name: Gareth Kyle Berg
Role: Right-hand bat, right-arm fast-medium bowler; all-rounder
Born: 18 January 1981, Cape Town, South Africa
Height: 6ft **Weight:** 13st 5lbs
Nickname: Bergy, Ice, Ford
County debut: 2008
Parents: Gina and Richard
Wife and date of marriage: Kelly, 1 April 2004
Children: Roman, 17 July 2007
Family links with cricket: 'Grandfather put cricket bat and ball in my hand at early age of three years old'
Education: South African College School (SACS)
Qualifications: Level 2 cricket coach, Level 1 hockey coach, Level 1 rugby coach, Level 1 athletics coach
Career outside cricket: Professional sports coach in schools
Career highlights to date: 'Playing alongside Hansie Cronje and Shaun Pollock in a friend's benefit game'

Cricket moments to forget: 'Being left out of South Africa U15 World Cup squad one week before the World Cup in England'
Cricket superstitions: 'Always put my right boot and pad on first. Look at the sun when stepping on to the field'
Cricketers particularly admired: Steve Waugh, Herschelle Gibbs
Young players to look out for: Steven Finn
Other sports played: Football (Western Province), rugby
Other sports followed: Football (Man Utd 'since three years old')
Favourite band: Red Hot Chili Peppers, Oasis, Beatles, Dean Martin
Relaxations: 'Surfing, sleeping'
Extras: Played for Western Province Academy and Western Province B. Has played for Northamptonshire 2nd XI and Middlesex 2nd XI in the 2nd XI Championship. In his first one-day game for the county in April 2008, he took four wickets (against Surrey).
Opinions on cricket: 'Love all the new formats that are coming out, which allow more specialist players to shine! Specialist forms of the game!'
Best batting: 35 Middlesex v Essex, Lord's, 2008
Best bowling: 3-38 Middlesex v Essex, Lord's, 2008

2008 Season

	M	Inn	NO	Runs	HS	Avg	100	50	Ct	St	Balls	Runs	Wkts	Avg	BB	5I	10M
Test																	
FC	3	5	0	118	35	23.60	-	-	1	-	312	171	5	34.20	3-38	-	-
ODI																	
List A	6	5	1	92	65	23.00	-	1	1	-	186	207	7	29.57	4-50	-	
20/20 Int																	
20/20																	

Career Performances

	M	Inn	NO	Runs	HS	Avg	100	50	Ct	St	Balls	Runs	Wkts	Avg	BB	5I	10M
Test																	
FC	3	5	0	118	35	23.60	-	-	1	-	312	171	5	34.20	3-38	-	-
ODI																	
List A	6	5	1	92	65	23.00	-	1	1	-	186	207	7	29.57	4-50	-	
20/20 Int																	
20/20																	

BIRCH, D. J. Derbyshire

Name: Daniel (Dan) John Birch
Role: Left-hand bat, right-arm medium bowler
Born: 21 January 1981, Nottingham
Height: 6ft 3in **Weight:** 16st
Nickname: Birchy
County debut: 2007
Place in batting averages: 97th av. 34.31 (2007 112th av. 33.71)
Marital status: Single
Family links with cricket: 'Dad John Birch played for Notts CCC in 1970s and 1980s and was [Notts] manager'
Education: Kimberley Comprehensive
Career outside cricket: 'Manager and coach at John Birch Sports Centre Ltd'
Overseas teams played for: Frankston Peninsula CC, Melbourne 2002-03
Cricketers particularly admired: Shane Warne, Brian Lara
Other sports followed: Football (Nottingham Forest)
Relaxations: 'Weight training, fishing, pub'
Extras: Scored century (130) on first-class debut v Cambridge UCCE at Fenner's 2007. Scored Derbyshire Premier League record 224* for Sandiacre v Alvaston & Boulton 2007. Scored over 800 runs in all competitions 2008. Signed new one-year contract in October 2008
Best batting: 130 Derbyshire v CUCCE, Fenner's 2007

2008 Season

	M	Inn	NO	Runs	HS	Avg	100	50	Ct	St	Balls	Runs	Wkts	Avg	BB	5I	10M
Test																	
FC	12	20	1	652	77	34.31	-	3	6	-	0	0	0		-	-	-
ODI																	
List A	8	7	0	170	76	24.28	-	1	1	-	0	0	0		-	-	
20/20 Int																	
20/20	10	9	2	108	25	15.42	-	-	2	-	0	0	0		-	-	

Career Performances

	M	Inn	NO	Runs	HS	Avg	100	50	Ct	St	Balls	Runs	Wkts	Avg	BB	5I	10M
Test																	
FC	16	27	1	888	130	34.15	1	4	7	-	0	0	0		-	-	-
ODI																	
List A	16	15	0	369	76	24.60	-	2	3	-	0	0	0		-	-	
20/20 Int																	
20/20	11	10	2	116	25	14.50	-	-	2	-	0	0	0		-	-	

BLACKWELL, I. D. — Durham

Name: Ian David Blackwell
Role: Left-hand bat, slow left-arm bowler; all-rounder/'team ball shiner'
Born: 10 June 1978, Chesterfield
Height: 6ft 2in
Nickname: Black Dog, Donk, Ying, Goatage**County debut:** 1997 (Derbyshire), 2000 (Somerset)
County cap: 2001 (Somerset)
Test debut: 2005-06
ODI debut: 2002-03
1000 runs in a season: 2
1st-Class 200s: 1
Place in batting averages: 39th av. 46.45 (2007 77th av. 39.23)
Place in bowling averages: 136th av. 44.45 (2007 63rd av. 29.65)
Parents: John and Marilyn
Wife and date of marriage: Elizabeth Rachel, 30 September 2006
Family links with cricket: 'Dad played for Derbyshire Over 50's.'
Education: Old Hall Primary; Manor School; Brookfield Community School
Qualifications: 9 GCSEs, 2 A-levels, Level 3 coaching award
Career outside cricket: 'None as yet'
Off-season: 'Training, playing golf'
Overseas tours: Somerset to Cape Town 2000, 2001; England VI to Hong Kong 2001; England to Sri Lanka (ICC Champions Trophy) 2002-03, to Australia 2002-03 (VB Series), to Africa (World Cup) 2002-03, to Bangladesh and Sri Lanka 2003-04 (one-day series), to West Indies 2003-04 (one-day series), to Pakistan 2005-06 (one-day series), to India 2005-06; ECB National Academy to Australia 2002-03
Overseas teams played for: Delacombe Park CC, Melbourne 1997, 1999; Spotswood CC, Melbourne

Career highlights to date: 'Playing for England. Winning the C&G Trophy 2001; winning the Twenty20 2005; promoted as champions of division two 2007'
Cricket moments to forget: 'All my noughts for England'
Cricket superstitions: 'Left pad first - always chew gum'
Cricketers particularly admired: Ricky Ponting, Graeme Smith, Jamie Cox, Marcus Trescothick, Andrew Caddick, Viv Richards, Ian Botham, Peter Trego
Young players to look out for: Liam Dawson, Dawid Malan, Adil Rashid
Other sports played: Golf (6 handicap), football (winter 5-a-side)
Other sports followed: Football (Chesterfield FC – 'Up the Spireites!')
Favourite band: The Ting Tings
Relaxations: 'PS3 and King.com'
Extras: Became first batsman in Championship history to score two centuries (103/122) in a match batting at No. 7, v Northants at Northampton 2001. Scored 134-ball double century (finishing with 247*) v Derbyshire at Taunton 2003, the fastest double century on record by an Englishman in terms of balls received. Won the Walter Lawrence Trophy 2005 (fastest first-class century of the season) for his 67-ball hundred (finishing with 107) v Derbyshire at Taunton. Captain of Somerset July 2005-2006, although absent injured for most of the 2006 season. Joined Durham for 2009
Opinions on cricket: 'Would like to see one of the league one-day competitions axed and the knockout cup brought back. If you play poorly, you're out and you play less cricket. If you keep winning, you don't mind the extra games. More Twenty20 cricket and day/night games.'
Best batting: 247* Somerset v Derbyshire, Taunton 2003
Best bowling: 7-90 Somerset v Glamorgan, Taunton 2004
7-90 Somerset v Nottinghamshire, Trent Bridge 2004

2008 Season

	M	Inn	NO	Runs	HS	Avg	100	50	Ct	St	Balls	Runs	Wkts	Avg	BB	5I	10M
Test																	
FC	17	25	1	1115	158	46.45	4	7	8	-	2406	978	22	44.45	4-74	-	-
ODI																	
List A	7	6	1	221	86 *	44.20	-	2	2	-	372	286	3	95.33	1-22	-	
20/20 Int																	
20/20	7	7	0	102	43	14.57	-	-	2	-	131	183	4	45.75	2-34	-	

Career Performances

	M	Inn	NO	Runs	HS	Avg	100	50	Ct	St	Balls	Runs	Wkts	Avg	BB	5I	10M
Test	1	1	0	4	4	4.00	-	-	-	-	114	71	0		-	-	-
FC	147	221	16	8154	247 *	39.77	21	41	55	-	21682	10076	239	42.15	7-90	7	-
ODI	34	29	2	403	82	14.92	-	1	8	-	1230	877	24	36.54	3-26	-	
List A	216	197	18	4951	134 *	27.65	3	30	55	-	7399	5912	162	36.49	5-26	1	
20/20 Int																	
20/20	30	29	5	498	82	20.75	-	1	10	-	577	694	23	30.17	4-26	-	

BLAIN, J. A. R. — Yorkshire

Name: John Angus Rae Blain
Role: Right-hand bat, right-arm fast-medium bowler
Born: 4 January 1979, Edinburgh, Scotland
Height: 6ft 2in **Weight:** 13st 7lbs
Nickname: Blainy, Haggis, William, JB
County debut: 1997 (Northamptonshire), 2004 (Yorkshire)
Parents: John and Elma
Marital status: Single
Education: Pencuik High School, Jewel and Esk Valley College
Qualifications: 8 GCSEs, 1 A-level, HNC Leisure and Recreation, Level 1 coaching award
Overseas tours: Northants CCC to Zimbabwe 1997, to Grenada 2001, 2002; Scotland U19 to Netherlands (International Youth Tournament) 1994-95, to Bermuda (International Youth Tournament) 1997, to South Africa (U19 World Cup) 1997-98 (captain); Scotland to Denmark (European Championships) 1996, to Malaysia (ICC Trophy) 1996-97, to Malaysia (Commonwealth Games) 1998-99, to Sharjah (World Cup warm-up) 1999, to Canada (ICC Trophy) 2001, to UAE (ICC Six Nations Challenge) 2003-04, to UAE (ICC Inter-Continental Cup) 2004, to Bangladesh (one-day series) 2006-07, to Kenya (including ICC World Cricket League) 2006-07, to Sharjah 2006-07, to West Indies (World Cup) 2006-07
Overseas teams played for: New Plymouth Old Boys, New Zealand 1998-99; Taranaki Cricket Association, New Zealand 1998-99
Career highlights to date: 'World Cup 1999, England. Signing for Yorkshire CCC'
Cricket moments to forget: 'Not qualifying for the 2003 World Cup, failing to qualify by losing the last match by six runs in Canada 2001; not qualifying for the Champions Trophy in England 2004, losing last game to the USA in Dubai 2004' (USA qualified for the Champions Trophy ahead of Scotland by virtue of a net run rate that was superior by just 0.028 runs)
Cricket superstitions: 'Keeping a tidy kitbag'
Cricketers particularly admired: Devon Malcolm, Darren Lehmann
Other sports played: Football (schoolboy forms with Hibernian FC and Falkirk FC, making youth and reserve team appearances)
Other sports followed: Rugby
Relaxations: 'Listening to music, going out for a beer; spending time with my girlfriend and going home to Scotland to see family; watching football, going to the gym, and sleeping!'

Extras: Has played for Scotland in first-class cricket and in the B&H and NatWest competitions; also played for Scottish Saltires in NCL. Took 5-24 on Sunday League debut for Northamptonshire v Derbyshire at Derby 1997. Represented Scotland in the 1999 World Cup, taking 10 wickets and finishing top of the strike rate chart for the tournament. Man of the Match in the final of the ICC Inter-Continental Cup v Canada in the UAE 2004, returning match figures of 7-55 (3-27/4-28). Released by Yorkshire at the end of the 2006 season. Has returned to Yorkshire for the 2009 season.
Best batting: 53 Scotland v Ireland, Aberdeen 2006
Best bowling: 6-42 Northamptonshire v Kent, Canterbury 2001

2008 Season

	M	Inn	NO	Runs	HS	Avg	100	50	Ct	St	Balls	Runs	Wkts	Avg	BB	5I	10M
Test																	
FC																	
ODI																	
List A	7	7	1	65	26	10.83	-	-	2	-	330	173	9	19.22	3-31	-	
20/20 Int																	
20/20																	

Career Performances

	M	Inn	NO	Runs	HS	Avg	100	50	Ct	St	Balls	Runs	Wkts	Avg	BB	5I	10M
Test																	
FC	42	47	16	495	93	15.96	-	2	12	-	5945	4266	120	35.55	6-42	4	-
ODI	31	23	6	241	30 *	14.17	-	-	6	-	1215	1062	38	27.94	5-22	1	
List A	95	59	23	542	32	15.05	-	-	22	-	3994	3336	126	26.47	5-22	3	
20/20 Int	6	3	1	4	3 *	2.00	-	-	1	-	120	108	6	18.00	2-23	-	
20/20	6	3	1	4	3 *	2.00	-	-	1	-	120	108	6	18.00	2-23	-	

10. How many runs did Don Bradman score on the first day of the Ashes Test at Headingley in 1930?

BLAKE, A. J. — Kent

Name: Alexander (<u>Alex</u>) James Blake
Role: Left-hand bat, right-arm fast-medium bowler; all-rounder
Born: 25 January 1989, Bromley, Kent
Height: 6ft 1in **Weight:** 13st 7lbs
Nickname: Blakey, Butler, Brakey
County debut: 2007 (one-day), 2008 (first-class)
Parents: Andrew and Michelle
Marital status: Single
Education: Hayes Secondary School; Leeds Metropolitan University
Qualifications: 8 GCSEs, 3 A-levels, Level 1 cricket coach, Level 1 hockey coach
Off-season: 'Studying for a BA (Hons) in Business Studies at Leeds Metropolitan University'
Overseas tours: England U19 to Malaysia 2006-07
Overseas teams played for: Balcatta CC, Perth 2007-08
Career highlights to date: 'Making my debut for Kent against Surrey in a Pro40 floodlit game on Sky Sports; taking my first Pro40 wicket v Glamorgan in 2007'
Cricket moments to forget: 'Being hit for three consecutive sixes by Inzamam-ul-Haq (Pro40 Kent v Yorkshire 2007)'
Cricket superstitions: 'Turn left at top of bowling mark'
Cricketers particularly admired: Brian Lara, Steve Waugh
Young players to look out for: James Goodman, Adam Ball
Other sports played: Hockey (HSBC 1st XI; Leeds Metropolitan University 1st XI)
Other sports followed: Football (Tottenham Hotspur)
Favourite band: Kings of Leon
Relaxations: 'FIFA, poker, Facebook'
Extras: Kent Academy Scholar of the Year 2005, 2006. Kent League Young Player of the Year 2007. Borough of Bromley Sports Personality of the Year 2007

2008 Season

	M	Inn	NO	Runs	HS	Avg	100	50	Ct	St	Balls	Runs	Wkts	Avg	BB	5I	10M
Test																	
FC	1	0	0	0	0		-	-	-	-	24	17	0		-	-	-
ODI																	
List A																	
20/20 Int																	
20/20																	

Career Performances

	M	Inn	NO	Runs	HS	Avg	100	50	Ct	St	Balls	Runs	Wkts	Avg	BB	5I	10M
Test																	
FC	1	0	0	0	0		-	-	-	-	24	17	0		-	-	-
ODI																	
List A	3	2	2	15	11 *		-	-	-	-	72	61	1	61.00	1-25	-	
20/20 Int																	
20/20																	

BOJE, N. Northamptonshire

Name: Nico (Nicky) Boje
Role: Left-hand bat, slow left-arm bowler; all-rounder, club captain
Born: 20 March 1973, Bloemfontein, South Africa
Nickname: Bodge
Height: 5ft 10in
County debut: 2002 (Nottinghamshire), 2007 (Northamptonshire)
Test debut: 1999-2000
ODI debut: 1995-96
Twenty20 Int debut: 2005-06
1st-Class 200s: 1
Place in batting averages: 63rd av. 40.25 (2007 61st av. 41.83)
Place in bowling averages: 108th av. 36.18 (2007 23rd av. 23.87)
Family links with cricket: Older brother Eduard (E.H.L.) Boje played for Orange Free State 1989-90 – 1990-91
Education: Grey College, Bloemfontein
Overseas tours: South Africa A to Zimbabwe 1994-95, to England 1996, to Sri Lanka 1998-99 (vc), to Australia 2002-03; South Africa U24 to Sri Lanka 1995-96; South Africa to Zimbabwe 1995-96 (one-day series), to India 1996-97, to Bangladesh (Wills International Cup) 1998-99, to New Zealand 1998-99, to UK, Ireland and Netherlands (World Cup) 1999, to India 1999-2000, to Sri Lanka 2000, to Kenya (ICC Knockout Trophy) 2000-01, to West Indies 2000-01, to Australia 2001-02, to Sri Lanka (ICC Champions Trophy) 2002-03, to New Zealand 2003-04, to Sri Lanka 2004, to England (ICC Champions Trophy) 2004, to West Indies 2004-05, to Australia 2005-06, to Sri Lanka 2006, plus other one-day series and tournaments in Sharjah, Australia, Singapore, Morocco and England; South Africa VI to Hong Kong 2006 (c)

Overseas teams played for: Orange Free State/Free State 1990-91 – 2002-03; Eagles 2003-04 – 2006-07; Hyderabad Heroes (ICL) 2007-08 –
Other sports played: Rugby, tennis
Extras: Represented South Africa Schools 1989-91. Attended South Africa Academy. One of *South African Cricket Annual*'s five Cricketers of the Year 2001. Represented South Africa in the 2002-03 World Cup. Represented African XI in the Afro-Asia Cup 2005-06. His series and match awards include Man of the [ODI] Series v New Zealand 2000-01 (had scores of 105*, 64 and 129 in the first three ODIs), Man of the Match in the second Test v India at Bangalore 1999-2000 (85 as nightwatchman plus 5-83 in India's second innings) and Man of the Match in the seventh ODI v Australia at Cape Town 2001-02 (49/5-21); Man of the Match in the final of the 2006 Hong Kong Sixes. Was Nottinghamshire's overseas player in 2002. Retired from international cricket in December 2006. Was a temporary overseas player with Northamptonshire during the 2007 season as a replacement for Johannes van der Wath; returned for 2008 as a non-overseas player. Scored century (125), then followed up with second innings figures of 6-110 v Leicestershire at Leicester 2007.
Best batting: 226* Northamptonshire v Worcestershire, Wantage Road, 2008
Best bowling: 8-93 Eagles v Dolphins, Durban, 2006

2008 Season

	M	Inn	NO	Runs	HS	Avg	100	50	Ct	St	Balls	Runs	Wkts	Avg	BB	5I	10M
Test																	
FC	13	17	1	644	226 *	40.25	2	1	9	-	2405	1194	33	36.18	4-26	-	-
ODI																	
List A	11	10	1	147	59	16.33	-	1	3	-	418	310	15	20.66	4-12	-	
20/20 Int																	
20/20	11	6	2	115	58 *	28.75	-	1	3	-	214	248	10	24.80	2-19	-	

Career Performances

	M	Inn	NO	Runs	HS	Avg	100	50	Ct	St	Balls	Runs	Wkts	Avg	BB	5I	10M
Test	43	62	10	1312	85	25.23	-	4	18	-	8620	4265	100	42.65	5-62	3	-
FC	188	278	49	7703	226 *	33.63	8	43	113	-	39070	17068	532	32.08	8-93	22	2
ODI	115	71	18	1414	129	26.67	2	4	33	-	4541	3415	96	35.57	5-21	1	
List A	258	182	46	3526	129	25.92	2	14	78	-	10986	7858	247	31.81	5-21	1	
20/20 Int	1	0	0	0	0		-	-	-	-	24	27	1	27.00	1-27	-	
20/20	30	20	7	382	58 *	29.38	-	2	8	-	544	660	24	27.50	3-31	-	

BOND, S. E. Hampshire

Name: Shane Edward Bond
Role: Right-hand bat, right-arm fast bowler
Born: 7 June 1975, Christchurch, New Zealand
Height: 6ft 2in
Nickname: Bondy
County debut: 2002 (Warwickshire), 2008 (Hampshire)
Test debut: 2001-02
Parents: John and Judith
Wife: Tracey
Children: Katie, Sophie
Education: Papanui High School, Christchurch
Career outside cricket: Police officer
Overseas tours: New Zealand A to India (Buchi Babu Tournament) 2001-02; New Zealand to Australia 2001-02, to West Indies 2002, to Sri Lanka (ICC Champions Trophy) 2002-03, to Africa (World Cup) 2002-03, to Sri Lanka 2003, to England 2004, to Zimbabwe 2005-06, to South Africa (one-day series) 2005-06, to India 2006-07 (Champions Trophy), to Australia 2006-07 (one-day), to West Indies 2006-07 (World Cup), to South Africa 2007-08 (World Twenty20 and full tour)
Overseas teams played for: Canterbury (New Zealand) 1996-97 – ; Delhi Giants (ICL) 2007-08 –
Extras: One of New Zealand Cricket Almanack's two Players of the Year 2002. Was forced home from New Zealand's 2004 tour of England with a persistent back injury. Has won several international awards, including Man of the [VB] Series in Australia 2001-02 (21 wickets; av. 16.38), of the [Test] Series v West Indies 2002 and of the [Test] Series v Zimbabwe 2005-06. Warwickshire's overseas player during August 2002 as a locum for Shaun Pollock. Attended same school in Christchurch as Andrew Caddick. Made Twenty20 international debut v South Africa at Johannesburg 2005-06. New Zealand Cricketer of the Year 2007. Problems over his registration were eventually overcome at the start of the 2008 season and he made a huge impact in the four first-class games he played - 19 wickets in 4 matches was an excellent return. Lost his New Zealand contract in 2008 when signing for the Indian Cricket League
Best batting: 100 Canterbury v Northern Districts, Christchurch 2004-05
Best bowling: 7-66 for Hampshire v Sussex, Rose Bowl, 2008

2008 Season

	M	Inn	NO	Runs	HS	Avg	100	50	Ct	St	Balls	Runs	Wkts	Avg	BB	5I	10M
Test																	
FC	4	5	0	33	17	6.60	-	-	-	-	595	365	19	19.21	7-66	2	-
ODI																	
List A	3	1	0	0	0	0.00	-	-	-	-	108	68	4	17.00	3-11	-	
20/20 Int																	
20/20																	

Career Performances

	M	Inn	NO	Runs	HS	Avg	100	50	Ct	St	Balls	Runs	Wkts	Avg	BB	5I	10M
Test	17	18	7	139	41 *	12.63	-	-	6	-	3079	1769	79	22.39	6-51	4	1
FC	58	67	20	774	100	16.46	1	2	22	-	9730	5177	211	24.53	7-66	11	1
ODI	67	28	14	200	31 *	14.28	-	-	15	-	3446	2416	125	19.32	6-19	4	
List A	106	53	25	386	40	13.78	-	-	18	-	5292	3798	168	22.60	6-19	5	
20/20 Int	9	6	1	19	8 *	3.80	-	-	1	-	207	244	12	20.33	2-12	-	
20/20	15	8	1	28	8 *	4.00	-	-	2	-	351	428	18	23.77	2-12	-	

BOPARA, R. S. — Essex

Name: Ravinder (Ravi) Singh Bopara
Role: Right-hand bat, right-arm medium bowler; batting all-rounder
Born: 4 May 1985, Forest Gate, London
Height: 5ft 10in **Weight:** 12st 7lbs
Nickname: Puppy, Bops
County debut: 2002
County cap: 2005
Test debut: 2007-08
ODI debut: 2006-07
Twenty20 Int debut: 2008
1st-Class 200s: 1
List A 200s: 1
Place in batting averages: 16th av. 54.60 (2007 13th av. 60.00)
Place in bowling averages: 101st av. 34.25 (2007 130th av. 44.41)
Parents: Baldish and Charanjit
Marital status: Single
Education: Brampton Manor School
Off-season: 'Touring with England'

Overseas tours: England U19 to Australia 2002-03, to Bangladesh (U19 World Cup) 2003-04; England A to West Indies 2005-06, to Bangladesh 2006-07; England to Australia 2006-07 (C'wealth Bank Series), to West Indies (World Cup) 2006-07, to Sri Lanka 2007-08, to New Zealand 2007-08 (one-day series): to India (one-day series) 2008; to West Indies (one-day series) 2009, England Lions to New Zealand 2009
Overseas teams played for: Rockingham-Mandurah CC, Perth 2004
Career highlights to date: 'Winning Sri Lanka [ODI] series away from home [2007-08]; the 2008 season'
Cricket moments to forget: 'My first Test tour'
Cricketers particularly admired: Sachin Tendulkar, Jacques Kallis, Viv Richards
Favourite band: Usher, Ne-Yo
Relaxations: 'Music, pets'
Player website: www.ravinderbopara.com
Extras: Played for Development of Excellence XI (South) v West Indies U19 2001. Represented England U19 2003 and 2004. C&G Man of the Match award v Devon at Exmouth 2005 (65*). Scored 135 v Australians in a two-day game at Chelmsford 2005. Represented England A v Sri Lankans and v Pakistanis 2006. ECB National Academy 2005-06, 2006-07. Man of the Match v Sri Lanka in Antigua in the World Cup 2006-07 (52). NBC Denis Compton Award for the most promising young Essex player 2007. Cricket Writers' Club Young Cricketer of the Year 2008.
Opinions on cricket: 'Make franchise teams'
Best batting: 229 Essex v Northamptonshire, Chelmsford 2007
Best bowling: 5-75 Essex v Surrey, Colchester 2006
Stop press: Bought by Kings XI Punjab for $450,00 in IPL Auction 2009

2008 Season

	M	Inn	NO	Runs	HS	Avg	100	50	Ct	St	Balls	Runs	Wkts	Avg	BB	5I	10M
Test																	
FC	15	26	3	1256	150	54.60	4	7	11	-	1619	959	28	34.25	4-33	-	-
ODI	6	5	0	129	58	25.80	-	1	3	-	24	26	0	-	-		
List A	22	21	4	878	201 *	51.64	2	5	5	-	566	561	20	28.05	4-52	-	
20/20 Int	1	0	0	0	0	-	-	-	-	-	0	0	0	-	-		
20/20	4	3	0	98	47	32.66	-	-	1	-	48	54	4	13.50	3-36	-	

Career Performances

	M	Inn	NO	Runs	HS	Avg	100	50	Ct	St	Balls	Runs	Wkts	Avg	BB	5I	10M
Test	3	5	0	42	34	8.40	-	-	1	-	156	81	1	81.00	1-39	-	-
FC	79	130	18	4572	229	40.82	10	19	53	-	6000	3946	90	43.84	5-75	1	-
ODI	28	24	7	459	58	27.00	-	2	10	-	235	198	4	49.50	2-43	-	
List A	116	107	27	2849	201 *	35.61	4	16	33	-	2394	2187	77	28.40	4-52	-	
20/20 Int	1	0	0	0	0	-	-	-	-	-	0	0	0	-	-		
20/20	34	26	3	511	83	22.21	-	2	8	-	410	524	23	22.78	3-18	-	

BORRINGTON, P. M. Derbyshire

Name: Paul Michael Borrington
Role: Right-hand opening bat, right-arm off-spin bowler, occasional wicket-keeper
Born: 24 May 1988, Nottingham
Height: 6ft **Weight:** 10st 4lbs
Nickname: Stuart Little, Pizza-face, Boz
County debut: 2005
Place in batting averages: 99th av. 33.56
Parents: Tony and Sharron
Marital status: Single
Family links with cricket: Father played for Derbyshire 1970-82
Education: Chellaston School; Repton School (sixth form); Loughborough University
Qualifications: GCSEs, A-levels
Overseas tours: Derbyshire U15 to South Africa 2003; England U16 to South Africa 2004; Repton School to Sri Lanka 2005; Derbyshire Academy to South Africa 2007

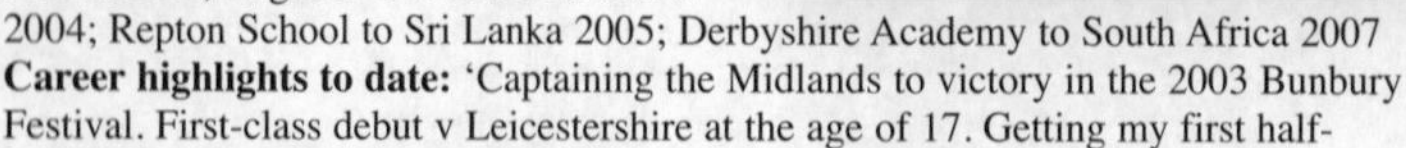

Career highlights to date: 'Captaining the Midlands to victory in the 2003 Bunbury Festival. First-class debut v Leicestershire at the age of 17. Getting my first half-century'
Cricket moments to forget: 'Leaving a straight ball on my first-class debut'
Cricket superstitions: 'Left pad on first'
Cricketers particularly admired: Mike Hendrick, John Morris, and my dad, Tony
Young players to look out for: Chris Paget, Dan Redfern
Other sports played: Football, occasional golf
Other sports followed: Football (Crewe Alexandra)
Favourite band: Razorlight
Relaxations: 'Spending time with my friends'
Extras: NBC Denis Compton Award for the most promising young Derbyshire player 2005. Derbyshire Academy Player of the Year 2006. Scored maiden first-class century for Loughborough University v Worcester in 2008.
Opinions on cricket: 'There's too much Twenty20 - should be more five-day first-class games so players like me have time to get in.'
Best batting: 102* LUCCE v Worcestershire, Kidderminster 2008

2008 Season

	M	Inn	NO	Runs	HS	Avg	100	50	Ct	St	Balls	Runs	Wkts	Avg	BB	5I	10M
Test																	
FC	12	20	4	537	102 *	33.56	1	3	10	-	6	5	0		-	-	-
ODI																	
List A																	
20/20 Int																	
20/20																	

Career Performances

	M	Inn	NO	Runs	HS	Avg	100	50	Ct	St	Balls	Runs	Wkts	Avg	BB	5I	10M
Test																	
FC	16	26	4	689	102 *	31.31	1	4	12	-	6	5	0		-	-	-
ODI																	
List A																	
20/20 Int																	
20/20																	

11. Jim Laker famously took nineteen wickets in the 1956 Old Trafford Test. Who took the other one?

BORTHWICK, S. G. Durham

Name: Scott George Borthwick
Role: Left-hand bat, leg-break bowler
Born: 19 April 1990
County debut: 2008 (one-day)
Family links with cricket: Uncle, David, played for Northumberland
Overseas tours: England U19 to South Africa 2009
Extras: Durham 2nd XI 2006. Durham Academy 2007-08. Entrusted with the last over of his debut game at Old Trafford, claiming three wickets in four impressive overs

2008 Season

	M	Inn	NO	Runs	HS	Avg	100	50	Ct	St	Balls	Runs	Wkts	Avg	BB	5I	10M
Test																	
FC																	
ODI																	
List A																	
20/20 Int																	
20/20	3	0	0	0	0		-	-	1	-	36	55	3	18.33	3-23	-	

Career Performances

	M	Inn	NO	Runs	HS	Avg	100	50	Ct	St	Balls	Runs	Wkts	Avg	BB	5I	10M
Test																	
FC																	
ODI																	
List A																	
20/20 Int																	
20/20	3	0	0	0	0		-	-	1	-	36	55	3	18.33	3-23	-	

BOTHA, A. G. — Warwickshire

Name: Anthony (Ant) Greyvensteyn Botha
Role: Left-hand bat, slow left-arm spin bowler
Born: 17 November 1976, Pretoria, South Africa
Height: 6ft **Weight:** 12st 7lbs
Nickname: Boats
County debut: 2004 (Derbyshire), 2007 (Warwickshire)
County cap: 2004 (Derbyshire)
50 wickets in a season: 1
Place in batting averages: 184th av. 21.76 (2007 217th av. 20.31)
Place in bowling averages: 138th av. 45.13 (2007 60th av. 29.43)
Parents: Elise and Ian
Marital status: Engaged
Education: Maritzburg College; Natal Tech
Qualifications: Marketing Manager Diploma; Coaching level 2
Off-season: 'Having our first child; Business called Playball! in Birmingham'
Overseas tours: South Africa U19 to India 1995-96
Overseas teams played for: Natal/KwaZulu-Natal 1995-96 – 1998-99; Easterns 1999-2000 – 2002-03; Joondalup CC, Perth 2005-06
Career highlights to date: 'Winning the four-day championship with Easterns 2002'
Cricket moments to forget: 'Getting badly injured in 2004 against Yorkshire'
Cricketers particularly admired: Steve Waugh
Young players to look out for: Chris Woakes
Other sports played: Hockey, tennis
Other sports followed: Football (Liverpool), Super 14 rugby (Natal Sharks)
Favourite band: Live
Relaxations: 'Watersports, beach'
Extras: Represented South African Schools 1995. Played for South Africa Academy 1997. Scored maiden first-class century (103) v Durham UCCE at Derby 2004, then took 5-55 in the DUCCE second innings to become the first Derbyshire player since 1937 to score a century and record a five-wicket innings return in the same first-class match. C&G Man of the Match award v Durham at Riverside 2005 (4-44/34*). Derbyshire Twenty20 player of the year 2005, 2006. Left Derbyshire towards the end of the 2007 season and joined Warwickshire. Is England-qualified.
Best batting: 156* Derbyshire v Yorkshire, Derby 2005
Best bowling: 8-53 Natal B v Northerns B, Centurion 1997-98

2008 Season

	M	Inn	NO	Runs	HS	Avg	100	50	Ct	St	Balls	Runs	Wkts	Avg	BB	5I	10M
Test																	
FC	13	16	3	283	62	21.76	-	3	16	-	1476	677	15	45.13	4-77	-	-
ODI																	
List A	13	10	2	139	32 *	17.37	-	-	7	-	437	382	12	31.83	5-43	1	
20/20 Int																	
20/20	11	6	2	67	35	16.75	-	-	7	-	186	163	14	11.64	3-15	-	

Career Perfomances

	M	Inn	NO	Runs	HS	Avg	100	50	Ct	St	Balls	Runs	Wkts	Avg	BB	5I	10M
Test																	
FC	113	176	25	3619	156 *	23.96	4	17	90	-	19393	9380	275	34.10	8-53	8	1
ODI																	
List A	122	94	27	1467	60 *	21.89	-	4	53	-	4379	3559	119	29.90	5-43	2	
20/20 Int																	
20/20	36	25	7	291	35	16.16	-	-	14	-	663	729	41	17.78	4-14	-	

BOYCE, M. A. G. — Leicestershire

Name: Matthew (Matt) Andrew Golding Boyce
Role: Left-hand opening bat, right-arm medium bowler
Born: 13 August 1985, Cheltenham
Height: 5ft 10in **Weight:** 11st 4lbs
Nickname: Boycey, Ferret
County debut: 2006
Place in batting averages: 150th av. 26.96
Parents: Anne and Andrew
Marital status: Single
Family links with cricket: 'Father played recreational cricket for over 20 years and coached youth cricket for ten years. Aunt played for Cambridge University. Brother played for Oakham School for three years in 1st XI'
Education: Oakham School; Nottingham University
Qualifications: 2.1 in Management and Economics
Overseas teams played for: Hoppers Crossing, Melbourne 2003-04

Career highlights to date: 'First-class debut and one-day debut. Scoring a double century [150-ball 225 for Rutland Championship side v Peterborough 2004]'
Cricket moments to forget: 'Going out to bat against Northants without a box on!'
Cricket superstitions: None
Cricketers particularly admired: Graham Thorpe, Mark Ramprakash, Paul Nixon
Young players to look out for: Tom New, Josh Cobb
Other sports played: Rugby (Oakham School *Daily Mail* Cup winner), hockey (Midlands U14 and U16),
Favourite band: The Fray, The Wallflowers
Relaxations: 'Poker, socialising, relaxing in general!'
Extras: County Council Special Award for Youth Cricket. *Rutland Times* Young Cricketer of the Year. Sporting Moment of the Year 2004 (225; *see above*). Rutland League Teenage Cricketer of the Year. Leading batsman in Leicestershire League 2007
Opinions on cricket: 'In a game where so much is said about Kolpak players, I believe the best young English players will still come through. Chances are for taking, not giving.'
Best batting: 106 Leicestershire v Warwickshire, Edgbaston, 2008

2008 Season

	M	Inn	NO	Runs	HS	Avg	100	50	Ct	St	Balls	Runs	Wkts	Avg	BB	5I	10M
Test																	
FC	17	26	1	674	106	26.96	1	4	2	-	36	61	0		-	-	-
ODI																	
List A	12	10	3	239	59	34.14	-	2	2	-	0	0	0		-	-	
20/20 Int																	
20/20	6	5	1	83	31	20.75	-	-	1	-	0	0	0		-	-	

Career Performances

	M	Inn	NO	Runs	HS	Avg	100	50	Ct	St	Balls	Runs	Wkts	Avg	BB	5I	10M
Test																	
FC	19	29	1	689	106	24.60	1	4	2	-	36	61	0		-	-	-
ODI																	
List A	13	11	3	275	59	34.37	-	2	2	-	0	0	0		-	-	
20/20 Int																	
20/20	6	5	1	83	31	20.75	-	-	1	-	0	0	0		-	-	

BRAGG, W. D. — Glamorgan

Name: William (Will) David Bragg
Role: Left-hand bat, wicket-keeper
Born: 24 October 1986, Gwent, South Wales
Height: 5ft 10in **Weight:** 12st 6lbs
Nickname: Braggy, Milf, Braggpot, Pottsy
County debut: 2007
Parents: Susan and Steven
Marital status: Single
Family links with cricket: 'Father and brother have both played for local sides (Malpas CC)'
Education: Rougemont Independent School; Cardiff University
Qualifications: 11 GCSEs, 4 A-levels
Career highlights to date: 'Playing for Glamorgan'
Cricket moments to forget: 'Dropping easy catches'
Cricket superstitions: 'Put box on last'
Cricketers particularly admired: Matthew Maynard, Alan Jones, Brian Lara
Young players to look out for: Tom Maynard, Ben Wright, Mike O'Shea, James Harris
Other sports played: Rugby (for school), football (Gwent County)
Other sports followed: Football (Tottenham)
Favourite band: Razorlight
Extras: Scored most runs by any batsman for Wales U15. Played for Wales Minor Counties in the C&G 2005 and in Minor Counties competitions 2004-06
Opinions on cricket: 'One-day cricket seems to pull in the crowds, exciting. Four-day cricket seems far slower and more boring.'
Best batting: 24 Glamorgan v Somerset, Taunton 2007

2008 Season

	M	Inn	NO	Runs	HS	Avg	100	50	Ct	St	Balls	Runs	Wkts	Avg	BB	5I	10M
Test																	
FC	2	4	0	51	24	12.75	-	-	-	-	0	0	0		-	-	-
ODI																	
List A																	
20/20 Int																	
20/20																	

Career Performances

	M	Inn	NO	Runs	HS	Avg	100	50	Ct	St	Balls	Runs	Wkts	Avg	BB	5I	10M
Test																	
FC	2	4	0	51	24	12.75	-	-	-	-	0	0	0		-	-	-
ODI																	
List A	1	1	1	41	41 *		-	-	1	-	0	0	0		-	-	
20/20 Int																	
20/20																	

BREESE, G. R. Durham

Name: Gareth Rohan Breese
Role: Right-hand bat, right-arm off-spin bowler; all-rounder
Born: 9 January 1976, Montego Bay, Jamaica
Height: 5ft 8in **Weight:** 13st
Nickname: Briggy
County debut: 2004
Test debut: 2002-03
Place in batting averages: (2007 241st av. 16.11)
Parents: Brian and Jean
Marital status: Single
Family links with cricket: Father played league cricket in Somerset and Wales; also played representative cricket for two parishes in Jamaica as wicket-keeper/batsman. He is currently the cricket operations officer of the Jamaica Cricket Association

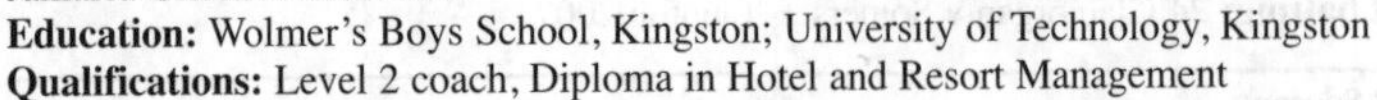

Education: Wolmer's Boys School, Kingston; University of Technology, Kingston
Qualifications: Level 2 coach, Diploma in Hotel and Resort Management
Overseas tours: West Indies U19 to Pakistan and Bangladesh 1995-96; Jamaica to Malaysia (Commonwealth Games) 1998-99; West Indies A to England 2002; West Indies to India 2002-03
Overseas teams played for: Jamaica 1995-96 – 2005-06
Career highlights to date: 'Playing at the highest level and representing Durham over the last five seasons'
Cricket moments to forget: 'My two Test innings'
Cricket superstitions: None
Cricketers particularly admired: Jimmy Adams, Courtney Walsh, Delroy Morgan (Jamaica), Dale Benkenstein, Gordon Muchall

Young players to look out for: Gordon Muchall, Nick Cook, Ben Harmison
Other sports played: Pool
Relaxations: 'My computer; music, shopping; hanging out with team-mates/friends'
Extras: Represented West Indies U19 1994-95. Second-highest wicket-taker in the Busta Cup 2000-01 with 36 (av. 15.11) and in 2001-02 with 44 (av. 20.18). Captain of Jamaica in first-class cricket 2003-04 and in one-day cricket 2004-05. Scored 165* as Durham made 453-9 to beat Somerset at Taunton 2004. Scored century (110) v Middlesex at Lord's 2006, in the process sharing with Dale Benkenstein (125) in a new record fifth-wicket partnership for Durham (222). Scored 121 not out in Durham's only innings as they defeated Kent to clinch title in Sept 2008. Is a British passport-holder and is not considered an overseas player
Best batting: 165* Durham v Somerset, Taunton 2004
Best bowling: 7-60 Jamaica v Barbados, Bridgetown 2000-01

2008 Season

	M	Inn	NO	Runs	HS	Avg	100	50	Ct	St	Balls	Runs	Wkts	Avg	BB	5I	10M
Test																	
FC	2	2	1	184	121 *	184.00	1	1	1	-	42	22	1	22.00	1-22	-	-
ODI																	
List A	17	16	7	188	34 *	20.88	-	-	6	-	598	519	18	28.83	5-41	1	
20/20 Int																	
20/20	11	5	2	72	21 *	24.00	-	-	4	-	156	166	8	20.75	3-17	-	

Career Performances

	M	Inn	NO	Runs	HS	Avg	100	50	Ct	St	Balls	Runs	Wkts	Avg	BB	5I	10M
Test	1	2	0	5	5	2.50	-	-	1	-	188	135	2	67.50	2-108	-	-
FC	112	180	20	4270	165 *	26.68	4	27	92	-	17852	8288	274	30.24	7-60	12	3
ODI																	
List A	122	92	23	1334	68 *	19.33	-	3	51	-	4716	3595	130	27.65	5-41	2	
20/20 Int																	
20/20	36	25	6	205	24 *	10.78	-	-	13	-	625	679	37	18.35	4-14		

BRESNAN, T. T. — Yorkshire

Name: Timothy (Tim) Thomas Bresnan
Role: Right-hand bat, right-arm fast bowler; all-rounder
Born: 28 February 1985, Pontefract
Height: 6ft 1in **Weight:** 14st 7lbs
Nickname: Brez, Brezzie, Tikka
County debut: 2001 (one-day), 2003 (first-class)
County cap: 2006
ODI debut: 2006
Twenty20 Int debut: 2006
Place in batting averages: 98th av. 33.73 (2007 38th av. 48.50)
Place in bowling averages: 63rd av. 28.40 (2007 91st av. 34.02)
Parents: Julie and Ray
Marital status: Single
Family links with cricket: 'Dad played local league cricket'

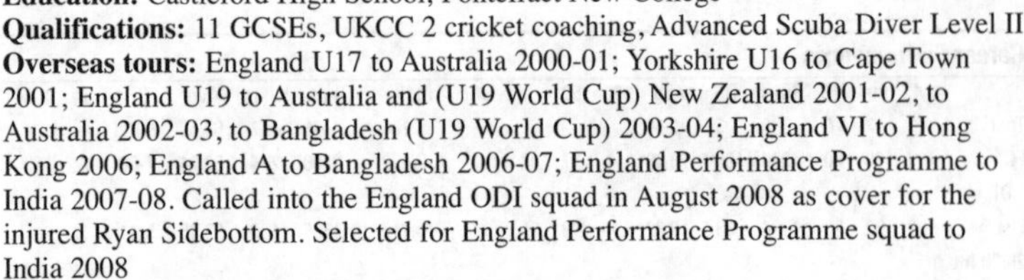

Education: Castleford High School; Pontefract New College
Qualifications: 11 GCSEs, UKCC 2 cricket coaching, Advanced Scuba Diver Level II
Overseas tours: England U17 to Australia 2000-01; Yorkshire U16 to Cape Town 2001; England U19 to Australia and (U19 World Cup) New Zealand 2001-02, to Australia 2002-03, to Bangladesh (U19 World Cup) 2003-04; England VI to Hong Kong 2006; England A to Bangladesh 2006-07; England Performance Programme to India 2007-08. Called into the England ODI squad in August 2008 as cover for the injured Ryan Sidebottom. Selected for England Performance Programme squad to India 2008
Overseas teams played for: Sutherland CC, Sydney 2005-06
Career highlights to date: 'Making England debut, Lord's 2006'
Cricket moments to forget: 'First big injury, June 2006'
Cricket superstitions: None
Cricketers particularly admired: Ian Botham
Young players to look out for: Jack Hughes
Other sports played: Golf
Other sports followed: Football (Sheffield United)
Favourite band: Razorlight, Snow Patrol
Relaxations: 'PlayStation, cinema'
Extras: Bunbury Festival Best All-rounder and Most Outstanding Player 2000. One-day debut v Kent at Headingley 2001 aged 16 years 102 days, the youngest player to represent Yorkshire since Paul Jarvis in 1981. NBC Denis Compton Award for the

most promising young Yorkshire player 2002, 2003. England U19 2002 and 2003. Scored maiden first-class century (116) v Surrey at The Oval 2007, while sharing with Jason Gillespie (123*) in a new record ninth-wicket partnership for Yorkshire (246). Only Rashid took more first-class wickets for the county in 2008. Member of the successful England Hong Kong Sixes team in November 2008.
Best batting: 126* England A v Indians, Chelmsford 2007
Best bowling: 5-42 Yorkshire v Worcestershire, Worcester 2005

2008 Season

	M	Inn	NO	Runs	HS	Avg	100	50	Ct	St	Balls	Runs	Wkts	Avg	BB	5I	10M
Test																	
FC	14	20	5	506	84 *	33.73	-	2	9	-	2526	1278	45	28.40	5-94	1	-
ODI																	
List A	17	9	2	134	55	19.14	-	1	3	-	715	513	24	21.37	4-31	-	
20/20 Int																	
20/20	9	8	3	58	15	11.60	-	-	4	-	204	244	8	30.50	2-12	-	

Career Performances

	M	Inn	NO	Runs	HS	Avg	100	50	Ct	St	Balls	Runs	Wkts	Avg	BB	5I	10M
Test																	
FC	73	99	19	2177	126 *	27.21	3	10	31	-	11131	6008	190	31.62	5-42	3	-
ODI	5	4	1	51	20	17.00	-	-	1	-	198	203	4	50.75	2-34	-	
List A	126	83	23	1105	61	18.41	-	2	33	-	5120	4240	121	35.04	4-25	-	
20/20 Int	1	1	1	6	6 *		-	-	-	-	12	20	0		-	-	
20/20	39	29	11	331	42	18.38	-	-	14	-	740	924	39	23.69	3-21	-	

12. In 1953 England re-gained the ashes for the first time since long before the War. Who was their captain?

BROAD, S. C. J. Nottinghamshire

Name: Stuart Christopher John Broad
Role: Left-hand bat, right-arm fast-medium bowler
Born: 24 June 1986, Nottingham
Height: 6ft 6in **Weight:** 13st
Nickname: Broady
County debut: 2005 (Leicestershire), 2008 (Nottinghamshire)
County cap: 2007 (Leicestershire)
Test debut: 2007
Test debut: 2007-08
ODI debut: 2006
Twenty20 Int debut: 2006
Place in batting averages: 91st av. 35.70
Place in bowling averages: 100th av. 34.09 (2007 35th av. 25.08)
Parents: Carole and Chris
Marital status: Single
Family links with cricket: 'Dad played for Gloucestershire, Nottinghamshire and England'
Education: Oakham School
Qualifications: 10 GCSEs, 3 A-levels
Overseas tours: Oakham School to South Africa 2000-01; England A to West Indies 2005-06, to Bangladesh 2006-07; England to Australia 2006-07 (C'wealth Bank Series), to West Indies (World Cup) 2006-07, to South Africa (World 20/20) 2007-08, to Sri Lanka 2007-08, to New Zealand 2007-08, to India (Test and one-day series) 2008, to West Indies (Test and one-day series) 2009
Overseas teams played for: Hoppers Crossing CC, Melbourne 2004-05
Career highlights to date: 'England ODI debut v Pakistan 2006. Winning Twenty20 Cup 2006 with Leicestershire'
Cricket superstitions: 'Three warm-up balls before I bowl a new spell'
Cricketers particularly admired: Glenn McGrath, Shaun Pollock
Young players to look out for: Mark Collier
Other sports played: Hockey (Midlands age groups), golf
Other sports followed: Football (Nottingham Forest), rugby (Leicester Tigers)
Relaxations: 'PSP, playing golf, films'
Extras: Leicestershire Young Cricketers' Batsman of the Year 2003. Represented England U19 2005. Cricket Writers' Club Young Cricketer of the Year 2006. Cricket Society Most Promising Young Cricketer of the Year 2006. ECB National Academy 2005-06, 2006-07. NBC Denis Compton Award for most promising young Leicestershire player 2005, 2006, 2007. Man of the Match in the fourth ODI v India at

Old Trafford 2007 (4-51/45*). Made Test debut in the second Test v Sri Lanka in Colombo 2007-08
Best batting: 91* Leicestershire v Derbyshire, Leicester 2007
Best bowling: 5-67 Leicestershire v Derbyshire, Leicester 2007

2008 Season

	M	Inn	NO	Runs	HS	Avg	100	50	Ct	St	Balls	Runs	Wkts	Avg	BB	5I	10M
Test	6	7	1	280	76	46.66	-	3	1	-	1208	697	15	46.46	3-44	-	-
FC	10	11	1	357	76	35.70	-	4	3	-	1924	1091	32	34.09	4-39	-	-
ODI	10	5	1	28	17	7.00	-	-	3	-	445	292	15	19.46	5-23	1	
List A	11	6	1	34	17	6.80	-	-	3	-	487	309	16	19.31	5-23	1	
20/20 Int	1	0	0	0	0		-	-	-	-	24	17	2	8.50	2-17	-	
20/20	1	0	0	0	0		-	-	-	-	24	17	2	8.50	2-17	-	

Career Performances

	M	Inn	NO	Runs	HS	Avg	100	50	Ct	St	Balls	Runs	Wkts	Avg	BB	5I	10M
Test	9	12	2	372	76	37.20	-	3	4	-	1928	1042	24	43.41	3-44	-	-
FC	46	56	13	1092	91 *	25.39	-	8	14	-	7897	4617	153	30.17	5-67	6	-
ODI	37	23	12	236	45 *	21.45	-	-	10	-	1813	1442	55	26.21	5-23	1	
List A	53	28	13	271	45 *	18.06	-	-	12	-	2571	2102	78	26.94	5-23	1	
20/20 Int	11	6	2	12	6	3.00	-	-	3	-	252	355	13	27.30	3-37	-	
20/20	20	6	2	12	6	3.00	-	-	4	-	462	527	27	19.51	3-13	-	

BROOKS, J. A. — Northamptonshire

Name: Jack Alexander Brooks
Role: Right-hand bat, right-arm fast-medium bowler
Born: 4 June 1984
Height: 6ft 2in
Nickname: Brooksy, Ferret
County debut: No first-team appearance
Career highlights to date: 'After playing village cricket until I was 20, signing a pro contract with Northants is pretty special!'
Cricket moments to forget: 'Whenever I bowl badly or drop a catch'
Favourite band: Hyper, Not My Day
Extras: On trial at Surrey and Northamptonshire, and playing for Oxfordshire, during the 2008 season before signing a one-year contract

BROPHY, G. L. Yorkshire

Name: Gerard Louis Brophy
Role: Right-hand bat, wicket-keeper
Born: 26 November 1975, Welkom, South Africa
Height: 5ft 11in **Weight:** 12st
Nickname: Scuba, Broph
County debut: 2002 (Northamptonshire), 2006 (Yorkshire)
Place in batting averages: 169th av. 23.73 (2007 117th av 32.94)
Parents: Gerard and Trish
Wife and date of marriage: Alison, 3 January 2004
Children: Georgia Beau, 22 December 2006
Education: Christian Brothers College, Boksburg; Wits Technikon (both South Africa)
Qualifications: Marketing Diploma, Level 2 coach
Overseas tours: South Africa U17 to England 1993; South Africa Academy to Zimbabwe 1998-99
Overseas teams played for: Gauteng 1996-97 – 1998-99; Free State 1999-2000 – 2000-01
Career highlights to date: 'Captaincy of Free State 2000-01. First dismissal [in collaboration] with Allan Donald'
Cricket moments to forget: 'Messing up a live TV interview'
Cricket superstitions: 'Right pad on first and right glove on first'
Cricketers particularly admired: Ray Jennings, Ian Healy, Allan Donald, Hansie Cronje
Other sports played: Golf, rugby
Other sports followed: Golf, rugby
Favourite band: Coldplay
Relaxations: 'Fishing, travelling, braais, scuba diving'
Extras: Captained South Africa U17. Played for Ireland in the NatWest 2000. Played hockey for East Transvaal in 1991. Holds a British passport and is not considered an overseas player.
Opinions on cricket: 'The introduction of IPL, ICL and Stanford is fantastic, the exposure for cricketers and potential for wealth is fantastic (as long as you can crack the 20/20 version)'
Best batting: 185 South Africa Academy v ZCU President's XI, Harare (S) 1998-99

2008 Season

	M	Inn	NO	Runs	HS	Avg	100	50	Ct	St	Balls	Runs	Wkts	Avg	BB	5I	10M
Test																	
FC	16	24	1	546	70	23.73	-	4	43	6	0	0	0		-	-	-
ODI																	
List A	17	15	5	238	61 *	23.80	-	2	24	2	0	0	0		-	-	
20/20 Int																	
20/20	9	9	1	177	57 *	22.12	-	1	6	3	0	0	0		-	-	

Career Performances

	M	Inn	NO	Runs	HS	Avg	100	50	Ct	St	Balls	Runs	Wkts	Avg	BB	5I	10M
Test																	
FC	92	145	16	3898	185	30.21	6	19	229	19	6	1	0				
ODI																	
List A	95	77	15	1476	66	23.80	-	8	90	18	0	0	0		-	-	
20/20 Int																	
20/20	32	29	7	539	57 *	24.50	-	2	14	4	0	0	0		-	-	

BROWN, A. D. Nottinghamshire

Name: Alistair Duncan Brown
Role: Right-hand bat, right-arm off-spin bowler, occasional wicket-keeper
Born: 11 February 1970, Beckenham
Height: 5ft 10in **Weight:** 12st 7lbs
Nickname: The Lord
County debut: 1990 (one-day, Surrey), 1992 (first-class, Surrey)
County cap: 1994 (Surrey)
Benefit: 2002 (Surrey)
ODI debut: 1996
1000 runs in a season: 8
1st-Class 200s: 3
List A 200s: 2
Place in batting averages: 87th av. 36.00 (2007 194th av. 23.08)
Parents: Robert and Ann
Wife and date of marriage: Sarah, 10 October 1998
Children: Max Charles, 9 March 2001; Joe Robert, 11 March 2003
Family links with cricket: Father played for Surrey Young Amateurs in the 1950s

Education: Caterham School
Qualifications: 5 O-levels, Level II coach
Overseas tours: England VI to Singapore 1993, 1994, 1995, to Hong Kong 1997; England to Sharjah (Champions Trophy) 1997-98, to Bangladesh (Wills International Cup) 1998-99
Overseas teams played for: North Perth, Western Australia 1989-90
Career highlights to date: '118 v India at Old Trafford 1996; 203 v Hampshire at Guildford 1997; 268 v Glamorgan at The Oval 2002'
Cricket moments to forget: 'A great couple of days in Ireland!'
Cricket superstitions: 'Always get to the ground before 11 a.m.'
Cricketers particularly admired: Ian Botham, Viv Richards
Other sports played: Football, golf
Other sports followed: Football (West Ham United), rugby union (London Wasps)
Favourite band: Roachford, Snow Patrol
Relaxations: 'Golf and sleep (when the children allow)'
Extras: Man of the Match for his 118 against India in the third ODI at Old Trafford 1996. Recorded the highest-ever score in the Sunday League with 203 off 119 balls against Hampshire at Guildford in 1997 and received an individual award at the PCA dinner for that achievement. Joint winner (with Carl Hooper) of the EDS Walter Lawrence Trophy for the fastest first-class 100 of the 1998 season (72 balls v Northants at The Oval). Surrey CCC Batsman of the Season 2001. Scored 160-ball 268 out of 438-5 v Glamorgan at The Oval in the C&G 2002; it set a new record for the highest individual score in professional one-day cricket worldwide and Brown also became the first batsman to have scored two double centuries in one-day cricket. Scored 154 v Lancashire at Old Trafford 2004 to complete full set of first-class hundreds against all 17 other counties. Scored 97-ball 176 v Gloucestershire at The Oval in the Friends Provident 2007, in the process sharing with James Benning (152) in a Surrey record one-day partnership (294) as the county posted a world record List A total of 496-4. Signed a two-year contract with Nottinghamshire in January 2009
Best batting: 295* Surrey v Leicestershire, Oakham School 2000
Best bowling: 3-25 Surrey v Somerset, Guildford 2006

2008 Season

	M	Inn	NO	Runs	HS	Avg	100	50	Ct	St	Balls	Runs	Wkts	Avg	BB	5I	10M
Test																	
FC	7	9	2	252	76 *	36.00	-	2	4	-	36	5	0		-	-	-
ODI																	
List A	7	6	2	140	40 *	35.00	-	-	1	-	31	37	0		-	-	
20/20 Int																	
20/20	9	9	0	192	51	21.33	-	1	5	-	0	0	0		-	-	

Career Performances

	M	Inn	NO	Runs	HS	Avg	100	50	Ct	St	Balls	Runs	Wkts	Avg	BB	5I	10M
Test																	
FC	247	388	43	14957	295 *	43.35	44	62	246	1	1224	635	5	127.00	3-25	-	-
ODI	16	16	0	354	118	22.12	1	1	6	-	6	5	0		-	-	
List A	376	360	19	10838	268	31.78	19	49	126	-	520	561	14	40.07	3-39	-	
20/20 Int																	
20/20	51	51	1	1170	83	23.40	-	7	33	-	2	2	0		-	-	

BROWN, B. C. Sussex

Name: Ben Christopher Brown
Role: Right-hand bat, wicket-keeper
Born: 23 November 1988, Crawley
Height: 5ft 8in **Weight:** 11st 10lbs
County debut: 2007
Parents: Diana and Chris
Marital status: Single
Education: Ardingly College
Qualifications: 9 GCSEs, 2 A-levels, Level 2 coaching, NVQ in Cricket
Off-season: 'Touring with England U19 to Sri Lanka and then on to Malaysia for U19 World Cup'
Overseas tours: Sussex Academy to Cape Town 2005; England U19 to Malaysia 2006-07, to Malaysia (U19 World Cup) 2007-08
Career highlights to date: 'Getting my first contract at Sussex'
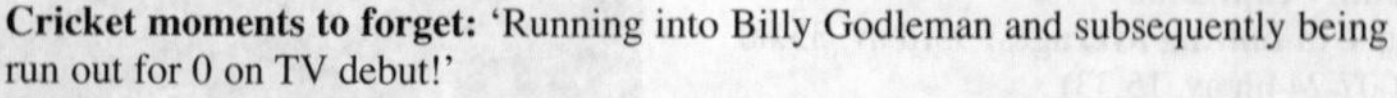
Cricket moments to forget: 'Running into Billy Godleman and subsequently being run out for 0 on TV debut!'
Cricket superstitions: None
Cricketers particularly admired: Alec Stewart, Adam Gilchrist
Young players to look out for: Matt Machan, Will Beer, Michael Thornely
Other sports played: Football
Other sports followed: Football (Chelsea FC)
Extras: Represented England U19 2007. Played for England U19 against New Zealand during the 2008 tour. Signed a new two-year contract in October 2008
Opinions on cricket: 'I would prefer to see fewer Kolpak players in county cricket and still have two overseas players for young players to learn from and compete against.'
Best batting: 46 Sussex v Sri Lanka A, Hove 2007

2008 Season

	M	Inn	NO	Runs	HS	Avg	100	50	Ct	St	Balls	Runs	Wkts	Avg	BB	5I	10M
Test																	
FC																	
ODI																	
List A	1	1	0	0	0	0.00	-	-	-	-	0	0	0		-	-	
20/20 Int																	
20/20	1	1	0	6	6	6.00	-	-	-	-	0	0	0		-	-	

Career Performances

	M	Inn	NO	Runs	HS	Avg	100	50	Ct	St	Balls	Runs	Wkts	Avg	BB	5I	10M
Test																	
FC	1	1	0	46	46	46.00	-	-	-	-	0	0	0		-	-	-
ODI																	
List A	2	2	0	4	4	2.00	-	-	-	-	0	0	0		-	-	
20/20 Int																	
20/20	1	1	0	6	6	6.00	-	-	-	-	0	0	0		-	-	

BROWN, D. O. Gloucestershire

Name: David Owen Brown
Role: Right-hand bat, right-arm medium bowler
Born: 8 December 1982, Burnley
Height: 6ft **Weight:** 13st 7lbs
Nickname: Wally, Bomber, Dangerous Dave
County debut: 2006
County cap: 2006
Place in batting averages: 93rd av. 35.00 (2007 244th av. 15.33)
Place in bowling averages: 49th av. 27.00
Parents: Peter and Valerie
Marital status: Single
Family links with cricket: 'Brother Michael played at Hampshire and Middlesex, now with Surrey. Dad played league cricket for many years, mum made 'cracking' teas.'
Education: Queen Elizabeth's Grammar School, Blackburn; Collingwood College, Durham University 2002-2005
Qualifications: 10 GCSEs, 4 A-levels, BA (Hons) Sport in the Community
Career outside cricket: 'Open to offers - haven't decided'

Off-season: 'Working on my game. Perth and India in February for some training'
Overseas tours: MCC B to Nepal 2003; MCC A to Canada 2005; Gloucestershire CCC to Pretoria 2006 and 2007
Overseas teams played for: Claremont-Nedlands, Perth 2001-02; Perth CC 2005-06, 2006-07; Northcote CC, Melbourne, 2007-08
Career highlights to date: 'C&G debut for Gloucsetershire v Surrey (*see Extras*); Championship debut for Gloucestershire. Any win'
Cricket moments to forget: 'Any dropped catch; any time I self-destruct; any loss'
Cricketers particularly admired: Dale Benkenstein, Michael Brown, Craig Spearman, Marcus North, Ian Harvey
Young players to look out for: Jonathan Clare, Steve Snell, Josh Cobb, Bharat Tripathi
Other sports played: Golf - 'great driver, terrible putter'; football - 'ex-centre forward, now play Owen Hargreaves role just in front of the back four'
Other sports followed: Football (Burnley FC)
Favourite band: Dire Straits, The Carpenters, Leona Lewis, Bon Jovi
Relaxations: 'Championship Manager, golf, going out.'
Extras: Part of the Burnley CC 2000 side that produced four current professional players (D. Brown, M. Brown, S. Anderson and J. Clare); played for Durham UCCE 2003-05. Represented British Universities 2005. Struck 26-ball 63* on one-day debut v Surrey at Bristol in the C&G 2006.
Opinions on cricket: 'We still play too much cricket - practice and preparation are neglected because of this. Too many Kolpaks. Would like to see a knock-out style 50-over competition, FA Cup style, i.e. how they used to have it.'
Best batting: 83 Gloucestershire v Worcestershire, Cheltenham, July 2008
Best bowling: 5-38 Gloucestershire v Derbyshire, Derby 2008

2008 Season

	M	Inn	NO	Runs	HS	Avg	100	50	Ct	St	Balls	Runs	Wkts	Avg	BB	5I	10M
Test																	
FC	9	15	4	385	83	35.00	-	3	5		693	432	16	27.00	5-38	1	-
ODI																	
List A	9	7	2	106	45 *	21.20	-	-	3		204	197	3	65.66	1-27	-	
20/20 Int																	
20/20																	

Career Performances

	M	Inn	NO	Runs	HS	Avg	100	50	Ct	St	Balls	Runs	Wkts	Avg	BB	5I	10M
Test																	
FC	23	39	4	975	83	27.85	-	7	12	-	1755	1251	28	44.67	5-38	1	-
ODI																	
List A	20	17	5	309	63 *	25.75	-	1	5	-	438	429	11	39.00	3-29	-	
20/20 Int																	
20/20	14	11	1	162	36	16.20	-	-	3	-	36	35	3	11.66	1-11	-	

BROWN, J. F. — Nottinghamshire

Name: Jason Fred Brown
Role: Right-hand bat, off-spin bowler
Born: 10 October 1974, Newcastle-under-Lyme
Height: 6ft **Weight:** 13st
Nickname: Cheese, Fish, Brownie
County debut: 1996 (Northamptonshire)
County cap: 2000 (Northamptonshire)
Benefit: 2008 (Northamptonshire)
50 wickets in a season: 3
Place in bowling averages: 149th av. 82.50 (2007 120th av. 41.16)
Parents: Peter and Cynthia
Wife and date of marriage: Sam, 26 September 1998
Children: Millie
Education: St Margaret Ward RC School, Stoke-on-Trent

Qualifications: 9 GCSEs, Level 1 coaching qualification
Overseas tours: Kidsgrove League U18 to Australia 1990; Northants CCC to Zimbabwe 1998, to Grenada 2000; England A to West Indies 2000-01; England to Sri Lanka 2000-01
Overseas teams played for: North East Valley, Dunedin, New Zealand 1996-97
Cricketers particularly admired: John Emburey, Carl Hooper
Other sports played: Golf
Other sports followed: Football (Port Vale)
Relaxations: 'Reading, listening to music'
Extras: Represented Staffordshire at all junior levels, in Minor Counties, and in the NatWest 1995. Once took 10-16 in a Kidsgrove League game against Haslington U18 playing for Sandyford U18. Took 100th first-class wicket in 23rd match, v Sussex at Northampton 2000, going on to take his 50th wicket of the season in the same game, only his seventh of the summer. Took 5-27 v Somerset at Northampton 2003, the best return by a Northants bowler in the Twenty20 Cup. C&G Man of the Match award for his 5-19 v Cambridgeshire at Northampton 2004. Joined Nottinghamshire for 2009
Best batting: 38 Northamptonshire v Hampshire, Northampton 2003
Best bowling: 7-69 Northamptonshire v Durham, Riverside 2003

2008 Season

	M	Inn	NO	Runs	HS	Avg	100	50	Ct	St	Balls	Runs	Wkts	Avg	BB	5I	10M
Test																	
FC	10	7	2	39	13	7.80	-	-	2	-	1690	825	10	82.50	2-33	-	-
ODI																	
List A	11	5	3	20	15 *	10.00	-	-	1	-	444	320	10	32.00	2-28	-	
20/20 Int																	
20/20	9	2	2	14	13 *		-	-	1	-	180	203	7	29.00	2-31	-	

Career Performances

	M	Inn	NO	Runs	HS	Avg	100	50	Ct	St	Balls	Runs	Wkts	Avg	BB	5I	10M
Test																	
FC	129	147	59	655	38	7.44	-	-	26	-	31140	14035	414	33.90	7-69	22	5
ODI																	
List A	153	56	34	136	16	6.18	-	-	29	-	7232	5260	137	38.39	5-19	1	
20/20 Int																	
20/20	42	4	3	23	13 *	23.00	-	-	9	-	833	1008	41	24.58	5-27	1	

BROWN, K. R. Lancashire

Name: Karl Robert Brown
Role: Right-hand bat, right-arm medium bowler
Born: 17 May 1988, Bolton
Height: 5ft 11in **Weight:** 11st 7lbs
Nickname: Brownie, Charlie
County debut: 2006
Parents: Paul and Lorraine
Marital status: Single
Family links with cricket: Father a club cricketer with Atherton CC for over 30 years and had two seasons as club professional at Clifton CC in the Bolton Association
Education: Hesketh Fletcher CE, Atherton, Lancashire
Qualifications: 8 GCSEs
Off-season: 'Going to Adelaide in January on ECB scholarship - also at the Darren Lehmann Academy'
Overseas tours: England U16 to South Africa 2003-04; England U19 to Bangladesh 2005-06, to Malaysia 2006-07
Overseas teams played for: Noble Park, Victoria, 2007-08

Career highlights: 'Walking out to bat in my first County Championship game in 2008
Cricket moments to forget: 'Walking back after about three minutes after getting a duck!'
Cricket superstitions: None
Cricketers particularly admired:
Andrew Flintoff, Stuart Law
Young players to look out for: Simon Kerrigan, Stephen Cheetham
Other sports played: 'Used to play football'; golf
Other sports followed: Football (Bolton Wanderers), golf
Favourite band/music: The Courteeners
Relaxations: 'My computer, music, Facebook, etc.'
Extras: Lancashire Junior Player of the Year 2004. Represented England U19 2007. Appeared in both first-class and one-day games in 2008. NBC Denis Compton Award for most promising young Lancashire player 2008.
Opinions on cricket: 'The game seems to be getting bigger and bigger - probably because of 20/20, but that must be a good thing for all forms of cricket'
Best batting: 40 Lancashire v Kent, Liverpool, September 2008

2008 Season

	M	Inn	NO	Runs	HS	Avg	100	50	Ct	St	Balls	Runs	Wkts	Avg	BB	5I	10M
Test																	
FC	3	4	1	55	40	18.33	-	-	1	-	0	0	0		-	-	-
ODI																	
List A	4	4	0	71	41	17.75	-	-	1	-	0	0	0		-	-	
20/20 Int																	
20/20																	

Career Performances

	M	Inn	NO	Runs	HS	Avg	100	50	Ct	St	Balls	Runs	Wkts	Avg	BB	5I	10M
Test																	
FC	5	8	1	116	40	16.57	-	-	2	-	18	7	0		-	-	-
ODI																	
List A	5	5	0	72	41	14.40	-	-	1	-	0	0	0		-	-	
20/20 Int																	
20/20																	

13. Up to and including the 2006-07 Ashes tour, how many series have been won by England?

BROWN, M. J. — Surrey

Name: Michael James Brown
Role: Right-hand bat, wicket-keeper
Born: 9 February 1980, Burnley
Height: 6ft **Weight:** 12st
Nickname: Fagmo, Weasel, Stone, Dawson
County debut: 1999 (Middlesex), 2004 (Hampshire)
County cap: 2007 (Hampshire)
1000 runs in a season: 1
Place in batting averages: 61st av. 40.86 (2007 57th av. 43.12)
Parents: Peter and Valerie
Marital status: Single
Family links with cricket: 'Father played league cricket for 30 years. Mum makes great tuna sandwiches.' Younger brother David played for DUCCE and now plays for Gloucestershire
Education: Queen Elizabeth's Grammar School, Blackburn; Durham University
Qualifications: 10 GCSEs, 4 A-levels, 2.1 Economics/Politics
Career outside cricket: 'Stockbroking'
Overseas teams played for: Western Province CC, Cape Town 1998-99; Fremantle CC 2002-05; South Perth CC 2005-06
Career highlights to date: 'Durham 2007 – 56* and 126* gained a draw for Hampshire'
Cricket moments to forget: 'Leaving straight balls'
Cricket superstitions: 'Always tap non-striker's end four times at end of over when at that end'
Cricketers particularly admired: Dale Benkenstein, Nic Pothas, Michael Yardy
Young players to look out for: Liam Dawson, Ben Howell
Other sports played: Football ('badly'), golf ('occasional bandit')
Other sports followed: Football (Burnley FC)
Favourite band: Goo Goo Dolls, Razorlight, The Killers, Oasis
Relaxations: 'Golf, shares'
Extras: Represented ECB U19 A v Pakistan U19 1998. Played for Durham UCCE and represented British Universities 2001, 2002. 'Was at non-striker's end as five wickets fell in one over, Middlesex 2nd XI v Glamorgan 2nd XI, July 2001.' Carried bat for 56* v Durham at Riverside 2007 (as Ottis Gibson took all ten Hampshire wickets), following up with 126* in the second innings (out of 262-9) to save the game. Joined Surrey for 2009.
Opinions on cricket: 'Less cricket. More practice. Forget 50-over cricket and replace

with 40-over cricket. All the players prefer it, but what do we know? ICC run by set of desk people rather than ex-cricketers.'

Best batting: 133 Hampshire v LUCCE, Rose Bowl 2006

2008 Season

	M	Inn	NO	Runs	HS	Avg	100	50	Ct	St	Balls	Runs	Wkts	Avg	BB	5I	10M
Test																	
FC	14	26	3	940	104 *	40.86	1	6	10	-	0	0	0		-	-	-
ODI																	
List A	6	5	2	137	96 *	45.66	-	1	4	-	0	0	0		-	-	
20/20 Int																	
20/20	6	6	1	130	44	26.00	-	-	4	-	0	0	0		-	-	

Career Performances

	M	Inn	NO	Runs	HS	Avg	100	50	Ct	St	Balls	Runs	Wkts	Avg	BB	5I	10M
Test																	
FC	76	136	15	4139	133	34.20	7	24	64	-	0	0	0		-	-	-
ODI																	
List A	15	14	2	365	96 *	30.41	-	2	7	-	0	0	0		-	-	
20/20 Int																	
20/20	10	10	1	184	44	20.44	-	-	4	-	0	0	0		-	-	

BUCK, N. L. — Leicestershire

Name: Nathan Liam Buck
Role: Right-hand bat, right-arm fast-medium bowler
Born: 26 April 1991, Leicester
County debut: No first-team appearances
Extras: Trained with Stuart Broad, Simon Jones and Graham Onions at the National Performance Centre in 2006, aged 15. Has represented England at U16 and U17 level. Plays club cricket for Loughborough Town CC. Took 28 wickets at an average of 20.46 in all competitions in 2007. Leicestershire 2nd XI 2007-08. Named for the England U19 squad to tour South Africa in January and February 2009. Has a summer contract for 2009

BURKE, J. Somerset

Name: James Burke
Role: Right-hand bat, right-arm fast bowler; all-rounder
County debut: No first-team appearances
Education: Plymouth College.
Overseas tours: England U17 to New Zealand 2008. England U19 to South Africa 2009.
Extras: Was the first Plymouth College pupil in over 20 years to score two centuries in a season at U12 level in 2003. Devon Cricket Board Youth Awards Cricketer of the Year 2005. Has played for Sidmouth CC (2007), Exmouth CC (2008), Devon CCC, Somerset Academy, Somerset Second XI and West of England

BURROWS, T. G. Hampshire

Name: Thomas (Tom) George Burrows
Role: Right-hand bat, wicket-keeper
Born: 5 May 1985, Reading, Berkshire
Height: 5ft 8in **Weight:** 10st 10lbs
Nickname: TB
County debut: 2005 (*see Extras*)
Parents: Tony and Victoria
Marital status: Single
Family links with cricket: 'My father was briefly on Gloucestershire groundstaff and played club cricket'
Education: Reading School; Solent University
Qualifications: 12 GCSEs, 4 AS-levels, 3 A-levels, Level 1 cricket coach
Overseas tours: MCC to Namibia and Uganda 2004-05

Overseas teams played for: Melville CC, Perth 2003-04
Career highlights to date: 'First-class debut v Kent, scoring 42 and putting on 131 with Shane Warne when we were 130-7'
Cricket moments to forget: 'Any dropped catch'
Cricket superstitions: 'Left pad on first'
Cricketers particularly admired: Adi Aymes, Jack Russell, Steve Waugh, John Crawley
Other sports played: Rugby, football
Other sports followed: Football (Chelsea), rugby (London Irish)
Favourite band: Gavin DeGraw
Relaxations: 'Watching films'
Extras: Appeared as substitute wicket-keeper for Hampshire v Yorkshire at The Rose Bowl 2002 but did not make full debut until 2005. Played for Berks in the C&G 2003.
Best batting: 42 Hampshire v Kent, Canterbury 2005

2008 Season

	M	Inn	NO	Runs	HS	Avg	100	50	Ct	St	Balls	Runs	Wkts	Avg	BB	5I	10M
Test																	
FC	2	3	2	30	13 *	30.00	-	-	8	-	0	0	0		-	-	-
ODI																	
List A																	
20/20 Int																	
20/20																	

Career Performances

	M	Inn	NO	Runs	HS	Avg	100	50	Ct	St	Balls	Runs	Wkts	Avg	BB	5I	10M
Test																	
FC	6	9	2	169	42	24.14	-	-	22	-	0	0	0		-	-	-
ODI																	
List A	3	3	1	18	16	9.00	-	-	3	2	0	0	0		-	-	
20/20 Int																	
20/20	1	0	0	0	0		-	-	-	-	0	0	0		-	-	

BURTON, D. A. — Middlesex

Name: David Alexander Burton
Role: Right-hand bat, right-arm fast-medium bowler
Born: 23 August 1985, Stockwell, London
Height: 5ft 11in **Weight:** 11st 11lbs
Nickname: Burts, Burtna, DB
County debut: 2006 (Gloucestershire); 2008 (Middlesex)
County cap: 2006 (Gloucestershire)
Parents: Denise Careless and Cuthbert Burton
Education: Sacred Heart RC Secondary School, Camberwell; Lambeth College, Vauxhall, both London
Qualifications: 2 GCSEs, First Diploma in Electronic Engineering, Diploma in Electronics and PC Systems, ECB Levels 1 and 2 coaching
Career highlights to date: '52* v Glamorgan [2006]'

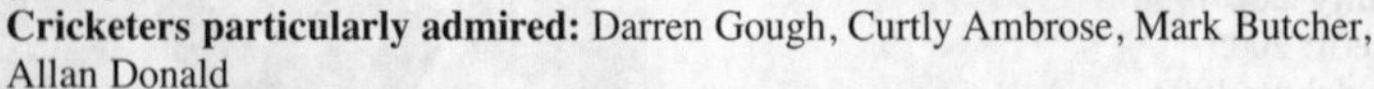

Cricketers particularly admired: Darren Gough, Curtly Ambrose, Mark Butcher, Allan Donald
Other sports followed: Mountain biking, basketball
Favourite band: Jagged Edge, Lil Jon, David Banner, Monica
Relaxations: 'Reading, cycling, running'
Extras: Played for South London Schools Hobbs Trophy runners-up side 2000. Dulwich CC Player of the Year 2006. Scored 52* on first-class debut at Cardiff 2006, in the process sharing with Mark Hardinges (101) in a record ninth-wicket partnership for Gloucestershire in matches v Glamorgan (128)
Opinions on cricket: 'Keep it simple and clear at all times, with the highest intensity of consistency.'
Best batting: 52* Gloucestershire v Glamorgan, Cardiff 2006
Best bowling: 1-97 Middlesex v South Africans, 2008

2008 Season

	M	Inn	NO	Runs	HS	Avg	100	50	Ct	St	Balls	Runs	Wkts	Avg	BB	5I	10M
Test																	
FC	1	0	0	0	0		-	-	-	-	138	97	1	97.00	1-97	-	-
ODI																	
List A																	
20/20 Int																	
20/20	2	0	0	0	0		-	-	1	-	30	38	2	19.00	1-17	-	

Career Performances

	M	Inn	NO	Runs	HS	Avg	100	50	Ct	St	Balls	Runs	Wkts	Avg	BB	5I	10M
Test																	
FC	2	2	1	53	52 *	53.00	-	1	-	-	258	226	1	226.00	1-97	-	-
ODI																	
List A																	
20/20 Int																	
20/20	2	0	0	0	0		-	-	1	-	30	38	2	19.00	1-17	-	

BUTCHER, M. A. Surrey

Name: Mark Alan Butcher
Role: Left-hand bat, right-arm medium bowler, county captain
Born: 23 August 1972, Croydon
Height: 5ft 11in **Weight:** 13st
Nickname: Butch, Baz
County debut: 1991 (one-day), 1992 (first-class)
County cap: 1996
Benefit: 2005
Test debut: 1997
1000 runs in a season: 8
1st-Class 200s: 3
Place in batting averages: 10th av. 57.88 (2007 73rd av. 39.57)
Parents: Alan and Elaine
Children: Alita, 1999
Family links with cricket: Father Alan played for Glamorgan, Surrey and England and was coach with Surrey; brother Gary played for Glamorgan and Surrey; uncle Ian played for Gloucestershire and Leicestershire; uncle Martin played for Surrey
Education: Trinity School; Archbishop Tenison's, Croydon
Qualifications: 5 O-levels, senior coaching award
Career outside cricket: Singer, guitar player
Overseas tours: England YC to New Zealand 1990-91; Surrey to Dubai 1990, 1993, to Perth 1995; England A to Australia 1996-97; England to West Indies 1997-98, to Australia 1998-99, to South Africa 1999-2000, to India and New Zealand 2001-02, to Australia 2002-03, to Bangladesh and Sri Lanka 2003-04, to West Indies 2003-04, to South Africa 2004-05
Overseas teams played for: South Melbourne, Australia 1993-94; North Perth 1994-95
Cricketers particularly admired: Ian Botham, David Gower, Viv Richards, Larry

Gomes, Graham Thorpe, Alec Stewart, Michael Holding, Andrew Flintoff
Other sports followed: Football (Crystal Palace)
Relaxations: 'Music, playing the guitar, novels, wine'
Favorite food: Sushi
Favourite TV programmes: *Nip/Tuck, Fawlty Towers*
Extras: Played his first game for Surrey in 1991 against his father's Glamorgan in the Refuge Assurance League at The Oval, the first-ever match of any sort between first-class counties in which a father and son have been in opposition. Captained England in the third Test v New Zealand at Old Trafford 1999, deputising for the injured Nasser Hussain. Scored match-winning 173* in the fourth Test v Australia at Headingley 2001, winning Man of the Match award, and was England's Man of the Series with 456 runs (more than any other batsman on either side) at an average of 50.66. His other Test awards include England's Man of the Series v Sri Lanka 2002 and v Zimbabwe 2003. Slazenger Sheer Instinct Award 2001 for the cricketer who has impressed the most in the recent season. Scored century in each innings (151/108) v Glamorgan at The Oval 2006, emulating achievement of his father, Alan (117*/114), in the corresponding fixture in 1984. Reached the final of BBC celebrity singing show *Just the Two of Us* in January 2007 with Sarah Brightman. Scored 179 at Hove 2007, in the process sharing with Mark Ramprakash (266*) in the highest partnership ever recorded against Sussex in the County Championship (403). Captain of Surrey since 2005. Knee operation in November 2008
Best batting: 259 Surrey v Leicestershire, Leicester 1999
Best bowling: 5-86 Surrey v Lancashire, Old Trafford 2000

2008 Season

	M	Inn	NO	Runs	HS	Avg	100	50	Ct	St	Balls	Runs	Wkts	Avg	BB	5I	10M
Test																	
FC	6	10	1	521	205	57.88	2	1	4	-	0	0	0		-	-	-
ODI																	
List A	6	5	1	281	139	70.25	1	1	4	-	0	0	0		-	-	
20/20 Int																	
20/20																	

Career Performances

	M	Inn	NO	Runs	HS	Avg	100	50	Ct	St	Balls	Runs	Wkts	Avg	BB	5I	10M
Test	71	131	7	4288	173 *	34.58	8	23	61	-	901	541	15	36.06	4-42	-	-
FC	275	470	37	17619	259	40.69	38	93	253	-	7703	4237	125	33.89	5-86	1	-
ODI																	
List A	191	171	31	4460	139	31.85	2	28	63	-	2527	2210	49	45.10	3-23	-	
20/20 Int																	
20/20	13	12	0	210	60	17.50	-	2	4	-	0	0	0		-	-	

BUTTLER, J. — Somerset

Name: Jos Buttler
Role: Right-handed batsman, wicket-keeper
County debut: No first-team appearances
Education: King's College, Taunton
Extras: Somerset Academy, Somerset 2nd XI. Played for Glastonbury CC 2008. Scored 71 in the second innings of his first game for Somerset Seconds in 2006 to help his county beat Nottinghamshire by 51 runs. In that same match Buttler claimed five catches. Scored a rapid 77 off 49 balls for the England U17 side against New Zealand U19s and 140 for Somerset Seconds v Hampshire, both 2008

CADDICK, A. R. — Somerset

Name: Andrew Richard Caddick
Role: Right-hand bat, right-arm fast-medium bowler, county vice-captain
Born: 21 November 1968, Christchurch, New Zealand
Height: 6ft 5in **Weight:** 14st 13lbs
Nickname: Des, Shack
County debut: 1990 (one-day), 1991 (first-class)
County cap: 1992
Benefit: 1999
Testimonial: 2009
Test debut: 1993
ODI debut: 1993
50 wickets in a season: 11
100 wickets in a season: 1
Place in batting averages: 217th av. 17.50 (2007 258th av. 13.36)
Place in bowling averages: 130th av. 41.88 (2007 17th av. 23.10)

Parents: Christopher and Audrey
Wife and date of marriage: Sarah, 27 January 1995
Children: Ashton Faye, 24 August 1998; Fraser Michael, 12 October 2001
Education: Papanui High School, Christchurch, New Zealand
Qualifications: Qualified plasterer and tiler. Qualified helicopter pilot
Overseas tours: New Zealand YC to Australia (U19 World Cup) 1987-88, to England 1988; England A to Australia 1992-93; England to West Indies 1993-94, to Zimbabwe and New Zealand 1996-97, to West Indies 1997-98, to South Africa and Zimbabwe 1999-2000, to Kenya (ICC Knockout Trophy) 2000-01, to Pakistan and Sri Lanka 2000-01, to India (one-day series) and New Zealand 2001-02, to Sri Lanka (ICC Champions Trophy) 2002-03, to Australia 2002-03, to Africa (World Cup) 2002-03
Career highlights to date: 'Bowling West Indies out at Lord's [2000] and thus getting my name up on the board'
Cricketers particularly admired: Dennis Lillee, Richard Hadlee, Robin Smith, Jimmy Cook
Other sports followed: 'Mostly all'
Relaxations: Golf
Extras: Whyte and Mackay Bowler of the Year 1997. Took 105 first-class wickets (av. 19.82) in 1998 season. Leading wicket-taker in the single-division four-day era of the County Championship with 422 wickets (av. 22.48) 1993-99. Cornhill England Player of the Year 1999-2000. Took 5-16 from 13 overs as West Indies were bowled out for 54 in their second innings in the second Test at Lord's 2000. Took 5-14 in the fourth Test v West Indies at Headingley 2000, including four wickets (Jacobs, McLean, Ambrose, King) in an over. One of *Wisden*'s Five Cricketers of the Year 2001. Took 200th Test wicket (Craig McMillan) in the third Test v New Zealand at Auckland 2001-02. His international awards include England's Man of the [Test] Series v New Zealand 1999 and joint Man of the Match (with Gary Kirsten) in the third Test v South Africa at Durban 1999-2000 (7-46). Retired from ODI cricket in March 2003. Took 1000th first-class wicket (Joe Sayers) v Yorkshire at Taunton 2005. Returned career-best match figures of 12-71 (7-30/5-41) v Gloucestershire at Bristol 2007. Appointed vice-captain of Somerset for 2008. His 2009 benefit will be his second
Best batting: 92 Somerset v Worcestershire, Worcester 1995
Best bowling: 9-32 Somerset v Lancashire, Taunton 1993

2008 Season

	M	Inn	NO	Runs	HS	Avg	100	50	Ct	St	Balls	Runs	Wkts	Avg	BB	5I	10M
Test																	
FC	10	12	4	140	35 *	17.50	-	-	2	-	1694	1047	25	41.88	5-118	1	-
ODI																	
List A	1	0	0	0	0		-	-	-	-	48	50	0		-	-	
20/20 Int																	
20/20																	

Career Performances

	M	Inn	NO	Runs	HS	Avg	100	50	Ct	St	Balls	Runs	Wkts	Avg	BB	5I	10M
Test	62	95	12	861	49 *	10.37	-	-	21	-	13558	6999	234	29.91	7-46	13	1
FC	270	353	69	4244	92	14.94	-	9	87	-	58876	30862	1170	26.37	9-32	78	17
ODI	54	38	18	249	36	12.45	-	-	9	-	2937	1965	69	28.47	4-19	-	
List A	262	135	59	810	39	10.65	-	-	44	-	12827	9085	341	26.64	6-30	5	
20/20 Int																	
20/20	16	1	0	0	0	0.00	-	-	1	-	306	468	15	31.20	2-12	-	

CAIRNS, C. L. Nottinghamshire

Name: Christopher (Chris) Lance Cairns
Role: Right-hand bat, right-arm fast-medium bowler, all-rounder
Born: 13 June 1970, Picton, Marlborough, New Zealand
Height: 6ft 2in **Weight:** 14st
County debut: 1988
County cap: 1993
Test debut: 1989-90
ODI debut: 1990-91
Twenty20 Int debut: 2004-05
1000 runs in a season: 1
50 wickets in a season: 3
Parents: Lance and Sue
Family links with cricket: Father played for New Zealand; uncle played first-class cricket in New Zealand
Education: Christchurch Boys' High School, New Zealand
Qualifications: Fifth and sixth form certificates
Overseas tours: New Zealand YC to Australia (U19 World Cup) 1987-88; New Zealand Young Internationals to Zimbabwe 1988-89; New Zealand to Australia 1989-90, 1993-94, to India 1995-96, to India and Pakistan (World Cup) 1995-96, to West Indies 1995-96, to Pakistan 1996-97, to Zimbabwe 1997-98, to Australia 1997-98, to Sri Lanka 1998, to UK, Ireland and Netherlands (World Cup) 1999, to England 1999, to India 1999-2000, to Zimbabwe and South Africa 2000-01, to Kenya (ICC Knockout Trophy) 2000-01, to Australia 2001-02, to Africa (World Cup) 2002-03, to Pakistan (one-day series) 2003-04, to England 2004, to England (ICC Champions Trophy) 2004, to Bangladesh 2004-05 (one-day series), to Australia 2004-05 (one-day series), plus other one-day tournaments in Sharjah, India, Singapore, Sri Lanka and Zimbabwe; ICC World XI to Australia (Tsunami Relief) 2004-05

Overseas teams played for: Northern Districts 1988-89; Canterbury 1990-91 - 2005-06; Chandigarh Lions (ICL) 2007-08 –
Cricketers particularly admired: Mick Newell, Richard Hadlee, Dennis Lillee
Extras: Won the Walter Lawrence Trophy for the fastest first-class hundred of the season 1995 (65 balls for Notts v Cambridge University at Fenner's). Cricket Society's Wetherell Award for leading all-rounder in English first-class cricket 1995. One of New Zealand Cricket Almanack's two Players of the Year 1998, 1999, 2000. One of Indian Cricket's five Cricketers of the Year 2000. One of Wisden's Five Cricketers of the Year 2000. Had match figures of 10-100 v West Indies at Hamilton 1999-2000 to make himself and his father Lance the first father and son to have taken ten wickets in a Test match; also won Man of the Match award. His other Test and ODI awards include New Zealand's Man of the Series v England 1999 and Man of the Match for his 102* in the ICC Knockout Trophy final v India in Kenya 2000-01. Took 200th ODI wicket (Tillakaratne Dilshan) v Sri Lanka at Christchurch 2005-06. An overseas player with Notts 1988-89, 1992-93, 1995-96, 2003 (one-day captain 2003) and as a locum for Stephen Fleming for the early part of 2006. Retired from Test cricket in 2004 after the third Test v England at Trent Bridge and from all international cricket in early 2006. His efforts in 2008 were confined to Twenty20
Best batting: 158 New Zealand v South Africa, Auckland 2003-04
Best bowling: 8-47 Nottinghamshire v Sussex, Arundel 1995

2008 Season

	M	Inn	NO	Runs	HS	Avg	100	50	Ct	St	Balls	Runs	Wkts	Avg	BB	5I	10M
Test																	
FC																	
ODI																	
List A																	
20/20 Int																	
20/20	9	9	1	153	50	19.12	-	1	1	-	0	0	0		-	-	

Career Performances

	M	Inn	NO	Runs	HS	Avg	100	50	Ct	St	Balls	Runs	Wkts	Avg	BB	5I	10M
Test	62	104	5	3320	158	33.53	5	22	14	-	11698	6410	218	29.40	7-27	13	1
FC	217	341	38	10702	158	35.32	13	71	78	-	34252	18322	647	28.31	8-47	30	6
ODI	215	193	25	4950	115	29.46	4	26	66	-	8168	6594	201	32.80	5-42	1	
List A	425	377	59	10364	143	32.59	9	55	118	-	16578	12711	455	27.93	6-12	6	
20/20 Int	2	2	0	3	2	1.50	-	-	1	-	48	52	1	52.00	1-28	-	
20/20	14	14	2	176	50	14.66	-	1	5	-	108	126	5	25.20	2-24	-	

14. Up to and including the 2006-07 Ashes tour, how many series have been won by Australia?

CARBERRY, M. A. Hampshire

Name: Michael Alexander Carberry
Role: Left-hand bat, right-arm medium bowler
Born: 29 September 1980, Croydon
Height: 5ft 11in **Weight:** 14st 7lbs
Nickname: Carbs
County debut: 2001 (Surrey), 2003 (Kent), 2006 (Hampshire)
County cap: 2006 (Hampshire)
1000 runs in a season: 2
Place in batting averages: 114th av. 31.34 (2007 31st av. 50.80)
Parents: Maria and Neville
Marital status: Single
Family links with cricket: 'My dad played club cricket'
Education: St John Rigby College
Qualifications: 10 GCSEs
Overseas tours: Surrey U17 to South Africa 1997; England U19 to New Zealand 1998-99, to Malaysia and (U19 World Cup) Sri Lanka 1999-2000; England A to Bangladesh 2006-07; England Lions to India 2007-08
Overseas teams played for: Portland CC, Melbourne; University CC, Perth 2005
Career highlights to date: 'Every day is a highlight'
Cricket moments to forget: None
Cricketers particularly admired: Ricky Ponting, Brian Lara
Relaxations: 'Sleeping'
Extras: Scored century (126*) for ECB U18 v Pakistan U19 at Abergavenny 1998. Represented England U19 1999, 2000. NBC Denis Compton Award for the most promising young Surrey player 1999, 2000. Scored century (137) on Kent debut v Cambridge UCCE at Fenner's 2003. Scored 112 as Kent scored a then county record fourth innings 429-5 to beat Worcestershire at Canterbury 2004. Scored career-best 192* as Hampshire scored 331-5 to beat Warwickshire with three balls to spare at The Rose Bowl 2007. Scored century in each innings (127/120) v Worcestershire at Kidderminster 2007. Scored a century (113*) v Yorkshire at Headingley 2007, in the process passing 1000 first-class runs in a season for the first time.
Best batting: 192* Hampshire v Warwickshire, Rose Bowl 2007
Best bowling: 2-85 Hampshire v Durham, Riverside 2006

2008 Season

	M	Inn	NO	Runs	HS	Avg	100	50	Ct	St	Balls	Runs	Wkts	Avg	BB	5I	10M
Test																	
FC	16	29	3	815	108	31.34	1	4	6	-	78	31	0		-	-	-
ODI																	
List A	13	13	1	394	67	32.83	-	5	7	-	0	0	0		-	-	
20/20 Int																	
20/20	10	10	1	334	58	37.11	-	4	6	-	0	0	0		-	-	

Career Performances

	M	Inn	NO	Runs	HS	Avg	100	50	Ct	St	Balls	Runs	Wkts	Avg	BB	5I	10M
Test																	
FC	83	147	14	5132	192 *	38.58	13	24	34	-	690	521	7	74.42	2-85	-	-
ODI																	
List A	93	88	7	2124	88	26.22	-	19	34	-	42	41	1	41.00	1-21	-	
20/20 Int																	
20/20	42	39	8	921	90	29.70	-	8	17	-	0	0	0		-	-	

CARTER, N. M. — Warwickshire

Name: Neil Miller Carter
Role: Left-hand bat, left-arm fast-medium bowler
Born: 29 January 1975, Cape Town, South Africa
Height: 6ft 2in **Weight:** 14st 8lbs
Nickname: Carts
County debut: 2001
County cap: 2005
Place in batting averages: 118th av. 30.71
Place in bowling averages: 78th av. 31.17 (2007 52nd av. 28.30)
Parents: John and Heather
Marital status: Single
Education: Hottentots Holland High School; Cape Technikon; ITI; stock market training
Qualifications: Certified Novell Engineer, Level 2 coaching
Career outside cricket: Investing and sports marketing
Overseas tours: SA Country Schools U15 to England 1992; Warwickshire to Cape Town 2001-03, to Grenada 2007

Overseas teams played for: Boland 1998-99 – 2003-04
Career highlights to date: 'Lord's finals and Championship win plus 2005 season'
Cricket moments to forget: 'Losing C&G final 2005'
Cricketers particularly admired: Allan Donald, Shaun Pollock
Young players to look out for: Chris Woakes, Moeen Ali
Other sports played: Swimming, golf, hockey, squash
Other sports followed: Rugby union (Stormers in Super 14; Springboks), football (Sheffield Wednesday), baseball (LA Angels), ice hockey (Anaheim Ducks)
Favourite band: Mike and the Mechanics
Relaxations: Gricing (steam train photography)
Extras: Won Man of the Match award in first one-day match for Warwickshire v Essex at Edgbaston in the C&G 2001 (4-21/43-ball 40). Warwickshire Player of the Year 2005 (1088 runs and 94 wickets in all cricket and, including Twenty20, equalled Allan Donald's club season record of 53 one-day wickets). Is England-qualified. Has played in every 20/20 game Warwickshire have played, 49 consecutive games. On loan to Middlesex for 2008 Stanford Series
Opinions on cricket: 'Wickets are becoming too slow, not only in county cricket, but worldwide... Somehow all wickets need to quicken up, but how?'
Best batting: 103 Warwickshire v Sussex, Hove 2002
Best bowling: 6-63 Boland v Griqualand West, Kimberley 2000-01

2008 Season

	M	Inn	NO	Runs	HS	Avg	100	50	Ct	St	Balls	Runs	Wkts	Avg	BB	5I	10M
Test																	
FC	13	14	0	430	84	30.71	-	4	3	-	2242	1278	41	31.17	6-100	2	-
ODI																	
List A	12	12	1	171	78	15.54	-	1	2	-	431	359	18	19.94	3-25	-	
20/20 Int																	
20/20	11	10	0	208	52	20.80	-	1	2	-	194	235	8	29.37	2-14	-	

Career Performances

	M	Inn	NO	Runs	HS	Avg	100	50	Ct	St	Balls	Runs	Wkts	Avg	BB	5I	10M
Test																	
FC	87	115	21	1937	103	20.60	1	7	24	-	14447	8425	230	36.63	6-63	8	-
ODI																	
List A	136	115	13	1950	135	19.11	1	6	14	-	5933	4736	189	25.05	5-31	2	
20/20 Int																	
20/20	49	46	2	794	58	18.04	-	2	8	-	964	1148	50	22.96	5-19	1	

CHAMBERS, M. A. — Essex

Name: Maurice Anthony Chambers
Role: Right-hand bat, right-arm fast bowler
Born: 14 September 1987, Portland, Jamaica
Height: 6ft 3in **Weight:** 13st
Nickname: Moza, Chungkid
County debut: 2005
Parents: Elaine Lewis
Marital status: Single
Education: Homerton College of Technology; Sir George Monoux College
Qualifications: BTEC Nat. Dip. in Business Studies
Career outside cricket: 'College and playing basketball with my mates'
Off-season: 'England Skill Set Programme to Florida for a month, then to India for two weeks (Denis Lillee's Academy)'
Overseas tours: Essex Academy to India 2006-07; England U19 to Malaysia 2006-07; Essex pre-season tour to Dubai 2008

Career highlights to date: 'Playing for Essex 2nd XI v Middlesex [2006] and bowling 16 overs, 7 maidens, and taking 3 wickets for 25 runs; playing 20/20 v Northants, it felt really good getting Matt Prior and Murray Goodwin out'
Cricket moments to forget: 'Playing for England U19 v India, we were 8 wickets down with 2 balls to go and I was the last batsman. I told myself I was not going to pad up, and then my mate was out and I went in to bat with no abdo guard or gloves'
Cricketers particularly admired: Courtney Walsh, Curtly Ambrose, Stuart Broad, Brian Lara, Kevin Pietersen, Brett Lee
Young players to look out for: Mervyn Westfield, Jahid Ahmed, Steve Finn, Andrew Miller, Ben Wright, Adil Rashid, Chris Jordan
Other sports played: 'Play basketball at college for the fun of it'
Other sports followed: Football (Manchester United)
Favourite band: Movado
Relaxations: 'Music, shopping, football and playing PS2'
Extras: London Schools Cricket Association Bowler of the Year 2004. Jack Petchey Award 2004. Played for MCC Young Cricketers 2004. Wanstead CC Bowler of the Year. Acquired British citizenship in 2007. Out for the whole of the 2007 season with a stress fracture in the lower back. Signed fresh two-year contract in November 2008. Attended Loughborough ECB fast bowling training camp which included a December trip to Florida
Opinions on cricket: 'It's the best game in the world...'
Best batting: 7 Essex v New Zealand, Chelmsford 2008
Best bowling: 3-37 Essex v New Zealand, Chelmsford 2008

2008 Season

	M	Inn	NO	Runs	HS	Avg	100	50	Ct	St	Balls	Runs	Wkts	Avg	BB	5I	10M
Test																	
FC	3	5	3	9	7	4.50	-	-	1	-	396	251	8	31.37	3-37	-	-
ODI																	
List A	2	1	1	1	1 *		-	-	1	-	54	54	2	27.00	1-26	-	
20/20 Int																	
20/20	11	6	4	19	10 *	9.50	-	-	5	-	162	221	10	22.10	3-31	-	

Career Performances

	M	Inn	NO	Runs	HS	Avg	100	50	Ct	St	Balls	Runs	Wkts	Avg	BB	5I	10M
Test																	
FC	4	6	4	11	7	5.50	-	-	1	-	492	335	9	37.22	3-37	-	-
ODI																	
List A	2	1	1	1	1 *		-	-	1	-	54	54	2	27.00	1-26	-	
20/20 Int																	
20/20	11	6	4	19	10 *	9.50	-	-	5	-	162	221	10	22.10	3-31	-	

CHANDERPAUL, S. — Durham

Name: Shivnarine Chanderpaul
Role: Left-hand bat, leg-break bowler
Born: 16 August 1974, Demerara, Guyana
Nickname: Shiv
County debut: 2007
Test debut: 1993-94
ODI debut: 1994-95
Twenty20 Int debut: 2005-06
1st-Class 200s: 4
1st-Class 300s: 1
Place in batting averages: 77th av. 37.36 (2007 4th av. 74.44)
Wife: Amy
Overseas tours: West Indies U19 to England 1993; West Indies to India 1994-95, to New Zealand 1994-95, to England 1995, to Australia 1995-96, to India, Pakistan and Sri Lanka (World Cup) 1995-96, to Australia 1996-97, to Pakistan 1997-98, to Bangladesh (Wills International Cup) 1998-99, to South Africa 1998-99, to UK, Ireland and Netherlands (World Cup) 1999, to Bangladesh 1999-2000, to New Zealand 1999-2000,

to England 2000, to Australia 2000-01, to Zimbabwe and Kenya 2001, to Sharjah (v Pakistan) 2001-02, to Sri Lanka (ICC Champions Trophy) 2002-03, to India and Bangladesh 2002-03, to Africa (World Cup) 2002-03, to Zimbabwe and South Africa 2003-04, to England 2004, to England (ICC Champions Trophy) 2004, to Sri Lanka 2005 (c), to Australia 2005-06 (c), to New Zealand 2005-06 (c), to India (ICC Champions Trophy) 2006-07, to Pakistan 2006-07, to England 2007, to South Africa (World 20/20) 2007-08, to Zimbabwe and South Africa 2007-08, to New Zealand 2008-09, plus other one-day tournaments and series in Sharjah, Singapore, Toronto, Bangladesh, Australia, Malaysia, India and Ireland
Overseas teams played for: Guyana 1991-92 – 2007-08; Bangalore Royal Challengers (IPL) 2007-08
Extras: Scored century (104) as West Indies made a Test record 418 in the fourth innings to beat Australia in Antigua 2002-03, winning Man of the Match award. His other series and match awards include Man of the [Test] Series v India 2001-02 (562 runs; av. 140.50), West Indies Man of the [Test] Series v England 2004 (437 runs; av. 72.83) and 2007 (446 runs; av 148.66) and overall Man of the [ODI] Series v England 2007 (202 runs; av. 202.00). Represented West Indies in the 2006-07 World Cup. Captain of West Indies from March 2005 to April 2006, scoring a double century (203*) in his first Test in charge, v South Africa 2004-05 in his home country of Guyana. In 2007 he scored 446 runs against England in three Tests. Named as one of *Wisden*'s Five Cricketers of the Year 2008. ICC Player of the Year 2008. Durham's overseas player for 2009
Best batting: 303* Guyana v Jamaica, Kingston 1995-96
Best bowling: 4-48 Guyana v Leeward Islands, Basseterre 1992-93

2008 Season

	M	Inn	NO	Runs	HS	Avg	100	50	Ct	St	Balls	Runs	Wkts	Avg	BB	5I	10M
Test																	
FC	8	12	1	411	138	37.36	1	2	2	-	24	19	0		-	-	-
ODI																	
List A	7	7	1	190	77	31.66	-	2	-	-	12	23	0		-	-	
20/20 Int																	
20/20	2	2	0	55	48	27.50	-	-	2	-	0	0	0		-	-	

Career Performances

	M	Inn	NO	Runs	HS	Avg	100	50	Ct	St	Balls	Runs	Wkts	Avg	BB	5I	10M
Test	112	193	30	8001	203 *	49.08	19	49	47	-	1680	845	8	105.62	1-2	-	-
FC	228	372	64	16363	303 *	53.12	46	83	135	-	4634	2453	56	43.80	4-48	-	-
ODI	235	221	34	7573	150	40.49	8	52	65	-	740	636	14	45.42	3-18	-	
List A	341	317	54	10843	150	41.22	9	79	98	-	1681	1388	56	24.78	4-22	-	
20/20 Int	6	6	1	133	41	26.60	-	-	4	-	0	0	0		-	-	
20/20	13	13	1	243	48	20.25	-	-	8	-	0	0	0		-	-	

CHAPPLE, G. Lancashire

Name: Glen Chapple
Role: Right-hand bat, right-arm fast-medium bowler; all-rounder; county captain
Born: 23 January 1974, Skipton, Yorkshire
Height: 6ft 1in **Weight:** 13st
Nickname: Chappy
County debut: 1992
County cap: 1994
Benefit: 2004
ODI debut: 2006
50 wickets in a season: 4
Place in batting averages: 153rd av. 26.18 (2007 198th av. 22.53)
Place in bowling averages: 15th av. 20.50 (2007 12th av. 21.85)
Parents: Mike and Eileen
Wife and date of marriage: Kerry, 31 January 2004
Children: Annie, 6 August 2003; Joe, 16 January 2006
Family links with cricket: Father played in Lancashire League for Nelson and was a professional for Darwen and Earby
Education: West Craven High School; Nelson and Colne College
Qualifications: 8 GCSEs, 2 A-levels
Overseas tours: England U18 to Canada (International Youth Tournament) 1991; England YC to New Zealand 1990-91; England U19 to Pakistan 1991-92, to India 1992-93; England A to India 1994-95, to Australia 1996-97; England VI to Hong Kong 2002, 2003, 2004, 2006
Cricket superstitions: None
Cricketers particularly admired: Dennis Lillee, Robin Smith
Other sports followed: Football (Liverpool), golf
Favourite band: U2, Oasis, Stone Roses
Relaxations: 'Golf'
Extras: Set record for fastest century in first-class cricket (21 minutes; against declaration bowling) v Glamorgan at Old Trafford 1993. Man of the Match in the 1996 NatWest final against Essex at Lord's (6-18). Lancashire Player of the Year 2002. Returned match figures of 10-86 (7-53/3-33) v Durham at Blackpool 2007. Topped the Lancashire wicket-takers for the 2008 first-class season with 42. Appointed county captain for 2009
Opinions on cricket: 'How long do people have to keep banging on about playing too much cricket? It's not difficult to see and it's annoying that nothing will change until my boots are in the bin! Cheers!'

Best batting: 155 Lancashire v Somerset, Old Trafford 2001
Best bowling: 7-53 Lancashire v Durham, Blackpool 2007

2008 Season

	M	Inn	NO	Runs	HS	Avg	100	50	Ct	St	Balls	Runs	Wkts	Avg	BB	5I	10M
Test																	
FC	11	13	2	288	52 *	26.18	-	1	4	-	1997	861	42	20.50	6-40	2	-
ODI																	
List A	7	6	2	82	33 *	20.50	-	-	-	-	246	184	8	23.00	3-30	-	
20/20 Int																	
20/20	5	2	1	26	22	26.00	-	-	2	-	96	95	5	19.00	2-23	-	

Career Performances

	M	Inn	NO	Runs	HS	Avg	100	50	Ct	St	Balls	Runs	Wkts	Avg	BB	5I	10M
Test																	
FC	227	310	57	6311	155	24.94	6	28	76	-	38518	19213	693	27.72	7-53	27	2
ODI	1	1	0	14	14	14.00	-	-	-	-	24	14	0	-	-	-	
List A	259	148	38	1951	81 *	17.73	-	9	55	-	11039	8295	286	29.00	6-18	4	
20/20 Int																	
20/20	28	17	5	176	55 *	14.66	-	1	10	-	480	614	26	23.61	2-13	-	

CHEETHAM, S. P. — Lancashire

Name: Steven Philip Cheetham
Role: Right-hand bat, right-arm fast bowler
Born: 5 September 1987, Oldham
Height: 6ft 5in **Weight:** 14st 6lbs
Nickname: Cheets, Bambi, Torres
County debut: 2007
Parents: Philip and Joan
Marital status: Single
Education: Bury Grammar School
Qualifications: 10 GCSEs, 4 A-levels
Off-season: 'Playing for Cheltenham CC in Melbourne'
Overseas teams played for: Cheltenham CC, Melbourne 2007-08, 2008-09
Career highlights to date: 'First-team debut for Lancashire v Durham UCCE. Representing England U17. Taking a hat-trick in the VTCA Cup semi-final v Old Mentonians in Melbourne, March 2008'

Cricket moments to forget: 'Two seasons of injuries – stress fracture of back and double hernia. Having my hat-trick ball and five-wicket haul dropped at Derby, first game of the 2008 season'
Cricket superstitions: 'Always right pad on first'
Cricketers particularly admired: Marcus Trescothick, Chris Gayle, Brett Lee, Andrew Flintoff
Young players to look out for: Karl Brown
Other sports played: Football (Bury GS Old Boys, trial for Oldham Athletic)
Other sports followed: Football (Oldham Athletic)
Favourite band: Arctic Monkeys, the Courteeners
Relaxations: 'Music, seeing friends'
Extras: Best figures of 5-11 for Radcliffe v Ramsbottom in the Inter League Club Challenge Trophy as a 17-year-old. Attended Dennis Lillee's MRF Pace Foundation, India 2007. Is a Lancashire Scholarship player and appeared in one first-class match for the county in 2007. Helped Cheltenham CC (Melbourne) to their first league win for 102 years in 2007-08
Opinions on cricket: '[Would like] to see more young players from the academies come through the counties to represent both counties and England.'
Best bowling: 1-44 Lancashire v DUCCE, Durham 2007

2008 Season

	M	Inn	NO	Runs	HS	Avg	100	50	Ct	St	Balls	Runs	Wkts	Avg	BB	5I	10M
Test																	
FC																	
ODI																	
List A	4	2	2	3	3*		-	-	-	-	168	126	7	18.00	3-25	-	
20/20 Int																	
20/20																	

Career Performances

	M	Inn	NO	Runs	HS	Avg	100	50	Ct	St	Balls	Runs	Wkts	Avg	BB	5I	10M
Test																	
FC	1	0	0	0	0		-	-	1	-	144	127	1	127.00	1-44	-	-
ODI																	
List A	4	2	2	3	3*	-	-	-	-	168	126	7	18.00	3-25	-		
20/20 Int																	
20/20																	

CHILTON, M. J. Lancashire

Name: Mark James Chilton
Role: Right-hand bat, right-arm medium bowler
Born: 2 October 1976, Sheffield
Height: 6ft 2in **Weight:** 13st 6lbs
Nickname: Chill, Peter, Roger, Dougie
County debut: 1997
County cap: 2002
1000 runs in a season: 1
Place in batting averages: 143rd av. 27.54 (2007 152nd av. 28.00)
Parents: Jim and Sue
Wife and date of marriage: Hayley, 29 December 2006
Children: Bethan, 31 October 2007
Family links with cricket: 'Dad played local leagues'
Education: Manchester Grammar School; Durham University
Qualifications: BA (Hons) Business Economics, Level III coach
Off-season: 'Playing for Melbourne University CC'
Overseas tours: Manchester Grammar School to Barbados 1993-94, to South Africa 1995-96; Durham University to Zimbabwe 1997-98
Overseas teams played for: East Torrens, Adelaide 2000-01; North Sydney CC, Sydney 2002-03
Career highlights to date: 'Playing for and captaining Lancashire'
Cricket moments to forget: 'Losing C&G final 2006'
Cricket superstitions: None
Cricketers particularly admired: John Crawley, David Gower
Young players to look out for: Karl Brown, Steve Mullaney
Other sports played: Golf
Other sports followed: Football (Manchester United)
Favourite band: The Charlatans
Relaxations: 'Guitar'
Extras: Represented England U14, U15, U17. England U15 Batsman of the Year award 1992. Played for North of England v New Zealand U19 1996. Played for British Universities in 1997 Benson and Hedges Cup, winning the Gold Award against Sussex at Fenner's (34/5-26). Captain of Lancashire 2005 until standing down in October 2007
Opinions on cricket: 'It's important to maintain a balance between the four-day game and Twenty20. These are exciting times, but let's not lose sight of all forms of the game.'

Best batting: 131 Lancashire v Kent, Old Trafford 2006
Best bowling: 1-1 Lancashire v Sri Lanka A, Old Trafford 1999

2008 Season

	M	Inn	NO	Runs	HS	Avg	100	50	Ct	St	Balls	Runs	Wkts	Avg	BB	5I	10M
Test																	
FC	7	12	1	303	102	27.54	1	1	1	-	0	0	0		-	-	-
ODI																	
List A	1	0	0	0	0		-	-	-	-	0	0	0		-	-	
20/20 Int																	
20/20																	

Career Performances

	M	Inn	NO	Runs	HS	Avg	100	50	Ct	St	Balls	Runs	Wkts	Avg	BB	5I	10M
Test																	
FC	150	245	17	7268	131	31.87	18	26	111	-	1311	664	10	66.40	1-1	-	-
ODI																	
List A	159	151	20	3885	115	29.65	4	19	49	-	1082	992	41	24.19	5-26	1	
20/20 Int																	
20/20	32	22	8	236	38	16.85	-	-	13	-	0	0	0		-	-	

CHOPRA, V. — Essex

Name: Varun Chopra
Role: Right-hand opening bat, right-arm swing/leg-spin bowler
Born: 21 June 1987, Barking, Essex
Height: 6ft 1in **Weight:** 12st 7lbs
Nickname: Chops, Chopper, Tiddles, Tidz
County debut: 2006
Place in batting averages: 132nd av. 29.23 (2007 151st av. 28.21)
Parents: Chander and Surinder
Marital status: Single
Education: Ilford County HS
Qualifications: 11 GCSEs, 4 A-levels
Off-season: 'Travelling in Europe and Asia, and working on my game at Essex.'
Overseas tours: England U19 to Bangladesh 2005-06 (c), to Sri Lanka (U19 World Cup) 2005-06; Essex to South Africa 2006, to Dubai 2007 and 2008

Overseas teams played for: Willetton CC, Perth 2006-07, 2007-08
Career highlights to date: 'Captaining England U19. Man of Series v India U19 2006. Century [106 plus 50* in second innings] on Championship debut v Gloucestershire [at Chelmsford 2006]. Winning the Friends Provident trophy, 2008'
Cricket moments to forget: 'Any dropped catch. England U19 [World Cup] semi-final v India [2005-06]' (*England lost by 234 runs, having been bowled out for 58*)
Cricketers particularly admired: Sachin Tendulkar, Shane Warne, Kevin Pietersen
Young players to look out for: Jaik Mickelburgh
Other sports played: 'Football – Spot!'
Other sports followed: Football (Manchester United)
Favourite band: Musiq Soulchild, Ginuwine, T.I., Lil Wayne, Kanye
Relaxations: 'Jamming with mates, poker, Pro Evo'
Extras: Lord's Taverners Player of the Year U13, U15, U19. Sony Sports Personality of the Year runner-up. Captained England U19 2005 and 2006; Man of the Match v Bangladesh U19 at Colombo in the quarter-finals of the U19 World Cup 2005-06 and Man of the Series v India U19 2006, scoring a century in each innings (123/164) in the second 'Test' at Taunton. Scored century (106) on Championship debut v Gloucestershire at Chelmsford 2006, in the process becoming the youngest player to score a Championship hundred for Essex. Scored his career best 155 in the final 2008 Championship game
Best batting: 155 Essex v Gloucestershire, Bristol 2008

2008 Season

	M	Inn	NO	Runs	HS	Avg	100	50	Ct	St	Balls	Runs	Wkts	Avg	BB	5I	10M
Test																	
FC	11	18	1	497	155	29.23	1	2	12	-	10	14	0		-	-	-
ODI																	
List A	8	7	0	205	79	29.28	-	2	1	-	0	0	0		-	-	
20/20 Int																	
20/20	5	5	0	52	18	10.40	-	-	-	-	0	0	0		-	-	

Career Performances

	M	Inn	NO	Runs	HS	Avg	100	50	Ct	St	Balls	Runs	Wkts	Avg	BB	5I	10M
Test																	
FC	36	60	5	1715	155	31.18	2	11	34	-	40	39	0		-	-	-
ODI																	
List A	20	19	0	488	102	25.68	1	3	5	-	0	0	0		-	-	
20/20 Int																	
20/20	7	7	2	58	18	11.60	-	-	1	-	0	0	0		-	-	

CHOUDHRY, S. H. Warwickshire

Name: Shaaiq Hussain Choudhry
Role: Right-hand bat, slow left-arm bowler
Born: 3 November 1985, Sheffield, Yorkshire
Height: 5ft 10in **Weight:** 11st 7lbs
Nickname: Shak, Chouds
County debut: No first-team appearance
Parents: Sabir and Badar-u-Nasa
Marital status: Single
Education: Fir Vale School; Rotherham College of Arts and Technology; University of Bradford
Qualifications: 9 GCSEs, BTEC National Diploma, BSc (Hons) degree ('currently studying final year')
Off-season: 'In the coming years I would like to go and play some cricket abroad to gain experience and further my skills and knowledge of the game, as I have not had the opportunity to do this in the past due to educational commitments'
Overseas tours: MCC Universities to Ireland 2006; Bradford/Leeds UCCE to India 2007; British Universities to South Africa 2008
Career highlights to date: '54* against West Indians for MCC in 2007. Six wickets against Surrey CCC at The Oval [for Bradford/Leeds UCCE 2007]. As a cricket fan, I have grown up watching cricketers like Mark Ramprakash and Vikram Solanki, and having the opportunity to play against them and get their wickets was a huge personal achievement for me'
Cricket moments to forget: 'Getting hit out of the ground by Rikki Clarke at The Oval'
Cricketers particularly admired: Shane Warne, Muttiah Muralitharan, Michael Vaughan, Sachin Tendulkar
Other sports followed: 'Follow a little of most sports'
Favourite band: Kanye West, Usher, Timbaland
Relaxations: 'Going to the gym, socialising with friends and family and listening to music'
Extras: Played for Bradford/Leeds UCCE 2006, 2007. Made first-class debut for MCC v West Indians at Durham 2007, scoring 54*
Opinions on cricket: 'I believe the game today is a faster-moving game as it is played in a more aggressive manner. I also think the standard of the game has developed and improved a great deal since I've been following it due to the help of the advanced technology that's around in this day and age.'
Best batting: 54* MCC v West Indians, Durham 2007

2008 Season (did not make any first-class or one-day appearances)

Career Performances

	M	Inn	NO	Runs	HS	Avg	100	50	Ct	St	Balls	Runs	Wkts	Avg	BB	5I	10M
Test																	
FC	1	2	2	61	54 *		-	1	-	-	72	43	0		-	-	-
ODI																	
List A																	
20/20 Int																	
20/20																	

CLARE, J. L. Derbyshire

Name: Jonathan Luke Clare
Role: Right-hand bat, right-arm fast-medium bowler; all-rounder
Born: 14 June 1986, Burnley, Lancashire
Height: 6ft 3in **Weight:** 15st
Nickname: JC, Unit, Beefy
County debut: 2007
Place in batting averages: 50th av. 42.69
Place in bowling averages: 61st av. 28.09 (2007 6th av. 20.30)
Parents: John and Elaine
Marital status: 'Single'
Family links with cricket: Grandfather and father played club cricket for Burnley CC
Education: St Theodores RC High School and Sixth Form
Qualifications: 10 GCSEs, 3 A-levels
Off-season: 'A month at the IMG Academy in Florida with the ECB Performance Programme'
Overseas tours: Derbyshire to Grenada, 2008
Overseas teams played for: Northern Districts, New Zealand; Hamilton Old Boys, New Zealand
Career highlights to date: 'Taking 5-90 on first-class debut v Notts. Scoring my maiden first-class century (129*) and taking 7-79 in game v Northamptonshire in 2008'
Cricket moments to forget: Not too many yet, but I'm sure there's one just around the corner!
Cricket superstitions: None
Cricketers particularly admired: Dale Benkenstein, Andrew Flintoff, Carl Hooper

Young players to look out for: Dan Redfern, Jamie Pipe
Other sports played: Football, golf ('handicap 14') 'any sports'
Other sports followed: Football (Burnley FC season ticket holder)
Favourite band: Glasvegas, Arctic Monkeys, 'any Manchester music'
Relaxations: 'Pub games - darts, pool and cribbage '
Extras: Was member of Burnley U15 with three other players currently playing county/international cricket – David Brown (Gloucestershire), Michael Brown (Hampshire), James Anderson (Lancashire/England). Recorded maiden first-class five-wicket return (5-90) on debut v Nottinghamshire at Chesterfield 2007. Was selected with six other fast bowlers for the 2008 ECB Skills Set trip to Florida which included tuition from Dennis Lillee in India
Opinions on cricket: 'Too many Championship games - not enough time to recover between games'
Best batting: 129* Derbyshire v Northamptonshire, Northampton 2008
Best bowling: 7-74 Derbyshire v Northamptonshire, Northampton 2008

2008 Season

	M	Inn	NO	Runs	HS	Avg	100	50	Ct	St	Balls	Runs	Wkts	Avg	BB	5I	10M
Test																	
FC	13	18	5	555	129 *	42.69	1	5	5	-	1546	871	31	28.09	7-74	1	-
ODI																	
List A	12	8	0	70	18	8.75	-	-	3	-	474	443	10	44.30	3-39	-	
20/20 Int																	
20/20	6	3	1	10	4 *	5.00	-	-	1	-	53	72	2	36.00	2-20	-	

Career Performances

	M	Inn	NO	Runs	HS	Avg	100	50	Ct	St	Balls	Runs	Wkts	Avg	BB	5I	10M
Test																	
FC	15	21	5	597	129 *	37.31	1	5	5	-	1842	1074	41	26.19	7-74	2	-
ODI																	
List A	15	11	0	87	18	7.90	-	-	4	-	582	560	14	40.00	3-39	-	
20/20 Int																	
20/20	6	3	1	10	4 *	5.00	-	-	1	-	53	72	2	36.00	2-20	-	

15. Who was the England captain in the 1936-37 Ashes series who had refused to bowl Bodyline in the 1932-33 series?

CLARKE, R. Warwickshire

Name: Rikki Clarke
Role: Right-hand bat, right-arm fast-medium bowler; all-rounder
Born: 29 September 1981, Orsett, Essex
Height: 6ft 4½in **Weight:** 14st
Nickname: Clarkey, Crouchy
County debut: 2001 (one-day, Surrey), 2002 (first-class, Surrey), 2008 (Derbyshire), 2008 (Warwickshire)
County cap: 2005 (Surrey)
Test debut: 2003-04
ODI debut: 2003
1000 runs in a season: 1
1st-Class 200s: 1
Place in batting averages: 155rd av. 25.90 (2007 193rd av. 23.15)
Place in bowling averages: 131st av. 42.00 (2007 122nd av. 42.20)
Parents: Bob and Janet
Marital status: Single
Family links with cricket: 'Dad played a bit but not any more'
Education: Broadwater; Godalming College
Qualifications: 5 GCSEs, GNVQ Leisure and Tourism
Overseas tours: Surrey U19 to Barbados; MCC Young Cricketers to Cape Town; England to Sri Lanka (ICC Champions Trophy) 2002-03, to Bangladesh and Sri Lanka 2003-04, to West Indies 2003-04, to India (ICC Champions Trophy) 2006-07; ECB National Academy to Australia and Sri Lanka 2002-03; England A to Sri Lanka 2004-05, to West Indies 2005-06
Career highlights to date: 'Playing for England'
Cricket moments to forget: None
Cricket superstitions: 'Left pad first'
Cricketers particularly admired: Andrew Flintoff, Darren Gough
Young players to look out for: Jade Dernbach, James Benning
Other sports played: Snooker, poker
Other sports followed: Football (Tottenham)
Favourite band: Ne-Yo
Relaxations: 'Watching films and playing poker'
Extras: Named after former Tottenham Hotspur and Argentina footballer Ricky Villa. Represented England U17. Scored maiden first-class century (107*) on first-class debut v Cambridge UCCE at Fenner's 2002. NBC Denis Compton Award for the most promising young Surrey player 2002. Cricket Writers' Club Young Player of the Year

2002. Surrey Supporters' Young Player of the Year 2002. Surrey Sponsors' Young Player of the Year 2002. Made ODI debut v Pakistan at Old Trafford in the NatWest Challenge 2003, taking the wicket of Imran Nazir with his first ball in international cricket. ECB National Academy 2004-05, 2005-06, 2006-07. Vice-captain of Surrey 2006 to June 2007. Scored 28-ball 82* v Gloucestershire at The Oval in the Friends Provident 2007 as Surrey posted a world record List A total of 496-4. Left Surrey at the end of the 2007 season and joined Derbyshire for 2008 as captain. Left Derbyshire in August 2008 and joined Warwickshire

Best batting: 214 Surrey v Somerset, Guildford 2006

Best bowling: 4-21 Surrey v Leicestershire, Leicester 2003

2008 Season

	M	Inn	NO	Runs	HS	Avg	100	50	Ct	St	Balls	Runs	Wkts	Avg	BB	5I	10M
Test																	
FC	13	20	0	518	81	25.90	-	3	26	-	974	630	15	42.00	4-87	-	-
ODI																	
List A	14	12	1	243	69	22.09	-	1	8	-	172	144	5	28.80	2-30	-	
20/20 Int																	
20/20	9	9	1	121	36	15.12	-	-	4	-	135	182	6	30.33	2-32	-	

Career Performances

	M	Inn	NO	Runs	HS	Avg	100	50	Ct	St	Balls	Runs	Wkts	Avg	BB	5I	10M
Test	2	3	0	96	55	32.00	-	1	1	-	174	60	4	15.00	2-7	-	-
FC	89	142	13	4719	214	36.58	10	20	113	-	7590	5215	125	41.72	4-21	-	-
ODI	20	13	0	144	39	11.07	-	-	11	-	469	415	11	37.72	2-28	-	
List A	124	109	14	2404	98 *	25.30	-	12	54	-	3041	2872	76	37.78	4-49	-	
20/20 Int																	
20/20	42	40	9	631	79 *	20.35	-	2	18	-	564	704	31	22.70	3-11	-	

CLAYDON, M. E. Durham

Name: Mitchell Eric Claydon
Role: Left-hand bat, right-arm fast bowler
Born: 25 November 1982, Fairfield, Australia
Height: 6ft 4in **Weight:** 15st 9lbs
Nickname: Lips
County debut: 2005 (Yorkshire), 2007 (Durham)
Parents: Robert (Tosh) and Sue
Marital status: Single
Children: Lachlan Robert Bickhoff-Claydon, 25 February 2004
Family links with cricket: Father played for Markington CC in the Nidderdale League
Education: Westfields Sports High School, Sydney
Qualifications: Level 1 coaching
Career outside cricket: 'Real estate agent'
Overseas teams played for: Campbelltown-Camden Ghosts 1999 –
Career highlights to date: 'Being a part of Durham 2007, even though I only played one game'
Cricket moments to forget: 'While participating in a fielding drill consisting of high catches, I misjudged the height of the ball; the next thing I knew I was lying on the physio table with an ice pack on my forehead'
Cricket superstitions: 'Must wear my gold chain that has a photo of my sister who died in 2003'
Cricketers particularly admired: Steve Waugh
Young players to look out for: Ben Harmison, Mark Stoneman
Other sports played: Rugby league, rugby union
Other sports followed: Rugby league (West Tigers), football (Leeds United)
Favourite band: Denham Reagh
Relaxations: 'Surfing whilst home in Australia; golf'
Extras: Only player in history of Campbelltown-Camden Ghosts to have taken two first grade hat-tricks. Played in all forms of the game for the first team during 2008 season. Holds a British passport and is not considered an overseas player
Best batting: 40 Durham v Lancashire, Old Trafford 2008
Best bowling: 3-26 Durham v DUCCE, Durham 2007

2008 Season

	M	Inn	NO	Runs	HS	Avg	100	50	Ct	St	Balls	Runs	Wkts	Avg	BB	5I	10M
Test																	
FC	1	2	0	44	40	22.00	-	-	-	-	168	94	1	94.00	1-64	-	-
ODI																	
List A	2	1	0	2	2	2.00	-	-	-	-	114	50	4	12.50	3-31	-	
20/20 Int																	
20/20	2	1	1	4	4 *		-	-	-	-	36	60	0		-	-	

Career Performances

	M	Inn	NO	Runs	HS	Avg	100	50	Ct	St	Balls	Runs	Wkts	Avg	BB	5I	10M
Test																	
FC	6	5	1	96	40	24.00	-	-	-	-	888	576	10	57.60	3-26	-	-
ODI																	
List A	9	3	0	17	9	5.66	-	-	-	-	456	343	12	28.58	3-31	-	
20/20 Int																	
20/20	9	3	3	18	12 *		-	-	2	-	175	248	5	49.60	2-6	-	

CLIFF, S. J. — Leicestershire

Name: Samuel (Sam) James Cliff
Role: Right-hand bat, right-arm fast-medium bowler
Born: 3 October 1987, Nottingham
Height: 6ft 2in **Weight:** 11st 8lbs
Nickname: Cliffy, Jacko
County debut: 2007
Parents: Colin Cliff and Julie Silverwood
Marital status: Single
Family links with cricket: 'Father plays village cricket "very well" and has scored over 60 centuries (he keeps reminding me)'
Education: Colonel Frank Seely Comprehensive, Calverton, Nottingham
Qualifications: 10 GCSEs
Career outside cricket: Painter and decorator
Off-season: 'In Perth'
Overseas tours: Leicestershire Young Cricketers to India 2005-06
Career highlights to date: 'Getting a contract. Playing Twenty20 and in the Championship! Taking 4-26 v Derbyshire in Pro40, August 2008'

Cricket moments to forget: 'None yet!'
Cricket superstitions: 'A few little ones but nothing specific'
Cricketers particularly admired: David Masters, HD Ackerman
Young players to look out for: Josh Cobb
Other sports played: Golf, football
Other sports followed: Ice hockey (Nottingham Panthers), football (Notts County), rugby (Nottingham)
Injuries: 'Shoulder injury - out for a month'
Relaxations: 'Going out, chilling'
Extras: Played for Leicestershire Academy v England U19 2007. Played in Loughborough Town's Leicestershire County Cup winning side 2007, taking 2-13 from eight overs in the final v Market Harborough at Leicester.
Opinions on cricket: 'Keep politics out of the changing room'
Best batting: 15 Leicestershire v Derbyshire, Grace Road 2008
Best bowling: 4-42 Leicestershire v Derbyshire, Grace Road 2008

2008 Season

	M	Inn	NO	Runs	HS	Avg	100	50	Ct	St	Balls	Runs	Wkts	Avg	BB	5I	10M
Test																	
FC	3	3	0	24	15	8.00	-	-	1	-	446	241	10	24.10	4-42	-	-
ODI																	
List A	4	1	1	0	0 *		-	-	1	-	168	151	5	30.20	4-26	-	
20/20 Int																	
20/20	3	0	0	0	0		-	-	1	-	66	78	1	78.00	1-24	-	

Career Performances

	M	Inn	NO	Runs	HS	Avg	100	50	Ct	St	Balls	Runs	Wkts	Avg	BB	5I	10M
Test																	
FC	5	6	2	45	15	11.25	-	-	1	-	614	367	11	33.36	4-42	-	-
ODI																	
List A	4	1	1	0	0 *		-	-	1	-	168	151	5	30.20	4-26	-	
20/20 Int																	
20/20	3	0	0	0	0		-	-	1	-	66	78	1	78.00	1-24	-	

16. Which England batsman took more than six hours to make a century against Australia in 1975?

CLINTON, R. S. — Surrey

Name: Richard Selvey Clinton
Role: Left-hand opening bat, right-arm medium bowler
Born: 1 September 1981, Sidcup, Kent
Height: 6ft 3in **Weight:** 15st 9lbs
Nickname: Clint
County debut: 2001 (Essex), 2004 (Surrey)
Parents: Cathy and Grahame
Marital status: Married
Family links with cricket: 'Father played for Surrey. Uncles, cousin and brother play high standard of club cricket in Kent Premier League'
Education: Colfes School, London; Loughborough University
Qualifications: 9 GCSEs, 3 A-levels
Overseas teams played for: Kensington CC, Adelaide; Valleys CC, Brisbane 2000-02
Cricket superstitions: 'Just a tried and tested routine'
Cricketers particularly admired: Graham Thorpe, Mark Butcher
Other sports played: Football, squash
Other sports followed: Motor racing (Formula One)
Favourite band: Aqua, The Sometime Maybes
Extras: Scored 36 and 58* on first-class debut v Surrey at Ilford 2001; scored 56 the following day on Norwich Union League debut v Durham at the same ground. Played for Loughborough UCCE 2004-06. Represented British Universities 2004, 2005, 2006. Joined Surrey during the 2004 season, scoring 73 on Championship debut v Worcestershire at The Oval
Best batting: 108* LUCCE v Essex, Chelmsford 2006
Best bowling: 2-30 Essex v Australians, Chelmsford 2001

2008 Season

	M	Inn	NO	Runs	HS	Avg	100	50	Ct	St	Balls	Runs	Wkts	Avg	BB	5I	10M
Test																	
FC	1	0	0	0	0	-	-	-	-	0	0	0		-	-	-	
ODI																	
List A																	
20/20 Int																	
20/20																	

Career Performances

	M	Inn	NO	Runs	HS	Avg	100	50	Ct	St	Balls	Runs	Wkts	Avg	BB	5I	10M
Test																	
FC	43	70	5	1837	108 *	28.26	4	9	24	-	295	207	2	103.50	2-30	-	-
ODI																	
List A	19	16	3	191	56	14.69	-	1	4	-	48	58	2	29.00	2-16	-	
20/20 Int																	

CLOUGH, G. D. Nottinghamshire

Name: Gareth David Clough
Role: Right-hand bat, right-arm medium bowler; all-rounder
Born: 23 May 1978, Leeds
Height: 6ft **Weight:** 12st
Nickname: Garth, Banga
County debut: 1998 (Yorkshire), 2001 (Nottinghamshire)
Parents: David and Gillian
Marital status: Single
Education: Pudsey Grangefield
Qualifications: 9 GCSEs, 3 A-levels, Level 1 cricket coach
Overseas tours: Yorkshire to Durban and Cape Town 1999; Nottinghamshire to Johannesburg 2001-03
Overseas teams played for: Somerset West, Cape Town 1996-97; Deepdene Bears, Melbourne 1999-2000, 2001-02
Career highlights to date: '2006 Twenty20 finals day'
Cricket moments to forget: 'Result at end of Twenty20 final'
Cricketers particularly admired: Ian Botham, Steve Waugh
Young players to look out for: Samit Patel
Other sports played: Golf, football, poker, darts
Other sports followed: 'All sports'; football (Everton), rugby league (Leeds Rhinos)
Favourite band: Razorlight
Relaxations: 'Dining out, socialising with friends, golf'
Extras: Took 6-25 v Sussex at Trent Bridge in the Pro40 2006, the best one-day return by a Nottinghamshire bowler since 1994.
Opinions on cricket: 'Just keeps on getting better and better.'
Best batting: 55 Nottinghamshire v India A, Trent Bridge 2003
Best bowling: 3-69 Nottinghamshire v Gloucestershire, Trent Bridge 2001

2008 Season

	M	Inn	NO	Runs	HS	Avg	100	50	Ct	St	Balls	Runs	Wkts	Avg	BB	5I	10M
Test																	
FC																	
ODI																	
List A																	
20/20 Int																	
20/20	5	1	0	7	7	7.00	-	-	1	-	60	68	1	68.00	1-12	-	

Career Perfomances

	M	Inn	NO	Runs	HS	Avg	100	50	Ct	St	Balls	Runs	Wkts	Avg	BB	5I	10M
Test																	
FC	12	17	2	156	55	10.40	-	1	4	-	1218	766	16	47.87	3-69	-	-
ODI																	
List A	96	53	18	625	42 *	17.85	-	-	28	-	3224	2815	86	32.73	6-25	1	
20/20 Int																	
20/20	39	22	5	285	40 *	16.76	-	-	10	-	611	788	31	25.41	4-24	-	

COBB, J. J. — Leicestershire

Name: Joshua (Josh) James Cobb
Role: Right-hand bat, leg-spin bowler; 'batter that bowls'
Born: 17 August 1990, Leicester
Height: 6ft 1in **Weight:** 12st 6lbs
Nickname: Cobby
County debut: 2007
Parents: Russell and Sharon
Family links with cricket: 'Father ex-Leicestershire player'
Education: Bosworth College; Oakham School
Qualifications: GCSEs
Overseas tours: Leicestershire U14 to South Africa 2003; Leicestershire U19 to India 2006. England U19 to South Africa 2009.
Career highlights to date: 'Making first-class debut v Northamptonshire [2007] having just turned 17'
Cricket superstitions: 'Putting on left pad before right pad'
Cricketers particularly admired: Shane Warne, Darren Stevens, Paul Nixon
Young players to look out for: Shiv Thakor
Other sports played: Badminton (Leicestershire U13-15), football ('played in goal

for Leicester District at U16')

Other sports followed: Football (Manchester United), rugby (Leicester Tigers)

Favourite band: D12

Relaxations: 'Listening to music, socialising with friends, playing sports and reading and writing books!'

Extras: Made 2nd XI Championship debut 2006. Played for Leicestershire Academy v Victoria Emerging Players at Leicester 2007, scoring 102*. Scored maiden century (148*) against Middlesex in August 2008.

Opinions on cricket: 'Should use more technology where possible, trying not to slow the game down in the process.'

Best batting: 148* Leicestershire v Middlesex 2008

Best bowling: 2-11 Leicestershire v Gloucestershire, Grace Road 2008

2008 Season

	M	Inn	NO	Runs	HS	Avg	100	50	Ct	St	Balls	Runs	Wkts	Avg	BB	5I	10M
Test																	
FC	8	10	3	419	148 *	59.85	1	2	5	-	120	90	4	22.50	2-11	-	-
ODI																	
List A	3	3	1	31	28	15.50	-	-	1	-	0	0	0		-	-	
20/20 Int																	
20/20	1	1	1	2	2 *		-	-	-	-	0	0	0		-	-	

Career Performances

	M	Inn	NO	Runs	HS	Avg	100	50	Ct	St	Balls	Runs	Wkts	Avg	BB	5I	10M
Test																	
FC	9	12	3	442	148 *	49.11	1	2	5	-	174	134	4	33.50	2-11	-	-
ODI																	
List A	3	3	1	31	28	15.50	-	-	1	-	0	0	0		-	-	
20/20 Int																	
20/20	1	1	1	2	2 *		-	-	-	-	0	0	0		-	-	

COETZER, K. J. Durham

Name: Kyle James Coetzer
Role: Right-hand bat, right-arm medium bowler
Born: 14 April 1984, Aberdeen
Height: 5ft 11in
Nickname: Costa
County debut: 2004
ODI debut: 2008
Twenty20 Int debut: 2008
Place in batting averages: (2007 85th av. 38.26)
Parents: Peter and Megan
Marital status: Single
Family links with cricket: 'All of my family plays, including two older brothers'
Education: Aberdeen Grammar School
Qualifications: Standard grades, 4 Intermediate 2s
Overseas tours: Scotland U19 to New Zealand (U19 World Cup) 2001-02, to Bangladesh (U19 World Cup) 2003-04 (c), plus other Scotland age-group and A tours; Scotland to UAE (ICC Inter-Continental Cup) 2004, to Ireland (ICC Trophy) 2005, to Barbados 2005-06; Durham to Dubai 2005, 2006, to Mumbai 2006
Overseas teams played for: Cape Town CC 2002-03, 2003-04, 2004, 2005-06; Gosnells CC 2005
Cricket moments to forget: 'Most of 2006 season'
Cricket superstitions: 'Touch bat in crease after "over" is called'
Cricketers particularly admired: Jacques Kallis, Michael Hussey
Young players to look out for: Andrew Smith, Moneeb Iqbal
Other sports played: Golf, basketball, football
Other sports followed: Football (Aberdeen, Arsenal)
Favourite band: Jack Johnson 'and a good mix of music'
Relaxations: 'Listening to music'
Extras: Man of the Match v Italy in the ECC U19 Championships at Deventer 2003 (146*). Has played for Scotland in first-class and one-day cricket, including NCL 2003 and C&G 2003, 2004 and 2006. Scored 67 on first-class debut, for Durham v Glamorgan at Cardiff 2004. Chosen by Scotland to face Pakistan in 2007, he opted to play for Durham instead
Best batting: 153* Durham v DUCCE, Durham 2007
Stop press: Delhi Daredevils in IPL paid $275,000 in auction for his services in 2009

2008 Season

	M	Inn	NO	Runs	HS	Avg	100	50	Ct	St	Balls	Runs	Wkts	Avg	BB	5I	10M
Test																	
FC	4	7	0	56	23	8.00	-	-	2	-	0	0	0	-	-	-	-
ODI																	
List A	7	7	0	93	61	13.28	-	1	1	-	0	0	0	-	-	-	
20/20 Int																	
20/20	1	1	0	10	10	10.00	-	-	-	-	0	0	0	-	-	-	

Career Performances

	M	Inn	NO	Runs	HS	Avg	100	50	Ct	St	Balls	Runs	Wkts	Avg	BB	5I	10M
Test																	
FC	27	48	6	1392	153 *	33.14	3	4	16	-	54	22	0	-	-	-	-
ODI	1	1	0	0	0	0.00	-	-	-	-	0	0	0	-	-	-	
List A	34	32	3	610	76	21.03	-	4	11	-	60	47	0	-	-	-	
20/20 Int	3	3	1	99	48 *	49.50	-	-	-	-	0	0	0	-	-	-	
20/20	6	5	1	110	48 *	27.50	-	-	-	-	0	0	0	-	-	-	

COLLINGWOOD, P. D. — Durham

Name: Paul David Collingwood
Role: Right-hand bat, right-arm medium bowler
Born: 26 May 1976, Shotley Bridge, Tyneside
Height: 5ft 11in **Weight:** 12st
Nickname: Colly
County debut: 1995 (one-day), 1996 (first-class)
County cap: 1998
Benefit: 2007
Test debut: 2003-04
ODI debut: 2001
Twenty20 Int debut: 2005
1000 runs in a season: 2
1st-Class 200s: 1
Place in batting averages: 111th av. 31.70 (2007 52nd av. 43.85)
Parents: David and Janet
Wife: Vicki
Children: Shannon, 2006

Family links with cricket: Father and brother play in the Tyneside Senior League for Shotley Bridge CC
Education: Blackfyne Comprehensive School; Derwentside College
Qualifications: 9 GCSEs, 2 A-levels
Overseas tours: Durham Cricket Academy to Sri Lanka 1996 (c); England VI to Hong Kong 2001, 2002; England to Zimbabwe (one-day series) 2001-02, to India and New Zealand 2001-02 (one-day series), to Australia 2002-03, to Africa (World Cup) 2002-03, to Bangladesh and Sri Lanka 2003-04, to West Indies 2003-04, to Zimbabwe (one-day series) 2004-05, to South Africa 2004-05, to Pakistan 2005-06, to India 2005-06, to India (ICC Champions Trophy) 2006-07, to Australia 2006-07, to West Indies (World Cup) 2006-07, to South Africa (World 20/20) 2007-08 (c), to Sri Lanka 2007-08 (ODI c), to New Zealand 2007-08 (ODI c), to India (Test and one-day series) 2008, to West Indies 2009
Overseas teams played for: Bulleen CC, Melbourne 1995-96, 1996-97 ('won flag on both occasions'); Cornwall CC, Auckland 1997-98; Alberton CC, Johannesburg 1998-99; Richmond CC, Melbourne 2000-01
Cricket moments to forget: 'Being Matthew Walker's (Kent) first first-class wicket'
Cricket superstitions: 'Left pad on first, and wearing them on the wrong legs'
Cricketers particularly admired: Steve Waugh, Jacques Kallis, Glenn McGrath, Shane Warne
Other sports played: Golf (9 handicap)
Other sports followed: Football ('The Red and Whites' – Sunderland)
Extras: Took wicket (David Capel) with first ball on first-class debut against Northants, then scored 91 in Durham's first innings. Durham Player of the Year 2000. Joint (and first English) winner of the Jack Ryder Medal, awarded by the umpires, for his performances in Victorian Premier Cricket 2000-01. Scored 112* and took England ODI record 6-31 v Bangladesh at Trent Bridge in the NatWest Series 2005, winning Man of the Match award. His other match awards include Man of the Match v Sri Lanka at Perth in the VB Series 2002-03 (100) and in three consecutive matches (including the two finals) in the Commonwealth Bank Series 2006-07; Man of the Match in the first Twenty20 Int v West Indies at The Oval 2007 (79). Vice-captain of Durham 2005-06. Slazenger Sheer Instinct Award 2005. Appointed MBE in 2006 New Year Honours as part of 2005 Ashes-winning England team. Scored 206 in the second Test at Adelaide 2006-07, becoming the first England batsman to score a Test double century in Australia since Wally Hammond in 1936-37 and sharing with Kevin Pietersen (158) in a record fourth-wicket stand for England v Australia (310). One of *Wisden*'s Five Cricketers of the Year 2007. Benefit year 2007. England 12-month central contract 2007-08. England one-day captain from June 2007 until relinquishing the position in 2008.
Best batting: 206 England v Australia, Adelaide 2006-07
Best bowling: 5-52 Durham v Somerset, Stockton 2005
Stop press: Delhi Daredevils (IPL) paid $275,000 for his services in 2009 auction

2008 Season

	M	Inn	NO	Runs	HS	Avg	100	50	Ct	St	Balls	Runs	Wkts	Avg	BB	5I	10M
Test	6	9	2	264	135	37.71	1	1	9	-	150	74	0	-	-	-	-
FC	8	13	3	317	135	31.70	1	1	15	-	252	136	5	27.20	3-17	-	-
ODI	8	5	0	163	64	32.60	-	1	1	-	197	151	7	21.57	4-15	-	
List A	15	12	2	377	78 *	37.70	-	3	4	-	407	371	15	24.73	4-15	-	
20/20 Int	1	0	0	0	0	-	-	-	-	-	12	17	1	17.00	1-17	-	
20/20	4	3	0	44	35	14.66	-	-	-	-	60	63	8	7.87	5-14	1	

Career Performances

	M	Inn	NO	Runs	HS	Avg	100	50	Ct	St	Balls	Runs	Wkts	Avg	BB	5I	10M
Test	39	72	8	2689	206	42.01	6	11	52	-	1287	687	14	49.07	3-23	-	-
FC	161	284	23	9301	206	35.63	20	45	178	-	9071	4584	119	38.52	5-52	1	-
ODI	149	134	29	3689	120 *	35.13	4	20	86	-	3854	3214	83	38.72	6-31	1	
List A	317	296	53	8063	120 *	33.18	6	48	163	-	8360	6750	196	34.43	6-31	1	
20/20 Int	14	13	0	330	79	25.38	-	2	2	-	150	237	13	18.23	4-22	-	
20/20	17	16	0	374	79	23.37	-	2	2	-	198	283	20	14.15	5-14	1	

COLLINS, P. T. Surrey

Name: Pedro Tyrone Collins
Role: Right-hand bat, left-arm fast-medium bowler
Born: 12 August 1976, Boscobelle, Barbados
County debut: 2008
Test debut: 1998-99
ODI debut: 1999-2000
Family links with cricket: Half-brother Fidel Edwards plays for Barbados and West Indies
Overseas tours: West Indies A to South Africa 1997-98, to Bangladesh and India 1998-99; West Indies to Bangladesh 1999-2000, to New Zealand 1999-2000, to Zimbabwe and Kenya 2001, to Sri Lanka 2001-02, to Sharjah (v Pakistan) 2001-02, to Sri Lanka (ICC Champions Trophy) 2002-03, to India and Bangladesh 2002-03, to Africa (World Cup) 2002-03, to England 2004, to Australia (VB Series) 2004-05, to South Africa (World 20/20) 2007-08, to South Africa 2007-08, plus one-day tournament in Sharjah
Overseas teams played for: Barbados 1996-97 –

Extras: Man of the Match v Windward Islands in Dominica in the Carib Beer Cup 2006-07 (6-24/1-15). Played for Benwell Hill in the North East Premier League 2007. Took 7-11 v West Indies U19 at Berbice in the KFC Cup 2007-08, winning Man of the Match award. Signed as a Surrey player just before the start of the 2008 season. he withdrew from the West Indies squad to play Sri Lanka in favour of his county. Only Saqlain Mushtaq took more first-class wickets for Surrey during 2008. Is not considered an overseas player
Best batting: 25 Barbados v Trinidad and Tobago, Pointe-a-Pierre 2003-04
Best bowling: 6-24 Barbados v Windward Islands, Portsmouth (BP) 2006-07

2008 Season

	M	Inn	NO	Runs	HS	Avg	100	50	Ct	St	Balls	Runs	Wkts	Avg	BB	5I	10M
Test																	
FC	12	13	4	53	21	5.88	-	-	2	-	1851	1121	27	41.51	4-111	-	-
ODI																	
List A	12	5	2	18	11	6.00	-	-	-	-	553	429	18	23.83	4-46	-	
20/20 Int																	
20/20	7	1	1	1	1 *		-	-	1	-	144	202	3	67.33	1-28	-	

Career Performances

	M	Inn	NO	Runs	HS	Avg	100	50	Ct	St	Balls	Runs	Wkts	Avg	BB	5I	10M
Test	32	47	7	235	24	5.87	-	-	7	-	6964	3671	106	34.63	6-53	3	-
FC	115	143	37	677	25	6.38	-	-	28	-	19723	10133	380	26.66	6-24	9	-
ODI	30	12	5	30	10 *	4.28	-	-	8	-	1577	1212	39	31.07	5-43	1	
List A	78	32	10	145	55 *	6.59	-	1	12	-	3993	2859	123	23.24	7-11	2	
20/20 Int																	
20/20	10	2	1	2	1 *	2.00	-	-	1	-	202	247	7	35.28	3-13	-	

17. Who was captain of Australia when the Aussies re-gained the Ashes in 1958-59?

COLLYMORE, C. D. Sussex

Name: Corey Dalanelo Collymore
Role: Right-hand bat, right-arm fast bowler
Born: 21 December 1977, Boscobelle, St. Peter, Barbados
Height: 6ft **Weight:** 13st 9lbs
Nickname: Screw, CC
County debut: 2003 (Warwickshire), 2008 (Sussex)
Test debut: 1998-99
ODI debut: 1999
Twenty20 debut: 2006
Parents: Maytred Collymore, Gordon Maxwell
Marital status: 'Married'
Children: 'Dionne, 24 December 2005; Dicoreya, 25 October 2006; Dicyrah, 5 March 2008'
Education: Alexandra Secondary School
Qualifications: 4 CXCs
Overseas tours: West Indies to Toronto (DMC Cup) 1999, to England 2000, to Zimbabwe 2001, to Kenya 2001, to Sri Lanka (LG Abans Triangular Series) 2001-02, to Sharjah (v Pakistan) 2001-02, to Sri Lanka (ICC Champions Trophy) 2002-03, to India 2002-03 (one-day series), to Bangladesh 2002-03, to Africa (World Cup) 2002-03, to Zimbabwe 2003-04, to South Africa 2003-04, to Australia 2005, to Malaysia, India and Pakistan 2006; to England 2007; to South Africa (World Cup) 2003; West Indies (World Cup) 2007
Overseas teams played for: Barbados 1998-99 –
Career highlights to date: 'Taking 11-134 v Pakistan, June 2005'
Cricket moments to forget: 'None!'
Cricket superstitions: None
Cricketers particularly admired: Courtney Walsh, Vasbert Drakes, Steve Waugh
Young players to look out for: Oliver Rayner, Will Beer
Other sports followed: Football (Arsenal, Brazil)
Relaxations: 'Listening to music, spending time with family and friends'
Extras: Represented West Indies U19 in home series v Pakistan U19 1996-97. Took 4-49 in the final of the Coca-Cola Cup v India at Harare 2001, winning the Man of the Match award. Took 5-51 v Sri Lanka at Colombo in the LG Abans Triangular Series 2001-02, winning the Man of the Match award. Player of the [Test] Series v Sri Lanka 2002-03, performances including 7-57 in the second Test at Kingston. Was an overseas player with Warwickshire in August and September 2003, replacing the injured Collins Obuya. Signed as a Kolpak player in May 2008.
Opinions on cricket: 'Need better wickets so as to keep fast bowlers in the game'

Best batting: 20 Barbados v West Indies B, Bridgetown 2002-03
20 Sussex v Hampshire, Arundel 2008
Best bowling: 7-57 West Indies v Sri Lanka, Kingston 2003

2008 Season

	M	Inn	NO	Runs	HS	Avg	100	50	Ct	St	Balls	Runs	Wkts	Avg	BB	5I	10M
Test																	
FC	9	12	5	57	20	8.14	-	-	2	-	1610	727	26	27.96	4-47	-	-
ODI																	
List A	2	1	1	1	1 *		-	-	-	-	96	107	0			-	
20/20 Int																	
20/20	3	1	0	4	4	4.00	-	-	1	-	47	90	1	90.00	1-35	-	

Career Performances

	M	Inn	NO	Runs	HS	Avg	100	50	Ct	St	Balls	Runs	Wkts	Avg	BB	5I	10M
Test	30	52	27	197	16 *	7.88	-	-	6	-	6337	3004	93	32.30	7-57	4	1
FC	97	141	65	594	20	7.81	-	-	34	-	16703	7851	290	27.07	7-57	10	2
ODI	84	35	17	104	13 *	5.77	-	-	12	-	4074	2924	83	35.22	5-51	1	
List A	125	46	22	146	13 *	6.08	-	-	17	-	5884	4223	134	31.51	5-27	2	
20/20 Int																	
20/20	6	2	1	5	4	5.00	-	-	4	-	95	133	3	44.33	1-21		

COMPTON, N. R. D. Middlesex

Name: Nicholas (Nick) Richard Denis Compton
Role: Right-hand bat, right-arm off-spin bowler
Born: 26 June 1983, Durban, South Africa
Height: 6ft 1in **Weight:** 13st 1lb
Nickname: Compo, Lord
County debut: 2001 (one-day), 2004 (first-class)
County cap: 2006
1000 runs in a season: 1
Place in batting averages: (2007 202nd av. 22.16)
Parents: Richard and Glynis
Marital status: Single
Family links with cricket: Grandfather Denis Compton played football and cricket for England
Education: Harrow; Durham University

Qualifications: 3 A-levels, ECB coach Level 1
Overseas tours: England U19 to Australia and (U19 World Cup) New Zealand 2001-02; MCC to Canada 2005-06; England A to Bangladesh 2006-07
Overseas teams played for: University of Western Australia, Perth 2001; Berea Rovers, Durban; University of Cape Town
Career highlights to date: 'Reaching 100 at Lord's with a six v Kent to score my first Championship century [2006] – champagne moment!'
Cricket moments to forget: 'Relegation to second division [2006]'
Cricketers particularly admired: Rahul Dravid, Jacques Kallis, Steve Waugh, Ed Joyce
Young players to look out for: Billy Godleman, Steve Finn
Other sports played: Golf (6 handicap), waterskiing, represented Natal at junior level at tennis
Other sports followed: Football (Arsenal), Super 14 rugby union (Sharks)
Favourite band: The Killers
Extras: Played for Natal U13 and U15. Natal Academy award 1997. Middlesex U17 Batsman of the Season 1999. Middlesex U19 Player of the Season 2000. NBC Denis Compton Award for the most promising young Middlesex player 2001, 2002, 2006. Represented England U19 2002. Scored maiden first-class century (101) v OUCCE at The Parks 2006 and maiden Championship century (124) in the following match v Kent at Lord's 2006. Carried bat for 105* v Nottinghamshire at Lord's 2006, in the process passing 1000 first-class runs for the season in his first full season of county cricket. Is England-qualified.
Best batting: 190 Middlesex v Durham, Lord's 2006
Best bowling: 1-94 Middlesex v Sussex, Southgate 2006

2008 Season

	M	Inn	NO	Runs	HS	Avg	100	50	Ct	St	Balls	Runs	Wkts	Avg	BB	5I	10M
Test																	
FC	5	8	0	68	27	8.50	-	-	2	-	0	0	0		-	-	-
ODI																	
List A																	
20/20 Int																	
20/20																	

Career Performances

	M	Inn	NO	Runs	HS	Avg	100	50	Ct	St	Balls	Runs	Wkts	Avg	BB	5I	10M
Test																	
FC	40	69	7	2128	190	34.32	6	9	20	-	66	123	1	123.00	1-94	-	-
ODI																	
List A	43	37	8	831	110 *	28.65	1	4	22	-	54	45	0		-	-	
20/20 Int																	
20/20	22	17	1	187	50 *	11.68	-	1	13	-	0	0	0		-	-	

COOK, A. N. Essex

Name: Alastair Nathan Cook
Role: Left-hand opening bat, right-arm off-spin bowler
Born: 25 December 1984, Gloucester
Height: 6ft 2in **Weight:** 12st 10lbs
Nickname: Ali, Cooky, Chef
County debut: 2003
County cap: 2005
Test debut: 2005-06
ODI debut: 2006
Twenty20 Int debut: 2007
1000 runs in a season: 3
Place in batting averages: 73rd av. 38.52 (2007 24th av. 54.70)
Parents: Graham and Elizabeth
Marital status: Single
Family links with cricket: 'Dad played for village side; brothers play for Maldon CC'
Education: Bedford School
Qualifications: 9 GCSEs, 3 A-levels
Overseas tours: Bedford School to Barbados 2001; England U19 to Bangladesh (U19 World Cup) 2003-04 (c); England A to Sri Lanka 2004-05, to West Indies 2005-06; England to Pakistan 2005-06, to India 2005-06, to Australia 2006-07, to Sri Lanka 2007-08, to New Zealand 2007-08, to India 2008, to West Indies 2009
Cricket moments to forget: 'Running myself out first ball in U15 World Cup game against India'
Cricket superstitions: 'A few!'
Cricketers particularly admired: Graham Thorpe, Andy Flower, Graham Gooch
Young players to look out for: James Hildreth, Mark Pettini
Other sports played: Squash, golf
Other sports followed: 'All sports'
Relaxations: 'Spending time with friends'
Extras: Played for England U15 in U15 World Cup 2000. Represented England U19 2003 and (as captain) 2004. Scored 69* on first-class debut v Nottinghamshire at Chelmsford 2003 and a further two half-centuries in his next two Championship matches. Had consecutive scores of 108*, 108* and 87 in the U19 World Cup 2003-04 in Bangladesh. NBC Denis Compton Award for the most promising young Essex player 2003, 2004, 2005 and 2006. ECB National Academy 2004-05 (part-time), 2005-06. Scored 214 v Australians at Chelmsford in a two-day game 2005. Cricket Writers' Club Young Player of the Year 2005. PCA Young Player of the Year 2005, 2006. Called up as a replacement to the England tour of India 2005-06, scoring century

(104*) on Test debut in the first Test at Nagpur (following 60 in first innings). Scored maiden Ashes century (116) in the third Test at Perth 2006-07, becoming the first England player to score four Test hundreds before his 22nd birthday. Man of the Match in the first Test v West Indies at Lord's 2007 (105/65). England 12-month central contract 2007-08. Man of the Match in the fourth ODI v Sri Lanka in Colombo 2007-08 (80). Became the youngest England player to achieve 2000 Test runs whilst in New Zealand 2008.
Best batting: 195 Essex v Northamptonshire, Northampton 2005
Best bowling: 3-13 Essex v Northamptonshire, Chelmsford 2005

2008 Season

	M	Inn	NO	Runs	HS	Avg	100	50	Ct	St	Balls	Runs	Wkts	Avg	BB	5I	10M
Test	7	11	0	443	76	40.27	-	5	5	-	6	1	0		-		-
FC	11	19	0	732	95	38.52	-	7	6	-	6	1	0		-	-	-
ODI	1	1	0	24	24	24.00	-	-	-	-	0	0	0		-	-	
List A	5	5	0	171	95	34.20	-	1	1	-	0	0	0		-	-	
20/20 Int																	
20/20	1	1	0	15	15	15.00	-	-	1	-	0	0	0		-	-	

Career Performances

	M	Inn	NO	Runs	HS	Avg	100	50	Ct	St	Balls	Runs	Wkts	Avg	BB	5I	10M
Test	34	62	2	2573	127	42.88	7	14	33	-	6	1	0		-	-	-
FC	88	158	11	6625	195	45.06	18	36	89	-	162	118	3	39.33	3-13	-	-
ODI	22	22	0	691	102	31.40	1	3	7	-	0	0	0		-	-	
List A	55	54	4	1657	125	33.14	2	8	24	-	18	10	0		-	-	
20/20 Int	2	2	0	24	15	12.00	-	-	1	-	0	0	0		-	-	
20/20	5	5	0	50	15	10.00	-	-	2	-	0	0	0		-	-	

18. Who completed his 7,000th Test run in the 1998-99 Ashes series?

COOK, S. J. — Kent

Name: Simon James Cook
Role: Right-hand bat, right-arm fast-medium bowler
Born: 15 January 1977, Oxford
Height: 6ft 4in **Weight:** 13st
Nickname: Cookie, Donk, Chef
County debut: 1997 (one-day, Middlesex), 1999 (first-class, Middlesex), 2005 (Kent)
County cap: 2003 (Middlesex), 2007 (Kent)
Place in batting averages: (2007 236th av. 16.77)
Place in bowling averages: (2007 86th av. 33.63)
Parents: Phil and Sue
Marital status: Single
Family links with cricket: Brothers played for Oxfordshire
Education: Matthew Arnold School
Qualifications: GCSEs, NVQ Business Administration II, Level 3 ECB coach
Career outside cricket: Coaching and property development
Overseas tours: Middlesex to South Africa 2000
Overseas teams played for: Rockingham, Perth 2001, 2002
Career highlights to date: 'Beating Australia in one-day game at Lord's; winning division two of NCL and equalling league record for wickets in a season (39); winning Twenty20 cup in 2007'
Cricket moments to forget: 'Being outside the circle in a one-day game when I was supposed to be in it. Danny Law was bowled, the ball went for four [off the stumps, making six no-balls in total] and he went on to win the game for Durham'
Cricket superstitions: None
Cricketers particularly admired: Angus Fraser, Glenn McGrath
Young players to look out for: Billy Godleman, Eoin Morgan, Joe Denly
Other sports followed: Football (Liverpool), 'any other ball sport'
Player website: www.vcamcricket.co.uk
Extras: Scored career best 93* v Nottinghamshire at Lord's 2001, helping Middlesex to avoid the follow-on, then took a wicket with the first ball of his opening spell. Equalled Adam Hollioake's record for the most wickets in a one-day league season (39) 2004.
Best batting: 93* Middlesex v Nottinghamshire, Lord's 2001
Best bowling: 8-63 Middlesex v Northamptonshire, Northampton 2002

2008 Season

	M	Inn	NO	Runs	HS	Avg	100	50	Ct	St	Balls	Runs	Wkts	Avg	BB	5I	10M
Test																	
FC	1	0	0	0	0		-	-	-	-	42	25	0	-	-	-	-
ODI																	
List A	13	3	0	44	42	14.66	-	-	3	-	523	410	12	34.16	3-41	-	
20/20 Int																	
20/20	12	1	1	0	0 *		-	-	4	-	276	379	11	34.45	3-21	-	

Career Perfomances

	M	Inn	NO	Runs	HS	Avg	100	50	Ct	St	Balls	Runs	Wkts	Avg	BB	5I	10M
Test																	
FC	104	133	18	1887	93 *	16.40	-	5	31	-	15859	8347	259	32.22	8-63	9	
ODI																	
List A	164	101	31	1193	67 *	17.04	-	2	26	-	7291	5744	205	28.01	6-37	2	
20/20 Int																	
20/20	39	13	6	106	25 *	15.14	-	-	7	-	835	1069	50	21.38	3-14		

CORK, D. G. Hampshire

Name: Dominic Gerald Cork
Role: Right-hand bat, right-arm fast-medium bowler
Born: 7 August 1971, Newcastle-under-Lyme, Staffordshire
Height: 6ft 2½in **Weight:** 14st
Nickname: Corky
County debut: 1990 (Derbyshire), 2004 (Lancashire)
County cap: 1993 (Derbyshire), 2004 (Lancashire)
Benefit: 2001 (Derbyshire)
Test debut: 1995
ODI debut: 1992
50 wickets in a season: 7
1st-Class 200s: 1
Place in batting averages: 227th av. 16.20 (2007 175th av. 25.30)
Place in bowling averages: 56th av. 27.60 (2007 88th av. 33.70)
Parents: Gerald and Mary
Wife and date of marriage: Donna, 28 August 2000
Children: Ashleigh, 28 April 1990; Gregory, 29 September 1994

Family links with cricket: 'Father and two brothers played in the same side at Betley CC in Staffordshire'
Education: St Joseph's College, Trent Vale, Stoke-on-Trent; Newcastle College
Qualifications: 2 O-levels, Level 2 coach
Overseas tours: England YC to Australia 1989-90; England A to Bermuda and West Indies 1991-92, to Australia 1992-93, to South Africa 1993-94, to India 1994-95; England to South Africa 1995-96, to India and Pakistan (World Cup) 1995-96, to New Zealand 1996-97, to Australia 1998-99, to Pakistan and Sri Lanka 2000-01, to Sri Lanka (ICC Champions Trophy) 2002-03; England VI to Hong Kong 2005, 2006 (c)
Overseas teams played for: East Shirley, Christchurch, New Zealand 1990-91
Career highlights to date: 'Making my debut for England'
Cricket moments to forget: 'Every time the team loses'
Cricket superstitions: None
Cricketers particularly admired: Kim Barnett, Mike Atherton, Ian Botham, Malcolm Marshall
Other sports played: Golf, football
Other sports followed: Football (Stoke City)
Favourite band: 'Anything R&B'
Relaxations: 'Listening to music'
Extras: Scored century (110) as nightwatchman for England Young Cricketers v Pakistan Young Cricketers at Taunton 1990. Took 8-53 before lunch on his 20th birthday, v Essex at Derby 1991. Selected for England A in 1991 – his first full season of first-class cricket. PCA Young Player of the Year 1991. Took 7-43 on Test debut against West Indies at Lord's 1995, the best innings figures ever by an England debutant. Took hat-trick (Richardson, Murray, Hooper) against the West Indies at Old Trafford in the fourth Test 1995. PCA Player of the Year 1995. Finished top of the Whyte and Mackay bowling ratings 1995. Cornhill England Player of the Year 1995-96. One of *Wisden*'s Five Cricketers of the Year 1996. Man of the Match in the second Test v West Indies at Lord's 2000; on his recall to the Test side he had match figures of 7-52 followed by a match-winning 33* in England's second innings. Derbyshire captain 1998-2003. Took Twenty20 hat-trick (Pietersen, Ealham, Patel) v Nottinghamshire at Old Trafford 2004. Has joined Hampshire for 2009
Best batting: 200* Derbyshire v Durham, Derby 2000
Best bowling: 9-43 Derbyshire v Northamptonshire, Derby 1995

2008 Season

	M	Inn	NO	Runs	HS	Avg	100	50	Ct	St	Balls	Runs	Wkts	Avg	BB	5I	10M
Test																	
FC	9	11	1	162	43	16.20	-	-	5	-	1218	552	20	27.60	3-33	-	-
ODI																	
List A																	
20/20 Int																	
20/20	8	5	3	37	19 *	18.50	-	-	2	-	156	188	8	23.50	2-24	-	

Career Performances

	M	Inn	NO	Runs	HS	Avg	100	50	Ct	St	Balls	Runs	Wkts	Avg	BB	5I	10M
Test	37	56	8	864	59	18.00	-	3	18	-	7678	3906	131	29.81	7-43	5	-
FC	287	418	55	9127	200 *	25.14	8	50	205	-	48489	23829	895	26.62	9-43	32	5
ODI	32	21	3	180	31 *	10.00	-	-	6	-	1772	1368	41	33.36	3-27	-	
List A	282	219	32	3995	93	21.36	-	19	105	-	13358	9452	343	27.55	6-21	4	
20/20 Int																	
20/20	37	30	6	304	28	12.66	-	-	8	-	582	698	30	23.26	4-16	-	

COSKER, D. A. — Glamorgan

Name: Dean Andrew Cosker
Role: Right-hand bat, left-arm spin bowler
Born: 7 January 1978, Weymouth, Dorset
Height: 5ft 11in **Weight:** 12st 7lbs
Nickname: Lurks, The Lurker, Bryn
County debut: 1996
County cap: 2000
Place in batting averages: 232nd av. 14.54
Place in bowling averages: 102nd av. 34.52 (2007 74th av. 32.37)
Parents: Des and Carol
Wife and date of marriage: Katie, 24 November 2006
Children: Jak Ruben, 19 February 2008
Family links with cricket: 'Brother dabbles in Welsh League when his missus lets him! Father still refuses to give his knees that much wanted rest, and plays for Thornford CC'
Education: Millfield School; 'University of Roath'
Qualifications: 10 GCSEs, 4 A-levels
Off-season: 'Pre-season in Cape Town with Glamorgan; revisiting Glamorgan's indoor school of death, which normally claims a few knee and back victims'
Overseas tours: West of England U15 to West Indies 1993-94; Millfield School to Sri Lanka 1994-95; England U17 to Netherlands 1995; England U19 to Pakistan 1996-97; England A to Kenya and Sri Lanka 1997-98, to Zimbabwe and South Africa 1998-99; Glamorgan CCC to Cape Town and Jersey
Overseas teams played for: Gordon CC, Sydney 1996-97; Crusaders, Durban 2001-02
Career highlights to date: 'Debut at Glamorgan in 1997; Championship medal 1997; England A caps; trophies with Glamorgan, and seeing the grimace on Gareth Rees's

face when he gets hit in short leg!'
Cricket moments to forget: 'Every time I bowl from the Taff End at the SWALEC Stadium in the Twenty20 with the wind with the batsmen...'
Cricketers particularly admired: Mike Kasprowic, Matt Elliott, Matt Maynard, Robert Croft, Steven Watkin, Graham Thorpe
Young players to look out for: Paul Lewis, 'Bones' Harris
Other sports played: Golf
Other sports followed: Football ('Spurs and the Swans'); WWF wrestling ('The Undertaker')
Favourite band: 'Bananarama'
Relaxations: 'Time with my son, Jak; long winter walks'
Extras: England U15, U17 and U19. Played for U19 TCCB Development of Excellence XI v South Africa U19 1995. NBC Denis Compton Award for most promising young Glamorgan player 1996. Leading wicket-taker on England A tour of Zimbabwe and South Africa 1998-99 (22; av. 22.90). Third youngest Glamorgan player to receive county cap
Opinions on cricket: 'Great to see more money coming into the game. Let's not see the young players at clubs not getting the opportunities because of Kolpaks...'
Best batting: 52 Glamorgan v Gloucestershire, Bristol 2005
Best bowling: 6-140 Glamorgan v Lancashire, Colwyn Bay 1998

2008 Season

	M	Inn	NO	Runs	HS	Avg	100	50	Ct	St	Balls	Runs	Wkts	Avg	BB	5I	10M
Test																	
FC	8	13	2	160	42	14.54	-	-	4	-	1118	656	19	34.52	5-81	1	-
ODI																	
List A	14	5	2	26	15 *	8.66	-	-	7	-	572	394	12	32.83	2-19	-	
20/20 Int																	
20/20	9	1	0	0	0	0.00	-	-	-	-	186	233	10	23.30	3-32	-	

Career Performances

	M	Inn	NO	Runs	HS	Avg	100	50	Ct	St	Balls	Runs	Wkts	Avg	BB	5I	10M
Test																	
FC	153	195	58	1784	52	13.02	-	1	98	-	28424	13897	366	37.96	6-140	4	-
ODI																	
List A	176	90	40	490	39 *	9.80	-	-	70	-	7532	5935	179	33.15	5-54	1	
20/20 Int																	
20/20	41	9	7	30	10 *	15.00	-	-	13	-	666	948	34	27.88	3-18	-	

19. Who took his 100th Test catch during the 1998-99 Ashes series?

CRAWLEY, J. P. Hampshire

Name: John Paul Crawley
Role: Right-hand bat, occasional wicket-keeper
Born: 21 September 1971, Maldon, Essex
Height: 6ft 2in **Weight:** 13st 7lbs
Nickname: Creepy, Jonty, JC
County debut: 1990 (Lancashire), 2002 (Hampshire)
County cap: 1994 (Lancashire), 2002 (Hampshire)
Benefit: 2008 (Hampshire)
Test debut: 1994
ODI debut: 1994-95
1000 runs in a season: 10
1st-Class 200s: 6
1st-Class 300s: 2
Place in batting averages: 141st av. 27.73 (2007 75th av. 39.36)
Parents: Frank and Jean (deceased)
Marital status: Married
Family links with cricket: Father played in Manchester Association; brother Mark played for Lancashire and Nottinghamshire; brother Peter plays for Warrington CC and has played for Scottish Universities and Cambridge University; uncle was excellent fast bowler; godfather umpires in Manchester Association
Education: Manchester Grammar School; Trinity College, Cambridge; Open University Business School
Qualifications: 10 O-levels, 2 AO-Levels, 3 A-levels, 2 S-levels, BA in History, MA (Cantab), Professional Certificate in Management
Overseas tours: England YC to Australia 1989-90, to New Zealand 1990-91 (c); England A to South Africa 1993-94, to West Indies 2000-01; England to Australia 1994-95, to South Africa 1995-96, to Zimbabwe and New Zealand 1996-97, to West Indies 1997-98, to Australia 1998-99, 2002-03
Overseas teams played for: Midland-Guildford, Perth 1990
Cricketers particularly admired: Michael Atherton, Neil Fairbrother, Graham Gooch, Alec Stewart, David Gower, Allan Donald, Ian Salisbury
Other sports followed: Football (Manchester United), golf
Relaxations: 'Playing or trying to play the guitar'
Extras: Sir John Hobbs Silver Jubilee Memorial Prize 1987. Played for England YC 1989, 1990 and (as captain) 1991; first to score 1000 runs in U19 'Tests'. Lancashire vice-captain 1998. Topped English first-class batting averages for 1998 season (1851 runs; av. 74.04). Lancashire Player of the Year 1998. Lancashire captain 1999-2001.

Scored 272 on debut for Hampshire v Kent at Canterbury 2002, a Hampshire debut record. Captain of Hampshire 2003. Hampshire Player of the Year 2006.
Best batting: 311* Hampshire v Nottinghamshire, Rose Bowl 2005
Best bowling: 1-7 Hampshire v Surrey, The Oval 2005

2008 Season

	M	Inn	NO	Runs	HS	Avg	100	50	Ct	St	Balls	Runs	Wkts	Avg	BB	5I	10M
Test																	
FC	9	16	1	416	104	27.73	1	2	3	-	0	0	0		-	-	-
ODI																	
List A	4	4	0	55	51	13.75	-	1	-	-	0	0	0		-	-	
20/20 Int																	
20/20																	

Career Performances

	M	Inn	NO	Runs	HS	Avg	100	50	Ct	St	Balls	Runs	Wkts	Avg	BB	5I	10M
Test	37	61	9	1800	156 *	34.61	4	9	29	-	0	0	0		-	-	-
FC	343	570	57	24053	311 *	46.88	54	131	214	1	215	283	2	141.50	1-7	-	-
ODI	13	12	1	235	73	21.36	-	2	1	1	0	0	0		-	-	
List A	304	290	23	8512	114	31.88	7	55	94	4	6	4	0		-	-	
20/20 Int																	
20/20	10	10	1	107	23	11.88	-	-	3	-	0	0	0		-	-	

CROFT, R. D. B. Glamorgan

Name: Robert Damien Bale Croft
Role: Right-hand bat, off-spin bowler
Born: 25 May 1970, Morriston, Swansea
Height: 5ft 11in **Weight:** 13st 7lbs
Nickname: Crofty
County debut: 1989
County cap: 1992
Benefit: 2000
Test debut: 1996
ODI debut: 1996
50 wickets in a season: 9
Place in batting averages: 128th av. 29.62 (2007 180th av. 24.79)
Place in bowling averages: 60th av. 28.04 (2007 85th av. 33.51)
Parents: Malcolm and Susan
Wife: Marie
Children: Callum James Bale Croft
Family links with cricket: Father and grandfather played league cricket
Education: St John Lloyd Catholic School, Llanelli; Neath Tertiary College; West Glamorgan Institute of Higher Education
Qualifications: 6 O-levels, OND Business Studies, HND Business Studies, NCA senior coaching certificate
Overseas tours: England A to Bermuda and West Indies 1991-92, to South Africa 1993-94; England to Zimbabwe and New Zealand 1996-97, to West Indies 1997-98, to Australia 1998-99, to Sharjah (Coca-Cola Cup) 1998-99, to Sri Lanka 2000-01, 2003-04; England VI to Hong Kong 2003, 2005 (c)
Career highlights to date: 'Playing for England and winning the Championship with Glamorgan in 1997'
Cricket moments to forget: 'None. This career is too short to forget any of it'
Cricketers particularly admired: Ian Botham, Viv Richards, Shane Warne
Other sports played: 'Give anything a go'
Other sports followed: Football (Liverpool FC), rugby (Llanelli and Wales)
Interests/relaxations: 'Everything'
Extras: Captained England South to victory in International Youth Tournament 1989 and was voted Player of the Tournament. Glamorgan Young Player of the Year 1992. Scored Test best 37* in the third Test at Old Trafford 1998, resisting for 190 minutes to deny South Africa victory. Represented England in the 1999 World Cup. Honorary fellow of West Glamorgan Institute of Higher Education. Scored 69-ball 119 v Surrey at The Oval in the C&G 2002 as Glamorgan made 429 in reply to Surrey's 438-5. Glamorgan Player of the Year 2003 (jointly with Michael Kasprowicz) and 2004.

Glamorgan vice-captain 2002-03; appointed captain during 2003, taking over from the injured Steve James; stood down as captain in mid-September 2006. Man of the Match in England's victory v Pakistan in the final of the Hong Kong Sixes 2003. Retired from international cricket in January 2004. Cricket Society's Wetherell Award 2004 for the leading all-rounder in English first-class cricket. Took 1000th first-class wicket (Niall O'Brien) v Northamptonshire at Northampton 2007 to become the first Welshman to have scored 10,000 runs and taken 1000 wickets in first-class cricket. Finished top of the county's first-class bowling averages in 2008
Best batting: 143 Glamorgan v Somerset, Taunton 1995
Best bowling: 8-66 Glamorgan v Warwickshire, Swansea 1992

2008 Season

	M	Inn	NO	Runs	HS	Avg	100	50	Ct	St	Balls	Runs	Wkts	Avg	BB	5I	10M
Test																	
FC	15	20	4	474	89 *	29.62	-	2	2	-	3062	1262	45	28.04	6-45	2	-
ODI																	
List A	9	9	0	101	25	11.22	-	-	1	-	396	267	9	29.66	3-23	-	
20/20 Int																	
20/20	9	6	1	145	50	29.00	-	1	3	-	190	213	9	23.66	3-12	-	

Career Performances

	M	Inn	NO	Runs	HS	Avg	100	50	Ct	St	Balls	Runs	Wkts	Avg	BB	5I	10M
Test	21	34	8	421	37 *	16.19	-	-	10	-	4619	1825	49	37.24	5-95	1	-
FC	365	541	96	11791	143	26.49	7	51	171	-	80174	37463	1049	35.71	8-66	48	9
ODI	50	36	12	345	32	14.37	-	-	11	-	2466	1743	45	38.73	3-51	-	
List A	394	331	59	6369	143	23.41	4	31	93	-	18049	13018	403	32.30	6-20	1	
20/20 Int																	
20/20	42	29	6	539	62 *	23.43	-	3	18	-	838	1064	42	25.33	3-12	-	

CROFT, S. J. — Lancashire

Name: Steven John Croft
Role: Right-hand bat, right-arm fast-medium bowler; all-rounder
Born: 11 October 1984, Blackpool
Height: 5ft 11in **Weight:** 14st
Nickname: Crofty
County debut: 2005
Place in batting averages: 105th av. 32.50 (2007 220th av. 19.29)
Place in bowling averages: 112th av. 36.62
Parents: Elizabeth and Lawrence
Marital status: Single
Family links with cricket: Father played for local team

Education: Highfield High, Blackpool; Myerscough College
Qualifications: 10 GCSEs, First Diploma in Sports Studies, Level 2 cricket coach
Career outside cricket: Coaching
Overseas teams played for: St Kilda, Melbourne 2005-06; Auckland 2008-09
Career highlights to date: 'Signing for Lancashire CCC'
Cricket moments to forget: 'Duck on 2nd XI debut'
Cricket superstitions: 'Left pad on first'
Cricketers particularly admired: Andrew Flintoff, Stuart Law, Jacques Kallis
Young players to look out for: Karl Brown, Tom Smith, Gareth Cross
Other sports played: Football ('played for Blackpool town team and trialled at Oldham FC and Wimbledon FC')
Other sports followed: Football (Newcastle)
Favourite band: Oasis, The Killers, Blink 182
Relaxations: 'Socialising with friends; music, movies, sport'
Extras: Played for Lancashire Board XI in the C&G 2003. Only third amateur to score over 1000 runs in a season in the Northern Premier League
Best batting: 122 Lancashire v Notinghamshire, Old Trafford 2008
Best bowling: 4-51 Lancashire v Nottinghamshire, Trent Bridge 2008

2008 Season

	M	Inn	NO	Runs	HS	Avg	100	50	Ct	St	Balls	Runs	Wkts	Avg	BB	5I	10M
Test																	
FC	13	19	1	585	122	32.50	1	3	6	-	966	586	16	36.62	4-51	-	-
ODI																	
List A	13	12	3	279	70	31.00	-	2	3	-	449	304	14	21.71	4-24	-	
20/20 Int																	
20/20	11	8	1	134	29	19.14	-	-	-	-	152	209	6	34.83	3-6	-	

Career Performances

	M	Inn	NO	Runs	HS	Avg	100	50	Ct	St	Balls	Runs	Wkts	Avg	BB	5I	10M
Test																	
FC	26	40	3	936	122	25.29	1	5	19	-	1506	921	22	41.86	4-51	-	-
ODI																	
List A	36	33	8	753	70	30.12	-	4	12	-	863	703	25	28.12	4-24	-	
20/20 Int																	
20/20	25	22	4	379	49	21.05	-	-	8	-	274	380	11	34.54	3-6	-	

CROOK, A. R. — Northamptonshire

Name: Andrew (Andy) Richard Crook
Role: Right-hand bat, right-arm off-spin bowler
Born: 14 October 1980, Adelaide, South Australia
Height: 6ft 4in **Weight:** 14st 5lbs
Nickname: Crooky, Gonk
County debut: 2004 (Lancashire), 2007 (Northamptonshire)
Place in batting averages: (2007 113th av. 33.62)
Parents: Sue (mother) and Doug (stepfather); Martyn (father)
Marital status: Engaged to Louise
Children: Harriet, 2007
Family links with cricket: 'Brother, Steve, also at Northants'
Education: Rostrevor College
Overseas teams played for: South Australia 1998-99; Northern Districts, South Australia; East Torrens CC, Adelaide
Career highlights to date: '2005 Twenty20 finals day'
Cricket moments to forget: 'Being the last man out on my Old Trafford debut, and my wicket meant Lancashire were relegated to Division Two of the County Championship'
Cricketers particularly admired: Gary Kirsten
Young players to look out for: Karl Brown
Other sports followed: Football (Blackburn Rovers), AFL (Essendon Bombers)
Favourite band: Snow Patrol, U2, Counting Crows
Extras: Made first-class debut for South Australia v England XI at Adelaide 1998-99. Made new Lancashire record individual one-day score (162*), v Buckinghamshire at Wormsley in the C&G 2005, winning Man of the Match award. Is not considered an overseas player
Best batting: 88 Lancashire v OUCCE, The Parks 2005
Best bowling: 3-71 Lancashire v Essex, Old Trafford 2005

2008 Season

	M	Inn	NO	Runs	HS	Avg	100	50	Ct	St	Balls	Runs	Wkts	Avg	BB	5I	10M
Test																	
FC	1	2	1	24	19 *	24.00	-	-	-	-	14	5	1	5.00	1-5	-	-
ODI																	

List A
20/20 Int
20/20

Career Performances

	M	Inn	NO	Runs	HS	Avg	100	50	Ct	St	Balls	Runs	Wkts	Avg	BB	5I	10M
Test																	
FC	11	18	2	493	88	30.81	-	3	8	-	896	574	8	71.75	3-71	-	-
ODI																	
List A	21	19	3	444	162 *	27.75	1	-	4	-	423	412	12	34.33	3-32	-	
20/20 Int																	
20/20	10	7	3	51	15	12.75	-	-	3	-	126	201	7	28.71	2-25	-	

CROOK, S.P. Northamptonshire

Name: Steven Paul Crook
Role: Right-hand bat, right-arm fast-medium bowler; all-rounder
Born: 28 May 1983, Adelaide, South Australia
Height: 5ft 11in **Weight:** 13st 3lbs
Nickname: Crooky, Crookster
County debut: 2003 (Lancashire), 2005 (Northamptonshire)
Place in batting averages: 80th av. 37.16 (2007 167th av. 26.46)
Place in bowling averages: (2007 102nd av. 36.13)
Parents: 'Dad Martyn, mum Sue and stepfather Doug'
Marital status: Single
Family links with sport: Brother Andrew also at Northamptonshire. Father, Martyn, played professional football
Education: Rostrevor College
Qualifications: Matriculation
Overseas tours: Lancashire to Cape Town 2003, 2004
Overseas teams played for: Northern Districts, South Australia
Career highlights to date: 'Playing semi-final of Twenty20 2004'
Cricket moments to forget: 'Getting beaten in semi of Twenty20 2004'
Cricketers particularly admired: Andrew Flintoff, Stuart Law
Young players to look out for: Tom Smith, Steve Croft, Andy Crook

Other sports followed: Football (Tottenham Hotspur FC)
Favourite band: The Doors, The Strokes
Relaxations: 'Hanging out with mates'
Extras: Attended South Australia Cricket Academy. Represented South Australia U13-U19. Selected for Australia U19 preliminary World Cup squad 2001-02. Is not considered an overseas player
Best batting: 97 Northamptonshire v Yorkshire, Northampton 2005
Best bowling: 4-56 Northamptonshire v Essex, Northampton 2007

2008 Season

	M	Inn	NO	Runs	HS	Avg	100	50	Ct	St	Balls	Runs	Wkts	Avg	BB	5I	10M
Test																	
FC	4	6	0	223	63	37.16	-	2	-	-	441	286	1	286.00	1-9	-	-
ODI																	
List A	2	1	0	1	1	1.00	-	-	-	-	78	58	2	29.00	1-24	-	
20/20 Int																	
20/20	10	3	1	38	26 *	19.00	-	-	2	-	96	158	3	52.66	1-24		

Career Performances

	M	Inn	NO	Runs	HS	Avg	100	50	Ct	St	Balls	Runs	Wkts	Avg	BB	5I	10M
Test																	
FC	33	44	7	1177	97	31.81	-	8	10	-	4015	2649	53	49.98	4-56	-	-
ODI																	
List A	27	17	2	153	23	10.20	-	-	6	-	960	966	20	48.30	4-20	-	
20/20 Int																	
20/20	28	14	3	171	27	15.54	-	-	5	-	222	336	9	37.33	2-24	-	

20. Which Waugh scored his debut Test century during the 1990 Ashes series?

CROSS, G. D. Lancashire

Name: Gareth David Cross
Role: Right-hand bat, wicket-keeper
Born: 20 June 1984, Bury
Height: 5ft 9in **Weight:** 11st 9lbs
Nickname: Crossy
County debut: 2005
Parents: Duncan and Margaret
Marital status: Single
Family links with cricket: 'Dad played for Prestwich. Brother Matthew plays for Monton and Weaste'
Education: Moorside High School; Eccles College
Qualifications: 9 GCSEs, GNVQ Science
Overseas teams played for: St Kilda, Melbourne 2002-04
Cricket moments to forget: 'Tim Rees top-edging the ball into my head whilst I was keeping for Salford against Bolton'
Cricket superstitions: 'Just putting batting gear on in the same order'
Cricketers particularly admired: Ian Healy, Adam Gilchrist, Graeme Rummans
Young players to look out for: Steven Croft, Steven Crook
Other sports played: Football ('had a trial for Man United when I was 13')
Other sports followed: Football (Man United)
Favourite band: Eminem, Oasis
Relaxations: 'Watching football; five-a-side football'
Extras: Manchester Association Young Player of the Year. Bolton Association Young Player of the Year 2000. ECB Premier League Young Player of the Year. Liverpool Competition Player of the Year 2004. Played for Lancashire Board XI in the C&G 2003. Made five dismissals in first innings of Championship debut v Leicestershire at Old Trafford 2005.
Best batting: 72 Lancashire v Kent, Canterbury 2006

2008 Season

	M	Inn	NO	Runs	HS	Avg	100	50	Ct	St	Balls	Runs	Wkts	Avg	BB	5I	10M
Test																	
FC	1	2	0	38	38	19.00	-	-	1	-	0	0	0		-	-	-
ODI																	
List A	12	11	0	139	41	12.63	-	-	9	1	36	26	2	13.00	2-26	-	
20/20 Int																	
20/20	11	7	3	97	42 *	24.25	-	-	7	4	0	0	0		-	-	

Career Performances

	M	Inn	NO	Runs	HS	Avg	100	50	Ct	St	Balls	Runs	Wkts	Avg	BB	5I	10M
Test																	
FC	8	13	1	309	72	25.75	-	3	27	8	0	0	0		-	-	-
ODI																	
List A	28	25	2	404	76	17.56	-	1	18	6	36	26	2	13.00	2-26	-	
20/20 Int																	
20/20	25	20	4	271	62	16.93	-	1	18	10	0	0	0		-	-	

CUMMINS, R. A. G. Northamptonshire

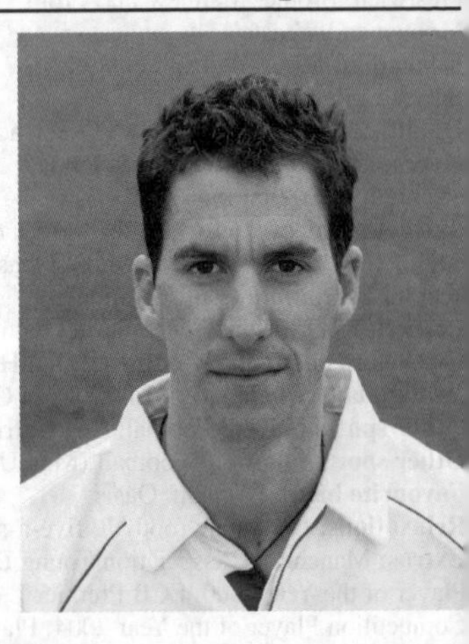

Name: Ryan Anthony Gilbert Cummins
Role: Right-hand bat, right-arm fast-medium bowler
Born: 14 April 1984, Sutton, Surrey
Height: 6ft 4in **Weight:** 13st 4lbs
Nickname: Rhino, Yummins
County debut: 2005 (Leicestershire)
Place in batting averages: (2007 233rd av. 17.33)
Place in bowling averages: (2007 109th av. 39.38)
Parents: Tony and Sheila
Marital status: Single
Family links with cricket: 'Great-grandfather, Gilly Reay, played for Surrey. Father played county 2nd XI and sister plays county cricket for Northants'
Education: Wallington County Grammar School for Boys; Loughborough University
Qualifications: 11 GCSEs, 4 A-levels, BSc (Hons) Geography (2.2), Level 2 cricket coach, Level 1 hockey coach
Overseas tours: Club Cricket Conference to Australia 2008; PCA Benevolent Fund Everest Trek 2007 - 'the highest game of cricket ever!'
Career highlights to date: 'Playing in the winning Twenty20 side of 2006'
Cricket moments to forget: 'Bowling in the Twenty20 final 2006'
Cricketers particularly admired: Phil DeFreitas, Brian Lara, Adam Hollioake
Other sports played: Hockey, golf
Other sports followed: Rugby (Leicester Tigers), golf
Favourite band: Counting Crows
Extras: Played for Loughborough UCCE 2003-05. Represented British Universities 2005. Signed from Leicestershire in October 2008

Opinions on cricket: 'Level of professionalism in the game must continue to improve, so as to improve both individuals and the standard of English cricket.'
Best batting: 34* Leicestershire v OUCCE, The Parks 2007
Best bowling: 5-60 Leicestershire v Northamptonshire, Leicester 2007

2008 Season

	M	Inn	NO	Runs	HS	Avg	100	50	Ct	St	Balls	Runs	Wkts	Avg	BB	5I	10M
Test																	
FC	2	2	0	44	22	22.00	-	-	2	-	506	268	7	38.28	3-73	-	-
ODI																	
List A	6	1	1	8	8 *		-	-	3	-	263	197	9	21.88	3-21	-	
20/20 Int																	
20/20																	

Career Performances

	M	Inn	NO	Runs	HS	Avg	100	50	Ct	St	Balls	Runs	Wkts	Avg	BB	5I	10M
Test																	
FC	22	27	11	221	34 *	13.81	-	-	7	-	3526	2184	49	44.57	5-60	1	-
ODI																	
List A	22	6	3	23	10	7.66	-	-	6	-	857	706	29	24.34	3-21	-	
20/20 Int																	
20/20	1	0	0	0	0		-	-	1	-	18	40	0		-	-	

DAGGETT, L. M. Northamptonshire

Name: Lee Martin Daggett
Role: Right-hand bat, right-arm fast-medium bowler
Born: 1 October 1982, Bury, Lancashire
Height: 6ft **Weight:** 13st 6lbs
Nickname: Terry, Dags, Dagsy, Daggers, Len Dugout
County debut: 2006 (Warwickshire; see extras)
Place in bowling averages: 79th av. 31.21
Parents: Peter and Kathleen
Marital status: Single
Family links with cricket: 'Father was captain of Ramsbottom CC in the Lancashire League. Also coached Ramsbottom CC and me'
Education: Woodhey High School, Bury; Holy Cross College, Bury; Durham University; Salford University
Qualifications: 10 GCSEs, 4 A-levels, BSc (Hons) Sport, Health and Exercise, ECB Level 2 coach, first aid
Career outside cricket: 'Studying physiotherapy at Salford Uni'
Overseas tours: BUSA to South Africa 2004; Warwickshire to Grenada 2007
Overseas teams played for: Joondalup CC, Perth 2001, 2006, 2007
Career highlights to date: '8-94 v Durham for DUCCE in 2004; 6-30 v Durham for Warwickshire in 2006'
Cricket moments to forget: 'First game on Sky – getting swept out of the ground three times by Mal Loye'
Cricket superstitions: 'To run inside my mark'
Cricketers particularly admired: Allan Donald, Graeme Fowler, Brett Lee
Young players to look out for: Chris Woakes
Other sports played: Football ('played for Bury School of Excellence and North-West'), squash, tennis, golf
Other sports followed: Football (Manchester United; 'watch Bury's progress')
Favourite band: Oasis, Ocean Colour Scene, Arctic Monkeys
Relaxations: 'Cinema/movies'
Extras: Played for Durham UCCE 2003-05. Durham University Sportsman of the Year 2004. Represented British Universities 2004-05. On loan with Leicestershire in 2008
Opinions on cricket: 'Young English cricketers trying to make their way in the game are suffering due to the amount of overseas-based cricketers who are playing county

cricket. I feel there are fewer young cricketers going to University because of Academies. Although Academies are great for cricketers' development, in the bigger scheme of things, young cricketers will suffer when careers end.'

Best batting: 33 Warwickshire v Durham, Riverside 2007
Best bowling: 8-94 DUCCE v Durham, Riverside 2004

2008 Season

	M	Inn	NO	Runs	HS	Avg	100	50	Ct	St	Balls	Runs	Wkts	Avg	BB	5I	10M
Test																	
FC	5	5	1	32	17	8.00	-	-	-	-	1014	593	19	31.21	4-41	-	-
ODI																	
List A	4	1	0	1	1	1.00	-	-	1	-	190	169	3	56.33	1-40	-	
20/20 Int																	
20/20																	

Career Performances

	M	Inn	NO	Runs	HS	Avg	100	50	Ct	St	Balls	Runs	Wkts	Avg	BB	5I	10M
Test																	
FC	22	29	13	132	33	8.25	-	-	1	-	3215	1959	53	36.96	8-94	2	-
ODI																	
List A	18	5	4	16	5 *	16.00	-	-	2	-	806	653	18	36.27	2-33		
20/20 Int																	
20/20	3	0	0	0	0		-	-	2	-	36	62	1	62.00	1-13	-	

21. Which Australian ground is the traditional venue for the Boxing Day Ashes Test?

DALRYMPLE, J. W. M. Glamorgan

Name: James (Jamie) William Murray Dalrymple
Role: Right-hand bat, off-spin bowler; county captain
Born: 21 January 1981, Nairobi, Kenya
Height: 6ft **Weight:** 13st 7lbs
Nickname: JD, Pest
County debut: 2000 (one-day, Middlesex), 2001 (first-class, Middlesex), 2008 (Glamorgan)
County cap: 2004 (Middlesex)
ODI debut: 2006
Twenty20 Int debut: 2006
1st-Class 200s: 2
Place in batting averages: 125th av. 30.12 (2007 216th av. 20.33)
Place in bowling averages: (2007 142nd av. 57.41)
Parents: Douglas and Patricia
Marital status: Single
Family links with cricket: 'Dad played lots of club cricket.' Brother Simon played for Oxford University in 2002 and 2004
Education: Radley College, Abingdon; St Peter's College, Oxford University
Qualifications: 10 GCSEs, 5 A-levels, degree in History
Overseas tours: Middlesex to South Africa 2000; England A to West Indies 2005-06; England to India (ICC Champions Trophy) 2006-07, to Australia 2006-07, to West Indies (World Cup) 2006-07; MCC to Uganda 2008 (captain)
Cricket moments to forget: 'Middlesex v Warwickshire at Edgbaston 2003 – being part of the loss of eight wickets in a session, and the match'
Cricketers particularly admired: David Gower, Carl Hooper, Ian Botham, Mark Waugh
Other sports played: Rugby (college), hockey (university)
Other sports followed: Rugby (Northampton RUFC)
Favourite band: 'Don't have a favourite'
Relaxations: Reading, golf
Extras: Represented England U19 2000. Played for Oxford UCCE 2001 and 2002 (c). Represented British Universities 2001 and 2002 (c). Oxford Blue 2001, 2002 (c) and 2003 (c). Scored double century (236*) in the Varsity Match at Fenner's 2003 and took 5-49 in the Cambridge first innings. C&G Man of the Match awards v Wales Minor Counties at Lamphey (104*; second fifty in 14 balls) and v Glamorgan at Lord's (107) 2004. ECB National Academy 2005-06, 2006-07. Left Middlesex at the end of the 2007 season and joined Glamorgan for 2008 - appointed county captain for 2009

Best batting: 244 Middlesex v Surrey, The Oval 2004
Best bowling: 5-49 Oxford University v Cambridge University, Fenner's 2003

2008 Season

	M	Inn	NO	Runs	HS	Avg	100	50	Ct	St	Balls	Runs	Wkts	Avg	BB	5I	10M
Test																	
FC	16	25	1	723	106	30.12	1	6	8	-	684	406	7	58.00	2-23	-	-
ODI																	
List A	15	15	1	314	54	22.42	-	2	3	-	370	376	10	37.60	3-47		
20/20 Int																	
20/20	9	7	2	152	38 *	30.40	-	-	4	-	84	102	5	20.40	2-22		

Career Performances

	M	Inn	NO	Runs	HS	Avg	100	50	Ct	St	Balls	Runs	Wkts	Avg	BB	5I	10M
Test																	
FC	91	147	13	4450	244	33.20	6	25	46	-	10332	5776	127	45.48	5-49	1	-
ODI	27	26	1	487	67	19.48	-	2	12	-	840	666	14	47.57	2-5		
List A	142	131	25	2833	107	26.72	2	16	55	-	4369	3689	104	35.47	4-14		
20/20 Int	3	3	0	60	32	20.00	-	-	1	-	30	39	2	19.50	1-10		
20/20	34	30	6	572	61	23.83	-	1	9	-	378	519	20	25.95	2-8		

DANISH KANERIA — Essex

Name: Danish Prabha Shanker Kaneria
Role: Right-hand bat, right-arm leg-spin and googly bowler
Born: 16 December 1980, Karachi, Pakistan
Height: 6ft 1in
Nickname: Danny Boy, Dani
County debut: 2004
County cap: 2004
Test debut: 2000-01
ODI debut: 2001-02
50 wickets in a season: 2
Place in batting averages: 254th av. 11.18 (2007 247th av. 14.40)
Place in bowling averages: 18th av. 21.30 (2007 13th av. 22.20)
Parents: Prabha Shanker Kaneria and Babita P. Kaneria
Wife and date of marriage: Dharmeta Danish Kaneria, 15 February 2004

Family links with cricket: Cousin, wicket-keeper Anil Dalpat, played nine Tests for Pakistan 1983-84
Education: St Patrick's High School, Karachi
Overseas tours: Pakistan U19 to Sri Lanka (U19 World Cup) 1999-2000; Pakistan A to Kenya 2000, to Sri Lanka 2001; Pakistan to Bangladesh 2001-02, to Sharjah (v West Indies) 2001-02, to Sharjah (v Australia) 2002-03, to New Zealand 2003-04, to Australia 2004-05, to India 2004-05, to West Indies 2004-05, to Sri Lanka 2005-06, to Scotland and England 2006, to South Africa 2006-07, to West Indies (World Cup) 2006-07, to India 2007-08, plus other one-day tournaments in Sharjah, Sri Lanka and England
Overseas teams played for: Several in Pakistan, including Karachi Whites 1998-99 – 2001-02; Habib Bank 1999-2000; Baluchistan Bears 2007-08 –
Career highlights to date: 'Playing for Pakistan. English county cricket'
Cricket superstitions: 'I kiss the ground when taking the field'
Cricketers particularly admired: Abdul Qadir, Viv Richards, Joel Garner
Other sports played: Football, table tennis
Other sports followed: Football (Brazil)
Favourite band: 'I like Indian music'
Relaxations: 'Listening to music and being with family'
Extras: Represented Pakistan U19 1998-99. The second Hindu to play in Tests for Pakistan, after his cousin Anil Dalpat. Had match figures of 12-94 (6-42/6-52) v Bangladesh at Multan in the first match of the Asian Test Championship 2001-02, winning Man of the Match award. His other international awards include Man of the [Test] Series v Bangladesh 2001-02 and Man of the Match in the second Test v Sri Lanka at Karachi 2004-05 (3-72/7-118). Became sixth Pakistan bowler to take 200 Test wickets when he dismissed Ashwell Prince in the first Test v South Africa in Karachi 2007-08, An overseas player with Essex 2004-05 and 2007-08. Signed central contract for Pakistan 2009. Essex's overseas player for 2009.
Best batting: 65 Essex v Nottinghamshire, Trent Bridge 2007
Best bowling: 7-39 Karachi Whites v Gujranwala, Karachi (C) 2000-01

2008 Season

	M	Inn	NO	Runs	HS	Avg	100	50	Ct	St	Balls	Runs	Wkts	Avg	BB	5I	10M
Test																	
FC	9	14	3	123	22	11.18	-	-	5	-	1892	852	40	21.30	7-157	4	-
ODI																	
List A	10	2	1	12	12	12.00	-	-	1	-	317	268	13	20.61	3-32	-	
20/20 Int																	
20/20	12	8	5	24	7 *	8.00	-	-	1	-	271	276	20	13.80	4-22	-	

Career Performances

	M	Inn	NO	Runs	HS	Avg	100	50	Ct	St	Balls	Runs	Wkts	Avg	BB	5I	10M
Test	51	69	31	260	29	6.84	-	-	16	-	14994	7458	220	33.90	7-77	12	2
FC	142	178	71	1090	65	10.18	-	1	48	-	37853	18144	680	26.68	7-39	47	6
ODI	18	10	8	12	6 *	6.00	-	-	2	-	854	682	15	45.46	3-31	-	
List A	118	57	28	225	33 *	7.75	-	-	22	-	5801	3986	184	21.66	5-21	5	
20/20 Int																	
20/20	34	14	6	39	7 *	4.87	-	-	6	-	690	797	44	18.11	4-22	-	

DAVIES, M. A. Durham

Name: Mark Anthony Davies
Role: Right-hand bat, right-arm fast-medium bowler
Born: 4 October 1980, Stockton-on-Tees
Height: 6ft 3in **Weight:** 13st
Nickname: Davo
County debut: 1998 (one-day), 2002 (first-class) (*see **Extras***)
County cap: 2005
50 wickets in a season: 1
Place in batting averages: (2007 263rd av. 12.75)
Place in bowling averages: 1st av. 14.63 (2007 25th av. 24.23)
Parents: Howard and Mandy
Marital status: Single
Education: Northfield School, Billingham; Stockton Sixth Form College
Qualifications: 5 GCSEs, NVQ Level 3 Sport and Recreation
Overseas tours: Durham to South Africa 2002; England Performance Programme Squad to India 2008; England Lions to New Zealand 2009
Overseas teams played for: North Kalgoorlie CC, Western Australia
Cricketers particularly admired: Glenn McGrath
Other sports played: Football, golf, boxing
Other sports followed: Football (Middlesbrough)
Relaxations: Socialising, golf
Extras: Represented England U19 2000. Attended Durham Academy. Was the first bowler to reach 50 first-class wickets in 2004. Played one first-class match for Nottinghamshire on loan 2007, returning then career-best innings figures of 7-59 v Northamptonshire at Trent Bridge. First in bowling averages 2008

Best batting: 62 Durham v Somerset, Stockton 2005
Best bowling: 8-24 Durham v Hampshire, Basingstoke, August 2008

2008 Season

	M	Inn	NO	Runs	HS	Avg	100	50	Ct	St	Balls	Runs	Wkts	Avg	BB	5I	10M
Test																	
FC	12	15	6	68	19	7.55	-	-	1	-	1526	600	41	14.63	8-24	4	2
ODI																	
List A	7	2	2	2	1 *		-	-	-	-	276	204	6	34.00	2-29	-	
20/20 Int																	
20/20																	

Career Performances

	M	Inn	NO	Runs	HS	Avg	100	50	Ct	St	Balls	Runs	Wkts	Avg	BB	5I	10M
Test																	
FC	66	93	34	658	62	11.15	-	1	15	-	10121	4722	223	21.17	8-24	12	2
ODI																	
List A	72	36	14	166	31 *	7.54	-	-	10	-	2934	2036	68	29.94	4-13	-	
20/20 Int																	
20/20	9	4	3	11	6	11.00	-	-	2	-	204	241	8	30.12	2-14	-	

DAVIES, S. M. — Worcestershire

Name: Steven (Steve) Michael Davies
Role: Left-hand bat, wicket-keeper
Born: 17 June 1986, Bromsgrove
Height: 5ft 11in **Weight:** 11st 8lbs
Nickname: Davo
County debut: 2004 (one-day), 2005 (first-class)
County colours: 2005
1000 runs in a season: 1
50 dismissals in a season: 2
Place in batting averages: 57th av. 41.55 (2007 133rd av. 31.37)
Parents: Lin and Michael
Marital status: Single
Education: King Charles I School, Kidderminster
Qualifications: 9 GCSEs, 1 A-level, 2 AS-levels
Overseas tours: England U17 to Netherlands 2003; England U19 to Bangladesh (U19 World Cup) 2003-04, to India 2004-05 (c); England A to West Indies 2005-06, to

Bangladesh 2006-07; England Performance Programme to India 2007-08; England Lions to India 2007-08. England to West Indies (one-day series) 2009. Selected for England Performance Programme squad to India 2008; England Lions to New Zealand 2009

Career highlights to date: 'Maiden first-class century against Somerset 2005. Pro40 champions 2007'

Cricket superstitions: None

Cricketers particularly admired: Adam Gilchrist, Michael Hussey, Matthew Hayden

Young players to look out for: Moeen Ali

Other sports played: Basketball (trials for England), tennis, golf

Other sports followed: Football (Arsenal)

Favourite band: Chris Brown

Relaxations: 'Playing golf and basketball; socialising with friends; listening to music'

Extras: Represented England U19 2004, 2005. NBC Denis Compton Award for most promising young Worcestershire player 2004, 2005, 2006, 2007, 2008. Took six catches in Leicestershire's first innings at Worcester 2006, equalling Worcestershire record for wicket-keeping catches in a first-class innings. Achieved double of 1000 (1052) runs and 50 (68) dismissals in first-class cricket 2006. ECB National Academy 2004-05 (part-time), 2005-06 (including visit to World Cricket Academy, India), 2006-07. Forced to withdraw from England Lions tour to India 2007-08 with a knee injury

Opinions on cricket: 'Increase in amount of Twenty20 games good for cricket. Only one overseas player allowed should create more opportunities for young players.'

Best batting: 192 Worcestershire v Gloucestershire, Bristol 2006

Stop press: Called up to join England tour party in West Indies 2009 when Matt Prior was given permission to return home

2008 Season

	M	Inn	NO	Runs	HS	Avg	100	50	Ct	St	Balls	Runs	Wkts	Avg	BB	5I	10M
Test																	
FC	16	24	6	748	99 *	41.55	-	5	72	-	0	0	0		-	-	-
ODI																	
List A	16	16	2	689	119	49.21	2	4	11	3	0	0	0		-	-	
20/20 Int																	
20/20	9	7	1	53	23 *	8.83	-	-	4	-	0	0	0		-	-	

Career Performances

	M	Inn	NO	Runs	HS	Avg	100	50	Ct	St	Balls	Runs	Wkts	Avg	BB	5I	10M
Test																	
FC	62	102	12	3258	192	36.20	4	14	197	12	0	0	0		-	-	-
ODI																	
List A	68	59	10	1552	119	31.67	2	8	61	17	0	0	0		-	-	
20/20 Int																	
20/20	24	19	5	224	30	16.00	-	-	10	2	0	0	0		-	-	

DAWSON, L. A. Hampshire

Name: Liam Andrew Dawson
Role: Right-hand bat, slow left-arm bowler; all-rounder
Born: 1 March 1990, Swindon
Height: 5ft 8in **Weight:** 11st
Nickname: Daws, Lemmy, Kimya, Chav
County debut: 2007
Place in batting averages: 142nd av. 27.57
Parents: Andy and Bev
Marital status: Single
Family links with cricket: 'Dad played club cricket for Goatacre and Cheltenham; brother also plays, for Wiltshire U14 /U15 and Goatacre'
Education: The John Bentley School, Calne
Qualifications: GCSEs
Overseas tours: West of England U15 to West Indies 2005; England U16 to South Africa 2006; England U19 to Malaysia 2006-07, to Malaysia (U19 World Cup) 2007-08, to South Africa 2009
Overseas teams played for: Melville, Perth 2006-07, 2007-08
Career highlights to date: 'Making my one-day and first-class debuts. Being Man of the Match at Lord's in the Pro40 v Middlesex'
Cricket moments to forget: 'Being hit for 20-odd in an over'
Cricket superstitions: None
Cricketers particularly admired: Shane Warne, Dan Vettori
Young players to look out for: James Vince
Other sports played: Football (Calne Town Youth)
Other sports followed: Football (Bury)
Favourite band: The Wombats, Coldplay
Relaxations: 'Rugby League'
Extras: Hampshire Academy Player of the Year 2005. Bunbury Festival All-rounder of the Tournament 2005. Represented England U19 2007. Made List A debut v Northamptonshire at Northampton in the Pro40 2007 aged 17, scoring a 31-ball 32. NBC Denis Compton Award for the most promising young Hampshire player 2007, 2008. Man of the Series for England U19 v New Zealand 2008. Made 100 not out in the final Championship fixture against Nottingham in September 2008.
Opinions on cricket: 'Pro40 should continue to be played, because most players think it's a good game'
Best batting: 100* Hampshire v Nottinghamshire, Trent Bridge, September 2008
Best bowling: 2-32 Hampshire v Surrey, The Oval, September 2008

2008 Season

	M	Inn	NO	Runs	HS	Avg	100	50	Ct	St	Balls	Runs	Wkts	Avg	BB	5I	10M
Test																	
FC	5	8	1	193	100 *	27.57	1	-	-	-	343	213	6	35.50	2-32	-	-
ODI																	
List A	7	7	1	158	45	26.33	-	-	6	-	186	174	11	15.81	4-45	-	
20/20 Int																	
20/20	4	3	3	15	11 *		-	-	-	-	24	34	2	17.00	1-14	-	

Career Performances

	M	Inn	NO	Runs	HS	Avg	100	50	Ct	St	Balls	Runs	Wkts	Avg	BB	5I	10M
Test																	
FC	6	8	1	193	100 *	27.57	1	-	-	-	343	213	6	35.50	2-32	-	-
ODI																	
List A	10	9	1	198	45	24.75	-	-	6	-	258	242	11	22.00	4-45	-	
20/20 Int																	
20/20	4	3	3	15	11 *		-	-	-	-	24	34	2	17.00	1-14		

DAWSON, R. K. J. Gloucestershire

Name: Richard Kevin James Dawson
Role: Right-hand bat, right-arm off-spin bowler
Born: 4 August 1980, Doncaster
Height: 6ft 4in **Weight:** 11st 4lbs
Nickname: Billy Dog
County debut: 2001 (Yorkshire), 2007 (Northamptonshire), 2008 (Gloucestershire)
County cap: 2004 (Yorkshire)
Test debut: 2001-02
Place in batting averages: 182nd av.22.00
Parents: Kevin and Pat
Marital status: Single
Family links with cricket: Brother Gareth plays for Doncaster Town CC
Education: Batley GS; Exeter University
Qualifications: 10 GCSEs, 4 A-levels, degree in Exercise and Sports Science
Overseas tours: England U18 to Bermuda 1997; England U19 to New Zealand 1998-99; England to India and New Zealand 2001-02, to Australia 2002-03; ECB

National Academy to Sri Lanka 2002-03; England A to Sri Lanka 2004-05
Cricketers particularly admired: Steve Waugh, Graeme Swann
Other sports played: Football
Other sports followed: Football (Doncaster Rovers FC)
Relaxations: Sleeping, listening to music
Extras: Captained England U15. Sir John Hobbs Silver Jubilee Memorial Prize 1995. Represented England U19 1999. Captained British Universities 2000. NBC Denis Compton Award for the most promising young Yorkshire player 2001. Made Test debut in the first Test v India at Mohali 2001-02, taking 4-134 in India's first innings. Released by Northamptonshire at the end of the 2007 season. Signed for Gloucestershire towards the end of the 2008 season
Best batting: 87 Yorkshire v Kent, Canterbury 2002
Best bowling: 6-82 Yorkshire v Glamorgan, Scarborough 2001

2008 Season

	M	Inn	NO	Runs	HS	Avg	100	50	Ct	St	Balls	Runs	Wkts	Avg	BB	5I	10M
Test																	
FC	5	7	1	132	40	22.00	-	-	3	-	522	346	1	346.00	1-113	-	-
ODI																	
List A	4	3	1	39	17 *	19.50	-	-	2	-	140	162	2	81.00	2-29	-	
20/20 Int																	
20/20																	

Career Performances

	M	Inn	NO	Runs	HS	Avg	100	50	Ct	St	Balls	Runs	Wkts	Avg	BB	5I	10M
Test	7	13	3	114	19 *	11.40	-	-	3	-	1116	677	11	61.54	4-134	-	-
FC	96	143	17	2673	87	21.21	-	11	51	-	14515	8160	187	43.63	6-82	5	-
ODI																	
List A	110	68	15	523	41	9.86	-	-	37	-	4249	3449	111	31.07	4-13	-	
20/20 Int																	
20/20	25	8	3	71	22	14.20	-	-	7	-	461	604	24	25.16	3-24	-	

22. The Brisbane Exhibition Ground staged only one Ashes Test. In which decade was this?

DEAN, K. J. Derbyshire

Name: Kevin James Dean
Role: Left-hand bat, left-arm medium bowler
Born: 16 October 1975, Derby
Height: 6ft 5in **Weight:** 14st
Nickname: Deany, Red Face, George, Dada
County debut: 1996
County cap: 1998
Benefit: 2006
50 wickets in a season: 2
Place in bowling averages: 5th av. 18.71 (2007 53rd av. 28.65)
Parents: Ken and Dorothy
Wife and date of marriage: Sharon, 20 October 2007
Education: Leek High School; Leek College of Further Education
Qualifications: 8 GCSEs, 1 AS-level, 3 A-levels, ECB Level 2 coaching, FA Level 7 referee
Career outside cricket: 'Director of BaileyDean Properties. Tipster at Uttoxeter racecourse. Betfair trading'
Overseas tours: MCC to Australia 2002-03
Overseas teams played for: Sturt CC, Adelaide 1996-97
Career highlights to date: 'Can't split – 1) Hitting the winning runs against Australia for Derbyshire in 1997; 2) Getting either hat-trick'
Cricket moments to forget: 'Being hit on the head [whilst] batting by Andy Bichel whilst unable to bend due to a back injury'
Cricket superstitions: 'Last person out of changing room for first session of fielding'
Cricketers particularly admired: Dominic Cork, Wasim Akram, Michael Holding
Young players to look out for: Dan Redfern, James Harris
Other sports played: Football, indoor cricket, golf, snooker
Other sports followed: Horse racing, football (Derby County)
Favourite band: Stereophonics, Pink, The Killers, Oasis
Relaxations: 'Horse racing, football'
Extras: Took Championship hat-trick (E. Smith, Hooper, Llong) v Kent at Derby 1998. Took second Championship hat-trick (DeFreitas, Kumble, Ormond) v Leicestershire at Leicester 2000. Joint leading wicket-taker in English first-class cricket 2002 (with Martin Saggers) with 83 wickets (av. 23.50). Derbyshire Player of the Year 2002 (jointly with Michael DiVenuto). Retired from first-class cricket at the end of the 2008 season
Best batting: 54* Derbyshire v Worcestershire, Derby 2002
Best bowling: 8-52 Derbyshire v Kent, Canterbury 2000

2008 Season

	M	Inn	NO	Runs	HS	Avg	100	50	Ct	St	Balls	Runs	Wkts	Avg	BB	5I	10M
Test																	
FC	4	5	2	46	25	15.33	-	-	-	-	537	262	14	18.71	6-46	1	-
ODI																	
List A	1	1	1	0	0 *		-	-	1	-	48	24	1	24.00	1-24	-	
20/20 Int																	
20/20	2	1	0	0	0	0.00	-	-	1	-	42	55	2	27.50	2-22	-	

Career Performances

	M	Inn	NO	Runs	HS	Avg	100	50	Ct	St	Balls	Runs	Wkts	Avg	BB	5I	10M
Test																	
FC	119	158	52	1222	54 *	11.52	-	2	22	-	18837	10470	401	26.10	8-52	17	4
ODI																	
List A	145	68	38	261	16 *	8.70	-	-	25	-	6425	4913	161	30.51	5-32	2	
20/20 Int																	
20/20	23	7	5	15	8 *	7.50	-	-	6	-	430	572	20	28.60	2-14	-	

DE BRUYN, Z. Somerset

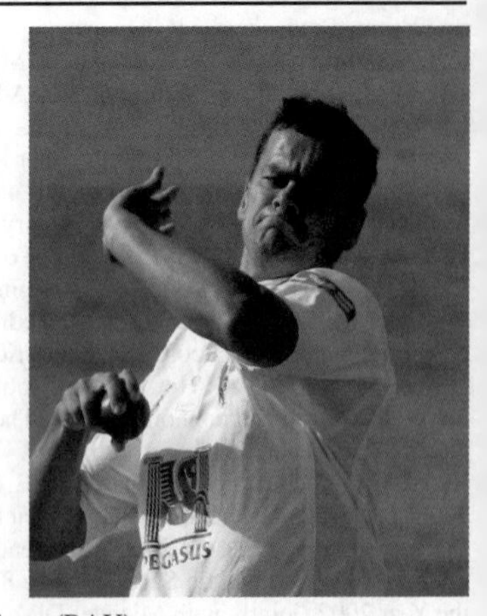

Name: Zander de Bruyn
Role: Right-hand bat, right-arm fast-medium bowler
Born: 5 July 1975, Johannesburg, South Africa
Height: 6ft 2in **Weight:** 12st 8lbs
Nickname: 'Z'
County debut: 2005 (Worcestershire), 2008 (Somerset)
County colours: 2005 (Worcestershire)
Place in batting averages: 45th av 45.31
Test debut: 2004-05
1st-Class 200s: 1
Parents: Hans and Ronel
Wife and date of marriage: Bronwyn, 13 April 2003
Children: Tyler James, 23 November 2007
Education: Hoerskool Helpmekaar; Hoerskool Randburg: University of Johannesburg (RAU)
Off-season: Playing in South Africa for Chevrolet Warriors in Eastern Cape
Overseas tours: South Africa A to Zimbabwe 2004, to Sri Lanka 2005-06; South Africa to India 2004-05

Overseas teams played for: Transvaal/Gauteng 1995-96 – 2000-01; Easterns 2002-03, 2003-04; Nashua Titans 2004-05; Chevrolet Warriors 2006-
Career highlights to date: 'Playing for South Africa'
Cricket moments to forget: 'Scoring my first pair'
Cricket superstitions: None
Cricketers particularly admired: Steve Waugh
Young players to look out for: James Hildreth
Other sports played: Rugby - played at provincial level up to U19
Other sports followed: Rugby (Lions and South Africa)
Favourite band: Live
Relaxations: 'Golf, gadgets, barbecues'
Extras: Represented South Africa Schools. Played for Surrey Board XI in the NatWest 2000 and C&G 2001. Scored 1015 runs (av. 72.50) in the SuperSport Series 2003-04, becoming only the second player (after Barry Richards) to record 1000 runs in a season in the South African domestic first-class competition. Has won numerous awards, including Man of the Match v Western Province in the semi-finals of the Standard Bank Cup at Cape Town 2003-04 (5-44/29) and v Yorkshire at Headingley in the C&G 2005 (3-24/82). An overseas player with Worcestershire 2005
Best batting: 266* Easterns v Griqualand West, Kimberley 2003-04
Best bowling: 6-120 Transvaal B v Western Province B, Cape Town 1996-97

2008 Season

	M	Inn	NO	Runs	HS	Avg	100	50	Ct	St	Balls	Runs	Wkts	Avg	BB	5I	10M
Test																	
FC	16	25	3	997	120	45.31	3	5	8	-	651	366	7	52.28	2-19	-	-
ODI																	
List A	13	12	1	389	79	35.36	-	2	4	-	254	276	7	39.42	2-20	-	
20/20 Int																	
20/20	4	4	1	17	10	5.66	-	-	-	-	0	0	0		-	-	

Career Performances

	M	Inn	NO	Runs	HS	Avg	100	50	Ct	St	Balls	Runs	Wkts	Avg	BB	5I	10M
Test	3	5	1	155	83	38.75	-	1	-	-	216	92	3	30.66	2-32	-	-
FC	119	201	23	7565	266 *	42.50	19	36	79	-	9808	5609	143	39.22	7-67	3	-
ODI																	
List A	131	120	23	3190	113 *	32.88	2	18	32	-	3167	2813	88	31.96	5-44	1	
20/20 Int																	
20/20	31	27	6	572	76 *	27.23	-	2	1	-	288	389	16	24.31	4-18	-	

DENLY, J. L. Kent

Name: Joseph (Joe) Liam Denly
Role: Right-hand bat, leg-spin bowler
Born: 16 March 1986, Canterbury
Height: 6ft **Weight:** 11st 9lbs
Nickname: No Pants
County debut: 2004
1000 runs in a season: 1
Place in batting averages: 123rd av 30.16 (2007 63rd av. 41.79)
Parents: Jayne and Nick
Marital status: Single
Family links with cricket: 'Dad and brother play local cricket'
Education: Chaucer Technology School
Qualifications: 10 GCSEs, Level 1 coach
Overseas tours: England U18 to Netherlands 2003; England U19 to India 2004-05; England Performance Programme to India 2007-08, 2008-09; England Lions to India 2007-08, to New Zealand 2009
Overseas teams played for: Hamersley Carine, Perth 2003; UTS Balmain Tigers, Sydney 2005-07
Career highlights to date: 'First first-class hundred'
Cricket moments to forget: 'Golden duck on first-class debut'
Cricket superstitions: 'Left pad on first'
Cricketers particularly admired: Steve Waugh
Young players to look out for: Sam Denly
Other sports played: Football (Charlton Athletic U14, U15)
Other sports followed: Football (Arsenal)
Favourite band: Westlife
Extras: Represented England U17, U18 and U19. Carried bat in scoring his first Championship century (115*) v Hampshire at Canterbury 2007. Represented England Lions 2007. In 2008, he scored over 1900 runs in all forms of cricket, including three centuries and eleven fifties.
Opinions on cricket: 'It's great!'
Best batting: 149 Kent v Somerset, Tunbridge Wells 2008
Best bowling: 2-13 Kent v Surrey, Canterbury 2007

2008 Season

	M	Inn	NO	Runs	HS	Avg	100	50	Ct	St	Balls	Runs	Wkts	Avg	BB	5I	10M
Test																	
FC	17	30	0	905	149	30.16	2	4	6	-	84	47	0		-	-	
ODI																	
List A	18	18	2	589	102	36.81	1	2	4	-	0	0	0		-	-	
20/20 Int																	
20/20	13	13	0	451	91	34.69	-	5	3	-	0	0	0		-	-	

Career Performances

	M	Inn	NO	Runs	HS	Avg	100	50	Ct	St	Balls	Runs	Wkts	Avg	BB	5I	10M
Test																	
FC	40	69	4	2359	149	36.29	6	12	16	-	703	354	10	35.40	2-13	-	-
ODI																	
List A	44	42	5	1037	102 *	28.02	2	4	11	-	6	6	0		-	-	
20/20 Int																	
20/20	28	25	1	736	91	30.66	-	6	11	-	0	0	0		-	-	

DERNBACH, J. W. — Surrey

Name: Jade Winston Dernbach
Role: Right-hand bat, right-arm fast bowler
Born: 3 March 1986, Johannesburg, South Africa
Height: 6ft 2in **Weight:** 13st
County debut: 2003
Place in bowling averages: 113th av 36.69
Parents: Carmen and Graeme
Marital status: Single
Education: St John the Baptist
Overseas tours: La Manga tournament, Spain 2003
Cricketers particularly admired: Jacques Kallis, Jonty Rhodes, James Anderson, Rikki Clarke
Other sports played: Rugby (Surrey U16)
Other sports followed: Football (Arsenal)
Favourite band: Usher
Relaxations: 'Going out with friends; swimming, playing football and rugby; listening to music'

Extras: Sir Jack Hobbs Fair Play Award. Surrey U19 Player of the Year. Made first-class debut v India A at The Oval 2003 aged 17, becoming the youngest player for 30 years to play first-class cricket for Surrey. Surrey Academy 2003, 2004.
Best batting: 16* Surrey v Nottinghamshire, Trent Bridge 2008
Best bowling: 6-72 Surrey v Somerset, The Whitgift School 2008

2008 Season

	M	Inn	NO	Runs	HS	Avg	100	50	Ct	St	Balls	Runs	Wkts	Avg	BB	5I	10M
Test																	
FC	10	12	3	78	16 *	8.66	-	-	-	-	1296	844	23	36.69	6-72	1	-
ODI																	
List A	16	8	3	51	19 *	10.20	-	-	2	-	743	751	35	21.45	5-31	1	
20/20 Int																	
20/20	8	2	0	9	9	4.50	-	-	1	-	165	244	7	34.85	3-32	-	

Career Performances

	M	Inn	NO	Runs	HS	Avg	100	50	Ct	St	Balls	Runs	Wkts	Avg	BB	5I	10M
Test																	
FC	20	23	8	112	16 *	7.46	-	-	2	-	2399	1679	41	40.95	6-72	1	-
ODI																	
List A	39	19	7	89	21	7.41	-	-	9	-	1589	1624	73	22.24	5-31	2	
20/20 Int																	
20/20	24	4	0	10	9	2.50	-	-	6	-	404	649	14	46.35	3-32	-	

23. Which other Test batsman accompanied David Gower when he flew over the Carrara Oval, Queensland, in a Tiger Moth during the 1990-91 Ashes tour?

DEXTER, N. J. — Middlesex

Name: Neil John Dexter
Role: Right-hand bat, right-arm medium bowler; all-rounder
Born: 21 August 1984, Johannesburg, South Africa
Height: 6ft **Weight:** 11st 4lbs
Nickname: Ted, Dex, Sexy Dexy
County debut: 2005 (Kent)
Place in batting averages: 133rd av 29.16 (2007 54th av. 43.75)
Parents: John and Susan
Marital status: Single
Education: Northwood School, Durban; UNISA (University of South Africa)
Qualifications: Matriculation
Overseas teams played for: Crusaders CC 2000-06
Career highlights to date: 'Scoring first ton, against Glamorgan 2006'
Cricket moments to forget: 'Being hit for 25 in one over against Worcester'
Cricketers particularly admired: Steve Waugh, Brett Lee
Young players to look out for: Alex Blake, Sam Northeast, Joe Denly
Other sports played: Golf, tennis, 'most sports'
Other sports followed: Football (Man Utd)
Favourite band: Simple Plan, Goo Goo Dolls
Relaxations: 'Lying around doing nothing'
Extras: Played for Natal U13-19, Natal Academy and Natal A. Loaned to Essex in 2008. Signed for Middlesex in September 2008. Is not considered an overseas player
Opinions on cricket: 'Very professional with lots of opportunities.'
Best batting: 131* Kent v Nottinghamshire, Canterbury 2006
Best bowling: 2-40 Kent v Lancashire, Old Trafford 2006
Stop press: Played for Middlesex in Stamford Twenty20 series

2008 Season

	M	Inn	NO	Runs	HS	Avg	100	50	Ct	St	Balls	Runs	Wkts	Avg	BB	5I	10M
Test																	
FC	10	13	1	350	105	29.16	1	2	6	-	12	9	0		-	-	-
ODI																	
List A	2	2	1	122	101 *	122.00	1	-	1	-	0	0	0		-	-	
20/20 Int																	
20/20	9	7	1	77	46	12.83	-	-	2	-	12	17	0		-	-	

Career Performances

	M	Inn	NO	Runs	HS	Avg	100	50	Ct	St	Balls	Runs	Wkts	Avg	BB	5I	10M
Test																	
FC	29	41	8	1339	131 *	40.57	3	8	19	-	816	523	9	58.11	2-40	-	-
ODI																	
List A	27	22	3	602	135 *	31.68	2	1	4	-	444	386	14	27.57	3-17	-	
20/20 Int																	
20/20	24	18	2	289	46	18.06	-	-	12	-	114	199	4	49.75	3-27	-	

DIBBLE, A. Somerset

Name: Adam Dibble
Role: Right-hand bat, right-arm fast-medium bowler
Born: 9 March 1991, Exeter, Devon
Height: 6ft 4in **Weight:** 14st
Nickname: Dibbs, Officer
County debut: No first-team appearances
Parents: Mike and Liz
Marital status: Single
Education: St John's School, Sidmouth; Taunton School
Cricketers particularly admired: Brett Lee, Andrew Flintoff
Other sports played: Rugby
Other sports followed: Rugby, football, tennis
Favourite band: Coldplay
Relaxations: 'Music, TV, computer, Starbuck's'
Extras: Elite Player Development 2008. Has played for Somerset Second XI and for Devon at U15 and U17 level. Played club cricket for Sidmouth CC 2007-08. Is due to join the county on a summer contract after completing A-Level studies in June 2009

DIPPENAAR, H. H. Leicestershire

Name: Hendrik Human (Boeta) Dippenaar
Role: Right-hand bat, right-arm off-break bowler
Born: 14 June 1977, Kimberley, South Africa
Height: 5ft 11in **Weight:** 11st 13lbs
Nickname: Dipps
County debut: 2008 (Leicestershire)
Test debut: 1999-2000
ODI debut: 1999-2000
Twenty20 Int debut: 2005-06
1st-Class 200s: 2
Place in batting averages: 158th av 25.35
Parents: Frank and Alet
Wife and date of marriage: Charleen, 16 April 2004
Education: Grey College, Bloemfontein
Career outside cricket: Commercial helicopter pilot
Off-season: Domestic cricket in South Africa
Overseas tours: South Africa U19 to England 1995, to India 1995-96; Free State to West Indies 1996-97; South Africa A to Zimbabwe 2004, to Zimbabwe 2007-08 (c), to India 2007-08 (c); South Africa to Kenya (LG Cup) 1999-2000, to Zimbabwe 1999-2000, to Kenya (ICC Knockout Trophy) 2000-01, to West Indies 2000-01, to Zimbabwe 2001-02, to Australia 2001-02, to Sri Lanka (ICC Champions Trophy) 2002-03, to Bangladesh 2003, to England 2003, to Pakistan 2003-04, to Sri Lanka 2004, to India 2004-05, to West Indies 2004-05, to Sri Lanka 2006, to India (ICC Champions Trophy) 2006-07, plus other one-day tournaments and series in Australia, Singapore, Morocco and New Zealand
Overseas teams played for: Free State 1995-96 – 2003-04; Eagles 2004-05 –
Career highlights to date: 'Test match at Lord's, 2003'
Cricket moments to forget: 'South Africa v Sri Lanka, World Cup 2003'
Cricketers particularly admired: Steve Waugh
Young players to look out for: Dean Elgar
Other sports played: Golf, tennis, rugby
Other sports followed: Golf, rugby (Cheetahs)
Favourite band: Hillsong
Relaxations: 'Fly fishing and hunting'
Extras: Represented South Africa in the 2002-03 World Cup. Scored 177* in the first Test v Bangladesh in Chittagong 2003, in the process sharing with Jacques Rudolph (222*) in the highest partnership for any wicket for South Africa in Tests (429*). One of *South African Cricket Annual*'s five Cricketers of the Year 2005. Played for an

African XI in the Afro-Asian Cup 2005-06, 2007. His numerous match and series awards include Man of the [ODI] Series v Pakistan 2003-04 and v West Indies 2004-05 (317 runs; av. 105.66). Announced his retirement from international cricket in 2008. Has joined Leicestershire as overseas player for 2009
Best batting: 250* Eagles v Warriors, Kimberley 2006-07

2008 Season

	M	Inn	NO	Runs	HS	Avg	100	50	Ct	St	Balls	Runs	Wkts	Avg	BB	5I	10M
Test																	
FC	12	19	2	431	84 *	25.35	-	3	19	-	0	0	0		-	-	-
ODI																	
List A	13	13	1	375	69	31.25	-	3	6	-	0	0	0		-	-	
20/20 Int																	
20/20	9	8	0	148	47	18.50	-	-	6	-	0	0	0		-	-	

Career Performances

	M	Inn	NO	Runs	HS	Avg	100	50	Ct	St	Balls	Runs	Wkts	Avg	BB	5I	10M
Test	38	62	5	1718	177 *	30.14	3	7	27	-	12	1	0		-	-	-
FC	148	245	21	9330	250 *	41.65	28	37	146	-	31	17	0		-	-	-
ODI	107	95	14	3421	125 *	42.23	4	26	36	-	0	0	0		-	-	
List A	210	191	27	6500	125 *	39.63	8	44	76	-	6	2	0		-	-	
20/20 Int	1	1	0	1	1	1.00	-	-	-	-	0	0	0		-	-	
20/20	30	26	2	387	47	16.12	-	-	15	-	0	0	0		-	-	

DIVENUTO, M. J. Durham

Name: Michael James DiVenuto
Role: Left-hand bat, right-arm medium/leg-break bowler
Born: 12 December 1973, Hobart, Tasmania
Height: 5ft 11in **Weight:** 12st 12lbs
Nickname: Diva
County debut: 1999 (Sussex), 2000 (Derbyshire), 2007 (Durham)
County cap: 1999 (Sussex), 2000 (Derbyshire)
ODI debut: 1996-97
1000 runs in a season: 7
1st-Class 200s: 3
Place in batting averages: 40th av 46.45 (2007 7th av. 66.45)
Parents: Enrico and Elizabeth
Wife and date of marriage: Renae, 31 December 2003
Children: Sophia Lily, 21 March 2005; Luca Michael, 3 September 2007
Family links with cricket: 'Dad and older brother Peter both played grade cricket in Tasmania.' Brother Peter also played for Italy
Education: St Virgil's College, Hobart
Qualifications: HSC (5 x Level III subjects), Level 3 cricket coach
Career outside cricket: 'Own a cafe, "Say Cheese Salamanca", in Hobart'
Off-season: 'Doing a bit of work in the cafe, and coaching with Tasmania from Juniors up to Senior squad.'
Overseas tours: Australian Cricket Academy to India and Sri Lanka 1993, to South Africa 1996; Australia A to Malaysia (Super 8s) 1997 (c), to Scotland and Ireland 1998 (c), to Los Angeles 1999; Australia to South Africa 1996-97 (one-day series), to Hong Kong (Super 6s) 1997, to Malaysia (Super 8s) 1998; Tasmania to Zimbabwe 1995-96
Overseas teams played for: North Hobart CC, Tasmania; Kingborough, Tasmania; Tasmania 1991-92 –
Career highlights to date: 'Playing for Australia. Man of the Match award v South Africa at Johannesburg 1997. Dismissing Jamie Cox at Taunton in 1999, my first wicket in first-class cricket. Winning Tasmania's first Pura Cup 2006-07. Winning Durham's first trophy and being part of the awesome 2007 season with Durham'
Cricket moments to forget: 'Being dismissed by Jamie Cox at Taunton in 1999, *his* first wicket in first-class cricket'
Cricketers particularly admired: David Boon, Dean Jones, Kepler Wessels, Mark and Steve Waugh

Young players to look out for: Kyle Coetzer, Mark Stoneman, Ben Harmison
Other sports played: Australian Rules (Tasmanian U15, U16 and Sandy Bay FC)
Other sports followed: Australian Rules football (Geelong Cats)
Favourite band: U2
Relaxations: Golf, sleeping and eating
Extras: Man of the Match in the fifth ODI v South Africa at Johannesburg 1997 (89). Was Sussex overseas player 1999; an overseas player with Derbyshire 2000-06; an overseas player with Durham 2007. Scored 173* v Derbyshire Board XI at Derby in NatWest 2000, a record for Derbyshire in one-day cricket. Carried bat for 192* v Middlesex at Lord's 2002; also scored 113 in the second innings. Derbyshire Player of the Year 2002 (jointly with Kevin Dean). First batsman to 1000 Championship runs 2003. Vice-captain of Derbyshire 2002-06 (was appointed captain for 2004 but was unable to take up post due to back surgery). Tasmania Pura Cup Player of the Year (David Boon Medal) 2006-07. Carried bat for 155* on Durham first-class debut v Worcestershire at Worcester 2007 and again for 204* v Kent at Riverside 2007. Made an invaluable 90 runs in Durham's title-clinching victory over Kent in September 2008. Retired from Tasmanian international cricket at the end of the 2007-08 season, and is now part-time batting coach with Tasmanian Cricket Association. Holds an Italian passport and is no longer considered an overseas player
Opinions on cricket: 'The game is in great shape.'
Best batting: 230 Derbyshire v Northamptonshire, Derby 2002
Best bowling: 1-0 Tasmania v Queensland, Brisbane (AB) 1999-2000

2008 Season

	M	Inn	NO	Runs	HS	Avg	100	50	Ct	St	Balls	Runs	Wkts	Avg	BB	5I	10M
Test																	
FC	16	28	4	1115	184	46.45	2	8	16	-	0	0	0		-	-	-
ODI																	
List A	16	16	2	559	138	39.92	2	3	12	-	0	0	0		-	-	
20/20 Int																	
20/20	10	10	0	115	40	11.50	-		5	-	0	0	0		-	-	

Career Performances

	M	Inn	NO	Runs	HS	Avg	100	50	Ct	St	Balls	Runs	Wkts	Avg	BB	5I	10M
Test																	
FC	281	501	32	21097	230	44.98	47	128	326	-	807	484	5	96.80	1-0	-	-
ODI	9	9	0	241	89	26.77	-	2	1	-	0	0	0				
List A	290	284	18	8832	173 *	33.20	15	45	120	-	200	181	5	36.20	1-10	-	
20/20 Int																	
20/20	40	38	4	842	95 *	24.76	-	6	9	-	78	88	5	17.60	3-19	-	

DOSHI, N. D. Derbyshire

Name: Nayan Dilip Doshi
Role: Right-hand bat, left-arm spin bowler
Born: 6 October 1978, Nottingham
Height: 6ft 4in
Nickname: Dosh, Troll, Turtlehead
County debut: 2004 (Surrey), 2008 (Derbyshire)
County cap: 2006 (Surrey)
50 wickets in a season: 1
Place in bowling averages: 148th av 63.30 (2007 140th av. 53.61)
Parents: Dilip and Kalindi
Marital status: Married
Family links with cricket: Father is former India Test and ODI spin bowler Dilip Doshi, who also played for Nottinghamshire and Warwickshire
Education: King Alfred School, London
Career outside cricket: Family business
Overseas teams played for: Saurashtra, India 2001-02 – 2006-07
Career highlights to date: 'Twenty20 semi-final 2004'
Cricket moments to forget: 'Too many'
Cricketers particularly admired: Viv Richards, Sachin Tendulkar, Garfield Sobers
Favourite band: 'Like lots of them'
Relaxations: Wildlife photography
Extras: Made first-class debut for Saurashtra v Baroda at Rajkot 2001-02. Recorded maiden first-class ten-wicket match return (5-125/6-57) v Lancashire at Old Trafford 2004 and another (3-73/7-110) v Sussex at Hove in the following Championship match. Took 21 wickets in the Twenty20 Cup 2006, breaking the competition season record of 20 held by Adam Hollioake. Became first bowler to 50 Twenty20 wickets, v Hampshire at The Oval 2007. Is England-qualified. Left Surrey during the 2007 season and joined Derbyshire for 2008. Released at the end of the 2008 season.
Best batting: 37 Saurashtra v Vidarbha, Rajkot (MS) 2005-06
Best bowling: 7-110 Surrey v Sussex, Hove 2004

2008 Season

	M	Inn	NO	Runs	HS	Avg	100	50	Ct	St	Balls	Runs	Wkts	Avg	BB	5I	10M
Test																	
FC	9	9	4	25	17 *	5.00	-	-	3	-	1548	825	13	63.46	3-84	-	-
ODI																	
List A	8	3	2	3	3 *	3.00	-	-	2	-	312	225	4	56.25	2-47	-	
20/20 Int																	
20/20	10	2	0	6	5	3.00	-	-	2	-	202	198	8	24.75	3-1	-	

Career Performances

	M	Inn	NO	Runs	HS	Avg	100	50	Ct	St	Balls	Runs	Wkts	Avg	BB	5I	10M
Test																	
FC	62	77	20	530	37	9.29	-	-	11	-	10872	5851	149	39.26	7-110	6	3
ODI																	
List A	69	31	8	200	38 *	8.69	-	-	18	-	2887	2619	59	44.38	5-30	1	
20/20 Int																	
20/20	44	9	5	10	5	2.50	-	-	12	-	868	975	61	15.98	4-22	-	

DREW, B. G. Gloucestershire

Name: Brendan Gerard Drew
Role: Right-hand bat, right-arm fast-medium bowler
Born: 16 December 1983, Lismore, New South Wales
Height: 6ft 4in
Nickname: Drewy
County debut: 2008 (one-day)
Education: St Joseph's, Alstonville; Alstonville High School
Overseas teams played for: Tasmania 2005 –
Extras: Played for New South Wales U17 2000-01, New South Wales U19 2002-03, New South Wales Colts 2003-04, Tasmania Second XI 2005-06 – 2008-09. In 2007-08 part of the Tasmania team that won the FR Cup (one-day competition) over Victoria. Selected for the ACA All-Star FR Cup team. Invited to the Australian Academy 2007. Played for Lancashire League side

Lowerhouse 2008. Joined Gloucestershire as an overseas player towards the end of the 2008 season, replacing Marcus North. Selected to represent Australia at the Hong Kong Sixes, October 2008.
Best batting: 28 Tasmania v Queensland, Brisbane 2007
Best bowling: 6-94 Tasmania v South Australia, Hobart 2006-07

2008 Season

	M	Inn	NO	Runs	HS	Avg	100	50	Ct	St	Balls	Runs	Wkts	Avg	BB	5I	10M
Test																	
FC																	
ODI																	
List A	2	2	0	26	22	13.00	-	-	2	-	84	110	1	110.00	1-60	-	
20/20 Int																	
20/20																	

Career Performances

	M	Inn	NO	Runs	HS	Avg	100	50	Ct	St	Balls	Runs	Wkts	Avg	BB	5I	10M
Test																	
FC	19	26	7	223	28	11.73	-	-	11		3276	2114	52	40.65	6-94	2	-
ODI																	
List A	26	19	7	203	33 *	16.91	-	-	10	-	1264	1212	39	31.07	5-36	1	
20/20 Int																	
20/20	11	7	3	86	25	21.50	-	-	11	-	216	301	11	27.36	3-24	-	

24. How many wickets did Dennis Lillee take in Ashes matches?

DU PLESSIS, F. — Lancashire

Name: Francois du Plessis
Role: Right-hand bat, leg-break bowler
Born: 13 July 1984, Pretoria, South Africa
Nickname: Faf
County debut: 2008
Place in batting averages: 159th av 25.16
Overseas tours: South Africa U19 to England 2003; South Africa Academy to Pakistan 2004-05; South Africa Emerging Players to Australia (Cricket Australia Emerging Players Tournament) 2007; South Africa VI to Hong Kong 2007
Overseas teams played for: Northerns 2003-04 – 2005-06; Titans 2005-06 –
Extras: Scored 177 v England U19 in the third 'Test' at Chelmsford 2003. Played for Nottinghamshire 2nd XI 2006, scoring 138-ball 203* v Minor Counties U25 at the Brian Wakefield Sports Ground, Nottingham, in the 2nd XI Trophy. Man of the Match v Warriors in East London in the MTN Domestic Championship 2006-07 (80). Played for Todmorden in the Lancashire League 2007. Is not considered an overseas player
Best batting: 156 Northerns v Gauteng, Johannesburg (WM) 2005-06
Best bowling: 4-39 Northerns v Free State, Pretoria (LCD) 2004-05

2008 Season

	M	Inn	NO	Runs	HS	Avg	100	50	Ct	St	Balls	Runs	Wkts	Avg	BB	5I	10M
Test																	
FC	12	19	1	453	57	25.16	-	4	4	-	702	354	8	44.25	3-61	-	-
ODI																	
List A	11	11	2	355	93 *	39.44	-	4	5	-	144	121	5	24.20	3-18	-	
20/20 Int																	
20/20	11	9	2	202	57 *	28.85	-	1	3	-	114	147	9	16.33	2-13	-	

Career Performances

	M	Inn	NO	Runs	HS	Avg	100	50	Ct	St	Balls	Runs	Wkts	Avg	BB	5I	10M
Test																	
FC	39	67	5	2195	156	35.40	3	15	30	-	1301	718	23	31.21	4-39	-	-
ODI																	
List A	51	47	8	1424	114	36.51	1	11	25	-	914	783	27	29.00	4-47	-	
20/20 Int																	
20/20	25	23	2	452	76	21.52	-	2	7	-	270	349	20	17.45	3-24	-	

DU PREEZ, D. Leicestershire

Name: Dillon du Preez
Role: Right-hand bat, right-arm fast-medium bowler; all-rounder
Born: 8 November 1981, Port Elizabeth, South Africa
Height: 6ft **Weight:** 14st 6lbs
Nickname: Dill
County debut: 2008
Place in batting averages: 247th av 12.20
Place in bowling averages: 22nd av 22.81
Parents: Denise and Leon
Wife: Nicola
Education: HTS Louis Botha
Qualifications: Level 1 and 2 coaching
Off-season: 'Playing for Diamond Eagles in South Africa.'
Overseas teams played for: Diamond Eagles 2003-04 –
Career highlights to date: 'Scoring 107* in Pro40 for Leicestershire v Yorkshire in 2008'
Cricket moments to forget: 'Went out to bat without a box and faced two balls before calling for it.'
Cricketers particularly admired: Allan Donald, Glen McGrath
Young players to look out for: Matthew Boyce, Greg Smith
Other sports followed: Rugby (Natal Sharks)
Favourite band: U2, Powderfinger
Relaxations: 'Movies, games'
Extras: Players' Player of the Year for Diamond Eagles in 2007-08. Signed as a Kolpak player in March 2008. South Africa Player of the Year 2008
Best batting: 122 Diamond Eagles v Cape Cobras, Cape Town 2007
Best bowling: 7-108 Diamond Eagles v Titans, Benoni, SA 2007

2008 Season

	M	Inn	NO	Runs	HS	Avg	100	50	Ct	St	Balls	Runs	Wkts	Avg	BB	5I	10M
Test																	
FC	10	13	3	122	22	12.20	-	-	1	-	1635	730	32	22.81	5-48	1	-
ODI																	
List A	13	11	5	236	107 *	39.33	1	-	1	-	582	543	12	45.25	3-65	-	
20/20 Int																	
20/20	5	5	1	71	33 *	17.75	-	-	-	-	114	157	6	26.16	2-31	-	

Career Performances

	M	Inn	NO	Runs	HS	Avg	100	50	Ct	St	Balls	Runs	Wkts	Avg	BB	5I	10M
Test																	
FC	41	56	6	910	122	18.20	1	3	9	-	7383	3323	144	23.07	7-108	5	1
ODI																	
List A	49	35	16	685	107 *	36.05	1	2	9	-	2327	1856	53	35.01	4-22	-	
20/20 Int																	
20/20	19	14	6	167	40 *	20.87	-	-	6	-	336	411	15	27.40	2-2	-	

DURSTON, W. J. Somerset

Name: Wesley (<u>Wes</u>) John Durston
Role: Right-hand bat, right-arm off-spin bowler, 'very occasional' wicket-keeper
Born: 6 October 1980, Taunton
Height: 5ft 10in **Weight:** 12st 7lbs
Nickname: Bestie
County debut: 2002
Parents: Gill and Steve
Wife and date of marriage: Christina, 4 October 2003
Children: Daisy, 4 July 2004; Joseph, 29 September 2006
Family links with cricket: 'Dad and my two brothers, Dan and Greg, all play. On occasions all four played in same local team (Compton Dundon)'
Education: Millfield School; University College Worcester
Qualifications: 3 A-levels, BSc Sport & Exercise Science, ECB Level II cricket coaching, Level 1 hockey coaching, Level 1 football coaching
Career outside cricket: 'Coaching at Millfield School'
Overseas tours: West of England to West Indies 1996; Somerset to Cape Town 2006
Career highlights to date: 'Winning the Twenty20 trophy with Somerset CCC in 2005. County Championship 2007' (*Somerset were division two champions*)
Cricket moments to forget: 'Being out lbw for first-ball duck on Sky Sports (v Kent 2006)'
Cricket superstitions: 'Right foot on to and off field first. Saluting magpies'
Cricketers particularly admired: Ian Botham
Young players to look out for: Joseph Buttler, Joseph Durston
Other sports played: Hockey (Firebrands HC), golf (12 handicap)
Other sports followed: Football (Man Utd)

Favourite band: Barenaked Ladies
Relaxations: 'Spending time with family and children'
Extras: Captained winning Lord's Taverners team v Shrewsbury School at Trent Bridge 1996. Wetherell Schools All-rounder Award 1999; scored 956 runs and took 35 wickets. Has captained Somerset 2nd XI on occasion. Scored 44-ball 55 on first-class debut at Taunton 2002 as Somerset, chasing 454 to win, tied with West Indies A. Attended World Cricket Academy, Mumbai, 2005
Opinions on cricket: 'With the success of Twenty20 it may be very easy to lose sight of the importance of Championship cricket, which would be very detrimental to the game, as it provides English cricket with the only specific grooming for the Test arena.'
Best batting: 146* Somerset v Derbyshire, Derby 2005
Best bowling: 3-23 Somerset v Sri Lanka A, Taunton 2004

2008 Season

	M	Inn	NO	Runs	HS	Avg	100	50	Ct	St	Balls	Runs	Wkts	Avg	BB	5I	10M
Test																	
FC	5	8	4	229	62 *	57.25	-	2	1	-	240	120	0		-	-	-
ODI																	
List A	10	8	3	198	60 *	39.60	-	1	4	-	24	34	0		-	-	
20/20 Int																	
20/20	3	3	0	26	24	8.66	-	-	-	-	24	55	2	27.50	2-20	-	

Career Performances

	M	Inn	NO	Runs	HS	Avg	100	50	Ct	St	Balls	Runs	Wkts	Avg	BB	5I	10M
Test																	
FC	33	55	11	1672	146 *	38.00	1	12	34	-	2145	1407	24	58.62	3-23	-	-
ODI																	
List A	53	46	15	952	62 *	30.70	-	6	13	-	804	827	19	43.52	3-44	-	
20/20 Int																	
20/20	35	27	5	299	34	13.59	-	-	11	-	214	338	17	19.88	3-25	-	

25. How many times did Australia lose an Ashes Test at Lord's during the twentieth century?

DU TOIT, J. Leicestershire

Name: Jacques du Toit
Role: Left-hand bat, left-arm medium bowler
Born: 2 January 1980, Port Elizabeth, South Africa
County debut: 2008
Place in batting averages: 162nd av 24.93
Overseas teams played for: Western Province, Boland, Impalas
Extras: Arrived in the Leicestershire First XI via the East Anglian leagues and the Second XI. Played in all competitions in 2008, scoring a couple of centuries in the process. After his maiden first-class century (103) against Northamptonshire, he went on to score 144 off 119 balls in the Pro40 game against Glamorgan in Colwyn Bay in August 2008, but couldn't prevent a four-wicket defeat
Best batting: 103 Leicestershire v Northamptonshire, Grace Road 2008
Best bowling: 3-31 Leicestershire v Gloucestershire, Grace Road 2008

2008 Season

	M	Inn	NO	Runs	HS	Avg	100	50	Ct	St	Balls	Runs	Wkts	Avg	BB	5I	10M
Test																	
FC	10	16	0	399	103	24.93	1	1	6	-	108	83	4	20.75	3-31	-	-
ODI																	
List A	14	13	2	319	144	29.00	1	-	5	-	0	0	0		-	-	
20/20 Int																	
20/20	9	9	0	117	25	13.00	-	-	3	-	26	32	2	16.00	2-15	-	

Career Performances

	M	Inn	NO	Runs	HS	Avg	100	50	Ct	St	Balls	Runs	Wkts	Avg	BB	5I	10M
Test																	
FC	13	20	1	558	103	29.36	1	3	7	-	348	246	5	49.20	3-31	-	-
ODI																	
List A	16	14	2	324	144	27.00	1	-	5	-	66	66	2	33.00	2-30	-	
20/20 Int																	
20/20	9	9	0	117	25	13.00	-	-	3	-	26	32	2	16.00	2-15	-	

EALHAM, M. A. Nottinghamshire

Name: Mark Alan Ealham
Role: Right-hand bat, right-arm medium bowler; all-rounder
Born: 27 August 1969, Ashford, Kent
Height: 5ft 10in **Weight:** 14st
Nickname: Ealy, Border, Skater
County debut: 1989 (Kent), 2004 (Nottinghamshire)
County cap: 1992 (Kent), 2004 (Nottinghamshire)
Benefit: 2003 (Kent)
Test debut: 1996
ODI debut: 1996
1000 runs in a season: 1
50 wickets in a season: 1
Place in batting averages: 194th av 20.56 (2007 179th av. 25.00)
Place in bowling averages: 67th av 29.56 (2007 49th av. 27.68)
Parents: Alan and Sue
Wife and date of marriage: Kirsty, 24 February 1996
Children: George, 8 March 2002
Family links with cricket: Father played for Kent
Education: Stour Valley Secondary School
Qualifications: 9 CSEs
Career outside cricket: Plumber
Overseas tours: England A to Australia 1996-97, to Kenya and Sri Lanka 1997-98; England VI to Hong Kong 1997, 2001; England to Sharjah (Champions Trophy) 1997-98, to Bangladesh (Wills International Cup) 1998-99, to Australia 1998-99 (CUB Series), to Sharjah (Coca-Cola Cup) 1998-99, to South Africa and Zimbabwe 1999-2000 (one-day series), to Kenya (ICC Knockout Trophy) 2000-01, to Pakistan and Sri Lanka 2000-01 (one-day series)
Overseas teams played for: Sth Perth, Australia 1992-93; University, Perth 1993-94
Cricketers particularly admired: Ian Botham, Viv Richards, Robin Smith, Steve Waugh, Paul Blackmore and Albert 'for his F and G'
Other sports followed: Football (Manchester United), 'and most other sports'
Relaxations: Playing golf and snooker, watching films
Extras: Set then record for fastest Sunday League century (44 balls), v Derbyshire at Maidstone 1995. Represented England in the 1999 World Cup. Returned a then England record ODI bowling analysis with his 5-15 v Zimbabwe at Kimberley in 1999-2000; all five were lbw. Vice-captain of Kent 2001. Won the Walter Lawrence

Trophy 2006 (fastest first-class century of the season) for his 45-ball hundred (finishing with 112*) v MCC at Lord's.
Best batting: 153* Kent v Northamptonshire, Canterbury 2001
Best bowling: 8-36 Kent v Warwickshire, Edgbaston 1996

2008 Season

	M	Inn	NO	Runs	HS	Avg	100	50	Ct	St	Balls	Runs	Wkts	Avg	BB	5I	10M
Test																	
FC	14	17	1	329	130 *	20.56	1	-	9	-	2176	887	30	29.56	7-59	1	1
ODI																	
List A	15	12	2	90	21	9.00	-	-	1	-	670	460	20	23.00	4-39	-	
20/20 Int																	
20/20	9	8	1	85	28	12.14	-	-	1	-	192	251	10	25.10	3-21	-	

Career Performances

	M	Inn	NO	Runs	HS	Avg	100	50	Ct	St	Balls	Runs	Wkts	Avg	BB	5I	10M
Test	8	13	3	210	53 *	21.00	-	2	4	-	1060	488	17	28.70	4-21	-	-
FC	267	402	60	10856	153 *	31.74	13	65	152	-	36112	16979	615	27.60	8-36	23	2
ODI	64	45	4	716	45	17.46	-	-	9	-	3227	2197	67	32.79	5-15	2	
List A	409	335	75	6211	112	23.88	1	26	109	-	18221	12437	470	26.46	6-53	4	
20/20 Int																	
20/20	42	36	6	519	91	17.30	-	1	5	-	923	1086	39	27.84	3-21	-	

EDWARDS, N. J. Somerset

Name: Neil James Edwards
Role: Left-hand bat, occasional right-arm medium bowler
Born: 14 October 1983, Truro, Cornwall
Height: 6ft 3in **Weight:** 14st 6lbs
Nickname: Toastie, Shanksy
County debut: 2002
1000 runs in a season: 1
1st-Class 200s: 1
Place in batting averages: 177th av 22.73 (2007 41st av. 48.11)
Parents: Lynn and John
Marital status: Single
Family links with cricket: 'Cousin played first-class cricket for Worcestershire'
Education: Cape Cornwall School; Richard Huish College
Qualifications: 11 GCSEs, 3 A-levels, Level 1 coach
Off-season: 'In Taunton.'
Overseas tours: Cornwall U13 to South Africa 1997; West of England to West Indies

1999; Somerset Academy to Australia 2002; England U19 to Australia 2002-03
Overseas teams played for: Richmond CC (Melbourne) 2007-08
Career highlights to date: 'Division 2 title 2007'
Cricket moments to forget: 'Duck on debut for Cornwall'
Cricket superstitions: 'Never change batting gloves when batting'
Cricketers particularly admired: Marcus Trescothick, Matthew Hayden
Young players to look out for: Jordan Lee
Other sports played: Football
Other sports followed: Football (Stoke City FC)
Favourite band: 'I listen to any music'
Extras: Scored 213 for Cornwall U19 v Dorset U19 at 16 years old. Scored a second innings 97 in England U19 victory over Australia U19 in the first 'Test' at Adelaide 2002-03. Represented England U19 2003. Somerset Wyverns Award for Best Performance by an Uncapped Player 2003 (160 v Hampshire).

Best batting: 212 Somerset v LUCCE, Taunton 2007
Best bowling: 1-16 Somerset v Derbyshire, Taunton 2004

2008 Season

	M	Inn	NO	Runs	HS	Avg	100	50	Ct	St	Balls	Runs	Wkts	Avg	BB	5I	10M
Test																	
FC	8	15	0	341	99	22.73	-	2	8	-	6	1	0		-	-	-
ODI																	
List A																	
20/20 Int																	
20/20																	

Career Performances

	M	Inn	NO	Runs	HS	Avg	100	50	Ct	St	Balls	Runs	Wkts	Avg	BB	5I	10M
Test																	
FC	49	82	0	2898	212	35.34	3	15	35	-	287	194	2	97.00	1-16	-	-
ODI																	
List A	5	5	0	113	65	22.60	-	1	1	-	0	0	0		-	-	
20/20 Int																	
20/20	1	1	0	1	1	1.00	-	-	-	-	0	0	0		-	-	

EDWARDS, P. D. Kent

Name: Philip Duncan Edwards
Role: Right-hand bat, right-arm fast-medium bowler
Born: 16 April 1984, Minster, Isle of Sheppey, Kent
County debut: No first-team appearance
Extras: His first-class career stretches back to 2004-05, although he has only played five first-class games in all. Played for Sussex Second XI 2006, and Kent Second XI 2008. Has also played for Cambridge UCCE 2004-05, Suffolk 2007-08
Best batting: 43 Cambridge UCCE v Middlesex, Fenners 2004
Best bowling: 1-31 Cambridge UCCE v Warwickshire, Fenners 2005

2008 Season (did not make any first-class or one-day appearances)

Career Performances

	M	Inn	NO	Runs	HS	Avg	100	50	Ct	St	Balls	Runs	Wkts	Avg	BB	5I	10M
Test																	
FC	5	8	5	96	43	32.00	-	-	1	-	708	495	5	99.00	1-31	-	-
ODI																	
List A																	
20/20 Int																	
20/20																	

26. During which Ashes series was the Waterford Crystal representation of the urn first employed as a trophy?

ERVINE, S. M. — Hampshire

Name: Sean Michael Ervine
Role: Left-hand bat, right-arm fast-medium bowler; all-rounder
Born: 6 December 1982, Harare, Zimbabwe
Height: 6ft 2in **Weight:** 14st
Nickname: Slug
County debut: 2005
County cap: 2005
Test debut: 2003
ODI debut: 2001-02
Place in batting averages: 139th av 27.95 (2007 106th av. 34.50)
Parents: Rory and Judy
Marital status: Single
Family links with cricket: 'Grandfather played cricket for Rhodesia and father and uncle both played for Rhodesia'
Education: Lomagundi College, Zimbabwe
Qualifications: 5 O-levels, Levels 1 and 2 coaching
Overseas tours: Zimbabwe U19 to Sri Lanka (U19 World Cup) 1999-2000, to New Zealand (U19 World Cup) 2001-02; Zimbabwe to Bangladesh 2001-02, to Sri Lanka 2001-02 (one-day series), to Sri Lanka (ICC Champions Trophy) 2002-03, to England 2003, to Australia 2003-04, plus one-day tournaments in Sharjah
Overseas teams played for: Midlands, Zimbabwe 2001-02 – 2003-04; Western Australia 2006-07 –
Cricket moments to forget: 'Fielding the ball off my own bowling and rupturing my knee, needing a total knee reconstruction'
Cricket superstitions: 'None'
Cricketers particularly admired: Andy Flower, Shane Warne
Young players to look out for: Shaun Marsh (Western Australia)
Other sports played: Golf, tennis, squash, fishing
Other sports followed: AFL (Kangaroos)
Favourite band: Snow Patrol
Relaxations: 'Music, art'
Extras: CFX [Zimbabwean] Academy 2000-01. Represented Zimbabwe in the World Cup 2002-03. Struck 99-ball century (100) at Adelaide in the VB Series 2003-04 as Zimbabwe fell just three runs short of India's 280-7. Man of the Match in the first Test v Bangladesh at Harare 2003-04 (86/74). C&G Man of the Match awards in the semi-final v Yorkshire at The Rose Bowl (100) and in the final v Warwickshire at Lord's (104) 2005. Holds an Irish passport and is not considered an overseas player
Opinions on cricket: 'No rest time for players in between games.'

Best batting: 126 Midlands v Manicaland, Mutare 2002-03
Best bowling: 6-82 Midlands v Mashonaland, Kwekwe 2002-03

2008 Season

	M	Inn	NO	Runs	HS	Avg	100	50	Ct	St	Balls	Runs	Wkts	Avg	BB	5I	10M
Test																	
FC	13	22	1	587	94 *	27.95	-	5	19	-	744	499	9	55.44	4-42	-	-
ODI																	
List A	11	10	2	278	103 *	34.75	1	1	5	-	270	325	7	46.42	2-38	-	
20/20 Int																	
20/20	9	9	1	173	46	21.62	-	-	2	-	42	83	2	41.50	1-30	-	

Career Performances

	M	Inn	NO	Runs	HS	Avg	100	50	Ct	St	Balls	Runs	Wkts	Avg	BB	5I	10M
Test	5	8	0	261	86	32.62	-	3	7	-	570	388	9	43.11	4-146	-	-
FC	83	132	13	3662	126	30.77	5	22	82	-	9346	5770	144	40.06	6-82	5	-
ODI	42	34	7	698	100	25.85	1	2	5	-	1649	1561	41	38.07	3-29	-	
List A	141	125	22	3162	134 *	30.69	5	14	40	-	5026	4646	138	33.66	5-50	2	
20/20 Int																	
20/20	31	28	5	488	56 *	21.21	-	2	13	-	252	382	14	27.28	3-18	-	

EVANS, D. Middlesex

Name: Daniel (Danny) Evans
Role: Right-hand bat, right-arm fast-medium bowler
Born: 24 July 1987, Hartlepool
Height: 6ft 6in **Weight:** 15st
Nickname: Hightower, Stella, Asbo
County debut: 2007
Place in bowling averages: 85th av 31.80
Parents: Richard and Barbara
Marital status: Single
Family links with cricket: 'Brother played for Durham; he now plays for Newcastle. My dad played a little bit, too; he said he was awesome'
Education: Brierton Comprehensive, Hartlepool
Qualifications: 9 GCSEs, GNVQ in IT
Overseas tours: England U17 to Netherlands 2003; MCC A to Papua New Guinea and New Zealand 2007

Overseas teams played for: Tea Tree Gully, Adelaide 2006
Career highlights to date: 'Making debut at Lord's, getting a wicket maiden first over'
Cricket moments to forget: 'Getting a run of ducks towards the end of the season in 2007'
Cricketers particularly admired: Brett Lee, Steve Harmison
Young players to look out for: Billy Godleman, Steve Finn, Eoin Morgan
Other sports played: Five-a-side football, rugby (West Hartlepool RUFC)
Other sports followed: Football (Newcastle)
Favourite band: Bloc Party, The Verve, Oasis
Relaxations: 'Poker, pool, films'
Extras: Attended Darren Lehmann Academy, Adelaide 2006. Dismissed Craig Spearman in wicket maiden first over on first-class debut v Gloucestershire at Lord's 2007
Opinions on cricket: 'Youngsters should be given more of a chance. I think we play too much as well, players not getting enough rest between games.'
Best batting: 12* Middlesex v Worcestershire, Lord's 2008
Best bowling: 6-35 Middlesex v Essex, Chelmsford 2008

2008 Season

	M	Inn	NO	Runs	HS	Avg	100	50	Ct	St	Balls	Runs	Wkts	Avg	BB	5I	10M
Test																	
FC	10	13	3	45	12 *	4.50	-	-	2	-	1446	954	30	31.80	6-35	2	-
ODI																	
List A	2	0	0	0	0		-	-	-	-	120	92	3	30.66	3-36	-	
20/20 Int																	
20/20																	

Career Performances

	M	Inn	NO	Runs	HS	Avg	100	50	Ct	St	Balls	Runs	Wkts	Avg	BB	5I	10M
Test																	
FC	14	18	4	52	12 *	3.71	-	-	3	-	1770	1123	35	32.08	6-35	2	-
ODI																	
List A	2	0	0	0	0		-	-	-	-	120	92	3	30.66	3-36	-	
20/20 Int																	
20/20																	

27. Name the England fast bowler who took 1-160 in the first Test of the 1954-55 series in Australia, before going on to much better things.

EVANS, L. J. Surrey

Name: Laurie John Evans
Role: Right-hand bat, right-arm fast-medium bowler; all-rounder
Born: 12 October 1987, Lambeth, London
Height: 6ft **Weight:** 13st 3lbs
Nickname: Lau, Evs, Augustus ('because I eat a lot')
County debut: No first-team appearance
Place in batting averages: (2007 29th av. 52.14)
Parents: Sue and Marcus
Marital status: Single
Education: John Fisher, Purley; Whitgift School, South Croydon; Durham University
Qualifications: BTEC Sport, 3 A-levels
Overseas tours: Surrey Academy to South Africa 2006
Cricket moments to forget: 'I only dropped three catches all season in 2005 and they were all in the U17 national final v Yorkshire'
Cricket superstitions: 'None'
Cricketers particularly admired: Mark Ramprakash
Young players to look out for: Simon King, Zafar Ansari
Other sports played: Rugby (Harlequins Academy; won U15 *Daily Mail* National Schools Cup with Whitgift v Millfield at Twickenham 2003)
Other sports followed: Football (Arsenal)
Favourite band: James Brown, 112, Usher, Arctic Monkeys
Relaxations: 'Love cooking, clothes'
Extras: Represented ECB Development of Excellence XI v India U19 2006. Played for Durham UCCE 2007, scoring 133* v Lancashire at Durham. Played for MCC v West Indians at Durham 2007, scoring 51
Opinions on cricket: 'The game today is more exciting than ever. It's got quicker and more interesting to spectators. However, I think that it shouldn't be changed too much, otherwise it will lose its history and essence.'
Best batting: 133* DUCCE v Lancashire, Durham 2007

2008 Season (did not make any first-class or one-day appearances)

Career Performances

	M	Inn	NO	Runs	HS	Avg	100	50	Ct	St	Balls	Runs	Wkts	Avg	BB	5I	10M
Test																	
FC	4	8	1	365	133 *	52.14	1	2	4	-	0	0	0		-	-	-
ODI																	
List A																	
20/20 Int																	
20/20																	

FERLEY, R. S. Kent

Name: Robert Steven Ferley
Role: Right-hand bat, left-arm spin bowler
Born: 4 February 1982, Norwich
Height: 5ft 8in **Weight:** 12st 4lbs
Nickname: Mr Shaky Shake, Billy Bob, Bob Turkey
County debut: 2003 (Kent), 2007 (Nottinghamshire)
Parents: Pam and Tim (divorced)
Marital status: Single
Education: King Edward VII High School; Sutton Valence School (A-levels); Grey College, Durham University
Qualifications: 10 GCSEs, 3 A-levels
Overseas tours: England U19 to India 2000-01; British Universities to South Africa 2002
Cricketers particularly admired: Steve Waugh, Steve Marsh, Min Patel, Charles Clarke
Other sports played: Rugby, hockey, tennis, football
Other sports followed: Football (Liverpool)
Relaxations: 'Films, interior design, keeping fit'
Extras: Represented England U17 1999. Played for Durham UCCE 2001, 2002 and 2003. Represented British Universities 2001, 2002 and 2003. Represented England U19 2001. Took 4-76 on Championship debut v Surrey at The Oval 2003. Rejoined Kent from Nottinghamshire in November 2008
Best batting: 78* DUCCE v Durham, Durham 2003
Best bowling: 6-136 Kent v Middlesex, Canterbury 2006

2008 Season

	M	Inn	NO	Runs	HS	Avg	100	50	Ct	St	Balls	Runs	Wkts	Avg	BB	5I	10M
Test																	
FC	1	1	1	26	26 *		-	-	1	-	331	136	2	68.00	1-60	-	-
ODI																	
List A	2	2	1	17	17 *	17.00	-	-	2	-	78	73	3	24.33	2-30	-	
20/20 Int																	
20/20	7	3	2	6	3 *	6.00	-	-	2	-	156	163	9	18.11	3-17	-	

Career Performances

	M	Inn	NO	Runs	HS	Avg	100	50	Ct	St	Balls	Runs	Wkts	Avg	BB	5I	10M
Test																	
FC	30	38	10	613	78 *	21.89	-	2	9	-	4477	2687	57	47.14	6-136	1	-
ODI																	
List A	42	21	6	256	42	17.06	-	-	18	-	1879	1518	54	28.11	4-33	-	
20/20 Int																	
20/20	17	7	4	23	16 *	7.66	-	-	4	-	321	391	14	27.92	3-17	-	

FERNANDO, C. R. D. Worcestershire

Name: Congenige Randhi Dilhara Fernando
Role: Right-hand bat, right-arm fast bowler
Born: 19 July 1979, Colombo, Sri Lanka
County debut: 2008
Test debut: 2000
ODI debut: 2000-01
Twenty20 Int debut: 2006
Overseas tours: Sri Lanka to South Africa 2000-01, to England 2002, to South Africa 2002-03, to Pakistan 2004-05, to India 2005-06, to New Zealand 2005-06, to Australia 2005-06, to Bangladesh 2005-06, to England 2006, to India 2006-07 (ICC Champions Trophy), New Zealand 2006-07, West Indies 2006-07 (World Cup), to Australia 2007, toSouth Africa 2007-08 (World Twenty20), to Zimbabwe 2008, to Bangladesh 2008-09
Overseas teams played for: Sinhalese Sports Club 1997-98 –; Mumbai Indians 2008
Extras: Made his first-class debut for the Sri Lankan Board President's XI against India in 1997. Named Man of the Match after taking 6-27 against England in the fifth ODI in Colombo Oct 2007. Named Man of the Match when taking four wickets for

Mumbai Indians in IPL game against Bangalore in May 2008. Joined Worcestershire as an overseas player for the duration of September 2008
Best batting: 42 Sinhalese Sports Club v Colts CC, Colombo (CCC) 1999
Best bowling: 6-27 Sri Lanka v England, Colombo (RPS) 2007-08

2008 Season

	M	Inn	NO	Runs	HS	Avg	100	50	Ct	St	Balls	Runs	Wkts	Avg	BB	5I	10M
Test																	
FC	1	2	0	11	11	5.50	-	-	-	-	145	130	2	65.00	1-27	-	-
ODI																	
List A																	
20/20 Int																	
20/20																	

Career Performances

	M	Inn	NO	Runs	HS	Avg	100	50	Ct	St	Balls	Runs	Wkts	Avg	BB	5I	10M
Test	31	39	12	184	36 *	6.81	-	-	10	-	4880	2928	86	34.04	5-42	3	-
FC	91	96	27	491	42	7.11	-	-	37	-	12542	7457	261	28.57	6-29	6	-
ODI	130	51	30	203	20	9.66	-	-	24	-	5628	4825	165	29.24	6-27	1	
List A	176	73	38	283	21 *	8.08	-	-	35	-	7730	6420	237	27.08	6-27	2	
20/20 Int	12	5	2	24	21	8.00	-	-	2	-	252	293	15	19.53	3-19	-	
20/20	19	7	4	26	21	8.66	-	-	4	-	420	531	26	20.42	4-18	-	

FINCH, J. M. — Yorkshire

Name: James Matthew Finch
Role: Right-hand lower-order bat, off-spin bowler
Born: 17 November 1988, Leeds
Height: 6ft 3in **Weight:** 15st
Nickname: Dog, Finchy
County debut: No first-team appearance
Parents: Paul and Mandy
Marital status: Single
Family links with cricket: 'Dad played local league cricket. Twin sister does a bit of scoring. Mum is a passionate fan'
Education: Guiseley School
Qualifications: 10 GCSEs, 2 A-levels, GNVQ in Cricket, Level 2 coach
Career outside cricket: 'Do a bit of coaching'
Overseas teams played for: St Andrews, Bloemfontein 2006-07; Old Andreans CC, Bloemfontein 2007-08

Career highlights to date: 'Getting a professional contract with Yorkshire and my time spent playing in Bloemfontein'
Cricket moments to forget: 'My grandad passing away whilst I was playing in South Africa in January 2007'
Cricket superstitions: 'Try to come out of the changing room either second or last'
Cricketers particularly admired: Daniel Vettori, Marcus Trescothick, Gareth Batty
Young players to look out for: Chris Allinson, Simon Tennant, Ian Hartley
Other sports played: Golf, snooker, five-a-side football
Other sports followed: Football (Man Utd), rugby league (Leeds Rhinos), rugby union (Free State Cheetahs)
Favourite band: Plain White T's
Relaxations: 'Going out with friends; watching films'
Extras: Returned the best figures by a Yorkshire Schoolboy as an U14 (17-4-24-8) v Northamptonshire at Oundle School. Attended Yorkshire Academy
Opinions on cricket: 'I think the general opinion that you have to be a wrist spinner to succeed as a spin bowler in the modern game is wrong.'

FINN, S. T. — Middlesex

Name: Steven Thomas Finn
Role: Right-hand bat, right-arm fast-medium bowler
Born: 4 April 1989, Watford
Height: 6ft 7in **Weight:** 13st 8lbs
Nickname: Finny, Lurch, Streak
County debut: 2005
Place in bowling averages: 122nd av 38.78 (2007 11th av. 21.72)
Parents: Diana and Terry
Marital status: Single
Family links with cricket: 'Dad played top-level club cricket/Minor Counties. Grandad played club cricket'
Education: Parmiter's School, Watford, Herts
Qualifications: 11 GCSEs, 3 A-levels
Career outside cricket: Journalism
Overseas tours: England U16 to South Africa 2004-05; England U19 to Malaysia 2006-07, to Malaysia (U19 World Cup) 2007-08, to Sri Lanka 2008; England Performance Programme to India 2007-08. Middlesex to Antigua 2008-09 for Stanford Super Series
Career highlights to date: 'First-class debut at 16. Debut at Lord's. Man of the Match award in TV play-off against Northamptonshire in 2007'

Cricket moments to forget: 'Third man out in a hat-trick v India U19 2006'
Cricket superstitions: 'Too many to mention'
Cricketers particularly admired: Glenn McGrath, Curtly Ambrose
Young players to look out for: Billy Godleman, Dan Housego, Adam London, David Malan
Other sports played: Basketball (county), football (district)
Other sports followed: Football (Watford)
Favourite band: Coldplay, Arctic Monkeys
Relaxations: 'Music'
Extras: Has represented England U15, U16, U17 and U19. Youngest person to play first-class cricket for Middlesex since Fred Titmus in 1949. Called up to the England Performance Programme in India 2007-08 as a replacement for the injured Luke Wright
Opinions on cricket: 'Pleased to see countless opportunities for young players to show what they can do. Technology enhancements are essential for the standard of the game.'
Best batting: 26* Middlesex v Worcestershire, Kidderminster 2008
Best bowling: 4-51 Middlesex v Gloucestershire, Bristol 2007

2008 Season

	M	Inn	NO	Runs	HS	Avg	100	50	Ct	St	Balls	Runs	Wkts	Avg	BB	5I	10M
Test																	
FC	13	15	5	87	26 *	8.70	-	-	5	-	1790	1086	28	38.78	4-80	-	-
ODI																	
List A	9	2	1	5	4	5.00	-	-	3	-	402	360	7	51.42	2-37	-	
20/20 Int																	
20/20	5	0	0	0	0		-	-	2	-	96	115	8	14.37	3-22	-	

Career Performances

	M	Inn	NO	Runs	HS	Avg	100	50	Ct	St	Balls	Runs	Wkts	Avg	BB	5I	10M
Test																	
FC	17	20	7	91	26 *	7.00	-	-	5	-	2347	1378	41	33.60	4-51	-	
ODI																	
List A	14	3	1	7	4	3.50	-	-	3	-	588	512	15	34.13	3-23	-	
20/20 Int																	
20/20	5	0	0	0	0		-	-	2	-	96	115	8	14.37	3-22	-	

FISHER, I. D. Worcestershire

Name: Ian Douglas Fisher
Role: Left-hand bat, left-arm spin bowler
Born: 31 March 1976, Bradford
Height: 5ft 11in **Weight:** 13st 6lbs
Nickname: Fish, Flash, Fishy
County debut: 1995-96 (Yorkshire), 2002 (Gloucestershire)
County cap: 2004 (Gloucestershire)
Place in batting averages: (2007 272nd av. 11.16)
Parents: Geoff and Linda
Marital status: Single
Family links with cricket: Father played club cricket
Education: Beckfoot Grammar School
Qualifications: 9 GCSEs, NCA coaching award, sports leader's award, lifesaver (bronze), YMCA gym instructor
Overseas tours: Yorkshire to Zimbabwe 1996, to South Africa 1998, 1999, 2001, to Perth 2000; MCC to Sri Lanka 2001
Overseas teams played for: Somerset West, Cape Town 1994-95; Petone Riverside, Wellington, New Zealand 1997-98
Career highlights to date: 'Winning the Championship with Yorkshire [2001]'
Cricket moments to forget: 'My pair'
Cricketers particularly admired: Darren Lehmann, Shane Warne
Other sports played: Football (Westbrook)
Other sports followed: Football (Leeds United)
Relaxations: Music, movies, catching up with friends, shopping, eating out
Extras: Played England U17 and Yorkshire Schools U15, U16 and Yorkshire U19. Bowled the last first-class ball delivered at Northlands Road, Southampton, September 2000. Recorded three Championship five-wicket returns in successive innings 2003, including his maiden ten-wicket match (5-30/5-93) v Durham at Bristol. After being on loan from Gloucestershire, signed for Worcestershire in October 2008
Best batting: 103* Gloucestershire v Essex, Gloucester 2002
Best bowling: 5-30 Gloucestershire v Durham, Bristol 2003

2008 Season

	M	Inn	NO	Runs	HS	Avg	100	50	Ct	St	Balls	Runs	Wkts	Avg	BB	5I	10M
Test																	
FC	1	1	0	4	4	4.00	-	-	-	-	48	7	0		-	-	-
ODI																	
List A	4	2	1	3	3	3.00	-	-	1	-	126	153	2	76.50	1-21	-	
20/20 Int																	
20/20	7	5	0	38	14	7.60	-	-	-	-	138	168	5	33.60	3-20	-	

Career Performances

	M	Inn	NO	Runs	HS	Avg	100	50	Ct	St	Balls	Runs	Wkts	Avg	BB	5I	10M
Test																	
FC	79	119	19	2201	103 *	22.01	1	7	27	-	12438	6713	157	42.75	5-30	7	1
ODI																	
List A	70	42	14	291	37 *	10.39	-	-	21	-	2697	2150	69	31.15	3-18	-	
20/20 Int																	
20/20	32	14	4	79	14	7.90	-	-	14	-	467	607	27	22.48	4-22	-	

FLETCHER, L. J. Nottinghamshire

Name: Luke Jack Fletcher
Role: Right-hand bat, right-arm fast-medium bowler
Born: 18 September 1988, Nottingham
Nickname: Fletch, Sloff
County debut: 2008
Parents: Alan and Jane
Marital status: Single
Family links with cricket: 'None'
Education: Henry Mellish School
Career highlights to date: 'Making my debut for Nottinghamshire in the Friends' Provident. Playing for England U19'
Cricketers particularly admired: Andrew Flintoff
Young players to look out for: Alex Hales, Ian Saxelby
Other sports played: Football (played for Notts County for a season)

Other sports followed: Football (Nottingham Forest)
Favourite band: Basshunter
Relaxations: 'Spending time with friends. Eating. Sleeping'
Best bowling: 1-70 Nottinghamshire v Oxford UCCE, Oxford 2008

2008 Season

	M	Inn	NO	Runs	HS	Avg	100	50	Ct	St	Balls	Runs	Wkts	Avg	BB	5I	10M
Test																	
FC	1	0	0	0	0		-	-	-	-	120	70	1	70.00	1-70	-	-
ODI+																	
List A	4	2	1	2	2 *	2.00	-	-	1	-	210	109	3	36.33	2-41	-	
20/20 Int																	
20/20																	

Career Performances

	M	Inn	NO	Runs	HS	Avg	100	50	Ct	St	Balls	Runs	Wkts	Avg	BB	5I	10M
Test																	
FC	1	0	0	0	0		-	-	-	-	120	70	1	70.00	1-70	-	-
ODI																	
List A	4	2	1	2	2 *	2.00	-	-	1	-	210	109	3	36.33	2-41	-	
20/20 Int																	
20/20																	

28. Which England fast bowler took five wickets without conceding a run, during the 1961 Ashes Test at Headingley?

FLINTOFF, A. Lancashire

Name: Andrew Flintoff
Role: Right-hand bat, right-arm fast-medium bowler; all-rounder
Born: 6 December 1977, Preston
Height: 6ft 4in
Nickname: Freddie
County debut: 1995
County cap: 1998
Benefit: 2006
Test debut: 1998
ODI debut: 1998-99
Twenty20 Int debut: 2005
Place in batting averages: 165th av 24.50
Place in bowling averages: 73rd av 30.18
Parents: Colin and Susan
Wife and date of marriage: Rachael, 5 March 2005
Children: Holly, 6 September 2004; Corey, 8 March 2006
Family links with cricket: Brother Chris and father both local league cricketers
Education: Ribbleton Hall High School, Preston
Qualifications: 9 GCSEs

Overseas tours: England Schools U15 to South Africa 1993; England U19 to West Indies 1994-95, to Zimbabwe 1995-96, to Pakistan 1996-97 (c); England A to Kenya and Sri Lanka 1997-98, to Zimbabwe and South Africa 1998-99; England to Sharjah (Coca-Cola Cup) 1998-99, to South Africa and Zimbabwe 1999-2000, to Kenya (ICC Knockout Trophy) 2000-01, to Pakistan and (one-day series) Sri Lanka 2000-01, to Zimbabwe (one-day series) 2001-02, to India and New Zealand 2001-02, to Australia 2002-03, to Africa (World Cup) 2002-03, to Bangladesh and Sri Lanka 2003-04, to West Indies 2003-04, to South Africa 2004-05, to Pakistan 2005-06, to India 2005-06, to India (ICC Champions Trophy) 2006-07 (c), to Australia 2006-07 (Test c), to West Indies (World Cup) 2006-07, to South Africa (World 20/20) 2007-08, to India 2008, to West Indies 2009; ECB National Academy to Australia 2001-02; England VI to Hong Kong 2001; ICC World XI to Australia (Super Series) 2005-06
Other sports/games played: Represented Lancashire Schools at chess
Extras: Represented England U14 to U19. NBC Denis Compton Award for the most promising young Lancashire player 1997. Cricket Writers' Club Young Player of the Year and PCA Young Player of the Year 1998. Scored first century before lunch by a Lancashire batsman in a Roses match, v Yorkshire at Old Trafford 1999. Won the EDS Walter Lawrence Trophy 1999 (for the fastest first-class century of the season). Lancashire Player of the Year 2000. Vice-captain of Lancashire 2002. BBC North West

Sports Personality of the Year 2003. One of *Wisden*'s Five Cricketers of the Year 2004. Vodafone England Cricketer of the Year 2003-04 and 2005-06. Shared with Andrew Strauss in a record stand for any wicket for England in ODIs (226), v West Indies at Lord's in the NatWest Series 2004. His Test awards include England's Man of the Series v West Indies 2004 and v Australia 2005 (plus the inaugural Compton-Miller Medal 2005 for Ashes Player of the Series), and Man of the Series v India 2005-06. His ODI awards include Man of the NatWest Series 2003 and Man of the Series v Bangladesh 2003-04. Winner of inaugural ICC One-Day Player of the Year award 2003-04. PCA Player of the Year award 2004, 2005. ICC Player of the Year award (jointly with Jacques Kallis) 2005. BBC Sports Personality of the Year 2005. Appointed MBE in 2006 New Year Honours as part of 2005 Ashes-winning England team. Lancashire benefit season 2006. Out for much of the 2007 season with a recurrence of an ankle problem. Named Man of the Series after England had beaten South Africa 4-0 in the ODI's 2008. There are now week-long cricket courses under the Flintoff name available at various venues around the UK.

Best batting: 167 England v West Indies, Edgbaston 2004

Best bowling: 5-24 Lancashire v Hampshire, Southampton 1999

Stop press: Chennai Super Kings paid $1.55m for his services in 2009 IPL auction

2008 Season

	M	Inn	NO	Runs	HS	Avg	100	50	Ct	St	Balls	Runs	Wkts	Avg	BB	5I	10M
Test	3	6	2	113	38	28.25	-	-	3	-	738	328	9	36.44	4-89	-	-
FC	8	14	4	245	62 *	24.50	-	1	8	-	1579	664	22	30.18	4-21	-	-
ODI	5	3	2	187	78 *	187.00	-	2	1	-	184	129	10	12.90	3-21	-	
List A	8	6	3	232	78 *	77.33	-	2	2	-	310	174	14	12.42	3-21	-	
20/20 Int																	
20/20	6	4	0	75	53	18.75	-	1	5	-	60	56	8	7.00	4-12	-	

Career Performances

	M	Inn	NO	Runs	HS	Avg	100	50	Ct	St	Balls	Runs	Wkts	Avg	BB	5I	10M
Test	70	116	8	3494	167	32.35	5	24	47	-	13300	6636	206	32.21	5-58	2	-
FC	171	271	22	8588	167	34.49	15	50	176	-	20762	10116	319	31.71	5-24	3	-
ODI	133	115	16	3277	123	33.10	3	18	43	-	5258	3815	159	23.99	5-56	1	
List A	274	244	28	6524	143	30.20	6	34	102	-	9050	6230	279	22.32	5-56	1	
20/20 Int	7	7	1	76	31	12.66	-	-	5	-	150	161	5	32.20	2-23	-	
20/20	21	19	1	393	85	21.83	-	2	12	-	341	365	22	16.59	4-12	-	

FLOWER, G. W. — Essex

Name: Grant William Flower
Role: Right-hand top-order bat, left-arm spin bowler; all-rounder
Born: 20 December 1970, Harare, Zimbabwe
Height: 5ft 10in **Weight:** 11st
Nickname: Gobby
County debut: 2002 (Leicestershire), 2005 (Essex)
County cap: 2005 (Essex)
Test debut: 1992-93
ODI debut: 1992-93
1st-Class 200s: 4
Place in batting averages: 246th av 12.42 (2007 66th av. 40.73)
Parents: Bill and Jean
Marital status: Single
Family links with cricket: Younger brother of Andy Flower (formerly of Zimbabwe and Essex and now England assistant coach)
Education: St George's College, Harare
Qualifications: 8 O-levels, 1 A-level, Level 3 coaching
Career outside cricket: Coaching
Off-season: 'Level 4 coaching course, Lashings tour to Abu Dhabi'
Overseas tours: Zimbabwe to India 1992-93, to Pakistan 1993-94, to Australia (one-day series) 1994-95, to New Zealand 1995-96, to India and Pakistan (World Cup) 1995-96, to Sri Lanka and Pakistan 1996-97, to Sri Lanka and New Zealand 1997-98, to Bangladesh (Wills International Cup) 1998-99, to Pakistan 1998-99, to UK, Ireland and Netherlands (World Cup) 1999, to South Africa 1999-2000, to West Indies 1999-2000, to England 2000, to Kenya (ICC Knockout Trophy) 2000-01, to India 2000-01, to New Zealand and Australia 2000-01, to Bangladesh, Sri Lanka and India 2001-02, to Sri Lanka (ICC Champions Trophy) 2002-03, to England 2003, to Australia 2003-04 (VB Series), plus other one-day tournaments in Sharjah, South Africa, Kenya, India, Bangladesh and Singapore
Overseas teams played for: Mashonaland 1994-95 – 2003-04
Career highlights to date: 'Scoring 201* v Pakistan in 1994-95 in our first Test match victory in Harare. Being named Man of the Match in the Friends Provident Trophy final against Kent at Lord's.'
Cricket moments to forget: 'Losing to Kenya in the 2002-03 World Cup for Zimbabwe'
Cricket superstitions: 'None'
Cricketers particularly admired: Graeme Hick, Sachin Tendulkar

Young players to look out for: Jake Mickelbrough
Other sports played: Squash, tennis
Other sports followed: Squash, tennis, football, rugby, golf
Relaxations: 'Reading, TV, films, fishing and drinking'
Extras: Appeared in Zimbabwe's inaugural Test, v India at Harare 1992-93. Scored 201* v Pakistan at Harare 1994-95 in Zimbabwe's first Test win, in the process sharing with Andy Flower (156) in a record fourth-wicket stand for Zimbabwe in Tests (269). Became the first player to score a hundred in each innings of a Test for Zimbabwe (104/151) in the first Test v New Zealand at Harare 1997-98. His Test awards include Man of the Series v New Zealand 1997-98. His ODI awards include Zimbabwe's Man of the Series v Pakistan 1996-97, as well as Man of the Match v England at Trent Bridge in the NatWest Series 2003 (96*) and v Australia at Adelaide in the VB Series 2003-04 (94). Was Leicestershire's overseas player during June 2002. Announced his retirement from international cricket in 2004. Is no longer considered an overseas player
Opinions on cricket: 'Risk of Twenty20 overkill?'
Best batting: 243* Mashonaland v Matabeleland, Harare (A) 1996-97
Best bowling: 7-31 Zimbabweans v Lahore City, Lahore 1998-99

2008 Season

	M	Inn	NO	Runs	HS	Avg	100	50	Ct	St	Balls	Runs	Wkts	Avg	BB	5I	10M
Test																	
FC	5	7	0	87	39	12.42	-	-	3	-	126	69	2	34.50	1-10	-	-
ODI																	
List A	13	10	3	369	75	52.71	-	5	3	-	48	44	1	44.00	1-14	-	
20/20 Int																	
20/20	12	11	2	203	39 *	22.55	-	-	3	-	12	21	3	7.00	3-21	-	

Career Performances

	M	Inn	NO	Runs	HS	Avg	100	50	Ct	St	Balls	Runs	Wkts	Avg	BB	5I	10M
Test	67	123	6	3457	201 *	29.54	6	15	43	-	3378	1537	25	61.48	4-41	-	-
FC	184	312	23	10766	243 *	37.25	23	58	171	-	12457	5573	165	33.77	7-31	3	-
ODI	219	212	18	6536	142 *	33.69	6	40	86	-	5420	4187	104	40.25	4-32	-	
List A	337	319	29	9885	148 *	34.08	11	67	130	-	8404	6234	177	35.22	4-32	-	
20/20 Int																	
20/20	28	20	4	350	40	21.87	-	-	7	-	154	215	13	16.53	3-20	-	

FOSTER, J. S. Essex

Name: James Savin Foster
Role: Right-hand bat, wicket-keeper, county vice-captain
Born: 15 April 1980, Whipps Cross, London
Height: 6ft **Weight:** 12st
Nickname: Fozzy, Chief
County debut: 2000
County cap: 2001
Test debut: 2001-02
ODI debut: 2001-02
1000 runs in a season: 1
50 dismissals in a season: 3
1st-Class 200s: 2
Place in batting averages: 47th av 44.09 (2007 89th av. 37.59)
Parents: Martin and Diana
Marital status: Single
Family links with cricket: 'Dad played for Essex Amateurs'
Education: Forest School; Durham University
Qualifications: 10 GCSEs, 3 A-levels, hockey and cricket Level 1 coaching awards
Overseas tours: BUSA to South Africa 1999; Durham University to South Africa 1999, to Vienna (European Indoor Championships) 1999; England A to West Indies 2000-01; England to Zimbabwe (one-day series) 2001-02, to India and New Zealand 2001-02, to Australia 2002-03; England Lions to India 2007-08
Overseas teams played for: Claremont-Nedlands, Perth 2006-07
Career highlights to date: 'Playing for my country'
Cricketers particularly admired: Nasser Hussain, Stuart Law, Robert Rollins, Ian Healy, Jack Russell, Alec Stewart, Adam Gilchrist
Other sports played: Hockey (Essex U21), tennis (played for GB U14 v Sweden U14; national training squad)
Other sports followed: Football
Relaxations: 'Socialising'
Extras: Essex U17 Player of the Year 1997. Represented ECB U19 1998 and England U19 1999. Represented BUSA 1999, 2000 and 2001. Voted Essex Cricket Society 2nd XI Player of the Year 2000. Played for Durham UCCE 2001. NBC Denis Compton Award for the most promising young Essex player 2001. Achieved double (1037 first-class runs plus 51 dismissals) 2004. Vice-captain of Essex since part-way through the 2007 season. Called up to squad for England Lions tour to India 2007-08 as a replacement for the injured Steve Davies. Finished the 2008 Championship season with a flourish, scoring 122 against Gloucestershire

Best batting: 212 Essex v Leicestershire, Chelmsford 2004
Best bowling: 1-122 Essex v Northamptonshire, Northampton 2008

2008 Season

	M	Inn	NO	Runs	HS	Avg	100	50	Ct	St	Balls	Runs	Wkts	Avg	BB	5I	10M
Test																	
FC	17	25	4	926	132 *	44.09	3	4	59	1	72	122	1	122.00	1-122	-	-
ODI																	
List A	17	14	2	323	61	26.91	-	1	20	5	0	0	0		-	-	
20/20 Int																	
20/20	12	11	3	295	50 *	36.87	-	1	6	4	0	0	0		-	-	

Career Performances

	M	Inn	NO	Runs	HS	Avg	100	50	Ct	St	Balls	Runs	Wkts	Avg	BB	5I	10M
Test	7	12	3	226	48	25.11	-	-	17	1	0	0	0		-	-	-
FC	140	206	26	6362	212	35.34	12	31	374	34	84	128	1	128.00	1-122	-	-
ODI	11	6	3	41	13	13.66	-	-	13	7	0	0	0		-	-	
List A	134	104	26	1845	69 *	23.65	-	6	164	37	0	0	0		-	-	
20/20 Int																	
20/20	46	38	8	669	62 *	22.30	-	3	19	15	0	0	0		-	-	

FRANCIS, J. D. Somerset

Name: John Daniel Francis
Role: Left-hand bat, slow left-arm bowler
Born: 13 November 1980, Bromley, Kent
Height: 5ft 11in **Weight:** 13st
Nickname: Long John, Franky, Junior
County debut: 2001 (Hampshire), 2004 (Somerset)
1000 runs in a season: 1
Parents: Linda and Daniel
Marital status: Single
Family links with cricket: Brother Simon played for Hampshire, Somerset and Nottinghamshire. Father played club cricket. Grandfather played in the services
Education: King Edward VI, Southampton; Durham and Loughborough Universities
Qualifications: 10 GCSEs, 3 A-levels, BSc Sports Science, ECB Level 1 coaching award

Career outside cricket: MD and co-owner of Universal Marquees Ltd.; co-owner of an events and weddings venue, and of Universal Mobile Creche
Off-season: 'Carrying on developing my business interests'
Overseas tours: Twyford School to Barbados 1993; West of England U15 to West Indies 1995; King Edward VI, Southampton to South Africa 1998; Durham University to South Africa 2000; British Universities to South Africa 2002
Career highlights to date: 'Scoring maiden first-class century for Somerset v Yorkshire at Scarborough 2004, sharing in a partnership of 197 runs with Ricky Ponting'
Cricket moments to forget: 'Getting first ever pair, in a match v Yorkshire'
Cricket superstitions: 'Too many to say'
Cricketers particularly admired: Graham Thorpe, Adam Hollioake, Mike Hussey, Simon Francis
Young players to look out for: James Hudson, Richard Daniell, Ben Riches
Other sports played: Hockey (England U18), golf, squash
Favourite band: Ray LaMontagne
Relaxations: Drawing and painting, socialising
Extras: Hampshire Young Sportsman of the Year 1995. Sir John Hobbs Silver Jubilee Memorial Prize for outstanding U16 player of the year 1996. Leading run-scorer in U15 World Cup 1996. Played for Loughborough UCCE 2001, 2002 and 2003. NBC Denis Compton Award for the most promising young Hampshire player 2002. Represented British Universities 2002 and 2003. Retired at the end of the 2008 season
Best batting: 125* Somerset v Yorkshire, Headingley 2005
Best bowling: 1-1 Hampshire v Leicestershire, Leicester 2002

2008 Season

	M	Inn	NO	Runs	HS	Avg	100	50	Ct	St	Balls	Runs	Wkts	Avg	BB	5I	10M
Test																	
FC	2	3	0	70	59	23.33	-	1	-	-	0	0	0		-	-	-
ODI																	
List A	5	4	1	82	48 *	27.33	-	-	2	-	0	0	0		-	-	
20/20 Int																	
20/20																	

Career Performances

	M	Inn	NO	Runs	HS	Avg	100	50	Ct	St	Balls	Runs	Wkts	Avg	BB	5I	10M
Test																	
FC	57	101	8	2748	125 *	29.54	6	15	32	-	273	164	4	41.00	1-1	-	-
ODI																	
List A	70	65	11	1827	103 *	33.83	1	12	17	-	0	0	0		-	-	
20/20 Int																	
20/20	14	14	4	271	49	27.10	-	-	1	-	0	0	0		-	-	

FRANKS, P. J. Nottinghamshire

Name: Paul John Franks
Role: Left-hand bat, right-arm fast-medium bowler; all-rounder
Born: 3 February 1979, Sutton-in-Ashfield
Height: 6ft 2in **Weight:** 14st
Nickname: Franksie, Pike
County debut: 1996
County cap: 1999
Benefit: 2007
ODI debut: 2000
50 wickets in a season: 2
Place in batting averages: 147th av 27.22 (2007 195th av. 22.91)
Place in bowling averages: 144th av 52.66 (2007 92nd av. 34.06)
Parents: Patricia and John
Wife and date of marriage: Helen, 1 October 2005
Family links with cricket: 'Dad was league legend for 25 years'
Education: Minster School, Southwell; West Notts College
Qualifications: 7 GCSEs, GNVQ (Advanced) Leisure Management, coaching Level 1
Overseas tours: England U19 to Pakistan 1996-97, to South Africa (including U19 World Cup) 1997-98; England A to Zimbabwe and South Africa 1998-99, to Bangladesh and New Zealand 1999-2000, to West Indies 2000-01, to Sri Lanka 2004-05; Notts CCC to South Africa 1998, 1999
Overseas teams played for: Bellville CC, Cape Town 2006
Career highlights to date: 'England debut. Notts Championship win 2005. Twenty20 finals day 2006'
Cricket moments to forget: 'Being injured'
Cricketers particularly admired: Ian Botham, Andrew Flintoff, Chris Cairns, Mark Ealham
Other sports played: Golf
Other sports followed: Football (Mansfield Town)
Favourite band: The Killers, Red Hot Chili Peppers
Relaxations: 'TV; temperature control of Guinness!'
Extras: Took Championship hat-trick (Penney, Brown, Welch) v Warwickshire at Trent Bridge 1997 (aged 18 years 163 days). NBC Denis Compton Award for most promising young Nottinghamshire player 1997, 1998, 1999. Won U19 World Cup winner's medal in Johannesburg 1998. Cricket Writers' Young Player of the Year 2000. Vice-captain of Nottinghamshire 2003-04. ECB National Academy 2004-05 'Youngest Notts player to be awarded a benefit year, aged 28'

Best batting: 123* Nottinghamshire v Leicestershire, Leicester 2003
Best bowling: 7-56 Nottinghamshire v Middlesex, Lord's 2000

2008 Season

	M	Inn	NO	Runs	HS	Avg	100	50	Ct	St	Balls	Runs	Wkts	Avg	BB	5I	10M
Test																	
FC	8	11	2	245	52	27.22	-	1	5	-	1032	632	12	52.66	2-25	-	
ODI																	
List A	7	5	2	62	34 *	20.66	-	-	2	-	144	153	2	76.50	1-10	-	
20/20 Int																	
20/20	3	2	1	4	2 *	4.00	-	-	-	-	30	29	2	14.50	2-12	-	

Career Performances

	M	Inn	NO	Runs	HS	Avg	100	50	Ct	St	Balls	Runs	Wkts	Avg	BB	5I	10M
Test																	
FC	154	221	43	4677	123 *	26.27	3	22	54	-	23289	13128	407	32.25	7-56	11	-
ODI	1	1	0	4	4	4.00	-	-	1	-	54	48	0		-	-	
List A	145	108	32	1604	84 *	21.10	-	4	22	-	5573	4544	163	27.87	6-27	2	
20/20 Int																	
20/20	30	19	8	200	29 *	18.18	-	-	4	-	165	230	11	20.90	2-12	-	

FROST, T. Warwickshire

Name: Tony Frost
Role: Right-hand bat
Born: 17 November 1975, Stoke-on-Trent
Height: 5ft 10in **Weight:** 10st 6lbs
County debut: 1997
County cap: 1999
50 dismissals in a season: 1
1000 runs in a season: 1
1st-Class 200s: 1
Parents: Ivan and Christine
Marital status: Single
Family links with cricket: Father played for Staffordshire
Education: James Brinkley High School; Stoke-on-Trent College
Qualifications: 5 GCSEs
Overseas tours: Kidsgrove U18 to Australia 1990-91
Other sports followed: Football, golf

Extras: Represented Staffordshire at all levels from U11 to U19. Won Texaco U16 competition with Staffordshire in 1992. Played for Development of Excellence XI U17, U18, and U19. Scored century (135*) v Sussex at Horsham 2004, in the process setting with Ian Bell (262*) a new Warwickshire record partnership for the seventh wicket (289*). C&G Man of the Match award in the semi-final v Lancashire at Edgbaston 2005. Retired at the end of the 2006 season; rejoined Warwickshire for 2008. Topped first-class batting averages
Best batting: 242* Warwickshire v Essex, Chelmsford 2008

2008 Season

	M	Inn	NO	Runs	HS	Avg	100	50	Ct	St	Balls	Runs	Wkts	Avg	BB	5I	10M
Test																	
FC	13	18	6	1003	242 *	83.58	2	4	26	2	12	3	0		-	-	-
ODI																	
List A	6	5	1	120	56	30.00	-	2	2	-	0	0	0		-	-	
20/20 Int																	
20/20	10	8	1	183	53	26.14	-	1	2	3	0	0	0		-	-	

Career Performances

	M	Inn	NO	Runs	HS	Avg	100	50	Ct	St	Balls	Runs	Wkts	Avg	BB	5I	10M
Test																	
FC	105	152	27	4181	242 *	33.44	5	20	251	18	24	18	0		-	-	-
ODI																	
List A	85	48	17	605	56	19.51	-	2	78	19	0	0	0		-	-	
20/20 Int																	
20/20	23	15	3	275	53	22.91	-	1	12	11	0	0	0		-	-	

GALE, A. W. Yorkshire

Name: Andrew William Gale
Role: Left-hand bat, right-arm off-spin bowler
Born: 28 November 1983, Dewsbury
Height: 6ft 2in **Weight:** 14st
Nickname: Galey, G-Dog, G-Unit, Bobby, Banger
County debut: 2004
Place in batting averages: 70th av 39.08 (2007 156th av. 27.87)
Parents: Denise and Alan
Marital status: 'Engaged'
Family links with cricket: 'Grandad was a good club cricketer'
Education: Whitcliffe Mount; Heckmondwike Grammar
Qualifications: 10 GCSEs, 3 A-levels, Level 3 cricket coaching
Career outside cricket: 'Cricket coaching'
Off-season: 'Football and business'
Overseas tours: England U17 to Australia 2001; England U19 to Australia 2002-03; Yorkshire to Grenada 2001, to India 2005
Overseas teams played for: Blacktown, Sydney 2004-05
Career highlights to date: 'Scoring maiden first-class hundred. Any hundred...'
Cricket moments to forget: 'Any ducks'
Cricket superstitions: 'Don't like odd numbers'
Cricketers particularly admired: Marcus Trescothick, Michael Vaughan
Young players to look out for: Adam Lyth, Gary Ballance
Other sports played: Football ('played for district')
Other sports followed: Football (Huddersfield Town)
Favourite band: Oasis, Simply Red
Relaxations: 'PlayStation'
Player website: www.procoachcricketacademy.co.uk
Extras: Played for England age groups from U15. Yorkshire League Young Batsman of the Year 2002. Yorkshire Player of the Year 2006. Jointly responsible for the Pro Cricket Coaching Academy, which casts its net over the North of England and the Midlands. Only Jacques Rudolph scored more first-class runs for Yorkshire in 2008
Opinions on cricket: 'Glad to see overseas players back down to one.'
Best batting: 150 Yorkshire v Surrey, The Oval 2008
Best bowling: 1-33 Yorkshire v LUCCE, Headingley 2007

2008 Season

	M	Inn	NO	Runs	HS	Avg	100	50	Ct	St	Balls	Runs	Wkts	Avg	BB	5I	10M
Test																	
FC	15	23	0	899	150	39.08	3	3	9	-	6	3	0		-	-	-
ODI																	
List A	18	17	1	450	89	28.12	-	3	-	-	0	0	0		-	-	
20/20 Int																	
20/20	9	9	2	106	45	15.14	-	-	2	-	0	0	0		-	-	

Career Performances

	M	Inn	NO	Runs	HS	Avg	100	50	Ct	St	Balls	Runs	Wkts	Avg	BB	5I	10M
Test																	
FC	30	47	0	1419	150	30.19	4	5	18	-	18	36	1	36.00	1-33	-	-
ODI																	
List A	60	52	7	1336	89	29.68	-	8	10	-	0	0	0		-	-	
20/20 Int																	
20/20	28	24	4	365	56	18.25	-	2	13	-	0	0	0		-	-	

GALLIAN, J. E. R. Essex

Name: Jason Edward Riche Gallian
Role: Right-hand bat, right-arm medium bowler
Born: 25 June 1971, Manly, NSW, Australia
Height: 6ft **Weight:** 14st 7lbs
Nickname: Gal
County debut: 1990 (Lancashire), 1998 (Nottinghamshire), 2008 (Essex)
County cap: 1994 (Lancashire), 1998 (Nottinghamshire)
Benefit: 2005 (Nottinghamshire)
Test debut: 1995
1000 runs in a season: 6
1st-Class 300s: 1
Place in batting averages: 145th av 27.35 (2007 88th av. 37.60)
Parents: Ray and Marilyn
Wife and date of marriage: Charlotte, 2 October 1999
Children: Tom, 11 May 2001; Harry, 8 September 2003; Emily, 6 October 2006
Family links with cricket: Father played for Stockport. 'Tom and Harry are showing a keen eye for a ball!'

Education: The Pittwater House Schools, Australia; Oxford University
Qualifications: Higher School Certificate, Diploma in Social Studies (Keble College, Oxford)
Career outside cricket: 'Working for Clydesdale Bank in London'
Off-season: 'Learning to be a private banker'
Overseas tours: Australia U20 to West Indies 1989-90; England A to India 1994-95, to Pakistan 1995-96, to Australia 1996-97; England to South Africa 1995-96; Nottinghamshire to Johannesburg 2000, to South Africa 2001; MCC to UAE and Oman 2004
Overseas teams played for: NSW U19 1988-89; NSW Colts and NSW 2nd XI 1990-91; Manly 1993-94
Career highlights to date: 'First Test match'
Cricket moments to forget: 'Breaking a finger in my first Test match'
Cricket superstitions: 'None'
Cricketers particularly admired: Desmond Haynes, Mike Gatting
Young players to look out for: Adam Wheater
Other sports played: Golf, shooting, darts (known as 'see it off')
Other sports followed: Rugby league and union, football
Favourite band: Midnight Oil, INXS
Relaxations: 'Looking after the kids'
Extras: Represented Australia YC 1988-90 (captain v England YC 1989-90); also represented Australia U20 and U21 1991-92. Took wicket of D. A. Hagan of Oxford University with his first ball in first-class cricket 1990. Played for Oxford University and Combined Universities 1992; captained Oxford University 1993. Qualified to play for England 1994. Recorded highest individual score in history of Old Trafford with his 312 v Derbyshire in 1996. Captain of Nottinghamshire from part-way through the 1998 season to 2002 and in 2004; Nottinghamshire club captain and captain in first-class cricket 2003. Left Nottinghamshire at the end of the 2007 season and joined Essex for 2008
Opinions on cricket: 'The changes to Championship cricket have been very positive in recreating Test cricket conditions to bring on up-and-coming players.'
Best batting: 312 Lancashire v Derbyshire, Old Trafford 1996
Best bowling: 6-115 Lancashire v Surrey, Southport 1996

2008 Season

	M	Inn	NO	Runs	HS	Avg	100	50	Ct	St	Balls	Runs	Wkts	Avg	BB	5I	10M
Test																	
FC	17	31	0	848	171	27.35	1	5	26	-	24	12	0		-	-	-
ODI																	
List A	15	15	3	614	117	51.16	3	2	5	-	0	0	0		-	-	
20/20 Int																	
20/20	8	8	0	163	55	20.37	-	1	4	-	0	0	0		-	-	

Career Performances

	M	Inn	NO	Runs	HS	Avg	100	50	Ct	St	Balls	Runs	Wkts	Avg	BB	5I	10M
Test	3	6	0	74	28	12.33	-	-	1	-	84	62	0		-	-	-
FC	252	430	35	15021	312	38.02	37	72	226	-	7162	4164	96	43.37	6-115	1	-
ODI																	
List A	228	224	18	6684	134	32.44	11	40	77	-	2049	1808	55	32.87	5-15	1	
20/20 Int																	
20/20	16	16	0	315	62	19.68	-	2	5	-	0	0	0		-	-	

GAZZARD, C. M. — Somerset

Name: Carl Matthew Gazzard
Role: Right-hand bat, wicket-keeper
Born: 15 April 1982, Penzance
Height: 6ft **Weight:** 13st
Nickname: Gazza, Larry
County debut: 2002
Parents: Paul and Alison
Wife and date of marriage: Laura, 29 September 2006
Children: Ruby and Noah, 17 September 2007
Family links with cricket: Father and brother both played for Cornwall Schools; mother's a keen follower
Education: Mounts Bay Comprehensive; Richard Huish College, Taunton
Qualifications: 10 GCSEs, 2 A-levels, Levels 1 and 2 coaching
Overseas tours: Cornwall Schools U13 to Johannesburg; West of England U15 to West Indies; Somerset Academy to Durban 1999
Overseas teams played for: Subiaco-Floreat, Perth 2000-01; Scarborough, Perth 2002-03
Career highlights to date: '157 v Derby in totesport game [2004]'
Cricket moments to forget: 'Dislocating my shoulder in Perth – kept me out for 2001 season'
Cricket superstitions: 'None'
Cricketers particularly admired: Marcus Trescothick, Graham Rose
Young players to look out for: James Hildreth
Other sports played: Football (played through the age groups for Cornwall)
Other sports followed: Football (West Ham United)

Favourite band: Red Hot Chili Peppers
Extras: Played for England U13, U14, U15, U19. Won the Graham Kersey Award for Best Wicket-keeper at Bunbury Festival. Played for Cornwall in Minor Counties aged 16. Scored 136-ball 157 (his maiden one-day century) v Derbyshire at Derby in the totesport League 2004. Man of the Match in Twenty20 Cup semi-final v Leicestershire at The Oval 2005.
Best batting: 74 Somerset v Worcestershire, Worcester 2005

2008 Season

	M	Inn	NO	Runs	HS	Avg	100	50	Ct	St	Balls	Runs	Wkts	Avg	BB	5I	10M
Test																	
FC	1	1	0	6	6	6.00	-	-	-	-	0	0	0		-	-	-
ODI																	
List A	1	1	1	30	30 *		-	-	3	1	0	0	0		-	-	
20/20 Int																	
20/20																	

Career Performances

	M	Inn	NO	Runs	HS	Avg	100	50	Ct	St	Balls	Runs	Wkts	Avg	BB	5I	10M
Test																	
FC	28	43	6	738	74	19.94	-	1	58	1	0	0	0		-	-	-
ODI																	
List A	53	45	5	954	157	23.85	1	4	51	7	0	0	0		-	-	
20/20 Int																	
20/20	27	17	4	221	39	17.00	-	-	14	6	0	0	0		-	-	

29. He captained Australia in ten consecutive Ashes Tests in the early nineteen-twenties, winning eight and drawing two. Can you name him?

GIBBS, H. H. Glamorgan

Name: Herschelle Herman Gibbs
Role: Right-hand bat, right-arm fast-medium leg-break bowler
Born: 23 February 1974, Green Point, Cape Town South Africa
Height: 5ft 8in
Nickname: Scooter
County debut: 2008 (one-day)
Test debut: 1997
ODI debut: 1996
Twenty20 Int debut: 2005
1st-Class 200s: 4
Parents: Herman and Barbara
Marital status: Divorced
Family links with cricket: Father Herman is a leading sports writer
Education: Diocesan College

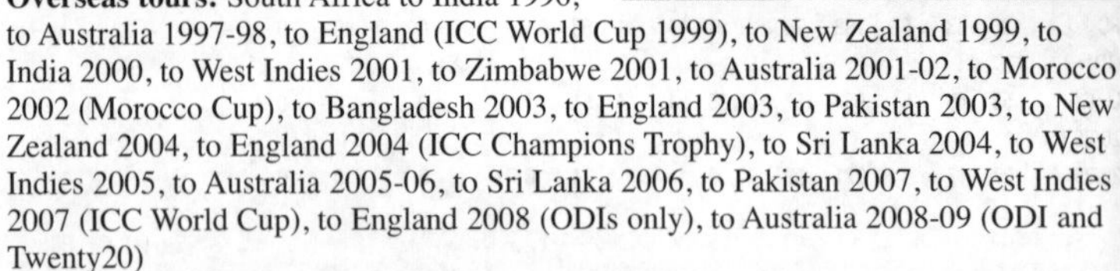

Overseas tours: South Africa to India 1996, to Australia 1997-98, to England (ICC World Cup 1999), to New Zealand 1999, to India 2000, to West Indies 2001, to Zimbabwe 2001, to Australia 2001-02, to Morocco 2002 (Morocco Cup), to Bangladesh 2003, to England 2003, to Pakistan 2003, to New Zealand 2004, to England 2004 (ICC Champions Trophy), to Sri Lanka 2004, to West Indies 2005, to Australia 2005-06, to Sri Lanka 2006, to Pakistan 2007, to West Indies 2007 (ICC World Cup), to England 2008 (ODIs only), to Australia 2008-09 (ODI and Twenty20)
Overseas teams played for: Western Province 1994-95 – 2003-04, Western Province Boland 2004-05, Cape Cobras 2005-06 – ; Deccan Chargers (IPL) 2007-08
Career highlights to date: '1999 World Cup semi-final at Edgbaston. It ended in a tie but could have gone either way; the complete one-day match that had everything.'
Cricket moments to forget: 'The game before, when I dropped Steve Waugh and we lost the game.'
Cricketers particularly admired: Peter Kirsten, Viv Richards
Other sports played: Golf ('I play off five')
Other sports followed: Football (Manchester United)
Favourite band: Luther Vandross, George Benson and Frank Sinatra
Relaxations: Shopping
Extras: In a World Cup match against the Netherlands in 2007 he hit six sixes in an over from Dan van Bunge, an international record. Has featured in three 300-plus opening partnerships with Graeme Smith in Test matches. Scored 175 off 111 balls to give South Africa victory over Australia in Johannesburg 2006. Signed with Glamorgan in 2008, finishing top of the county's batting averages. He will return in 2009, and will play from July until the end of the season

Best batting: 228 South Africa v Pakistan, Cape Town 2003
Best bowling: 2-14 South Africa A v Somerset, Taunton 1996

2008 Season

	M	Inn	NO	Runs	HS	Avg	100	50	Ct	St	Balls	Runs	Wkts	Avg	BB	5I	10M
Test																	
FC																	
ODI	5	5	0	136	74	27.20	-	1	2	-	0	0	0		-	-	
List A	7	7	0	245	81	35.00	-	2	2	-	0	0	0		-	-	
20/20 Int																	
20/20	8	6	1	281	98	56.20	-	2	4	-	0	0	0		-	-	

Career Performances

	M	Inn	NO	Runs	HS	Avg	100	50	Ct	St	Balls	Runs	Wkts	Avg	BB	5I	10M
Test	90	154	7	6167	228	41.95	14	26	94	-	6	4	0		-	-	-
FC	185	319	13	13076	228	42.73	31	58	164	-	138	78	3	26.00	2-14	-	-
ODI	232	225	16	7589	175	36.31	20	35	100	-	0	0	0		-	-	
List A	350	335	27	10724	175	34.81	24	57	157	-	66	57	2	28.50	1-16	-	
20/20 Int	9	9	1	182	90 *	22.75	-	2	2	-	0	0	0		-	-	
20/20	35	33	2	747	98	24.09	-	5	16	-	0	0	0		-	-	

GIDMAN, A. P. R. Gloucestershire

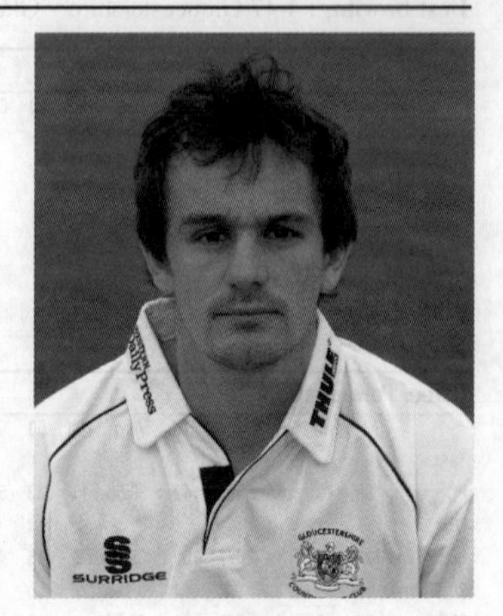

Name: Alexander (Alex) Peter Richard Gidman
Role: Right-hand bat, right-arm medium bowler, county captain
Born: 22 June 1981, High Wycombe
Height: 6ft 2in **Weight:** 15st 7lbs
Nickname: G, Giddo
County debut: 2001 (one-day), 2002 (first-class)
County cap: 2004
1000 runs in a season: 3
Place in batting averages: 166th av 24.05 (2007 72nd av. 40.12)
Parents: Alistair and Jane
Marital status: Engaged
Family links with cricket: Brother Will is at Durham CCC
Education: Wycliffe College, Stonehouse, Gloucestershire

Qualifications: 6 GCSEs, 1 A-level, GNVQ Level 2 in Leisure and Tourism
Off-season: 'Playing my guitar, learning piano'
Overseas tours: MCC Young Cricketers to Cape Town 1999; Gloucestershire to South Africa; England A to Malaysia and India 2003-04 (c), to Sri Lanka 2004-05, to Bangladesh 2006-07
Overseas teams played for: Albion CC, New Zealand 2001; Otago, New Zealand 2007-08
Career highlights to date: 'England A tours. Two C&G Trophy final victories. Academy captain'
Cricket moments to forget: '2008'
Cricketers particularly admired: Steve Waugh
Young players to look out for: Will Gidman
Other sports played: Golf
Other sports followed: Football (Wolves), rugby (Gloucester)
Favourite band: Oasis, Pink Floyd
Relaxations: 'Just chilling out; movies, golf, playing guitar'
Extras: Gloucestershire Young Player of the Year 2002, 2003. NBC Denis Compton Award for the most promising young Gloucestershire player 2002, 2003. ECB National Academy 2003-04, 2004-05. Included in England's preliminary squad for ICC Champions Trophy in 2004. Gloucestershire Players' Player of the Year 2006. Vice-captain of Gloucestershire since 2006. Scored century in each innings (130/105*) v Northamptonshire at Gloucester 2007. Represented England Lions 2007. Gloucestershire county captain for 2009
Opinions on cricket: 'None – just enjoy. Cricket is not the be-all and end-all...'
Best batting: 142 Gloucestershire v Surrey, Bristol 2005
Best bowling: 4-47 Gloucestershire v Glamorgan, Cardiff 2005

2008 Season

	M	Inn	NO	Runs	HS	Avg	100	50	Ct	St	Balls	Runs	Wkts	Avg	BB	5I	10M
Test																	
FC	13	23	3	481	73	24.05	-	2	2	-	421	226	9	25.11	3-35	-	-
ODI																	
List A	11	10	0	169	105	16.90	1	-	3	-	252	185	3	61.66	1-17	-	
20/20 Int																	
20/20	3	3	0	31	22	10.33	-	-	-	-	0	0	0		-	-	

Career Performances

	M	Inn	NO	Runs	HS	Avg	100	50	Ct	St	Balls	Runs	Wkts	Avg	BB	5I	10M
Test																	
FC	98	173	20	5595	142	36.56	11	33	54	-	6094	3832	83	46.16	4-47	-	-
ODI																	
List A	126	117	13	2677	105	25.74	2	15	41	-	2362	2049	51	40.17	5-42	1	
20/20 Int																	
20/20	39	33	7	540	61	20.76	-	2	9	-	186	237	6	39.50	2-24	-	

GIDMAN, W. R. S. Durham

Name: William (Will) Robert Simon Gidman
Role: Left-hand bat, right-arm medium bowler; all-rounder
Born: 14 February 1985, High Wycombe
Height: 6ft 2in **Weight:** 12st 7lbs
Nickname: Gidders, Giddo, Rev, PT
County debut: 2007
Parents: Alistair and Jane
Marital status: Single
Family links with cricket: Brother of Alex Gidman, vice-captain of Gloucestershire
Education: Wycliffe College, Stonehouse, Gloucestershire; Berkshire College of Agriculture
Qualifications: 7 GCSEs, Level 2 cricket coaching, Level 1 rugby and football coaching
Career outside cricket: 'Part-time teacher'
Overseas tours: Wycliffe College to South Africa 2000; MCC YC to Sri Lanka 2004, to India 2005, to Lanzarote 2006; Durham to Cape Town 2007
Overseas teams played for: Gold Coast Dolphins, Australia 2004-05
Career highlights to date: 'Signing for Durham CCC'
Cricket moments to forget: 'Giving away four overthrows off Freddie Flintoff's bowling whilst doing 12th man duties for England against Bangladesh'
Cricket superstitions: 'None'
Cricketers particularly admired: Garfield Sobers, Graham Thorpe, Mike Hussey, Alex Gidman
Young players to look out for: Garry Park
Other sports played: Football (Stroud and District), rugby, golf, table tennis
Other sports followed: Football (Wolves), rugby (Gloucester)
Favourite band: Embrace
Relaxations: 'Music, TV, walking the dog, Sudoku'
Extras: Was first Gloucestershire U10 to score a hundred. Played for Gloucestershire Board XI in the 2003 C&G. MCC YC cap. Brother is captain of Gloucestershire
Opinions on cricket: 'I love the traditions of our game and the prospect of things like drop-in pitches and taking too many decisions away from the umpires in the middle, I am not sure about.'
Best batting: 8 Durham v Sri Lanka A, Riverside 2007
Best bowling: 3-37 Durham v Sri Lanka A, Riverside 2007

2008 Season

	M	Inn	NO	Runs	HS	Avg	100	50	Ct	St	Balls	Runs	Wkts	Avg	BB	5I	10M
Test																	
FC																	
ODI																	
List A	2	2	0	21	21	10.50	-	-	1	-	84	61	4	15.25	2-21	-	
20/20 Int																	
20/20																	

Career Performances

	M	Inn	NO	Runs	HS	Avg	100	50	Ct	St	Balls	Runs	Wkts	Avg	BB	5I	10M
Test																	
FC	1	2	0	8	8	4.00	-	-	-	-	138	86	4	21.50	3-37	-	-
ODI																	
List A	3	3	0	33	21	11.00	-	-	1	-	84	61	4	15.25	2-21	-	
20/20 Int																	
20/20																	

GILLESPIE, J. N. Glamorgan

Name: Jason Neil Gillespie
Role: Right-hand bat, right-arm fast bowler
Born: 19 April 1975, Darlinghurst, Australia
Height: 6ft 5in **Weight:** 14st 8lbs
Nickname: Dizzy
County debut: 2006 (Yorkshire), 2008 (Glamorgan)
County cap: 2007 (Yorkshire)
Test debut: 1996-97
ODI debut: 1996
Twenty20 Int debut: 2005
1st-Class 200s: 1
Place in batting averages: 180th av 22.13 (2007 111th av. 33.75)
Place in bowling averages: 115th av 37.58 (2007 97th av. 34.91)
Parents: Neil and Vicki
Wife and date of marriage: Anna, 20 September 2003
Children: Sapphire, 2 March 1995; Jackson Anderson, 1 February 2006; Brandon Ryder, October 2007

Education: Cabra College, Adelaide
Career outside cricket: 'Property investments and developments; radio'
Off-season: 'ICL and beach cricket. Studying Strength and Conditioning. Obtaining Level 3 coaching.'
Overseas tours: Australia U19 to India 1993-94; Australia A to Scotland and Ireland 1998, to Pakistan 2007-08; Australia to Sri Lanka (Singer World Series) 1996, to South Africa 1996-97, to England 1997, to West Indies 1998-99, to Sri Lanka 1999, to Kenya (ICC Knockout Trophy) 2000-01, to India 2000-01, to England 2001, to South Africa 2001-02, to Sri Lanka (ICC Champions Trophy) 2002-03, to Sri Lanka and Sharjah (v Pakistan) 2002-03, to Africa (World Cup) 2002-03, to West Indies 2002-03, to Sri Lanka 2003-04, to England (ICC Champions Trophy) 2004, to India 2004-05, to New Zealand 2004-05, to England 2005, to Bangladesh 2005-06, plus other one-day series and tournaments in India, Kenya, Zimbabwe, Netherlands and England
Overseas teams played for: Adelaide CC 1986 – ; South Australia 1994-95 – 2007-08; Ahmedabad Rockets (ICL) 2007-08 –
Career highlights to date: 'Winning cricket matches – that is what we play for'
Cricket moments to forget: 'Colliding with Steve Waugh in a Test match' (*During the first Test v Sri Lanka in Kandy 1999, Waugh and Gillespie collided attempting a catch. Waugh's nose was broken; Gillespie suffered a broken leg and wrist*)
Cricket superstitions: 'Not any more'
Cricketers particularly admired: Michael Kasprowicz, Darren Lehmann, Dennis Lillee, Merv Hughes, Glenn McGrath, Dean Cosker
Young players to look out for: James Harris, Gareth Rees
Other sports played: 'Will play social basketball when I finish playing cricket'
Other sports followed: AFL (Western Bulldogs), NRL (Sydney Roosters), basketball (Adelaide 36ers) - 'Can watch most sports except rugby union and hockey'
Favourite band: Metallica - 'Whatever is on radio'
Relaxations: 'Time with family and friends, a couple of beers with mates.'
Extras: Is the first known male cricketer of indigenous descent (great-grandson of a Kamilaroi warrior) to have played Test cricket for Australia. One of *Wisden*'s Five Cricketers of the Year 2002. Is sixth in the all-time list of Australia's Test wicket-takers. Scored 201* batting as nightwatchman in the second Test v Bangladesh at Chittagong 2005-06, reaching his double century on his 31st birthday. His match awards include Man of the Match v England in the fourth Test at Headingley 1997 (7-37/2-65) and v India at Centurion in the 2002-03 World Cup (3-13 from 10 overs). An overseas player with Yorkshire 2006-07. Scored century (123*) v Surrey at The Oval 2007, in the process sharing with Tim Bresnan (116) in a new record ninth-wicket partnership for Yorkshire (246). Joined Glamorgan as an overseas player for 2008, departing at the end of the season.
Opinions on cricket: 'ICL should be embraced, not banned - it's giving more opportunities for younger players to play and learn from experienced cricketers. BCCI has yet to give an argument as to why this is a bad thing. I'd also like to see Wales achieve Test status!'
Best batting: 201* Australia v Bangladesh, Chittagong (B) 2005-06
Best bowling: 8-50 South Australia v New South Wales, Sydney 2001-02

2008 Season

	M	Inn	NO	Runs	HS	Avg	100	50	Ct	St	Balls	Runs	Wkts	Avg	BB	5I	10M
Test																	
FC	13	20	5	332	52	22.13	-	1	4	-	2093	902	24	37.58	4-32	-	-
ODI																	
List A	13	8	7	50	9 *	50.00	-	-	3	-	504	345	17	20.29	5-13	1	
20/20 Int																	
20/20																	

Career Performances

	M	Inn	NO	Runs	HS	Avg	100	50	Ct	St	Balls	Runs	Wkts	Avg	BB	5I	10M
Test	71	93	28	1218	201 *	18.73	1	2	27	-	14234	6770	259	26.13	7-37	8	-
FC	189	256	65	3742	201 *	19.59	3	10	68	-	35372	16540	613	26.98	8-50	22	2
ODI	97	39	16	289	44 *	12.56	-	-	10	-	5144	3611	142	25.42	5-22	3	
List A	192	88	43	640	44 *	14.22	-	-	31	-	10048	6987	255	27.40	5-13	4	
20/20 Int	1	1	0	24	24	24.00	-	-	-	-	24	49	1	49.00	1-49	-	
20/20	21	7	4	55	24	18.33	-	-	5	-	403	532	19	28.00	2-19	-	

GITSHAM, M. T. Gloucestershire

Name: Matthew Thomas Gitsham
Role: Right-hand bat, right-arm leg-spin bowler
Born: 1 February 1982, Truro, Cornwall
Height: 5ft 10in **Weight:** 14st
Nickname: Gitchie
County debut: 2008
Parents: Colin and Marilyn
Marital status: Single ('long-term girlfriend Tamsyn')
Family links with cricket: 'Brother Simon plays good club cricket for Wembdon CC'
Education: Queen's College, Taunton; College of St Mark and St John, Plymouth
Qualifications: GCSEs, 2 A-levels, BA (Hons) Sports Science and IT
Career outside cricket: Builder
Overseas tours: England U17 to Northern Ireland (ECC Colts Festival) 1999
Overseas teams played for: Wanneroo DCC, Perth 2000-01; Sturt Hill, Adelaide 2006-07

Career highlights to date: 'Gaining a professional contract'
Cricket moments to forget: 'Knee injury 2005-06'
Cricketers particularly admired: Shane Warne, Ricky Ponting
Young players to look out for: Alex Bailey
Other sports played: Hockey, surfing
Other sports followed: Football (Tottenham Hotspur FC)
Favourite band: Jack Johnson, Jason Mraz
Relaxations: 'Playing the guitar'
Extras: Brian Johnston Memorial Trust Scholarship to Adelaide (with Terry Jenner) 1999. NBC Denis Compton Award for the most promising young Gloucestershire player 2007
Best batting: 35* Gloucestershire v Loughborough UCCE, Bristol 2008
Best bowling: 1-12 Gloucestershire v Worcestershire, Worcester 2008

2008 Season

	M	Inn	NO	Runs	HS	Avg	100	50	Ct	St	Balls	Runs	Wkts	Avg	BB	5I	10M
Test																	
FC	4	6	2	58	35 *	14.50	-	-	1	-	573	271	3	90.33	1-12	-	-
ODI																	
List A																	
20/20 Int																	
20/20																	

Career Performances

	M	Inn	NO	Runs	HS	Avg	100	50	Ct	St	Balls	Runs	Wkts	Avg	BB	5I	10M
Test																	
FC	4	6	2	58	35 *	14.50	-	-	1	-	573	271	3	90.33	1-12	-	-
ODI																	
List A	2	1	0	15	15	15.00	-	-	-	-	0	0	0		-	-	
20/20 Int																	
20/20																	

30. England were whitewashed 5-0 in the Ashes tour of 2006-07. During which tour of Australia had that happened previously?

GODDARD, L. J. Durham

Name: Lee James Goddard
Role: Right-hand bat, wicket-keeper
Born: 22 October 1982, Dewsbury
Height: 5ft 10½in **Weight:** 11st 4lbs
Nickname: Godders, Goddy
County debut: 2004 (Derbyshire), 2007 (Durham)
Parents: Steve and Lynda
Marital status: Engaged to Kelly Moore
Family links with cricket: 'Dad is a cricket badger!'
Education: Batley Grammar School; Loughborough University
Qualifications: GCSEs, Foundation degree in Sports Science, ECB Level 1 coaching
Career outside cricket: 'Relaxing; bit of this, bit of that'
Overseas teams played for: Parramatta DCC, Sydney 2001-02
Career highlights to date: 'Five catches in first innings on Championship debut for Derbyshire [v Hampshire 2004]. Fifty off 31 balls (fastest first-class fifty in Durham history) on first-class debut for Durham [v Sri Lanka A 2007]. Friends Provident win [2007] (Durham's first trophy)'

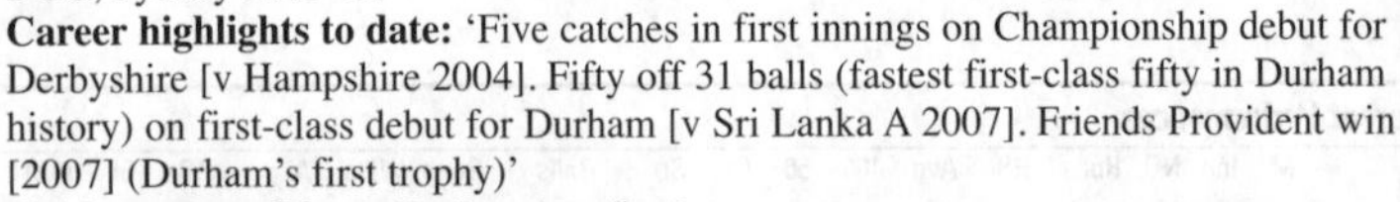

Cricket superstitions: 'Left pad on first'
Cricketers particularly admired: Adam Gilchrist, Damien Martyn, Paul Nixon
Young players to look out for: Scott Borthwick, Karl Turner, Rich Hopwood
Other sports played: Squash, golf, football (Huddersfield Town aged 9-15)
Other sports followed: Football (Leeds United), rugby league (Leeds Rhinos)
Favourite band: Jack Johnson
Relaxations: 'Gym; planning the wedding!'
Extras: Played in Yorkshire's U17 County Championship winning side. Played for Yorkshire Board XI in the 2003 C&G. Played for Loughborough UCCE in 2003. Was in British Universities squad for match v Zimbabweans 2003. Derbyshire CCC 2nd XI Player of the Year 2004. Shared with Graham Wagg in a new record seventh-wicket partnership for Derbyshire in matches v Surrey (181) at Derby 2006. Scored 31-ball fifty on first-class debut for Durham v Sri Lanka A at Riverside 2007, breaking record (jointly held by Ian Botham, Martin Speight and Phil Mustard) for fastest first-class fifty for the county
Opinions on cricket: 'Limit on Kolpaks per squad (there must be some way to limit the intrusion). More opportunities for youth! That's what academies are there for!'
Best batting: 91 Derbyshire v Surrey, Derby 2006

2008 Season

	M	Inn	NO	Runs	HS	Avg	100	50	Ct	St	Balls	Runs	Wkts	Avg	BB	5I	10M
Test																	
FC																	
ODI																	
List A	2	2	1	31	16	31.00	-	-	5	-	0	0	0		-	-	
20/20 Int																	
20/20																	

Career Performances

	M	Inn	NO	Runs	HS	Avg	100	50	Ct	St	Balls	Runs	Wkts	Avg	BB	5I	10M
Test																	
FC	10	14	4	324	91	32.40	-	2	22	-	0	0	0		-	-	-
ODI																	
List A	8	7	3	100	36	25.00	-	-	13	-	0	0	0		-	-	
20/20 Int																	
20/20	1	0	0	0	0		-	-	-	-	0	0	0		-	-	

GODLEMAN, B-A. Middlesex

Name: Billy-Ashley (Billy) Godleman
Role: Left-hand opening bat, right-arm leg-spin bowler
Born: 11 February 1989, Islington, London
Height: 6ft 2in **Weight:** 13st
Nickname: G
County debut: 2005
Place in batting averages: 129th av 29.44 (2007 84th av. 38.27)
Parents: Ashley Fitzgerald and John Godleman
Marital status: Single
Family links with cricket: 'Dad played club cricket for Hampstead'
Education: Central Foundation School; Islington Green School
Qualifications: 7 GCSEs
Overseas tours: England U16 to South Africa 2004-05; England U19 to Malaysia 2006-07, to Malaysia (U19 World Cup) 2007-08; England Performance Programme to India 2007-08

Career highlights to date: 'Maiden first-class century – 113* v Somerset'
Cricketers particularly admired: Graeme Smith, Andy Flower, Matthew Hayden
Young players to look out for: Steven Finn, Eoin Morgan, Tom Westley, Ben Brown, Alex Wakely
Other sports played: Football
Other sports followed: Football (Liverpool FC), cricket (Brondesbury)
Favourite band: Pink Floyd, Led Zeppelin, Fleetwood Mac
Relaxations: 'Spending time with my little brother Johnny and family; reading; watching Liverpool FC'
Extras: Named best player in country U13, U14 and U15 at regional tournaments; scored 168-ball 143 for South v West at Bunbury U15 Festival at Nottingham 2004. Made 2nd XI Trophy debut for Middlesex 2003. Scored 69* on first-class debut v Cambridge UCCE at Fenner's 2005. NBC Denis Compton Award for the most promising young Middlesex player 2005, 2007. Represented England U19 2006, 2007, 2008. Scored maiden first-class century (113*) on Championship debut v Somerset at Taunton 2007. Made over 1000 runs in all forms of cricket in 2008
Opinions on cricket: 'You get out what you put in.'
Best batting: 113* Middlesex v Somerset, Taunton 2007

2008 Season

	M	Inn	NO	Runs	HS	Avg	100	50	Ct	St	Balls	Runs	Wkts	Avg	BB	5I	10M
Test																	
FC	15	25	0	736	106	29.44	1	3	5	-	0	0	0		-	-	-
ODI																	
List A	6	6	1	151	48	30.20	-	-	3	-	0	0	0		-	-	
20/20 Int																	
20/20	11	11	0	201	69	18.27	-	2	7	-	0	0	0		-	-	

Career Performances

	M	Inn	NO	Runs	HS	Avg	100	50	Ct	St	Balls	Runs	Wkts	Avg	BB	5I	10M
Test																	
FC	31	50	3	1647	113 *	35.04	2	10	27	-	30	35	0		-	-	-
ODI																	
List A	8	8	1	184	48	26.28	-	-	3	-	0	0	0		-	-	
20/20 Int																	
20/20	15	14	0	272	69	19.42	-	2	7	-	0	0	0		-	-	

GOODWIN, M. W. Sussex

Name: Murray William Goodwin
Role: Right-hand bat, right-arm medium/ leg-spin bowler
Born: 11 December 1972, Harare, Zimbabwe
Height: 5ft 9in **Weight:** 11st 2lbs
Nickname: Muzza, Fuzz, Goodie
County debut: 2001
County cap: 2001
Test debut: 1997-98
ODI debut: 1997-98
1000 runs in a season: 6
1st-Class 200s: 6
1st-Class 300s: 1
Place in batting averages: 10th av 58.39 (2007 23rd av. 55.18)
Parents: Penny and George
Wife and date of marriage: Tarsha, 13 December 1997
Children: Jayden William; Ashton George, 19 November 2006
Family links with cricket: 'Dad is a coach. Eldest brother played for Zimbabwe'
Education: St John's, Harare, Zimbabwe; Newtonmoore Senior High, Bunbury, Western Australia
Qualifications: Level II coach
Overseas tours: Australian Cricket Academy to South Africa 1992, to Sri Lanka and India 1993; Zimbabwe to Sri Lanka and New Zealand 1997-98, to Bangladesh (Wills International Cup) 1998-99, to Pakistan 1998-99, to UK, Ireland and Netherlands (World Cup) 1999, to South Africa 1999-2000, to West Indies 1999-2000, to England 2000
Overseas teams played for: Excelsior, Netherlands 1997; Mashonaland 1997-98 – 1998-99; Western Australia 1994-95 – 1996-97, 2000-01 – 2005-06; Warriors 2006-07; Ahmedabad Rockets (ICL) 2007-08 –
Career highlights to date: 'Becoming the highest individual scorer in Sussex's history – 335* v Leicestershire, September 2003 at Hove. Broke Duleepsinhji's record of 333 in 1930'
Cricketers particularly admired: Allan Border, Steve Waugh, Curtly Ambrose, Sachin Tendulkar
Other sports played: Hockey (WA Country), golf, tennis
Other sports followed: 'All'
Favourite band: 'No real favourites; I have a very eclectic collection'
Relaxations: 'Socialising with friends'

Extras: Attended Australian Cricket Academy. Scored 166* v Pakistan at Bulawayo 1997-98, in the process sharing with Andy Flower (100*) in the highest partnership for Zimbabwe for any wicket in Tests (277*). His international awards include Man of the Match in the second ODI v Sri Lanka at Colombo 1997-98 (111) and in the second Test v England at Trent Bridge 2000 (148*). Retired from international cricket in 2000. Scored double century (203*) and century (115) v Nottinghamshire at Trent Bridge 2001 and again (119/205*) v Surrey at Hove 2007. Joint Sussex Player of the Year (with Richard Montgomerie) 2001. Scored 335* v Leicestershire at Hove 2003, surpassing K. S. Duleepsinhji's 333 in 1930 to set a new record for the highest individual score for Sussex (and winning the Sussex Outstanding Performance of the Year Award 2003). Scored 214* v Warwickshire at Hove 2006, in the process sharing with Michael Yardy (159*) in a new Sussex record partnership for the third wicket (385*). Overseas player with Sussex 2001-04. His 87* against Nottinghamshire in the final Pro40 Division 1 game of 2008 helped Sussex secure the trophy. Finished top of the Sussex first-class batting averages 2008. Is no longer considered an overseas player
Best batting: 335* Sussex v Leicestershire, Hove 2003
Best bowling: 2-23 Zimbabweans v Lahore City, Lahore 1998-99

2008 Season

	M	Inn	NO	Runs	HS	Avg	100	50	Ct	St	Balls	Runs	Wkts	Avg	BB	5I	10M
Test																	
FC	16	25	2	1343	184	58.39	6	5	3	-	0	0	0		-	-	-
ODI																	
List A	12	10	4	348	87 *	58.00	-	3	3	-	0	0	0		-	-	
20/20 Int																	
20/20	10	10	2	345	79 *	43.12	-	3	2	-	0	0	0		-	-	

Career Perfomances

	M	Inn	NO	Runs	HS	Avg	100	50	Ct	St	Balls	Runs	Wkts	Avg	BB	5I	10M
Test	19	37	4	1414	166 *	42.84	3	8	10	-	119	69	0		-	-	-
FC	234	408	32	18380	335 *	48.88	58	77	133	-	701	363	7	51.85	2-23	-	-
ODI	71	70	3	1818	112 *	27.13	2	8	20	-	248	210	4	52.50	1-12	-	
List A	311	299	36	9309	167	35.39	12	59	97	-	351	306	7	43.71	1-9	-	
20/20 Int																	
20/20	46	41	5	993	102 *	27.58	1	5	7	-	0	0	0		-	-	

31. Name the batsman who made 'a pair' in his only Test against Australia, in 1880. He had a rather famous brother.

GOUGH, D. Yorkshire

Name: Darren Gough
Role: Right-hand bat, right-arm fast bowler;
Born: 18 September 1970, Barnsley
Height: 5ft 11in **Weight:** 13st 9lbs
Nickname: Rhino, Dazzler
County debut: 1989 (Yorkshire), 2004 (Essex)
County cap: 1993 (Yorkshire), 2004 (Essex)
Benefit: 2001 (Yorkshire)
Test debut: 1994
ODI debut: 1994
Twenty20 Int debut: 2005
50 wickets in a season: 4
Place in batting averages: 242nd av. 15.64
Place in bowling averages: 20th av. 23.67 (2006 35th av. 28.96)
Parents: Trevor and Christine
Children: Liam James, 24 November 1994; Brennan Kyle, 9 December 1997
Education: Priory Comprehensive; Airedale and Wharfedale College (part-time)

Qualifications: 2 O-levels, 5 CSEs, BTEC Leisure, NCA coaching award
Overseas tours: England YC to Australia 1989-90; Yorkshire to Barbados 1989-90, to South Africa 1991-92, 1992-93; England A to South Africa 1993-94; England to Australia 1994-95, to South Africa 1995-96, to India and Pakistan (World Cup) 1995-96, to Zimbabwe and New Zealand 1996-97, to Australia 1998-99, to Sharjah (Coca-Cola Cup) 1998-99, to South Africa and Zimbabwe 1999-2000, to Kenya (ICC Knockout Trophy) 2000-01, to Pakistan and Sri Lanka 2000-01, to India and New Zealand 2001-02 (one-day series), to Australia 2002-03, to West Indies 2003-04 (one-day series), to Zimbabwe (one-day series) 2004-05, to South Africa 2004-05 (one-day series); ICC World XI to Australia (Tsunami Relief) 2004-05; England VI to Hong Kong 2006
Overseas teams played for: East Shirley, Christchurch, New Zealand 1991-92
Cricketers particularly admired: Shane Warne, Steve Waugh, Ian Botham, Michael Atherton, Malcolm Marshall
Other sports played: Golf, football
Other sports followed: Football (Barnsley and Tottenham Hotspur)
Relaxations: Golf, cinema
Extras: Yorkshire Sports Personality of the Year 1994. Cornhill England Player of the Year 1994-95, 1998-99. Whyte and Mackay Bowler of the Year 1996. Took hat-trick (Healy, MacGill, Miller) in the fifth Test v Australia at Sydney 1998-99. *Sheffield Star* Sports Personality of the Year. One of *Wisden*'s Five Cricketers of the Year 1999. Won Freeserve Fast Ball award 2000 for a delivery timed at 93.1 mph during the first Test v

Zimbabwe at Lord's. Vodafone England Cricketer of the Year 2000-01. *GQ* Sportsman of the Year 2001. Took 200th Test wicket (Rashid Latif) v Pakistan at Lord's 2001 in his 50th Test. His international awards include Man of the [Test] Series v Sri Lanka 2000-01 and England's Man of the [Test] Series v West Indies 2000. Retired from Test cricket during the 2003 season. Granted Freedom of the City of London in March 2004. Took 200th ODI wicket (Harbhajan Singh) v India at Lord's in the NatWest Challenge 2004, becoming the first England bowler to reach the milestone. Winner, with Lilia Kopylova, of *Strictly Come Dancing*, December 2005. Vice-captain of Essex 2005-06. Rejoined Yorkshire for 2007 as captain. Retired at the end of the 2008 season

Best batting: 121 Yorkshire v Warwickshire, Headingley 1996
Best bowling: 7-28 Yorkshire v Lancashire, Headingley 1995

2008 Season

	M	Inn	NO	Runs	HS	Avg	100	50	Ct	St	Balls	Runs	Wkts	Avg	BB	5I	10M
Test																	
FC	8	11	1	148	34	14.80	-	-	4	-	894	528	9	58.66	2-34	-	-
ODI																	
List A	17	3	1	38	33	19.00	-	-	4	-	632	510	21	24.28	3-17	-	
20/20 Int																	
20/20	9	4	3	26	20 *	26.00	-	-	1	-	204	242	8	30.25	2-28	-	

Career Performances

	M	Inn	NO	Runs	HS	Avg	100	50	Ct	St	Balls	Runs	Wkts	Avg	BB	5I	10M
Test	58	86	18	855	65	12.57	-	2	13	-	11821	6503	229	28.39	6-42	9	-
FC	248	326	60	4607	121	17.31	1	20	51	-	44023	23217	855	27.15	7-28	33	3
ODI	159	87	38	609	46 *	12.42	-	-	25	-	8470	6209	235	26.42	5-44	2	
List A	421	225	75	2092	72 *	13.94	-	2	73	-	20665	14457	598	24.17	7-27	7	
20/20 Int	2	0	0	0	0	-	-	-	-	-	41	49	3	16.33	3-16	-	
20/20	32	18	5	205	37	15.76	-	-	2	-	665	830	33	25.15	3-16	-	

32. Which wicketkeeper was responsible for a record 148 dismissals in Ashes Tests?

GRANT, R. N. Glamorgan

Name: Richard Neil Grant
Role: Right-hand bat, right-arm medium bowler; 'batter who bowls a little'
Born: 5 June 1984, Neath
Height: 5ft 10in **Weight:** 13st 8lbs
Nickname: Pingu, Wig, Shelf, Big-nose
County debut: 2004 (one-day), 2005 (first-class)
Place in batting averages: 185th av 21.72 (2007 164th av. 26.92)
Parents: Kevin ('Sven-Göran Eriksson') and Moira
Marital status: Single ('long-term girlfriend Samantha')
Family links with cricket: 'Brother Glamorgan 2nd XI, MCC YC (groundstaff); Dad local cricket (not very good, though)'
Education: Cefn Saeson Comprehensive, Neath; Neath Port Talbot College
Qualifications: 6 GCSEs, NVQ Level II Carpentry, Level II coaching award
Career outside cricket: '12-month contract'
Overseas tours: South Wales Junior League to Australia 1998; Wales U16 to Jersey 2000; Neath Port Talbot College to Goa 2001, to Malta 2002, to South Africa 2003
Overseas teams played for: Havelock North, Napier, New Zealand 2003-04; Balmain Tigers, Sydney 2007-08
Cricket moments to forget: 'None, they have all been great'
Cricket superstitions: 'Left pad on first'
Young players to look out for: James Harris, Sam Davies
Other sports played: Golf
Other sports followed: Football (Swansea City, Blackburn), rugby (Ospreys)
Favourite band: Timbaland
Relaxations: 'Spending time with girlfriend Samantha. Playing golf and swimming'
Extras: Neath Port Talbot College Sportsman of the Year 2002; Neath Port Talbot County Borough Council Sportsman of the Year 2002. Glamorgan 2nd XI Player of the Year 2005. Released at the end of the 2008 season
Opinions on cricket: 'Ninety overs in the day plus longer tea break.'
Best batting: 79 Glamorgan v Northamptonshire, Colwyn Bay 2007
Best bowling: 1-7 Glamorgan v Somerset, Taunton 2007

2008 Season

	M	Inn	NO	Runs	HS	Avg	100	50	Ct	St	Balls	Runs	Wkts	Avg	BB	5I	10M
Test																	
FC	6	11	0	239	75	21.72	-	2	5	-	102	44	1	44.00	1-8	-	-
ODI																	
List A	2	2	0	17	13	8.50	-	-	-	-	0	0	0		-	-	
20/20 Int																	
20/20	3	3	1	55	39 *	27.50	-	-	1	-	0	0	0		-	-	

Career Performances

	M	Inn	NO	Runs	HS	Avg	100	50	Ct	St	Balls	Runs	Wkts	Avg	BB	5I	10M
Test																	
FC	25	42	1	888	79	21.65	-	4	10	-	345	268	6	44.66	1-7	-	-
ODI																	
List A	41	38	2	679	45	18.86	-	-	9	-	247	315	7	45.00	2-21	-	
20/20 Int																	
20/20	19	17	2	388	77	25.86	-	2	7	-	63	130	7	18.57	4-38	-	

GREENIDGE, C. G. Gloucestershire

Name: Carl Gary Greenidge
Role: Right-hand bat, right-arm fast-medium bowler
Born: 20 April 1978, Basingstoke
Height: 5ft 10in **Weight:** 12st 8lbs
Nickname: Carlos, Gs, Jackal
County debut: 1998 (one-day, Surrey), 1999 (first-class, Surrey), 2002 (Northamptonshire), 2005 (Gloucestershire)
County cap: 2005 (Gloucestershire)
50 wickets in a season: 1
Place in bowling averages: 44th av. 26.85
Parents: Gordon and Anita
Marital status: Single
Family links with cricket: Father Gordon played for Hampshire and West Indies, as did cousin (on mother's side) Andy Roberts
Education: St Michael's, Barbados; Heathcote School, Chingford; City of Westminster College
Qualifications: GNVQ Leisure and Tourism, NCA senior coaching award

Cricket moments to forget: 'Yorkshire v Northants, April 2003, first game of the season – easily my worst ever game' (*Northants conceded 673 runs and lost by an innings*)
Cricket superstitions: 'None'
Cricketers particularly admired: Malcolm Marshall, Michael Holding, Viv Richards
Other sports played: Football ('PlayStation!')
Other sports followed: Football (Arsenal), basketball (LA Lakers)
Favourite band: Bob Marley and the Wailers
Relaxations: 'PlayStation, movies, reading, music'
Extras: Spent a year on Lord's groundstaff. Took 5-60 (8-124 the match) on Championship debut for Surrey, v Yorkshire at The Oval 1999. Was released by Gloucestershire at the end of September 2008
Best batting: 46 Northamptonshire v Derbyshire, Derby 2002
Best bowling: 6-40 Northamptonshire v Durham, Riverside 2002

2008 Season

	M	Inn	NO	Runs	HS	Avg	100	50	Ct	St	Balls	Runs	Wkts	Avg	BB	5I	10M
Test																	
FC	1	1	0	1	1	1.00	-	-	-	-	126	62	5	12.40	5-62	1	-
ODI																	
List A	2	1	0	7	7	7.00	-	-	-	-	60	61	0		-	-	
20/20 Int																	
20/20	2	1	1	0	0*		-	-	-	-	36	71	0		-	-	

Career Performances

	M	Inn	NO	Runs	HS	Avg	100	50	Ct	St	Balls	Runs	Wkts	Avg	BB	5I	10M
Test																	
FC	50	61	8	444	46	8.37	-	-	18	-	7500	5034	145	34.71	6-40	6	-
ODI																	
List A	67	29	11	147	29	8.16	-	-	16	-	2849	2683	77	34.84	4-15	-	
20/20 Int																	
20/20	31	10	6	34	20	8.50	-	-	11	-	621	914	32	28.56	3-15	-	

-

33. Which two Australian players received official reprimands for betting during the 'Botham Test' at Headingley in 1981?

GRIFFITHS, D. A. Hampshire

Name: David Andrew Griffiths
Role: Left-hand bat, right-arm fast-medium bowler
Born: 10 September 1985, Newport, Isle of Wight
Height: 6ft **Weight:** 12st 7lbs
Nickname: Griff
County debut: 2006
Place in bowling averages: 93rd av. 34.25
Parents: Adrian Griffiths and Lizbeth Porter; Dave Porter (stepfather); Sharon Griffiths (stepmother)
Marital status: Single ('girlfriend Sophie')
Family links with cricket: 'Father captained Wales. Stepfather captained Isle of Wight. Uncles play league cricket'
Education: Sandown High School, Isle of Wight
Qualifications: Levels 1 and 2 cricket coaching
Career outside cricket: 'Coaching and odd jobs'
Overseas tours: West of England U15 to West Indies 2001; England U19 to India 2004-05
Overseas teams played for: Melville, Perth 2007
Career highlights to date: 'Making Championship debut against Durham [2007]'
Cricket moments to forget: 'The first ball in Championship cricket – Ottis Gibson hitting me on the head'
Cricket superstitions: 'Turn right at end of run-up'
Cricketers particularly admired: Darren Gough, Brett Lee
Young players to look out for: Liam Dawson, Benny Howell
Other sports played: Football (Isle of Wight U11-U18), rugby (IOW)
Other sports followed: Football (Man Utd), rugby league (St Helens)
Favourite band: 'No band – R&B music'
Relaxations: Golf
Extras: Represented England U19 2004. Southern League Young Player of the Year 2004. Took 3-13 on Twenty20 debut v Essex at The Rose Bowl 2007
Best batting: 31* Hampshire v Surrey, Rose Bowl 2007
Best bowling: 4-46 Hampshire v Durham, Riverside 2007

2008 Season

	M	Inn	NO	Runs	HS	Avg	100	50	Ct	St	Balls	Runs	Wkts	Avg	BB	5I	10M
Test																	
FC	1	1	0	4	4	4.00	-	-	-	-	252	178	2	89.00	1-38	-	-
ODI																	
List A	3	1	1	3	3 *	-	-	-	1	-	126	142	1	142.00	1-53	-	
20/20 Int																	
20/20																	

Career Performances

	M	Inn	NO	Runs	HS	Avg	100	50	Ct	St	Balls	Runs	Wkts	Avg	BB	5I	10M
Test																	
FC	7	10	4	62	31 *	10.33	-	-	1	-	891	618	14	44.14	4-46	-	-
ODI																	
List A	3	1	1	3	3 *	-	-	-	1	-	126	142	1	142.00	1-53	-	
20/20 Int																	
20/20	3	1	1	4	4 *	-	-	-	-	-	42	55	3	18.33	3-13	-	

GROENEWALD, T. D. Derbyshire

Name: Timothy (Tim) Duncan Groenewald
Role: Right-hand bat, right-arm fast-medium bowler; bowling all-rounder
Born: 10 January 1984, Pietermaritzburg, South Africa
Height: 6ft 2in **Weight:** 13st 2lbs
Nickname: Groeners
County debut: 2006 (Warwickshire)
Place in batting averages: (2007 223rd av. 19.00)
Place in bowling averages: 55th av 27.54
Parents: Neil and Tessa
Wife and date of marriage: Michelle, 5 January 2008
Education: Maritzburg College, Natal; University of South Africa
Qualifications: Matric, degree (BComm) in Marketing
Career outside cricket: Part-time student
Off-season: 'Three months in South Africa with family. January at Edgbaston, training, February and March in Bloemfontein with Warwickshire'

Overseas tours: Natal U15 to UK 1999; Warwickshire to Grenada 2007
Overseas teams played for: Zingari CC, Natal 1999-2005; Natal Dolphins 2002-03; KZN Inland 2004-05; Rovers CC 2006
Career highlights to date: 'Getting Kevin Pietersen out in the Friends Provident semi-final [2007]. Playing Twenty20 against Gloucestershire in 2008, putting on 95 with Tony Frost in six overs to tie the game - I was 39 not out off 18 balls'
Cricket moments to forget: 'Double relegation in 2007. Every six I've ever been hit for. Losing to Kent in the Twenty20 quarter-final in 2008'
Cricketers particularly admired: Allan Donald, Steve Waugh, Hansie Cronje, Brett Lee
Young players to look out for: Richard Johnson
Other sports played: Hockey (Midlands U21 A 2003), tennis and golf ('socially')
Other sports followed: Super 14 rugby (Natal Sharks)
Favourite band: Coldplay, Mika
Relaxations: 'Golf, and fishing on the Natal south coast.'
Extras: Leading wicket-taker at National U19 Week and represented South African Schools Colts U19. Seventh in the Sky Sports Sixes League 2007 with 20. In October 2008 joined Derbyshire from Warwickshire for the 2009 season.
Opinions on cricket: 'The game has moved towards my preferred format, Twenty20, but I don't think anything should be taken away from Test or first-class cricket, they're still very important for player development. I don't think too much Twenty20 should be played because of overkill, but if it's run properly it will be great for the future.'
Best batting: 78 Warwickshire v Bangladesh A, Edgbaston 2008
Best bowling: 5-24 Warwickshire v Cambridge UCCE, Fenners 2008

2008 Season

	M	Inn	NO	Runs	HS	Avg	100	50	Ct	St	Balls	Runs	Wkts	Avg	BB	5I	10M
Test																	
FC	3	3	0	78	78	26.00	-	1	2	-	552	303	11	27.54	5-24	1	-
ODI																	
List A	9	6	1	85	33	17.00	-	-	2	-	200	218	5	43.60	2-18	-	
20/20 Int																	
20/20	11	6	4	87	39 *	43.50	-	-	5	-	150	218	10	21.80	3-40	-	

Career Performances

	M	Inn	NO	Runs	HS	Avg	100	50	Ct	St	Balls	Runs	Wkts	Avg	BB	5I	10M
Test																	
FC	17	21	4	368	78	21.64	-	2	11	-	2049	1129	26	43.42	5-24	1	-
ODI																	
List A	27	19	3	217	36	13.56	-	-	6	-	754	771	19	40.57	3-25	-	
20/20 Int																	
20/20	21	13	6	227	41	32.42	-	-	10	-	288	426	16	26.62	3-40	-	

GUY, S. M. Yorkshire

Name: Simon Mark Guy
Role: Right-hand bat, wicket-keeper
Born: 17 November 1978, Rotherham
Height: 5ft 7in **Weight:** 10st 7lbs
Nickname: Rat
County debut: 2000
Parents: Darrell and Denise
Wife and date of marriage: Suzanne, 13 October 2001
Children: Isaac Simon, 15 January 2004; Rowan Joseph, 25 March 2007
Family links with cricket: 'Father played for Nottinghamshire and Worcestershire 2nd XI and for Rotherham Town CC. Brothers play local cricket for Treeton CC'
Education: Wickersley Comprehensive School
Qualifications: GNVQ in Leisure and Recreation, Level 3 coaching award
Overseas tours: Yorkshire to South Africa 1999, 2001, to Grenada 2002
Overseas teams played for: Orange CYMS, NSW 1999-2000
Career highlights to date: 'Playing the last ever County Championship game at Southampton [Northlands Road in 2000] and winning off the last ball with 13 Yorkshire and past Yorkshire men on the pitch at the same time'
Cricket moments to forget: 'On my debut against the Zimbabweans, smashing a door after getting out – but I still say it was an accident'
Cricket superstitions: 'Just a lot of routines'
Cricketers particularly admired: Jack Russell, Darren Lehmann
Young players to look out for: Joe Root
Other sports played: 'I like to play all sports', rugby (played for South Yorkshire and Yorkshire)
Other sports followed: Rugby (Rotherham RUFC), 'Treeton Welfare CC, where all my family play'
Favourite band: My Chemical Romance
Relaxations: 'Playing all sports, socialising with friends, watching cartoons, and eating a lot'
Extras: Topped Yorkshire 2nd XI batting averages 1998 (106.00). Awarded 2nd XI cap 2000. Took five catches in an innings for first time for Yorkshire 1st XI v Surrey at Scarborough 2000
Opinions on cricket: 'The division structure has improved the standard of competitiveness of the county championship.'
Best batting: 52* Yorkshire v Durham, Headingley 2006

2008 Season

	M	Inn	NO	Runs	HS	Avg	100	50	Ct	St	Balls	Runs	Wkts	Avg	BB	5I	10M
Test																	
FC																	
ODI																	
List A	1	1	0	6	6	6.00	-	-	-	-	0	0	0		-	-	
20/20 Int																	
20/20	4	2	0	11	7	5.50	-	-	1	-	0	0	0		-	-	

Career Performances

	M	Inn	NO	Runs	HS	Avg	100	50	Ct	St	Balls	Runs	Wkts	Avg	BB	5I	10M
Test																	
FC	36	50	6	727	52 *	16.52	-	1	97	12	24	8	0		-	-	-
ODI																	
List A	26	19	3	260	40	16.25	-	-	23	7	0	0	0		-	-	
20/20 Int																	
20/20	4	2	0	11	7	5.50	-	-	1	-	0	0	0		-	-	

HALES, A. D. Nottinghamshire

Name: Alexander (Alex) Daniel Hales
Role: Right-hand bat, off-spin bowler, part-time wicket-keeper
Born: 3 January 1989, Hillingdon, Middlesex
Height: 6ft 5in **Weight:** 13st 6lbs
Nickname: Halesy, Trigg
County debut: 2008
Parents: Gary and Lisa
Marital status: Single
Education: Chesham High School, Chesham, Buckinghamshire
Qualifications: 10 GCSEs, 3 AS-levels
Overseas tours: London County CC to Cape Town 2006; MCC YC to St Kitts and Nevis 2007
Overseas teams played for: Pennant Hills District CC, Sydney 2007
Cricket moments to forget: 'Dropping a sitter against Kent 2nd XI for MCC Young Cricketers – if I had held the catch we would have won the game and qualified for the semi-finals!'
Cricket superstitions: 'Always put my left pad on before my right one'

Cricketers particularly admired: Ian Bell, Nick Lines, Vinnie Fazio
Young players to look out for: Lee Hodgson, Luke Fletcher, Dave Cranfield-Thompson
Other sports played: 'Play a bit of football in the winter for my local team. Used to play county tennis and table tennis'
Other sports followed: Football (Arsenal)
Favourite band: Oasis
Relaxations: 'Enjoy playing poker and socialising with mates'
Extras: Once scored 52 in one over on the Lord's Nursery ground – over included eight sixes and a four plus three no-balls for an overall total of 55. Played for Buckinghamshire in Minor Counties competitions 2006, 2007. Played for MCC YC 2006, 2007. NBC Denis Compton Award for the most promising young Nottinghamshire player 2008. 'Grandfather once took Rod Laver to five sets at Wimbledon'
Opinions on cricket: 'The tempo of cricket has become a lot higher with the introduction of Twenty20 and Pro40 and this is changing the overall image of the game.'

2008 Season

	M	Inn	NO	Runs	HS	Avg	100	50	Ct	St	Balls	Runs	Wkts	Avg	BB	5I	10M
Test																	
FC	1	0	0	0	0		-	-	-	-	0	0	0		-	-	-
ODI																	
List A	1	0	0	0	0		-	-	-	-	0	0	0		-	-	
20/20 Int																	
20/20																	

Career Performances

	M	Inn	NO	Runs	HS	Avg	100	50	Ct	St	Balls	Runs	Wkts	Avg	BB	5I	10M
Test																	
FC	1	0	0	0	0		-	-	-	-	0	0	0		-	-	-
ODI																	
List A	1	0	0	0	0		-	-	-	-	0	0	0		-	-	
20/20 Int																	
20/20																	

34. Name the Australian who scored his 5,000th run during an innings of 196 at Lord's in 1985.

HALL, A. J. Northamptonshire

Name: Andrew James Hall
Role: Right-hand bat, right-arm fast-medium bowler; all-rounder
Born: 31 July 1975, Johannesburg, South Africa
Height: 6ft **Weight:** 14st
Nickname: Hally
County debut: 2003 (Worcestershire), 2005 (Kent), 2008 (Northamptonshire)
County cap: 2003 (Worcestershire colours), 2005 (Kent)
Test debut: 2001-02
ODI debut: 1998-99
Twenty20 Int debut: 2005-06
Place in batting averages: 106th av 32.12 (2007 145th av. 29.33)
Place in bowling averages: 19th av 22.29 (2007 118th av. 40.66)
Parents: John and Frances
Wife and date of marriage: Leanie, 2 September 2000
Education: Hoërskool Alberton
Qualifications: Level 3 coaching
Off-season: 'Playing ICL in India, and beach cricket in Australia'
Overseas tours: South Africa to Sri Lanka (Singer Triangular Series) 2000, to Australia (Super Challenge) 2000, to Singapore (Godrej Singapore Challenge) 2000-01, to Kenya (ICC Knockout Trophy) 2000-01, to Bangladesh (TVS Cup) 2003, to England 2003, to Pakistan 2003-04, to India 2004-05, to West Indies 2004-05, to India (one-day series) 2005-06, to Australia 2005-06 (VB Series), to Sri Lanka 2006, to India (ICC Champions Trophy) 2006-07, to West Indies (World Cup) 2006-07, to Ireland (one-day series v India) 2007; South Africa A to Zimbabwe 2007-08
Overseas teams played for: Transvaal/Gauteng 1994-95 – 2000-01; Easterns 2001-02 – 2003-04; Lions 2004-05 – 2005-06; Dolphins 2006-07; Chandigarh Lions (ICL) 2007-08 –
Career highlights to date: 'Scoring 163 against India in Kanpur, and taking 5-18 against England in the 2007 World Cup'
Cricket moments to forget: 'Losing to Australia in the World Cup semi-final in 2007'
Cricketers particularly admired: Ray Jennings, Clive Rice, Jimmy Cook
Young players to look out for: Alex Wakely
Other sports played: Golf (12 handicap)
Other sports followed: Formula One (Ferrari), rugby (Golden Lions)

Favourite band: Crowded House
Relaxations: 'Movies and shopping with Leanie'
Extras: Played for South Africa Academy 1997. Was shot in the hand and face by a mugger in Johannesburg in 1999 and was car-jacked in 2002. Man of the Match in the tied second indoor ODI v Australia at Melbourne 2000 (37/2-8). His other international awards include Man of the Match in the first Test v India at Kanpur 2004-05 (163), in the fifth ODI v New Zealand at Centurion 2005-06 (4-23) and v England at Bridgetown in the 2006-07 World Cup (5-18). One of *South African Cricket Annual*'s five Cricketers of the Year 2002. His South African domestic awards include Man of the SuperSport Series 2002-03 and Man of the Match in the final (6-77/5-22). An overseas player with Worcestershire 2003-04. Man of the Match v Lancashire in the C&G semi-final at Worcester 2003. An overseas player with Kent 2005-07. Retired from international cricket in late summer 2007. Left Kent at the end of the 2007 season and joined Northamptonshire for 2008. Took 20 wickets in Twenty20 matches at a fairly economical rate. Is no longer considered an overseas player
Opinions on cricket: 'I don't think four-day first-class cricket should be shortened to three days as it would only increase the gap between Test and first-class.'
Best batting: 163 South Africa v India, Kanpur 2004-05
Best bowling: 6-77 Easterns v Western Province, Benoni 2002-03

2008 Season

	M	Inn	NO	Runs	HS	Avg	100	50	Ct	St	Balls	Runs	Wkts	Avg	BB	5I	10M
Test																	
FC	10	9	1	257	58	32.12	-	2	19	-	1042	535	24	22.29	5-81	1	-
ODI																	
List A	8	5	0	93	72	18.60	-	1	1	-	270	296	11	26.90	3-39	-	
20/20 Int																	
20/20	9	8	1	233	66 *	33.28	-	3	2	-	205	271	20	13.55	6-21	2	

Career Performances

	M	Inn	NO	Runs	HS	Avg	100	50	Ct	St	Balls	Runs	Wkts	Avg	BB	5I	10M
Test	21	33	4	760	163	26.20	1	3	16	-	3001	1617	45	35.93	3-1	-	-
FC	136	193	26	5610	163	33.59	5	38	110	-	22252	10528	406	25.93	6-77	14	1
ODI	88	56	13	905	81	21.04	-	3	29	-	3341	2515	95	26.47	5-18	1	
List A	250	194	34	4779	129 *	29.86	5	26	71	-	10182	7720	288	26.80	5-18	1	
20/20 Int	2	1	0	11	11	11.00	-	-	-	-	48	60	3	20.00	3-22	-	
20/20	40	37	3	829	66 *	24.38	-	4	12	-	829	1086	57	19.05	6-21	2	

HAMILTON-BROWN, R. J. Sussex

Name: Rory James Hamilton-Brown
Role: Right-hand bat, right-arm off-spin bowler
Born: 3 September 1987, London
Height: 6ft **Weight:** 13st 7lbs
Nickname: Bear, Stewi, RHB
County debut: 2005 (Surrey), 2008 (Sussex)
Parents: Roger and Holly
Marital status: Single
Family links with cricket: 'Dad played for Warwickshire'
Education: Millfield School
Qualifications: 9 GCSEs, 3 A-levels
Overseas tours: England U16 to South Africa; England U19 to Bangladesh 2005-06, to Sri Lanka (U19 World Cup) 2005-06
Career highlights to date: 'Facing Mushtaq Ahmed on debut against Sussex in the totesport League'

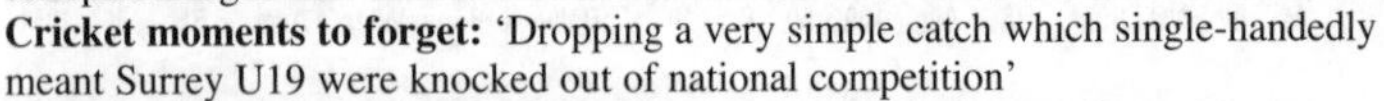

Cricket moments to forget: 'Dropping a very simple catch which single-handedly meant Surrey U19 were knocked out of national competition'
Cricket superstitions: 'None'
Cricketers particularly admired: Damien Martyn, Mark Ramprakash, Alec Stewart
Young players to look out for: Billy Godleman, Ben Wright
Other sports played: Rugby (England U16, England Junior National Academy)
Other sports followed: Football (Birmingham City)
Favourite band: Donell Jones, Trey Songz
Relaxations: 'Relaxing with friends'
Extras: Captained England U15. *Daily Telegraph* Bunbury Scholar (Batsman) 2003. Broke Millfield batting record 2004 at 16. Made 2nd XI Championship debut 2004, scoring 43 and 84 v Sussex 2nd XI at Hove. Represented England U19 2006 and (as captain) 2007. Left Surrey at the end of the 2007 season and joined Sussex for 2008
Best batting: 62 Sussex v Durham, Hove 2008 (on Sussex debut)
Best bowling: 2-54 Sussex v Surrey, The Oval 2008

2008 Season

	M	Inn	NO	Runs	HS	Avg	100	50	Ct	St	Balls	Runs	Wkts	Avg	BB	5I	10M
Test																	
FC	2	3	0	108	62	36.00	-	1	-	-	137	85	3	28.33	2-54	-	-
ODI																	
List A	9	5	0	90	35	18.00	-	-	3	-	235	198	7	28.28	2-30	-	
20/20 Int																	
20/20	10	8	0	68	36	8.50	-	-	1	-	84	119	4	29.75	2-17	-	

Career Performances

	M	Inn	NO	Runs	HS	Avg	100	50	Ct	St	Balls	Runs	Wkts	Avg	BB	5I	10M
Test																	
FC	3	5	0	122	62	24.40	-	1	1	-	137	85	3	28.33	2-54	-	-
ODI																	
List A	18	13	1	161	35	13.41	-	-	6	-	403	357	13	27.46	3-28	-	
20/20 Int																	
20/20	10	8	0	68	36	8.50	-	-	1	-	84	119	4	29.75	2-17	-	

HANNON-DALBY, O. J. Yorkshire

Name: Oliver James Hannon-Dalby
Role: Left-hand bat, right-arm fast-medium bowler
Born: 20 June 1989, Halifax
Height: 6ft 7in **Weight:** 13st 8lbs
Nickname: Bunse, Dave, Shaggy
County debut: 2008
Parents: Sally Hannon and Stephen Dalby
Marital status: Single
Family links with cricket: 'Whole family on both sides play and support cricket'
Education: The Brooksbank School Sports College and Sixth Form; Leeds Metropolitan University
Qualifications: 13 GCSEs, 3 A-levels, 1 NVQ, Community Sports Leader Award and Higher Sports Leader Award
Career outside cricket: 'Teacher, coach'
Off-season: 'Studying at Leeds Met'
Overseas tours: Yorkshire Schools Cricket Association to Cape Town 2007; Yorkshire to Abu Dhabi 2008

Overseas teams played for: St Andrews, Bloemfontein 2008; Old Andreans, Bloemfontein 2008
Career highlights to date: 'Taking 6-32 v Scotland for Yorkshire 2nd XI 2007. First-class debut, May 2008'
Cricket moments to forget: 'Jersey Cricket Festival final 2005'
Cricket superstitions: 'None'
Cricketers particularly admired: Fred Hemmingway, Peter Blake, Brett Lee
Young players to look out for: Gary Ballance, Chris Allinson, Johnny Bairstow
Other sports played: Football (Hebden Bridge Saints, Copley United)
Other sports followed: Football (Leeds United), 'all England teams'
Injuries: Two weeks out mid-season with an Achilles impingement
Favourite band: Stone Roses, Arctic Monkeys, Oasis, The Verve
Relaxations: 'Snooker, guitar playing, golf'
Extras: Ian Steen Memorial Award 2004 for Most Improved U15 Player. YCB Alec Holdsworth U17 Bowling Award 2006. YCCSA Young Player of the Year 2007
Opinions on cricket: 'With the development of much larger bats and with shorter boundaries being used in recent years, it's definitely a batsman's game.'
Best batting: 1 Yorkshire v Surrey, The Oval 2008
Best bowling: 1-58 Yorkshire v Surrey, The Oval 2008

2008 Season

	M	Inn	NO	Runs	HS	Avg	100	50	Ct	St	Balls	Runs	Wkts	Avg	BB	5I	10M
Test																	
FC	1	1	0	1	1	1.00	-	-	-	-	174	114	1	114.00	1-58	-	-
ODI																	
List A																	
20/20 Int																	
20/20																	

Career Performances

	M	Inn	NO	Runs	HS	Avg	100	50	Ct	St	Balls	Runs	Wkts	Avg	BB	5I	10M
Test																	
FC	1	1	0	1	1	1.00	-	-	-	-	174	114	1	114.00	1-58	-	-
ODI																	
List A																	
20/20 Int																	
20/20																	

35. Which England bowler took six wickets in the first innings of the 2005 Old Trafford Test?

HARDINGES, M. A. Gloucestershire

Name: Mark Andrew Hardinges
Role: Right-hand bat, right-arm fast-medium bowler
Born: 5 February 1978, Gloucester
Height: 6ft 1in **Weight:** 13st 7lbs
Nickname: Dinges
County debut: 1999
County cap: 2004
Place in batting averages: 74th av 38.28 (2007 187th av. 23.92)
Place in bowling averages: 111th av 36.60 (2007 138th av. 51.37)
Parents: David and Jean
Marital status: Single
Family links with cricket: Brother and father played club cricket
Education: Malvern College; Bath University
Qualifications: 10 GCSEs, 3 A-levels, BSc (Hons) Economics and Politics
Overseas tours: Malvern College to South Africa 1996; Gloucestershire to South Africa 1999, 2000
Overseas teams played for: Newtown and Chilwell, Geelong, Australia 1997
Career highlights to date: 'Norwich Union debut v Notts 2001 – scored 65 and set [then] domestic one-day seventh-wicket partnership record (164) with J. Snape. Also Lord's final v Surrey'
Cricket moments to forget: 'Glos v Somerset [Norwich Union 2001] – bowled three overs for 30 and was run out for 0 on Sky TV'
Cricketers particularly admired: Kim Barnett, Steve Waugh, Mark Alleyne
Other sports played: Golf, tennis (Gloucester U14), football (university first team)
Other sports followed: Football (Tottenham)
Relaxations: Golf
Extras: Represented British Universities 2000. C&G Man of the Match award for his 4-19 v Shropshire at Shrewsbury School 2002. Scored maiden one-day century (111*) v Lancashire at Old Trafford in the totesport League 2005, in the process sharing with Ramnaresh Sarwan (118*) in a new competition record fifth-wicket partnership (221*). Released at the end of September 2008
Best batting: 172 Gloucestershire v OUCCE, The Parks 2002
Best bowling: 5-51 Gloucestershire v Kent, Maidstone 2005

2008 Season

	M	Inn	NO	Runs	HS	Avg	100	50	Ct	St	Balls	Runs	Wkts	Avg	BB	5I	10M
Test																	
FC	6	9	2	268	82	38.28	-	2	4	-	597	366	10	36.60	2-13	-	-
ODI																	
List A	12	8	4	218	80*	54.50	-	1	4	-	450	416	12	34.66	3-60	-	
20/20 Int																	
20/20	7	6	1	94	33*	18.80	-	-	1	-	144	170	7	24.28	4-30	-	

Career Performances

	M	Inn	NO	Runs	HS	Avg	100	50	Ct	St	Balls	Runs	Wkts	Avg	BB	5I	10M
Test																	
FC	50	76	9	1778	172	26.53	4	6	26	-	6396	3851	95	40.53	5-51	1	-
ODI																	
List A	85	74	14	1318	111*	21.96	1	7	32	-	2996	2744	77	35.63	4-19	-	
20/20 Int																	
20/20	43	31	6	529	94*	21.16	-	2	10	-	641	908	33	27.51	4-30	-	

HARINATH, A. Surrey

Name: Arun Harinath
Role: Left-hand bat, off-spin bowler
Born: 26 March 1987, Carshalton, Surrey
Height: 5ft 11in **Weight:** 11st 10lbs
Nickname: The Baron
County debut: No first-team appearance
Parents: Mala and Suppiah
Marital status: Single
Family links with cricket: Brother Muhunthan played for Surrey 2nd XI 2006
Education: Tiffin Boys Grammar School; Loughborough University
Overseas tours: Surrey U19 to Sri Lanka 2002, to Cape Town 2005; Surrey Academy to Perth 2004; England U17 to Netherlands 2004
Overseas teams played for: Randwick Petersham, Sydney 2005-06
Cricket moments to forget: 'Dropping Samit Patel against Nottinghamshire Seconds at Sutton'
Cricketers particularly admired: Steve Waugh, Michael Hussey, Justin Langer, Brian Lara, Rahul Dravid, Mohammad Yousuf

Young players to look out for: Muhunthan Harinath
Other sports played: Rugby, badminton
Other sports followed: Rugby (Bath), NFL (Atlanta Falcons)
Relaxations: 'Films and music mainly'
Extras: Made 2nd XI Championship debut 2003. Played for Loughborough UCCE 2007
Opinions on cricket: 'The harder you work, the more you will get out of the game.'
Best batting: 69 LUCCE v Worcestershire, Worcester 2007

2008 Season

	M	Inn	NO	Runs	HS	Avg	100	50	Ct	St	Balls	Runs	Wkts	Avg	BB	5I	10M
Test																	
FC	1	1	0	33	33	33.00	-	-	1	-	0	0	0		-	-	-
ODI																	
List A																	
20/20 Int																	
20/20																	

Career Performances

	M	Inn	NO	Runs	HS	Avg	100	50	Ct	St	Balls	Runs	Wkts	Avg	BB	5I	10M
Test																	
FC	4	6	0	161	69	26.83	-	2	4	-	0	0	0		-	-	-
ODI																	
List A																	
20/20 Int																	
20/20																	

36. He scored a century in the first match of the 1997 Ashes series, and this probably kept him his place in the side. Name him.

HARMISON, B. W. Durham

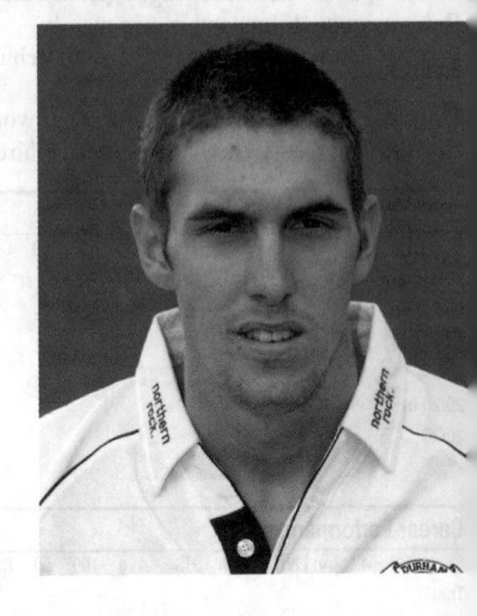

Name: Ben William Harmison
Role: Left-hand bat, right-arm fast-medium bowler; all-rounder
Born: 9 January 1986, Ashington, Northumberland
Height: 6ft 5in **Weight:** 14st
Nickname: Harmy
County debut: 2005 (one-day), 2006 (first-class)
Place in batting averages: 225th av 16.52 (2007 174th av. 25.57)
Place in bowling averages: 52nd av 16.27
Parents: Jimmy and Margaret
Marital status: Single
Family links with cricket: Brother Stephen plays for Durham and England. Father Jim and brother James play league cricket for Ashington CC
Education: Ashington High School
Overseas tours: England U19 to Bangladesh (U19 World Cup) 2003-04, to India 2004-05; Durham to India 2005
Career highlights to date: 'Two hundreds in my first two [first-class] games for Durham'
Cricket moments to forget: 'Getting a first-baller v Bangladesh A in a one-dayer'
Cricket superstitions: 'Left pad first'
Cricketers particularly admired: Andrew Flintoff
Young players to look out for: Moeen Ali 'and Durham Academy lads'
Other sports played: Golf, fishing, football
Other sports followed: Football (Newcastle United)
Relaxations: 'Fishing, listening to music'
Extras: NBC Denis Compton Award for the most promising young Durham player 2004, 2006, 2008. Represented England U19 2005. Scored century (110) on first-class debut v Oxford UCCE at The Parks 2006 and another (105) in his next first-class match v West Indies A at Riverside 2006
Opinions on cricket: 'More time for rest and preparation for the next game!'
Best batting: 110 Durham v OUCCE, The Parks 2006
Best bowling: 4-27 Durham v Surrey, Guildford 2008

2008 Season

	M	Inn	NO	Runs	HS	Avg	100	50	Ct	St	Balls	Runs	Wkts	Avg	BB	5I	10M
Test																	
FC	12	18	1	281	39	16.52	-	-	10	-	681	437	16	27.31	4-27	-	-
ODI																	
List A	15	13	2	206	31 *	18.72	-	-	2	-	295	256	9	28.44	3-43	-	
20/20 Int																	
20/20	7	3	2	21	21	21.00	-	-	4	-	42	63	1	63.00	1-21	-	

Career Performances

	M	Inn	NO	Runs	HS	Avg	100	50	Ct	St	Balls	Runs	Wkts	Avg	BB	5I	10M
Test																	
FC	30	51	5	1202	110	26.13	3	5	22	-	1001	723	19	38.05	4-27	-	-
ODI																	
List A	28	24	3	381	57	18.14	-	1	10	-	385	335	11	30.45	3-43	-	
20/20 Int																	
20/20	12	7	2	41	21	8.20	-	-	6	-	42	63	1	63.00	1-21	-	

HARMISON, S. J. Durham

Name: Stephen James Harmison
Role: Right-hand bat, right-arm fast bowler
Born: 23 October 1978, Ashington, Northumberland
Height: 6ft 4in **Weight:** 14st
Nickname: Harmy
County debut: 1996
County cap: 1999
Test debut: 2002
ODI debut: 2002-03
Twenty20 Int debut: 2005
50 wickets in a season: 4
Place in batting averages: 210th av 19.11 (2007 246th av. 14.72)
Place in bowling averages: 23rd av 22.86 (2007 15th av. 22.33)
Parents: Jimmy and Margaret
Wife and date of marriage: Hayley, 8 October 1999
Children: Emily Alice, 1 June 1999; Abbie Meg; Isabel Grace, May 2006
Family links with cricket: Brother James has played for Northumberland; brother Ben played for England U19 and is now at Durham

Education: Ashington High School
Overseas tours: England U19 to Pakistan 1996-97; England A to Zimbabwe and South Africa 1998-99; ECB National Academy to Australia 2001-02; England to Australia 2002-03, to Africa (World Cup) 2002-03, to Bangladesh 2003-04, to West Indies 2003-04, to South Africa 2004-05, to Pakistan 2005-06, to India 2005-06, to India (ICC Champions Trophy) 2006-07, to Australia 2006-07, to Sri Lanka 2007-08, to New Zealand 2007-08, to India (Test and one-day series) 2008, to West Indies (Test and one-day series) 2009; ICC World XI to Australia (Super Series) 2005-06
Overseas teams played for: Highveld Lions, South Africa 2007-08
Cricketers particularly admired: David Boon, Courtney Walsh
Other sports played: Football (played for Ashington in Northern League), golf, snooker
Other sports followed: Football (Newcastle United)
Relaxations: Spending time with family
Extras: Man of the [Test] Series v West Indies 2003-04 (23 wickets at 14.86, including 7-12 at Kingston) and England's Man of the [Test] Series v New Zealand 2004 (21 wickets at 22.09). Had match figures of 9-121 (6-46/3-75) in the fourth Test v West Indies at The Oval 2004 to go to the top of the PricewaterhouseCoopers ratings for Test bowlers. His other international awards include Man of the Match in the second Test v Pakistan at Old Trafford 2006 (6-19/5-57). Became second England bowler (after James Anderson) to take an ODI hat-trick (Kaif, Balaji, Nehra), v India at Trent Bridge in the NatWest Challenge 2004. One of *Wisden*'s Five Cricketers of the Year 2005. Became first bowler to take a first-class hat-trick for Durham (Pipe, Mason, Wigley) v Worcestershire at Riverside 2005. Appointed MBE in 2006 New Year Honours as part of 2005 Ashes-winning England team. Retired from ODI cricket in December 2006 - was enticed back by (then England captain) Kevin Pietersen in 2008
Best batting: 49* England v South Africa, The Oval 2008
Best bowling: 7-12 England v West Indies, Kingston 2003-04

2008 Season

	M	Inn	NO	Runs	HS	Avg	100	50	Ct	St	Balls	Runs	Wkts	Avg	BB	5I	10M
Test	1	1	1	49	49 *		-	-	-	-	258	133	4	33.25	2-49	-	-
FC	14	15	6	172	49 *	19.11	-	-	1	-	2833	1486	65	22.86	6-122	2	-
ODI	5	0	0	0	0		-	-	-	-	144	110	5	22.00	2-4	-	
List A	19	8	2	62	25 *	10.33	-	-	1	-	821	640	35	18.28	4-31	-	
20/20 Int																	
20/20	7	0	0	0	0		-	-	-	-	124	144	9	16.00	4-38	-	

Career Performances

	M	Inn	NO	Runs	HS	Avg	100	50	Ct	St	Balls	Runs	Wkts	Avg	BB	5I	10M
Test	58	78	20	691	49 *	11.91	-	-	7	-	12663	6788	216	31.42	7-12	8	1
FC	168	225	62	1675	49 *	10.27	-	-	25	-	32784	17189	607	28.31	7-12	22	1
ODI	51	22	13	67	13 *	7.44	-	-	8	-	2587	2167	72	30.09	5-33	1	
List A	128	59	29	230	25 *	7.66	-	-	19	-	6202	5027	174	28.89	5-33	1	
20/20 Int	2	0	0	0	0		-	-	1	-	39	42	1	42.00	1-13	-	
20/20	13	2	0	5	5	2.50	-	-	2	-	241	294	14	21.00	4-38	-	

HARRIS, A. J. — Nottinghamshire

Name: Andrew James Harris
Role: Right-hand bat, right-arm fast-medium bowler
Born: 26 June 1973, Ashton-under-Lyne, Lancashire
Height: 6ft **Weight:** 11st 9lbs
Nickname: AJ, Honest
County debut: 1994 (Derbyshire), 2000 (Nottinghamshire)
County cap: 1996 (Derbyshire), 2000 (Nottinghamshire)
Benefit: 2008 (Nottinghamshire)
50 wickets in a season: 1
Parents: Norman (deceased) and Joyce
Wife and date of marriage: Kate, 7 October 2000
Children: Jacob Alexander, 28 August 2002
Education: Hadfield Comprehensive School; Glossopdale Community College
Qualifications: 6 GCSEs, 1 A-level
Overseas tours: England A to Australia 1996-97
Overseas teams played for: Ginninderra West Belconnen, Australian Capital Territory 1992-93; Victoria University of Wellington CC, New Zealand 1997-98
Cricket superstitions: 'None'
Cricketers particularly admired: Merv Hughes, Allan Donald
Other sports played: Golf, snooker, football
Other sports followed: Football (Man City)
Relaxations: 'Good food, good wine and the odd game of golf'
Extras: Nottinghamshire Player of the Year 2002. Had the misfortune to be 'timed out' v Durham UCCE at Trent Bridge 2003 (was suffering from groin injury). On loan at Worcestershire for part of the 2008 season

Best batting: 41* Nottinghamshire v Northamptonshire, Northampton 2002
Best bowling: 7-54 Nottinghamshire v Northamptonshire, Trent Bridge 2002

2008 Season

	M	Inn	NO	Runs	HS	Avg	100	50	Ct	St	Balls	Runs	Wkts	Avg	BB	5I	10M
Test																	
FC	4	4	2	14	11 *	7.00	-	-	-	-	336	192	1	192.00	1-31	-	-
ODI																	
List A	5	2	1	1	1 *	1.00	-	-	1	-	192	182	8	22.75	4-47	-	
20/20 Int																	
20/20	3	2	1	6	6 *	6.00	-	-	-	-	72	78	5	15.60	2-19	-	

Career Performances

	M	Inn	NO	Runs	HS	Avg	100	50	Ct	St	Balls	Runs	Wkts	Avg	BB	5I	10M
Test																	
FC	127	171	43	1083	41 *	8.46	-	-	36	-	21503	12909	407	31.71	7-54	16	3
ODI																	
List A	145	55	24	217	34	7.00	-	-	28	-	6442	5421	190	28.53	5-35	1	
20/20 Int																	
20/20	23	7	4	12	6 *	4.00	-	-	4	-	417	599	21	28.52	2-13	-	

37. Of whom did Ian Chappell say: 'The good thing about his bowling is that when he's doing it he's not fielding'?

HARRIS, J. A. R. Glamorgan

Name: James Alexander Russell Harris
Role: Right-hand bat, right-arm fast-medium bowler; bowling all-rounder
Born: 16 May 1990, Morriston, Swansea
Height: 6ft 1in **Weight:** 11st
Nickname: Bones, Lloyd Christmas
County debut: 2007
Place in batting averages: 168th av 23.85 (2007 239th av. 16.33)
Place in bowling averages: 95th av 32.90 (2007 30th av. 24.57)
Parents: Helen and Russ
Marital status: Single
Family links with cricket: 'Dad played for British Universities'
Education: Pontarddulais Comprehensive; Gorseinon College
Qualifications: 9 GCSEs, 3 A-levels
Career outside cricket: 'Entrepreneur'
Off-season: 'Recovering from some small injuries, working hard on my fitness and my game, and also some golf as well'
Overseas tours: West of England U15 to West Indies 2004-05 (c); England U16 to South Africa 2005-06 (c); England Performance Programme to India 2007-08; England U19 to Malaysia (U19 World Cup) 2007-08, to South Africa 2009.
Career highlights to date: 'Taking 12 wickets in a match May 2007, becoming the youngest player in Championship history to do so'
Cricket moments to forget: 'None, they've all been brilliant'
Cricket superstitions: 'Put left pad on first, then right before batting'
Cricketers particularly admired: Glenn McGrath, Ricky Ponting, Jason Gillespie
Young players to look out for: Liam Dawson, Dan Redfern
Favourite band: Lighthouse Family, the Killers
Relaxations: 'Shopping for clothes, music, golf '
Extras: ESCA Bunbury Scholarship 2005. Signed professional contract aged 16 years 9 days. Youngest Glamorgan player to take a Championship wicket, v Nottinghamshire at Trent Bridge 2007 aged 16 years 351 days. Youngest player in Championship history to take ten wickets in a match – 7-66/5-52 v Gloucestershire at Bristol 2007 on only his second first-class appearance, aged 17 years 3 days. Youngest Glamorgan player to score a Championship fifty – 87* v Nottinghamshire at Swansea 2007. Represented England U19 2007. Glamorgan Young Player of the Year 2007, BBC Wales Young Sports Personality of the Year 2007. NBC Denis Compton Award for the most promising young Glamorgan player 2007, 2008

Opinions on cricket: 'I think the game today is pretty well balanced... it would be difficult to play less cricket in the summer, especially with how much play we lose to the weather. I'm really looking forward to the coming summer...'
Best batting: 87* Glamorgan v Nottinghamshire, Swansea 2007
Best bowling: 7-66 Glamorgan v Gloucestershire, Bristol 2007

2008 Season

	M	Inn	NO	Runs	HS	Avg	100	50	Ct	St	Balls	Runs	Wkts	Avg	BB	5I	10M
Test																	
FC	5	9	2	167	46	23.85	-	-	-	-	656	362	11	32.90	3-40	-	-
ODI																	
List A	6	4	1	28	15	9.33	-	-	2	-	234	169	12	14.08	4-48	-	
20/20 Int																	
20/20	4	1	0	8	8	8.00	-	-	1	-	60	89	4	22.25	3-41	-	

Career Performances

	M	Inn	NO	Runs	HS	Avg	100	50	Ct	St	Balls	Runs	Wkts	Avg	BB	5I	10M
Test																	
FC	14	23	4	363	87 *	19.10	-	1	4	-	2143	1173	44	26.65	7-66	2	1
ODI																	
List A	9	7	1	43	15	7.16	-	-	3	-	348	289	16	18.06	4-48	-	
20/20 Int																	
20/20	4	1	0	8	8	8.00	-	-	1	-	60	89	4	22.25	3-41	-	

HARRISON, D. S. — Glamorgan

Name: David Stuart Harrison
Role: Right-hand bat, right-arm fast-medium bowler
Born: 31 July 1981, Newport, Gwent
Height: 6ft 4in **Weight:** 16st
Nickname: Harry, Hazza, Des, Moorehead, Butter, Pass Me, Get Off My Train, Your Eyes, Gangster
County debut: 1999
County cap: 2006
50 wickets in a season: 1
Place in batting averages: 200th av 20.31
Place in bowling averages: 120th av 38.33
Parents: Stuart and Susan
Marital status: Single
Family links with cricket: Father played for Glamorgan in the 1970s. Brother Adam also played for Glamorgan. 'Mum tea lady for local club'
Education: West Monmouth School; Pontypool College; UWIC
Qualifications: 8 GCSEs, 2 A-levels, Levels 1 and 2 cricket coaching, 'qualified school caretaker'
Career outside cricket: 'Coaching/developing CV'
Overseas tours: Wales U15 to Ireland; Gwent YC to South Africa 1996; Wales U16 to Jersey 1997, 1998; England U19 to Malaysia and (U19 World Cup) Sri Lanka 1999-2000; Glamorgan to Cape Town 2002; England A to Sri Lanka 2004-05; MCC to Bahrain 2005-06, to Papua New Guinea and New Zealand 2007, to Uganda 2008
Overseas teams played for: Claremont, Cape Town 2002 (one game during Glamorgan tour)
Career highlights to date: 'Glamorgan debut 1999. Winning National League 2002 at Canterbury with friends and family. England A selection'
Cricket superstitions: 'Always wear a cap so don't burn my head!'
Cricketers particularly admired: Matthew Maynard, Mike Kasprowicz
Other sports played: Squash (Wales junior squads), rugby (East Wales U11 caps), boxing (Welsh champion at U14; 'still have odd spar')
Other sports followed: 'All sports (i.e. Sky Sports)', rugby (Pontypool), football (Man Utd), darts (Terry Jenkins)
Extras: Has played for Glamorgan from U12. Represented England at U17, U18 and U19. Glamorgan Young Player of the Year 2003, 2004. ECB National Academy 2004-05. NBC Denis Compton Award for the most promising young Glamorgan player 2004. Spent the whole of the 2007 season out of the game because of a serious back injury

Best batting: 88 Glamorgan v Essex, Chelmsford 2004
Best bowling: 5-48 Glamorgan v Somerset, Swansea 2004

2008 Season

	M	Inn	NO	Runs	HS	Avg	100	50	Ct	St	Balls	Runs	Wkts	Avg	BB	5I	10M
Test																	
FC	14	18	2	325	64 *	20.31	-	2	2	-	2188	1150	30	38.33	4-49		-
ODI																	
List A	11	7	4	20	7 *	6.66	-	-	-	-	443	413	10	41.30	2-36		
20/20 Int																	
20/20	9	2	1	1	1 *	1.00	-	-	1	-	162	205	8	25.62	2-28	-	

Career Performances

	M	Inn	NO	Runs	HS	Avg	100	50	Ct	St	Balls	Runs	Wkts	Avg	BB	5I	10M
Test																	
FC	82	116	16	1666	88	16.66	-	6	26	-	12821	7350	200	36.75	5-48	6	
ODI																	
List A	69	44	16	377	37 *	13.46	-	-	6	-	2889	2263	78	29.01	5-26	2	
20/20 Int																	
20/20	19	5	1	6	4	1.50	-	-	4	-	339	457	17	26.88	2-17	-	

HARVEY, I. J. — Hampshire

Name: Ian Joseph Harvey
Role: Right-hand bat, right-arm fast-medium bowler
Born: 10 April 1972, Wonthaggi, Victoria, Australia
Height: 5ft 9in **Weight:** 12st 8lbs
Nickname: Freak
County debut: 1999 (Gloucestershire), 2004 (Yorkshire), 2007 (Derbyshire), 2008 (Hampshire, one-day)
County cap: 1999 (Gloucestershire), 2005 (Yorkshire)
ODI debut: 1997-98
1st-Class 200s: 1
Marital status: Married
Family links with cricket: Brothers club cricketers in Australia
Education: Wonthaggi Technical College

Overseas tours: Australian Academy to New Zealand 1994-95; Australia to Sharjah (Coca-Cola Cup) 1997-98, to New Zealand 1999-2000 (one-day series), to Kenya (ICC Knockout Trophy) 2000-01, to India 2000-01 (one-day series), to England 2001 (one-day series), to South Africa 2001-02 (one-day series), to Africa (World Cup) 2002-03, to West Indies 2002-03 (one-day series), to India (TVS Cup) 2003-04, to Sri Lanka 2003-04 (one-day series), to Zimbabwe (one-day series) 2004, to Netherlands (Videocon Cup) 2004, to England (ICC Champions Trophy) 2004; Australia A to South Africa 2002-03; FICA World XI to New Zealand 2004-05
Overseas teams played for: Victoria 1993-94 – 2004-05; Cape Cobras 2005-06 – ; Chennai Superstars (ICL) 2007-08 –
Extras: The nickname 'Freak' is a reference to his brilliant fielding and was reportedly coined by Shane Warne. Attended Commonwealth Bank [Australian] Cricket Academy 1994. An overseas player with Gloucestershire 1999-2003 and in 2006; an overseas player with Yorkshire 2004-05. Man of the Match in the Carlton Series first final v West Indies at Sydney 2000-01 (47*/2-5). Won the Walter Lawrence Trophy 2001 for the season's fastest first-class hundred with his 61-ball century v Derbyshire at Bristol; also took 5-89 in Derbyshire's second innings. Has won numerous Australian and English domestic awards, including C&G Man of the Match in the final v Worcestershire at Lord's 2003 (2-37/36-ball 61). Scored the first ever century in the Twenty20 Cup (100* from 50 balls), v Warwickshire at Edgbaston 2003. One of *Wisden*'s Five Cricketers of the Year 2004. Appeared as an overseas player for Derbyshire 2007; left Derbyshire at the end of the 2007 season. Played only Twenty20 games in 2008
Best batting: 209* Yorkshire v Somerset, Headingley 2005
Best bowling: 8-101 Australia A v South Africa A, Adelaide 2002-03

2008 Season

	M	Inn	NO	Runs	HS	Avg	100	50	Ct	St	Balls	Runs	Wkts	Avg	BB	5I	10M
Test																	
FC																	
ODI																	
List A																	
20/20 Int																	
20/20	9	9	0	197	34	21.88	-	-	3	-	156	189	7	27.00	2-20	-	

Career Performances

	M	Inn	NO	Runs	HS	Avg	100	50	Ct	St	Balls	Runs	Wkts	Avg	BB	5I	10M
Test																	
FC	165	272	29	8409	209 *	34.60	15	46	114	-	24274	11693	425	27.51	8-101	15	2
ODI	73	51	11	715	48 *	17.87	-	-	17	-	3279	2577	85	30.31	4-16	-	
List A	304	267	27	5973	112	24.88	2	28	83	-	13601	9949	445	22.35	5-19	9	
20/20 Int																	
20/20	41	40	3	1190	109	32.16	3	4	11	-	785	1033	40	25.82	3-28	-	

HAYWARD, N. — Hampshire

Name: Mortnantau (Nantie) Hayward
Role: Right-hand bat, right arm fast bowler
Born: 6 March 1977, Uitenhage, Cape Province, South Africa
Nickname: Nantie
County debut: 2003 (Worcestershire), 2004 (Middlesex), 2008 (Hampshire)
Test debut: 1999
ODI debut: 1998
Overseas teams played for: Eastern Province B 1995-96; Eastern Province 1996-97 – 2003-04; Warriors 2004-05 – 2007-08; Dolphins 2005-06; Kolkata Tigers (ICL) 2005 – ; Chennai Superstars (ICL) 2008-09
Overseas tours: South Africa to England 1998; India 1999-2000; Sri Lanka 2000; to Australia 2001-02; to Sri Lanka 2004
Other sports played: Baseball (Provincial level in South Africa)
Extras: South African Cricket Annual Cricketer of the Year 2000. Signed for Worcestershire in 2003 season, then moved to Middlesex in 2004. Played as an overseas player for Ireland in the Friends Provident Trophy 2007. Signed for Hampshire as a Kolpak player in May 2008, but played in only one first-class match for the county all season
Best batting: 55* Eastern Province v Boland, Port Elizabeth 1997
Best bowling: 6-31 Eastern Province v Easterns, Port Elizabeth 1999

2008 Season

	M	Inn	NO	Runs	HS	Avg	100	50	Ct	St	Balls	Runs	Wkts	Avg	BB	5I	10M
Test																	
FC	1	2	1	24	17 *	24.00	-	-	-	-	151	101	3	33.66	2-87	-	-
ODI																	
List A																	
20/20 Int																	
20/20	10	2	0	6	5	3.00	-	-	5	-	210	278	13	21.38	3-22	-	

Career Performances

	M	Inn	NO	Runs	HS	Avg	100	50	Ct	St	Balls	Runs	Wkts	Avg	BB	5I	10M
Test	16	17	8	66	14	7.33	-	-	4	-	2821	1609	54	29.79	5-56	1	-
FC	128	145	53	1060	55 *	11.52	-	1	35	-	22938	12263	431	28.45	6-31	9	2
ODI	21	5	1	12	4	3.00	-	-	4	-	993	858	21	40.85	4-31	-	
List A	149	45	23	206	19 *	9.36	-	-	30	-	6528	5431	201	27.01	5-37	3	
20/20 Int																	
20/20	20	4	0	11	5	2.75	-	-	7	-	381	527	18	29.27	3-21	-	

HEMP, D. L. Glamorgan

Name: David Lloyd Hemp
Role: Left-hand bat, right-arm medium bowler
Born: 15 November 1970, Hamilton, Bermuda
Height: 6ft 1in **Weight:** 12st 7lbs
Nickname: Hempy, Gramps, Mad Dog
County debut: 1991 (Glamorgan), 1997 (Warwickshire)
County cap: 1994 (Glamorgan), 1997 (Warwickshire)
Benefit: 2008 (Glamorgan)
ODI debut: 2006-07
1000 runs in a season: 6
1st-Class 200s: 1
Place in batting averages: 95th av. 34.68 (2007 107th av. 34.45)
Parents: Clive and Elisabeth
Wife and date of marriage: Angela, 16 March 1996
Children: Cameron, January 2002; Kendal Noa, 6 September 2007
Family links with cricket: Father and brother both played for Swansea CC
Education: Olchfa Comprehensive School; Millfield School; Birmingham University
Qualifications: 5 O-levels, 2 A-levels, MBA, Level 3 coaching award
Career outside cricket: PR/marketing; coaching
Off-season: 'Playing with Bermuda; Level 4 coaching award'
Overseas tours: Welsh Cricket Association U18 to Barbados 1986; Welsh Schools U19 to Australia 1987-88; Glamorgan to Trinidad 1990; South Wales Cricket Association to New Zealand and Australia 1991-92; England A to India 1994-95; Bermuda to Kenya 2006-07, to South Africa (ICC Associates Tri-Series) 2006-07, to West Indies (World Cup) 2006-07, to Kenya and UAE 2007-08

Overseas teams played for: Crusaders, Durban 1992-98
Career highlights to date: '99* England A v India A, Calcutta "Test" match 1994-95. World Cup 2007 – playing for Bermuda'
Cricket moments to forget: 'None'
Cricket superstitions: 'None'
Cricketers particularly admired: Brian Lara, Graeme Hick, Mark Ramprakash
Other sports played: Football, golf
Other sports followed: Football (Swansea City, West Ham United)
Favourite band: Manic Street Preachers, Stereophonics
Relaxations: Golf, reading
Extras: In 1989 scored 104* and 101* for Welsh Schools U19 v Scottish Schools U19 and 120 and 102* v Irish Schools U19. Scored 258* for Wales v MCC 1991. Scored two centuries (138/114*) v Hampshire at Southampton 1997. Vice-captain of Warwickshire 2001. Left Warwickshire in the 2001-02 off-season and rejoined Glamorgan for 2002. Scored 88-ball 102 v Surrey at The Oval in the C&G 2002 as Glamorgan made 429 in reply to Surrey's 438-5. Won Glamorgan's Byron Denning Award 2004. Glamorgan Player of the Year 2005. Has played first-class and ODI cricket for Bermuda. Recorded highest score by a Bermuda player at the 2006-07 World Cup – 76* v India at Port of Spain. Glamorgan captain since mid-September 2006. Released at the end of the 2008 season, during which he had scored over 1200 runs in all competitions, when he took up a coaching post at Solihull School. Continues to play for Bermuda, being appointed vice-captain in January 2009
Opinions on cricket: 'Slightly reduce amount of cricket played, which would allow for more quality practices. Practice facilities, although improving, still need to get better. No overseas players as the best are not available, which would therefore hopefully give more opportunities to home-grown players. Larger fines for clubs for playing more than one Kolpak player per team, placing more emphasis on developing home-grown talent.'
Best batting: 247* Bermuda v Netherlands, Pretoria (LCD) 2006
Best bowling: 3-23 Glamorgan v South Africa A, Cardiff 1996

2008 Season

	M	Inn	NO	Runs	HS	Avg	100	50	Ct	St	Balls	Runs	Wkts	Avg	BB	5I	10M
Test																	
FC	15	25	3	763	104	34.68	2	5	10	-	0	0	0		-	-	-
ODI																	
List A	14	14	0	364	95	26.00	-	2	7	-	0	0	0		-	-	
20/20 Int																	
20/20	9	8	1	146	38 *	20.85	-	-	4	-	0	0	0		-	-	

Career Performances

	M	Inn	NO	Runs	HS	Avg	100	50	Ct	St	Balls	Runs	Wkts	Avg	BB	5I	10M
Test																	
FC	268	456	43	15250	247 *	36.92	30	83	181	-	1134	821	17	48.29	3-23	-	-
ODI	20	20	2	458	76 *	25.44	-	3	5	-	114	119	1	119.00	1-25	-	
List A	291	260	29	6097	121	26.39	5	32	106	-	303	297	12	24.75	4-32	-	
20/20 Int	2	2	0	20	20	10.00	-	-	-	-	0	0	0		-	-	
20/20	45	41	7	905	74	26.61	-	4	23	-	0	0	0		-	-	

HEMPHREY, C. R. Kent

Name: Charles (Charlie) Richard Hemphrey
Role: Right-hand bat, right-arm offbreak bowler
Born: 31 August 1989, Doncaster, Yorkshire
County debut: No first-team appearances
Education: Harvey Grammar School
Overseas teams played for: Redlands Tigers, Brisbane 2008-09
Extras: Played for Kent in the Second XI Championship: 2005-08. Spent six months in Brisbane, Australia in preparation for the 2009 season on the ECB Scholarship Programme. Spent 2008 on a Development Contract with Kent; has signed a second Development Contract for 2009

38. In which decade was a Test held at Bramall Lane, Sheffield?

HENDERSON, C. W. Leicestershire

Name: Claude William Henderson
Role: Right-hand bat, left-arm spin bowler
Born: 14 June 1972, Worcester, South Africa
Height: 6ft 2in **Weight:** 14st 2lbs
Nickname: Hendy, Hendo
County debut: 2004
County cap: 2004
Test debut: 2001-02
ODI debut: 2001-02
Place in batting averages: 195th av. 20.52 (2007 178th av. 25.07)
Place in bowling averages: 81st av. 31.56 (2007 111th av. 39.80)
Parents: Henry and Susan
Wife and date of marriage: Nicci, 29 March 2003
Children: Mia, 2007
Family links with cricket: Brother James played first-class cricket
Education: Worcester High School
Qualifications: Level 2 coaching, basic computer skills, basic bookkeeping skills
Career outside cricket: 'Family business'
Overseas tours: South Africa A to Sri Lanka 1998; South Africa to Zimbabwe 2001-02, to Australia 2001-02
Overseas teams played for: Boland 1990-91 – 1997-98; Western Province 1998-99 – 2003-04; Highveld Lions 2006-07; Cape Cobras 2008-09
Career highlights to date: 'Playing for South Africa'
Cricket moments to forget: 'Losing to Devon in C&G 2004'
Cricket superstitions: 'None'
Cricketers particularly admired: Shane Warne, Jacques Kallis
Other sports played: Golf, tennis, fishing
Other sports followed: Rugby (Leicester Tigers)
Favourite band: U2
Relaxations: 'Cinema, travelling, spending time with family'
Extras: Has won several match awards in South African domestic cricket. Scored fifty (63) and recorded five-wicket innings return (5-28) on Championship debut for Leicestershire v Glamorgan at Leicester 2004; recorded a further five-wicket return (5-24) on one-day debut v Yorkshire at Headingley in the totesport League 2004. Appointed player/coach at Leicestershire for 2008 with responsibility for spin bowling. Is not considered an overseas player
Best batting: 81 Leicestershire v Gloucestershire, Leicester 2007
Best bowling: 7-57 Boland v Eastern Province, Paarl (PCC) 1994-95

2008 Season

	M	Inn	NO	Runs	HS	Avg	100	50	Ct	St	Balls	Runs	Wkts	Avg	BB	5I	10M
Test																	
FC	16	21	4	349	66	20.52	-	4	2	-	3273	1294	41	31.56	5-39	1	-
ODI																	
List A	15	10	3	115	30	16.42	-	-	3	-	689	573	21	27.28	4-30	-	
20/20 Int																	
20/20	9	7	2	28	9	5.60	-	-	3	-	201	205	8	25.62	2-15	-	

Career Performances

	M	Inn	NO	Runs	HS	Avg	100	50	Ct	St	Balls	Runs	Wkts	Avg	BB	5I	10M
Test	7	7	0	65	30	9.28	-	-	2	-	1962	928	22	42.18	4-116	-	-
FC	204	277	62	4082	81	18.98	-	14	72	-	49145	21131	673	31.39	7-57	23	1
ODI	4	0	0	0	0		-	-	-	-	217	132	7	18.85	4-17	-	
List A	213	120	58	1043	45	16.82	-	-	50	-	9567	6785	263	25.79	6-29	2	
20/20 Int																	
20/20	34	15	4	48	9 *	4.36	-	-	10	-	538	609	24	25.37	3-26	-	

HENDERSON, T. Middlesex

Name: Tyron Henderson
Role: Right-hand bat, right-arm fast-medium bowler; all-rounder
Born: 1 August 1974, Durban, South Africa
Nickname: The Blacksmith
County debut: 2006 (Kent), 2007 (one-day, Middlesex)
Twenty20 Int debut: 2006-07
Family links with cricket: Grandfather (J. K. Henderson) and great-uncle (W. A. Henderson) played first-class cricket for North Eastern Transvaal
Overseas tours: South Africa Academy to Ireland and Scotland 1999; South Africa A to Sri Lanka 2005-06
Overseas teams played for: Border 1998-99 – 2003-04; Eastern Cape 2003-04; Warriors 2004-05 – 2005-06; Lions 2006-07; Cape Cobras 2007-08 – ; Boland 2007-08 –
Extras: Played for Berkshire in the 2003 C&G. Has represented South Africa A. His awards include Man of the Match v Griqualand West at Kimberley in the Standard

Bank Cup 2003-04 (3-45/126*) and v Dolphins at Port Elizabeth in the Standard Bank Pro20 Series 2004-05 (3-24/44). An overseas player with Kent from June to September 2006; was a temporary overseas player with Middlesex during the 2007 season as a locum for Chaminda Vaas. One of the heroes of the Twenty20 Cup final win over Kent in 2008, scoring 43 runs and running out Justin Kemp off the final ball of the game, Signed by Rajasthan for IPL 2009 – leading Twenty20 wicket-taker
Best batting: 81 Border v Gauteng, Johannesburg 2000
Best bowling: 7-67 Boland v Western Province, Paarl 2007

2008 Season

	M	Inn	NO	Runs	HS	Avg	100	50	Ct	St	Balls	Runs	Wkts	Avg	BB	5I	10M
Test																	
FC																	
ODI																	
List A	8	8	0	90	50	11.25	-	1	2	-	354	296	11	26.90	2-21	-	
20/20 Int																	
20/20	12	11	4	281	64 *	40.14	-	2	5	-	282	349	21	16.61	4-29	-	

Career Performances

	M	Inn	NO	Runs	HS	Avg	100	50	Ct	St	Balls	Runs	Wkts	Avg	BB	5I	10M
Test																	
FC	86	137	17	1897	81	15.80	-	6	31	-	15744	7024	262	26.80	7-67	10	1
ODI																	
List A	106	87	16	1500	126 *	21.12	1	8	25	-	4689	3391	124	27.34	5-5	3	
20/20 Int	1	1	0	0	0	0.00	-	-	-	-	24	31	0		-	-	
20/20	60	53	8	1048	85	23.28	-	7	10	-	1310	1520	73	20.82	4-29	-	

39. The final Test of the 2005 Ashes series ended in a draw, but who took twelve England wickets in their two innings?

HICK, G. A. Worcestershire

Name: Graeme Ashley Hick
Role: Right-hand bat, off-spin bowler
Born: 23 May 1966, Harare, Zimbabwe
Height: 6ft 3in **Weight:** 14st 4lbs
Nickname: Hicky, Ash
County debut: 1984
County cap: 1986; colours 2002
Benefit: 1999; testimonial 2006
Test debut: 1991
ODI debut: 1991
1000 runs in a season: 19
1st-Class 200s: 13
1st-Class 300s: 2
1st-Class 400s: 1
Place in batting averages: 42nd av. 45.93 (2007 60th av. 41.86)
Parents: John and Eve
Wife and date of marriage: Jackie, 5 October 1991
Children: Lauren Amy, 12 September 1992; Jordan Ashley, 5 September 1995
Family links with cricket: Father has served on Zimbabwe Cricket Union Board of Control and played representative cricket in Zimbabwe
Education: Prince Edward Boys' High School, Zimbabwe
Qualifications: 4 O-levels, NCA coaching award
Overseas tours: Zimbabwe to England (World Cup) 1983, to Sri Lanka 1983-84, to England 1985; England to Australia and New Zealand (World Cup) 1991-92, to India and Sri Lanka 1992-93, to West Indies 1993-94, to Australia 1994-95, to South Africa 1995-96, to India and Pakistan (World Cup) 1995-96, to Sharjah (Champions Trophy) 1997-98, to West Indies 1997-98 (one-day series), to Bangladesh (Wills International Cup) 1998-99, to Australia 1998-99, to Sharjah (Coca-Cola Cup) 1998-99, to South Africa and Zimbabwe 1999-2000 (one-day series), to Kenya (ICC Knockout Trophy) 2000-01, to Pakistan and Sri Lanka 2000-01; FICA World XI to New Zealand 2004-05
Overseas teams played for: Old Hararians, Zimbabwe 1982-90; Northern Districts, New Zealand 1987-89; Queensland 1990-91; Auckland 1997-98; Chandigarh Lions (ICL) 2008-09
Cricketers particularly admired: Steve Waugh, Glenn McGrath
Other sports played: Golf ('relaxation'), hockey (played for Zimbabwe)
Other sports followed: Football (Liverpool FC), golf, tennis, squash, hockey
Extras: One of *Wisden*'s Five Cricketers of the Year 1987. In 1988 he made 405* v Somerset at Taunton and scored 1000 first-class runs by the end of May. PCA Player of the Year 1988. Qualified to play for England 1991. Scored 100th first-class century

(132) v Sussex at Worcester 1998; at the age of 32, he became the second youngest player after Wally Hammond to score 100 centuries. Scored 200* v Durham at Riverside 2001, in the process achieving the feat of having recorded centuries against each of the other 17 counties, both home and away. Became leading run-scorer in the history of the one-day league, v Middlesex at Lord's 2005. Took eight catches in match v Essex at Chelmsford 2005, equalling the Worcestershire record. Scored 130th career first-class century (139) v Northamptonshire at Worcester 2006 to move into eighth spot on the all-time first-class century-makers' list and become the eighth batsman (the first for Worcestershire) to register 100 first-class centuries for a single county. Became fifth quickest batsman to reach 40,000 runs in first-class cricket (in terms of innings played) v Warwickshire at Edgbaston 2007. His series and match awards include England's Man of the CUB Series 1998-99 and Man of the Match v Zimbabwe, the country of his birth, for his match-winning 87* at Bulawayo and his 80 and 5-33 at Harare 1999-2000. Captain of Worcestershire 2000-02. Winner of Sky Sports Sixes Award 2007. Retired from first-class cricket at end of 2008 season
Best batting: 405* Worcestershire v Somerset, Taunton 1988
Best bowling: 5-18 Worcestershire v Leicestershire, Worcester 1995

2008 Season

	M	Inn	NO	Runs	HS	Avg	100	50	Ct	St	Balls	Runs	Wkts	Avg	BB	5I	10M
Test																	
FC	11	18	3	689	149	45.93	2	2	25	-	0	0	0		-	-	-
ODI																	
List A	10	10	1	178	40	19.77	-	-	8	-	0	0	0		-	-	
20/20 Int																	
20/20	9	9	1	272	88 *	34.00	-	3	2	-	0	0	0		-	-	

Career Performances

	M	Inn	NO	Runs	HS	Avg	100	50	Ct	St	Balls	Runs	Wkts	Avg	BB	5I	10M
Test	65	114	6	3383	178	31.32	6	18	90	-	3057	1306	23	56.78	4-126	-	-
FC	526	871	84	41112	405 *	52.23	136	158	709	-	20889	10308	232	44.43	5-18	5	1
ODI	120	118	15	3846	126 *	37.33	5	27	64	-	1236	1026	30	34.20	5-33	1	
List A	651	630	96	22059	172 *	41.30	40	139	289	-	8603	6649	225	29.55	5-19	4	
20/20 Int																	
20/20	37	36	3	1201	116 *	36.39	2	10	10	-	0	0	0		-	-	

HILDRETH, J. C. Somerset

Name: James Charles Hildreth
Role: Right-hand bat, right-arm medium bowler; all-rounder
Born: 9 September 1984, Milton Keynes
Height: 5ft 10in **Weight:** 12st
Nickname: Hildy, Hildz
County debut: 2003
County cap: 2007
1000 runs in a season: 1
1st-Class 200s: 1
Place in batting averages: 108th av. 32.06 (2007 26th av. 52.91)
Parents: David and Judy
Marital status: Single
Family links with cricket: 'Dad played county league cricket in Kent and Northants'
Education: Millfield School
Qualifications: 10 GCSEs, 3 A-levels, ECB Level 1 coaching
Overseas tours: 'West' to West Indies 1999, 2000; Millfield to Sri Lanka 2001; England U19 to Bangladesh (U19 World Cup) 2003-04; England Performance Programme to India 2007-08; England Lions to India 2007-08
Cricket moments to forget: 'Being bowled first ball by Shoaib Akhtar'
Cricket superstitions: 'Left pad before right when getting padded up'
Other sports played: Hockey (West of England), squash (South of England), tennis (South of England), football (England Independent Schools, Luton Town), rugby (Millfield)
Other sports followed: Football (Charlton Athletic)
Favourite band: Jack Johnson
Relaxations: Travelling, snowboarding, music
Extras: NBC Denis Compton Award for the most promising young Somerset player 2003, 2004, 2005. Scored maiden first-class century (101) plus 72 in the second innings v Durham at Taunton 2004 in his second Championship match. Represented England U19 v Bangladesh U19 2004, scoring 210 in second 'Test' at Taunton. Cricket Society's Most Promising Young Cricketer of the Year 2004. Scored maiden first-class double century (227*) at Taunton 2006, setting a new record for the highest score by a Somerset batsman v Northamptonshire. ECB National Academy 2004-05 (part-time). Scored almost 1000 first-class runs in 2008
Best batting: 227* Somerset v Northamptonshire, Taunton 2006
Best bowling: 2-39 Somerset v Hampshire, Taunton 2004

2008 Season

	M	Inn	NO	Runs	HS	Avg	100	50	Ct	St	Balls	Runs	Wkts	Avg	BB	5I	10M
Test																	
FC	18	32	2	962	158	32.06	1	6	8	-	48	38	0		-	-	-
ODI																	
List A	15	14	1	264	112 *	20.30	1	-	2	-	36	47	3	15.66	2-26	-	
20/20 Int																	
20/20	4	4	0	3	2	.75	-	-	2	-	0	0	0		-	-	

Career Performances

	M	Inn	NO	Runs	HS	Avg	100	50	Ct	St	Balls	Runs	Wkts	Avg	BB	5I	10M
Test																	
FC	79	133	11	4736	227 *	38.81	10	26	61	-	396	316	4	79.00	2-39	-	-
ODI																	
List A	92	88	13	2148	122	28.64	2	7	24	-	150	185	6	30.83	2-26	-	
20/20 Int																	
20/20	38	37	4	568	71	17.21	-	3	15	-	169	247	10	24.70	3-24	-	

HINDMARCH, P. Durham

Name: Paul Robert Hindmarch
Role: Right-hand bat; right-arm fast-medium bowler; all-rounder
Born: 8 February 1988, Carlisle
County debut: No first-team appearances
Education: Keswick School
Extras: Made his debut for Durham 2nd XI v Surrey 2nd XI, Guildford, August 2006. Has played for Cumbria U17s Signed a development contract with Durham for 2009

HINDS, W. W. Derbyshire

Name: Wavell Wayne Hinds
Role: Left-hand bat, right-arm medium bowler
Born: 7 September 1976, Kingston, Jamaica
County debut: 2008
Test debut: 1999-2000
ODI debut: 1999
Twenty20 Int debut: 2005-06
1st-Class 200s: 1
Place in batting averages: 115th av. 31.30
Place in bowling averages: 41st av. 26.10
Overseas tours: West Indies U19 to Pakistan 1995-96; West Indies A to South Africa 1997-98, to Bangladesh and India 1998-99; West Indies to Singapore (Coca-Cola Singapore Challenge) 1999, to Bangladesh 1999-2000, to New Zealand 1999-2000, to England 2000, to Kenya (ICC Knockout Trophy) 2000-01, to Australia 2000-01, to Zimbabwe and Kenya 2001, to Sharjah (v Pakistan) 2001-02, to Sri Lanka (ICC Champions Trophy) 2002-03, to India and Bangladesh 2002-03, to Africa (World Cup) 2002-03, to Zimbabwe and South Africa 2003-04, to England (ICC Champions Trophy) 2004, to Australia 2005-06, to India (ICC Champions Trophy) 2006-07, plus other one-day tournaments and series in Toronto, Sharjah, Australia, New Zealand and Malaysia
Overseas teams played for: Jamaica 1995-96 – ; Ahmedabad Rockets (ICL) 2007-08
Extras: Scored 213 in the first Test at Georgetown 2004-05, in the process sharing with Shivnarine Chanderpaul (203*) in a record fourth-wicket partnership for West Indies in Tests against South Africa (284). His match and series awards include Man of the [Test] Series v Pakistan 1999-2000 and of the [ODI] Series v Australia 2002-03. Is not considered an overseas player
Best batting: 213 West Indies v South Africa, Georgetown 2004-05
Best bowling: 3-9 Jamaica v West Indies B, Montego Bay 2000-01

2008 Season

	M	Inn	NO	Runs	HS	Avg	100	50	Ct	St	Balls	Runs	Wkts	Avg	BB	5I	10M
Test																	
FC	9	13	0	407	76	31.30	-	3	1	-	528	261	10	26.10	3-22	-	-
ODI																	
List A	8	8	0	218	84	27.25	-	2	1	-	192	193	5	38.60	2-43	-	
20/20 Int																	
20/20	10	10	2	283	72 *	35.37	-	2	1	-	108	124	4	31.00	2-14	-	

Career Performances

	M	Inn	NO	Runs	HS	Avg	100	50	Ct	St	Balls	Runs	Wkts	Avg	BB	5I	10M
Test	45	80	1	2608	213	33.01	5	14	32	-	1123	590	16	36.87	3-79	-	-
FC	137	233	9	7778	213	34.72	18	39	65	-	2926	1388	39	35.58	3-9	-	-
ODI	114	107	9	2835	127 *	28.92	5	14	28	-	945	837	28	29.89	3-24	-	
List A	194	183	14	4769	127 *	28.21	6	26	45	-	1490	1339	49	27.32	4-35	-	
20/20 Int	1	1	0	14	14	14.00	-	-	-	-	0	0	0		-	-	
20/20	17	15	3	374	72 *	31.16	-	2	2	-	120	137	4	34.25	2-14	-	

HOCKLEY, J. B. Kent

Name: James Bernard Hockley
Role: Right-hand bat, right-arm offbreak bowler; all-rounder
Born: 16 April 1979, Beckenham
Height: 6ft 2in
Nickname: Hickers, Ice
County debut: 1998 (Kent)
Parents: Bernard and Joan
Education: Churchfields Primary School, Beckenham; Kelsey Park Secondary School, Beckenham
Qualifications: 7 GCSEs, NCA Level 1 coaching award
Career outside cricket: Teaching
Overseas tours: Kent to Jamaica 1999, to South Africa 2001
Overseas teams played for: North City, Wellington, New Zealand 1999-2000
Career highlights to date: 'Winning the Norwich Union League Trophy with Kent in 2001'
Cricket moments to forget: 'Playing at Lord's for the first time - out for a duck and dropped a catch.'
Other sports played: Football, golf, snooker
Other sports followed: Football (Arenal)
Extras: ACKL Player of the Year Award 1995. Equalled Trevor Ward's Kent U15 batting record with a total of 1000 runs in the season. Kent Schools Player of the Year 1996. Played for Kent 2nd XI 1996-98, Kent 1998-2002. Represented Kent Cricket Board in the Minor Counties Trophy 1998-2000. Scored a 102-ball 90 in the title-clinching Norwich Union League victory v Warwickshire at Edgbaston 2001. B&H Gold Award for his 32-ball 33* v Middlesex at Canterbury 2002. C&G Man of the Match Award for his 107-ball 121 (his maiden one-day century) v Warwickshire at

Canterbury 2002. After being releasd by Kent in 2002, combined a career in teaching with a return to club cricket, playing for Kent Cricket League sides Bexley CC (2003-05) and Hartley Country Club (2006-08). Was a member of Hartley's Kent Premier League championship side 2008
Best batting: 74 Kent v Zimbabweans, Canterbury 2000
Best batting: 1-21 Kent v Glamorgan, Hove 2001

2008 Season (Did not make any first-class or one-day appearances)

Career Performances

	M	Inn	NO	Runs	HS	Avg	100	50	Ct	St	Balls	Runs	Wkts	Avg	BB	5I	10M
Test																	
FC	19	30	2	423	74	15.11	0	1	9	-	366	233	3	77.67	1-21	-	-
ODI																	
List A	57	55	5	1329	121	26.58	1	6	20	-	24	35	1	35.00	1-35	-	
20/20 Int																	
20/20																	

HODD, A. J. Sussex

Name: Andrew John Hodd
Role: Right-hand bat, wicket-keeper
Born: 12 January 1984, Chichester
Height: 5ft 9½in **Weight:** 11st 8lbs
Nickname: Hoddy
County debut: 2002 (one-day, Sussex), 2003 (first-class, Sussex), 2005 (Surrey)
Parents: Karen and Adrian
Marital status: Single
Family links with cricket: 'Long line of enthusiastic club cricketers'
Education: Bexhill High School; Bexhill College; 'short stint at Loughborough Uni'
Qualifications: 9 GCSEs, 4 A-levels, Level 1 coach
Career outside cricket: Coaching
Overseas tours: South of England U14 to West Indies 1998; Sussex Academy to Cape Town 1999, to Sri Lanka 2001; England U17 to Australia 2000-01; England U19 to Australia 2002-03

Cricket superstitions: 'Too many! Must drink coffee the morning of a game'

Cricketers particularly admired: David Hussey, Matt Prior
Young players to look out for: Luke Wright, Ollie Rayner, Ben Brown
Other sports played: Golf, football, boxing
Other sports followed: Football (Brighton & Hove Albion)
Favourite band: Hard-Fi
Relaxations: 'Cinema, DVDs, gym, going out'
Extras: Played for England U14, U15, U17 and U19. Graham Kersey Trophy, Bunbury 1999. Several junior Player of the Year awards at Sussex. Sussex County League Young Player of the Year 2002. Sussex 2nd XI Player of the Year 2003. Joined Surrey for 2004, leaving at the end of the 2005 season to rejoin Sussex for 2006
Best batting: 123 Sussex v Yorkshire, Hove 2007

2008 Season

	M	Inn	NO	Runs	HS	Avg	100	50	Ct	St	Balls	Runs	Wkts	Avg	BB	5I	10M
Test																	
FC	3	4	0	99	81	24.75	-	1	7	-	0	0	0		-	-	-
ODI																	
List A	3	2	0	36	33	18.00	-	-	1	-	0	0	0		-	-	
20/20 Int																	
20/20	6	4	0	34	16	8.50	-	-	6	1	0	0	0		-	-	

Career Performances

	M	Inn	NO	Runs	HS	Avg	100	50	Ct	St	Balls	Runs	Wkts	Avg	BB	5I	10M
Test																	
FC	22	31	7	868	123	36.16	2	5	39	7	0	0	0		-	-	-
ODI																	
List A	17	14	2	228	42	19.00	-	-	9	-	0	0	0		-	-	
20/20 Int																	
20/20	15	6	0	50	16	8.33	-	-	9	4	0	0	0		-	-	

40. Armed robber George Davis was innocent. At which ground, during the 1975 Ashes series, did his supporters cause the Test to be abandoned when they damaged the pitch?

HODGE, B. J. Lancashire

Name: Bradley (Brad) John Hodge
Role: Right-hand bat, right-arm off-spin bowler
Born: 29 December 1974, Sandringham, Melbourne, Australia
Height: 5ft 7½in **Weight:** 12st 8lbs
Nickname: Bunk
County debut: 2002 (Durham), 2003 (Leicestershire), 2005 (Lancashire)
County cap: 2003 (Leicestershire), 2006 (Lancashire)
Test debut: 2005-06
ODI debut: 2005-06
Twenty20 Int debut: 2007-08
1000 runs in a season: 2
1st-Class 200s: 8
1st-Class 300s: 1
Parents: John and Val
Wife: Megan
Children: Jesse
Education: St Bede's College, Mentone; Deakin University
Overseas tours: Australia U19 to New Zealand 1992-93; Commonwealth Bank [Australian] Cricket Academy to Zimbabwe 1998-99; Australia A to Los Angeles (Moov America Challenge) 1999, to Pakistan 2005-06; Australia to India 2004-05, to New Zealand 2004-05, to England 2005, to New Zealand (one-day series) 2005-06, 2006-07, to West Indies (World Cup) 2006-07, to South Africa (World 20/20) 2007-08, to India (one-day series) 2007-08
Overseas teams played for: Victoria 1993-94 – ;Kolkata Knight Riders (IPL) 2007-08
Cricketers particularly admired: Allan Border, Dennis Lillee, Dean Jones, Sachin Tendulkar
Other sports played/followed: Australian Rules football (Melbourne), golf, tennis, soccer, skiing
Extras: Attended Commonwealth Bank [Australian] Cricket Academy 1993. Leading run-scorer for Victoria in the Sheffield Shield in his first season (1993-94) with 903 runs (av. 50.16). Victoria's Pura Cup Player of the Year 2000-01 and 2001-02; winner of the national Pura Cup Player of the Season Award 2001-02 (jointly with Jimmy Maher of Queensland). Was Durham's overseas player 2002 from late July; an overseas player with Leicestershire 2003-04 (appointed vice-captain for 2004; assumed the captaincy in July on the resignation of Phillip DeFreitas). Scored 202* v Loughborough UCCE at Leicester 2003, in the process

sharing with Darren Maddy (229*) in a record partnership for any wicket for Leicestershire (436*). His 302* v Nottinghamshire at Trent Bridge 2003 was the then highest individual first-class score by a Leicestershire player. ING Cup Player of the Year 2003-04. Has won numerous Australian and English domestic awards, including Man of the Match in the Twenty20 Cup final at Edgbaston 2004 for his 53-ball 77*. Man of the Match in the first Test v South Africa at Perth 2005-06 (41/203*) and v Netherlands in St Kitts in the 2006-07 World Cup (123). An overseas player with Lancashire since 2005

Best batting: 302* Leicestershire v Nottinghamshire, Trent Bridge 2003

Best bowling: 4-17 Australia A v West Indians, Hobart 2000-01

2008 Season

	M	Inn	NO	Runs	HS	Avg	100	50	Ct	St	Balls	Runs	Wkts	Avg	BB	5I	10M
Test																	
FC	2	2	1	44	43 *	44.00	-	-	1	-	60	26	2	13.00	2-24	-	-
ODI																	
List A																	
20/20 Int																	
20/20																	

Career Performances

	M	Inn	NO	Runs	HS	Avg	100	50	Ct	St	Balls	Runs	Wkts	Avg	BB	5I	10M
Test	6	11	2	503	203 *	55.88	1	2	9	-	12	8	0		-	-	-
FC	211	370	37	16005	302 *	48.06	48	59	123	-	5175	2881	72	40.01	4-17	-	-
ODI	25	21	2	575	123	30.26	1	3	16	-	66	51	1	51.00	1-17	-	
List A	214	204	25	7322	164	40.90	19	35	87	-	1482	1308	38	34.42	5-28	1	
20/20 Int	8	5	2	94	36	31.33	-	-	3	-	12	20	0		-	-	
20/20	50	47	5	1661	106	39.54	1	11	24	-	396	500	24	20.83	4-17	-	

HODGSON, L. J. — Yorkshire

Name: Lee John Hodgson
Role: Right-hand bat, right-arm fast-medium bowler; all-rounder
Born: 29 June 1986, Middlesbrough
County debut: 2008 (Surrey)
Extras: Played for Saltburn CC in North Yorkshire and South Durham League. MCC Young Cricketer 2006. On first-class debut scored 63, including 13 fours, v Nottinghamshire. Has joined Yorkshire for 2009.
Best batting: 63 Surrey v Nottinghamshire, The Oval 2008

2008 Season

	M	Inn	NO	Runs	HS	Avg	100	50	Ct	St	Balls	Runs	Wkts	Avg	BB	5I	10M
Test																	
FC	1	2	0	66	63	33.00	-	1	2	-	54	58	0		-	-	
ODI																	
List A	2	0	0	0	0		-	-	2	-	48	52	0		-	-	
20/20 Int																	
20/20																	

Career Performances

	M	Inn	NO	Runs	HS	Avg	100	50	Ct	St	Balls	Runs	Wkts	Avg	BB	5I	10M
Test																	
FC	1	2	0	66	63	33.00	-	1	2	-	54	58	0		-	-	
ODI																	
List A	2	0	0	0	0		-	-	2	-	48	52	0		-	-	
20/20 Int																	
20/20																	

HODNETT, G. P. — Gloucestershire

Name: Grant Phillip Hodnett
Role: Right-hand top-order bat, right-arm leg-spin bowler, occasional wicket-keeper
Born: 17 August 1982, Johannesburg, South Africa
Height: 6ft 4in **Weight:** 14st
Nickname: Hodders, Hoddy
County debut: 2005
County cap: 2005
Parents: Phillip and Julia
Marital status: Single
Family links with cricket: Brother Kyle an MCC Young Cricketer
Education: Northwood High School, Durban
Qualifications: Matriculation, ECB Level 1 coach, GFA Fitness Instructor
Overseas tours: Gloucestershire to South Africa 2006
Overseas teams played for: Durban Collegians 2005-06
Cricket superstitions: 'None'
Cricketers particularly admired: Hansie Cronje, Jonty Rhodes, Steve Waugh, Andrew Flintoff, Michael Atherton
Other sports played: Golf, squash, bodyboarding, football, rugby
Other sports followed: Rugby union (England), football (Newcastle United)
Favourite band: Blink-182
Relaxations: 'Going to gym; swimming; reading sports magazines'
Extras: Represented KwaZulu-Natal Schools. West of England Premier League Batsman of the Year 2004. Limited appearances in 2008. Is not considered an overseas player
Best batting: 168 Gloucestershire v Derbyshire, Bristol 2007
Best bowling: 2-91 Gloucestershire v Loughborough UCCE, Bristol 2008

2008 Season

	M	Inn	NO	Runs	HS	Avg	100	50	Ct	St	Balls	Runs	Wkts	Avg	BB	5I	10M
Test																	
FC	3	5	0	75	57	15.00	-	1	5	-	114	132	2	66.00	2-91	-	-
ODI																	
List A																	
20/20 Int																	
20/20																	

Career Performances

	M	Inn	NO	Runs	HS	Avg	100	50	Ct	St	Balls	Runs	Wkts	Avg	BB	5I	10M
Test																	
FC	19	32	1	1020	168	32.90	2	7	14	-	129	142	2	71.00	2-91	-	-
ODI																	
List A	4	4	0	114	50	28.50	-	1	2	-	0	0	0	-	-	-	
20/20 Int																	
20/20																	

HOGG, K. W. — Lancashire

Name: Kyle William Hogg
Role: Left-hand bat, right-arm fast-medium bowler; all-rounder
Born: 2 July 1983, Birmingham
Height: 6ft 4in **Weight:** 13st
Nickname: Boss, Hoggy
County debut: 2001
Place in batting averages: (2006 92nd av. 36.28)
Place in bowling averages: (2006 81st av. 35.20)
Parents: Sharon and William
Marital status: Single
Family links with cricket: Father played for Lancashire and Warwickshire; grandfather Sonny Ramadhin played for Lancashire and West Indies
Education: Saddleworth High School, Oldham
Qualifications: GCSEs
Overseas tours: England U19 to India 2000-01, to Australia and (U19 World Cup) New Zealand 2001-02; Lancashire to South Africa, to Grenada; ECB National Academy to Australia and Sri Lanka 2002-03
Overseas teams played for: Otago 2006-07
Cricket moments to forget: '[B&H 2002] semi-final v Warwickshire'
Cricket superstitions: 'None'
Cricketers particularly admired: Andrew Flintoff, David Byas, Stuart Law, Carl Hooper
Other sports played: Football
Other sports followed: Football (Man Utd)
Favourite band: Stone Roses, Red Hot Chili Peppers, Bob Marley

Relaxations: 'Relaxing with friends'
Extras: Represented England U19 2001, 2002. NBC Denis Compton Award for the most promising young Lancashire player 2001. Recorded maiden first-class five-wicket return (5-48) on Championship debut v Leicestershire at Old Trafford 2002. Included in provisional England squad of 30 for the 2002-03 World Cup. Played two first-class and four List A matches for Worcestershire on loan 2007 and two first-class and three List A matches for Nottinghamshire on loan 2007. In recent years, has suffered a series of injuries that have damaged his career
Best batting: 71 Otago v Central Districts, Napier 2006-07
Best bowling: 5-48 Lancashire v Leicestershire, Old Trafford 2002

2008 Season

	M	Inn	NO	Runs	HS	Avg	100	50	Ct	St	Balls	Runs	Wkts	Avg	BB	5I	10M
Test																	
FC	2	2	0	33	33	16.50	-	-	-	-	132	60	4	15.00	3-26	-	-
ODI																	
List A	11	9	1	175	66 *	21.87	-	1	1	-	413	310	10	31.00	3-27	-	
20/20 Int																	
20/20	11	8	1	120	44	17.14	-	-	3	-	174	219	6	36.50	2-31	-	

Career Performances

	M	Inn	NO	Runs	HS	Avg	100	50	Ct	St	Balls	Runs	Wkts	Avg	BB	5I	10M
Test																	
FC	41	50	5	1015	71	22.55	-	7	11	-	5222	2756	70	39.37	5-48	1	-
ODI																	
List A	98	62	17	761	66 *	16.91	-	1	16	-	3574	2817	96	29.34	4-20	-	
20/20 Int																	
20/20	20	15	2	209	44	16.07	-	-	3	-	259	359	12	29.91	2-10	-	

41. Which England wicketkeeper took 97 minutes to get off the mark in the Adelaide Test of 1947?

HOGGARD, M. J. Yorkshire

Name: Matthew James Hoggard
Role: Right-hand bat, right-arm fast-medium bowler
Born: 31 December 1976, Leeds
Height: 6ft 2in **Weight:** 14st
Nickname: Oggie
County debut: 1996
County cap: 2000
Benefit: 2008
Test debut: 2000
ODI debut: 2001-02
50 wickets in a season: 2
Place in batting averages: 245th av. 1283 (2007 257th av. 13.44)
Place in bowling averages: 32nd av. 24.35 (2007 9th av. 21.40)
Parents: Margaret and John
Wife and date of marriage: Sarah, 2 October 2004
Children: Ernie, May 2007
Family links with cricket: 'Dad is a cricket badger'
Education: Pudsey Grangefield School, West Yorkshire
Qualifications: GCSEs and A-levels
Overseas tours: Yorkshire CCC to South Africa; England U19 to Zimbabwe 1995-96; England to Kenya (ICC Knockout Trophy) 2000-01, to Pakistan and Sri Lanka 2000-01, to Zimbabwe (one-day series) 2001-02, to India and New Zealand 2001-02, to Sri Lanka (ICC Champions Trophy) 2002-03, to Australia 2002-03, to Africa (World Cup) 2002-03, to Bangladesh and Sri Lanka 2003-04, to West Indies 2003-04, to South Africa 2004-05, to Pakistan 2005-06, to India 2005-06, to Australia 2006-07, to Sri Lanka 2007-08, to New Zealand 2007-08
Overseas teams played for: Pirates, Johannesburg 1995-97; Free State 1998-2000
Cricketers particularly admired: Allan Donald, Courtney Walsh
Other sports played: Rugby
Other sports followed: Rugby league (Leeds Rhinos)
Relaxations: Dog walking
Extras: NBC Denis Compton Award for most promising young Yorkshire player 1998. Was top wicket-taker in the 2000 National League competition with 37 wickets at 12.37. PCA Young Player of the Year 2000. Took 7-63 v New Zealand in the first Test at Christchurch 2001-02, the best innings return by an England pace bowler in Tests v New Zealand. Took hat-trick (Sarwan, Chanderpaul, Ryan Hinds) in the third Test v West Indies at Bridgetown 2003-04. His international awards include Man of the [Test]

Series v Bangladesh 2003-04 and Man of the Match in the fourth Test v South Africa at Johannesburg 2004-05 (5-144/7-61) and in the first Test v India at Nagpur 2005-06 (6-57). Appointed MBE in 2006 New Year Honours as part of 2005 Ashes-winning England team. One of *Wisden*'s Five Cricketers of the Year 2006. Took 200th Test wicket (Farveez Maharoof) in the first Test v Sri Lanka at Lord's 2006. Took 237th Test wicket (Dwayne Bravo) in the fourth Test v West Indies at Riverside 2007 to move into sixth place in the England list of Test wicket-takers. England 12-month central contract 2007-08. Briefly returned to the England squad in 2008
Best batting: 89* Yorkshire v Glamorgan, Headingley 2004
Best bowling: 7-49 Yorkshire v Somerset, Headingley 2003

2008 Season

	M	Inn	NO	Runs	HS	Avg	100	50	Ct	St	Balls	Runs	Wkts	Avg	BB	5I	10M
Test																	
FC	14	18	6	154	28 *	12.83	-	-	3	-	2237	1096	45	24.35	6-57	1	-
ODI																	
List A	2	1	1	1	1 *		-	-	-	-	96	67	3	22.33	3-26	-	
20/20 Int																	
20/20	9	0	0	0	0		-	-	3	-	192	251	6	41.83	2-22	-	

Career Performances

	M	Inn	NO	Runs	HS	Avg	100	50	Ct	St	Balls	Runs	Wkts	Avg	BB	5I	10M
Test	67	92	27	473	38	7.27	-	-	24	-	13903	7564	248	30.50	7-61	7	1
FC	179	229	67	1458	89 *	9.00	-	3	50	-	32679	16802	622	27.01	7-49	20	1
ODI	26	6	2	17	7	4.25	-	-	5	-	1306	1152	32	36.00	5-49	1	
List A	127	39	21	67	7 *	3.72	-	-	14	-	6001	4452	177	25.15	5-28	4	
20/20 Int																	
20/20	15	2	1	19	18	19.00	-	-	4	-	324	472	13	36.30	3-23	-	

42. In 1884, who scored the first double century in Test cricket?

HOLE, S. M. Warwickshire

Name: Stuart Mark Hole
Role: Right-hand bat, right-arm seam bowler
Born: 17 July 1985, Oxford
Height: 6ft 1in **Weight:** 12st 7lbs
Nickname: Holey
County debut: 2007
Parents: Les and Sally
Marital status: Single
Education: Bartholomew School, Eynsham
Qualifications: Premier Training personal trainer, gym instructor and sports masseur
Career outside cricket: Personal trainer
Career highlights to date: 'First-class debut against Yorkshire [2007]'
Cricket moments to forget: 'None as yet'
Cricketers particularly admired: Matthew Hoggard
Young players to look out for: Chris Woakes
Other sports played: Football ('played at Wycombe Wanderers FC for four years'), golf
Other sports followed: Football (Liverpool, Wycombe Wanderers)
Favourite band: 112
Relaxations: 'Music, PlayStation 3'
Extras: Played for Oxfordshire in Minor Counties competitions 2005-06
Best batting: 24 Warwickshire v Yorkshire, Scarborough 2007
Best bowling: 2-29 Warwickshire v Cambridge UCCE, Fenner's 2008

2008 Season

	M	Inn	NO	Runs	HS	Avg	100	50	Ct	St	Balls	Runs	Wkts	Avg	BB	5I	10M
Test																	
FC	1	0	0	0	0	-	-	-	-		108	40	2	20.00	2-29	-	-
ODI																	
List A																	
20/20 Int																	
20/20																	

Career Performances

	M	Inn	NO	Runs	HS	Avg	100	50	Ct	St	Balls	Runs	Wkts	Avg	BB	5I	10M
Test																	
FC	2	2	1	24	24	24.00	-	-	-	-	198	105	2	52.50	2-29	-	-
ODI																	
List A	2	0	0	0	0		-	-	-	-	18	16	1	16.00	1-16	-	
20/20 Int																	
20/20																	

HOPKINSON, C. D. — Sussex

Name: Carl Daniel Hopkinson
Role: Right-hand bat, right-arm fast-medium bowler; 'batter that bowls'
Born: 14 September 1981, Brighton
Height: 5ft 11in
Nickname: Hoppo
County debut: 2001 (one-day), 2002 (first-class)
Place in batting averages: 102nd av. 32.87 (2007 214th av. 20.41)
Parents: Jane and Jerry
Marital status: Single
Family links with cricket: 'Dad played in the local team, which got me interested, and coached me from a young age'
Education: Chailey; Brighton College
Qualifications: 7 GCSEs, 3 A-levels, Level 1 coaching
Overseas tours: Tours to India 1997-98, to South Africa 1999
Overseas teams played for: Rockingham-Mandurah, Western Australia 2000-01
Cricketers particularly admired: Dennis Lillee, Ian Botham, Viv Richards, Graham Thorpe
Other sports played: Rugby ('won Rosslyn Park National Sevens'), squash, football
Other sports followed: Football (West Ham)
Favourite band: 50 Cent
Extras: South of England and England squads until U17. Sussex Young Player of the Year 2000. Sussex 2nd XI Fielder of the Year 2001, 2003. Took wicket (John Wood) with his third ball on county debut, in the Norwich Union League v Lancashire at Hove 2001. C&G Man of the Match award v Nottinghamshire at Hove 2005 (51 plus run-out of Stephen Fleming)
Best batting: 106 Sussex v Hampshire, Arundel 2008
Best bowling: 1-20 Sussex v LUCCE, Hove 2004

2008 Season

	M	Inn	NO	Runs	HS	Avg	100	50	Ct	St	Balls	Runs	Wkts	Avg	BB	5I	10M
Test																	
FC	17	27	3	789	106	32.87	1	4	12	-	12	16	0	-	-	-	-
ODI																	
List A	13	9	3	165	48	27.50	-	-	3	-	18	21	0	-	-	-	
20/20 Int																	
20/20	6	4	1	41	26 *	13.66	-	-	6	-	0	0	0	-	-	-	

Career Performances

	M	Inn	NO	Runs	HS	Avg	100	50	Ct	St	Balls	Runs	Wkts	Avg	BB	5I	10M
Test																	
FC	55	90	4	2262	106	26.30	1	15	37	-	340	262	2	131.00	1-20	-	-
ODI																	
List A	91	71	11	1390	123 *	23.16	1	6	39	-	566	560	15	37.33	3-19	-	
20/20 Int																	
20/20	28	18	5	165	26 *	12.69	-	-	11	-	0	0	0	-	-	-	

HORTON, P. J. Lancashire

Name: Paul James Horton
Role: Right-hand bat, right-arm medium/off-spin bowler
Born: 20 September 1982, Sydney, Australia
Height: 5ft 10in **Weight:** 11st 3lbs
Nickname: Horts, Ozzy
County debut: 2003
County cap: 2007
1000 runs in a season: 2
Place in batting averages: 33rd av. 47.26 (2007 37th av. 48.52)
Parents: Donald William and Norma
Marital status: Single
Education: Colo High School, Sydney/Broadgreen Comprehensive, Liverpool; St Margaret's High School, Liverpool
Qualifications: 11 GCSEs, 3 A-levels, Level 2 ECB coach
Overseas tours: Hawkesbury U15 to New Zealand 1997; Lancashire to Cape Town 2002-03, to Grenada 2003

Overseas teams played for: Hawkesbury, Sydney 1992-93 – 1997-98; Penrith, NSW 2002-03
Cricket moments to forget: 'First 2nd XI game for Lancashire at Old Trafford – out for 0'
Cricket superstitions: 'None'
Cricketers particularly admired: Dean Jones, Sachin Tendulkar, Mark Waugh
Other sports played: Football, golf, squash, tennis, badminton
Other sports followed: Football (Liverpool)
Favourite band: Red Hot Chili Peppers
Relaxations: 'Golf, socialising with friends, watching sport'
Extras: Captained Lancashire U17 and U19. Captained Lancashire Board XI in the C&G 2003. Lancashire Young Player of the Year Award 2001, 2002. Leading run-scorer for Lancashire 2nd XI in the 2nd XI Championship 2003 (861 runs; av. 50.65). Lancashire Player of the Year 2007. Scored over 1000 runs in 2008.
Best batting: 152 Lancashire v Hampshire, Old Trafford 2007

2008 Season

	M	Inn	NO	Runs	HS	Avg	100	50	Ct	St	Balls	Runs	Wkts	Avg	BB	5I	10M
Test																	
FC	16	26	3	1087	152	47.26	3	7	10	-	0	0	0		-	-	-
ODI																	
List A	8	8	0	128	56	16.00	-	1	3	-	0	0	0		-	-	
20/20 Int																	
20/20																	

Career Performances

	M	Inn	NO	Runs	HS	Avg	100	50	Ct	St	Balls	Runs	Wkts	Avg	BB	5I	10M
Test																	
FC	42	69	8	2804	152	45.96	6	16	33	1	0	0	0		-	-	-
ODI																	
List A	26	23	0	424	56	18.43	-	1	4	-	0	0	0		-	-	
20/20 Int																	
20/20	5	4	1	28	11	9.33	-	-	2	-	0	0	0		-	-	

HOUSEGO, D. M. Middlesex

Name: Daniel (Dan) Mark Housego
Role: Right-hand top-order bat, right-arm off-spin bowler
Born: 12 October 1988, Windsor
Height: 5ft 9in **Weight:** 11st 4lbs
Nickname: Harry Housego, Housey
County debut: 2008
Parents: Beryl and Jim
Marital status: Single
Education: The Oratory School, Reading
Qualifications: 8 GCSEs, 3 A-levels, Level 1 coaching
Career outside cricket: 'Golf'
Off-season: 'Three months in Adelaide'
Overseas tours: England U15 to South Africa; England U16 to South Africa and Barbados
Overseas teams played for: Adelaide CC, 2007-08; Prospect, North Adelaide, 2008-09
Career highlights to date: 'Making my first-class debut against Derbyshire'
Cricket moments to forget: 'Two low scores at Lord's'
Cricket superstitions: 'None'
Cricketers particularly admired: Ian Bell
Young players to look out for: Josh Cobb, Eoin Morgan
Other sports played: Football (Oxford United Academy 1998-2003), athletics (age-group 200m national champion 2002), golf, fishing
Other sports followed: Football (Chelsea), golf (Tiger Woods)
Favourite band: Chris Brown, T-Pain, Lil Wayne
Relaxations: 'Fishing, golf, reading'
Extras: Neil Lloyd Trophy (Bunbury Festival). Represented England U15, U16, U17. Played for Berkshire in the Minor Counties Championship 2006, making a personal best 170* against Shropshire
Opinions on cricket: 'You only get what you give.'
Best batting: 36 Middlesex v Derbyshire, Derby 2008

2008 Season

	M	Inn	NO	Runs	HS	Avg	100	50	Ct	St	Balls	Runs	Wkts	Avg	BB	5I	10M
Test																	
FC	2	4	0	66	36	16.50	-	-	-	-	0	0	0		-	-	-
ODI																	
List A																	
20/20 Int																	
20/20	4	3	0	36	18	12.00	-	-	-	-	0	0	0		-	-	

Career Performances

	M	Inn	NO	Runs	HS	Avg	100	50	Ct	St	Balls	Runs	Wkts	Avg	BB	5I	10M
Test																	
FC	2	4	0	66	36	16.50	-	-	-	-	0	0	0		-	-	-
ODI																	
List A																	
20/20 Int																	
20/20	4	3	0	36	18	12.00	-	-	-	-	0	0	0		-	-	

HOWELL, B. A. C. — Hampshire

Name: Benjamin (Benny) Alexander Cameron Howell
Role: Right-hand opening bat, right-arm medium bowler
Born: 5 October 1988, Bordeaux, France
Height: 5ft 11in **Weight:** 12st
Nickname: Growler, Howly, Schofield
County debut: No first-team appearance
Parents: Jonathan and Julie
Marital status: Single
Family links with cricket: 'Dad played one game for Warwickshire first team; made a half-century. Brother Nick played county age-group cricket for Berkshire'
Education: The Oratory School, Reading
Qualifications: 9 GCSEs, 3 A-levels
Overseas tours: Oratory School to Barbados 2003, 2004
Overseas teams played for: Melville, Perth 2007-08
Career highlights to date: '172 not out in a 50-over game for Hampshire Cricket Academy, August 2007'

Cricket moments to forget: 'Every time I bowl!'
Cricketers particularly admired: Shane Warne, Nic Pothas, Brett Lee, Steve Waugh, Sachin Tendulkar, Brian Lara
Young players to look out for: Liam Dawson, Hamza Riazuddin, James Vince, Dan Housego
Other sports played: Football, rugby, golf, tennis, squash, basketball, real tennis, snooker, darts
Other sports followed: Football (Everton FC), AFL (Melbourne Demons)
Favourite band: Justin Timberlake, 50 Cent, Timbaland, Chris Brown, Akon, Eminem, Kanye West
Relaxations: 'Movies, music, sports (playing and watching), sleeping'
Extras: Hampshire Academy Player of the Year 2006. Southern Electric Premier League Player of the Month, August 2007. Awarded a development contract 2009
Opinions on cricket: 'At the end of the day, cricket is all about enjoying playing and entertaining the spectators. Twenty20 does that; it is exciting, explosive and highly skilful. This brings in the crowds and money to develop the game. It has to be played more often.'

HOWGEGO, B. H. N. — Northamptonshire

Name: Benjamin Harry Nicholas Howgego
Role: Left-hand bat, right-arm fast-medium bowler
Born: 3 March 1988, Norfolk
County debut: 2008
Education: The King's School, Ely; Stowe School
Extras: Made 2nd XI Championship debut 2005. Represented both ECB Development of Excellence XI and ECB Schools v India U19 2006. A student, he and Richard Browning were offered 2008 summer contracts to tie in with their studies. Howgego made his first-class debut for Northamptonshire as an opening batsman against Gloucestershire in August 2008, having played in the Second XI Championship just once up to that point in the season
Best batting: 15 Northamptonshire v Gloucestershire, Bristol 2008

2008 Season

	M	Inn	NO	Runs	HS	Avg	100	50	Ct	St	Balls	Runs	Wkts	Avg	BB	5I	10M
Test																	
FC	1	2	1	16	15	16.00	-	-	-	-	0	0	0		-	-	-
ODI																	
List A																	
20/20 Int																	
20/20																	

Career Performances

	M	Inn	NO	Runs	HS	Avg	100	50	Ct	St	Balls	Runs	Wkts	Avg	BB	5I	10M
Test																	
FC	1	2	1	16	15	16.00	-	-	-	-	0	0	0		-	-	-
ODI																	
List A																	
20/20 Int																	
20/20																	

HUNTER, I. D. Derbyshire

Name: Ian David Hunter
Role: Right-hand bat, right-arm fast-medium bowler
Born: 11 September 1979, Durham City
Height: 6ft 2in **Weight:** 13st
Nickname: Sticks, Hunts, Kingsley
County debut: 1999 (one-day, Durham), 2000 (first-class, Durham), 2004 (Derbys)
Parents: Ken and Linda
Marital status: Single
Family links with cricket: Brother local village cricketer
Education: Fyndoune Community College, Sacriston; New College, Durham
Qualifications: 9 GCSEs, 1 A-level (PE), BTEC National Diploma in Sports Science, Level I and II cricket coaching awards
Overseas tours: Durham U21 to Sri Lanka 1996; Durham to Cape Town 2002
Career highlights to date: 'Taking 5-63 against Durham at Riverside [2005]'
Cricket moments to forget: 'All of 2007 season – out through knee injuries'

Cricket superstitions: 'Always put my left pad on first'
Cricketers particularly admired: Allan Donald, Graeme Welch, Steve Waugh
Young players to look out for: Dan Redfern, Gary Ballance
Other sports played: Football, golf
Other sports followed: Football (Newcastle United FC), rugby league (St Helens)
Favourite band: Arctic Monkeys
Relaxations: 'Golf, gym, socialising with friends'
Extras: Set a then Durham best analysis for the 2nd XI Championship with his 11-155 v Lancashire 2nd XI at Great Crosby 1999. Represented England U19 1999. Out for most of the 2007 season with torn cartilage and patellar tendonopathy of the right knee. Signed a new one-year contract in October 2008
Opinions on cricket: 'Too much one-day cricket played; not enough time to recover between games.'
Best batting: 65 Durham v Northamptonshire, Northampton 2002
Best bowling: 5-63 Derbyshire v Durham, Riverside 2005

2008 Season

	M	Inn	NO	Runs	HS	Avg	100	50	Ct	St	Balls	Runs	Wkts	Avg	BB	5I	10M
Test																	
FC	6	6	1	37	17	7.40	-	-	1	-	795	332	8	41.50	2-12	-	-
ODI																	
List A	6	3	1	33	24	16.50	-	-	2	-	246	202	10	20.20	3-18	-	
20/20 Int																	
20/20																	

Career Performances

	M	Inn	NO	Runs	HS	Avg	100	50	Ct	St	Balls	Runs	Wkts	Avg	BB	5I	10M
Test																	
FC	56	74	18	935	65	16.69	-	2	16	-	8715	5242	129	40.63	5-63	1	-
ODI																	
List A	82	49	12	310	39	8.37	-	-	16	-	3545	2909	91	31.96	4-29	-	
20/20 Int																	
20/20	15	6	2	41	25 *	10.25	-	-	3	-	318	453	17	26.64	3-26	-	

43. Who kept wicket for both Australia and England in Test matches?

IMRAN ARIF Worcestershire

Name: Imran Arif
Role: Right-hand bat, right-arm fast-medium bowler
Born: 15 January 1984, Kotli, Pakistan
Height: 5ft 11in **Weight:** 11st 2lbs
Nickname: Immy, Ice Man
County debut: 2008
Place in bowling averages: 42nd av. 26.13
Education: Government High School, Saidpur, Kotli (AK), Bradford College
Qualifications: 5 GCSEs
Career highlights to date: 'Making my first-class debut'
Other sports followed: Football (Liverpool), tennis, snooker
Relaxations: 'Watching football, listening to music, computer games, movies, spending time with friends and family.'

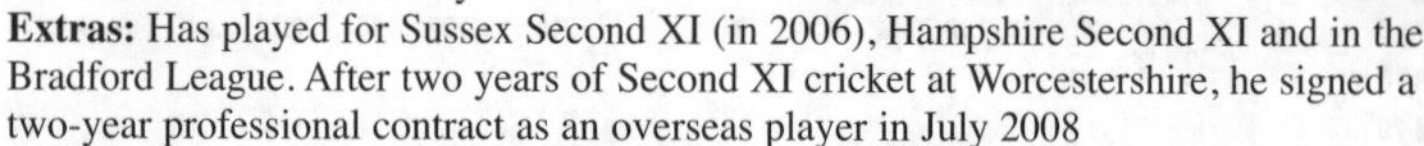

Extras: Has played for Sussex Second XI (in 2006), Hampshire Second XI and in the Bradford League. After two years of Second XI cricket at Worcestershire, he signed a two-year professional contract as an overseas player in July 2008
Best batting: 5 Worcestershire v Middlesex, Lord's 2008
Best bowling: 5-50 Worcestershire v Glamorgan, New Road 2008 (on debut)

2008 Season

	M	Inn	NO	Runs	HS	Avg	100	50	Ct	St	Balls	Runs	Wkts	Avg	BB	5I	10M
Test																	
FC	6	3	1	13	5	6.50	-	-	1	-	953	575	22	26.13	5-50	1	1
ODI																	
List A	5	2	2	17	16 *	-	-	-	0	-	182	198	5	39.60	1-17	-	
20/20 Int																	
20/20																	

Career Performances

	M	Inn	NO	Runs	HS	Avg	100	50	Ct	St	Balls	Runs	Wkts	Avg	BB	5I	10M
Test																	
FC	6	3	1	13	5	6.50	-	-	1	-	953	575	22	26.13	5-50	1	1
ODI																	
List A	5	2	2	17	16 *	-	-	-	0	-	182	198	5	39.60	1-17	-	
20/20 Int																	
20/20																	

IMRAN TAHIR Hampshire

Name: Mohammad Imran Tahir
Role: Right-hand bat, right-arm leg-spin bowler
Born: 27 March 1979, Lahore, Pakistan
County debut: 2003 (Middlesex), 2007 (Yorkshire), 2008 (Hampshire)
Place in bowling averages: 2nd av. 16.68 (2007 33rd av. 47.26)
Overseas tours: Pakistan U19 to South Africa 1996-97, to Australia 1997-98, to South Africa (U19 World Cup) 1997-98; Pakistan A to Sri Lanka 2004-05
Overseas teams played for: Lahore City 1996-97 – 1997-98, Pakistan International Airlines 2004-05 – 2006-07 (and others in Pakistan); Titans, South Africa 2007-08 –
Extras: Played for Staffordshire in the C&G 2004 and 2005, winning Man of the Match award v Lancashire at Stone 2004 (3-31/18-ball 41*). Represented both Pakistan A and a PCB Patron's XI v England XI 2005-06. Was a temporary overseas player with Middlesex in 2003, and with Yorkshire in 2007. Joined Hampshire in July 2008 and will rejoin them as their overseas player from June 2009
Best batting: 48 REDCO v KRL, Rawalpindi (KRL) 1999-2000
Best bowling: 8-76 REDCO v Karachi Blues, Lahore (C) 1999-2000

2008 Season

	M	Inn	NO	Runs	HS	Avg	100	50	Ct	St	Balls	Runs	Wkts	Avg	BB	5I	10M
Test																	
FC	7	8	4	85	24 *	21.25	-	-	3	-	1550	734	44	16.68	7-66	3	1
ODI																	
List A	7	2	1	4	3	4.00	-	-	1	-	276	244	12	20.33	5-27	1	
20/20 Int																	
20/20																	

Career Performances

	M	Inn	NO	Runs	HS	Avg	100	50	Ct	St	Balls	Runs	Wkts	Avg	BB	5I	10M
Test																	
FC	73	89	18	770	48	10.84	-	-	38	-	13472	7055	284	24.84	8-76	17	4
ODI																	
List A	48	18	7	155	41 *	14.09	-	-	12	-	2227	1608	74	21.72	5-27	2	
20/20 Int																	
20/20	7	4	2	25	13	12.50	-	-	4	-	150	133	8	16.62	3-13	-	

IRELAND, A. J. Gloucestershire

Name: Anthony John Ireland
Role: Right-hand bat, right-arm medium bowler
Born: 30 August 1984, Masvingo, Zimbabwe
County debut: 2007
County cap: 2007
ODI debut: 2005-06
Twenty20 Int debut: 2006-07
Place in bowling averages: 114th av. 36.78
Overseas tours: ZCU President's XI to India (Duleep Trophy) 2005-06; Zimbabwe A to Bangladesh 2006-07; Zimbabwe to West Indies (one-day series) 2006, to South Africa (one-day series) 2006-07, to India (ICC Champions Trophy) 2006-07, to Bangladesh (one-day series) 2006-07, to West Indies (World Cup) 2006-07

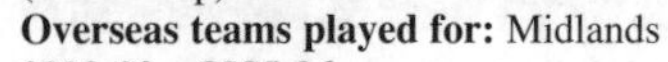

Overseas teams played for: Midlands 2002-03 – 2005-06
Extras: Retired from international cricket in April 2007. Is not considered an overseas player
Best batting: 16* Gloucestershire v Middlesex, Bristol 2008
Best bowling: 7-36 Zimbabwe A v Bangladesh A, Mirpur 2006-07

2008 Season

	M	Inn	NO	Runs	HS	Avg	100	50	Ct	St	Balls	Runs	Wkts	Avg	BB	5I	10M
Test																	
FC	9	13	6	30	16 *	4.28	-	-	3	-	1309	846	23	36.78	3-33	-	-
ODI																	
List A	7	2	1	8	7 *	8.00	-	-	-	-	241	243	4	60.75	2-43	-	
20/20 Int																	
20/20	2	0	0	0	0		-	-	1	-	19	44	1	44.00	1-32	-	

Career Perfomances

	M	Inn	NO	Runs	HS	Avg	100	50	Ct	St	Balls	Runs	Wkts	Avg	BB	5I	10M
Test																	
FC	21	34	12	93	16 *	4.22	-	-	7	-	2974	1823	56	32.55	7-36	1	1
ODI	26	13	5	30	8 *	3.75	-	-	2	-	1326	1115	38	29.34	3-41	-	
List A	49	24	13	77	17	7.00	-	-	8	-	2235	1926	67	28.74	4-16	-	
20/20 Int	1	1	1	2	2 *		-	-	-	-	18	33	1	33.00	1-33	-	
20/20	10	4	2	20	8 *	10.00	-	-	3	-	165	247	14	17.64	3-10	-	

JAMES, N.A. Warwickshire

Name: Nicholas (Nick) Alexander James
Role: Left-hand bat, slow left-arm bowler; all-rounder
Born: 17 September 1986, Sandwell, West Midlands
Height: 5ft 10in **Weight:** 12st 2lbs
Nickname: Jaymo
County debut: 2006 (one-day), 2008 (first-class)
Parents: Ann and Mike
Marital status: Single
Family links with cricket: 'Dad and brother Chris play at Aldridge CC. Dad also coaches'
Education: King Edward VI Aston School, Birmingham
Qualifications: 10 GCSEs, 3 A-levels
Off-season: 'In Australia - playing and improving my game'
Overseas tours: England U19 to Bangladesh 2005-06, to Sri Lanka (U19 World Cup) 2005-06; CCC to Australia 2007-08
Overseas teams played for: Tea Tree Gully (Adelaide) 2008-09
Career highlights to date: 'Representing England U19. Reaching semi-final of 2006 U19 World Cup. Playing for Warwickshire first team in C&G, Pro40 and Twenty20'
Cricket moments to forget: 'Fracturing hand diving to stop ball (against Lancashire) 2006 – unavailable for six weeks. Watching ball I had just hit for six bounce and smash through rear window of my car (while bringing my 150 up) v Hampshire 2nd XI at Basingstoke 2007'
Cricketers particularly admired: Kevin Pietersen, Kumar Sangakkara
Young players to look out for: Andrew Miller, Chris Woakes, Richard Johnson
Other sports played: 'Recreational football, golf'
Other sports followed: Football (Aston Villa and Nottingham Forest)
Favourite band: Coldplay
Relaxations: 'Relaxing with friends'
Extras: Captain of Warwickshire U17 County Championship winning side 2004. Member of ECB U18 Development Squad 2004. Represented England U19 and captained ECB Development of Excellence XI v Sri Lanka U19 2005. Has won eight Warwickshire youth awards, including Tiger Smith Memorial Award for the most promising young player 2005. Acted as 12th man (one day only) for England A v Sri Lankans at Worcester 2006. Attended ECB Elite Skills Set Spin Programme at Loughborough 2006-07. Birmingham Premier League Young Player of the Year 2007. ECB Scholarship for Club Cricket Conference tour to Australia 2007-08. Released by Warwickshire in September 2008

Opinions on cricket: 'It's faster and more exciting now...'
Best batting: 34 Warwickshire v Cambridge UCCE, Fenner's 2008
Best bowling: 1-6 Warwickshire v Cambridge UCCE, Fenner's 2008

2008 Season

	M	Inn	NO	Runs	HS	Avg	100	50	Ct	St	Balls	Runs	Wkts	Avg	BB	5I	10M
Test																	
FC	1	1	0	34	34	34.00	-	-	1	-	18	6	1	6.00	1-6	-	-
ODI																	
List A	1	1	0	3	3	3.00	-	-	-	-	0	0	0	-	-		
20/20 Int																	
20/20																	

Career Performances

	M	Inn	NO	Runs	HS	Avg	100	50	Ct	St	Balls	Runs	Wkts	Avg	BB	5I	10M
Test																	
FC	1	1	0	34	34	34.00	-	-	1	-	18	6	1	6.00	1-6	-	-
ODI																	
List A	9	6	2	102	30	25.50	-	-	2	-	210	141	6	23.50	2-34	-	
20/20 Int																	
20/20	2	2	1	13	12*	13.00	-	-	2	-	0	0	0	-	-		

JAVID, A. — Warwickshire

Name: Ateeq Javid
Role: Right-hand bat, right-arm seam and occasional leg-spin bowler
Born: 15 October 1991, Birmingham
County debut: No first-team appearances
Extras: Played for Aston Manor CC in the Birmingham League 2008. Represented Warwickshire Academy and Warwickshire 2nd XI 2008. Played for England U16 Elite Player Development side at the Bunbury Festival, August 2008, scoring 45 from 29 balls. Has made a century for Warwickshire U17's, and three 50's for U19's. Called up to England U18 squad October 2008. Signed a two-year contract for the county in September 2008. Part of the ECB Development Group 2008

JEFFERSON, W. I. Nottinghamshire

Name: William (Will) Ingleby Jefferson
Role: Right-hand opening bat
Born: 25 October 1979, Derby ('but native of Norfolk')
Height: 6ft 10½in **Weight:** 15st 2lbs
Nickname: Santa, Lemar, Jeffo
County debut: 2000 (Essex), 2007 (Nottinghamshire)
County cap: 2002 (Essex)
1000 runs in a season: 1
1st-Class 200s: 1
Place in batting averages: 181st av. 22.10 (2007 102nd av. 35.11)
Parents: Richard
Marital status: Single
Family links with cricket: Grandfather Jefferson played for the Army and Combined Services in the 1920s. Father, R. I. Jefferson, played for Cambridge University 1961 and Surrey 1961-66
Education: Oundle School, Northants; Durham University
Qualifications: 9 GCSEs, 3 A-levels, BA (Hons) Sport in the Community, Level 3 cricket coach
Off-season: 'In Australia - playing and improving my game'
Overseas tours: Oundle School to South Africa 1995; England A to Bangladesh 2006-07
Overseas teams played for: Young People's Club, Paarl, South Africa 1998-99; South Perth, Western Australia 2002-03
Career highlights to date: 'Being awarded [Essex] county cap on final day of the 2002 season. Scoring 165* to help beat Notts and secure 2002 second division Championship. 222 v Hampshire at Rose Bowl [2004]'
Cricket moments to forget: 'Any dropped catch; any time bowled playing across the line'
Cricket superstitions: 'Put batting gear on in the same order'
Cricketers particularly admired: Andy Flower, Nasser Hussain
Young players to look out for: Samit Patel, Jake Mickleburgh
Other sports played: Golf (12 handicap), tennis ('occasionally')
Other sports followed: Rugby (British & Irish Lions, England), golf (Ryder Cup)
Favourite band: Coldplay, U2, The Verve
Relaxations: 'Reading, pilates, listening to music, spending time with family'
Extras: Holmwoods School Cricketer of the Year 1998. Represented British Universities 2000, 2001 and 2002. Played for Durham UCCE 2001 and 2002. NBC

Denis Compton Award for the most promising young Essex player 2002. Scored century before lunch on the opening day for Essex v Cambridge UCCE at Fenner's 2003. C&G Man of the Match awards for his 97 v Scotland at Edinburgh 2004 and for his 126 v Nottinghamshire at Trent Bridge in the next round. Essex Player of the Year 2004. Essex Boundary Club Trophy for scoring most runs for Essex 1st XI 2004. Represented England Lions 2007

Opinions on cricket: 'Standard of cricket is getting nearer first-class played in Australia, which is where we want to be. Last step is still to reduce number of days during the summer to improve quality further. System in good health - look how tight all the tables were right up to the end of 2008 domestic season. Twenty20 skills converted into Pro40, which will convert more into 50-over cricket in the future'

Best batting: 222 Essex v Hampshire, Rose Bowl 2004

Best bowling: 1-16 Essex v Yorkshire, Headingley 2005

2008 Season

	M	Inn	NO	Runs	HS	Avg	100	50	Ct	St	Balls	Runs	Wkts	Avg	BB	5I	10M
Test																	
FC	13	21	1	442	98	22.10	-	2	19	-	0	0	0		-	-	-
ODI																	
List A	11	11	0	280	53	25.45	-	1	6	-	0	0	0		-	-	
20/20 Int																	
20/20	9	9	0	209	43	23.22	-	-	6	-	0	0	0		-	-	

Career Performances

	M	Inn	NO	Runs	HS	Avg	100	50	Ct	St	Balls	Runs	Wkts	Avg	BB	5I	10M
Test																	
FC	87	153	12	5111	222	36.24	11	20	81	-	120	60	1	60.00	1-16	-	-
ODI																	
List A	85	84	5	2767	132	35.02	4	15	40	-	24	9	2	4.50	2-9	-	
20/20 Int																	
20/20	25	25	2	417	51	18.13	-	1	10	-	0	0	0		-	-	

44. How many wickets did Ian Botham take in Ashes Tests?

JEWELL, T. M. Surrey

Name: Tom Melvin Jewell
Role: Right-hand bat, right-arm fast-medium bowler; all-rounder
Born: 13 January 1991, Reading, Berkshire
Height: 6ft 4in **Weight:** 13st 6lbs
Nickname: TJ
County debut: 2008
Parents: Melvin and Caroline
Marital status: Single
Education: Bradfield College
Qualifications: 8 GCSEs, 3 A-levels
Career outside cricket: Student
Off-season: 'School, and a cricket tour to India and South Africa'
Career highlights: 'Making my first-class debut against Loughborough'
Cricketers particularly admired: Steve Waugh
Young players to look out for: Matthew Dunn
Other sports followed: Football (Reading)
Favourite band: Kings of Leon
Relaxations: 'Spending time with my girlfriend. The odd episode of *Friends*'
Extras: Won the Sir Jack Hobbs Award (for the best U15 cricketer in England) 2007. Features in the book *Training for Success - Cricket*
Opinions on cricket: 'Twenty20 cricket has reduced the number of county championship hundreds'
Best bowling: 1-16 Surrey v Loughborough UCCE, The Oval 2008

2008 Season

	M	Inn	NO	Runs	HS	Avg	100	50	Ct	St	Balls	Runs	Wkts	Avg	BB	5I	10M
Test																	
FC	1	0	0	0	0		-	-	-	-	42	16	1	16.00	1-16	-	-
ODI																	
List A																	
20/20 Int																	
20/20																	

Career Performances

	M	Inn	NO	Runs	HS	Avg	100	50	Ct	St	Balls	Runs	Wkts	Avg	BB	5I	10M
Test																	
FC	1	0	0	0	0		-	-	-	-	42	16	1	16.00	1-16	-	-
ODI																	
List A																	
20/20 Int																	
20/20																	

JOHNSON, R. M. — Warwickshire

Name: Richard Matthew Johnson
Role: Right-hand bat, wicket-keeper
Born: 1 September 1988, Solihull
Height: 5ft 10in **Weight:** 11st
Nickname: Johnno
County debut: 2008 (*see below*)
Parents: Barry and Lorraine
Marital status: Single
Family links with cricket: 'Dad played club cricket'
Education: Solihull School
Qualifications: 3 A-levels, ECB Level 2 coaching award
Off-season: 'Hopefully a pre-season tour to South Africa'
Overseas tours: England U16 to Cape Town 2005; Warwickshire Academy to Cape Town 2005; Solihull School to Barbados 2007

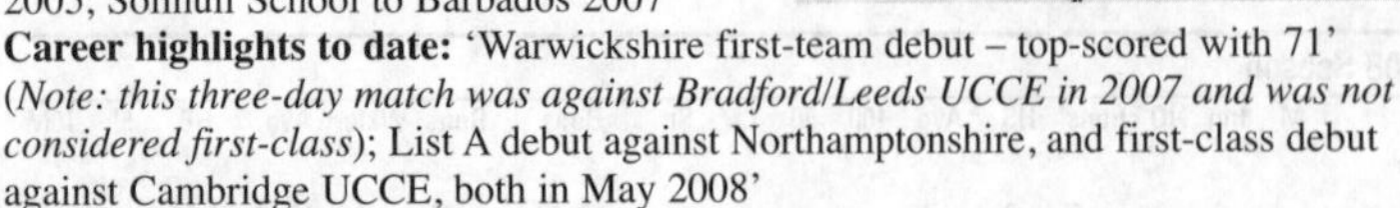

Career highlights to date: 'Warwickshire first-team debut – top-scored with 71' (*Note: this three-day match was against Bradford/Leeds UCCE in 2007 and was not considered first-class*); List A debut against Northamptonshire, and first-class debut against Cambridge UCCE, both in May 2008'
Cricket moments to forget: 'Breaking a bone in my thumb before playing for England U15'
Cricket superstitions: 'Pack playing kit in same position'
Cricketers particularly admired: Keith Piper, Sachin Tendulkar
Young players to look out for: Chris Woakes, Callum MacLeod
Other sports played: Football (Wolverhampton Wanderers U10, U11, U12), rugby (Solihull School 1st XV)
Other sports followed: Football (Aston Villa)
Favourite band: Oasis

Relaxations: 'Music, TV, computer, friends, watching Aston Villa'
Extras: Best Wicket-keeper Award at Bunbury Festival 2005. Warwickshire Second XI most improved player 2008
Opinions on cricket: 'Second XI one-day cricket should be played with coloured kits and white ball, in preparation for first team cricket.'
Best batting: 72 Warwickshire v Cambridge UCCE, Fenners 2008

2008 Season

	M	Inn	NO	Runs	HS	Avg	100	50	Ct	St	Balls	Runs	Wkts	Avg	BB	5I	10M
Test																	
FC	1	1	0	72	72	72.00	-	1	1	-	0	0	0		-	-	-
ODI																	
List A	2	2	0	26	20	13.00	-	-	2	-	0	0	0		-	-	
20/20 Int																	
20/20																	

Career Performances

	M	Inn	NO	Runs	HS	Avg	100	50	Ct	St	Balls	Runs	Wkts	Avg	BB	5I	10M
Test																	
FC	1	1	0	72	72	72.00	-	1	1	-	0	0	0		-	-	-
ODI																	
List A	2	2	0	26	20	13.00	-	-	2	-	0	0	0		-	-	
20/20 Int																	
20/20																	

JONES, A. J. Glamorgan

Name: Alexander (Alex) John Jones
Role: Right-hand bat, left-arm seam bowler
Born: 10 November 1988, Bridgend,
Nickname: AJ
County debut: No first-team appearance
Education: Cowbridge Comprehensive School, UWIC (Degree course in Sport and Physical Education)
Cricket moments to forget: 'Getting hit in the box!'
Cricketers particularly admired: Kevin Pietersen, Chris Gayle
Young players to look out for: Chris Ashling, Will Owen, Kyle Tudge
Other sports followed: Rugby
Extras: Glamorgan and Wales Academy U17s 2005, Glamorgan U17s 2006, Glamorgan U19s 2008, Glamorgan and Wales Academy 2005-08, Glamorgan Second XI 2006-08, Wales Minor Counties 2007-08
Opinions on cricket: 'Under-rated... great game, great game!'

45. Who fell just two runs short of a century in his final innings of the 1932-33 Bodyline series, and did not play for England again?

JONES, C. — Somerset

Name: Christopher (Chris) Jones
Role: Right-hand bat
Born: November 1991
County debut: No first-team appearances
Education: Richard Huish College, Taunton
Extras: Ex-Somerset Academy. Has played for Poole CC and Bashley CC (Southern League): Represented Somerset at U17 level in 2008, finishing with an average of 162.5. Played for England U17 v New Zealand U19 in August 2008. Will sign a professional contract with the county after completing his A-Level studies in June 2009

JONES, E. P. — Derbyshire

Name: Edward (Ed) Peter Jones
Role: Right-hand bat, right-arm slow-medium bowler
Born: 23 October 1989, Stoke-on-Trent
County debut: No first-team appearances
Extras: Played for Staffordshire in the Minor Counties Championship 2007. Became first Derbyshire player to take up free University degree course in business and sports management, September 2008. The Donald Carr scholarship, as it is called, will be available on a yearly basis to two or three Derbyshire players, after a deal was struck with the University of Derby

JONES, G. O. Kent

Name: Geraint Owen Jones
Role: Right-hand bat, wicket-keeper
Born: 14 July 1976, Kundiawa, Papua New Guinea
Height: 5ft 10in **Weight:** 12st
Nickname: Joner, Jonesy, 'G'
County debut: 2001
County cap: 2003
Test debut: 2003-04
ODI debut: 2004
Twenty20 Int debut: 2005
50 dismissals in a season: 1
Place in batting averages: 121st av. 30.36 (2007 104th av. 34.61)
Parents: Emrys, Carol (deceased), Maureen (stepmother)
Wife and date of marriage: 'Jennifer, 30 September 2006'
Family links with cricket: 'Father was star off-spinner in local school side'
Education: Harristown State High School, Toowoomba, Queensland; MacGregor SHS, Brisbane
Qualifications: Level 1 coach; pharmacy technician
Career outside cricket: Hobby farming
Off-season: 'Making sure the pigs, lambs and chickens fatten up nicely!'
Overseas tours: Beenleigh-Logan U19 to New Zealand 1995; Kent to Port Elizabeth 2001-02; England to Bangladesh and Sri Lanka 2003-04, to West Indies 2003-04, to Zimbabwe (one-day series) 2004-05, to South Africa 2004-05, to Pakistan 2005-06, to India 2005-06, to Australia 2006-07
Overseas teams played for: Beenleigh-Logan, Brisbane 1995-98, 2006-07; Valleys, Brisbane 2001-02
Career highlights to date: 'Ashes 2005, Twenty20 final 2007'
Cricket moments to forget: 'Last Test played, finals of 2008'
Cricket superstitions: 'Left pad first'
Cricketers particularly admired: Adam Gilchrist
Young players to look out for: Joe Denly, Neil Dexter, Robbie Joseph
Other sports played: Golf
Other sports followed: Football (Liverpool), Rugby (Crickhowell RFC)
Favourite band: Newton Faulkner
Relaxations: 'Rearing my own animals for meat and sausage production'

Extras: Set new competition record for a season's tally of wicket-keeping dismissals in the one-day league (33; 27/6) 2003; also equalled record for number of wicket-keeping catches in one match, six v Leicestershire at Canterbury 2003. Made 59 first-class dismissals plus 985 first-class runs in his first full season of county cricket 2003. Man of the Match in the second Test v New Zealand at Headingley 2004, in which he scored his maiden Test century (100). His other international awards include Man of the Match v Australia in the tied final of the NatWest Series 2005 (71 plus five catches). Appointed MBE in 2006 New Year Honours as part of 2005 Ashes-winning England team. Made 100th Test dismissal (Mahela Jayawardene, caught) in the first Test v Sri Lanka at Lord's 2006, becoming the fastest England wicket-keeper to the milestone (27 matches)
Opinions on cricket: 'The authorities need to sort out the worldwide Twenty20 situation, as it seems that the only ones missing out are the English players. Also, don't overkill the concept.'
Best batting: 108* Kent v Essex, Chelmsford 2003

2008 Season

	M	Inn	NO	Runs	HS	Avg	100	50	Ct	St	Balls	Runs	Wkts	Avg	BB	5I	10M
Test																	
FC	17	26	4	668	106	30.36	1	3	64	3	0	0	0		-	-	-
ODI																	
List A	17	12	2	231	86	23.10	-	1	22	6	0	0	0		-	-	
20/20 Int																	
20/20	13	11	3	59	28	7.37	-	-	7	3	0	0	0		-	-	

Career Performances

	M	Inn	NO	Runs	HS	Avg	100	50	Ct	St	Balls	Runs	Wkts	Avg	BB	5I	10M
Test	34	53	4	1172	100	23.91	1	6	128	5	0	0	0		-	-	-
FC	109	161	20	4351	108 *	30.85	7	24	341	22	18	18	0		-	-	-
ODI	49	41	8	815	80	24.69	-	4	68	4	0	0	0		-	-	
List A	137	115	20	2227	86	23.44	-	8	162	26	0	0	0		-	-	
20/20 Int	2	2	1	33	19	33.00	-	-	2	-	0	0	0		-	-	
20/20	33	26	7	225	28	11.84	-	-	18	7	0	0	0		-	-	

JONES, P. S. Somerset

Name: Philip Steffan Jones
Role: Right-hand bat, right-arm fast-medium bowler
Born: 9 February 1974, Llanelli
Height: 6ft 1in **Weight:** 15st 2lbs
Nickname: Jona
County debut: 1997 (Somerset), 2004 (Northamptonshire), 2006 (Derbyshire)
50 wickets in a season: 2
Place in batting averages: 204th av. 19.90 (2007 128th av. 31.87)
Place in bowling averages: 80th av. 31.40 (2007 115th av. 40.57)
Parents: Lyndon and Ann
Wife and date of marriage: Alex, 12 October 2002
Children: Seren, 2006
Family links with cricket: 'Father played locally in South Wales'
Education: Ysgol Gyfun y Strade, Llanelli; Loughborough University; Homerton College, Cambridge University
Qualifications: BSc Sports Science, PGCE in Physical Education
Career outside cricket: 'Sports conditioner'
Overseas tours: Wales Minor Counties to Barbados 1996; Somerset CCC to South Africa 1999, 2000, 2001
Overseas teams played for: Clarence CC, Tasmania 2005
Career highlights to date: 'C&G final 2001 with Somerset. 6-25 v Glamorgan for Derbyshire [at Cardiff 2006]' (*His full second innings figures were 20-14-25-6*)
Cricket moments to forget: '2003-04'
Cricket superstitions: 'Getting early to the ground'
Cricketers particularly admired: 'Pop' Welch, Brett Lee
Other sports played: Rugby union ('professionally for Bristol and Moseley 1997-99')
Other sports followed: Rugby union
Favourite band: Pussycat Dolls, Black Eyed Peas
Relaxations: 'Going to the cinema'
Extras: Took nine wickets (6-67/3-81) in the Varsity Match at Lord's 1997. Derbyshire's Championship Player of the Year 2006. Left Derbyshire at the end of the 2006 season and rejoined Somerset for 2007. Took over 40 wickets in championhip and one-day games in 2008.
Opinions on cricket: 'Overkill on Twenty20! Moderation is the key to bringing the crowds in and keeping them interested. Wickets have also become too flat!'

Best batting: 114 Somerset v Leicestershire, Leicester 2007
Best bowling: 6-25 Derbyshire v Glamorgan, Cardiff 2006

2008 Season

	M	Inn	NO	Runs	HS	Avg	100	50	Ct	St	Balls	Runs	Wkts	Avg	BB	5I	10M
Test																	
FC	9	12	2	199	27 *	19.90	-	-	-	-	1364	848	27	31.40	5-53	2	-
ODI																	
List A	10	4	0	54	42	13.50		-	1		487	455	16	28.43	3-36	-	
20/20 Int																	
20/20	2	2	2	2	1 *		-	-	2	-	42	75	0		-	-	

Career Performances

	M	Inn	NO	Runs	HS	Avg	100	50	Ct	St	Balls	Runs	Wkts	Avg	BB	5I	10M
Test																	
FC	122	144	36	2003	114	18.54	2	5	24	-	19893	11953	319	37.47	6-25	9	1
ODI																	
List A	176	94	44	628	42	12.56	-	-	30	-	7977	7006	237	29.56	6-56	3	
20/20 Int																	
20/20	26	12	6	62	24 *	10.33	-	-	5	-	532	776	27	28.74	3-26	-	

JONES, R. A. — Worcestershire

Name: Richard Alan Jones
Role: Right-hand bat, right-arm fast-medium bowler
Born: 6 November 1986, Wordsley, West Midlands
Height: 6ft 2in **Weight:** 13st
Nickname: Jonesy, Jonah
County debut: 2007
County colours: 2007
Parents: Bob and Julie
Marital status: Single
Education: The Grange School, Stourbridge; King Edward VI College, Stourbridge
Qualifications: 13 GCSEs, 3 A-levels
Off-season: 'Staying in England to work hard on my fitness and game. Also plan to start a part-time educational course in Business.'

Overseas tours: England U19 to Bangladesh 2005-06
Overseas teams played for: Subiaco Floreat (Perth) 2007-08
Career highlights to date: 'Making first-class debut for Worcestershire against Warwickshire 2007'
Cricket moments to forget: 'Opening over against Sussex in last game of 2007 season – it went for plenty!'
Cricket superstitions: 'None'
Cricketers particularly admired: Ian Botham, Andrew Flintoff, Brett Lee
Young players to look out for: Chris Bending, Adam Bending, Keith Bradley
Other sports played: Football (district schools), golf
Other sports followed: Football (West Bromwich Albion)
Favourite band: Arctic Monkeys
Relaxations: 'Football, listening to music, staying fit, chatting with friends'
Extras: Scored first league hundred aged 17 for local side Old Hill (Birmingham & District Premier League)
Opinions on cricket: 'Going back to one overseas per team will give more younger players a chance to shine in county cricket, which can only be a good thing. The emergence and success of Twenty20 cricket at international level will eventually see it becoming the leading form of cricket in the future.'
Best batting: 24 Worcestershire v LUCCE, Worcester 2007
Best bowling: 3-37 Worcestershire v LUCCE, Worcester 2007

2008 Season

	M	Inn	NO	Runs	HS	Avg	100	50	Ct	St	Balls	Runs	Wkts	Avg	BB	5I	10M
Test																	
FC	2	1	0	2	2	2.00	-	-	-	-	218	140	1	140.00	1-20	-	-
ODI																	
List A	2	1	0	6	6	6.00	-	-	1	-	36	43	0	-	-		
20/20 Int																	
20/20																	

Career Performances

	M	Inn	NO	Runs	HS	Avg	100	50	Ct	St	Balls	Runs	Wkts	Avg	BB	5I	10M
Test																	
FC	5	6	1	40	24	8.00	-	-	1	-	596	435	8	54.37	3-37	-	-
ODI																	
List A	2	1	0	6	6	6.00	-	-	1	-	36	43	0	-	-		
20/20 Int																	
20/20																	

JONES, S. P. Worcestershire

Name: Simon Philip Jones
Role: Left-hand bat, right-arm fast bowler
Born: 25 December 1978, Morriston, Swansea
Height: 6ft 3in **Weight:** 15st
Nickname: Horse
County debut: 1998 (Glamorgan), 2008 (Worcestershire)
County cap: 2002 (Glamorgan)
Test debut: 2002
ODI debut: 2004-05
Place in batting averages: 236th av. 13.85 (2007 249th av. 14.33)
Place in bowling averages: 3rd av. 18.02
Parents: Irene and Jeff
Marital status: Single
Family links with cricket: 'Father played for England [1963-64 – 1967-68]'
Education: Coedcae Comprehensive School; Millfield School
Qualifications: 12 GCSEs, 1 A-level, basic and senior coaching awards
Overseas tours: Dyfed Schools to Zimbabwe 1994; Glamorgan to South Africa 1998; ECB National Academy to Australia 2001-02; England to Australia 2002-03, to West Indies 2003-04, to Zimbabwe (one-day series) 2004-05, to South Africa 2004-05, to India 2005-06; England A to Malaysia and India 2003-04
Career highlights to date: 'Winning Ashes series 2005'
Cricket moments to forget: 'Every injury'
Cricket superstitions: 'Right boot on first'
Cricketers particularly admired: Allan Donald
Young players to look out for: Ben Wright
Other sports played: Football (trials with Leeds United)
Favourite band: Eminem
Extras: NBC Denis Compton Award for the most promising young Glamorgan player 2001. Made Test debut in the first Test v India at Lord's 2002, striking a 43-ball 44 (more runs than his father scored in his 15-Test career); the Joneses are the eleventh father and son to have played in Tests for England. ECB National Academy 2003-04. Recorded maiden Test five-wicket return (5-57) in the second Test v West Indies at Port-of-Spain 2003-04; the Joneses thus became the first father and son to have taken five-wicket hauls for England. Had best strike rate among Test bowlers taking 20 or more wickets in the calendar year 2005 (38.50 balls/wicket). Appointed MBE in 2006 New Year Honours as part of 2005 Ashes-winning England team. One of *Wisden*'s Five Cricketers of the Year 2006. Left Glamorgan at the end of the 2007 season and

joined Worcestershire for 2008. Selected for England Lions against South Africa in August 2008, but had to withdraw due to a knee injury that curtailed his season
Best batting: 46 Glamorgan v Yorkshire, Scarborough 2001
Best bowling: 6-45 Glamorgan v Derbyshire, Cardiff 2002

2008 Season

	M	Inn	NO	Runs	HS	Avg	100	50	Ct	St	Balls	Runs	Wkts	Avg	BB	5I	10M
Test																	
FC	9	11	4	97	25	13.85	-	-	-	-	1266	757	42	18.02	5-30	4	-
ODI																	
List A	4	0	0	0	0		-	-	-	-	192	140	9	15.55	5-32	1	
20/20 Int																	
20/20	4	2	1	22	11 *	22.00	-	-	-	-	92	150	2	75.00	1-36	-	

Career Performances

	M	Inn	NO	Runs	HS	Avg	100	50	Ct	St	Balls	Runs	Wkts	Avg	BB	5I	10M
Test	18	18	5	205	44	15.76	-	-	4	-	2821	1666	59	28.23	6-53	3	-
FC	88	108	35	899	46	12.31	-	-	17	-	12999	7947	260	30.56	6-45	15	1
ODI	8	1	0	1	1	1.00	-	-	-	-	348	275	7	39.28	2-43	-	
List A	34	13	8	76	26	15.20	-	-	2	-	1454	1239	31	39.96	5-32	1	
20/20 Int																	
20/20	4	2	1	22	11 *	22.00	-	-	-	-	92	150	2	75.00	1-36	-	

JORDAN, C. J. — Surrey

Name: Christopher (Chris) James Jordan
Role: Right-hand bat, right-arm fast bowler; all-rounder
Born: 4 October 1988, Barbados
Height: 6ft 2in
Nickname: CJ
County debut: 2007
Place in batting averages: 216th av. 17.57
Place in bowling averages: 141st av. 47.50 (2007 28th av. 24.50)
Parents: Robert and Rosie
Marital status: Single
Education: Dulwich College
Qualifications: 2 A-levels
Overseas tours: Barbados U15 to St Vincent 2004
Cricket superstitions: 'Have to touch my box, my thigh pad and my pads before I settle down to bat'

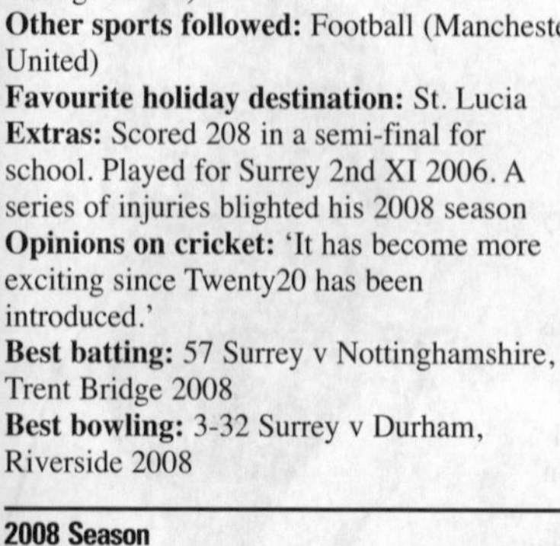

Cricketers particularly admired: Dwayne Bravo, Brian Lara, Brett Lee
Young players to look out for: Dwayne Smith
Other sports played: Football (Dulwich College 1st XI)
Other sports followed: Football (Manchester United)
Favourite holiday destination: St. Lucia
Extras: Scored 208 in a semi-final for school. Played for Surrey 2nd XI 2006. A series of injuries blighted his 2008 season
Opinions on cricket: 'It has become more exciting since Twenty20 has been introduced.'
Best batting: 57 Surrey v Nottinghamshire, Trent Bridge 2008
Best bowling: 3-32 Surrey v Durham, Riverside 2008

2008 Season

	M	Inn	NO	Runs	HS	Avg	100	50	Ct	St	Balls	Runs	Wkts	Avg	BB	5I	10M
Test																	
FC	8	9	2	123	57	17.57	-	1	2	-	954	570	12	47.50	3-32		-
ODI																	
List A	7	4	0	48	38	12.00	-	-	2	-	313	291	9	32.33	3-53	-	
20/20 Int																	
20/20	7	6	2	57	31	14.25	-	-	3	-	102	147	1	147.00	1-23	-	

Career Performances

	M	Inn	NO	Runs	HS	Avg	100	50	Ct	St	Balls	Runs	Wkts	Avg	BB	5I	10M
Test																	
FC	13	15	4	220	57	20.00	-	1	3	-	1789	1060	32	33.12	3-32	-	-
ODI																	
List A	14	8	0	61	38	7.62	-	-	4	-	625	561	22	25.50	3-28	-	
20/20 Int																	
20/20	7	6	2	57	31	14.25	-	-	3	-	102	147	1	147.00	1-23	-	

JOSEPH, R. H. — Kent

Name: Robert Hartman Joseph Jnr
Role: Right-hand bat, right-arm fast-medium bowler
Born: 20 January 1982, Antigua
Height: 6ft 1in **Weight:** 13st 7lbs
Nickname: RJ, Blueie
County debut: 2004
Place in bowling averages: 40th av. 26.05
Education: Sutton Valence School; St Mary's University College
Overseas tours: Antigua Young Lions to England 1997; Antigua and Leeward Islands U15 to Trinidad and St Lucia. England Performance Programme to India, 2008-09
Cricket moments to forget: 'Local school final – getting out on 47 needing one to win with four wickets in hand and losing'
Cricketers particularly admired: Sir Vivian Richards, Andy Roberts
Other sports played: Golf
Other sports followed: Football (Arsenal)
Favourite band: Maroon 5
Relaxations: Listening to music
Extras: Made first-class debut for First-Class Counties XI v New Zealand A at Milton Keynes 2000. Took 55 first-class wickets in 2008 to top the county's bowling averages
Best batting: 36* Kent v Sussex, Hove 2007
Best bowling: 6-32 Kent v Durham, Riverside 2008

2008 Season

	M	Inn	NO	Runs	HS	Avg	100	50	Ct	St	Balls	Runs	Wkts	Avg	BB	5I	10M
Test																	
FC	15	18	5	118	23 *	9.07	-	-	1	-	2515	1433	55	26.05	6-32	2	-
ODI																	
List A	10	2	2	3	2 *		-	-	-	-	395	314	16	19.62	5-13	1	
20/20 Int																	
20/20	1	1	1	1	1 *		-	-	-	-	24	24	2	12.00	2-24	-	

Career Performances

	M	Inn	NO	Runs	HS	Avg	100	50	Ct	St	Balls	Runs	Wkts	Avg	BB	5I	10M
Test																	
FC	37	48	18	330	36 *	11.00	-	-	8	-	5718	3446	111	31.04	6-32	4	-
ODI																	
List A	26	9	7	26	15	13.00	-	-	3	-	1043	830	34	24.41	5-13	1	
20/20 Int																	
20/20	1	1	1	1	1 *		-	-	-	-	24	24	2	12.00	2-24	-	

JOYCE, E. C. Sussex

Name: Edmund (Ed) Christopher Joyce
Role: Left-hand bat, occasional right-arm medium bowler
Born: 22 September 1978, Dublin
Height: 5ft 10in **Weight:** 12st 7lbs
Nickname: Joycey, Spud, Piece
County debut: 1999 (Middlesex)
County cap: 2002 (Middlesex)
ODI debut: 2006
Twenty20 Int debut: 2006
1st-Class 200s: 1
1000 runs in a season: 5
Place in batting averages: 89th av. 35.77 (2007 78th av. 39.11)
Parents: Maureen and Jimmy
Marital status: Single
Family links with cricket: Two brothers and two sisters have represented Ireland
Education: Presentation College, Bray, County Wicklow; Trinity College, Dublin
Qualifications: Irish Leaving Certificate, BA (Hons) Economics and Geography, Level II coach
Overseas tours: Ireland U19 to Bermuda (International Youth Tournament) 1997, to South Africa (U19 World Cup) 1997-98; Ireland to Zimbabwe (ICC Emerging Nations Tournament) 1999-2000, to Canada (ICC Trophy) 2001; MCC to Namibia and Uganda 2004-05; England A to West Indies 2005-06; England to India (ICC Champions Trophy) 2006-07, to Australia 2006-07, to West Indies (World Cup) 2006-07; England Lions to India 2007-08
Overseas teams played for: Coburg CC, Melbourne 1996-97; University CC, Perth 2001-02
Cricket superstitions: 'None'
Cricketers particularly admired: Larry Gomes, Brian Lara

Young players to look out for: Eoin Morgan, Nick Compton
Other sports played: Golf, rugby, soccer, snooker
Other sports followed: Rugby (Leinster), football (Manchester United)
Favourite band: The Mars Volta
Relaxations: Cinema, eating out, listening to music
Extras: NBC Denis Compton Award for the most promising young Middlesex player 2000. Became the first Irish-born-and-bred player to record a century in the County Championship with his 104 v Warwickshire at Lord's 2001. C&G Man of the Match award for his 72 v Northamptonshire at Northampton 2003. Vice-captain of Middlesex June 2004 to end of 2004 season (captaining the county in the absence of Andrew Strauss on international duty) and from 2007 to end 2008. First batsman to 1000 first-class runs in 2005 (18 June). Has represented Ireland in first-class and one-day cricket. Made England ODI debut in Belfast 2006 v Ireland, for whom his brother Dominick was also making his ODI debut. Has also represented England in Twenty20 International cricket. ECB National Academy 2005-06. Scored maiden ODI century (107) v Australia at Sydney in the Commonwealth Bank Series 2006-07, winning Man of the Match award. Man of the Match v Kenya in St Lucia in the World Cup 2006-07 (75). Captained Middlesex to Twenty20 Cup Final win in 2008. Signed for Sussex November 2008
Best batting: 211 Middlesex v Warwickshire, Edgbaston 2006
Best bowling: 2-34 Middlesex v CUCCE, Fenner's 2004

2008 Season

	M	Inn	NO	Runs	HS	Avg	100	50	Ct	St	Balls	Runs	Wkts	Avg	BB	5I	10M
Test																	
FC	17	28	1	966	101	35.77	1	7	12	-	0	0	0		-	-	-
ODI																	
List A	14	13	0	393	99	30.23	-	3	6	-	24	39	0		-	-	
20/20 Int																	
20/20	13	12	3	227	47	25.22	-	-	6	-	0	0	0		-	-	

Career Performances

	M	Inn	NO	Runs	HS	Avg	100	50	Ct	St	Balls	Runs	Wkts	Avg	BB	5I	10M
Test																	
FC	127	210	17	8661	211	44.87	19	50	97	-	1275	1016	10	101.60	2-34	-	-
ODI	17	17	0	471	107	27.70	1	3	6	-	0	0	0		-	-	
List A	165	156	17	4757	115 *	34.22	4	33	62	-	264	309	6	51.50	2-10	-	
20/20 Int	2	1	0	1	1	1.00	-	-	-	-	0	0	0		-	-	
20/20	31	29	5	407	47	16.95	-	-	10	-	6	12	0		-	-	

KARTIK, M. Middlesex

Name: Murali Kartik
Role: Left-hand bat, orthodox left-arm spin bowler
Born: 11 September 1976, Chennai (Madras), India
Height: 6ft **Weight:** 12st
Nickname: Pirate, Gary, Karts, Trickster, Special K
County debut: 2005 (Lancashire), 2007 (Middlesex)
County cap: 2007 (Middlesex)
Test debut: 1999-2000
ODI debut: 2001-02
Twenty20 ODI debut: 2007
50 wickets in a season: 1
Place in batting averages: 202nd av. 20.12 (2007 222nd av. 19.00)
Place in bowling averages: 99th av. 34.06 (2007 34th av. 24.96)
Parents: Mr R. Murali and the late Mrs Shanta Murali
Wife and date of marriage: Shweta Kartik, 11 September 2002
Education: Sardar Patel Vidyalaya, New Delhi; Hindu College, Delhi University
Qualifications: BCom (Hons); Masters in Computer Application
Career outside cricket: Broadcasting
Off-season: 'Playing for my first-class side, Railways, in India'
Overseas tours: India A to Pakistan 1997-98, to West Indies 1999-2000, to South Africa 2001-02, to Sri Lanka 2002, to England 2003; India to Bangladesh 2000-01, to Australia 2003-04, to Pakistan 2003-04, to Bangladesh 2004-05, to Zimbabwe 2005-06 (Videocon Tri-Series), to Pakistan 2005-06 (one-day series)
Overseas teams played for: Railways, India 1996-97 – ; Kolkata Knight Riders (IPL) 2007-08
Career highlights to date: 'My Test debut in 1999 v South Africa. Our Test victories in Australia and Pakistan in 2003-04. 9-70 v Bombay in the Irani Trophy. 6-27 v Australia in 2007 ODIs'
Cricket moments to forget: 'Being dropped the day after being named as Man of the Match against Australia in 2004'
Cricket superstitions: 'Lots of them!'
Cricketers particularly admired: Sir Garfield Sobers, Steve Waugh, Matthew Hayden, Anil Kumble
Young players to look out for: Eoin Morgan, Michael Lumb
Other sports played: Golf, table-tennis

Other sports followed: Formula One, tennis, golf, football (Chelsea)
Favourite band: Simon & Garfunkel
Relaxations: 'Photography, travelling, sleeping'
Extras: Represented India U19. Broke Ravi Shastri's 20-year-old record when taking 9-70 for Rest of India v Mumbai in October 2000. Spinner of the Year award in India 2001. Man of the Match in the fourth Test v Australia at Mumbai (Bombay) 2004-05 (4-44/3-32). Was a temporary overseas player with Lancashire during the 2005 and 2006 seasons, taking 10-168 (5-93/5-75) on Championship debut v Essex at Chelmsford 2005; an overseas player with Middlesex since 2007. Took 6-27 (world record figures for a left-arm spinner) and Man of the Match award in the seventh ODI v Australia in 2007. Played in both the Stanford Series and IPL in 2008
Opinions on cricket: 'Too much cricket played in England (the volume of county cricket). Two overseas players would help the English game more than one, and there are too many Kolpaks'
Best batting: 96 Railways v Rest of India, Delhi (KS) 2005-06
Best bowling: 9-70 Rest of India v Mumbai, Mumbai (Bombay) 2000-01

2008 Season

	M	Inn	NO	Runs	HS	Avg	100	50	Ct	St	Balls	Runs	Wkts	Avg	BB	5I	10M
Test																	
FC	7	10	2	161	44	20.12	-	-	9	-	1344	545	16	34.06	4-101	-	-
ODI																	
List A	6	6	3	37	12 *	12.33	-	-	-	-	288	198	6	33.00	2-22	-	
20/20 Int																	
20/20	11	0	0	0	0		-	-	4	-	252	282	14	20.14	2-15	-	

Career Performances

	M	Inn	NO	Runs	HS	Avg	100	50	Ct	St	Balls	Runs	Wkts	Avg	BB	5I	10M
Test	8	10	1	88	43	9.77	-	-	2	-	1932	820	24	34.16	4-44	-	-
FC	125	150	21	2420	96	18.75	-	11	86	-	27323	11053	424	26.06	9-70	23	3
ODI	37	14	5	126	32 *	14.00	-	-	10	-	1907	1612	37	43.56	6-27	1	
List A	158	75	26	541	37 *	11.04	-	-	48	-	8093	5862	194	30.21	6-27	2	
20/20 Int	1	0	0	0	0		-	-	-	-	24	27	0		-	-	
20/20	24	5	1	31	17	7.75	-	-	12	-	466	533	26	20.50	5-13	1	

KEEDY, G. Lancashire

Name: Gary Keedy
Role: Left-hand bat, left-arm spin bowler
Born: 27 November 1974, Wakefield
Height: 5ft 11in **Weight:** 13st
Nickname: Keeds, Phil Mitchell, Minty
County debut: 1994 (Yorkshire), 1995 (Lancashire)
County cap: 2000 (Lancashire)
50 wickets in a season: 3
Place in batting averages: 218th av. 17.35
Place in bowling averages: 127th av. 41.32 (2007 89th av. 33.87)
Parents: Roy and Pat
Wife and date of marriage: Andrea, 12 October 2002
Children: Erin Grace, 8 September 2006
Education: Garforth Comprehensive; Open University
Qualifications: 8 GCSEs, Level 2 cricket coach, Certificate in Natural Sciences
Overseas tours: England U18 to South Africa 1992-93, to Denmark 1993; England U19 to Sri Lanka 1993-94; Lancashire to Portugal 1995, to Jamaica 1996, to South Africa 1997; MCC to UAE and Oman 2004
Overseas teams played for: Frankston, Melbourne 1995-96
Career highlights to date: 'County cap; playing for Lancashire. Fourteen wickets in match v Glos at Old Trafford 2004. Five wickets v Yorks at Headingley'
Cricket superstitions: 'None'
Cricketers particularly admired: Graham Gooch, Shane Warne
Other sports followed: Rugby league (Leeds Rhinos), football (Leeds United)
Relaxations: 'Wine tasting; looking after family'
Extras: Player of the Series for England U19 v West Indies U19 1993; also played v India U19 1994. Had match figures of 14-227 (7-95/7-132) v Gloucestershire at Old Trafford 2004, the best return by an English spinner since Martyn Ball's 14-169 in 1993. Leading English wicket-taker (second overall) in the Championship 2004 (72 at 25.68). Lancashire Player of the Year 2004. Voted 'best county player never to have played for England' in *All Out Cricket*'s October 2006 edition. Took over 40 wickets in all competitions in 2008
Best batting: 64 Lancashire v Sussex, Hove 2008
Best bowling: 7-95 Lancashire v Gloucestershire, Old Trafford 2004

2008 Season

	M	Inn	NO	Runs	HS	Avg	100	50	Ct	St	Balls	Runs	Wkts	Avg	BB	5I	10M
Test																	
FC	13	18	4	243	64	17.35	-	1	2	-	2529	1157	28	41.32	5-56	1	-
ODI																	
List A	8	6	2	69	33	17.25	-	-	3	-	274	175	7	25.00	2-31	-	
20/20 Int																	
20/20	5	1	1	4	4 *		-	-	1	-	70	81	6	13.50	4-15	-	

Career Performances

	M	Inn	NO	Runs	HS	Avg	100	50	Ct	St	Balls	Runs	Wkts	Avg	BB	5I	10M
Test																	
FC	170	194	97	1138	64	11.73	-	2	46	-	34674	16270	509	31.96	7-95	24	5
ODI																	
List A	51	18	8	121	33	12.10	-	-	5	-	1990	1543	54	28.57	5-30	1	
20/20 Int																	
20/20	34	6	3	19	9 *	6.33	-	-	3	-	663	700	33	21.21	4-15	-	

KEMP, J. M. Ken

Name: Justin Miles Kemp
Role: Right-hand bat, right-arm fast medium bowler
Born: 2 October 1977, Queenstown, Cape Province, South Africa
Height: 6ft 4in **Weight:** 15st 2lbs
Nickname: Kempy
County debut: 2003 (Worcestershire), 2005 (Kent)
County cap: 2003 (Worcestershire colours), 2006 (Kent)
Test debut: 2000-01
ODI debut: 2000-01
Twenty20 Int debut: 2005-06
Place in batting averages: 157th av. 25.75
Family links with cricket: 'Grandfather (J. M. Kemp) played for Border 1947-48; father (J. W. Kemp) played for Border 1975-76 – 1976-77; cousin of former South Africa ODI player Dave Callaghan'
Education: Queens College; University of Port Elizabeth
Overseas tours: South Africa U19 to India 1995-96; South African Academy to

Zimbabwe 1998-99; South Africa A to West Indies 2000, to Australia 2002-03, to Zimbabwe 2004; South Africa to West Indies 2000-01, to Zimbabwe 2001-02, to Australia 2001-02 (VB Series), to West Indies 2004-05 (one-day series), to India (one-day series) 2005-06, to Australia 2005-06, to India (ICC Champions Trophy) 2006-07
Overseas teams played for: Eastern Province 1996-97 – 2002-03; Northerns 2003-04 – 2004-05; Titans 2004-05 – 2006-07; Hyderabad Heroes (ICL) 2007-08 – ; Cape Cobras 2007-08
Extras: An overseas player with Worcestershire during the 2003 season as a locum for Andrew Hall; an overseas player with Kent 2005-06. Played for African XI v Asian Cricket Council XI in ODI series 2005-06. Has won numerous awards in domestic and international cricket, including Player of the [ODI] Series v New Zealand 2005-06 and Man of the Match v England in the fifth ODI at East London 2004-05 (50-ball 80)
Best batting: 188 Eastern Province v North West, Port Elizabeth 2000-01
Best bowling: 6-56 Eastern Province v Border, Port Elizabeth 2000-01

2008 Season

	M	Inn	NO	Runs	HS	Avg	100	50	Ct	St	Balls	Runs	Wkts	Avg	BB	5I	10M
Test																	
FC	10	17	1	412	102	25.75	1	3	16	-	0	0	0		-	-	-
ODI																	
List A	12	10	1	267	68 *	29.66	-	3	5	-	6	12	0		-	-	
20/20 Int																	
20/20	11	11	0	201	49	18.27	-	-	6	-	0	0	0		-	-	

Career Performances

	M	Inn	NO	Runs	HS	Avg	100	50	Ct	St	Balls	Runs	Wkts	Avg	BB	5I	10M
Test	4	6	0	80	55	13.33	-	1	3	-	479	222	9	24.66	3-33	-	-
FC	109	177	21	5445	188	34.90	12	27	140	-	10637	4996	186	26.86	6-56	5	-
ODI	85	66	18	1512	100 *	31.50	1	10	33	-	1303	1015	32	31.71	3-20	-	
List A	243	205	55	5365	107 *	35.76	3	39	102	-	6545	5205	179	29.07	6-20	3	
20/20 Int	8	7	3	203	89 *	50.75	-	1	3	-	6	5	0		-	-	
20/20	40	36	9	771	89 *	28.55	-	2	16	-	324	419	23	18.21	3-19	-	

46. Including the game which was abandoned without a ball being bowled, how many matches were played in Australia in the 1970-71 Ashes series?

KERRIGAN, S. C. Lancashire

Name: Simon Christopher Kerrigan
Role: Left-hand bat, slow left-arm orthodox bowler
Born: 10 May 1989, Preston, Lancashire
Height: 5ft 9in
County debut: No first-team appearance
Extras: Former Lancashire Academy player. Played for Fulwood & Broughton CC 2005-07 and for Ormskirk CC in 2008, taking 69 wickets in their Liverpool Competition Premier League title-winning campaign. Has represented Lancashire at U15 and U17 level. Lancashire Second XI 2007-08. Signed a two-year contract in September 2008

KERVEZEE, A. N. Worcestershire

Name: Alexei Nicolaas Kervezee
Role: Right-hand bat, right-arm medium bowler
Born: 11 September 1989, Walvis Bay, Namibia
Nickname: Rowdy
County debut: 2008
ODI debut: 2006
Overseas tours: Netherlands to UAE (EurAsia Series) 2006, to Scotland (European Championship) 2006, to South Africa (ICC Associates Tri-Series) 2006-07, to Kenya (ICC World Cricket League) 2006-07, to West Indies (World Cup) 2006-07, to Canada 2007, to Ireland (Quadrangular Series) 2007, plus various Netherlands age-group tours
Overseas teams played for: HBS, Netherlands

:xtras: Made first-class debut for Netherlands v Scotland at Utrecht in the ICC Inter-:ontinental Cup 2005, aged 15. Made ODI debut for Netherlands v Sri Lanka at ımstelveen 2006, aged 16, scoring 47. Attended ICC Winter Training Camp in South ıfrica 2006-07. Was still only 17 when playing in the World Cup in 2007

:est batting: 98 Netherlands v Canada, Toronto (MSE) 2007

:est bowling: 1-14 Netherlands v Namibia, Windhoek 2008

:008 Season

	M	Inn	NO	Runs	HS	Avg	100	50	Ct	St	Balls	Runs	Wkts	Avg	BB	5I	10M
est																	
:	1	1	0	41	41	41.00	-	-	1	-	0	0	0		-	-	-
DI																	
st A																	
)/20 Int																	
0/20																	

:areer Performances

	M	Inn	NO	Runs	HS	Avg	100	50	Ct	St	Balls	Runs	Wkts	Avg	BB	5I	10M
est																	
:	11	16	2	424	98	30.28	-	2	4	-	120	59	2	29.50	1-14	-	-
DI	18	15	2	341	62	26.23	-	1	6	-	6	8	0		-	-	
st A	20	17	2	392	62	26.13	-	1	7	-	30	47	0		-	-	
)/20 Int																	
0/20																	

47. How old was Don Bradman when he died?

Name: Robert William Trevor Key
Role: Right-hand bat, off-spin bowler, county captain
Born: 12 May 1979, Dulwich, London
Height: 6ft 1in **Weight:** 12st 7lbs
Nickname: Keysy
County debut: 1998
County cap: 2001
Test debut: 2002
ODI debut: 2003
1000 runs in a season: 5
1st-Class 200s: 1
Place in batting averages: 75th av. 38.25 (2007 17th av. 56.81)
Parents: Trevor and Lynn
Wife and date of marriage: Fleur, 2006
Children: Aaliyah, September 2006
Family links with cricket: Mother played for Kent Ladies. Father played club cricket in Derby. Sister Elizabeth played for her junior school side
Education: Langley Park Boys' School
Qualifications: 10 GCSEs, NCA coaching award, GNVQ Business Studies
Overseas tours: Kent U13 to Netherlands; England U17 to Bermuda (International Youth Tournament) 1997 (c); England U19 to South Africa (including U19 World Cup 1997-98; England A to Zimbabwe and South Africa 1998-99; ECB National Academy to Australia 2001-02, to Sri Lanka 2002-03; England to Australia 2002-03, to South Africa 2004-05. England Performance Programme to India 2008-09; England Lions to New Zealand 2009 (c)
Overseas teams played for: Greenpoint CC, Cape Town 1996-97
Cricketers particularly admired: Min Patel, Neil Taylor, Alan Wells, Mark Ealham
Other sports played: Hockey, football, snooker, tennis (played for county)
Other sports followed: Football (Chelsea), basketball (Chicago Bulls)
Extras: Represented England U19 1997 and was England U19 Man of the Series v Pakistan U19 1998 (award shared with Graeme Swann). NBC Denis Compton Award for the most promising young Kent player 2001. Scored 221 in the first Test v West Indies 2004, in the process sharing with Andrew Strauss (137) in a record second-wicket stand for Test cricket at Lord's (291). Leading run-scorer in English first-class cricket 2004 with 1896 runs at 79.00, including nine centuries. One of *Wisden*'s Five Cricketers of the Year 2005. Scored twin centuries (112/189) v Surrey at Tunbridge Wells 2005, in the second innings sharing with Martin van Jaarsveld (168) in a new Kent record third-wicket partnership (323). Carried bat for 75* v Surrey at

Canterbury 2007. ECB National Academy 2005-06, 2006-07. Enjoyed a successful 2008 season, accumulating over 1750 runs, including three hundreds and eight fifties. Captain of Kent since 2006

Best batting: 221 England v West Indies, Lord's 2004

2008 Season

	M	Inn	NO	Runs	HS	Avg	100	50	Ct	St	Balls	Runs	Wkts	Avg	BB	5I	10M
Test																	
FC	16	27	3	918	178 *	38.25	2	4	5	-	12	2	0		-	-	-
ODI																	
List A	17	17	1	594	120 *	37.12	1	4	5	-	0	0	0		-	-	
20/20 Int																	
20/20	13	13	0	345	52	26.53	-	1	5	-	0	0	0		-	-	

Career Performances

	M	Inn	NO	Runs	HS	Avg	100	50	Ct	St	Balls	Runs	Wkts	Avg	BB	5I	10M
Test	15	26	1	775	221	31.00	1	3	11	-	0	0	0		-	-	-
FC	191	330	21	12818	221	41.48	37	50	109	-	164	94	0		-	-	-
ODI	5	5	0	54	19	10.80	-	-	-	-	0	0	0		-	-	
List A	173	166	12	4927	120 *	31.99	5	32	34	-	0	0	0		-	-	
20/20 Int																	
20/20	35	35	5	889	68 *	29.63	-	6	9	-	0	0	0		-	-	

KHAN, A. Kent

Name: Amjad Khan
Role: Right-hand bat, right-arm fast bowler
Born: 14 October 1980, Copenhagen, Denmark
Height: 6ft **Weight:** 11st 6lbs
Nickname: Ammy
County debut: 2001
County cap: 2005
50 wickets in a season: 2
Place in bowling averages: 16th av. 20.61
Parents: Aslam and Raisa
Marital status: Single
Education: Skolen på Duevej, Denmark; Falkonĕrgårdens Gymnasium
Overseas tours: Denmark U19 to Canada 1996, to Bermuda 1997, to South Africa (U19 World Cup) 1997-98, to Wales 1998, to Ireland 1999; Denmark to Netherlands 1998, to Zimbabwe (ICC Emerging Nations Tournament) 1999-2000, to Canada (ICC Trophy) 2001; England A to Bangladesh 2006-07; England to India 2008; England Performance Programme to India, 2008-09; England Lions to New Zealand 2009
Overseas teams played for: Kjøbenhavns Boldklub, Denmark
Cricket moments to forget: 'I try to forget most of the games where I didn't perform as well as I would like'
Cricketers particularly admired: Wasim Akram, Dennis Lillee
Other sports followed: Football (Denmark)
Favourite band: Marvin Gaye, George Michael, Nerd (Neptunes)
Relaxations: 'Music, sleeping, reading'
Extras: Made debut for Denmark at the age of 17. Took over 50 (63) first-class wickets in his first full season 2002. NBC Denis Compton Award for the most promising young Kent player 2002. Out for the whole of the 2007 season with a knee injury. Is England-qualified
Best batting: 78 Kent v Middlesex, Lord's 2003
Best bowling: 6-52 Kent v Yorkshire, Canterbury 2002

2008 Season

	M	Inn	NO	Runs	HS	Avg	100	50	Ct	St	Balls	Runs	Wkts	Avg	BB	5I	10M
Test																	
FC	6	7	1	46	21 *	7.66	-	-	1	-	871	433	21	20.61	3-10	-	-
ODI																	
List A	3	1	0	4	4	4.00	-	-	-	-	94	81	4	20.25	2-23	-	
20/20 Int																	
20/20																	

Career Performances

	M	Inn	NO	Runs	HS	Avg	100	50	Ct	St	Balls	Runs	Wkts	Avg	BB	5I	10M
Test																	
FC	63	72	24	870	78	18.12	-	3	10	-	10209	6625	211	31.39	6-52	6	-
ODI																	
List A	54	29	6	269	65 *	11.69	-	1	13	-	2201	1899	60	31.65	4-26	-	
20/20 Int																	
20/20	17	7	2	30	15	6.00	-	-	1	-	313	466	22	21.18	3-11	-	

KIESWETTER, C. Somerset

Name: Craig Kieswetter
Role: Right-hand bat, wicket-keeper
Born: 28 November 1987, Johannesburg, South Africa
Height: 5ft 11in **Weight:** 13st 5lbs
Nickname: Bangle, Hobnob, Shnitz, Kitchen Utensil
County debut: 2007
Place in batting averages: 134th av. 28.86 (2007 146th av. 29.00)
Parents: Wayne and Belinda
Marital status: Single
Education: Diocesan College (Bishops), Cape Town; Millfield School
Overseas tours: South Africa U19 to Sri Lanka (U19 World Cup) 2005-06
Overseas teams played for: Alma Marist CC, Cape Town 2005-06
Career highlights to date: 'Making first-class and List A debuts in first year aged 19'
Cricket superstitions: 'Routine to put gear on; mark guard after every ball; certain amount of taps when bowler running in'

Cricketers particularly admired: Marcus Trescothick, Andrew Caddick, Ian Blackwell, Justin Langer, Neil McKenzie, Damien Martyn, Adam Gilchrist
Other sports played: Hockey (provincial)
Other sports followed: Football (Aston Villa)
Favourite band: Justin Timberlake, Ne-Yo, R&B, NDubz, Plan B
Relaxations: 'PlayStation B, Pro Evolution Soccer, music, girlfriend'
Extras: Represented South Africa Schools 2005. Man of the Match v USA U19 at Colombo in the U19 World Cup 2005-06 (80). Struck 58-ball 69* on List A debut v Glamorgan at Taunton in the Friends Provident 2007. Magic Moment v Warwickshire at Edgbaston in the Twenty20 2007. NBC Denis Compton Award for the most promising young Somerset player 2007, 2008. Although he has played for South Africa at U19 level, he has committed himself to an England future. Claimed more than 70 victims from behind the stumps in all competitions in 2008
Best batting: 93 Somerset v Glamorgan, Taunton 2007

2008 Season

	M	Inn	NO	Runs	HS	Avg	100	50	Ct	St	Balls	Runs	Wkts	Avg	BB	5I	10M
Test																	
FC	17	26	4	635	67 *	28.86	-	2	48	2	0	0	0		-	-	-
ODI																	
List A	14	13	0	537	121	41.30	1	3	16	3	0	0	0		-	-	
20/20 Int																	
20/20	8	8	1	165	42	23.57	-	-	2	1	0	0	0		-	-	

Career Performances

	M	Inn	NO	Runs	HS	Avg	100	50	Ct	St	Balls	Runs	Wkts	Avg	BB	5I	10M
Test																	
FC	31	42	7	1012	93	28.91	-	5	94	2	0	0	0		-	-	-
ODI																	
List A	29	28	3	866	121	34.64	1	5	34	5	0	0	0		-	-	
20/20 Int																	
20/20	14	14	3	246	48	22.36	-	-	3	1	0	0	0		-	-	

48. How old was England batsman Ken Barrington when he died of a heart attack in Barbados?

KILLEEN, N. Durham

Name: Neil Killeen
Role: Right-hand bat, right-arm fast-medium bowler
Born: 17 October 1975, Shotley Bridge
Height: 6ft 1in **Weight:** 15st
Nickname: Killer, Bully, Quinny, Squeaky, Bull
County debut: 1995
County cap: 1999
Benefit: 2006
50 wickets in a season: 1
Parents: Glen and Thora
Wife and date of marriage: Clare Louise, 5 February 2000
Children: Jonathan David
Family links with cricket: 'Dad best armchair player in the game'
Education: Greencroft Comprehensive School; Derwentside College, University of Teesside
Qualifications: 8 GCSEs, 2 A-levels, first year Sports Science, Level III coaching award, Level I staff coach
Career outside cricket: Cricket coaching
Overseas tours: Durham CCC to Zimbabwe 1992; England U19 to West Indies 1994-95; MCC to Bangladesh 1999-2000
Career highlights to date: 'My county cap and first-class debut'
Cricket moments to forget: 'Injury causing me to miss most of 2001 season'
Cricketers particularly admired: Ian Botham, Curtly Ambrose, Courtney Walsh, David Boon
Other sports played: Athletics (English Schools javelin)
Sports followed: Football (Sunderland AFC), cricket (Anfield Plain CC)
Relaxations: 'Good food, good wine; golf; spending time with wife and family'
Extras: Was first Durham bowler to take five wickets in a Sunday League game (5-26 v Northamptonshire at Northampton 1995). Scored 35 batting at No. 10 as Durham made 453-9 to beat Somerset at Taunton 2004. Had figures of 8.3-7-5-2 v Derbyshire at Riverside in the totesport League 2004
Best batting: 48 Durham v Somerset, Riverside 1995
Best bowling: 7-70 Durham v Hampshire, Riverside 2003

2008 Season

	M	Inn	NO	Runs	HS	Avg	100	50	Ct	St	Balls	Runs	Wkts	Avg	BB	5I	10M
Test																	
FC	2	2	1	5	4 *	5.00	-	-	1	-	228	65	8	8.12	5-15	1	-
ODI																	
List A	7	5	2	39	16	13.00	-	-	-	-	295	185	7	26.42	3-45	-	
20/20 Int																	
20/20	3	0	0	0	0		-	-	-	-	54	91	3	30.33	2-39	-	

Career Performances

	M	Inn	NO	Runs	HS	Avg	100	50	Ct	St	Balls	Runs	Wkts	Avg	BB	5I	10M
Test																	
FC	102	145	31	1302	48	11.42	-	-	26	-	16499	8215	262	31.35	7-70	9	-
ODI																	
List A	221	117	45	683	32	9.48	-	-	38	-	10421	7177	295	24.32	6-31	4	
20/20 Int																	
20/20	33	14	10	85	17 *	21.25	-	-	6	-	657	833	35	23.80	4-7	-	

KING, S. J. Surrey

Name: Simon James King
Role: Right-hand bat, right-arm off-spin bowler
Born: 4 September 1987, Lambeth, London
Height: 6ft 1in **Weight:** 11st
Nickname: Kingy
County debut: No first-team appearance
Parents: Angela Pocock and David King
Marital status: Single
Family links with cricket: 'Brother plays'
Education: Warlingham Secondary School; John Fisher Sixth Form College
Qualifications: GCSEs, BTEC National Diploma in Sport, ECB Level 2 coaching
Overseas tours: Surrey Academy to South Africa 2005; Surrey CCC to India 2006
Overseas teams played for: Mildura West CC, Victoria; Millewa CC, Victoria (both Australia)
Career highlights to date: 'Receiving first contract at the end of the 2006 season. First five-wicket haul, v Sussex 2nd XI 2005, when I was 17'

Cricket moments to forget: 'Dropping a skyer into my face in an England regional match'
Cricketers particularly admired: Alec Stewart, Shane Warne, Mark Ramprakash, Phil Matthews
Young players to look out for: Zafar Ansari, Daryl King, Harry Allen
Other sports played: Football (Warlingham FC, Hamsey Rangers FC)
Other sports followed: Football (Fulham)
Favourite band: Goo Goo Dolls, Oasis, U2, Lifehouse
Relaxations: 'Sleeping'
Extras: Surrey U15 Player of the Year 2003. Surrey Academy Player of the Year 2006

KIRBY, S. P. Gloucestershire

Name: Steven Paul Kirby
Role: Right-hand bat, right-arm fast bowler
Born: 4 October 1977, Bury, Lancashire
Height: 6ft 3in **Weight:** 13st 5lbs
Nickname: Tango
County debut: 2001 (Yorkshire), 2005 (Gloucestershire)
County cap: 2003 (Yorkshire), 2005 (Gloucestershire)
50 wickets in a season: 1
Place in bowling averages: 64th av. 28.72 (2007 18th av. 23.43)
Parents: Paul and Alison
Wife and date of marriage: Sasha, 11 October 2003
Children: Joel, 2005; Aleisha, 2007
Education: Elton High School, Walshaw, Bury, Lancs; Bury College
Qualifications: 10 GCSEs, BTEC/GNVQ Advanced Leisure and Tourism
Overseas tours: Yorkshire to Grenada 2001; ECB National Academy to Australia 2001-02; England A to India 2003-04; England Lions to India 2007-08
Overseas teams played for: Egmont Plains, New Zealand 1997-98
Cricket moments to forget: 'Being knocked out by Nixon McLean trying to take a return catch'
Cricketers particularly admired: Steve Waugh, Richard Hadlee, Glenn McGrath, Michael Atherton, Curtly Ambrose, Sachin Tendulkar
Other sports played: Basketball, table tennis, squash, golf – 'anything sporty and competitive'
Other sports followed: Football (Manchester United), rugby (Leicester Tigers)

Extras: Formerly with Leicestershire but did not appear for first team. Took 14 wickets (41-18-47-14) in one day for Egmont Plains v Hawera in a New Zealand club match 1997-98. Took 7-50 in Kent's second innings at Headingley 2001, the best bowling figures by a Yorkshire player on first-class debut; Kirby had replaced Matthew Hoggard (called up by England) halfway through the match. Took 13-154 (5-74/8-80) v Somerset at Taunton 2003, the best match return by a Yorkshire bowler for 36 years. Took over 60 wickets in all forms of cricket in 2008
Best batting: 57 Yorkshire v Hampshire, Headingley 2002
Best bowling: 8-80 Yorkshire v Somerset, Taunton 2003

2008 Season

	M	Inn	NO	Runs	HS	Avg	100	50	Ct	St	Balls	Runs	Wkts	Avg	BB	5I	10M
Test																	
FC	13	17	6	84	28	7.63	-	-	3	-	2317	1149	40	28.72	5-60	1	-
ODI																	
List A	12	3	2	8	4 *	8.00	-	-	3	-	576	487	22	22.13	4-27	-	
20/20 Int																	
20/20	5	3	1	4	3 *	2.00	-	-	1	-	114	145	4	36.25	1-20	-	

Career Performances

	M	Inn	NO	Runs	HS	Avg	100	50	Ct	St	Balls	Runs	Wkts	Avg	BB	5I	10M
Test																	
FC	102	139	44	775	57	8.15	-	1	20	-	18319	10618	364	29.17	8-80	14	4
ODI																	
List A	56	24	9	72	15	4.80	-	-	11	-	2371	2229	67	33.26	5-36	1	
20/20 Int																	
20/20	16	6	2	5	3 *	1.25	-	-	2	-	330	434	17	25.52	2-15	-	

KIRTLEY, R. J. Sussex

Name: Robert James Kirtley
Role: Right-hand bat, right-arm fast-medium bowler
Born: 10 January 1975, Eastbourne
Height: 6ft **Weight:** 12st
Nickname: Ambi
County debut: 1995
County cap: 1998
Benefit: 2006
Test debut: 2003
ODI debut: 2001-02
Twenty20 Int debut: 2007-08
50 wickets in a season: 7
Parents: Bob and Pip
Wife and date of marriage: Jenny, 26 October 2002
Children: Robert Oliver (known as Oliver), 12 June 2008
Family links with cricket: Brother plays league cricket
Education: St Andrew's School, Eastbourne; Clifton College, Bristol
Qualifications: 9 GCSEs, 2 A-levels, NCA coaching first level
Overseas tours: Sussex YC to Barbados 1993, to Sri Lanka 1995; Sussex to Grenada 2001; England A to Bangladesh and New Zealand 1999-2000, to Bangladesh 2006-07; England to Zimbabwe (one-day series) 2001-02, to Sri Lanka (ICC Champions Trophy) 2002-03, to Australia 2002-03 (VB Series), to Bangladesh and Sri Lanka 2003-04, to West Indies 2003-04 (one-day series), to South Africa (World 20/20) 2007-08
Overseas teams played for: Mashonaland, Zimbabwe 1996-97; Namibian Cricket Board/Wanderers, Windhoek, Namibia 1998-99
Career highlights to date: 'My Test debut at Trent Bridge, the County Championship 2003, the C&G Final 2006'
Cricket moments to forget: 'The three times I've bagged a pair'
Cricket superstitions: 'Put my left boot on first!'
Cricketers particularly admired: Curtly Ambrose, Jim Andrew, Darren Gough
Other sports followed: Rugby (England), football (Brighton & Hove Albion)
Relaxations: 'Inviting friends round for a braai (barbeque) and enjoying a cold beer with them'
Extras: Played in the Mashonaland side which defeated England on their 1996-97 tour of Zimbabwe, taking seven wickets in the match. NBC Denis Compton Award for the most promising young Sussex player 1997. Leading wicket-taker in English first-class cricket 2001 with 75 wickets (av. 23.32). Sussex Player of the Year 2002. Made Test debut in the third Test v South Africa at Trent Bridge 2003, taking 6-34 in South

Africa's second innings and winning Man of the Match award. Vice-captain of Sussex 2001-05. C&G Man of the Match award for his 5-27 in the final v Lancashire at Lord's 2006. Took 600th first-class wicket (Yuvraj Singh) v Indians at Hove 2007

Best batting: 59 Sussex v Durham, Eastbourne 1998

Best bowling: 7-21 Sussex v Hampshire, Southampton 1999

2008 Season

	M	Inn	NO	Runs	HS	Avg	100	50	Ct	St	Balls	Runs	Wkts	Avg	BB	5I	10M
Test																	
FC	2	2	0	19	19	9.50	-	-	-	-	252	130	2	65.00	2-88	-	-
ODI																	
List A	13	3	2	23	20 *	23.00	-	-	4	-	558	529	16	33.06	3-25	-	
20/20 Int																	
20/20	9	3	1	1	1 *	.50	-	-	3	-	174	305	5	61.00	2-16	-	

Career Performances

	M	Inn	NO	Runs	HS	Avg	100	50	Ct	St	Balls	Runs	Wkts	Avg	BB	5I	10M
Test	4	7	1	32	12	5.33	-	-	3	-	1079	561	19	29.52	6-34	1	-
FC	167	228	75	1995	59	13.03	-	4	58	-	31575	16422	608	27.00	7-21	29	4
ODI	11	2	0	2	1	1.00	-	-	5	-	549	481	9	53.44	2-33	-	
List A	231	85	42	419	30 *	9.74	-	-	64	-	10188	7922	344	23.02	5-27	7	
20/20 Int	1	1	1	2	2 *		-	-	-	-	6	17	0		-		
20/20	40	13	5	10	2 *	1.25	-	-	10	-	747	1038	34	30.52	4-22		

49. By what margin did Australia win the 1958-59 Ashes series?

KLEINVELDT, R. K. Hampshire

Name: Rory Keith Kleinveldt
Role: Right-hand bat, right-arm fast-medium bowler; all-rounder
Born: 15 March 1983, Cape Town, South Africa
County debut: 2008
Twenty20 Int debut: 2008-09
Overseas tours: South Africa A to India 2007
Overseas teams played for: Western Province 2002-03 – 2005-06; Cape Cobras 2005-06 –
Extras: Was part of the South Africa U19 squad that reached the final of the 2002 World Cup. Released by Hampshire at the end of the 2008 season. Made his Twenty20 International debut against Bangladesh in Johannesburg in November 2008
Best batting: 115* Western Province v KwaZulu-Natal, Chatsworth Stadium 2005
Best bowling: 8-47 Cape Cobras v Warriors, Stellenbosch University Ground 2006

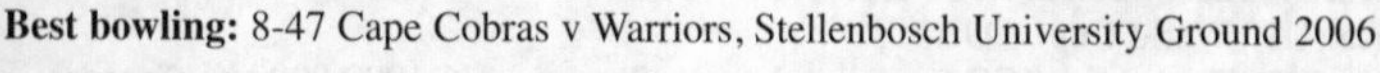

2008 Season

	M	Inn	NO	Runs	HS	Avg	100	50	Ct	St	Balls	Runs	Wkts	Avg	BB	5I	10M
Test																	
FC	1	2	0	20	16	10.00	-	-	-	-	54	42	1	42.00	1-17	-	-
ODI																	
List A																	
20/20 Int																	
20/20																	

Career Performances

	M	Inn	NO	Runs	HS	Avg	100	50	Ct	St	Balls	Runs	Wkts	Avg	BB	5I	10M
Test																	
FC	40	62	7	1097	115 *	19.94	1	5	22	-	6623	3337	107	31.18	8-47	4	1
ODI																	
List A	45	33	6	491	54 *	18.18	-	1	6	-	1969	1486	55	27.01	4-29	-	
20/20 Int																	
20/20	28	24	8	305	46	19.06	-	-	6	-	562	658	24	27.41	3-18		

KLOKKER, F. A. Derbyshire

Name: Frederik Andreas Klokker
Role: Left-hand bat, wicket-keeper
Born: 13 March 1983, Odense, Denmark
Height: 5ft 11in **Weight:** 14st 2lbs
Nickname: Kloks, J-Lo, The Great Dane
County debut: 2006 (Warwickshire), 2007 (Derbyshire)
Parents: Peter Palle and Ingermarie
Marital status: Single
Family links with cricket: 'Dad played for Denmark for many years and is now head coach of Danish cricket. My two sisters played a bit when they were younger'
Education: Hindsholmskolen, Denmark
Qualifications: Levels 1 and 2 coaching. Levels 1 and 2 fitness instructor
Career outside cricket: Philatelist
Overseas tours: Denmark U19 to South Africa (U19 World Cup) 1997-98; Denmark to Zimbabwe (ICC Emerging Nations Tournament) 1999-2000, to Canada (ICC Trophy) 2001, to Ireland (ICC Trophy) 2005, to Kenya 2007, to Namibia (ICC World Cricket League) 2007-08, plus various other tours and tournaments with Denmark and Denmark age groups; MCC YC to Sri Lanka 2003-04
Overseas teams played for: Kerteminde CC, Denmark 1989-99; Skanderborg CC, Denmark 2000-01; South Perth CC 2001-02 – 2003-04; Prospect CC, Adelaide 2006-07
Career highlights to date: 'Playing in the 1997 U19 World Cup in South Africa. Debut for Denmark. Debut for Warwickshire. Breaking record for most runs by an MCC Young Cricketer. Hundred for Derbyshire on my first-class debut for them'
Cricket moments to forget: 'The game against the West Indies in the 1997 U19 World Cup'
Cricket superstitions: 'Not really'
Cricketers particularly admired: Waugh twins, Dominic Ostler
Young players to look out for: Michael Pedersen (MCC YC)
Other sports played: 'Played handball in the winter before I started going to Australia'
Other sports followed: Handball (GOG)
Favourite band: Live
Relaxations: 'Can't beat a good movie'
Extras: MCC Young Cricketer 2002-05, acting as substitute fielder for England in the first Test v New Zealand at Lord's 2004. Has represented Denmark in one-day cricket,

including NatWest/C&G. Man of the Match v USA at Armagh in the ICC Trophy 2005 (149-ball 138*). Played for European XI v MCC at Rotterdam 2006. Played one first-class match and one C&G match for Warwickshire 2006 as injury cover in the wicket-keeping department, scoring 40 as nightwatchman v Sussex at Hove. Played two first-class matches for Derbyshire 2007, scoring century (100*) on debut for the county v Cambridge UCCE at Fenner's. Played four first-class games for Derbyshire in 2008, scoring a century in one of them

Best batting: 103* Derbyshire v Warwickshire, Derby 2008

2008 Season

	M	Inn	NO	Runs	HS	Avg	100	50	Ct	St	Balls	Runs	Wkts	Avg	BB	5I	10M
Test																	
FC	4	8	1	160	103 *	22.85	1	-	10	-	60	99	0		-	-	-
ODI																	
List A	3	1	0	11	11	11.00	-	-	4	-	0	0	0		-	-	
20/20 Int																	
20/20																	

Career Performances

	M	Inn	NO	Runs	HS	Avg	100	50	Ct	St	Balls	Runs	Wkts	Avg	BB	5I	10M
Test																	
FC	7	12	2	371	103 *	37.10	2	-	16	-	60	99	0		-	-	-
ODI																	
List A	21	17	2	568	138 *	37.86	1	4	22	5	0	0	0		-	-	
20/20 Int																	
20/20																	

KLUSENER, L. Northamptonshire

Name: Lance Klusener
Role: Left-hand bat, right-arm fast-medium bowler; all-rounder
Born: 4 September 1971, Durban, South Africa
Height: 5ft 10in **Weight:** 12st 4lbs
Nickname: Zulu
County debut: 2002 (Nottinghamshire), 2004 (Middlesex), 2006 (Northamptonshire)
County cap: 2006 (Northamptonshire)
Test debut: 1996-97
ODI debut: 1995-96
1000 runs in a season: 3
1st-Class 200s: 1
Place in batting averages: 4th av. 73.00 (2007 40th av. 48.23)
Place in bowling averages: (2007 105th av. 38.78)
Parents: Peter and Dawn
Wife and date of marriage: Isabelle, 13 May 2000
Children: Matthew, 23 January 2002; Thomas, 1 July 2006
Education: Durban High School; Technikon Natal
Career outside cricket: 'Farming – sugar'
Overseas tours: South Africa U24 to Sri Lanka 1995; South Africa A to England 1996; South Africa to India 1996-97, to Pakistan 1997-98, to Australia 1997-98, to England 1998, to New Zealand 1998-99, to UK, Ireland and Netherlands (World Cup) 1999, to Zimbabwe 1999-2000, to India 1999-2000, to Sri Lanka 2000, to Kenya (ICC Knockout Trophy) 2000-01, to West Indies 2000-01, to Zimbabwe 2001-02, to Australia 2001-02, to Sri Lanka (ICC Champions Trophy) 2002-03, to New Zealand 2003-04 (one-day series), to Sri Lanka 2004, to England (ICC Champions Trophy) 2004, plus other one-day tournaments in Kenya, Sharjah, Australia, Singapore and Morocco; FICA World XI to New Zealand 2004-05
Overseas teams played for: Natal/KwaZulu-Natal 1993-94 – 2003-04; Dolphins 2004-05 – 2006-07; Kolkata Tigers (ICL) 2007-08 –
Career highlights to date: 'World Cup Man of the Tournament [1999]'
Cricketers particularly admired: Malcolm Marshall, Shaun Pollock
Young players to look out for: Hashim Amla
Other sports played: Golf
Other sports followed: Rugby (Natal Sharks, Springboks)
Relaxations: 'Fishing, hunting'
Extras: Returned the best innings analysis by a South African on Test debut – 8-64 in the second Test v India at Kolkata 1996-97. One of *South African Cricket Annual*'s

five Cricketers of the Year 1997, 1999. Scored 174 in the second Test v England at Port Elizabeth 1999-2000, winning Man of the Match award. His other Test awards include Man of the Series v Sri Lanka 2000. One of *Wisden*'s Five Cricketers of the Year 2000. Has won numerous ODI awards, including Player of the Tournament in the World Cup 1999. His domestic awards include Man of the Match in the SuperSport Series final v Western Province at Cape Town 2003-04 (7-70/5-90). An overseas player with Nottinghamshire at the start of the 2002 season; an overseas player with Middlesex 2004. Is no longer considered an overseas player. Scored 126* and 62 and had first innings figures of 4-50 on Championship debut for Northamptonshire v Essex at Chelmsford 2006; scored century (122) and followed up with first innings figures of 5-62 v Leicestershire at Oakham School 2006. Signed for the Kolkata Tigers (ICL) in 2007. Finished the 2008 season with over 1000 first-class runs. Parted company with Northamptonshire at the end of September 2008
Best batting: 202* Northamptonshire v Glamorgan, Northampton 2008
Best bowling: 8-34 Natal v Western Province, Durban 1995-96

2008 Season

	M	Inn	NO	Runs	HS	Avg	100	50	Ct	St	Balls	Runs	Wkts	Avg	BB	5I	10M
Test																	
FC	14	20	5	1095	202 *	73.00	2	9	3	-	1100	638	6	106.33	1-21	-	-
ODI																	
List A	10	9	4	199	60 *	39.80	-	1	1	-	306	283	4	70.75	2-20	-	
20/20 Int																	
20/20	11	8	2	116	41 *	19.33	-	-	2	-	60	82	3	27.33	2-8	-	

Career Performances

	M	Inn	NO	Runs	HS	Avg	100	50	Ct	St	Balls	Runs	Wkts	Avg	BB	5I	10M
Test	49	69	11	1906	174	32.86	4	8	34	-	6887	3033	80	37.91	8-64	1	-
FC	197	283	60	9521	202 *	42.69	21	48	99	-	31735	15447	508	30.40	8-34	20	4
ODI	171	137	50	3576	103 *	41.10	2	19	35	-	7336	5751	192	29.95	6-49	6	
List A	323	267	101	6623	142 *	39.89	3	34	81	-	13433	10502	332	31.63	6-49	8	
20/20 Int																	
20/20	49	42	16	930	111 *	35.76	1	3	14	-	702	1018	26	39.15	2-8	-	

KNAPPETT, J. P. T. Worcestershire

Name: Joshua (Josh) Philip Thomas Knappett
Role: Right-hand bat, wicket-keeper
Born: 15 April 1985, Westminster, London
Height: 6ft **Weight:** 12st 4lbs
Nickname: Badger, Edwin (van der Sar)
County debut: 2007
County colours: 2007
Parents: Phil and Janie
Marital status: Single
Family links with cricket: Father is Youth and Coaching Manager at Middlesex and has played club cricket. 'Brother, Jon, plays socially'
Education: East Barnet School; Oxford Brookes University
Qualifications: 10 GCSEs, 3 A-levels, Level 3 ECB, tutor-trained and assessor-trained cricket coach to level 2, swimming, football and rugby Level 1 coaching qualifications
Off-season: 'Touring, and training in Worcester.'
Career outside cricket: Coaching and coach education
Overseas tours: MCC A to Canada 2005; MCC B to Botswana and Zambia 2006, to Fiji and Samoa 2008
Career highlights to date: 'My championship debut v Sussex in 2007'
Cricket moments to forget: 'Being hit on the head by Jimmy Ormond on first-class debut for OUCCE. Getting out to Mushtaq twice in a day for 7 and 4.'
Cricketers particularly admired: Jack Russell, Adam Gilchrist
Young players to look out for: Phil Mellish, Keith Bradley, Jack Manual
Other sports played: Squash, trampolining
Other sports followed: Football (Tottenham Hotspur)
Favourite band: 'Architecture In Helsinki, Cold War Kids, The New Pornographers, Bernard Fanning, Bob Dylan, Daft Punk, Elbow, The Whitlams'
Relaxations: 'Listening to music, films, eating'
Extras: Played for Oxford UCCE 2004-06. Represented British Universities 2005, 2006. Attended training camp in Mumbai, India 2005 (World Cricket Academy). Despite having made his first-class debut in 2007, he did not make an appearance in 2008
Opinions on cricket: 'Test match cricket is the pinnacle of the game.'
Best batting: 100* OUCCE v Durham, The Parks 2006

2008 Season (did not make any first-class or one-day appearances for his county)

Career Performances

	M	Inn	NO	Runs	HS	Avg	100	50	Ct	St	Balls	Runs	Wkts	Avg	BB	5I	10M
Test																	
FC	11	18	2	518	100 *	32.37	1	3	21	3	0	0	0	-	-	-	-
ODI																	
List A																	
20/20 Int																	
20/20																	

KRUGER, G. J-P. Glamorgan

Name: Garnett John-Peter Kruger
Role: Right-hand bat, right-arm fast-medium bowler
Born: 5 January 1977, Port Elizabeth, South Africa
Height: 6ft 3in
County debut: 2007 (Leicestershire)
ODI debut: 2005-06
Twenty20 Int debut: 2005-06
Place in bowling averages: 74th av. 30.31 (2007 33rd av. 24.92)
Family links with cricket: Father played cricket in Eastern Province
Education: Gelvan High School; Russell Road College
Qualifications: Fitting and machinery; architecture
Overseas tours: South Africa A to West Indies 2000-01, to Zimbabwe 2004, to Sri Lanka 2005-06; South Africa VI to Hong Kong 2003; South Africa to Australia 2005-06; South Africa Emerging Players to Australia (Cricket Australia Emerging Players Tournament) 2006
Overseas teams played for: Eastern Province 1997-98 – 2002-03; Gauteng 2003-04; Lions 2003-04 –
Cricketers particularly admired: Glenn McGrath
Other sports played: Basketball

Extras: Has represented South Africa A against various touring teams. His match awards include Man of the Match v North West at Port Elizabeth in the Standard Bank Cup 1999-2000 (6-23), v Dolphins at Durban in the SuperSport Series 2005-06 (8-112) and v Warriors at Johannesburg in the SuperSport Series 2005-06 (7-44/4-46). Was due to join Leicestershire as an overseas player in 2004 but was forced to pull out through injury; is no longer considered an overseas player. Man of the Match v Dolphins at Durban in the SuperSport Series 2007-08 (6-49). Took over 50 wickets for Leicestershire in all competitions in 2008. Signed for Glamorgan in December 2008

Best batting: 58 South Africa A v Windward Islands, Arnos Vale 2000-01

Best bowling: 8-112 Lions v Dolphins, Durban 2005-06

2008 Season

	M	Inn	NO	Runs	HS	Avg	100	50	Ct	St	Balls	Runs	Wkts	Avg	BB	5I	10M
Test																	
FC	10	12	1	39	7	3.54	-	-	1	-	1801	970	32	30.31	5-47	2	-
ODI																	
List A	11	2	0	2	2	1.00	-	-	3	-	508	418	16	26.12	3-25	-	
20/20 Int																	
20/20	6	2	2	0	0 *		-	-	1	-	114	172	4	43.00	1-26	-	

Career Performances

	M	Inn	NO	Runs	HS	Avg	100	50	Ct	St	Balls	Runs	Wkts	Avg	BB	5I	10M
Test																	
FC	90	112	30	896	58	10.92	-	2	20	-	15741	8817	300	29.39	8-112	13	2
ODI	3	2	1	0	0 *	0.00	-	-	1	-	138	139	2	69.50	1-43	-	
List A	114	33	16	115	20 *	6.76	-	-	18	-	5047	4031	158	25.51	6-23	4	
20/20 Int	1	1	0	3	3	3.00	-	-	-	-	24	29	0		-	-	
20/20	29	8	7	37	19 *	37.00	-	-	4	-	598	786	30	26.20	4-10	-	

KRUIS, G. J. Yorkshire

Name: Gideon (Deon) Jacobus Kruis
Role: Right-hand bat, right-arm fast-medium bowler
Born: 9 May 1974, Pretoria, South Africa
Height: 6ft 3in **Weight:** 14st 7lbs
Nickname: Kruisie, Chicken Head
County debut: 2005
County cap: 2006
50 wickets in a season: 1
Place in batting averages: 120th av. 30.50
Place in bowling averages: 126th av. 41.04
Parents: Fanie and Hester
Wife and date of marriage: Marna, 29 June 2002
Children: Elé, 5 October 2006
Family links with cricket: Brother-in-law P. J. Koortzen plays first-class cricket in South Africa
Education: St Alban's College, Pretoria; University of Pretoria
Qualifications: BCom (Hotel and Catering Management)
Off-season: 'Got a sports clothing manufacturing business in Kimberley. Doing commentary on SuperSport in South Africa. Coaching at St Andrew's School in Bloemfontein'
Overseas tours: MCC to Bermuda, to Denmark; South African Invitation XI to Malawi
Overseas teams played for: Northern Transvaal 1993-97; Griqualand West 1997-2004; Goodyear Eagles 2004-05
Career highlights to date: 'Playing for Yorkshire and being Player of the Year in 2005'
Cricket moments to forget: 'The 2007 season – too many injuries!'
Cricket superstitions: 'Left boot on first; four knots when batting, five when bowling on left boot'
Cricketers particularly admired: Allan Donald, Clive Rice, Richard Hadlee, Dennis Lillee, Glenn McGrath, Steve Waugh
Young players to look out for: Chris Woakes, Joe Denly
Other sports played: Golf, squash
Other sports followed: Golf, football (Liverpool)
Favourite band: The Killers
Relaxations: Golf, falconry
Extras: Yorkshire Player of the Year 2005. Is not considered an overseas player

Opinions on cricket: 'I feel that first-division cricket is very strong and competitive. We have to guard against Twenty20 overkill, but it has brought some money into the game. I think the proposed changes to the 2010 season will benefit all players, as it will better prepare them for international cricket. From a bowling point of view, I'd like to see better balls for four-day cricket.'
Best batting: 59 Griqualand West v Bangladeshis, Kimberley 2000-01
Best bowling: 7-58 Griqualand West v Northerns, Centurion 1997-98

2008 Season

	M	Inn	NO	Runs	HS	Avg	100	50	Ct	St	Balls	Runs	Wkts	Avg	BB	5I	10M
Test																	
FC	10	14	8	183	50 *	30.50	-	1	2	-	1773	903	22	41.04	5-47	1	-
ODI																	
List A	12	1	1	3	3 *		-	-	-	-	480	300	13	23.07	4-32	-	
20/20 Int																	
20/20																	

Career Performances

	M	Inn	NO	Runs	HS	Avg	100	50	Ct	St	Balls	Runs	Wkts	Avg	BB	5I	10M
Test																	
FC	121	171	56	1718	59	14.93	-	3	44	-	24151	11988	384	31.21	7-58	19	1
ODI																	
List A	119	52	19	407	31 *	12.33	-	-	27	-	5489	4235	144	29.40	4-17	-	
20/20 Int																	
20/20	14	2	1	6	5 *	6.00	-	-	3	-	289	317	13	24.38	2-15	-	

50. Who captained England when the Ashes were won in Australia at the end of the bad-tempered 1970-71 series?

LAMB, G. A. — Hampshire

Name: Gregory (Greg) Arthur Lamb
Role: Right-hand bat, right-arm off-spin or medium bowler; all-rounder
Born: 4 March 1981, Harare, Zimbabwe
Height: 6ft **Weight:** 12st
Nickname: Lamby
County debut: 2004
Parents: Terry and Jackie
Marital status: Single
Children: Isabella Grace Saskia Lamb
Education: Lomagundi College; Guildford College (both Zimbabwe)
Qualifications: School and coaching qualifications
Overseas tours: Zimbabwe U19 to South Africa (U19 World Cup) 1997-98, to Sri Lanka (U19 World Cup) 1999-2000; Zimbabwe A to Sri Lanka 1999-2000
Overseas teams played for: CFX [Zimbabwe] Academy 1999-2000; Mashonaland A 2000-01
Career highlights to date: 'Playing against Australia. Making my first first-class hundred'
Cricket superstitions: 'Every time I hit a four I have to touch the other side of the pitch'
Cricketers particularly admired: Aravinda de Silva
Other sports played: 'All sports'
Favourite band: Matchbox Twenty
Relaxations: 'Fishing, playing sport'
Extras: Played for Zimbabwe U12, U15 and U19. Represented CFX [Zimbabwe] Academy, ZCU President's XI and Zimbabwe A against various touring sides. Scored 94 on Championship debut for Hampshire v Derbyshire at Derby 2004. Released at the end of September 2008
Best batting: 100* CFX Academy v Manicaland, Mutare 1999-2000
Best bowling: 7-73 CFX Academy v Midlands, Kwekwe 1999-2000

2008 Season

	M	Inn	NO	Runs	HS	Avg	100	50	Ct	St	Balls	Runs	Wkts	Avg	BB	5I	10M
Test																	
FC	9	15	2	272	54 *	20.92	-	1	7	-	844	571	8	71.37	2-69	-	-
ODI																	
List A	10	7	2	128	84	25.60	-	1	2	-	405	382	8	47.75	4-47	-	
20/20 Int																	
20/20	10	8	2	62	22 *	10.33	-	-	3	-	201	265	8	33.12	2-25	-	

Career Performances

	M	Inn	NO	Runs	HS	Avg	100	50	Ct	St	Balls	Runs	Wkts	Avg	BB	5I	10M
Test																	
FC	38	59	7	1175	100 *	22.59	1	6	31	-	2304	1425	39	36.53	7-73	1	-
ODI																	
List A	56	47	7	954	100 *	23.85	1	5	29	-	953	869	26	33.42	4-38	-	
20/20 Int																	
20/20	38	31	4	462	67	17.11	-	2	11	-	367	523	19	27.52	4-28	-	

LANGER, J. L. — Somerset

Name: Justin Lee Langer
Role: Left-hand top order bat, right-arm medium bowler, county captain
Born: 21 November 1970, Subiaco, Western Australia
Height: 5ft 8in **Weight:** 12st 4lbs
Nickname: JL, Alfie
County debut: 1998 (Middlesex), 2006 (Somerset)
County cap: 1998 (Middlesex), 2007 (Somerset)
Test debut: 1992-93
ODI debut: 1993-94
1000 runs in a season: 5
1st-Class 200s: 10
1st-Class 300s: 2
Place in batting averages: 48th av. 43.32 (2007 20th av. 55.95)
Parents: Colin and Joy-Anne
Wife and date of marriage: Sue, 13 April 1996
Children: Jessica, 28 March 1997; Ali-Rose, November 1998; Sophie, April 2001;

Grace, November 2005
Family links with cricket: Uncle, Robbie Langer, played Sheffield Shield cricket for Western Australia and World Series for Australia; father played A Grade cricket in Western Australia
Education: Liwara Catholic School; Aquinas College, Perth; University of Western Australia
Career outside cricket: Journalism, writing and public speaking
Overseas tours: Young Australia to England 1995; Australia A to South Africa 2002-03 (c); Australia to New Zealand 1992-93, to Pakistan 1994-95, to West Indies 1994-95, to South Africa 1996-97, to England 1997, to Pakistan 1998-99, to West Indies 1998-99, to Sri Lanka and Zimbabwe 1999-2000, to New Zealand 1999-2000, to India 2000-01, to England 2001, to South Africa 2001-02, to Sri Lanka and Sharjah (v Pakistan) 2002-03, to West Indies 2002-03, to Sri Lanka 2003-04, to India 2004-05, to New Zealand 2004-05, to England 2005, to South Africa 2005-06, plus other one-day tournaments in Sharjah, Sri Lanka and Pakistan
Overseas teams played for: Scarborough CC, Perth; Western Australia 1991-92 –
Career highlights to date: 'Winning back the Ashes 2006-07. Being paid to play cricket and keep fit for the past 18 years - I'm the luckiest man in the world!'
Cricket moments to forget: 'Losing the Ashes in 2005, although it was the best series I played in.'
Cricket superstitions: 'Right pad on first - two chewies when I bat'
Cricketers particularly admired: 'Too many to single them out...'
Young players to look out for: James Hildreth, Craig Kieswetter, Jos Butler, Neil Edwards, Arul Suppiah, Luke Pomersbach
Other sports played: Tennis, golf, Australian Rules, martial arts (has black belt in zen do kai). 'Football and touch rugby in warm-ups.'
Other sports followed: Australian Rules (West Coast Eagles), football (Manchester United, Subiaco), the Australian cricket team.
Favourite band: U2
Relaxations: Family, writing, fishing, crabbing, gardening
Extras: Scored 54 (Australia's only fifty of the match) in the second innings of his debut Test v West Indies at Adelaide 1992-93. Overseas player with Middlesex 1998-2000; county vice-captain 1999 and captain 2000. Scored 166 for Middlesex v Essex at Southgate 1998, in the process sharing with Mike Gatting (241) in a new Middlesex record partnership for the first wicket (372). Put on 238 for the sixth wicket with Adam Gilchrist as Australia successfully chased 369 to beat Pakistan in the second Test at Hobart 1999-2000; his 127 (coupled with 59 in the first innings) won him the Man of the Match award. His numerous other awards include Man of the [Test] Series v New Zealand 2001-02, and Man of the Match in the fourth Test v England at Melbourne 2002-03 (250) and in the first Test v West Indies at Georgetown 2002-03 (146/78*). One of *Wisden*'s Five Cricketers of the Year 2001. Became first Western Australian to make 100 Test appearances, in the third Test v South Africa at Johannesburg 2005-06. A temporary overseas player with Somerset during the 2006 season and an overseas player with the county and captain since 2007. Scored 342 v Surrey at Guildford 2006, setting a new record for the highest individual first-class

score by a Somerset player. Retired from international cricket after the fifth Test v England at Sydney 2006-07. Has written three books, *From Outback To Outfield*, *The Power of Passion*, and *See the Sunrise*, the most recent, published in February 2008. Member of the Order of Australia 2008. In the 2008 season he again scored over 1000 first-class runs. Announced in November 2008 that he intends to continue playing until he reaches 40

Opinions on cricket: 'English cricket has worked hard to boast a world-class domestic system. Now the first division provides this, so I don't see any reason to change it. The only thing I would change is the competitiveness of the pitches being played on. As a general rule, I believe they are too flat to produce consistent outright results.'

Best batting: 342 Somerset v Surrey, Guildford 2006

Best bowling: 2-17 Australia A v South Africans, Brisbane 1997-98

2008 Season

	M	Inn	NO	Runs	HS	Avg	100	50	Ct	St	Balls	Runs	Wkts	Avg	BB	5I	10M
Test																	
FC	15	26	1	1083	188	43.32	3	7	15	-	12	6	0		-	-	
ODI																	
List A	14	13	1	418	117	34.83	2	1	6	-	0	0	0		-	-	
20/20 Int																	
20/20	8	8	0	205	62	25.62	-	1	1	-	0	0	0				

Career Performances

	M	Inn	NO	Runs	HS	Avg	100	50	Ct	St	Balls	Runs	Wkts	Avg	BB	5I	10M
Test	105	182	12	7696	250	45.27	23	30	73	-	6	3	0		-	-	-
FC	345	601	55	27551	342	50.45	84	106	306	-	386	210	5	42.00	2-17	-	-
ODI	8	7	2	160	36	32.00	-	-	2	1	0	0	0		-	-	
List A	225	217	21	7603	146	38.79	14	51	106	2	193	215	7	30.71	3-51	-	
20/20 Int																	
20/20	24	24	1	788	97	34.26	-	5	6	-	0	0	0		-	-	

51. He was a great England batsman, but he made 'a pair' on his Test debut in the 1975 Ashes series. Who is he?

LANGEVELDT, C. K. Derbyshire

Name: Charl Kenneth Langeveldt
Role: Right-hand bat, right-arm fast-medium bowler
Born: 17 December 1974, Stellenbosch, South Africa
County debut: 2005 (Somerset), 2007 (Leicestershire), 2008 (Derbyshire)
County cap: 2005 (Somerset)
Test debut: 2004-05
ODI debut: 2001-02
Twenty20 Int debut: 2005-06
Place in batting averages: 219th av. 17.33
Place in bowling averages: 20th av. 22.50
Career outside cricket: Formerly a prison officer
Overseas tours: South Africa Academy to Zimbabwe 1998-99; South Africa A to West Indies 2000, to Australia 2002-03, to Zimbabwe 2004, 2006-07, 2007-08, to India 2007-08; South Africa to Zimbabwe 2001-02, to England (ICC Champions Trophy) 2004, to West Indies 2004-05, to Australia 2005-06, to India (ICC Champions Trophy) 2006-07, to West Indies (World Cup) 2006-07, to Pakistan 2007-08, plus other one-day series and tournaments in Australia, England, Sri Lanka, India and Ireland
Overseas teams played for: Boland 1997-98 – 2002-03; Border 2003-04; Lions 2003-04 – 2006-07; Cape Cobras 2007-08 –
Extras: Represented South Africa in the 2002-03 World Cup. Took 5-46 on Test debut in the third Test v England at Cape Town 2004-05. Took 5-62 in the third ODI v West Indies at Bridgetown 2004-05, including a hat-trick (Bradshaw, Powell, Collymore) to secure a one-run win and series victory, winning the Man of the Match award. His other match awards include Man of the Match v Bangladesh at Edgbaston in the ICC Champions Trophy 2004 (3-17) and (shared with Lasith Malinga) v Sri Lanka at Providence Stadium, Guyana, in the 2006-07 World Cup (5-39). Was joint leading wicket-taker (with Andrew Hall) for South Africa in the 2006-07 World Cup (14; av. 25.78). Was a temporary overseas player with Somerset during the 2005 season; was a temporary overseas player with Leicestershire during the 2007 season, as a replacement for RP Singh. South African Player of the Year 2007. One of *South African Cricket Annual*'s five Cricketers of the Year 2007. Signed for Derbyshire in April 2008. Should have toured with South Africa in 2008, but withdrew due to controversy over selection policy
Best batting: 56 Boland v Eastern Province, Port Elizabeth 1999-2000
Best bowling: 6-48 Lions v Titans, Potchefstroom 2006-07

2008 Season

	M	Inn	NO	Runs	HS	Avg	100	50	Ct	St	Balls	Runs	Wkts	Avg	BB	5I	10M
Test																	
FC	12	15	3	208	40	17.33	-	-	5	-	2509	1238	55	22.50	5-40	3	-
ODI																	
List A	9	5	1	34	26	8.50	-	-	-	-	385	297	16	18.56	4-28	-	
20/20 Int																	
20/20	7	4	3	7	3 *	7.00	-	-	3	-	126	118	8	14.75	4-9	-	

Career Performances

	M	Inn	NO	Runs	HS	Avg	100	50	Ct	St	Balls	Runs	Wkts	Avg	BB	5I	10M
Test	6	4	2	16	10	8.00	-	-	2	-	999	593	16	37.06	5-46	1	-
FC	87	109	38	1039	56	14.63	-	1	25	-	16258	8064	283	28.49	6-48	9	1
ODI	59	14	5	41	12	4.55	-	-	9	-	2811	2334	82	28.46	5-39	2	
List A	170	66	23	311	33 *	7.23	-	-	29	-	8003	6060	259	23.39	5-7	6	
20/20 Int	3	2	1	2	2	2.00	-	-	1	-	60	67	4	16.75	2-14	-	
20/20	22	8	6	9	3 *	4.50	-	-	11	-	456	464	32	14.50	5-16	1	

LATOUF, K. J. Hampshire

Name: Kevin John Latouf
Role: Right-hand bat, right-arm medium bowler
Born: 7 September 1985, Pretoria, South Africa
Height: 5ft 10in **Weight:** 12st
Nickname: Poindexter, Mushy, Latsy, Kev
County debut: 2005 (one-day), 2006 (first-class)
Parents: Colin and Josephine
Marital status: Single
Education: Millfield School; Barton Peveril Sixth Form College
Qualifications: 11 GCSEs, 4 AS-Levels
Overseas tours: West of England U15 to West Indies 2000, 2001
Overseas teams played for: Melville CC, Perth ('briefly')
Cricket moments to forget: 'Golden duck in England U15 trial match'
Cricket superstitions: 'Don't believe in superstition'
Cricketers particularly admired: Ricky Ponting, Jonty Rhodes, Allan Donald

Other sports played: Tennis (county trials), rugby (Bristol and Somerset trials), golf ('fun'), surfing, snowboarding
Other sports followed: Rugby (Natal Sharks), football (Arsenal), AFL (Collingwood)
Favourite band: Coldplay
Extras: Played for West of England U13, U14 and U15. Played for ECB U17 and ECB U19. Played in Hampshire's 2nd XI Trophy winning side 2003. Represented England U19 2005. NBC Denis Compton award for most promising young Hampshire player 2005. Released at the end of September 2008
Best batting: 29 Hampshire v LUCCE, Rose Bowl 2006

2008 Season

	M	Inn	NO	Runs	HS	Avg	100	50	Ct	St	Balls	Runs	Wkts	Avg	BB	5I	10M
Test																	
FC																	
ODI																	
List A	1	1	0	14	14	14.00	-	-	-	-	0	0	0	-	-		
20/20 Int																	
20/20																	

Career Performances

	M	Inn	NO	Runs	HS	Avg	100	50	Ct	St	Balls	Runs	Wkts	Avg	BB	5I	10M
Test																	
FC	1	1	0	29	29	29.00	-	-	-	-	0	0	0	-	-	-	
ODI																	
List A	11	10	2	90	25	11.25	-	-	6	-	0	0	0	-	-		
20/20 Int																	
20/20																	

52. Who made a century against Australia on his Test match debut when he scored 114 in the second innings at Trent Bridge in 1993?

LAW, S. G. — Lancashire

Name: Stuart Grant Law
Role: Right-hand bat
Born: 18 October 1968, Brisbane, Australia
Height: 6ft 1in **Weight:** 13st 7lbs
Nickname: Lawman, Judge
County debut: 1996 (Essex), 2002 (Lancashire)
County cap: 1996 (Essex), 2002 (Lancashire)
Benefit: 2007 (Lancashire)
Test debut: 1995-96
ODI debut: 1994-95
1000 runs in a season: 10
1st-Class 200s: 6
Place in batting averages: 81st av. 37.05 (2007 8th av. 63.85)
Parents: Grant and Pam
Wife and date of marriage: Debbie-Lee, 31 December 1998
Children: Max, 9 January 2002
Family links with cricket: 'Dad, grandad and uncles played'
Education: Craigslea State High School, Brisbane
Qualifications: Level 2 cricket coach
Overseas tours: Australia B to Zimbabwe 1991-92; Young Australia (Australia A) to England and Netherlands 1995 (c); Australia to India and Pakistan (World Cup) 1995-96, to Sri Lanka (Singer World Series) 1996, to India (Titan World Series) 1996-97, to South Africa 1996-97 (one-day series), to New Zealand (one-day series) 1997-98
Overseas teams played for: Queensland Bulls 1988-89 – 2003-04
Career highlights to date: 'Playing for Australia. Winning first ever Sheffield Shield trophy with Queensland as captain [1994-95]'
Cricket superstitions: 'None'
Cricketers particularly admired: Greg Chappell, Viv Richards
Young players to look out for: Steve Croft, Gareth Cross, 'Max Law'
Other sports played: Golf ('very socially')
Other sports followed: Rugby league
Favourite band: Red Hot Chili Peppers, Foo Fighters
Relaxations: 'Beach'
Extras: Sheffield Shield Player of the Year 1990-91. Captain of Queensland 1994-95 – 1996-97 and 1999-2000 – 2001-02; is the most successful captain in modern-day Australian domestic cricket, having captained his state to five Sheffield Shield/Pura Cup titles and to three one-day titles, and has a stand named after him at Queensland's

Allan Border Field in Brisbane. One of *Wisden*'s Five Cricketers of the Year 1998. PCA Player of the Year 1999. Scored century (168) v Warwickshire at Edgbaston 2003, sharing with Carl Hooper (177) in a Lancashire record fifth-wicket partnership of 360 as the county scored 781. Lancashire Player of the Year 2003. Retired from Australian cricket at the end of 2003-04. Vice-captain of Lancashire 2005-07; appointed captain of Lancashire for 2008. Awarded Medal of the Order of Australia (OAM) in Australia Day Honours list 2007 for service to cricket as a state, national and international player. Is a UK citizen and not considered an overseas player. Released at the end of the 2008 season

Opinions on cricket: 'Very lucky to do what I do.'

Best batting: 263 Essex v Somerset, Chelmsford 1999

Best bowling: 5-39 Queensland v Tasmania, Brisbane 1995-96

2008 Season

	M	Inn	NO	Runs	HS	Avg	100	50	Ct	St	Balls	Runs	Wkts	Avg	BB	5I	10M
Test																	
FC	13	21	2	704	158 *	37.05	1	4	11	-	0	0	0		-	-	
ODI																	
List A	11	11	1	171	65	17.10	-	1	3	-	0	0	0		-	-	
20/20 Int																	
20/20	11	10	1	192	54	21.33	-	1	5	-	0	0	0		-	-	

Career Performances

	M	Inn	NO	Runs	HS	Avg	100	50	Ct	St	Balls	Runs	Wkts	Avg	BB	5I	10M
Test	1	1	1	54	54 *		-	1	1	-	18	9	0		-	-	-
FC	365	597	65	27041	263	50.82	79	128	406	-	8433	4236	83	51.03	5-39	1	
ODI	54	51	5	1237	110	26.89	1	7	12	-	807	635	12	52.91	2-22	-	
List A	386	365	27	11590	163	34.28	20	62	153	-	3855	3166	90	35.17	5-26	1	
20/20 Int																	
20/20	41	40	3	1013	101	27.37	1	6	15	-	6	10	0		-	-	

LAWSON, J. J. C. — Leicestershire

Name: Jermaine Jay Charles Lawson
Role: Right-hand bat, right-arm fast-medium bowler
Born: 13 January 1982, Spanish Town, St Catherine, Jamaica
County debut: 2004
Test debut: 2002
ODI debut: 2001
Overseas tours: West Indies to Sri Lanka (LG Albans Triangular Series) 2001, to Bangladesh 2002, to England 2004, to Australia 2005
Extras: Took 6-3 for West Indies against Bangladesh at Dhaka in only his third Test match. Took a career best 7-78 in the third Test against Australia in Antigua 2003. In a career overshadowed by controversy surrounding his bowling action, has also played for West Indies A, West Indies B, University of West Indies and Jamaica. Signed for Leicestershire in March 2008.
Best batting: 35 Leicester v Northamptonshire, Grace Road 2008
Best bowling: 7-78 West Indies v Australia, St Johns, Antigua 2003

2008 Season

	M	Inn	NO	Runs	HS	Avg	100	50	Ct	St	Balls	Runs	Wkts	Avg	BB	5I	10M
Test																	
FC	2	2	0	35	35	17.50	-	-	1	-	228	188	2	94.00	1-41	-	-
ODI																	
List A																	
20/20 Int																	
20/20																	

Career Performances

	M	Inn	NO	Runs	HS	Avg	100	50	Ct	St	Balls	Runs	Wkts	Avg	BB	5I	10M
Test	13	21	6	52	14	3.46	-	-	3	-	2364	1512	51	29.64	7-78	2	-
FC	54	75	22	434	35	8.18	-	-	15	-	8331	5100	174	29.31	7-78	6	-
ODI	13	5	2	18	8	6.00	-	-	-	-	558	498	17	29.29	4-57	-	
List A	34	15	5	32	8	3.20	-	-	2	-	1579	1159	60	19.31	5-66	1	
20/20 Int																	
20/20	3	0	0	0	0		-	-	-	-	60	60	4	15.00	3-29	-	

LAWSON, M. A. K. Derbyshire

Name: Mark Anthony Kenneth Lawson
Role: Right-hand bat, right-arm leg-spin bowler
Born: 24 November 1985, Leeds
Height: 5ft 8in **Weight:** 12st ('approx')
Nickname: Sauce
County debut: 2004 (Yorkshire), 2008 (Derbyshire)
Place in batting averages: (2006 238th av. 15.50)
Place in bowling averages: (2006 78th av. 34.50)
Parents: Anthony and Dawn
Marital status: Single
Family links with cricket: 'Father played local league cricket and encouraged me to take up the game'
Education: Castle Hall Language College, Mirfield, West Yorkshire
Qualifications: 11 GCSEs

Overseas tours: England U19 to Australia 2002-03, to Bangladesh (U19 World Cup) 2003-04, to India 2004-05
Cricketers particularly admired: Shane Warne, Gareth Batty
Other sports played: Football (school), rugby union (school, Cleckheaton 'in early teens'), rugby league (Dewsbury Moor ARLFC 'in early teens')
Other sports followed: Rugby league (Bradford Bulls)
Relaxations: Music, dining out, cinema
Extras: Played for Yorkshire Schools U11-U16 (captain U13-U15); ESCA North of England U14 and U15; North of England Development of Excellence U17 and U19. Represented England U15, U17 and U19. Awarded Brian Johnston Scholarship. Voted Yorkshire Supporters' Young Player of the Year 2003. 2nd XI cap 2006. Spent 2007 in the shadow of rising star Adil Rashid, making only two appearances. On loan at Middlesex in 2008. Released by Yorkshire in August 2008. Agreed a short-term deal with Derbyshire in time to appear in their final championship game of 2008 and will play for the county in 2009
Best batting: 44 Yorkshire v Hampshire, Rose Bowl 2006
Best bowling: 6-88 Yorkshire v Middlesex, Scarborough 2006

2008 Season

	M	Inn	NO	Runs	HS	Avg	100	50	Ct	St	Balls	Runs	Wkts	Avg	BB	5I	10M
Test																	
FC	2	2	1	8	5	8.00	-	-	-	-	96	83	0		-	-	-
ODI																	
List A																	
20/20 Int																	
20/20																	

Career Performances

	M	Inn	NO	Runs	HS	Avg	100	50	Ct	St	Balls	Runs	Wkts	Avg	BB	5I	10M
Test																	
FC	17	23	6	205	44	12.05	-	-	7	-	2427	1782	42	42.42	6-88	4	-
ODI																	
List A	4	4	0	30	20	7.50	-	-	1	-	118	141	3	47.00	2-50	-	
20/20 Int																	
20/20	2	1	1	4	4 *		-	-	1	-	48	87	3	29.00	2-34	-	

LAXMAN, V. V. S. Lancashire

Name: Vangipurappu Venkata Sai (VVS) Laxman
Role: Right-hand bat, right-arm off-break bowler
Born: 1 November 1974, Hyderabad, India
County debut: 2007
Test debut: 1996-97
ODI debut: 1997-98
1st-Class 200s: 4
1st-Class 300s: 2
Place in batting averages: 49th av. 44.56
Overseas tours: India U19 to England 1994; India to South Africa 1996-97, to West Indies 1996-97, to New Zealand 1998-99; to Australia 1999-2000, to Zimbabwe 2001, to South Africa 2001-02, to West Indies 2001-02, to England 2002, to Sri Lanka (ICC Champions Trophy) 2002-03, to New Zealand 2002-03, to Australia 2003-04, to Pakistan 2003-04, to England (ICC Champions Trophy) 2004, to Bangladesh 2004-05, to Zimbabwe 2005-06, to Pakistan 2005-06, to West Indies 2006, to South Africa 2006-07, to England 2007, to Australia

2007-08, plus other one-day tournaments in Sharjah, Malaysia, Sri Lanka, Netherlands and England

Overseas teams played for: Hyderabad, India 1992-93 –

Extras: Popularly nicknamed 'Very Very Special'. One of *Wisden*'s Five Cricketers of the Year 2002. Scored 281 in the second Test v Australia in Kolkata 2000-01 (following a first-innings 59), in the process sharing with Rahul Dravid (180) in a record fifth-wicket partnership for India in Tests (376) and winning Man of the Match award. Scored 178 in the fourth Test v Australia in Sydney 2003-04, in the process sharing with Sachin Tendulkar (241) in a record fourth-wicket partnership for India in Tests (353). His other series and match awards include Man of the [Test] Series v New Zealand 2003-04 and Man of the Match v Australia in Brisbane in the VB Series 2003-04 (103*) and v Pakistan in the fifth ODI in Lahore 2003-04 (107). Was a temporary overseas player with Lancashire during the 2007 season as a replacement for Brad Hodge. Scored a double century in the third Test against Australia in October 2008

Best batting: 353 Hyderabad v Karnataka, Bangalore 1999-2000

Best bowling: 3-11 Hyderabad v Railways, Delhi (KS) 1999-2000

2008 Season (Did not make any first-class or one-day appearances)

Career Performances

	M	Inn	NO	Runs	HS	Avg	100	50	Ct	St	Balls	Runs	Wkts	Avg	BB	5I	10M
Test	96	158	21	6000	281	43.79	12	35	102	-	324	126	2	63.00	1-2	-	-
FC	209	340	38	15450	353	51.15	44	71	223	-	1754	728	21	34.66	3-11	-	-
ODI	86	83	7	2338	131	30.76	6	10	39	-	42	40	0		-	-	
List A	167	161	18	4944	131	34.57	9	27	73	-	698	548	8	68.50	2-42	-	
20/20 Int																	
20/20	6	6	1	155	52	31.00	-	1	1	-	0	0	0		-	-	

53. By how many runs did Australia lead England in the first innings at The Gabba in November 2006?

LEE, J. E. — Yorkshire

Name: James Edward Lee
Role: Left-hand bat, right-arm fast-medium bowler
Born: 23 December 1988, Sheffield
Height: 6ft 1in **Weight:** 12st
Nickname: Binga
County debut: 2006
Parents: Diane and Steven
Marital status: Single
Family links with cricket: Father played Yorkshire Colts
Education: Immanuel College, Bradford
Qualifications: 8 GCSEs, 2 AS-levels
Overseas tours: England U19 to Malaysia (U19 World Cup) 2007-08
Career highlights to date: 'First-class debut v Lancashire in Roses match 2006'
Cricket superstitions: 'Tap three times'
Cricketers particularly admired: Brett Lee
Young players to look out for: Joe Root
Other sports followed: Football (Arsenal FC)
Favourite band: Reverend And The Makers
Relaxations: 'TV'
Best batting: 21* Yorkshire v Lancashire, Old Trafford 2006

2008 Season (did not make any first-class or one-day appearances)

Career Performances

	M	Inn	NO	Runs	HS	Avg	100	50	Ct	St	Balls	Runs	Wkts	Avg	BB	5I	10M
Test																	
FC	1	2	1	22	21 *	22.00	-	-	-	-	54	36	0		-	-	-
ODI																	
List A																	
20/20 Int																	
20/20																	

LEE, W. W. Kent

Name: Warren Wain Lee
Role: Right-hand bat, right-arm fast-medium bowler
Born: 27th August 1987, Delhi, India
County debut: No first-team appearances.
Education: Eaglesfield School, Shooters Hill
Extras: Debut for Kent 2nd XI v Derbyshire 2nd XI, Beckenham, August 2005, debut for Middlesex 2nd XI v Hampshire 2nd XI, Ealing, May 2008, debut for Surrey 2nd XI v Lancashire 2nd XI, Great Crosby, September 2008. Blackheath CC 2002-08.

LETT, R. J. H. Somerset

Name: Robin Jonathan Hugh Lett
Role: Right-hand bat, right-arm fast-medium bowler
Born: 23 December 1986, London
County debut: 2006
Family links with cricket: Grandfather is PH Jaques, who played for Leicestershire, 1949
Education: Millfield School; Oxford Brookes University
Extras: Played for Oxford UCCE in 2007 and 2008
Best batting: 57 Oxford UCCE v Glamorgan, The Parks, 2007

2008 Season

	M	Inn	NO	Runs	HS	Avg	100	50	Ct	St	Balls	Runs	Wkts	Avg	BB	5I	10M
Test																	
FC	3	3	0	55	50	18.33	-	1	1	-	0	0	0		-	-	-
ODI																	
List A																	
20/20 Int																	
20/20																	

Career Performances

	M	Inn	NO	Runs	HS	Avg	100	50	Ct	St	Balls	Runs	Wkts	Avg	BB	5I	10M
Test																	
FC	9	13	1	263	57	21.91	-	4	3	-	0	0	0		-	-	-
ODI																	
List A																	
20/20 Int																	
20/20																	

LEWIS, C. C. Surrey

Name: Christopher (Chris) Clairmonte Lewis
Role: Right-hand bat, right-arm fast-medium bowler
Born: 14 February 1968, Georgetown, Guyana
Height: 6ft 2in **Weight:** 13st
Nickname: Carl
County debut: 1987 (Leics), 1992 (Notts), 1996 (Surrey)
County cap: 1990 (Leics), 1994 (Notts), 1996 (Surrey)
Test debut: 1990
50 wickets in a season: 2
1st-Class 200s: 2
Education: Willesden High School
Qualifications: 2 O-levels
Overseas tours: England YC to Australia (Youth World Cup) 1987-88; England A to Kenya and Zimbabwe 1989-90; England to West Indies 1989-90, to Australia 1990-91, to New Zealand 1991-92, to India and Sri Lanka 1992-93, to West Indies 1993-94, to Australia 1994-95; England XI to New Zealand (Cricket Max) 1997

Other sports followed: Snooker, football, darts, American football, basketball
Relaxations: Music, sleeping
Extras: Suffers from Raynaud's disease, a problem of blood circulation. Left Leicestershire at the end of 1991 season and signed for Nottinghamshire. Hit first Test century v India at Madras on 1992-93 tour to India and Sri Lanka. Cornhill England Player of the Year (jointly with Alec Stewart) 1992-93. His 247 v Durham at Chester-le-Street in 1993 is the highest score by a Nottinghamshire batsman since World War II. Left Nottinghamshire and joined Surrey for the 1996 season. Rejoined Leicestershire as vice-captain for the 1998 season and captained the club for much of the season in the absence through injury of James Whitaker. Scored 71* in 33 balls as Leicestershire made 204 in 19 overs and one ball to beat Northamptonshire at Grace Road in 1998. A persistent hip injury forced him to announce his retirement during the 2000-01 off-season. Rejoined Surrey in 2008 to play in 20-over matches
Best batting: 247 Nottinghamshire v Durham, Chester-le-Street 1993
Best bowling: 6-22 Leicestershire v Oxford University, The Parks 1988

2008 Season

	M	Inn	NO	Runs	HS	Avg	100	50	Ct	St	Balls	Runs	Wkts	Avg	BB	5I	10M
Test																	
FC																	
ODI																	
List A	1	1	0	33	33	33.00	-	-	-	-	36	51	0		-	-	
20/20 Int																	
20/20	1	1	0	2	2	2.00	-	-	-	-	12	29	0		-	-	

Career Performances

	M	Inn	NO	Runs	HS	Avg	100	50	Ct	St	Balls	Runs	Wkts	Avg	BB	5I	10M
Test	32	51	3	1105	117	23.02	1	4	25	-	6852	3490	93	37.52	6-111	3	-
FC	189	275	34	7406	247	30.73	9	34	154	-	32003	16225	543	29.88	6-22	20	3
ODI	53	40	14	374	33	14.38	-	-	20	-	2625	1942	66	29.42	4-30	-	
List A	266	217	56	3959	116 *	24.59	1	14	104	-	11846	8232	312	26.38	5-19	2	
20/20 Int																	
20/20	1	1	0	2	2	2.00	-	-	-	-	12	29	0		-	-	

LEWIS, J. Gloucestershire

Name: Jonathan (Jon) Lewis
Role: Right-hand bat, right-arm fast-medium bowler
Born: 26 August 1975, Aylesbury
Height: 6ft 3in **Weight:** 14st
Nickname: Lewy, JJ
County debut: 1995
County cap: 1998
Benefit: 2007
Test debut: 2006
ODI debut: 2005
Twenty20 Int debut: 2005
50 wickets in a season: 6
Place in batting averages: 222nd av. 16.86 (2007 262nd av. 13.00)
Place in bowling averages: 65th av. 28.82 (2007 108th av. 39.33)
Parents: John and Jane
Wife and date of marriage: Kate, 16 October 2004
Children: Jacob, 28 April 2007
Education: Churchfields Comprehensive School, Swindon; Swindon College
Qualifications: 9 GCSEs, BTEC in Leisure and Hospitality, ECB Level 3 coach
Career outside cricket: Coaching
Off-season: 'Daddy Day Care!'
Overseas tours: Bath Schools to New South Wales 1993; England A to West Indies 2000-01, to Sri Lanka 2004-05; England to South Africa 2004-05, to India (ICC Champions Trophy) 2006-07, to Australia 2006-07 (C'wealth Bank Series), to West Indies (World Cup) 2006-07
Overseas teams played for: Marist, Christchurch, New Zealand 1994-95; Richmond City, Melbourne 1995-96; Wanderers, Johannesburg 1996-98; Techs CC, Cape Town 1998-99; Randwick-Petersham, Sydney 2003-04
Career highlights to date: 'Every time I've pulled on an England shirt'
Cricket moments to forget: 'Any injury'
Cricket superstitions: 'I always get a haircut if I go for a gallon'
Cricketers particularly admired: Courtney Walsh, Jack Russell, Jonty Rhodes
Other sports played: Golf (7 handicap), football (Bristol North West FC)
Other sports followed: Football (Swindon Town FC)
Favourite band: Brand New Heavies
Relaxations: Movies
Extras: Was on Northamptonshire staff in 1994 but made no first-team appearance. Took Championship hat-trick (Gallian, Afzaal, Morris) v Nottinghamshire at Trent

Bridge 2000. Leading first-class wicket-taker among English bowlers in 2000 with 72 wickets (av. 20.91). Gloucestershire Player of the Year 2000. C&G Man of the Match award for his 4-39 v Hampshire at Bristol 2004. ECB National Academy 2004-05, 2006-07. Took 4-24 v Australia at The Rose Bowl in Twenty20 International 2005. Captain of Gloucestershire since 2006. Relinquished captaincy in November 2008
Best batting: 62 Gloucestershire v Worcestershire, Cheltenham 1999
Best bowling: 8-95 Gloucestershire v Zimbabweans, Gloucester 2000

2008 Season

	M	Inn	NO	Runs	HS	Avg	100	50	Ct	St	Balls	Runs	Wkts	Avg	BB	5I	10M
Test																	
FC	14	20	5	253	51	16.86	-	1	1	-	2357	1009	35	28.82	5-64	1	
ODI																	
List A	11	4	1	22	8	7.33	-	-	1	-	501	378	14	27.00	3-17	-	
20/20 Int																	
20/20	4	3	0	10	4	3.33	-	-	1	-	84	131	4	32.75	3-22	-	

Career Performances

	M	Inn	NO	Runs	HS	Avg	100	50	Ct	St	Balls	Runs	Wkts	Avg	BB	5I	10M
Test	1	2	0	27	20	13.50	-	-	-	-	246	122	3	40.66	3-68	-	-
FC	180	250	53	2857	62	14.50	-	6	41		33025	16681	621	26.86	8-95	32	5
ODI	13	8	2	50	17	8.33	-	-	-	-	716	500	18	27.77	4-36	-	
List A	183	104	40	657	40	10.26	-	-	31	-	8599	6436	239	26.92	5-19	2	
20/20 Int	2	2	1	1	1	1.00	-	-	1	-	42	55	4	13.75	4-24	-	
20/20	27	13	4	144	43	16.00	-	-	5	-	559	764	33	23.15	4-24	-	

54. Which Australian fast bowler took six wickets as England slumped to 52 all out in Don Bradman's last Test in 1948?

LEWRY, J. D. — Sussex

Name: Jason David Lewry
Role: Left-hand bat, left-arm fast-medium bowler
Born: 2 April 1971, Worthing
Height: 6ft 3in **Weight:** 'Going up'
Nickname: Lew, Lewie
County debut: 1994
County cap: 1996
Benefit: 2002
50 wickets in a season: 5
Place in bowling averages: 71st av. 30.09 (2007 70th av. 30.81)
Parents: David and Veronica
Wife and date of marriage: Naomi Madeleine, 18 August 1997
Children: William, 14 February 1998; Louis, 20 November 2000; Ruby and Poppy (identical twins!), 8 March 2007
Family links with cricket: Father coaches
Education: Durrington High School, Worthing; Worthing Sixth Form College
Qualifications: 6 O-levels, 3 GCSEs, City and Guilds, NCA Award
Career outside cricket: 'Still looking, but with more urgency with each passing year!'
Overseas tours: Goring CC to Isle of Wight 1992, 1993; England A to Zimbabwe and South Africa 1998-99
Cricket moments to forget: 'King pair, Eastbourne 1995'
Cricketers particularly admired: David Gower, Martin Andrews, Darren Lehmann
Other sports played: Golf, squash; darts, pool ('anything you can do in a pub')
Other sports followed: Football (West Ham United)
Favourite band: REM
Relaxations: Golf, pub games, films
Extras: Took seven wickets in 14 balls v Hampshire at Hove 2001, the second most (most by a seamer) outstanding spell of wicket-taking in first-class cricket (after Pat Pocock's seven in 11 for Surrey v Sussex at Eastbourne in 1972). His 5-75 v Lancashire at Liverpool 2006 included his 500th first-class wicket (Glen Chapple). Leading wicket-taker for the county in first-class matches in 2008 with 41
Opinions on cricket: 'More points should be awarded for a four-day win – 14 not enough.'
Best batting: 72 Sussex v Surrey, The Oval 2004
Best bowling: 8-106 Sussex v Leicestershire, Hove 2003

2008 Season

	M	Inn	NO	Runs	HS	Avg	100	50	Ct	St	Balls	Runs	Wkts	Avg	BB	5I	10M
Test																	
FC	15	18	3	101	27	6.73	-	-	7	-	2327	1234	41	30.09	4-56	-	-
ODI																	
List A	1	0	0	0	0		-	-	-	-	48	56	0		-	-	
20/20 Int																	
20/20																	

Career Performances

	M	Inn	NO	Runs	HS	Avg	100	50	Ct	St	Balls	Runs	Wkts	Avg	BB	5I	10M
Test																	
FC	181	237	62	1783	72	10.18	-	2	52	-	30940	16299	611	26.67	8-106	31	4
ODI																	
List A	79	44	15	217	16 *	7.48	-	-	13	-	3579	2768	100	27.68	4-29	-	
20/20 Int																	
20/20	11	4	1	10	8 *	3.33	-	-	4	-	197	239	14	17.07	3-34	-	

LIDDLE, C. J. Sussex

Name: Christopher (Chris) John Liddle
Role: Right-hand bat, left-arm fast-medium bowler
Born: 1 February 1984, Middlesbrough
Height: 6ft 4in **Weight:** 13st
Nickname: Lids, Chuck, Ice Man, Dolce
County debut: 2005 (Leicestershire), 2007 (Sussex)
Parents: Pat and John
Marital status: Single
Family links with cricket: 'Brother plays cricket'
Education: Nunthorpe Comprehensive School, Middlesbrough; TTE Modern Apprenticeship
Qualifications: 9 GCSEs, fully qualified instrument artificer, Level 1 coaching
Overseas teams played for: Balcatta CC, Perth
Cricket superstitions: 'Too many to list'
Cricketers particularly admired: Mushtaq Ahmed, Naved-ul-Hasan, Jason Lewry

Young players to look out for: Ben Brown, Mike Thornely, Tom Smith, Mike Gould
Other sports played: Football
Other sports followed: Football (Middlesbrough)
Favourite band: The Killers
Extras: Yorkshire Area Bowler of the Year 2001-02. Has attended Paul Terry Academy, Perth
Best batting: 53 Sussex v Worcestershire, Hove 2007
Best bowling: 3-42 Leicestershire v Somerset, Leicester 2006

2008 Season

	M	Inn	NO	Runs	HS	Avg	100	50	Ct	St	Balls	Runs	Wkts	Avg	BB	5I	10M
Test																	
FC	2	3	1	8	4 *	4.00	-	-	-	-	192	74	1	74.00	1-39	-	-
ODI																	
List A	8	1	0	1	1	1.00	-	-	4	-	228	243	5	48.60	2-46	-	
20/20 Int																	
20/20	5	2	1	10	10 *	10.00	-	-	2	-	116	165	10	16.50	4-15	-	

Career Performances

	M	Inn	NO	Runs	HS	Avg	100	50	Ct	St	Balls	Runs	Wkts	Avg	BB	5I	10M
Test																	
FC	14	14	5	113	53	12.55	-	1	5	-	1706	962	17	56.58	3-42	-	-
ODI																	
List A	14	3	0	13	11	4.33	-	-	6	-	504	532	10	53.20	3-60	-	
20/20 Int																	
20/20	5	2	1	10	10 *	10.00	-	-	2	-	116	165	10	16.50	4-15	-	

LOGAN, R. J. Northamptonshire

Name: Richard James Logan
Role: Right-hand bat, right-arm fast bowler
Born: 28 January 1980, Cannock, Staffordshire
Height: 6ft 1in **Weight:** 14st
Nickname: Bungle
County debut: 1999 (Northants), 2001 (Notts), 2005 (Hants)
Parents: Margaret and Robert
Marital status: Single
Family links with cricket: 'Dad played local cricket for Cannock'
Education: Wolverhampton Grammar School
Qualifications: 11 GCSEs, 1 A-level
Overseas tours: England U17 to Bermuda (International Youth Tournament) 1997; England U19 to South Africa (including U19 World Cup) 1997-98, to New Zealand 1998-99
Overseas teams played for: St George, Sydney 1999-2000; Lancaster Park, New Zealand; Rovers, Durban; Northerns Goodwood, Cape Town
Career highlights to date: 'Winning junior World Cup'
Cricketers particularly admired: Malcolm Marshall, Dennis Lillee
Other sports played: Hockey
Other sports followed: Football (Wolverhampton Wanderers)
Relaxations: 'Spending time with my mates. Training'
Extras: Played for Staffordshire U11-U19 (captain U13-U17); Midlands U14 and U15 (both as captain); HMC Schools U15. 1995 *Daily Telegraph*/Lombard U15 Midlands Bowler and Batsman of the Year. Played for Northamptonshire U17 and U19 national champions 1997. Played for England U15, U17 and U19. C&G Man of the Match award for his 5-24 v Suffolk at Mildenhall 2001. Took 5-26 v Lancashire at Trent Bridge 2003, the best return by a Nottinghamshire bowler in the Twenty20 Cup. Returned to Northamptonshire for 2007 season. Released September 2008
Best batting: 37* Nottinghamshire v Hampshire, Trent Bridge 2001
Best bowling: 6-93 Nottinghamshire v Derbyshire, Trent Bridge 2001

2008 Season

	M	Inn	NO	Runs	HS	Avg	100	50	Ct	St	Balls	Runs	Wkts	Avg	BB	5I	10M
Test																	
FC	1	1	0	1	1	1.00	-	-	-	-	114	117	1	117.00	1-87	-	-
ODI																	
List A																	
20/20 Int																	
20/20																	

Career Performances

	M	Inn	NO	Runs	HS	Avg	100	50	Ct	St	Balls	Runs	Wkts	Avg	BB	5I	10M
Test																	
FC	54	73	16	527	37 *	9.24	-	-	16	-	7936	5246	133	39.44	6-93	4	-
ODI																	
List A	65	30	11	215	28 *	11.31	--		21	-	2548	2464	70	35.20	5-24	1	
20/20 Int																	
20/20	17	8	4	39	11 *	9.75	-	-	-	-	244	315	17	18.52	5-26	1	

LONDON, A. B. Middlesex

Name: Adam Brian London
Role: Left-hand bat, right-arm off-break bowler
Born: 12 October 1988, Surrey
Extras: Former Sunbury CC and Middlesex Second XI player. Signed summer contract with Middlesex in June 2008

LOUW, J. — Northamptonshire

Name: Johann Louw
Role: Right-hand bat, right-arm fast-medium bowler; all-rounder
Born: 12 April 1979, Cape Town
County debut: 2004 (Northamptonshire), 2006 (Middlesex)
ODI debut: 2008
Twenty20 Int debut: 2005
Place in bowling averages: 109th av. 36.33
Overseas teams played for: Griqualand West 2000-01 – 2002-03; Eastern Province 2003-04; Dolphins 2004-05, 2006-07 - ; Eagles 2005-06
Extras: Scored over 1000 runs and took 75 wickets with Heywood (Central Lancashire League) 2001. Part of the East Lancashire side that took the Lancashire League title 2003. Played as a Kolpak player for Northamptonshire 2004, 2005. Northamptonshire Player of the Year 2004. Returned to South African domestic cricket in 2005-06, so now regarded as an overseas player. Overseas player with Middlesex 2006, and Northamptonshire 2008
Best batting: 124 Eastern Province v Boland Port Elizabeth 2003-04
Best bowling: 3-39 Dolphins v Eagles Bloemforntein 2007-08

2008 Season

	M	Inn	NO	Runs	HS	Avg	100	50	Ct	St	Balls	Runs	Wkts	Avg	BB	5I	10M
Test																	
FC	7	8	3	281	82	56.20	-	2	1	-	1074	545	15	36.33	3-42	-	-
ODI																	
List A	8	6	1	76	35 *	15.20	-	-	2	-	317	278	6	46.33	2-53	-	
20/20 Int																	
20/20	11	4	1	59	21 *	19.66	-	-	3	-	234	325	17	19.11	3-18	-	

Career Perfomances

	M	Inn	NO	Runs	HS	Avg	100	50	Ct	St	Balls	Runs	Wkts	Avg	BB	5I	10M
Test																	
FC	105	153	23	2855	124	21.96	1	15	35	-	18396	9670	298	32.44	6-39	11	1
ODI																	
List A	115	85	19	1191	72	18.04	-	3	16	-	5266	4202	169	24.86	5-27	4	
20/20 Int																	
20/20	39	21	4	148	21 *	8.70	-	-	9	-	826	1070	52	20.57	4-18	-	

LOYE, M. B. — Lancashire

Name: Malachy (Mal) Bernard Loye
Role: Right-hand bat, occasional wicket-keeper
Born: 27 September 1972, Northampton
Height: 6ft 2in **Weight:** 13st 12lbs
Nickname: Malcolm
County debut: 1991 (Northamptonshire), 2003 (Lancashire)
County cap: 1994 (Northamptonshire), 2003 (Lancashire)
Benefit: 2008 (Lancashire)
ODI debut: 2006-07
1000 runs in a season: 5
1st-Class 200s: 2
1st-Class 300s: 1
Place in batting averages: 238th av. 13.53 (2007 100th av. 35.58)
Parents: Patrick and Anne
Marital status: Single
Family links with cricket: 'Brother and Dad played for Cogenhoe CC in Northampton'
Education: Moulton Comprehensive, Northampton
Qualifications: GCSEs, coaching Levels 1-3
Overseas tours: England U18 to Canada (International Youth Tournament) 1991; England U19 to Pakistan 1991-92; England A to South Africa 1993-94, to Zimbabwe and South Africa 1998-99; Northamptonshire to Cape Town 1993, to Zimbabwe 1995, 1998, to Johannesburg 1996, to Grenada 2001, 2002; England VI to Hong Kong 2006; England to Australia 2006-07 (C'wealth Bank Series)
Overseas teams played for: Riccarton, Christchurch 1992-93 – 1994-95; Canterbury B 1993; Onslow, Wellington 1995-96; North Perth 1997-98, 1999-2000; Claremont, Western Australia 2000-01; Auckland 2006-07
Career highlights to date: 'PCA Player of the Year 1998'
Cricket moments to forget: '[C&G] semi-final against Worcester 2003'
Cricketers particularly admired: Gordon Greenidge, Wayne Larkins, Peter Carlstein, Graeme Hick, John Crawley
Young players to look out for: Gareth Cross, Steven Croft
Other sports played: 'Muck about at anything'
Other sports followed: Football (Northampton Town, Liverpool), rugby union
Favourite band: U2
Player website: www.malloyebenefit.com
Extras: Played for England YC and for England U19. PCA Young Player of the Year

and Whittingdale Young Player of the Year 1993. Scored 322* v Glamorgan at Northampton 1998 (the then highest individual first-class score for the county), in the process sharing with David Ripley in a new record partnership for any wicket for Northamptonshire (401). PCA Player of the Year 1998. Scored century (126) on Championship debut for Lancashire v Surrey at The Oval 2003 and another (113) in the next match v Nottinghamshire at Old Trafford to become the first batsman to score centuries in his first two matches for the county. Finished top of Lancashire's Twenty20 averages for 2008

Best batting: 322* Northamptonshire v Glamorgan, Northampton 1998

Best bowling: 1-8 Lancashire v Kent, Blackpool 2003

2008 Season

	M	Inn	NO	Runs	HS	Avg	100	50	Ct	St	Balls	Runs	Wkts	Avg	BB	5I	10M
Test																	
FC	10	16	1	203	61	13.53	-	1	6	-	0	0	0		-	-	-
ODI																	
List A	9	9	0	203	77	22.55	-	2	-	-	0	0	0		-	-	
20/20 Int																	
20/20	10	10	2	275	54 *	34.37	-	2	5	-	0	0	0		-	-	

Career Performances

	M	Inn	NO	Runs	HS	Avg	100	50	Ct	St	Balls	Runs	Wkts	Avg	BB	5I	10M
Test																	
FC	232	370	33	13520	322 *	40.11	39	54	115	-	55	61	1	61.00	1-8	-	-
ODI	7	7	0	142	45	20.28	-	-	-	-	0	0	0		-	-	
List A	287	281	31	8586	127	34.34	10	56	63	-	0	0	0		-	-	
20/20 Int																	
20/20	38	38	4	1131	100	33.26	1	7	14	-	0	0	0		-	-	

55. Which Indian prince scored a century on his Test match debut for England against Australia in 1932?

LUCAS, D. S. Northamptonshire

Name: David Scott Lucas
Role: Right-hand bat, left-arm fast-medium bowler
Born: 19 August 1978, Nottingham
Height: 6ft 3in **Weight:** 13st
Nickname: Muke, Lukey
County debut: 1999 (Nottinghamshire), 2005 (Yorkshire), 2007 (Northamptonshire)
Place in batting averages: (2007 188th av. 23.88)
Place in bowling averages: 132nd av. 42.58 (2007 110th av. 39.52)
Parents: Mary and Terry
Wife and date of marriage: Donna-Marie, 22 November 2004
Children: 'Gizmo and Missy'
Education: Horsendale Primary School, Djanogly City Technology College, Nottingham
Qualifications: 6 GCSEs, pass in Computer-Aided Design, Level 2 coaching award
Career outside cricket: 'I have a cleaning business that I currently run'
Off-season: 'Growing my business, holiday, football'
Overseas tours: England (Indoor) to Australia (Indoor Cricket World Cup) 1998
Overseas teams played for: Bankstown-Canterbury Bulldogs, Sydney 1996-97; Wanneroo, Perth 2001-02
Career highlights to date: 'The crack in the dressing room; lunches at Lord's'
Cricket superstitions: 'Always walk back to the left of my mark when bowling. Always put left pad on first. Can't bowl without my watch!'
Cricketers particularly admired: Chaminda Vaas, Brett Lee
Young players to look out for: Samit Patel, Chris Wright
Other sports played: Indoor cricket, football, golf
Other sports followed: Football (Arsenal and Stenhousemuir), ice hockey (Nottingham Panthers)
Favourite band: Michael Jackson, Snow Patrol, Bee Gees
Relaxations: 'PlayStation, running, eating, drinking'
Opinions on cricket: 'Not enough consistent rest between 4-day games. If the game is dead on the last day, call it off latest at tea, if captains agree. Quarters, semis and finals shouldn't be played under lights, as conditions change drastically. Pro40 games should start a lot earlier to stop bad light issues.'
Extras: Won Yorkshire League with Rotherham in 1996. NBC Denis Compton Award for the most promising young Nottinghamshire player 2000. Only J. J. van der Wath took more first-class wickets for the county in 2008

Best batting: 49 Nottinghamshire v DUCCE, Trent Bridge 2002
Best bowling: 5-30 Northamptonshire v Gloucestershire, Northampton 2008

2008 Season

	M	Inn	NO	Runs	HS	Avg	100	50	Ct	St	Balls	Runs	Wkts	Avg	BB	5I	10M
Test																	
FC	16	16	4	112	35	9.33	-	-	3	-	2542	1533	36	42.58	5-30	1	-
ODI																	
List A	7	5	2	20	9 *	6.66	-	-	5	-	246	191	6	31.83	2-19	-	
20/20 Int																	
20/20	2	1	1	3	3 *		-	-	1	-	18	31	0		-	-	

Career Performances

	M	Inn	NO	Runs	HS	Avg	100	50	Ct	St	Balls	Runs	Wkts	Avg	BB	5I	10M
Test																	
FC	48	57	16	763	49	18.60	-	-	8	-	7068	4277	115	37.19	5-30	4	-
ODI																	
List A	51	21	6	150	32	10.00	-	-	10	-	1986	1894	59	32.10	4-27	-	
20/20 Int																	
20/20	9	3	3	10	5 *		-	-	1	-	108	173	5	34.60	2-37	-	

LUMB, M. J. — Hampshire

Name: Michael John Lumb
Role: Left-hand bat, right-arm medium bowler
Born: 12 February 1980, Johannesburg, South Africa
Height: 6ft **Weight:** 13st
Nickname: China, Joe
County debut: 2000 (Yorkshire), 2007 (Hampshire)
County cap: 2003 (Yorkshire)
1000 runs in a season: 1
Place in batting averages: 104th av. 32.72 (2007 139th av. 31.00)
Parents: Richard and Sue
Marital status: Single
Family links with cricket: Father played for Yorkshire. Uncle played for Natal
Education: St Stithians College
Qualifications: Matriculation

Overseas tours: Transvaal U19 to Barbados; Yorkshire to Cape Town 2001, to Grenada 2002; England A to Malaysia and India 2003-04
Overseas teams played for: Pirates CC, Johannesburg; Wanderers CC, Johannesburg
Cricket moments to forget: 'Relegation in 2002 [with Yorkshire]'
Cricket superstitions: 'None'
Cricketers particularly admired: Graham Thorpe, Darren Lehmann, Craig White, Stephen Fleming
Other sports played: Golf
Other sports followed: Rugby union (Sharks in Super 14, Leeds Carnegie)
Favourite band: Oasis
Relaxations: 'Golf, socialising with friends'
Extras: Scored maiden first-class century (122) v Leicestershire at Headingley 2001; the Lumbs thus became only the fourth father and son to have scored centuries for Yorkshire. Yorkshire Young Player of the Year 2002, 2003. ECB National Academy 2003-04. C&G Man of the Match award in the quarter-final v Northamptonshire at Headingley 2005 (89). Scored 98 v Durham at Headingley 2006, in the process sharing with Darren Lehmann (339) in a new record fourth-wicket partnership for Yorkshire (358)
Best batting: 144 Yorkshire v Middlesex, Southgate 2006
Best bowling: 2-10 Yorkshire v Kent, Canterbury 2001

2008 Season

	M	Inn	NO	Runs	HS	Avg	100	50	Ct	St	Balls	Runs	Wkts	Avg	BB	5I	10M
Test																	
FC	16	27	2	818	107	32.72	1	6	17	-	0	0	0		-	-	-
ODI																	
List A	14	14	1	498	88	38.30	-	4	6	-	0	0	0		-	-	
20/20 Int																	
20/20	10	10	0	315	63	31.50	-	2	3	-	0	0	0		-	-	

Career Performances

	M	Inn	NO	Runs	HS	Avg	100	50	Ct	St	Balls	Runs	Wkts	Avg	BB	5I	10M
Test																	
FC	113	193	14	5879	144	32.84	9	39	78	-	318	242	6	40.33	2-10	-	-
ODI																	
List A	139	133	9	3801	108	30.65	1	28	44	-	12	28	0		-	-	
20/20 Int																	
20/20	43	43	3	828	84 *	20.70	-	6	11	-	36	65	3	21.66	3-32	-	

LUNGLEY, T. Derbyshire

Name: Tom Lungley
Role: Left-hand bat, right-arm medium bowler
Born: 25 July 1979, Derby
Height: 6ft 2in **Weight:** 13st
Nickname: Lungfish, Monkfish, Sweaty, Full Moon, Half Moon, Lungo
County debut: 2000
County cap: 2007
50 wickets in a season: 1
Place in batting averages: (2007 270th av. 11.26)
Place in bowling averages: (2007 42nd av. 26.35)
Parents: Richard and Christina
Marital status: 'Taken'
Family links with cricket: 'Dad was captain of Derby Road CC. Grandad was bat maker in younger days'
Education: Saint John Houghton School, Kirk Hallam; South East Derbyshire College
Qualifications: 9 GCSEs, Sport and Recreation Levels 1 and 2, pool lifeguard qualification, coaching qualifications in cricket, tennis, basketball, football and volleyball
Career outside cricket: Painter and decorator
Overseas teams played for: Delacombe Park, Melbourne 1999-2000
Cricket moments to forget: 'Unable to speak when interviewed by Sybil Ruscoe on *Channel 4 Cricket Roadshow* (live)'
Cricketers particularly admired: Ian Botham, Dennis Lillee, Courtney Walsh, Curtly Ambrose, Brian Lara, Richard Hadlee, Glenn McGrath
Other sports played: 'Enjoy playing most sports, mainly football and basketball'
Other sports followed: Football (Derby County), basketball
Extras: First home-grown cricketer to become professional from Ockbrook and Borrowash CC (for whom he struck the Derbyshire Premier League 2006 season's best, 213 v Marehay). NBC Denis Compton Award for the most promising young Derbyshire player 2003
Best batting: 50 Derbyshire v Warwickshire, Derby 2008
Best bowling: 5-20 Derbyshire v Leicestershire, Derby 2007

2008 Season

	M	Inn	NO	Runs	HS	Avg	100	50	Ct	St	Balls	Runs	Wkts	Avg	BB	5I	10M
Test																	
FC	4	4	1	108	50	36.00	-	1	2	-	511	326	9	36.22	4-70	-	-
ODI																	
List A	6	2	0	5	3	2.50	-	-	1	-	265	218	8	27.25	3-31	-	
20/20 Int																	
20/20	1	0	0	0	0		-	-	-	-	18	34	0		-	-	

Career Performances

	M	Inn	NO	Runs	HS	Avg	100	50	Ct	St	Balls	Runs	Wkts	Avg	BB	5I	10M
Test																	
FC	42	61	13	701	50	14.60	-	1	15	-	5634	3623	117	30.96	5-20	3	-
ODI																	
List A	73	42	11	371	45	11.96	-	-	18	-	2794	2386	82	29.09	4-28	-	
20/20 Int																	
20/20	23	12	4	105	25	13.12	-	-	6	-	382	488	21	23.23	4-11	-	

LYTH, A. — Yorkshire

Name: Adam Lyth
Role: Left-hand bat, right-arm medium bowler
Born: 25 September 1987, Whitby, North Yorkshire
Height: 5ft 9in **Weight:** 10st
Nickname: Peanut
County debut: 2006 (one-day), 2007 (first-class)
Place in batting averages: 117th av. 30.71
Parents: Alistair and Christine
Marital status: Single
Family links with cricket: 'Grandfather – wicket-keeper; father and brother played cricket'
Education: Caedmon School; Whitby Community College
Qualifications: GCSEs
Overseas tours: England U16 to South Africa 2004; England U19 to Malaysia 2006-07
Career highlights to date: 'Getting hundred [122] for England U19 on home ground

at Scarborough in the first 'Test' against Pakistan [2007]'
Cricket moments to forget: 'Getting caught by my brother when we played against each other'
Cricket superstitions: 'None'
Cricketers particularly admired: Craig White, Darren Lehmann, Graham Thorpe
Young players to look out for: Adil Rashid
Other sports played: Football (represented district and North Yorkshire; had trials with Man City and Sunderland); golf
Other sports followed: Football (Arsenal), 'follow all sports – sports mad'
Favourite band: Jay-Z
Relaxations: 'Socialising'
Extras: North Player of Tournament at Taunton at U13. Played in Bunbury Festival 2003. Led Yorkshire to U17 County Championship 2005. Represented England at U15, U16, U17 and U19 levels, scoring 64 and 113 on U19 "Test" debut v India U19 at Canterbury 2006. Scarborough and District Best Male Achiever award. Promising Yorkshire Young Cricketer award
Best batting: 132 Yorkshire v Nottinghamshire, Trent Bridge 2008
Best bowling: 1-12 Yorkshire v LUCCE, Headingley 2007

2008 Season

	M	Inn	NO	Runs	HS	Avg	100	50	Ct	St	Balls	Runs	Wkts	Avg	BB	5I	10M
Test																	
FC	14	21	0	645	132	30.71	1	5	11	-	181	105	1	105.00	1-20	-	-
ODI																	
List A	15	10	1	162	38 *	18.00	-	-	5	-	6	3	0		-	-	
20/20 Int																	
20/20	1	1	0	0	0	0.00	-	-	-	-	0	0	0		-	-	

Career Performances

	M	Inn	NO	Runs	HS	Avg	100	50	Ct	St	Balls	Runs	Wkts	Avg	BB	5I	10M
Test																	
FC	15	22	0	676	132	30.72	1	5	11	-	187	117	2	58.50	1-12	-	-
ODI																	
List A	18	13	2	196	38 *	17.81	-	-	8	-	6	3	0		-	-	
20/20 Int																	
20/20	1	1	0	0	0	0.00	-	-	-	-	0	0	0		-	-	

MacLEOD, C. S. — Warwickshire

Name: Calum Scott MacLeod
Role: Right-hand bat, right-arm fast-medium bowler
Born: 15 November 1988, Rutherglen, Glasgow
Height: 6ft 2in **Weight:** 13st 5lbs
Nickname: Cloudy, Highlander, Scot
County debut: 2007
ODI debut: 2008
Parents: Donald and Morag
Marital status: Single
Family links with cricket: 'Two brothers playing at Uddingston CC - Allan also represented West District U15 and U18 and Niall represented West District U13 and U15 and Scotland U12 and U13. Our mother Morag managed Scotland U12 for four years'
Education: Hillpark Secondary School, Glasgow
Qualifications: 8 Standard Grades, 2 Higher Grades
Off-season: 'Preparing for next season at home in Scotland, and in Birmingham'
Overseas tours: West District to Australia 2004-05; Warwickshire Academy to South Africa 2005-06; Scotland U19 to Sri Lanka (U19 World Cup) 2005-06, plus other Scotland age-group tours to Holland, Ireland and Denmark
Overseas teams played for: Penrith CC, Sydney 2007-08
Career highlights to date: 'Making first-class Scotland debut against UAE on 27 June 2007 at Ayr as youngest ever player for Scotland at full international level. Signing a two-year contract with Warwickshire. Scotland v England ODI, August 2008'
Cricket moments to forget: 'Love them all!'
Cricket superstitions: 'Scratch my guard mark on the crease nine times before batting'
Cricketers particularly admired: Glenn McGrath
Young players to look out for: Chris Woakes (Warwickshire)
Other sports played: Hockey (Stepps HC Glasgow; represented West District and Scotland Select, and Scotland U16s)
Other sports followed: Football (Celtic FC)
Favourite band: Kings of Leon
Relaxations: 'Like to go shopping, spend time with friends and listen to music'
Extras: City of Glasgow Young Sportsperson of the Year 2005 and North Lanarkshire Male Youth Sportsperson of the Year 2005. Has twice been European U19

Championship Player of the Year. Cricket Scotland National Young Player of the Year 2006, 2007. Warwickshire Most Improved 2nd XI Player 2007. Made first-class debut for Scotland v UAE in the ICC Inter-Continental Cup 2007 at Ayr

Opinions on cricket: 'Cricket is in a pretty good state, with growing interest through Twenty20, Stanford and IPL in particular, leading to what looks like an exciting future for fans and players alike. In domestic cricket, make it easier for U16s to watch or be involved, especially if they bring an adult!'

Best bowling: 3-36 Warwickshire v Cambridge UCCE, Fenner's 2008

2008 Season

	M	Inn	NO	Runs	HS	Avg	100	50	Ct	St	Balls	Runs	Wkts	Avg	BB	5I	10M
Test																	
FC	1	0	0	0	0	-	-	-	1	-	109	56	4	14.00	3-36	-	-
ODI																	
List A	4	2	0	8	7	4.00	-	-	2	-	114	100	1	100.00	1-44	-	
20/20 Int																	
20/20																	

Career Performances

	M	Inn	NO	Runs	HS	Avg	100	50	Ct	St	Balls	Runs	Wkts	Avg	BB	5I	10M
Test																	
FC	2	0	0	0	0	-	-	-	1	-	157	86	4	21.50	3-36	-	-
ODI	1	1	1	10	10 *	-	-	-	-	-	0	0	0		-	-	
List A	5	3	1	18	10 *	9.00	-	-	2	-	114	100	1	100.00	1-44	-	
20/20 Int																	
20/20																	

56. In the 1970-71 Ashes series, how many Australians were out leg before wicket?

MADDY, D. L. Warwickshire

Name: Darren Lee Maddy
Role: Right-hand bat, right-arm medium bowler
Born: 23 May 1974, Leicester
Height: 5ft 9in **Weight:** 12st 7lbs
Nickname: Madds
County debut: 1993 (one-day, Leicestershire), 1994 (first-class, Leicestershire), 2007 (Warwickshire)
County cap: 1996 (Leicestershire), 2007 (Warwickshire)
Benefit: 2006 (Leicestershire)
Test debut: 1999
ODI debut: 1998
Twenty20 Int debut: 2007-08
1000 runs in a season: 4
1st-Class 200s: 2
Place in batting averages: 60th av. 40.94 (2007 43rd av. 46.82)
Place in bowling averages: 39th av. 26.00 (2007 46th av. 27.26)
Parents: William Arthur and Hilary Jean
Wife and date of marriage: Justine Marie, 7 October 2000
Children: George William, 13 October 2005, Isaac James, 12 July 2008
Family links with cricket: Father and younger brother, Greg, play club cricket
Education: Roundhill, Thurmaston; Wreake Valley, Syston
Qualifications: 8 GCSEs, Level 1 coach
Career outside cricket: Fitness advisor
Off-season: 'Spending time with my family; studying and building an extension.'
Overseas tours: Leicestershire to Bloemfontein 1995, to Western Transvaal 1996, to Durban 1997, to Barbados 1998, to Anguilla 2000, to Potchefstroom 2001; England A to Kenya and Sri Lanka 1997-98, to Zimbabwe and South Africa 1998-99; England to South Africa and Zimbabwe 1999-2000, to South Africa (World 20/20) 2007-08; England VI to Hong Kong 2003, 2004, 2005, 2006, 2007, 2008; Lord's Taverners to Dubai 2006, 2007, 2008; Warwickshire to Grenada 2007
Overseas teams played for: Wanderers, Johannesburg 1992-93; Northern Free State, South Africa 1993-95; Rhodes University, South Africa 1995-97; Sunshine CC, Grenada 2002; Perth CC, 2002-04
Career highlights to date: 'Winning two Championship medals. Playing for England. Winning Twenty20 final 2004 and 2006. Being awarded the Warwickshire captaincy 2007'
Cricket moments to forget: 'Being relegated in two competitions in 2007'
Cricket superstitions: 'Always put my left pad on first'

Cricketers particularly admired: 'Anyone who has made a success of their career'
Young players to look out for: Chris Woakes
Other sports played: Touch rugby, golf, squash, 5-a-side football, soccer volley ball
Other sports followed: Rugby (Leicester Tigers), football (Leicester City), baseball, golf, boxing – 'most sports really except for horse racing and motor racing'
Favourite band: 'Too many to mention – Two Tone Deaf, Bon Jovi, Def Leppard, Stereophonics, Aerosmith, Red Hot Chili Peppers'
Relaxations: 'Going to the gym, playing sport, spending time with my wife, Justine; listening to music, TV, holidaying, scuba diving, bungee jumping, playing the drums'
Player website: www.darrenmaddy.com
Extras: Rapid Cricketline 2nd XI Championship Player of the Year 1994. Was leading run-scorer on England A's 1997-98 tour (687; av. 68.7). In 1998, broke the season record for runs scored in the B&H (629; av. 125.80), winning five Gold Awards. Scored 229* v Loughborough UCCE at Leicester 2003, in the process sharing with Brad Hodge (202*) in a record partnership for any wicket for Leicestershire (436*). Struck 60-ball 111 v Yorkshire at Headingley in the Twenty20 2004, in the process sharing with Brad Hodge (78) in a then competition record partnership for any wicket (167). Scored 86* (also took a wicket and two catches) in the final of the Twenty20 Cup at Trent Bridge 2006, becoming the first player to pass 1000 career runs in the competition and winning the Man of the Match award. President of the Leicestershire School Sports Federation. Vice-captain of Leicestershire July 2004-2005. Made captain of Warwickshire in 2007, he relinquished the post towards the end of 2008
Opinions on cricket: 'Regional cricket against touring sides. Two one-day competitions – Twenty20 and 50-over cricket.'
Best batting: 229* Leicestershire v LUCCE, Leicester 2003
Best bowling: 5-37 Leicestershire v Hampshire, Rose Bowl 2002

2008 Season

	M	Inn	NO	Runs	HS	Avg	100	50	Ct	St	Balls	Runs	Wkts	Avg	BB	5I	10M
Test																	
FC	14	22	3	778	138	40.94	3	3	9	-	924	442	17	26.00	4-25	-	-
ODI																	
List A	12	11	0	334	77	30.36	-	3	5	-	222	206	8	25.75	2-25	-	
20/20 Int																	
20/20	1	1	0	27	27	27.00	-	-	-	-	3	7	1	7.00	1-7	-	

Career Performances

	M	Inn	NO	Runs	HS	Avg	100	50	Ct	St	Balls	Runs	Wkts	Avg	BB	5I	10M
Test	3	4	0	46	24	11.50	-	-	4	-	84	40	0		-	-	-
FC	242	392	27	12247	229 *	33.55	26	58	251	-	12372	6585	205	32.12	5-37	5	-
ODI	8	6	0	113	53	18.83	-	1	1	-	0	0	0		-	-	
List A	322	297	29	8263	167 *	30.83	11	50	126	-	6464	5470	188	29.09	4-16	-	
20/20 Int	4	4	0	113	50	28.25	-	1	1	-	18	26	3	8.66	2-6	-	
20/20	48	48	5	1418	111	32.97	1	11	28	-	563	735	26	28.26	2-6	-	

MAGOFFIN, S. J. — Worcestershire

Name: Steven (Steve) James Magoffin
Role: Left-hand bat, right-arm fast-medium bowler
Born: 17 December 1979, Corinda, Queensland, Australia
Height: 6ft 4in
Nickname: Mal
County debut: 2007 (Surrey), 2008 (Worcestershire)
Education: Indooroopilly HS, Brisbane; Curtin University, Western Australia
Overseas tours: Australian Cricket Academy to India 2003-04; University of Western Australia to India 2006-07
Overseas teams played for: Western Australia 2004-05 –
Extras: Played for Queensland Colts, Queensland Academy of Sport and Australian Cricket Academy. Man of the Match v South Australia at Perth in the Pura Cup 2006-07 (3-18/4-13). Was a temporary overseas player with Surrey during the 2007 season as a locum for Matthew Nicholson. Played for Worcestershire as overseas player for the first half of 2008
Best batting: 45 Western Australia v Tasmania, Hobart 2007-08
Best bowling: 8-47 Western Australia v South Australia, Perth 2005-06

2008 Season

	M	Inn	NO	Runs	HS	Avg	100	50	Ct	St	Balls	Runs	Wkts	Avg	BB	5I	10M
Test																	
FC	7	9	2	85	33	12.14	-	-	-	-	1212	755	23	32.82	4-49	-	-
ODI																	
List A	8	5	5	64	24 *		-	-	1	-	350	245	10	24.50	3-19	-	
20/20 Int																	
20/20	5	2	1	12	11 *	12.00	-	-	1	-	108	157	3	52.33	1-12	-	

Career Performances

	M	Inn	NO	Runs	HS	Avg	100	50	Ct	St	Balls	Runs	Wkts	Avg	BB	5I	10M
Test																	
FC	47	63	18	611	45	13.57	-	-	14	-	9183	4460	153	29.15	8-47	4	-
ODI																	
List A	40	24	16	189	24 *	23.62	-	-	12	-	1998	1597	55	29.03	4-58	-	
20/20 Int																	
20/20	6	2	1	12	11 *	12.00	-	-	1	-	126	172	5	34.40	2-15	-	

MAHMOOD, S. I. — Lancashire

Name: Sajid Iqbal Mahmood
Role: Right-hand bat, right-arm fast-medium bowler
Born: 21 December 1981, Bolton
Height: 6ft 4in **Weight:** 12st 7lbs
Nickname: Saj, King
County debut: 2002
County cap: 2007
Test debut: 2006
ODI debut: 2004
Twenty20 Int debut: 2006
Place in batting averages: 258th av. 10.27 (2007 256th av. 13.45)
Place in bowling averages: 91st av. 32.77 (2007 71st av. 31.83)
Parents: Shahid and Femida
Marital status: Single
Family links with cricket: Father played in Bolton League; younger brother plays in Bolton League
Education: Smithills School; North College, Bolton (sixth form)
Qualifications: 9 GCSEs, 3 A-levels
Overseas tours: Lancashire to South Africa 2003; England A to Malaysia and India 2003-04, to Sri Lanka 2004-05, to West Indies 2005-06; England to India 2005-06 (one-day series), to India (ICC Champions Trophy) 2006-07, to Australia 2006-07, to West Indies (World Cup) 2006-07, to India (one-day series) 2008. England Performance Programe to India, 2008-09. England Lions to New Zealand 2009
Overseas teams played for: Napier, New Zealand 2002-03
Cricket moments to forget: 'None'
Cricket superstitions: 'None'
Cricketers particularly admired: Brett Lee, Shoaib Akhtar
Favourite band: Nelly, Eminem

Relaxations: 'Music and chillin' with mates'
Extras: NBC Denis Compton Award for the most promising young Lancashire player 2003. Man of the Match in the fifth ODI v Pakistan at Edgbaston 2006 (10-2-24-2) and v Bangladesh in Bridgetown in the World Cup 2006-07 (3-27). ECB National Academy 2003-04, 2004-05, 2005-06. Played in the winning England Lions team against the visiting South Africans in 2008. Is cousin of boxer Amir Khan
Best batting: 94 Lancashire v Sussex, Old Trafford 2004
Best bowling: 5-37 Lancashire v DUCCE, Durham 2003

2008 Season

	M	Inn	NO	Runs	HS	Avg	100	50	Ct	St	Balls	Runs	Wkts	Avg	BB	5I	10M
Test																	
FC	12	15	4	113	33	10.27	-	-	3	-	1937	1147	35	32.77	5-76	1	-
ODI																	
List A	8	5	2	23	16 *	7.66	-	-	-	-	318	260	4	65.00	1-35	-	
20/20 Int																	
20/20	9	2	1	1	1 *	1.00	-	-	1	-	186	193	12	16.08	3-12	-	

Career Performances

	M	Inn	NO	Runs	HS	Avg	100	50	Ct	St	Balls	Runs	Wkts	Avg	BB	5I	10M
Test	8	11	1	81	34	8.10	-	-	-	-	1130	762	20	38.10	4-22	-	-
FC	66	86	14	975	94	13.54	-	2	13	-	9602	5902	185	31.90	5-37	4	-
ODI	25	15	4	85	22 *	7.72	-	-	1	-	1155	1128	29	38.89	4-50	-	
List A	103	59	17	355	29	8.45	-	-	11	-	4440	3830	146	26.23	5-16	1	
20/20 Int	2	1	1	0	0*	-	-	-	-	42	63	1	63.00	1-34	-		
20/20	21	8	3	39	21	7.80	-	-	1	-	438	525	18	29.16	3-12	-	

MAHOMED, U. — Durham

Name: Uzair Mahomed
Role: Right-hand bat, right-arm off-spin bowler; batting all-rounder
Born: 20 August 1987, Johannesburg, South Africa
Height: 5ft 9in **Weight:** 11st 6lbs
Nickname: Uzi
County debut: No first-team appearance
Parents: Ishtiyak and Faghmida
Marital status: Single
Family links with cricket: Father captained Transvaal Schools and represented South Africa Schools. Brother played for Yorkshire Schools and Yorkshire Academy
Education: Woodhouse Grove; Bradford Grammar School
Qualifications: 10 GCSEs, 3 A-levels

Overseas tours: Two school tours to West Indies; Durham to Mumbai (World Cricket Academy), to Cape Town
Overseas teams played for: Delfos CC, Johannesburg 2005, 2006, 2007
Career highlights to date: '118 off 114 balls for Durham 2nd XI v Lancashire 2nd XI [2006]; 144 for Durham 2nd XI v MCC YC [2007]'
Cricket moments to forget: 'None. Every moment is an experience you can learn from'
Cricket superstitions: 'None'
Cricketers particularly admired: Jonty Rhodes, Hansie Cronje, Shaun Pollock
Young players to look out for: Paul Hindmarch
Other sports played: Golf
Other sports followed: Football (Liverpool)
Favourite band: Dr Dre, Eminem, Gwen Stefani
Relaxations: 'Watching sport on TV; gym'
Extras: Youngest centurion for Bradford Grammar School (record previously held by Ashley Metcalfe). National U15 championship winner (Yorkshire Schools). Played for Northumberland in the Minor Counties Championship 2005. Released at the end of the 2008 season
Opinions on cricket: '[Cricket is] becoming more aggressive and attacking with the success of Twenty20.'

2008 Season

	M	Inn	NO	Runs	HS	Avg	100	50	Ct	St	Balls	Runs	Wkts	Avg	BB	5I	10M
Test																	
FC																	
ODI																	
List A	1	1	0	3	3	3.00	-	-	-	-	0	0	0		-	-	
20/20 Int																	
20/20																	

Career Performances

	M	Inn	NO	Runs	HS	Avg	100	50	Ct	St	Balls	Runs	Wkts	Avg	BB	5I	10M
Test																	
FC																	
ODI																	
List A	1	1	0	3	3	3.00	-	-	-	-	0	0	0		-	-	
20/20 Int																	
20/20																	

MALAN, D. J. Middlesex

Name: Dawid Johannes Malan
Role: Left-hand bat, right-arm leg-spin bowler
Born: 3 September 1987, Roehampton, London
Height: 6ft **Weight:** 12st 12lbs
Nickname: AC ('as in AC Milan')
County debut: 2006 (one-day)
Place in batting averages: 65th av. 39.71
Parents: Dawid and Janet
Family links with cricket: Father played for the University of Stellenbosch and for Western Province B. Brother (Charl) an MCC Young Cricketer
Education: Paarl Boys' High, South Africa; UNISA
Overseas tours: Performance Programe to India, 2008-09.
Overseas teams played for: Wellington CC 2005-06 – 2006-07; Boland 2005-06; Western Province/Boland Cricket Academy 2006; Belville CC
Career highlights to date: 'Playing for Middlesex in a Twenty20 game against Surrey at The Oval in front of a packed house'
Cricket moments to forget: 'Getting a first-ball in my school's yearly interschool match in my final year at school'
Cricket superstitions: 'The way I pack my cricket bag'
Cricketers particularly admired: Gary Kirsten
Young players to look out for: Billy Godleman, Steve Finn, Eoin Morgan
Other sports played: Rugby, golf
Other sports followed: Rugby (Blue Bulls)
Favourite band: The Killers
Relaxations: 'Fishing'
Extras: Boland U19 Provincial Player of the Year 2005. Wellington CC Player of the Year 2005-06. Western Province/Boland Academy Player of the Year 2006. Is not considered an overseas player
Opinions on cricket: 'In my opinion the game has changed dramatically in the past few years. The introduction of Twenty20 has changed the mindset of batsmen and caused them to become more attacking in all forms of the game, which in turn has made cricket more exciting.'
Best batting: 132* Middlesex v Northamptonshire, Uxbridge 2008
Best bowling: 2-26 Middlesex v Northamptonshire, Uxbridge 2008

2008 Season

	M	Inn	NO	Runs	HS	Avg	100	50	Ct	St	Balls	Runs	Wkts	Avg	BB	5I	10M
Test																	
FC	10	16	2	556	132 *	39.71	1	4	3	-	350	204	4	51.00	2-26	-	-
ODI																	
List A	8	8	1	106	30	15.14	-	-	4	-	42	37	1	37.00	1-24	-	
20/20 Int																	
20/20	12	10	5	306	103	61.20	1	1	4	-	42	54	1	54.00	1-29	-	

Career Performances

	M	Inn	NO	Runs	HS	Avg	100	50	Ct	St	Balls	Runs	Wkts	Avg	BB	5I	10M
Test																	
FC	14	23	2	714	132 *	34.00	1	5	5	-	509	356	7	50.85	2-26	-	-
ODI																	
List A	13	13	1	196	42	16.33	-	-	4	-	48	50	1	50.00	1-24	-	
20/20 Int																	
20/20	13	11	5	317	103	52.83	1	1	4	-	42	54	1	54.00	1-29	-	

MALCOLM-HANSEN, R. J. A. Leicestershire

Name: Richard Johan Anders Malcolm-Hansen
Role: Right-hand bat, right-arm off-break bowler
Born: 22 April 1986, Farnborough, Kent
County debut: 2008
Place in batting averages: 58th av. 41.33
Extras: Beckenham (Kent Cricket League) 2002-08; Kent U21's 2003; Kent 2nd XI 2003-07; Denmark (List A and ICC) 2005-08; Loughborough UCCE 2007-08; Made his first-class debut for Loughborough UCCE against Yorkshire in May 2007; Leicestershire 2nd XI 2008
Best batting: 93 Loughborough UCCE v Surrey, The Oval 2008
Best bowling: 1-40 Loughborough UCCE v Worcestershire, Kidderminster 2008

2008 Season

	M	Inn	NO	Runs	HS	Avg	100	50	Ct	St	Balls	Runs	Wkts	Avg	BB	5I	10M
Test																	
FC	5	7	1	248	93	41.33	-	2	2	-	216	100	1	100.00	1-40	-	-
ODI																	
List A	2	0	0	0	0		-	-	-	-	18	23	1	23.00	1-23	-	
20/20 Int																	
20/20																	

Career Performances

	M	Inn	NO	Runs	HS	Avg	100	50	Ct	St	Balls	Runs	Wkts	Avg	BB	5I	10M
Test																	
FC	6	9	1	283	93	35.37	-	2	2	-	240	128	1	128.00	1-40	-	-
ODI																	
List A	14	11	0	157	71	14.27	-	1	4	-	422	381	8	47.62	3-38	-	
20/20 Int																	
20/20																	

MALIK, M. N. — Leicestershire

Name: Muhammad Nadeem Malik
Role: Right-hand bat, right-arm fast-medium bowler
Born: 6 October 1982, Nottingham
Height: 6ft 5in **Weight:** 14st 7lbs
Nickname: Nad, Busta, Nigel, Gerz
County debut: 2001 (Nottinghamshire), 2004 (Worcestershire), 2008 (Leicestershire)
County colours: 2004 (Worcestershire)
Place in batting averages: 250th av. 11.86
Place in bowling averages: 105th av. 35.11 1 (2007 43rd av. 58.80)
Parents: Abdul and Arshad
Marital status: Single
Family links with cricket: Brother plays club cricket for Carrington
Education: Wilford Meadows Secondary School; Bilborough College
Qualifications: 9 GCSEs
Career outside cricket: Personal trainer
Overseas tours: ZRK to Pakistan 2000; Nottinghamshire to South Africa 2001;

England U19 to India 2000-01, to Australia and (U19 World Cup) New Zealand 2001-02
Career highlights to date: '5-57 against Derbyshire 2001. Pro40 winners 2007 [Worcestershire]'
Cricket moments to forget: 'Norwich Union match v Yorkshire at Scarborough 2001 – Lehmann 191'
Cricketers particularly admired: Glenn McGrath, Wasim Akram, Curtly Ambrose
Young players to look out for: Mehraj Ahmed, James Taylor
Other sports played: Football
Other sports followed: 'Most major sports'
Relaxations: Music, games consoles
Extras: Made Nottinghamshire 2nd XI debut in 1999, aged 16, and took 15 wickets at an average of 19.40 for the 2nd XI 2000. Represented England U19 2001 and 2002. Played one first-class and one List A match for Nottinghamshire on loan 2007. Left Worcestershire at the end of the 2007 season and joined Leicestershire for 2008. Finished top of the Leicestershire first-class bowling averages in 2008, subsequently winning the Frank S. Smith bowling award
Best batting: 41 Leicestershire v Essex, Grace Road 2008
Best bowling: 6-46 Leicestershire v Essex, Chelmsford 2008

2008 Season

	M	Inn	NO	Runs	HS	Avg	100	50	Ct	St	Balls	Runs	Wkts	Avg	BB	5I	10M
Test																	
FC	15	20	5	178	41	11.86	-	-	2	-	2801	1475	42	35.11	6-46	3	-
ODI																	
List A	11	4	1	3	2	1.00	-	-	2	-	492	400	12	33.33	3-21	-	
20/20 Int																	
20/20	9	2	1	2	2	2.00	-	-	-	-	192	216	11	19.63	4-16	-	

Career Performances

	M	Inn	NO	Runs	HS	Avg	100	50	Ct	St	Balls	Runs	Wkts	Avg	BB	5I	10M
Test																	
FC	66	87	30	558	41	9.78	-	-	10	-	10570	6467	179	36.12	6-46	7	
ODI																	
List A	69	28	18	97	11	9.70	-	-	10	-	2711	2371	66	35.92	4-42	-	
20/20 Int																	
20/20	24	6	3	6	3 *	2.00	-	-	2	-	474	650	28	23.21	4-16	-	

MARSHALL, H. J. H. — Gloucestershire

Name: Hamish John Hamilton Marshall
Role: Right-hand bat, right-arm medium bowler
Born: 15 February 1979, Warkworth, Auckland, New Zealand
Nickname: Marshy
County debut: 2006
County cap: 2006
Test debut: 2000
ODI debut: 2003
Twenty20 Int debut: 2004-05
1000 runs in a season: 1
Place in batting averages: 122nd av. 30.35 (2007 65th av. 40.85)
Parents: Kate and Drew
Family links with cricket: Twin brother James Marshall also plays for Northern Districts and has represented New Zealand
Education: Mahurangi College; King's College
Off-season: 'Playing in India and going to New Zealand'
Overseas tours: New Zealand U19 to South Africa (U19 World Cup) 1997-98; New Zealand to South Africa 2000-01, to Pakistan (one-day series) 2003-04, to England 2004 (NatWest Series), to England (ICC Champions Trophy) 2004, to Bangladesh 2004-05, to Australia 2004-05, to Zimbabwe 2005-06, to South Africa 2005-06, to India (ICC Champions Trophy) 2006-07, to Australia (C'wealth Bank Series) 2006-07, to West Indies (World Cup) 2006-07
Overseas teams played for: Northern Districts 1998-99 – 2006-07 and 2008-09; Chandigarh Lions (ICL) 2007-08; Royal Bengal Tigers (ICL) 2008-09
Career highlights to date: '146 against Australia [Christchurch, March 2005]'
Cricket moments to forget: 'Any golden duck'
Cricketers particularly admired: Mark Waugh
Young players to look out for: Daniel Flynn, Tim Southee
Other sports followed: Rugby (North Harbour, Auckland Blues, Bristol)
Favourite band: U2
Relaxations: 'Golf, fishing'
Extras: MCC Young Cricketer 1998. Attended New Zealand Cricket Academy 1999. Played for Buckinghamshire in the 2004 C&G competition. Represented New Zealand v FICA World XI 2004-05. One of *New Zealand Cricket Almanack*'s two Players of the Year 2005. His match awards include Man of the Match v West Indies at Cardiff in the NatWest Series 2004 (75*) and v Australia in the first ODI at Melbourne 2004-05 (50*). An overseas player with Gloucestershire 2006-07; is no longer considered an

overseas player. Refused a contract with New Zealand 2007-08 to pursue his county career. Topped the county 40-over and Twenty20 batting averages in 2008
Best batting: 168 Gloucestershire v Leicestershire, Cheltenham 2006
Best bowling: 1-6 Northern Districts v Central Districts, Gisborne 2006-07

2008 Season

	M	Inn	NO	Runs	HS	Avg	100	50	Ct	St	Balls	Runs	Wkts	Avg	BB	5I	10M
Test																	
FC	16	29	1	850	121	30.35	2	5	6	-	372	204	1	204.00	1-31	-	-
ODI																	
List A	13	12	1	416	102 *	37.81	1	2	4	-	37	39	1	39.00	1-15	-	
20/20 Int																	
20/20	7	7	0	203	59	29.00	-	1	2	-	0	0	0		-	-	

Career Performances

	M	Inn	NO	Runs	HS	Avg	100	50	Ct	St	Balls	Runs	Wkts	Avg	BB	5I	10M
Test	13	19	2	652	160	38.35	2	2	1	-	6	4	0		-	-	-
FC	113	192	13	6346	168	35.45	15	30	55	-	1344	697	11	63.36	1-6	-	-
ODI	66	62	9	1454	101 *	27.43	1	12	18	-	0	0	0		-	-	
List A	194	185	22	4620	122	28.34	5	30	77	-	121	140	2	70.00	1-14	-	
20/20 Int	3	3	0	12	8	4.00	-	-	1	-	0	0	0		-	-	
20/20	20	20	1	532	100	28.00	1	2	13	-	0	0	0		-	-	

57. Name the Kent and England wicketkeeper who made his 200th Test dismissal during the 1974-75 Ashes series.

MARSHALL, S. J. Lancashire

Name: Simon James Marshall
Role: Right-hand bat, right-arm leg-spin bowler; all-rounder
Born: 20 September 1982, Arrowe Park, Wirral
Height: 6ft 3in **Weight:** 13st 2lbs
Nickname: Tron, David Dickinson
County debut: 2005
Parents: Jim and Dinah
Marital status: Single
Family links with cricket: Father captained Radley School and Liverpool University
Education: Birkenhead School; Cambridge University
Qualifications: 9 GCSEs, 4 A-levels, BA (Cantab) Land Economy
Overseas tours: ESCA and ECB age-group tours 1996-2001; British Universities to South Africa 2004

Overseas teams played for: Adelaide Buffalos CC, Adelaide 2004-05; West Torrens Eagles, Adelaide 2005-06
Career highlights to date: 'First-class debut for Lancashire CCC'
Cricket moments to forget: 'Losing the C&G final to Sussex 2006'
Cricket superstitions: 'Like to give the bat a few spins before facing up'
Cricketers particularly admired: Carl Hooper, Brad Hodge, Mal Loye, Gary Keedy
Other sports played: Hockey (Cambridge Blue)
Other sports followed: Football (Everton FC), hockey (Cambridge University HC)
Favourite band: Dire Straits, Man From Michael
Extras: Played for Cheshire in the C&G 2002, 2003. Played for Cambridge UCCE 2002, (as captain) 2003, and 2004; took 6-128 then followed up with 99 in CUCCE's second innings v Essex at Fenner's 2002. Cambridge Blue 2002-04. Represented British Universities 2004. Cambridge University Sportsman of the Year 2004. Topped the Lancashire Twenty20 bowling averages 2008. Released at the end of the 2008 season.
Opinions on cricket: 'Heavy scheduling makes it very difficult to achieve and maintain an intensity of performance in all competitions throughout the season. A straight knockout format in one of the limited-over competitions would be preferable.'
Best batting: 126* Cambridge University v Oxford University, Fenner's 2003
Best bowling: 6-128 CUCCE v Essex, Fenner's 2002

2008 Season

	M	Inn	NO	Runs	HS	Avg	100	50	Ct	St	Balls	Runs	Wkts	Avg	BB	5I	10M
Test																	
FC	2	1	1	29	29 *		-	-	1	-	270	171	2	85.50	1-47	-	-
ODI																	
List A	5	2	0	9	6	4.50	-	-	1	-	168	111	2	55.50	2-37	-	
20/20 Int																	
20/20	9	2	1	1	1 *	1.00	-	-	1	-	157	190	14	13.57	4-21	-	

Career Performances

	M	Inn	NO	Runs	HS	Avg	100	50	Ct	St	Balls	Runs	Wkts	Avg	BB	5I	10M
Test																	
FC	21	31	7	809	126 *	33.70	1	3	6	-	4004	2147	32	67.09	6-128	1	-
ODI																	
List A	26	12	0	63	22	5.25	-	-	8	-	1011	782	17	46.00	3-36	-	
20/20 Int																	
20/20	17	8	3	98	47	19.60	-	-	6	-	341	376	26	14.46	4-20	-	

MARTIN, C. S. Warwickshire

Name: Christopher (Chris) Stewart Martin
Role: Right-hand bat, right-arm fast-medium bowler
Born: 10 December 1974
County debut: 2008
Test debut: 2000
ODI debut: 2001
Twenty20 Int debut: 2007
Place in bowling averages: 121st av. 38.53
Overseas tours: New Zealand Academy to Australia 1998-99, 1999-2000, to India (Buchi Babu Invitation Tournament) 2000; New Zealand A to Netherlands 2000, to South Africa 2005; New Zealand to South Africa 2000, 2006, 2007, to Australia 2001, 2004, 2008, to Pakistan 2002, to England 2004, 2008, to Zimbabwe 2005
Overseas teams played for: Canterbury Wizards 1997-2004; Auckland Aces 2005 –
Extras: Has represented New Zealand Academy, New Zealand A and New Zealand. Is one of only 11 New Zealand Test cricketers to have taken 100 wickets. Joined Warwickshire as an overseas player in June 2008

Best batting: 25 Canterbury v Northern Districts, Gisborne (NZ) 2001
Best bowling: 6-54 New Zealand v Sri Lanka, Wellington 2005

2008 Season

	M	Inn	NO	Runs	HS	Avg	100	50	Ct	St	Balls	Runs	Wkts	Avg	BB	5I	10M
Test	3	5	3	0	0 *	0.00	-	-	-	-	462	235	4	58.75	2-76	-	-
FC	11	8	4	4	4 *	1.00	-	-	2	-	1759	1002	26	38.53	5-84	1	-
ODI																	
List A	3	3	1	9	7	4.50	-	-	2	-	108	69	3	23.00	2-16	-	
20/20 Int																	
20/20	11	0	0	0	0		-	-	1	-	216	226	9	25.11	3-33	-	

Career Performances

	M	Inn	NO	Runs	HS	Avg	100	50	Ct	St	Balls	Runs	Wkts	Avg	BB	5I	10M
Test	43	61	30	74	12 *	2.38	-	-	9	-	8206	4678	140	33.41	6-54	8	1
FC	130	160	76	345	25	4.10	-	-	25	-	24681	12575	407	30.89	6-54	18	1
ODI	20	7	2	8	3	1.60	-	-	7	-	948	804	18	44.66	3-62	-	
List A	108	44	23	78	13	3.71	-	-	22	-	5325	4192	146	28.71	6-24	2	
20/20 Int	6	1	1	5	5 *		-	-	1	-	138	193	7	27.57	2-14	-	
20/20	32	3	3	10	5 *		-	-	7	-	702	904	27	33.48	3-33	-	

MARTIN-JENKINS, R. S. C. Sussex

Name: Robin Simon Christopher Martin-Jenkins
Role: Right-hand bat, right-arm fast-medium bowler; all-rounder
Born: 28 October 1975, Guildford
Height: 6ft 5in **Weight:** 14st
Nickname: Tucker
County debut: 1995
County cap: 2000
Benefit: 2008
1000 runs in a season: 1
1st-Class 200s: 1
Place in batting averages: 92nd av. 35.66 (2007 120th av. 32.56)
Place in bowling averages: 94th av. 32.87 (2007 10th av. 21.41)
Parents: Christopher and Judy
Wife and date of marriage: Flora, 19 February 2000

Family links with cricket: Father was *The Times* senior cricket columnist until May 2008 and BBC *TMS* commentator. Brother plays for the Radley Rangers
Education: Radley College, Oxon; Durham University
Qualifications: 10 GCSEs, 3 A-levels, 1 AS-level, Grade 3 bassoon (with merit), BA (Hons) Social Sciences, Don MacKenzie School of Professional Photography Certificate, SWPP (Society of Wedding and Portrait Photographers), BPPA (British Professional Photographers Associates), Wine and Spirit Education Trust Intermediate and Advanced Certificates
Career outside cricket: Land agent
Overseas tours: Radley College to Barbados 1992; Sussex U19 to Sri Lanka 1995; Durham University to Vienna 1995; MCC to Kenya 1999; Sussex to Grenada 2001, 2002
Overseas teams played for: Lima CC, Peru 1994; Bellville CC, Cape Town 2000-01
Career highlights to date: 'Maiden first-class ton and double ton; three Championship titles; C&G Trophy final 2006 – the last six or seven years at Sussex in general'
Cricket superstitions: 'Never bowl first at Colwyn Bay'
Young players to look out for: Matt Machan, Will Beer
Other sports played: Golf, tennis, Rugby fives
Other sports followed: Rugby, football (Liverpool)
Favourite band: Keane
Relaxations: 'Wine, food, guitar'
Extras: Played for ESCA U15-U19. European Player of the Year, Vienna 1995. Best Performance Award for Sussex 1998. NBC Denis Compton Award for the most promising young Sussex player 1998, 1999, 2000. Scored 205* v Somerset at Taunton 2002, in the process sharing with Mark Davis (111) in a record eighth-wicket stand for Sussex (291); the stand fell one run short of the record eighth-wicket partnership in English first-class cricket, set in 1896. BBC South Cricketer of the Year 2002
Opinions on cricket: 'Scrap all 50-over cricket and replace with 40-over. Forty-over cricket produces more exciting finishes and reduces the workload on bowlers and players generally. Twenty 40-over international matches a year would mean 400 fewer overs for the players (equivalent of eight 50-over innings).'
Best batting: 205* Sussex v Somerset, Taunton 2002
Best bowling: 7-51 Sussex v Leicestershire, Horsham 2002

2008 Season

	M	Inn	NO	Runs	HS	Avg	100	50	Ct	St	Balls	Runs	Wkts	Avg	BB	5I	10M
Test																	
FC	17	23	5	642	73 *	35.66	-	6	4	-	2325	1052	32	32.87	3-36	-	-
ODI																	
List A	13	8	5	87	39 *	29.00	-	-	1	-	534	457	13	35.15	2-22	-	
20/20 Int																	
20/20	8	5	1	42	24	10.50	-	-	2	-	180	199	4	49.75	1-17	-	

Career Performances

	M	Inn	NO	Runs	HS	Avg	100	50	Ct	St	Balls	Runs	Wkts	Avg	BB	5I	10M
Test																	
FC	162	246	36	6520	205 *	31.04	3	35	46	-	21886	10867	331	32.83	7-51	6	-
ODI																	
List A	208	155	31	1865	68 *	15.04	-	3	43	-	9104	6459	219	29.49	4-22	-	
20/20 Int																	
20/20	31	19	5	205	56 *	14.64	-	1	9	-	625	781	24	32.54	4-20	-	

MASCARENHAS, D. A. Hampshire

Name: Dimitri Adrian Mascarenhas
Role: Right-hand bat, right-arm medium bowler, county captain
Born: 30 October 1977, Chiswick, London
Height: 6ft 1in **Weight:** 12st 2lbs
Nickname: Dimi, D-Train
County debut: 1996
County cap: 1998
Benefit: 2007
ODI debut: 2007
Twenty20 Int debut: 2007
50 wickets in a season: 1
Place in batting averages: 119th av. 30.59 (2007 103rd av. 34.92)
Place in bowling averages: 29th av. 23.82 (2007 73rd av. 32.06)
Parents: Malik and Pauline
Marital status: Single
Family links with cricket: Uncle played in Sri Lanka and brothers both play for Melville CC in Perth, Western Australia
Education: Trinity College, Perth
Qualifications: Level 2 coaching
Career outside cricket: Personal trainer
Overseas tours: England VI to Hong Kong 2004, 2005; England to South Africa (World 20/20) 2007-08, to Sri Lanka 2007-08 (one-day series), to New Zealand 2007-08 (one-day series), to West Indies 2009 (one-day series)
Overseas teams played for: Melville CC, Perth 1991 – ; Rajasthan Royals 2007-08; Otago 2008-09
Cricketers particularly admired: Sir Viv Richards, Malcolm Marshall, Shane Warne
Other sports followed: Australian Rules (Collingwood)

Favourite band: Red Hot Chili Peppers
Relaxations: Tennis, golf, Australian Rules
Extras: Played for Western Australia at U17 and U19 level as captain. Took 6-88 on first-class debut, for Hampshire v Glamorgan at Southampton 1996. Won NatWest Man of the Match awards in semi-final v Lancashire at Southampton 1998 (3-28/73) and in quarter-final v Middlesex at Lord's 2000 (4-25). Scorer of the first Championship century at The Rose Bowl (104) v Worcestershire 2001. Took Hampshire competition best 5-14 v Sussex at Hove in the Twenty20 2004, including the competition's first hat-trick (Davis, Mushtaq Ahmed, Lewry). Struck 15-ball 36* in the sixth ODI v India at The Oval 2007, including a six off each of the last five balls of the England innings. Played against New Zealand in ODI and Twenty20 games in 2008. Captained England to victory in the Hong Kong Sixes tournament 2008 - named Player of the Tournament. In 2008 became the first England player to sign with the IPL
Best batting: 131 Hampshire v Kent, Canterbury 2006
Best bowling: 6-25 Hampshire v Derbyshire, Rose Bowl 2004

2008 Season

	M	Inn	NO	Runs	HS	Avg	100	50	Ct	St	Balls	Runs	Wkts	Avg	BB	5I	10M
Test																	
FC	15	24	2	673	99	30.59	-	3	8	-	2368	977	41	23.82	6-67	2	-
ODI	1	1	0	23	23	23.00	-	-	-	-	6	10	0		-	-	
List A	13	11	5	277	56 *	46.16	-	3	3	-	546	437	15	29.13	3-37	-	
20/20 Int	1	0	0	0	0		-	-	-	-	12	10	0		-	-	
20/20	5	4	1	32	9	10.66	-	-	-	-	108	128	8	16.00	3-12	-	

Career Performances

	M	Inn	NO	Runs	HS	Avg	100	50	Ct	St	Balls	Runs	Wkts	Avg	BB	5I	10M
Test																	
FC	171	260	28	5931	131	25.56	7	22	68	-	24735	11200	405	27.65	6-25	16	-
ODI	11	7	2	150	52	30.00	-	1	3	-	426	317	6	52.83	3-23	-	
List A	215	187	39	3622	79	24.47	-	24	56	-	9015	6402	252	25.40	5-27	1	
20/20 Int	10	9	3	81	31	13.50	-	-	6	-	186	247	10	24.70	3-18	-	
20/20	37	36	12	506	52	21.08	-	1	15	-	707	873	48	18.18	5-14	1	

MASON, M. S. Worcestershire

Name: Matthew (Matt) Sean Mason
Role: Right-hand bat, right-arm fast-medium bowler
Born: 20 March 1974, Claremont, Perth, Western Australia
Height: 6ft 5in **Weight:** 16st
Nickname: Mase, Moose
County debut: 2002
County colours: 2002
50 wickets in a season: 3
Place in bowling averages: 69th av. 29.90
Parents: Bill and Sue
Wife and date of marriage: Kellie, 8 October 2005
Children: Evie, 27 March 2007
Family links with cricket: Brother plays first-grade for Claremont-Nedlands in Western Australia
Education: Mazenod College, Perth; Edith Cowan University, Perth
Qualifications: Level 1 ACB coach
Career outside cricket: 'Would love to become a fast-bowling coach'
Overseas tours: Worcestershire to South Africa 2003
Overseas teams played for: Western Australia 1996-97 – 1997-98; Wanneroo District CC 1999-2001; Claremont-Nedlands CC, Perth 2007-08
Career highlights to date: 'Back-to-back Lord's finals 2003 and 2004'
Cricket moments to forget: 'Losing back-to-back Lord's finals 2003 and 2004'
Cricketers particularly admired: Dennis Lillee, Darren Gough, Justin Langer
Young players to look out for: Moeen Ali
Other sports played: Golf ('badly'), tennis, Australian Rules football
Other sports followed: Australian Rules football (West Coast Eagles), rugby union (Worcester Warriors)
Favourite band: Snow Patrol
Relaxations: 'Love being at home with my family'
Extras: Scored maiden first-class fifty (50) from 27 balls v Derbyshire at Worcester 2002. Dick Lygon Award for the [Worcestershire] Clubman of the Year 2003. Took up position of Worcestershire CC bowling coach 2008. Signed a new contract for the 2009 season in August 2008. Is England-qualified
Opinions on cricket: 'I do not believe that we play too many matches. We need to return to the old C&G format. Would not like Twenty20 to take over cricket.'
Best batting: 63 Worcestershire v Warwickshire, Worcester 2004
Best bowling: 8-45 Worcestershire v Gloucestershire, Worcester 2006

2008 Season

	M	Inn	NO	Runs	HS	Avg	100	50	Ct	St	Balls	Runs	Wkts	Avg	BB	5I	10M
Test																	
FC	7	3	0	37	25	12.33	-	-	2	-	862	329	11	29.90	2-26	-	-
ODI																	
List A	2	1	1	5	5 *		-	-	1	-	60	77	1	77.00	1-34	-	
20/20 Int																	
20/20																	

Career Performances

	M	Inn	NO	Runs	HS	Avg	100	50	Ct	St	Balls	Runs	Wkts	Avg	BB	5I	10M
Test																	
FC	76	92	23	976	63	14.14	-	3	15	-	13865	6375	237	26.89	8-45	8	1
ODI																	
List A	72	33	13	158	25	7.90	-	-	15	-	3314	2388	85	28.09	4-34	-	
20/20 Int																	
20/20	10	4	2	18	8 *	9.00	-	-	2	-	220	290	9	32.22	3-42	-	

MASTERS, D. D. — Essex

Name: David Daniel Masters
Role: Right-hand bat, right-arm fast-medium bowler
Born: 22 April 1978, Chatham, Kent
Height: 6ft 4ins **Weight:** 12st 5lbs
Nickname: Hod, Race Horse, Hoddy
County debut: 2000 (Kent), 2003 (Leicestershire), 2008 (Essex)
County cap: 2007 (Leicestershire)
Place in batting averages: 256th av. 10.50 (2007 234th av. 17.28)
Place in bowling averages: 27th av. 23.33 (2007 16th av. 22.53)
Parents: Kevin and Tracey
Marital status: Single
Family links with cricket: 'Dad was on staff at Kent 1983-86'
Education: Fort Luton High School, Chatham; Mid-Kent College
Qualifications: 8 GCSEs, GNVQ in Leisure and Tourism, qualified coach in cricket, football and athletics, bricklayer and plasterer

Career outside cricket: Builder
Overseas teams played for: Doubleview, Perth 1998-99
Cricketers particularly admired: Ian Botham
Other sports played: Football, boxing 'and most other sports'
Other sports followed: Football (Manchester United)
Relaxations: 'Going out with mates'
Extras: Joint Kent Player of the Year 2000 (with Martin Saggers). NBC Denis Compton Award for the most promising young Kent player 2000. Leicestershire Player of the Year 2005. Left Leicestershire at the end of the 2007 season and joined Essex for 2008
Best batting: 119 Leicestershire v Sussex, Hove 2003
Best bowling: 6-24 Essex v Leicestershire, Chelmsford 2008

2008 Season

	M	Inn	NO	Runs	HS	Avg	100	50	Ct	St	Balls	Runs	Wkts	Avg	BB	5I	10M
Test																	
FC	14	17	3	147	27	10.50	-	-	3	-	2655	980	42	23.33	6-24	2	-
ODI																	
List A	16	6	3	54	21	18.00	-	-	2	-	680	414	22	18.81	5-17	1	
20/20 Int																	
20/20	12	8	2	42	14	7.00	-	-	3	-	234	256	10	25.60	2-17	-	

Career Performances

	M	Inn	NO	Runs	HS	Avg	100	50	Ct	St	Balls	Runs	Wkts	Avg	BB	5I	10M
Test																	
FC	103	127	25	1342	119	13.15	1	2	30	-	17294	8457	278	30.42	6-24	10	-
ODI																	
List A	107	58	23	437	39	12.48	-	-	13	-	4311	3255	98	33.21	5-17	2	
20/20 Int																	
20/20	44	15	6	58	14	6.44	-	-	13	-	795	968	40	24.20	3-7	-	

58. Who did Shane Warne dismiss with his first ever ball in an Ashes match?

MAUNDERS, J. K. Essex

Name: John Kenneth Maunders
Role: Left-hand opening bat, right-arm medium bowler
Born: 4 April 1981, Ashford, Middlesex
Height: 5ft 10in **Weight:** 13st
Nickname: Rod, Weaz
County debut: 1999 (Middlesex), 2003 (Leicestershire), 2008 (Essex)
Place in batting averages: (2007 170th av. 26.13)
Parents: Lynn and Kenneth
Marital status: Single
Family links with cricket: Grandfather and two uncles club cricketers for Thames Valley Ramblers
Education: Ashford High School; Spelthorne College
Qualifications: 10 GCSEs, coaching certificates
Career outside cricket: Cricket coach
Overseas tours: England U19 to New Zealand 1998-99, to Malaysia and (U19 World Cup) Sri Lanka 1999-2000
Overseas teams played for: University CC, Perth 2001-02
Career highlights to date: 'Scoring maiden first-class hundred v Surrey at Grace Road'
Cricket moments to forget: 'Not any one in particular; getting 0 and dropping catches are not great moments!'
Cricket superstitions: 'Just a few small ones'
Cricketers particularly admired: Brad Hodge, Justin Langer
Other sports played: Football, hockey, squash
Other sports followed: Horse racing
Extras: Has been Seaxe Player of Year. Represented England U17 and U19. NBC Denis Compton Award 1999. Released by Leicestershire at the end of the 2007 season. Signed a new one-year contract with Essex in November 2008
Best batting: 180 Leicestershire v Gloucestershire, Cheltenham 2006
Best bowling: 4-15 Leicestershire v Worcestershire, Worcester 2006

2008 Season

	M	Inn	NO	Runs	HS	Avg	100	50	Ct	St	Balls	Runs	Wkts	Avg	BB	5I	10M
Test																	
FC	3	5	0	217	105	43.40	1	1	-	-	0	0	0	-	-	-	
ODI																	
List A	1	1	0	11	11	11.00	-	-	-	-	0	0	0	-	-		
20/20 Int																	
20/20																	

Career Performances

	M	Inn	NO	Runs	HS	Avg	100	50	Ct	St	Balls	Runs	Wkts	Avg	BB	5I	10M
Test																	
FC	72	129	3	3761	180	29.84	6	19	38	-	1525	928	24	38.66	4-15	-	-
ODI																	
List A	31	31	3	640	109 *	22.85	1	1	9	-	139	103	4	25.75	2-16	-	
20/20 Int																	
20/20	14	7	3	24	10	6.00	-	-	2	-	12	14	2	7.00	2-14	-	

MAYNARD, T. L. Glamorgan

Name: Thomas (Tom) Lloyd Maynard
Role: Right-hand bat, right-arm medium bowler
Born: 25 March 1989, Cardiff
Height: 6ft 2in **Weight:** 15st
Nickname: George, Squirrel
County debut: 2007
Place in batting averages: 251st av. 11.71
Parents: Matthew and Sue
Marital status: Single
Family links with cricket: 'Dad used to play [for Glamorgan and England]. Uncle plays'
Education: Millfield School; Whitchurch High
Qualifications: 11 GCSEs, 3 A-levels
Overseas tours: England U15 to South Africa 2003-04
Career highlights to date: 'Debut for Glamorgan'
Cricket moments to forget: 'None'
Cricket superstitions: 'None'

Cricketers particularly admired: Brian Lara, Kevin Pietersen
Young players to look out for: Ed Jackson, Richard Davies, Alex Nielsen
Other sports played: Rugby (Bath Youth/Cardiff Youth)
Other sports followed: Football (Man City)
Favourite band: Oasis
Relaxations: 'Golf'
Extras: Played for Wales Minor Counties 2006-07. Scored 75-ball 71 on List A debut v Gloucestershire at Colwyn Bay in the Friends Provident 2007
Opinions on cricket: 'Twenty20 is a good form of the game and is good for cricket on the whole.'
Best batting: 26 Glamorgan v Leicestershire, Cardiff 2008

2008 Season

	M	Inn	NO	Runs	HS	Avg	100	50	Ct	St	Balls	Runs	Wkts	Avg	BB	5I	10M
Test																	
FC	5	7	0	82	26	11.71	-	-	5	-	0	0	0		-	-	-
ODI																	
List A	15	15	0	321	67	21.40	-	2	4	-	0	0	0		-	-	
20/20 Int																	
20/20	1	1	0	9	9	9.00	-	-	2	-	0	0	0		-	-	

Career Performances

	M	Inn	NO	Runs	HS	Avg	100	50	Ct	St	Balls	Runs	Wkts	Avg	BB	5I	10M
Test																	
FC	7	10	0	117	26	11.70	-	-	5	-	12	18	0		-	-	-
ODI																	
List A	17	17	0	393	71	23.11	-	3	4	-	0	0	0		-	-	
20/20 Int																	
20/20	5	4	0	35	11	8.75	-	-	4	-	0	0	0		-	-	

McGRATH, A. Yorkshire

Name: Anthony McGrath
Role: Right-hand bat, right-arm medium bowler, county captain
Born: 6 October 1975, Bradford
Height: 6ft 2in **Weight:** 14st 7lbs
Nickname: Gripper, Mags, Terry
County debut: 1995
County cap: 1999
Benefit: 2009
Test debut: 2003
ODI debut: 2003
1000 runs in a season: 2
Place in batting averages: 96th av. 34.66 (2007 45th av. 46.55)
Parents: Terry and Kath
Marital status: Single
Education: Yorkshire Martyrs Collegiate School
Qualifications: 9 GCSEs, BTEC National Diploma in Leisure Studies, senior coaching award
Overseas tours: England U19 to West Indies 1994-95; England A to Pakistan 1995-96, to Australia 1996-97; MCC to Bangladesh 1999-2000; England to Bangladesh and Sri Lanka 2003-04 (one-day series), to West Indies 2003-04 (one-day series)
Overseas teams played for: Deep Dene, Melbourne 1998-99; Wanneroo, Perth 1999-2001
Cricket moments to forget: 'Losing semi-final to Lancashire 1996. Relegation to Division Two 2002'
Cricketers particularly admired: Darren Lehmann, Robin Smith
Other sports followed: 'Most sports', football (Manchester United)
Relaxations: 'Music; spending time with friends; eating out'
Extras: Captained Yorkshire Schools U13, U14, U15, U16; captained English Schools U17. Bradford League Young Cricketer of the Year 1992 and 1993. Played for England U17 and U19. Captain of Yorkshire 2003; vice-captain of Yorkshire 2007, 2008; captain again for 2009
Best batting: 188* Yorkshire v Warwickshire, Edgbaston 2007
Best bowling: 5-39 Yorkshire v Derbyshire, Derby 2004

2008 Season

	M	Inn	NO	Runs	HS	Avg	100	50	Ct	St	Balls	Runs	Wkts	Avg	BB	5I	10M
Test																	
FC	14	21	0	728	144	34.66	2	3	11	-	601	282	9	31.33	2-27	-	-
ODI																	
List A	17	15	3	489	105 *	40.75	1	3	7	-	190	164	10	16.40	3-16	-	
20/20 Int																	
20/20	9	9	2	392	72 *	56.00	-	4	4	-	56	76	3	25.33	1-14	-	

Career Perfomances

	M	Inn	NO	Runs	HS	Avg	100	50	Ct	St	Balls	Runs	Wkts	Avg	BB	5I	10M
Test	4	5	0	201	81	40.20	-	2	3	-	102	56	4	14.00	3-16	-	-
FC	198	333	25	11475	188 *	37.25	27	55	144	-	7332	3728	109	34.20	5-39	1	-
ODI	14	12	2	166	52	16.60	-	1	4	-	228	175	4	43.75	1-13	-	
List A	262	241	34	6760	148	32.65	7	38	85	-	2892	2429	75	32.38	4-41	-	
20/20 Int																	
20/20	38	37	7	928	72 *	30.93	-	7	12	-	337	494	15	32.93	3-27	-	

McKENZIE, N. D. Durham

Name: Neil Douglas McKenzie
Role: Right-hand bat, right-arm medium bowler
Born: 24 November 1975, Johannesburg, South Africa
Nickname: Bertie
County debut: 2007 (Somerset), Durham (2008)
Test debut: 2000
ODI debut: 1999-2000
Twenty20 Int debut: 2005-06
1st-Class 200s: 1
Place in batting averages: 107th av. 32.11
Family links with cricket: Father Kevin played for North Eastern Transvaal and Transvaal
Education: King Edward VII School, Johannesburg; RAU, Johannesburg
Overseas tours: South Africa U19 to England 1995 (c); Transvaal to Australia 1997-98; South Africa to India 1999-2000 (one-day series), to Sri Lanka 2000, to West Indies 2000-01, to Zimbabwe 2001-02, to Australia 2001-02, to Bangladesh 2003, to

England 2003, to Pakistan 2003-04, to New Zealand 2003-04, to Bangladesh 2008, to Australia 2008-09, plus other one-day tournaments in Sharjah, Australia and Singapore; South Africa A to Zimbabwe 2002-03, 2004; South Africa Emerging Players to Australia (Cricket Australia Emerging Players Tournament) 2006 (c)
Overseas teams played for: Transvaal 1994-95 – 1996-97; Gauteng 1997-98 – 1998-99; Northerns 1999-2000 – 2003-04; Lions 2003-04 –
Extras: Captained South Africa Schools. One of *South African Cricket Annual*'s five Cricketers of the Year 2001. His match awards include Man of the Match in the second Test v New Zealand in Port Elizabeth 2000-01 (120) and in the second ODI v Sri Lanka in East London 2000-01 (120*). Captain of Highveld Lions. Was a temporary overseas player with Somerset during the 2007 season as a replacement for Cameron White; joined Durham as an overseas player for 2008 as a locum for Shivnarine Chanderpaul. Man of the Match v Dolphins at Potchefstroom in the SuperSport Series 2007-08 (164). Recalled to South Africa Test side for the second Test v West Indies at Cape Town 2007-08. Shared in a world-record opening stand of 415 with Graeme Smith (South Africa v Bangladesh, Chittagong, March 2008) on the way to making a career-best 226 first-class runs
Best batting: 226 South Africa v Bangladesh, Chittagong 2008
Best bowling: 2-13 Lions v Eagles, Kimberley 2007

2008 Season

	M	Inn	NO	Runs	HS	Avg	100	50	Ct	St	Balls	Runs	Wkts	Avg	BB	5I	10M
Test	4	8	1	339	138	48.42	1	1	2	-	0	0	0		-	-	-
FC	10	19	2	546	138	32.11	1	2	10	-	30	19	0		-	-	-
ODI																	
List A	9	9	0	235	77	26.11	-	2	1	-	0	0	0		-	-	
20/20 Int																	
20/20																	

Career Performances

	M	Inn	NO	Runs	HS	Avg	100	50	Ct	St	Balls	Runs	Wkts	Avg	BB	5I	10M
Test	51	82	6	2988	226	39.31	5	15	44	-	84	67	0		-	-	-
FC	170	287	32	11139	226	43.68	28	56	137	-	660	364	7	52.00	2-13	-	-
ODI	59	51	10	1580	131 *	38.53	2	9	19	-	46	27	0		-	-	
List A	202	181	28	5519	131 *	36.07	7	37	57	-	255	248	4	62.00	2-19	-	
20/20 Int	1	0	0	0	0		-	-	-	-	0	0	0		-	-	
20/20	24	23	7	591	85 *	36.93	-	4	9	-	12	19	0		-	-	

59. Who played his last Test match during the 1974-75 Ashes series, and went on to become an umpire and coach of the England side - before walking his dog in-between commentaries for Sky Sports?

McLAREN, R. Kent

Name: Ryan McLaren
Role: Left-hand bat, right-arm fast-medium bowler
Born: 9 February 1983, Kimberley, South Africa
County debut: 2007
County cap: 2007
Place in batting averages: 173rd av. 23.20 (2007 208th av. 20.92)
Place in bowling averages: 28th av. 23.58 (2007 29th av. 24.52)
Family links with cricket: Father (Paul McLaren) and uncle (Keith McLaren) played for Griqualand West. Cousin (Adrian McLaren) plays for Griqualand West
Overseas tours: South Africa U19 to New Zealand (U19 World Cup) 2001-02
Overseas teams played for: Free State 2003-04 – 2004-05; Eagles 2004-05 –
Extras: SuperSport Series Cricketer of the Year 2007. Took hat-trick (H. Marshall, Adshead, Fisher) v Gloucestershire in the final of the Twenty20 Cup at Edgbaston 2007, winning Man of the Match award. His other awards include Man of the Match v Canada U19 at Auckland in the U19 World Cup 2001-02 (4-9; full figures 10-4-9-4), v Warriors at Bloemfontein in the Supersport Series 2005-06 (140; 3-31/4-50) and v Dolphins at Bloemfontein in the SuperSport Series 2006-07 (53*; 5-57/4-59). Selected for South Africa ODI squad to face Bangladesh and Kenya 2008, but was not released by Kent. Is not considered an overseas player
Best batting: 140 Eagles v Warriors, Bloemfontein 2005-06
Best bowling: 8-38 Eagles v Cape Cobras, Stellenbosch (US) 2006-07
Stop press: Signed to play in IPL 2008-09 by Mumbai Indians

2008 Season

	M	Inn	NO	Runs	HS	Avg	100	50	Ct	St	Balls	Runs	Wkts	Avg	BB	5I	10M
Test																	
FC	16	23	3	464	65 *	23.20	-	2	6	-	2400	1179	50	23.58	6-75	2	-
ODI																	
List A	15	11	6	222	63	44.40	-	1	2	-	609	525	19	27.63	5-46	1	
20/20 Int																	
20/20	13	9	4	63	19 *	12.60	-	-	4	-	263	334	15	22.26	3-28	-	

Career Performances

	M	Inn	NO	Runs	HS	Avg	100	50	Ct	St	Balls	Runs	Wkts	Avg	BB	5I	10M
Test																	
FC	71	104	17	2450	140	28.16	2	13	37	-	11336	5593	230	24.31	8-38	10	1
ODI																	
List A	77	56	21	1309	82 *	37.40	-	8	27	-	2792	2268	77	29.45	5-46	1	
20/20 Int																	
20/20	45	31	13	327	46 *	18.16	-	-	18	-	790	957	38	25.18	3-22	-	

MEAKER, S. C. — Surrey

Name: Stuart Christopher Meaker
Role: Right-hand bat, right-arm fast bowler
Born: 21 January 1989, Durban, South Africa
Height: 5ft 11in **Weight:** 13st
Nickname: Meaksy, Herc
County debut: 2008
Parents: Vivien White
Marital status: Single
Education: Cranleigh School
Qualifications: GCSEs, 4 A-levels
Overseas tours: England U16 to South Africa; England U19 to Malaysia (U19 World Cup) 2007-08
Career highlights to date: 'Being given a contract by Surrey CCC, and making my first-class debut'
Cricket moments to forget: 'Playing against Kent CCC for Surrey in a pre-season friendly and going for an astonishing amount of runs. Being taken out of the attack for bowling a couple of beamers'
Cricket superstitions: 'Wearing my helmet way before I go in to bat. Left pad on first'
Cricketers particularly admired: Allan Donald, Mark Ramprakash
Young players to look out for: James Halton
Other sports played: Rugby, hockey, water polo, athletics, swimming, golf - 'as many sports as possible'
Other sports followed: Rugby (Natal Sharks, Sale Sharks)
Favourite band: Kings of Leon
Relaxations: 'Watching TV, stretching'
Extras: Lord's fielding award. Represented England U19 2007. NBC Denis Compton Award for the most promising young Surrey player 2008
Opinions on cricket: 'Stick with local players. No need for Kolpaks.'

Best batting: 16 Surrey v Nottinghamshire, The Oval 2008
Best bowling: 3-86 Surrey v Nottinghamshire, The Oval 2008

2008 Season

	M	Inn	NO	Runs	HS	Avg	100	50	Ct	St	Balls	Runs	Wkts	Avg	BB	5I	10M
Test																	
FC	2	2	0	22	16	11.00	-	-	-	-	211	139	4	34.75	3-86	-	-
ODI																	
List A	2	0	0	0	0		-	-	-	-	48	57	1	57.00	1-57	-	
20/20 Int																	
20/20																	

Career Performances

	M	Inn	NO	Runs	HS	Avg	100	50	Ct	St	Balls	Runs	Wkts	Avg	BB	5I	10M
Test																	
FC	2	2	0	22	16	11.00	-	-	-	-	211	139	4	34.75	3-86	-	-
ODI																	
List A	2	0	0	0	0		-	-	-	-	48	57	1	57.00	1-57	-	
20/20 Int																	
20/20																	

60. When Len Hutton made the then record Test score of 364 in 1938, who eventually got him out?

MICKLEBURGH, J. C. Essex

Name: Jaik Charles Mickleburgh
Role: Right-hand bat, right-arm fast-medium bowler
Born: 30 March 1990, Norwich, Norfolk
County debut: 2008
Overseas tours: England U19 to South Africa 2009
Extras: Made 2nd XI Championship debut 2006. Attended World Cricket Academy, Mumbai 2007. Played for Norfolk in Minor Counties competitions 2007. Played for Essex in the Twenty20 Floodlit Cup 2007. First-class debut 2008.
Best batting: 72 Essex v Warwickshire, Chelmsford 2008

2008 Season

	M	Inn	NO	Runs	HS	Avg	100	50	Ct	St	Balls	Runs	Wkts	Avg	BB	5I	10M
Test																	
FC	3	4	0	150	72	37.50	-	2	3	-	24	11	0		-	-	-
ODI																	
List A																	
20/20 Int																	
20/20																	

Career Performances

	M	Inn	NO	Runs	HS	Avg	100	50	Ct	St	Balls	Runs	Wkts	Avg	BB	5I	10M
Test																	
FC	3	4	0	150	72	37.50	-	2	3	-	24	11	0		-	-	-
ODI																	
List A																	
20/20 Int																	
20/20																	

Name: James Daniel Middlebrook
Role: Right-hand bat, off-spin bowler
Born: 13 May 1977, Leeds
Height: 6ft 1in **Weight:** 13st
Nickname: Midhouse, Midi, Midders
County debut: 1998 (Yorkshire), 2002 (Essex)
County cap: 2003 (Essex)
50 wickets in a season: 1
Place in batting averages: 156th av. 25.87 (2007 123rd av. 32.38)
Place in bowling averages: 104th av. 35.03 (2007 123rd av. 42.50)
Parents: Ralph and Mavis
Marital status: Single
Family links with cricket: 'Dad is a senior staff coach'
Education: Crawshaw, Pudsey
Qualifications: NVQ Level 2 in Coaching Sport and Recreation, ECB senior coach
Off-season: 'Cape Town, January 2009'
Overseas tours: Yorkshire CCC to Guernsey
Overseas teams played for: Stokes Valley CC, New Zealand; Gold Coast Dolphins, Brisbane; Surfers Paradise CC, Brisbane; Upper Valley CC, Wellington, New Zealand 2006-07
Career highlights to date: 'Winning the Friends Provident, 2008. Pro40, 2008'
Cricket superstitions: 'Always put my batting gear on the same way'
Cricketers particularly admired: John Emburey, Ian Botham
Young players to look out for: Jaik Mickleburgh, Joe Denly
Other sports played: Golf, tennis, squash, badminton
Other sports followed: Football (Leeds United), Formula 1, golf
Favourite band: Hed Kandi, Ministry of Sound
Relaxations: 'Any music - MTV - sleeping, socialising, catching up with old friends'
Extras: Played for Yorkshire from U11 to 1st XI. His 6-82 v Hampshire at Southampton 2000 included a spell of four wickets in five balls. Took Championship hat-trick (Saggers, Muralitharan, Sheriyar) v Kent at Canterbury 2003
Opinions on cricket: 'Too much cricket without rest in between games so you can practise at your skill level.'
Best batting: 127 Essex v Middlesex, Lord's 2007
Best bowling: 6-82 Yorkshire v Hampshire, Southampton 2000

2008 Season

	M	Inn	NO	Runs	HS	Avg	100	50	Ct	St	Balls	Runs	Wkts	Avg	BB	5I	10M
Test																	
FC	14	19	3	414	75	25.87	-	1	8	-	2066	1086	31	35.03	5-69	1	-
ODI																	
List A	16	12	6	126	26	21.00	-	-	7	-	384	327	8	40.87	2-29	-	
20/20 Int																	
20/20	12	9	2	65	17 *	9.28	-	-	2	-	120	180	4	45.00	3-13	-	

Career Performances

	M	Inn	NO	Runs	HS	Avg	100	50	Ct	St	Balls	Runs	Wkts	Avg	BB	5I	10M
Test																	
FC	135	191	25	4209	127	25.35	4	16	70	-	22724	11861	305	38.88	6-82	8	1
ODI																	
List A	139	93	27	1235	47	18.71	-	-	41	-	4849	3740	109	34.31	4-27	-	
20/20 Int																	
20/20	39	31	7	303	43	12.62	-	-	8	-	420	592	13	45.53	3-13	-	

MILLER, A. S. — Warwickshire

Name: Andrew Stephen Miller
Role: Right-hand bat, right-arm fast-medium bowler
Born: 27 September 1987, Preston
Height: 6ft 4in **Weight:** 13st 3lbs
Nickname: Millsy, Donk
County debut: 2008
Parents: Steve and Sharon
Family links with cricket: 'Dad and brother played club cricket at Longridge CC'
Education: St Cecilia's RC High School; Preston College
Qualifications: 10 GCSEs, BTEC National Diploma in Sport Fitness and Development, coaching Levels 1 and 2
Overseas tours: England U16 to South Africa 2004; England U19 to India 2004-05, to Bangladesh 2005-06, to Sri Lanka (U19 World Cup) 2005-06, to Malaysia 2006-07
Overseas teams played for: Yarroweyah United CC, Victoria 2007-08
Career highlights to date: 'Playing in an U19 Cricket World Cup and getting a full-time contract at Warwickshire CCC'

Cricket moments to forget: 'Being super-subbed for England U19 in the semi-final of the U19 World Cup on TV after seven overs of the first innings of the match. Going out to bat with two right-hand gloves'
Cricket superstitions: 'Always step over the boundary rope; never split it'
Cricketers particularly admired: Glenn McGrath, Curtly Ambrose
Young players to look out for: Nick James
Other sports played: Golf, football, swimming
Other sports followed: Football (Blackburn Rovers)
Favourite band: Arctic Monkeys
Relaxations: 'Watching TV, music, eating and sleeping'
Extras: Represented England U19 2005, 2006, 2007. NBC Denis Compton Award for the most promising young Warwickshire player 2006
Best batting: 4* Warwickshire v Bangladesh A, Edgbaston 2008
Best bowling: 2-35 Warwickshire v Bangladesh A, Edgbaston 2008

2008 Season

	M	Inn	NO	Runs	HS	Avg	100	50	Ct	St	Balls	Runs	Wkts	Avg	BB	5I	10M
Test																	
FC	1	1	1	4	4 *		-	-	-	-	120	45	3	15.00	2-35	-	-
ODI																	
List A																	
20/20 Int																	
20/20																	

Career Performances

	M	Inn	NO	Runs	HS	Avg	100	50	Ct	St	Balls	Runs	Wkts	Avg	BB	5I	10M
Test																	
FC	1	1	1	4	4 *		-	-	-	-	120	45	3	15.00	2-35	-	-
ODI																	
List A																	
20/20 Int																	
20/20																	

MITCHELL, D. K. H. Worcestershire

Name: Daryl Keith Henry Mitchell
Role: Right-hand bat, right-arm medium bowler; batting all-rounder
Born: 25 November 1983, Evesham
Height: 5ft 10in **Weight:** 11st 10lbs
Nickname: Mitch, Peggy, Toucan
County debut: 2005
County colours: 2005
Place in batting averages: 64th av. 40.08 (2007 56th av. 43.33)
Parents: Keith and Jane
Marital status: Single
Family links with cricket: 'Dad played club cricket and coaches WYC (Worcestershire Young Cricketers) U13'
Education: Prince Henry's High, Evesham; University of Worcester
Qualifications: 10 GCSEs, 4 A-levels, BSc (Hons) Sports Studies and Geography (2.2), ECB Level 1 coaching
Career outside cricket: 'Coaching'
Off-season: 'At home for the winter. Plenty of gym work, indoor nets, coaching and decorating.'
Overseas tours: Worcestershire to Guernsey 2007
Overseas teams played for: Midland-Guildford, Perth 2005-08
Career highlights to date: '134* v Glamorgan – maiden first-class century 2006. Winning Pro40 2007'
Cricket moments to forget: 'Run out first ball by a Monty direct hit v Northants, Twenty20 2006. Bowling at Taunton!'
Cricket superstitions: 'Put gloves on before helmet'
Cricketers particularly admired: Michael Atherton, Graeme Hick
Young players to look out for: Jack Manual, Alexi Kervezee
Other sports played: Football, golf ('badly'), pool, darts, skittles
Other sports followed: Football (Aston Villa), rugby (Worcester), AFL (West Coast Eagles)
Favourite band: Oasis
Relaxations: 'Music, movies, PlayStation'
Extras: Scored 210* for Worcestershire v Bradford/Leeds UCCE at Harrogate 2006. Carried bat for 70* v Sussex at Hove 2007
Opinions on cricket: 'The Twenty20 tournaments are great entertainment and it's good to see money coming into cricket. However, Test cricket must remain the pinnacle of a career, so the first-class structure in England should remain unchanged.'

Best batting: 134* Worcestershire v Glamorgan, Colwyn Bay 2006
Best bowling: 3-50 Worcestershire v Sussex, Hove 2007

2008 Season

	M	Inn	NO	Runs	HS	Avg	100	50	Ct	St	Balls	Runs	Wkts	Avg	BB	5I	10M
Test																	
FC	16	29	6	922	102	40.08	1	4	9	-	186	65	0	-	-	-	
ODI																	
List A	16	12	2	339	92	33.90	-	3	3	-	330	351	7	50.14	2-29	-	
20/20 Int																	
20/20	9	6	2	73	31 *	18.25	-	-	5	-	185	205	12	17.08	4-11	-	

Career Performances

	M	Inn	NO	Runs	HS	Avg	100	50	Ct	St	Balls	Runs	Wkts	Avg	BB	5I	10M
Test																	
FC	31	55	12	1660	134 *	38.60	3	9	25	-	525	280	7	40.00	3-50	-	-
ODI																	
List A	26	20	3	453	92	26.64	-	4	8	-	528	559	13	43.00	4-42	-	
20/20 Int																	
20/20	26	12	5	83	31 *	11.85	-	-	9	-	479	624	23	27.13	4-11	-	

MOHAMMAD SAMI — Sussex

Name: Mohammad Sami
Role: Right-hand bat, right-arm fast bowler
Born: 24 February 1981, Karachi, Sind, Pakistan
County debut: 2003 (Kent), 2008 (Sussex)
Test debut: 2001
ODI debut: 2001
Overseas tours: Pakistan U19 to Sri Lanka (U19 World Cup) 1999-2000; Pakistan to New Zealand 2000-01, to England 2001, to Bangladesh 2001-02, to Sharjah (v West Indies) 2001-02, to Sri Lanka (ICC Champions Trophy) 2002-03, to Sri Lanka and Sharjah (v Australia) 2002-03, to Zimbabwe 2002-03, to South Africa 2002-03, to Africa (World Cup) 2002-03, to England (NatWest Challenge) 2003, to New Zealand 2003-04, to Holland (Videocon Cup) 2004, to England (ICC Champions Trophy) 2004,

to Australia 2004-05, to India 2004-05, to England 2006, to India 2007, plus other one-day tournaments in Sharjah, Australia, Morocco, Kenya and Sri Lanka
Overseas teams played for: Pakistan Customs 1999-2000; Karachi Whites 2000-01 – 2007-08; National Bank of Pakistan 2001-02 – 2006-07; Karachi 2003-04; Karachi Blues 2004-05; Karachi Dolphins 2005-06 – 2006-07; Sind 2006-07; Lahore Badshahs
Extras: Had match figures of 8-106 (3-70/5-36) on Test debut in the first Test v New Zealand at Auckland 2000-01, winning Man of the Match award. Took hat-trick (T. C. B. Fernando, Zoysa, Muralitharan) v Sri Lanka in the final of the Asian Test Championship at Lahore 2001-02. Was an overseas player with Kent late June and early July 2003 before injuring an ankle; returned for 2004; left Kent at the end of the 2004 season. Took 15-114 (8-64/7-50) v Nottinghamshire at Maidstone 2003, the best match figures by a Kent bowler since 1939. ODI Man of the Match awards v South Africa at Lahore 2003-04 (3-20) and v New Zealand at Lahore 2003-04 (5-10). Spent the last month only of the 2008 season at Sussex
Best batting: 49 Pakistan v India, Rawalpindi 2004
Best bowling: 8-39 Karachi Whites v Sialkot, Karachi 2007

2008 Season

	M	Inn	NO	Runs	HS	Avg	100	50	Ct	St	Balls	Runs	Wkts	Avg	BB	5I	10M
Test																	
FC	3	4	1	38	28 *	12.66	-	-	-	-	498	265	9	29.44	5-95	1	-
ODI																	
List A	2	1	1	32	32 *		-	-	-	-	84	78	3	26.00	2-48	-	
20/20 Int																	
20/20																	

Career Performances

	M	Inn	NO	Runs	HS	Avg	100	50	Ct	St	Balls	Runs	Wkts	Avg	BB	5I	10M
Test	33	51	13	458	49	12.05	-	-	7	-	6984	4161	81	51.37	5-36	2	
FC	94	127	37	1326	49	14.73	-	-	36	-	17416	10070	318	31.66	8-39	17	2
ODI	83	46	19	314	46	11.62	-	-	18	-	4094	3357	118	28.44	5-10	1	
List A	117	67	27	474	46	11.85	-	-	24	-	5791	4774	169	28.24	6-20	2	
20/20 Int																	
20/20	10	5	1	26	8	6.50	-	-	5	-	233	283	7	40.42	2-14	-	

MOHAMMAD YOUSUF Lancashire

Name: Mohammad Yousuf (formerly known as Yousuf Youhana)
Role: Right-hand bat, right-arm off-break bowler
Born: 27 August 1974, Lahore, Pakistan
County debut: 2008
Test debut: 1998
ODI debut: 1998
1st-Class 200s: 5
Overseas tours: Pakistan to South Africa 1997-98, to Zimbabwe 1997-98, to India 1998-99, to UK, Ireland and Holland (World Cup) 1999, to Australia 1999-2000, to West Indies 1999-2000, to Sri Lanka 2000, to Kenya (ICC Knockout Trophy) 2000-01, to New Zealand 2000-01, to England 2001, to Bangladesh 2001-02, to Sharjah (v West Indies) 2001-02, to Sri Lanka (ICC Champions Trophy) 2002-03, to Zimbabwe 2002-03, to South Africa 2002-03, to Africa (World Cup) 2002-03, to New Zealand 2003-04, to England (ICC Champions Trophy) 2004, to Australia 2004-05, to India 2004-05, to West Indies 2005, to Sri Lanka 2005-06, to England 2006, to South Africa 2006-07, to India 2007-08 plus other one-day tournaments and series in India, Sharjah, Toronto, Bangladesh, Singapore, Australia, Morocco, Sri Lanka, England and Holland; Asian Cricket Council to Australia (Tsunami Relief) 2004-05, to South Africa (Afro-Asia Cup) 2005-06
Overseas teams played for: Bahawalpur 1996-97; Water and Power Development Authority 1997-98 – 2007-08; Lahore City 1997-98; Lahore Blues 2000-01; Pakistan International Airlines 2001-02; Lahore 2002-03 – 2003-04; Zarai Taraqiati Bank Ltd. 2002-03; Lahore Lions 2004-05 – 2008-09; Punjab (Pakistan) 2007-08
Extras: Known as Yousuf Youhana until his conversion from Christianity to Islam in September 2005. His numerous international awards include Man of the [Test] Series v England 2000-01, Man of the Match v India at Edgbaston in the ICC Champions Trophy 2004 (81*) and Man of the Match v West Indies at Perth in the VB Series 2004-05 (105). Prevented from joining Derbyshire for 2006 due to ECB regulations concerning overseas players. One of *Wisden*'s Five Cricketers of the Year 2007. Joined Lancashire on short-term contract, 2008, replacing Brad Hodge
Best batting: 223 Pakistan v England, Lahore 2005
Stop press: Signed to play in ICL in 2007, before changing mind. Was prevented from joining the IPL before finally making his debut for Lahore Badshahs in the ICL in 2008-09

2008 Season

	M	Inn	NO	Runs	HS	Avg	100	50	Ct	St	Balls	Runs	Wkts	Avg	BB	5I	10M
Test																	
FC	2	3	1	248	205 *	124.00	1	-	-	-	0	0	0		-	-	-
ODI																	
List A	5	5	0	62	32	12.40	-	-	1	-	0	0	0		-	-	
20/20 Int																	
20/20																	

Career Performances

	M	Inn	NO	Runs	HS	Avg	100	50	Ct	St	Balls	Runs	Wkts	Avg	BB	5I	10M
Test	79	134	12	6770	223	55.49	23	28	59	-	6	3	0		-	-	-
FC	122	202	20	9354	223	51.39	28	44	77	-	18	24	0		-	-	-
ODI	269	254	40	9242	141 *	43.18	15	62	53	-	2	1	1	1.00	1-0	-	
List A	305	289	45	10032	141 *	41.11	15	67	63	-	8	13	1	13.00	1-0	-	
20/20 Int	1	1	0	20	20	20.00	-	-	-	-	0	0	0		-	-	
20/20	8	7	0	135	30	19.28	-	-	1	-	1	1	0		-	-	

MOORE, S. C. — Worcestershire

Name: Stephen Colin Moore
Role: Right-hand opening bat, right-arm medium bowler
Born: 4 November 1980, Johannesburg, South Africa
Height: 6ft 1in **Weight:** 13st
Nickname: Mandy, Circles, Mork
County debut: 2003
County colours: 2003
1000 runs in a season: 2
1st-Class 200s: 1
Place in batting averages: 15th av. 55.80 (2007 95th av. 36.75)
Parents: Shane and Carrol
Wife and date of marriage: Ruth, 4 October 2008
Education: St Stithians College, South Africa; Exeter University
Qualifications: MEng (Hons) Electronic Engineering
Off-season: 'Training and working in and around Worcester'

Overseas tours: England Performance Programme to India, 2008-09; England Lions to New Zealand 2009
Overseas teams played for: Midland-Guildford, Perth 2002-04; Northern Districts, Adelaide
Career highlights to date: 'First-class debut and Lord's final 2004'
Cricket moments to forget: 'Losing Lord's final 2004 and getting a duck!'
Cricket superstitions: 'Left pad first!'
Other sports played: Hockey, tennis (both Exeter University 1st team), golf, squash
Other sports followed: Tennis
Favourite band: Jack Johnson
Relaxations: 'My music (guitar and saxophone); watersports and wildlife'
Extras: Scored 1000 first-class runs in his first full season 2004. Is not considered an overseas player. One of three Worcestershire batsmen to score over 1000 first-class runs in 2008
Opinions on cricket: 'These are exciting times. Hopefully the right decisions can be made to further the development of cricket in England and we can all benefit in the future.'
Best batting: 246 Worcestershire v Derbyshire, Worcester 2005
Best bowling: 1-13 Worcestershire v Lancashire, Worcester 2004

2008 Season

	M	Inn	NO	Runs	HS	Avg	100	50	Ct	St	Balls	Runs	Wkts	Avg	BB	5I	10M
Test																	
FC	16	30	4	1451	156	55.80	6	6	8	-	0	0	0		-	-	-
ODI																	
List A	13	12	1	111	46	10.09	-	-	4	-	0	0	0		-	-	
20/20 Int																	
20/20	9	8	0	215	51	26.87	-	1	1	-	0	0	0		-	-	

Career Performances

	M	Inn	NO	Runs	HS	Avg	100	50	Ct	St	Balls	Runs	Wkts	Avg	BB	5I	10M
Test																	
FC	84	151	15	5793	246	42.59	13	28	41	-	342	321	5	64.20	1-13		-
ODI																	
List A	77	75	7	1857	105 *	27.30	2	10	19	-	35	42	1	42.00	1-1	-	
20/20 Int																	
20/20	35	30	4	585	53	22.50	-	2	12	-	0	0	0		-	-	

MORGAN, C.G.W Hampshire

Name: Christopher George Wakefield Morgan
Role: Right-hand batsman; right-arm leg-break bowler
Born: 28 October 1989, Portsmouth
County debut: No first-team appearances
Overseas teams played for: Joondalup (Western Australia) 2008-09
Extras: Hampshire Academy Player of the Year for 2008; also played for Durham UCCE

MORGAN, E. J. G. Middlesex

Name: Eoin Joseph Gerard Morgan
Role: Left-hand bat, right-arm medium bowler
Born: 10 September 1986, Dublin
Height: 5ft 10in **Weight:** 11st 11lbs
Nickname: Moggie
County debut: 2005 (one-day), 2006 (first-class)
County cap: 2008
ODI debut: 2006
1st-Class 200s: 1
Place in batting averages: 29th av. 49.31 (2007 122nd av. 32.42)
Parents: Joseph and Olivia
Marital status: Single
Family links with cricket: 'My father, three brothers, two sisters, grandfather and great-grandfather all played'
Education: Catholic University School, Dublin

Overseas tours: Ireland U19 to Bangladesh (U19 World Cup) 2003-04, to Sri Lanka (U19 World Cup) 2005-06; Ireland to Namibia (ICC Inter-Continental Cup) 2005, to Scotland (European Championship) 2006, to Kenya (ICC World Cricket League) 2006-07, to West Indies (World Cup) 2006-07, plus Ireland age-group tours. England Performance Programme to India 2008-09; England Lions to New Zealand 2009
Overseas teams played for: St Henry's Marist School U19, Durban 2003
Career highlights to date: 'Winning the Inter-Continental Cup with Ireland in Namibia [2005]'
Cricketers particularly admired: Ricky Ponting, Brian Lara
Young players to look out for: Billy Godleman
Other sports played: Rugby (Schools), Gaelic football
Other sports followed: Gaelic football (Dublin GAA – 'The Dubs'), rugby, snooker, darts
Favourite band: Aslan
Relaxations: 'Watching sports and listening to music'
Extras: Capped for Ireland at every level from U13 up. Player of the Tournament at European U15 Championships 2000, 2002 and at European U17 Championships 2002. Became then youngest player to represent Ireland 2003. NBC Denis Compton Award for the most promising young Middlesex player 2003. C&G Man of the Match award for Ireland v Yorkshire in Belfast 2005 (59). Made ODI debut for Ireland v Scotland at Ayr in the European Championship 2006, winning Man of the Match award (99). Scored maiden first-class double century (209*) v UAE in Abu Dhabi in the 2006 ICC Inter-Continental Cup, winning Man of the Match award
Best batting: 209* Ireland v United Arab Emirates, Abu Dhabi (SZ) 2006-07
Best bowling: 2-24 Middlesex v Nottinghamshire, Lord's 2007

2008 Season

	M	Inn	NO	Runs	HS	Avg	100	50	Ct	St	Balls	Runs	Wkts	Avg	BB	5I	10M
Test																	
FC	17	29	7	1085	137 *	49.31	3	5	19	-	0	0	0		-	-	-
ODI																	
List A	14	13	1	457	100	38.08	1	1	5	-	0	0	0		-	-	
20/20 Int																	
20/20	13	12	1	279	62	25.36	-	1	7	-	0	0	0		-	-	

Career Performances

	M	Inn	NO	Runs	HS	Avg	100	50	Ct	St	Balls	Runs	Wkts	Avg	BB	5I	10M
Test																	
FC	36	60	9	2095	209 *	41.07	5	10	29	1	79	46	2	23.00	2-24	-	-
ODI	21	21	1	600	115	30.00	1	3	8	-	0	0	0		-	-	
List A	76	71	8	2104	115	33.39	3	11	24	-	30	44	0		-	-	
20/20 Int																	
20/20	27	25	2	572	66	24.86	-	2	12	-	0	0	0		-	-	

MORKEL, J. A. Durham

Name: Johannes Albertus (Albie) Morkel
Role: Left-hand bat, right-arm fast-medium bowler; all-rounder
Born: 10 June 1981, Vereeniging, South Africa
County debut: 2008
ODI debut: 2003-04
Twenty20 Int debut: 2005-06
1st-Class 200s: 1
Family links with cricket: Father Albert played for Southern Transvaal Country Districts; brother Morne plays for Titans and South Africa, played for Yorkshire 2008
Overseas tours: South Africa U19 to Sri Lanka (U19 World Cup) 1999-2000; South Africa A to Zimbabwe 2002-03, to Australia 2002-03, to Zimbabwe 2004, to Sri Lanka (Triangular A Team Tournament) 2005-06, to Zimbabwe 2006-07; South Africa to New Zealand 2003-04, to India (one-day series) 2005-06, to Zimbabwe (one-day series) 2007-08, to Pakistan 2007-08 (one-day series), Bangladesh (one-day series) 2007-08, England (one-day series) 2008 to Australia (one-day series) 2008-09; African XI to India (Afro-Asia Cup) 2007
Overseas teams played for: Easterns 1999-2000 – 2005-06; Titans 2003-04 – ; Chennai (IPL) 2007-08 –
Extras: Represented South Africa in the Twenty20 World Championship 2007-08. His match awards include Man of the Match for South Africa A v New Zealand A at Johannesburg 2004-05 (67*). Man of the Match for Titans v Eagles at Benoni in the SuperSport Series 2007-08 (44/151). Joined Durham as an overseas player for 2008 as a locum for Shivnarine Chanderpaul. South African Player of the Year 2008
Best batting: 204* Titans v Western Province Boland, Paarl 2004-05
Best bowling: 6-36 Easterns v Griqualand West, Kimberley 1999-2000

2008 Season

	M	Inn	NO	Runs	HS	Avg	100	50	Ct	St	Balls	Runs	Wkts	Avg	BB	5I	10M
Test																	
FC	1	1	0	37	37	37.00	-	-	2	-	0	0	0		-	-	-
ODI	2	2	0	22	16	11.00	-	-	-	-	30	30	1	30.00	1-30	-	
List A	4	4	0	45	16	11.25	-	-	1	-	72	105	1	105.00	1-30	-	
20/20 Int																	
20/20	9	8	3	150	54 *	30.00	-	1	1	-	114	154	6	25.66	4-30	-	

Career Performances

	M	Inn	NO	Runs	HS	Avg	100	50	Ct	St	Balls	Runs	Wkts	Avg	BB	5I	10M
Test																	
FC	55	78	14	2718	204 *	42.46	4	17	22	-	8585	4388	144	30.47	6-36	3	-
ODI	26	16	1	258	97	17.20	-	1	4	-	1014	872	30	29.06	4-29	-	
List A	126	93	25	1814	97	26.67	-	8	22	-	5174	4083	144	28.35	4-23	-	
20/20 Int	11	8	1	196	43	28.00	-	-	4	-	156	163	6	27.16	2-12	-	
20/20	64	53	12	1021	71	24.90	-	3	10	-	1092	1389	54	25.72	4-30	-	

MORKEL, M. Yorkshire

Name: Morne Morkel
Role: Left-hand bat, right-arm fast bowler
Born: 6 October 1984, Vereeniging, South Africa
County debut: 2007 (Kent, one-day), 2008 (Yorkshire, first-class)
Test debut: 2006-07
ODI debut: 2007
Twenty20 Int debut: 2007-08
Place in batting averages: 82nd av. 31.61
Family links with cricket: Father Albert played for Southern Transvaal Country Districts; brother Albie plays for Titans and South Africa
Overseas tours: South Africa Academy to Pakistan 2005-06; African XI to India (Afro-Asia Cup) 2007; South Africa Emerging Players to Australia (Cricket Australia Emerging Players Tournament) 2007; South Africa to Zimbabwe (one-day series) 2007-08, to Pakistan 2007-08, Bangladesh 2007-08, to India 2007-08, to England 2008, to Australia 2008-09
Overseas teams played for: Easterns 2003-04 – 2006-07; Titans 2004-05 –
Extras: His match awards include Man of the Match v Eagles at Centurion in the SuperSport Series 2006-07 (22/57; 4-76/2-58). Made ODI debut for African XI v Asian Cricket Council XI in Bangalore 2007; has also played in ODIs for South Africa. Was a temporary overseas player with Kent during the 2007 season as a replacement for Andrew Hall. Represented South Africa in the Twenty20 World Championship 2007-08. Signed to play in IPL for Rajasthan Royals although not appear in 2007-08. Joined Yorkshire as an overseas player for 2008 as a locum for Rana Naved - injury restricted him to just one first-class appearance for the county

Best batting: 57 Titans v Eagles, Centurion 2006-07
Best bowling: 6-66 Easterns/Northerns XI v Zimbabweans, Benoni 2004-05

2008 Season

	M	Inn	NO	Runs	HS	Avg	100	50	Ct	St	Balls	Runs	Wkts	Avg	BB	5I	10M
Test	4	5	0	51	18	10.20	-	-	-	-	842	502	15	33.46	4-52	-	-
FC	7	8	0	62	18	7.75	-	-	2	-	1096	664	21	31.61	4-52	-	-
ODI	3	1	0	6	6	6.00	-	-	-	-	84	83	1	83.00	1-32	-	
List A	4	1	0	6	6	6.00	-	-	-	-	126	110	1	110.00	1-32	-	
20/20 Int																	
20/20																	

Career Performances

	M	Inn	NO	Runs	HS	Avg	100	50	Ct	St	Balls	Runs	Wkts	Avg	BB	5I	10M
Test	10	12	1	163	35	14.81	-	-	-	-	1699	1052	32	32.87	5-50	1	-
FC	32	40	6	524	57	15.41	-	1	15	-	5234	3099	103	30.08	6-66	4	-
ODI	13	5	2	58	25	19.33	-	-	3	-	656	542	21	25.80	4-36		
List A	29	11	5	108	35	18.00	-	-	6	-	1357	1056	41	25.75	4-36	-	
20/20 Int	6	1	1	1	1 *		-	-	-	-	144	142	10	14.20	4-17	-	
20/20	28	6	4	18	7 *	9.00	-	-	4	-	581	668	31	21.54	4-17	-	

MUCHALL, G. J. Durham

Name: Gordon James Muchall
Role: Right-hand bat, right-arm medium bowler
Born: 2 November 1982, Newcastle upon Tyne
Height: 6ft 2in **Weight:** 13st
Nickname: Much, Muchy, Hank, Melon
County debut: 2002
County cap: 2005
1st-Class 200s: 1
Parents: Mary and Arthur
Marital status: Single
Family links with cricket: 'Dad and brother Matthew play for South Shields CC; brother Paul for Tynemouth and Durham Academy'
Education: Durham School
Qualifications: 7 GCSEs, 2 A-levels, Level 2 cricket coach

Career outside cricket: Coaching
Overseas tours: England U19 to India 2000-01, to Australia and (U19 World Cup) New Zealand 2001-02; ECB National Academy to Australia and Sri Lanka 2002-03
Overseas teams played for: Fremantle 2001-02; Claremont-Nedlands, Perth 2005-06
Career highlights to date: '100 at Lord's. 200 against Kent. 250 for England U19. Winning Friends Provident Trophy [2007]'
Cricket moments to forget: 'With the opposition needing four off the last ball to win, going into the long barrier position and the ball bouncing over my head for four'
Cricketers particularly admired: Dale Benkenstein, Mike Hussey, Jimmy Maher, Paul Collingwood, Jon Lewis
Young players to look out for: Luke Evans, Paul Muchall, Scott Borthwick
Other sports played: Rugby (Durham School – played in *Daily Mail* Cup final at Twickenham)
Other sports followed: Rugby (Newcastle Falcons)
Favourite band: Mika, The Killers
Relaxations: Listening to music, socialising with friends
Extras: Represented England U19, scoring 254 in the first 'Test' v India U19 at Cardiff 2002. Cricket Society's Most Promising Young Cricketer of the Year Award 2002. NBC Denis Compton Award for the most promising young Durham player 2002. Durham Batsman of the Year 2004. Scored maiden first-class double century (219) v Kent at Canterbury 2006, in the process sharing with Phil Mustard (130) in a new Durham record partnership for the sixth wicket (249)
Best batting: 219 Durham v Kent, Canterbury 2006
Best bowling: 3-26 Durham v Yorkshire, Headingley 2003

2008 Season

	M	Inn	NO	Runs	HS	Avg	100	50	Ct	St	Balls	Runs	Wkts	Avg	BB	5I	10M
Test																	
FC	1	1	0	12	12	12.00	-	-	-	-	0	0	0		-	-	-
ODI																	
List A	5	5	1	95	54 *	23.75	-	1	6	-	0	0	0		-	-	
20/20 Int																	
20/20	2	2	0	11	10	5.50	-	-	1	-	0	0	0		-	-	

Career Performances

	M	Inn	NO	Runs	HS	Avg	100	50	Ct	St	Balls	Runs	Wkts	Avg	BB	5I	10M
Test																	
FC	92	166	7	4541	219	28.55	7	23	60		890	615	15	41.00	3-26	-	-
ODI																	
List A	77	68	12	1649	101 *	29.44	1	8	25	-	162	137	1	137.00	1-15	-	
20/20 Int																	
20/20	31	27	6	578	64 *	27.52	-	1	11	-	12	8	1	8.00	1-8	-	

MUCHALL, P. B. Durham

Name: Paul Bernard Muchall
Role: Right-hand bat, right-arm fast-medium bowler; all-rounder
Born: 17 March 1987, Newcastle upon Tyne
Height: 6ft 2in **Weight:** 13st
Nickname: Much
County debut: No first-team appearance
Parents: Arthur and Mary
Marital status: Single
Family links with cricket: 'Grandad played for Northumberland in the Minor Counties Championship, Dad plays for Durham Over-50s and brother Gordon currently plays for Durham'
Education: Durham School
Qualifications: 10 GCSEs, 3 AS-levels, 2 A-levels, Level 2 personal trainer
Career outside cricket: Personal trainer
Overseas teams played for: Fremantle DCC 2005-06, 2007-08
Career highlights to date: 'Scoring a century [107*] on debut for Durham 2nd XI, and receiving a contract for the coming 2008 season with Durham'
Cricket moments to forget: 'Getting a pair for Northumberland'
Cricket superstitions: 'Always put left pad on first'
Cricketers particularly admired: Steve Waugh, Gordon Muchall, Malcolm Marshall
Young players to look out for: Patrick Molinari (Fremantle), Theo Doropoulos (Western Australia), Michael Turns, Ben Stokes
Other sports played: Checkers, golf, football, rugby
Other sports followed: Football (Newcastle United), rugby (Newcastle Falcons, Westoe)
Favourite band: U2, Sneaky Sound System
Relaxations: 'Golf, beach'
Extras: Played for Northumberland in the Minor Counties Championship 2006, 2007, 2008. Has also appeared for Durham U17 2004, Durham Academy 2005-08, Tynemouth 2006 and South Shields 2008. Development contract with Durham for 2009
Opinions on cricket: 'Free hits in four-day games.'

MULLANEY, S. J. Lancashire

Name: Steven John Mullaney
Role: Right-hand bat, right-arm medium bowler; all-rounder
Born: 19 November 1986, Warrington
Height: 5ft 10in **Weight:** 12st
Nickname: Mull, Cadet Mahoney, Tony
County debut: 2006
Parents: Andrew and Elaine
Marital status: Single - 'Girlfriend, Nicola'
Family links with cricket: 'Dad was club professional in 1980s and 1990s'
Education: St Mary's RC High School, Astley
Career outside cricket: PE teacher
Qualifications: 9 GCSEs
Off-season: 'In Australia with South Caulfield CC, Melbourne.'
Overseas tours: England U19 to India 2004-05, to Sri Lanka (U19 World Cup) 2005-06
Overseas teams played for: McKinnon, Melbourne 2006-08; South Caulfield, Melbourne, 2008-09
Career highlights to date: '165* for Lancashire v Durham UCCE 2007 (maiden first-class hundred)' (*Scored in his only first-class innings of 2007*)
Cricket moments to forget: 'None'
Cricket superstitions: 'Put left pad on first'
Cricketers particularly admired: Andrew Flintoff
Young players to look out for: Karl Brown, Tom Smith, Moeen Ali, Gareth Cross
Other sports played: Rugby league (formerly; 'toured France with England U15')
Other sports followed: Football (Manchester City FC), rugby league (St Helens)
Favourite band: Westlife
Relaxations: 'Watching TV and other sports'
Extras: Scored 208 for Lancashire U17. Represented England U19 2005, 2006. Signed new contract in September 2008
Opinions on cricket: 'The standard is getting higher and higher so you have got to work harder and harder.'
Best batting: 165* Lancashire v DUCCE, Durham 2007
Best bowling: 1-3 Lancashire v DUCCE, Durham 2008

2008 Season

	M	Inn	NO	Runs	HS	Avg	100	50	Ct	St	Balls	Runs	Wkts	Avg	BB	5I	10M
Test																	
FC	2	3	0	48	33	16.00	-	-	-	-	59	35	1	35.00	1-3	-	-
ODI																	
List A	1	1	1	4	4 *		-	-	-	-	12	18	0		-	-	
20/20 Int																	
20/20																	

Career Performances

	M	Inn	NO	Runs	HS	Avg	100	50	Ct	St	Balls	Runs	Wkts	Avg	BB	5I	10M
Test																	
FC	4	5	1	257	165 *	64.25	1	-	3	-	161	84	1	84.00	1-3	-	-
ODI																	
List A	6	3	1	26	12	13.00	-	-	1	-	116	97	6	16.16	3-13	-	
20/20 Int																	
20/20	2	1	0	5	5	5.00	-	-	1	-	0	0	0		-	-	

MUNDAY, M. K. Somerset

Name: Michael Kenneth Munday
Role: Right-hand bat, leg-spin bowler
Born: 22 October 1984, Nottingham
Height: 5ft 8in **Weight:** 12st
County debut: 2005
Place in bowling averages: 125th av. 41.00 (2007 1st av. 13.71)
Parents: John and Maureen
Marital status: Single
Family links with cricket: 'Dad, brother and sister have played league cricket in Cornwall'
Education: Truro School; Corpus Christi College, Oxford University
Qualifications: 10 GCSEs, 3 A-levels, MChem (Oxon)
Off-season: 'Training in Taunton'
Overseas tours: Cornwall Schools U13 to South Africa 1998; ESCA West U15 to West Indies 2000
Overseas teams played for: Glenelg DCC, Adelaide 2006-08
Career highlights to date: 'Taking 8-55 on the last day of the 2007 season'

Cricket moments to forget: 'Being hit on the point of the elbow by Steffan Jones's "skiddy" bouncer, OUCCE v Derbyshire 2006'
Cricket superstitions: 'Always wear an arm guard'
Cricketers particularly admired: Shane Warne, Marcus Trescothick
Young players to look out for: Max Waller, Andy Sutton, Mark Turner, Jos Buttler
Other sports played: Chess ('Yes, it is a sport')
Other sports followed: Football (Liverpool)
Favourite band: Coldplay, The Killers
Relaxations: 'Swimming, reading, crosswords'
Extras: Played for Cornwall in the C&G 2001. Played for Oxford UCCE 2003-06. Oxford Blue 2003-06, returning match figures of 11-143 v Cambridge University in the Varsity Match at The Parks 2006. Represented England U19 2004. Returned match figures of 10-65 (2-10/8-55) v Nottinghamshire at Taunton 2007
Best batting: 21 Somerset v Lancashire, Old Trafford 2008
Best bowling: 8-55 Somerset v Nottinghamshire, Taunton 2007

2008 Season

	M	Inn	NO	Runs	HS	Avg	100	50	Ct	St	Balls	Runs	Wkts	Avg	BB	5I	10M
Test																	
FC	5	5	1	35	21	8.75	-	-	1	-	608	410	10	41.00	3-18	-	-
ODI																	
List A																	
20/20 Int																	
20/20																	

Career Performances

	M	Inn	NO	Runs	HS	Avg	100	50	Ct	St	Balls	Runs	Wkts	Avg	BB	5I	10M
Test																	
FC	27	24	10	106	21	7.57	-	-	11	-	3325	2182	76	28.71	8-55	4	2
ODI																	
List A	1	0	0	0	0		-	-	-	-	30	39	1	39.00	1-39	-	
20/20 Int																	
20/20																	

MURPHY, D. — Northamptonshire

Name: David Murphy
Role: Right-hand bat, wicket-keeper
Born: 24 July 1989, Welwyn Garden City, Hertfordshire
County debut: No first-team appearance
Extras: Northampton Academy. Played for Hertfordshire U17 2005-06, Northamptonshire Cricket Board U19s 2007-08, Northamptonshire Second XI 2006-08

MURTAGH, C. P. — Surrey

Name: Christopher (Chris) Paul Murtagh
Role: Right-hand bat
Born: 14 October 1984, Lambeth, London
Height: 5ft 11in **Weight:** 11st 9lbs
Nickname: Murts, Baby, Brow
County debut: 2005 (one-day)
County cap: 2008
Parents: Dominic and Elizabeth
Marital status: Single
Family links with cricket: Elder brother Tim played for Surrey and is now with Middlesex; Uncle Andy (A. J. Murtagh) played for Hampshire
Education: John Fisher, Purley, Surrey; Loughborough University
Qualifications: 10 GCSEs, 2 A-levels, BSc (Hons) Sport and Exercise Science
Off-season: 'Playing for Parramatta in Sydney and training for the new season.'

Overseas tours: Surrey U19 to Sri Lanka 2002, to Perth 2004
Overseas teams played for: Parramatta, Sydney 2004 –
Cricket superstitions: 'Left pad on first'
Cricketers particularly admired: Sachin Tendulkar, Andrew Flintoff, Curtly Ambrose
Other sports played: Rugby, football, golf
Other sports followed: Football (Liverpool FC)
Relaxations: 'Playing golf; watching sport'
Extras: Played for Surrey age groups and attended Surrey Academy. Made 2nd XI Championship debut 2002. Played for Loughborough UCCE 2005, 2006, 2007, scoring century (107) v Yorkshire at Headingley 2007
Best batting: 107 LUCCE v Yorkshire, Headingley 2007

2008 Season

	M	Inn	NO	Runs	HS	Avg	100	50	Ct	St	Balls	Runs	Wkts	Avg	BB	5I	10M
Test																	
FC	4	5	0	28	12	5.60	-	-	2	-	0	0	0		-	-	-
ODI																	
List A	2	1	0	74	74	74.00	-	1	1	-	0	0	0		-	-	
20/20 Int																	
20/20	2	2	0	0	0	0.00	-	-	4	-	0	0	0		-	-	

Career Performances

	M	Inn	NO	Runs	HS	Avg	100	50	Ct	St	Balls	Runs	Wkts	Avg	BB	5I	10M
Test																	
FC	12	18	2	287	107	17.93	1	-	7	-	6	8	0		-	-	-
ODI																	
List A	4	3	2	108	74	108.00	-	1	3	-	0	0	0		-	-	
20/20 Int																	
20/20	2	2	0	0	0	0.00	-	-	4	-	0	0	0		-	-	

61. Who dismissed Don Bradman for a duck in Bradman's last Test innings?

MURTAGH, T. J. Middlesex

Name: Timothy (Tim) James Murtagh
Role: Left-hand bat, right-arm fast-medium bowler
Born: 2 August 1981, Lambeth, London
Height: 6ft 2in **Weight:** 12st
County debut: 2000 (one-day, Surrey), 2001 (first-class, Surrey), 2007 (Middlesex)
Place in batting averages: 211th av. 18.27 (2007 231st av. 17.80)
Place in bowling averages: 50th av. 27.09 (2007 32nd av. 24.85)
Parents: Dominic and Elizabeth
Marital status: Single
Family links with cricket: Younger brother Chris plays for Surrey; Uncle Andy (A. J. Murtagh) played for Hampshire
Education: John Fisher, Purley, Surrey; St Mary's University, Twickenham
Qualifications: 10 GCSEs, 2 A-levels

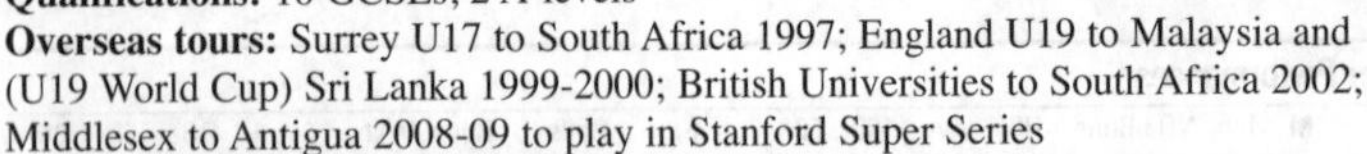

Overseas tours: Surrey U17 to South Africa 1997; England U19 to Malaysia and (U19 World Cup) Sri Lanka 1999-2000; British Universities to South Africa 2002; Middlesex to Antigua 2008-09 to play in Stanford Super Series
Overseas teams played for: Eastern Suburbs, Sydney 2006-07
Cricketers particularly admired: Darren Gough, Glenn McGrath
Other sports played: Rugby (was captain of John Fisher 2nd XV), skiing ('in the past')
Other sports followed: Football (Liverpool FC), rugby
Relaxations: Playing golf, watching sport, films, reading
Extras: Represented British Universities 2000, 2001, 2002 and 2003. Represented England U19 2000. NBC Denis Compton Award for the most promising young Surrey player 2001. Took 6-24 v Middlesex at Lord's 2005, the best return in the history of the Twenty20 Cup
Best batting: 74* Surrey v Middlesex, The Oval 2004
74* Surrey v Warwickshire, Croydon 2005
Best bowling: 7-95 Middlesex v Glamorgan, Lord's 2008

2008 Season

	M	Inn	NO	Runs	HS	Avg	100	50	Ct	St	Balls	Runs	Wkts	Avg	BB	5I	10M
Test																	
FC	17	25	3	402	49	18.27	-	-	4	-	3035	1734	64	27.09	7-95	3	1
ODI																	
List A	13	11	4	122	35 *	17.42	-	-	3	-	621	539	20	26.95	4-29	-	
20/20 Int																	
20/20	13	6	3	22	10 *	7.33	-	-	2	-	300	400	20	20.00	3-15	-	

Career Performances

	M	Inn	NO	Runs	HS	Avg	100	50	Ct	St	Balls	Runs	Wkts	Avg	BB	5I	10M
Test																	
FC	69	94	26	1602	74 *	23.55	-	6	23	-	9485	5596	182	30.74	7-95	7	1
ODI																	
List A	95	65	23	550	35 *	13.09	-	-	27	-	4358	3746	139	26.94	4-14	-	
20/20 Int																	
20/20	48	24	9	159	40 *	10.60	-	-	7	-	973	1387	59	23.50	6-24	1	

MURTAZA HUSSAIN Surrey

Name: Murtaza Hussain
Role: Right-hand bat, right-arm off-break bowler
Born: 20 December 1974, Bahawalpur, Pakistan
Height: 5ft 11in **Weight:** 12st 12lbs
Nickname: Murty
County debut: 2007
Place in bowling averages: 38th av. 25.63
Parents: Sakina Begum and Mohammed Mukhtiar Hussain
Wife and date of marriage: Christine, 29 July 1999
Education: Abbassia High School, Bahawalpul
Qualifications: ECB level 2 coaching
Off-season: Playing first-class cricket in Pakistan
Overseas teams played for: Several in Pakistan, including Bahawalpur 1990-91 – 1997-98, 2001-02, Khan Research Laboratories 1997-98 – 1999-2000, Pakistan Customs 2004-05 – , Multan Tigers 2005-06

Career highlights to date: 'Taking 6 wickets for Surrey against Lancashire in the 2007 championship, helping us to win the game.'
Cricket moments to forget: 'Breaking my thumb when playing for Walsall CC in 2001. It was broken in three places, and it was on my bowling hand. Thankfully, the expertise of the doctors at Lister hospital helped me to make a full recovery and continue with my cricketing career.'
Cricketers particularly admired: Imran Khan, Wasim Akram
Young players to look out for: Chris Jordan, „Jade Dernbach, Matthew Spriegel
Other sports followed: Football (Manchester United)
Favourite band: 'Indian music in general'
Relaxations: Watching Hindi films, listening to music
Extras: Prior to obtaining British Citizenship in 2007, played club cricket in the UK as an overseas player for Vickers 1998-99, Stevenage 2000, 2002, Walsall 2001, Pyrford 2003, 2004, Byfleet 2005, Welwyn Garden City 2006 and Londonderry 2007. In Pakistani domestic cricket, held the record for the number of first-class wickets taken in a season (105) from 1995-96 until 1998-99. Holds the recod for the highest number of wickets taken in the Qaid-i-Azam trophy (72 wickets in 10 matches, 1995-96). Represented Pakistan U19 1991-92. Played for Combined XI v New Zealanders 1996-97, Dr Abdul Qadeer Khan's XI v West Indians 1997-98 and Pakistan A v India A at Karachi 1997-98. Has played for Derbyshire 2nd XI and Middlesex 2nd XI. Now holds a British passport and is no longer considered an overseas player
Best batting: 117 Pakistan Customs v Attock, Karachi (UBL) 2006-07
Best bowling: 9-54 Bahawalpur v Islamabad, Bahawalpur 1995-96

2008 Season

	M	Inn	NO	Runs	HS	Avg	100	50	Ct	St	Balls	Runs	Wkts	Avg	BB	5I	10M
Test																	
FC	4	7	2	83	56	16.60	-	1	1	-	739	365	7	52.14	3-82	-	-
ODI																	
List A	2	2	2	3	2*	-	-	-	-	96	118	0		-	-		
20/20 Int																	
20/20																	

Career Performances

	M	Inn	NO	Runs	HS	Avg	100	50	Ct	St	Balls	Runs	Wkts	Avg	BB	5I	10M
Test																	
FC	138	198	39	3432	117	21.58	1	12	69	-	31520	13137	544	24.14	9-54	36	7
ODI																	
List A	106	71	18	774	85	14.60	-	1	34	-	4815	3371	131	25.73	5-18	1	
20/20 Int																	
20/20																	

MUSHTAQ AHMED Sussex

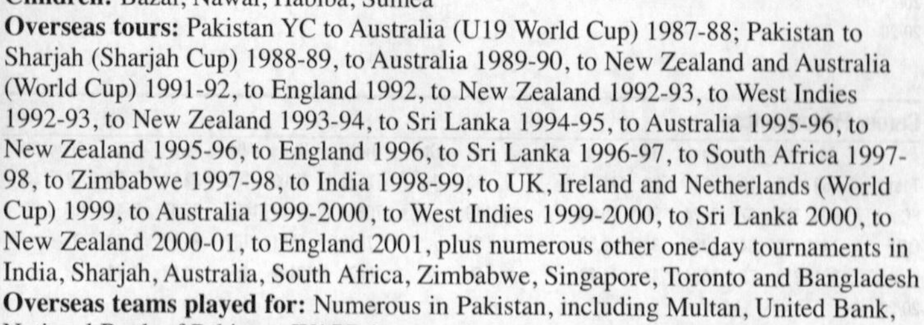

Name: Mushtaq Ahmed
Role: Right-hand bat, leg-spin bowler
Born: 28 June 1970, Sahiwal, Pakistan
Height: 5ft 4in
Nickname: Mushie
County debut: 1993 (Somerset), 2002 (Surrey), 2003 (Sussex)
County cap: 1993 (Somerset), 2003 (Sussex)
Test debut: 1989-90
ODI debut: 1988-89
50 wickets in a season: 6
100 wickets in a season: 2
Place in batting averages: (2007 267th av. 12.14)
Place in bowling averages: 124th av. 40.89 (2007 39th av. 25.66)
Wife and date of marriage: Uzma, 18 December 1994
Children: Bazal, Nawal, Habiba, Sumea
Overseas tours: Pakistan YC to Australia (U19 World Cup) 1987-88; Pakistan to Sharjah (Sharjah Cup) 1988-89, to Australia 1989-90, to New Zealand and Australia (World Cup) 1991-92, to England 1992, to New Zealand 1992-93, to West Indies 1992-93, to New Zealand 1993-94, to Sri Lanka 1994-95, to Australia 1995-96, to New Zealand 1995-96, to England 1996, to Sri Lanka 1996-97, to South Africa 1997-98, to Zimbabwe 1997-98, to India 1998-99, to UK, Ireland and Netherlands (World Cup) 1999, to Australia 1999-2000, to West Indies 1999-2000, to Sri Lanka 2000, to New Zealand 2000-01, to England 2001, plus numerous other one-day tournaments in India, Sharjah, Australia, South Africa, Zimbabwe, Singapore, Toronto and Bangladesh
Overseas teams played for: Numerous in Pakistan, including Multan, United Bank, National Bank of Pakistan, WAPDA
Career highlights to date: 'Winning the 1992 cricket World Cup final'
Cricket moments to forget: 'Losing the 1996 World Cup quarter-final to India at Bangalore'
Cricket superstitions: 'None'
Other sports followed: Hockey, football (Brazil)
Relaxations: 'Spending time with family, prayer'
Extras: Somerset's overseas player 1993-95 and 1997-98; Player of the Year 1993. Had match figures of 9-198 and 9-186 in successive Tests (Man of the Match in the latter) v Australia 1995-96, following up with 10-171 in next Test v New Zealand eight days later, winning Man of the Match award. His other international awards include Man of the [Test] Series v England 1996 and v South Africa 1997-98. One of *Wisden*'s

Five Cricketers of the Year 1997. Was Surrey's overseas player during August 2002; an overseas player with Sussex since 2003. Took 103 Championship wickets (av. 24.65) 2003. Sussex Player of the Year 2003, 2006. PCA Player of the Year 2003. Took 1000th first-class wicket (Martin Bicknell) v Surrey at The Oval 2004. Took 9-48 (13-108 in the match) v Nottinghamshire at Trent Bridge 2006 to finish the season with 102 Championship wickets (av. 19.91). Took 7-132 (13-225 in the match) v Worcestershire at Hove 2007 to finish the season with 90 Championship wickets (av. 25.66) and as the competition's leading wicket-taker for the fifth consecutive season. Joined the ICL team Lahore Badshahs in February 2008. Injury forced him to announce his retirement from county cricket in August 2008. He was immediately approached by the ECB to become England's bowling coach, and will be fulfilling the same role with Sussex in 2009

Best batting: 90* Sussex v Kent, Hove 2005

Best bowling: 9-48 Sussex v Nottinghamshire, Trent Bridge 2006

2008 Season

	M	Inn	NO	Runs	HS	Avg	100	50	Ct	St	Balls	Runs	Wkts	Avg	BB	5I	10M
Test																	
FC	6	10	1	65	20	7.22	-	-	1	-	1357	777	19	40.89	5-83	1	-
ODI																	
List A	1	0	0	0	0		-	-	-	-	60	55	0		-	-	
20/20 Int																	
20/20																	

Career Performances

	M	Inn	NO	Runs	HS	Avg	100	50	Ct	St	Balls	Runs	Wkts	Avg	BB	5I	10M
Test	52	72	16	656	59	11.71	-	2	23	-	12532	6100	185	32.97	7-56	10	3
FC	309	389	57	5124	90 *	15.43	-	20	119	-	70859	36127	1407	25.67	9-48	104	32
ODI	144	76	34	399	34 *	9.50	-	-	30	-	7543	5361	161	33.29	5-36	1	
List A	381	219	75	1624	41	11.27	-	-	59	-	18973	13182	461	28.59	7-24	4	
20/20 Int																	
20/20	29	10	2	55	20 *	6.87	-	-	3	-	591	580	42	13.80	5-11	1	

62. When did the original Ashes urn last visit Australia?

MUSTARD, P. Durham

Name: Philip (Phil) Mustard
Role: Left-hand bat, wicket-keeper
Born: 8 October 1982, Sunderland
Height: 5ft 11in **Weight:** 13st 3lbs
Nickname: Colonel
County debut: 2002
ODI debut: 2007-08
50 dismissals in a season: 2
Place in batting averages: 173rd av. 25.62 (2006 123rd av. 32.64)
Parents: Maureen
Marital status: Single
Children: Haydon Samuel, 12 July 2006
Education: Usworth Comprehensive, Washington, Tyne and Wear
Overseas tours: England to Sri Lanka 2007-08, to New Zealand 2007-08
Overseas teams played for: Bulleen, Melbourne 2002; Glenorchy, Tasmania 2003; Bankstown, Sydney 2004; Tea Tree Gully, South Australia

Career highlights to date: 'First century 2006. Playing for England U19'
Cricket moments to forget: 'First ball against Jimmy Anderson on debut in C&G' *(Caught Flintoff, bowled Anderson)*
Cricketers particularly admired: Alec Stewart
Young players to look out for: Ben Harmison
Other sports played: 'Golf, football' (he spent time as a schoolboy player with both Middlesbrough and Manchester United, and is still an enthusiastic participant)
Other sports followed: Football (Newcastle)
Favourite band: Bee Gees
Relaxations: 'Socialising'
Extras: Scored 77-ball 75 on first-class debut v Sri Lankans at Riverside 2002. Represented England U19 2002. Scored maiden first-class century (130) v Kent at Canterbury 2006, in the process sharing with Gordon Muchall (219) in a new Durham record partnership for the sixth wicket (249). Made 50 (54) dismissals in a season for the first time and also scored 816 runs in first-class cricket 2006. Scored 21-ball fifty (ending with 40-ball 78) v Leicestershire at Riverside in the Pro40 2007, setting a new Durham record for fastest one-day fifty. Made ODI debut in the first ODI v Sri Lanka in Dambulla 2007-08. Top of Durham's Twenty20 batting averages in 2008
Best batting: 130 Durham v Kent, Canterbury 2006

2008 Season

	M	Inn	NO	Runs	HS	Avg	100	50	Ct	St	Balls	Runs	Wkts	Avg	BB	5I	10M
Test																	
FC	16	24	1	483	92	21.00	-	4	56	2	0	0	0		-	-	-
ODI																	
List A	16	16	0	367	82	22.93	-	2	18	5	0	0	0		-	-	
20/20 Int																	
20/20	11	11	0	303	61	27.54	-	1	7	2	0	0	0		-	-	

Career Performances

	M	Inn	NO	Runs	HS	Avg	100	50	Ct	St	Balls	Runs	Wkts	Avg	BB	5I	10M
Test																	
FC	83	134	7	3329	130	26.21	2	17	277	12	0	0	0		-	-	-
ODI	10	10	0	233	83	23.30	-	1	9	2	0	0	0		-	-	
List A	102	88	6	2156	108	26.29	1	12	108	21	0	0	0		-	-	
20/20 Int	2	2	0	60	40	30.00	-	-	-	-	0	0	0		-	-	
20/20	42	42	2	964	67 *	24.10	-	5	14	13	0	0	0		-	-	

NAIK, J. K. H. Leicestershire

Name: Jigar Kumar Hakumatrai Naik
Role: Right-hand bat, right-arm off-break bowler
Born: 10 August 1984, Leicester
Height: 6ft 2in **Weight:** 14st
Nickname: Jigs, Jiggy, Jigsy
County debut: 2006
Parents: Hakumatrai and Daxa
Marital status: Single
Education: Rushey Mead; Gateway College; Nottingham Trent University; Loughborough University
Qualifications: BSc (Hons) Multimedia Technology, MSc Computer Science
Career outside cricket: Technical systems engineer
Overseas tours: Leicestershire to India and Sri Lanka 2007
Career highlights to date: 'Making my Championship and Pro40 debuts'
Cricketers particularly admired: Sachin Tendulkar, Erapalli Prasanna
Other sports played: Golf, tennis, football

Other sports followed: Tennis, football (Liverpool FC)
Favourite band: Nickelback
Relaxations: 'Music, movies, going to the gym'
Extras: Played for Leicestershire Board XI in the 2003 C&G. Attended World Cricket Academy 2007. Played for Loughborough UCCE 2007. First Leicester-born player of Asian origin to represent the county
Opinions on cricket: 'The new ruling of having only one overseas player can only be better for English cricket, so long as the overseas player has enough experience and talent at the highest level to provide input to the club and be helpful to the younger members of the squad.'
Best batting: 15 LUCCE v Yorkshire, Headingley 2007
Best bowling: 3-70 Leicestershire v Bangladesh A, Leicester 2008

2008 Season

	M	Inn	NO	Runs	HS	Avg	100	50	Ct	St	Balls	Runs	Wkts	Avg	BB	5I	10M
Test																	
FC	1	0	0	0	0		-	-	1	-	150	70	3	23.33	3-70	-	-
ODI																	
List A	2	2	1	14	13	14.00	-	-	-	-	60	55	1	55.00	1-38	-	
20/20 Int																	
20/20	5	3	2	6	3 *	6.00	-	-	1	-	72	100	1	100.00	1-18	-	

Career Performances

	M	Inn	NO	Runs	HS	Avg	100	50	Ct	St	Balls	Runs	Wkts	Avg	BB	5I	10M
Test																	
FC	7	7	3	60	15	15.00	-	-	5	-	732	514	7	73.42	3-70	-	-
ODI																	
List A	6	3	1	15	13	7.50	-	-	1	-	260	207	7	29.57	3-24	-	
20/20 Int																	
20/20	5	3	2	6	3 *	6.00	-	-	1	-	72	100	1	100.00	1-18	-	

NAPIER, G. R. Essex

Name: Graham Richard Napier
Role: Right-hand bat, right-arm fast-medium bowler; all-rounder
Born: 6 January 1980, Colchester
Height: 5ft 9in **Weight:** 14st 2lbs
Nickname: George, Napes
County debut: 1997
Place in batting averages: 197th av. 20.50 (2007 47th av. 45.28)
Place in bowling averages: 37th av. 25.77 (2007 144th av. 58.90)
Parents: Roger and Carol
Marital status: Single
Family links with cricket: Father played for Palmers Boys School 1st XI (1965-68), Essex Police divisional teams, and Harwich Immigration CC
Education: Gilberd School, Colchester
Qualifications: City & Guilds Digital Imaging, NCA coaching award
Career outside cricket: Sports photography
Off-season: 'Going back to Wellington to play for Wellington Firebirds and Hutt District CC'
Overseas tours: England U17 to Bermuda (International Youth Tournament) 1997; England U19 to South Africa (including U19 World Cup) 1997-98; England A to Malaysia and India 2003-04; England VI to Hong Kong 2004; MCC to Namibia and Uganda 2004-05
Overseas teams played for: Campbelltown CC, Sydney 2000-01; North Perth, Western Australia 2001-02; Upper Valley CC, Wellington, New Zealand 2007-08; Wellington Firebirds, New Zealand 2008-09; Hutt District CC, New Zealand 2008-09
Career highlights to date: 'Testing myself against the world's best and scoring some runs. Winning the Friends Provident Trophy. Scoring 152*, including 16 sixes, in Twenty20' [Essex v Sussex, Chelmsford, 2008 - the 16 sixes set a new Twenty20 world record for a single innings]
Cricket moments to forget: 'Being run out in a Lord's final'
Young players to look out for: Jake Mickleburgh
Other sports followed: Golf
Favourite band: Elton John
Relaxations: 'Fly fishing (only a beginner)'
Extras: Represented England U19 1999. Man of the Match award for Essex Board XI v Lancashire Board XI in the NatWest 2000. ECB National Academy 2003-04. Included in preliminary England one-day squad of 30 for ICC Champions Trophy

2004. Took part in 'highest game of cricket ever played' at Everest base camp in 2007 in aid of the PCA's Benevolent Fund.
Opinions on cricket: 'A balance needs to be found between Twenty20, 50-over and Test cricket to ensure that all three formats have a place in the professional game.'
Best batting: 125 Essex v Nottinghamshire, Chelmsford 2007
Best bowling: 6-103 Essex v Glamorgan, Southend 2008
Stop press: Signed to play in IPL 2009 by Mumbai Indians

2008 Season

	M	Inn	NO	Runs	HS	Avg	100	50	Ct	St	Balls	Runs	Wkts	Avg	BB	5I	10M
Test																	
FC	7	8	0	164	76	20.50	-	1	-	-	1037	567	22	25.77	6-103	1	-
ODI																	
List A	15	10	1	163	61	18.11	-	1	1	-	577	459	19	24.15	3-22	-	
20/20 Int																	
20/20	12	11	1	326	152 *	32.60	1	-	3	-	241	282	16	17.62	4-10	-	

Career Performances

	M	Inn	NO	Runs	HS	Avg	100	50	Ct	St	Balls	Runs	Wkts	Avg	BB	5I	10M
Test																	
FC	85	116	21	2910	125	30.63	3	18	34	-	10236	6555	164	39.96	6-103	3	-
ODI																	
List A	158	119	17	1701	79	16.67	-	8	36	-	4665	3920	158	24.81	6-29	1	
20/20 Int																	
20/20	39	26	3	515	152 *	22.39	1	-	6	-	806	975	45	21.66	4-10	-	

63. The 1902 Ashes tour of England, which Australia won 2-1, is generally regarded as having been one of the very best series. Who were the two team captains?

NASH, C. D. Sussex

Name: Christopher (Chris) David Nash
Role: Right-hand bat, right-arm off-spin bowler
Born: 19 May 1983, Cuckfield
Height: 5ft 11½in **Weight:** 13st
Nickname: Nashy, Nashdog, Hero, Beaut, Pointless
County debut: 2002
County cap: 2008
Place in batting averages: 76th av. 37.69 (2007 157th av. 27.83)
Parents: Nick and Jane
Marital status: Single ('girlfriend, Amy')
Family links with cricket: 'Brother played for Sussex 2nd XI and Horsham First XI'
Education: Tanbridge House; Collyers Sixth Form College; Loughborough University
Qualifications: 11 GCSEs, 4 A-levels, BSc (Hons) in Sports Science, Level II squash and cricket coaching
Career outside cricket: 'Traveller, after-dinner speaker'
Off-season: 'Playing for Richmond CC in Melbourne'
Overseas tours: England U17 to Northern Ireland (ECC Colts Festival) 1999; Sussex U19 to Cape Town 1999; Horsham CC to Barbados 2005; Sussex to Dubai 2006-07
Overseas teams played for: Subiaco Marist, Perth 2004-05, 2005-06; Cornwall CC, Auckland 2007-08; Richmond CC, Melbourne 2008-09
Career highlights to date: 'Winning the Championship 2006. First championship century at Old Trafford, 2008.'
Cricket moments to forget: 'Every time I come on to bowl, I get a barrage of abuse from my team-mates (Lewry, Yardy, Hodd, Jenkins and everyone else). Getting a pair at Taunton, much to the amusement of the Swann brothers.'
Cricketers particularly admired: Murray Goodwin, Mushtaq Ahmed, Dr John Dew
Young players to look out for: Mark Nash, Philip Hudson, Ryan Leverton, Richard Hawkes, Alex Harding
Other sports played: Squash (county and national U11-15), football (Sussex CCC FC, PureTown FC, Horsham YMCA), tennis (county)
Other sports followed: Football (Brighton & Hove Albion, Horsham, PureTown)
Favourite band: Kings of Leon
Extras: 'Smallest ears in Sussex squad.' Represented England U15, U17, U18, U19, captaining at U17 and U18 levels. Sussex League Young Player of the Year 2001, 2003. Played for Loughborough UCCE 2002, 2003, 2004. Represented British Universities 2004. Man of the Match in the 2nd XI Trophy final v Nottinghamshire at

Horsham 2005 (2-21/72*). Scored 82 v Warwickshire in the Pro40 at Hove 2006, winning Man of the Match award. Sussex Most Improved Player (Umer Rashid Memorial Award) 2006. Signed a new contract with Sussex in October 2008.
Opinions on cricket: 'Mirror international cricket in the domestic game. The game is in great shape. Overseas players play a key role, if they are committed to the county, in helping to produce future England players'
Best batting: 108 Sussex v Lancashire, Old Trafford 2008
Best bowling: 3-7 Sussex v Surrey, The Oval 2008

2008 Season

	M	Inn	NO	Runs	HS	Avg	100	50	Ct	St	Balls	Runs	Wkts	Avg	BB	5I	10M
Test																	
FC	17	30	4	980	108	37.69	2	5	2	-	141	63	3	21.00	3-7	-	-
ODI																	
List A	9	8	0	156	34	19.50	-	-	1	-	71	51	4	12.75	3-8		
20/20 Int																	
20/20	8	8	0	101	52	12.62	-	1	3	-	0	0	0		-	-	

Career Performances

	M	Inn	NO	Runs	HS	Avg	100	50	Ct	St	Balls	Runs	Wkts	Avg	BB	5I	10M
Test																	
FC	47	79	6	2362	108	32.35	2	17	17	-	914	647	12	53.91	3-7	-	
ODI																	
List A	29	27	0	618	82	22.88	-	3	4	-	221	202	6	33.66	3-8	-	
20/20 Int																	
20/20	20	20	2	288	52	16.00	-	1	8	-	0	0	0				

64. Which grey-haired batsman was voted BBC Sports Personality of the Year in 1975, after he had scored 250 runs in three Tests against Australia to help England draw the series?

NASH, D. C. Middlesex

Name: David Charles Nash
Role: Right-hand bat, wicket-keeper
Born: 19 January 1978, Chertsey, Surrey
Height: 5ft 7in **Weight:** 11st 5lbs
Nickname: Nashy, Knocker
County debut: 1995 (one-day), 1997 (first-class)
County cap: 1999
Benefit: 2007
50 dismissals in a season: 1
Place in batting averages: (2007 11th av. 60.85)
Parents: David and Christine
Marital status: Single
Family links with cricket: 'Father played club cricket; brother plays now and again for Ashford CC; mother is avid watcher and tea lady'
Education: Sunbury Manor; Malvern College
Qualifications: 9 O-levels, 1 A-level, Levels 1 and 2 cricket coaching, qualified football referee
Career outside cricket: Qualified cricket coach
Overseas tours: England U15 to South Africa 1993; British Airways Youth Team to West Indies 1993-94; England U19 to Zimbabwe 1995-96, to Pakistan 1996-97; England A to Kenya and Sri Lanka 1997-98
Overseas teams played for: Fremantle, Perth 2000-01, 2002-03
Career highlights to date: 'Touring with England A and scoring first hundred for Middlesex at Lord's v Somerset'
Cricket moments to forget: 'All golden ducks'
Cricket superstitions: 'Too many to mention'
Cricketers particularly admired: Angus Fraser
Other sports played: Rugby, football ('played for Millwall U15 and my district side'), 'and most other sports'
Other sports followed: Rugby (London Irish), football (Chelsea)
Relaxations: 'Listening to music, watching sport and socialising with friends'
Extras: Represented Middlesex at all ages. Played for England U14, U15, U17 and U19. Once took six wickets in six balls, aged 11 – 'when I could bowl!' Seaxe Young Player of the Year 1993
Best batting: 114 Middlesex v Somerset, Lord's 1998
Best bowling: 1-8 Middlesex v Essex, Chelmsford 1997

2008 Season

	M	Inn	NO	Runs	HS	Avg	100	50	Ct	St	Balls	Runs	Wkts	Avg	BB	5I	10M
Test																	
FC	4	7	3	351	100 *	87.75	1	3	9	-	0	0	0	-	-	-	-
ODI																	
List A																	
20/20 Int																	
20/20																	

Career Performances

	M	Inn	NO	Runs	HS	Avg	100	50	Ct	St	Balls	Runs	Wkts	Avg	BB	5I	10M
Test																	
FC	135	195	43	5532	114	36.39	11	27	281	23	90	105	2	52.50	1-8	-	-
ODI																	
List A	120	89	18	1480	67	20.84	-	6	91	18	0	0	0	-	-		
20/20 Int																	
20/20																	

NAVED-UL-HASAN Yorkshire

Name: Rana Naved-ul-Hasan
Role: Right-hand bat, right-arm fast bowler
Born: 28 February 1978, Sheikhupura City, Pakistan
Height: 5ft 11in **Weight:** 12st 12lbs
County debut: 2005 (Sussex), 2008 (Yorkshire)
County cap: 2005 (Sussex)
Test debut: 2004-05
ODI debut: 2002-03
Twenty20 Int debut: 2006
50 wickets in a season: 2
Place in batting averages: 245th av. 14.76 (2006 232nd av. 16.75)
Place in bowling averages: 56th av. 29.08 (2006 2nd av. 16.71)
Parents: Rana Mehdi Hassan Khan
Wife and date of marriage: Najma Naveed, 29 April 1997
Children: Aqsa, Rimsha, Naima, Maha

Education: Government High School, Sheikhupura
Career outside cricket: 'With family'
Overseas tours: Pakistan U19 to New Zealand 1994-95; Pakistan to Sharjah (Cherry Blossom Sharjah Cup) 2002-03, to England (ICC Champions Trophy) 2004, to Australia 2004-05, to India 2004-05, to West Indies 2004-05, to Sri Lanka 2005-06, to UAE (DLF Cup) 2006, to England 2006, to India (ICC Champions Trophy) 2006-07, to South Africa 2006-07, to West Indies (World Cup) 2006-07, plus other one-day matches in England and India
Overseas teams played for: Lahore Division 1999-2000; Pakistan Customs 2000-01; Sheikhupura 2000-01 – 2001-02; Allied Bank 2001-02; WAPDA 2002-03 – 2003-04, 2006-07; Sialkot/Sialkot Stallions 2003-04 – 2006-07; Lahore Badshahs (ICL) 2008
Cricket moments to forget: 'When we lost the World Cup match against Ireland'
Cricketers particularly admired: Brian Lara
Young players to look out for: Adil Rashid
Other sports played: Hockey
Other sports followed: Football (Manchester United)
Favourite band: 'Any music'
Relaxations: 'Music'
Extras: Played for Herefordshire in the 2003 C&G competition. Was selected in the World One-Day Team of the Year at the ICC Awards 2005. Has won several match and series awards, including Player of the [ODI] Series v India 2004-05 and Player of the [ODI] Series v West Indies 2006-07. An overseas player with Sussex 2005-07; joined Yorkshire as an overseas player for 2008. Played for a Pakistan XI against a World XI, November 2008
Best batting: 139 Sussex v Middlesex, Lord's 2005
Best bowling: 7-49 Sheikhupura v Sialkot, Muridke 2001-02

2008 Season

	M	Inn	NO	Runs	HS	Avg	100	50	Ct	St	Balls	Runs	Wkts	Avg	BB	5I	10M
Test																	
FC	7	10	3	114	22	16.28	-	-	3	-	919	606	16	37.87	4-86	-	-
ODI																	
List A	9	8	0	212	74	26.50	-	2	-	-	348	307	14	21.92	2-26	-	
20/20 Int																	
20/20																	

Career Performances

	M	Inn	NO	Runs	HS	Avg	100	50	Ct	St	Balls	Runs	Wkts	Avg	BB	5I	10M
Test	9	15	3	239	42 *	19.91	-	-	3	-	1565	1044	18	58.00	3-30	-	-
FC	108	153	18	3058	139	22.65	3	9	54	-	20042	11357	470	24.16	7-49	26	4
ODI	62	41	14	359	29	13.29	-	-	13	-	2854	2630	95	27.68	6-27	1	
List A	141	105	29	1551	74	20.40	-	7	37	-	6570	5662	221	25.61	6-27	3	
20/20 Int	2	1	1	17	17 *		-	-	1	-	42	55	1	55.00	1-26	-	
20/20	28	18	10	258	40 *	32.25	-	-	16	-	572	661	24	27.54	3-9	-	

NEEDHAM, J. Derbyshire

Name: Jake Needham
Role: Right-hand bat, right-arm off-spin bowler; all-rounder
Born: 30 September 1986, Portsmouth, Hampshire
Height: 6ft 1in **Weight:** 11st 7lbs
County debut: 2005
Extras: Man of the Match playing for Ockbrook & Borrowash v Kibworth in the Cockspur Cup final at Lord's 2004 (51/4-27). Derbyshire Academy Player of the Year 2005. Represented England U19 2006. Is committed to Derbyshire until the end of the 2009 season
Best batting: 48 Derbyshire v Nottinghamshire, Chesterfield 2007
Best bowling: 6-49 Derbyshire v Leicestershire, Grace Road 2008

2008 Season

	M	Inn	NO	Runs	HS	Avg	100	50	Ct	St	Balls	Runs	Wkts	Avg	BB	5I	10M
Test																	
FC	8	14	6	168	36	21.00	-	-	5	-	973	503	19	26.47	6-49	1	-
ODI																	
List A	6	4	3	26	12 *	26.00	-	-	2	-	151	145	4	36.25	2-42	-	
20/20 Int																	
20/20	10	4	2	16	7 *	8.00	-	-	3	-	126	172	4	43.00	1-4	-	

Career Performances

	M	Inn	NO	Runs	HS	Avg	100	50	Ct	St	Balls	Runs	Wkts	Avg	BB	5I	10M
Test																	
FC	14	24	9	329	48	21.93	-	-	7	-	1653	915	28	32.67	6-49	1	-
ODI																	
List A	28	21	10	203	42	18.45	-	-	8	-	795	725	12	60.41	2-36	-	
20/20 Int																	
20/20	13	5	3	16	7 *	8.00	-	-	3	-	135	191	4	47.75	1-4	-	

NEL, A. Essex

Name: Andre Nel
Role: Right-hand bat, right-arm fast-medium bowler
Born: 15 July 1977, Germiston, Gauteng, South Africa
County debut: 2003 (Northants), 2005 (Essex)
County cap: 2003 (Northants)
Test debut: 2001-02
ODI debut: 2000-01
Twenty20 Int debut: 2005-06
Place in bowling averages: 93rd av. 32.84 (2007 106th av. 39.10)
Education: Hoërskool Dr E.G. Jansen, Boksburg
Overseas tours: South Africa Academy to Ireland and Scotland 1999; South Africa A to Zimbabwe 2002-03, to Australia 2002-03, to Zimbabwe 2007-08; South Africa to West Indies 2000-01, to Zimbabwe 2001-02, to England 2003 (NatWest Series), to Pakistan 2003-04, to New Zealand 2003-04, to West Indies 2004-05, to India (one-day series) 2005-06, to Australia 2005-06, to Sri Lanka 2006, to India (ICC Champions Trophy) 2006-07, to West Indies (World Cup) 2006-07, to Ireland (one-day series v India) 2007, to Pakistan 2007-08, to England 2008
Overseas teams played for: Easterns 1996-97 – 2005-06; Titans 2003-04 –
Extras: Was an overseas player with Northamptonshire 2003. One of *South African Cricket Annual*'s five Cricketers of the Year 2004, 2005. His match awards include Man of the Match in the fourth ODI v Pakistan at Rawalpindi 2003-04 (4-39) and in the third Test v West Indies in Barbados 2004-05 (4-56/6-32). Was an overseas player with Essex during the 2005 season as a locum for André Adams, taking a wicket (Matthew Wood) with his first ball for the county, v Somerset at Colchester; returned for part of the 2007 season. Represented South Africa in the Twenty20 World Championship 2007-08. Released by Essex at the end of the 2008 season
Best batting: 56 South Africa v Bangladesh A, Worcester 2008
Best bowling: 6-25 Easterns v Gauteng, Johannesburg 2001-02

2008 Season

	M	Inn	NO	Runs	HS	Avg	100	50	Ct	St	Balls	Runs	Wkts	Avg	BB	5I	10M
Test	2	3	1	7	4	3.50	-	-	-	-	368	203	4	50.75	3-47	-	-
FC	7	7	3	68	56	17.00	-	1	1	-	1328	624	19	32.84	3-25	-	-
ODI	4	2	0	23	13	11.50	-	-	-	-	89	78	0		-	-	
List A	10	4	1	34	13	11.33	-	-	1	-	397	333	7	47.57	2-40	-	
20/20 Int																	
20/20																	

Career Performances

	M	Inn	NO	Runs	HS	Avg	100	50	Ct	St	Balls	Runs	Wkts	Avg	BB	5I	10M
Test	36	42	8	337	34	9.91	-	-	16	-	7630	3919	123	31.86	6-32	3	1
FC	107	120	37	1127	56	13.57	-	1	39	-	21215	9928	368	26.97	6-25	12	1
ODI	79	22	12	127	30 *	12.70	-	-	21	-	3801	2935	106	27.68	5-45	1	
List A	193	74	41	375	30 *	11.36	-	-	46	-	9494	6774	267	25.37	6-27	4	
20/20 Int	2	1	1	0	0 *		-	-	1	-	48	42	2	21.00	2-19	-	
20/20	19	10	1	51	12	5.66	-	-	6	-	420	418	18	23.22	2-13	-	

NELSON, M. A. G. Northamptonshire

Name: Mark Anthony George Nelson
Role: Left-hand bat, right-arm fast-medium bowler
Born: 24 September 1986, Milton Keynes
Height: 5ft 11in **Weight:** 11st 7lbs
Nickname: Nelo, Nelly
County debut: 2006 (one-day), 2007 (first-class)
Parents: George and Janet
Marital status: Single
Education: Lord Grey School, Milton Keynes; Stowe School
Qualifications: 3 A-levels
Overseas tours: England U19 to Sri Lanka (U19 World Cup) 2005-06
Cricket moments to forget: 'Batting for U19, the ball hit my bat and a piece of bat broke off, knocked on to a stump and I was declared out'
Cricket superstitions: 'Nobody can touch my bat before I go in'
Cricketers particularly admired: Brian Lara 'for his skill'

Young players to look out for: Alex Wakely, Ben Howgego
Other sports played: Football 'for recreational purposes only'
Other sports followed: Football (Manchester United)
Favourite band: Tupac, Notorious B.I.G.
Relaxations: 'Music and dancing'
Extras: NBC Denis Compton Award for the most promising young Northamptonshire player 2006. Represented England at U17, U18 and U19 levels
Best batting: 42 Northamptonshire v Middlesex, Northampton 2007
Best bowling: 2-62 Northamptonshire v Warwickshire, Edgbaston 2008

2008 Season

	M	Inn	NO	Runs	HS	Avg	100	50	Ct	St	Balls	Runs	Wkts	Avg	BB	5I	10M
Test																	
FC	2	3	0	51	42	17.00	-	-	-	-	48	62	0		-	-	-
ODI																	
List A	2	2	0	43	24	21.50	-	-	-	-	16	26	1	26.00	1-26	-	
20/20 Int																	
20/20																	

Career Performances

	M	Inn	NO	Runs	HS	Avg	100	50	Ct	St	Balls	Runs	Wkts	Avg	BB	5I	10M
Test																	
FC	3	4	0	64	42	16.00	-	-	1	-	96	124	2	62.00	2-62	-	-
ODI																	
List A	9	7	2	113	26	22.60	-	-	-	-	94	100	2	50.00	1-26	-	
20/20 Int																	
20/20																	

65. Who opened the batting and made 99 not out against Australia in 1980?

NEW, T. J. Leicestershire

Name: Thomas (Tom) James New
Role: Left-hand bat, wicket-keeper, right-arm slow-medium bowler
Born: 18 January 1985, Sutton-in-Ashfield
Height: 5ft 9in **Weight:** 10st
Nickname: Newy, P
County debut: 2003 (one-day), 2004 (first-class)
Place in batting averages: 154th av. 26.04 (2007 94th av. 36.80)
Parents: Martin and Louise
Marital status: Engaged
Family links with cricket: 'Dad played local cricket'
Education: Quarrydale Comprehensive
Qualifications: GCSEs
Overseas tours: England U19 to Bangladesh (U19 World Cup) 2003-04
Overseas teams played for: Geelong Cement, Victoria 2001-02
Cricket moments to forget: 'Losing semi-final of Costcutter World Challenge 2000 to Pakistan'
Cricket superstitions: 'None'
Cricketers particularly admired: Ian Healy, Jack Russell
Other sports played: Golf, football
Other sports followed: Football (Mansfield Town)
Relaxations: 'Golf, music'
Extras: Played for Nottinghamshire U12, U13, U15, U16 and Midlands U13, U14, U15. Captained England U15 in Costcutter World Challenge [U15 World Cup] 2000. Sir John Hobbs Silver Jubilee Memorial Prize 2000. Represented England U19 2003 and 2004. NBC Denis Compton Award for the most promising young Leicestershire player 2003, 2004. On loan at Derbyshire for part of 2008 season
Best batting: 125 Leicestershire v OUCCE, The Parks 2007
Best bowling: 2-18 Leicestershire v Gloucestershire, Leicester 2007

2008 Season

	M	Inn	NO	Runs	HS	Avg	100	50	Ct	St	Balls	Runs	Wkts	Avg	BB	5I	10M
Test																	
FC	16	25	3	573	109	26.04	1	1	26	2	12	7	1	7.00	1-7	-	-
ODI																	
List A	10	10	3	202	39	28.85	-	-	6	1	0	0	0		-	-	
20/20 Int																	
20/20	1	1	0	18	18	18.00	-	-	1	1	0	0	0		-	-	

Career Performances

	M	Inn	NO	Runs	HS	Avg	100	50	Ct	St	Balls	Runs	Wkts	Avg	BB	5I	10M
Test																	
FC	50	84	10	2367	125	31.98	2	17	66	5	181	175	5	35.00	2-18	-	-
ODI																	
List A	34	32	3	751	68	25.89	-	3	7	2	0	0	0		-	-	
20/20 Int																	
20/20	1	1	0	18	18	18.00	-	-	1	1	0	0	0		-	-	

NEWBY, O. J. Lancashire

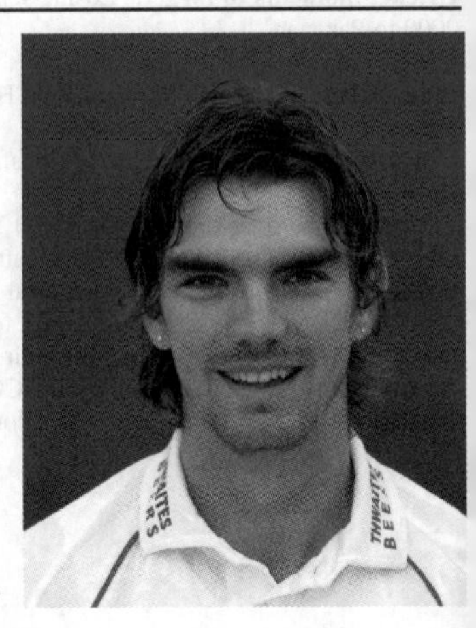

Name: Oliver James Newby
Role: Right-hand bat, right-arm fast-medium bowler
Born: 26 August 1984, Blackburn
Height: 6ft 5in **Weight:** 13st
Nickname: Newbz, Uncle, Flipper
County debut: 2003 (*see Extras*)
Place in bowling averages: 84th av. 31.72 (2007 67th av. 30.45)
Parents: Frank and Carol
Marital status: Single
Family links with cricket: 'Dad played league cricket for Read CC'
Education: Ribblesdale High School; Myerscough College
Qualifications: 10 GCSEs, ND Sports Science, Level 1 coaching
Career highlights to date: 'First-class debut'
Other sports played: Golf
Favourite band: Eminem, Counting Crows
Relaxations: Music

Extras: Took a wicket in each of his first two overs on one-day debut for Lancashire v India A at Blackpool 2003. Played two Championship matches for Nottinghamshire on loan 2005. Spent a month on loan at Gloucestershire, August 2008, during which he recorded his best bowling figures of 5-69 in a championship game against Northamptonshire. Signed a new contract with Lancashire in September 2008
Best batting: 38* Nottinghamshire v Kent, Trent Bridge 2005
Best bowling: 5-69 Gloucestershire v Northamptonshire, Bristol 2008

2008 Season

	M	Inn	NO	Runs	HS	Avg	100	50	Ct	St	Balls	Runs	Wkts	Avg	BB	5I	10M
Test																	
FC	10	7	2	26	13	5.20	-	-	3	-	1163	793	25	31.72	5-69	1	-
ODI																	
List A	3	3	1	5	3 *	2.50	-	-	-	-	84	78	1	78.00	1-39	-	
20/20 Int																	
20/20																	

Career Performances

	M	Inn	NO	Runs	HS	Avg	100	50	Ct	St	Balls	Runs	Wkts	Avg	BB	5I	10M
Test																	
FC	30	26	7	174	38 *	9.15	-	-	6	-	3726	2398	74	32.40	5-69	1	-
ODI																	
List A	15	11	6	24	7 *	4.80	-	-	2	-	560	546	10	54.60	2-37	-	
20/20 Int																	
20/20	10	4	2	14	6 *	7.00	-	-	3	-	162	216	6	36.00	2-34	-	

66. In which year did Australia record their 100th Test-match victory against England?

NEWMAN, S. A. Surrey

Name: Scott Alexander Newman
Role: Left-hand bat
Born: 3 November 1979, Epsom
Height: 6ft 1in **Weight:** 13st 7lbs
Nickname: Ronaldo
County debut: 2001 (one-day), 2002 (first-class)
County cap: 2005
1000 runs in a season: 3
1st-Class 200s: 1
Place in batting averages: 55th av. 41.76 (2007 121st av. 32.48)
Parents: Ken and Sandy
Marital status: Married
Children: Lemoy, 1985; Brandon, 8 September 2002
Family links with cricket: 'Dad and brother both played'
Education: Trinity School, Croydon; Brighton University
Qualifications: 10 GCSEs, GNVQ (Advanced) Business Studies
Overseas tours: SCB to Barbados; England A to Malaysia and India 2003-04
Overseas teams played for: Mount Lawley CC, Perth
Career highlights to date: 'First one-day century'
Cricket moments to forget: 'Any time I fail'
Cricket superstitions: 'None'
Cricketers particularly admired: 'All of Surrey CCC'
Other sports played: 'Most sports'
Other sports followed: Football (Man Utd)
Favourite band: Nas
Relaxations: 'Music, relaxing with family'
Extras: Scored 99 on first-class debut v Hampshire at The Oval 2002. Scored 284 v Derbyshire 2nd XI at The Oval 2003, in the process sharing with Nadeem Shahid (266) in an opening partnership of 552, just three runs short of the English all-cricket record first-wicket stand of 555 set in 1932. Scored 117 and 219 v Glamorgan at The Oval 2005, becoming the first Surrey batsman to score a double hundred and a hundred in the same Championship match. ECB National Academy 2003-04
Best batting: 219 Surrey v Glamorgan, The Oval 2005

2008 Season

	M	Inn	NO	Runs	HS	Avg	100	50	Ct	St	Balls	Runs	Wkts	Avg	BB	5I	10M
Test																	
FC	15	25	0	1044	129	41.76	2	8	8	-	0	0	0		-	-	-
ODI																	
List A	15	15	0	422	65	28.13	-	3	3	-	0	0	0		-	-	
20/20 Int																	
20/20	10	10	0	188	52	18.80	-	1	3	-	0	0	0		-	-	

Career Performances

	M	Inn	NO	Runs	HS	Avg	100	50	Ct	St	Balls	Runs	Wkts	Avg	BB	5I	10M
Test																	
FC	88	151	3	6305	219	42.60	13	38	70	-	24	22	0		-	-	
ODI																	
List A	74	73	3	1817	106	25.95	1	11	17	-	0	0	0		-	-	
20/20 Int																	
20/20	31	29	3	540	59	20.76	-	3	11	-	0	0	0		-	-	

NICHOLSON, M. J. Surrey

Name: Matthew James Nicholson
Role: Right-hand bat, right-arm fast-medium bowler
Born: 2 October 1974, Sydney, Australia
Height: 6ft 6in
Nickname: Nicho
County debut: 2006 (Northamptonshire), 2007 (Surrey)
County cap: 2007 (Surrey)
Test debut: 1998
Place in batting averages: 24th av. 50.33 (2007 142nd av. 30.00)
Place in bowling averages: 145th av. 56.54 (2007 59th av. 29.29)
Wife: Natalie
Children: 2 (twin boys)
Overseas tours: Australia U19 to New Zealand 1992-93, to India 1993-94; Australia to Zimbabwe 1999-2000
Overseas teams played for: Western Australia 1996-97 – 2002-03; New South Wales 2003-04 –

Extras: Australia U19 Player of the Year 1992-93. Attended Commonwealth Bank [Australian] Cricket Academy 1994-95. Had first innings figures of 7-77 (and scored 58*) for Western Australia v England XI at Perth 1998-99; it was his first first-class match after 18 months out with glandular fever and chronic fatigue syndrome (CFS). Played in his only Test match against England in Melbourne, December 1998. Man of the Match v South Australia at Adelaide in the Pura Cup 2001-02 (4-58/4-60). Had second innings figures of 5-60 v Queensland at Brisbane in the final of the Pura Cup 2004-05. Has played for Australia A against touring sides. An overseas player with Northamptonshire 2006; was an overseas player with Surrey 2007. Man of the Match v Queensland at Brisbane in the Pura Cup 2007-08 (2-46/3-25 plus 80). Left Surrey before the end of the 2008 season.
Best batting: 133 Surrey v Yorkshire, The Oval 2008
Best bowling: 7-62 Northamptonshire v Gloucestershire, Northampton 2006

2008 Season

	M	Inn	NO	Runs	HS	Avg	100	50	Ct	St	Balls	Runs	Wkts	Avg	BB	5I	10M
Test																	
FC	9	12	3	453	133	50.33	1	1	4	-	1134	625	11	56.81	3-44	-	-
ODI																	
List A	11	6	1	63	24	12.60	-	-	1	-	474	402	15	26.80	3-37	-	
20/20 Int																	
20/20	1	1	0	7	7	7.00	-	-	1	-	18	22	1	22.00	1-22	-	

Career Performances

	M	Inn	NO	Runs	HS	Avg	100	50	Ct	St	Balls	Runs	Wkts	Avg	BB	5I	10M
Test	1	2	0	14	9	7.00	-	-	-	-	150	115	4	28.75	3-56	-	-
FC	124	171	34	3258	133	23.78	4	6	70	-	23366	12150	406	29.92	7-62	11	-
ODI																	
List A	79	47	15	485	57 *	15.15	-	1	19	-	3530	3123	85	36.74	3-23	-	
20/20 Int																	
20/20	24	9	4	76	20 *	15.20	-	-	5	-	457	608	28	21.71	3-12	-	

67. Which England batsman scored a total of 732 runs in the 1985 Ashes series?

NIXON, P. A. — Leicestershire

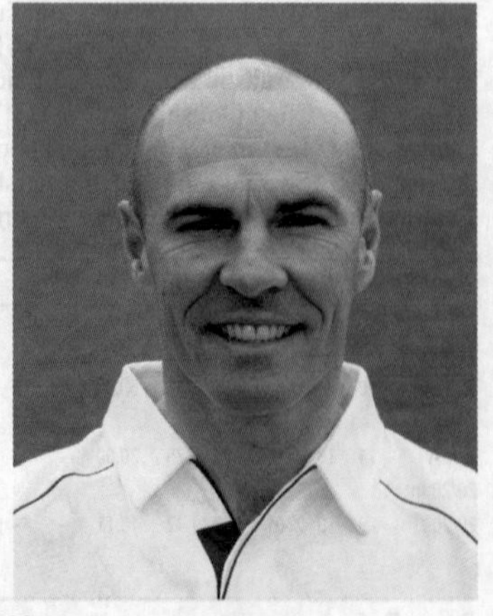

Name: Paul Andrew Nixon
Role: Left-hand bat, wicket-keeper, county captain
Born: 21 October 1970, Carlisle
Height: 6ft **Weight:** 12st 10lbs
Nickname: Badger, Nico, Nobby
County debut: 1989 (Leicestershire), 2000 (Kent)
County cap: 1994 (Leicestershire), 2000 (Kent)
Benefit: 2007 (Leicestershire)
ODI debut: 2006-07
Twenty20 Int debut: 2006-07
1000 runs in a season: 1
50 dismissals in a season: 7
Place in batting averages: 36th av. 48.83 (2006 20th av. 59.66)
Parents: Brian and Sylvia
Wife and date of marriage: Jen, 9 October 1999
Children: Isabella Rose, 13 May 2008
Family links with cricket: 'Grandad and father played local league cricket. Mum made the teas for Edenhall CC, Penrith'
Education: Ullswater High
Qualifications: 2 O-levels, 6 GCSEs, coaching certificates
Overseas tours: Cumbria Schools U15 to Denmark 1985; Leicestershire to Barbados, to Jamaica, to Netherlands, to Johannesburg, to Bloemfontein; MCC to Bangladesh 1999-2000; England A to India and Bangladesh 1994-95; England to Pakistan and Sri Lanka 2000-01, to Australia 2006-07 (C'wealth Bank Series), to West Indies (World Cup) 2006-07
Overseas teams played for: Melville, Western Australia; North Fremantle, Western Australia; Mitchells Plain, Cape Town 1993; Primrose CC, Cape Town 1995-96; Delhi Giants (ICL) 2008
Career highlights to date: 'Winning the Championship in 1996 with Leicestershire. Receiving phone call from David Graveney advising me of England [tour] selection'
Cricket moments to forget: 'Losing Lord's one-day finals'
Cricketers particularly admired: David Gower, Ian Botham, Ian Healy, Viv Richards
Other sports played: Golf, football (played for Carlisle United)
Other sports followed: Football (Leicester City, Carlisle United, Liverpool), rugby (Leicester Tigers)
Relaxations: Watching England rugby
Extras: Played for England U15. Played in Minor Counties Championship for Cumberland at 16. MCC Young Pro 1988. Took eight catches in debut match v

Warwickshire at Hinckley 1989. Leicestershire Young Player of the Year two years running. In 1994 became only second Leicestershire wicket-keeper to score 1000 (1046) first-class runs in a season; also made 62 first-class dismissals to achieve double. Voted Cumbria Sports Personality of the Year 1994-95. Captained First-Class Counties Select XI v New Zealand A at Milton Keynes 2000. Released by Kent at the end of the 2002 season and rejoined Leicestershire for 2003. Took over as captain of county in the Championship in July 2007, scoring century (126) and taking eight catches in his first match in charge; appointed captain of Leicestershire at the end of August 2007. Second-highest Leicestershire run-maker in 2008.
Best batting: 144* Leicestershire v Northamptonshire, Northampton 2006

2008 Season

	M	Inn	NO	Runs	HS	Avg	100	50	Ct	St	Balls	Runs	Wkts	Avg	BB	5I	10M
Test																	
FC	16	24	6	954	106 *	53.00	1	6	53	1	30	41	0		-	-	-
ODI																	
List A	14	13	1	360	75	30.00	-	3	21	6	0	0	0		-	-	
20/20 Int																	
20/20	9	9	0	163	42	18.11	-	-	4	2	0	0	0		-	-	

Career Performances

	M	Inn	NO	Runs	HS	Avg	100	50	Ct	St	Balls	Runs	Wkts	Avg	BB	5I	10M
Test																	
FC	326	482	108	12955	144 *	34.63	19	63	875	67	105	141	0		-	-	-
ODI	19	18	4	297	49	21.21	-	-	20	3	0	0	0		-	-	
List A	390	335	69	6938	101	26.08	1	32	413	98	3	1	0		-	-	
20/20 Int	1	1	1	31	31 *	-	-	-	-	1	0	0	0		-	-	
20/20	50	47	10	887	65	23.97	-	3	24	13	0	0	0		-	-	

NOFFKE, A. A. Middlesex

Name: Ashley Allan Noffke
Role: Right-hand bat, right-arm fast bowler; all-rounder
Born: 30 April 1977, Sunshine Coast, Queensland, Australia
Height: 6ft 3in **Weight:** 14st
Nickname: Noffers, Wombat
County debut: 2002 (Middlesex), 2005 (Durham), 2007 (Gloucestershire)
County cap: 2003 (Middlesex), 2007 (Gloucestershire)
Twenty20 Int debut: 2007
Place in bowling averages: (2007 14th av. 22.33)
Parents: Rob and Lesley Simpson, and Allan Noffke
Wife and date of marriage: Michelle, 8 April 2000
Family links with cricket: Father played club cricket
Education: Immanuel Lutheran College; Sunshine Coast University
Qualifications: Bachelor of Business, ACB Level 2 coaching certificate
Overseas tours: Commonwealth Bank [Australian] Cricket Academy to Zimbabwe 1998-99; Australia to England 2001, to West Indies 2002-03; Australia A to Pakistan 2007-08, to India 2008-09
Overseas teams played for: Queensland 1999-2000 – ; Banglalore Royal Challengers (IPL) 2007-08
Career highlights to date: 'Man of the Match in a winning Pura Cup final for Queensland. Being selected for Australia for 2001 Ashes tour'
Cricket moments to forget: 'Rolling my ankle playing for Australia v Sussex, forcing me home from the [2001] Ashes tour'
Cricket superstitions: 'None'
Cricketers particularly admired: Steve Waugh
Other sports played: Golf
Other sports followed: Rugby league, rugby union, 'enjoy all sports'
Favourite band: Powderfinger
Relaxations: Fishing
Extras: Queensland Academy of Sport Player of the Year 1998-99. Awarded an ACB contract 2001-02 after just six first-class matches. Has represented Australia A. Sunshine Coast Sportstar of the Year 2001. His awards include Man of the Match in the Pura Cup final v Victoria 2000-01 for his 7-120 match return and 43 runs batting as nightwatchman and v South Australia at Brisbane in the Pura Cup 2003-04 (4-48/2-37; 114*). Was Middlesex overseas player for two periods during the 2002

season; returned as an overseas player for 2003. Was an overseas player with Durham in 2005 but was ruled out with a back injury from late July. Was a temporary overseas player with Gloucestershire during the 2007 season. Made Twenty20 Int debut v New Zealand at Perth, December 2007. Man of the Match v Tasmania at Brisbane in the Pura Cup 2007-08 (5-33/2-114 plus 100*). Joined Middlesex as an overseas player for 2009 season

Best batting: 114* Queensland v South Australia, Brisbane 2003-04

Best bowling: 8-24 Middlesex v Derbyshire, Derby 2002

2008 Season (Did not make any first-class or one-day appearances for his county)

Career Performances

	M	Inn	NO	Runs	HS	Avg	100	50	Ct	St	Balls	Runs	Wkts	Avg	BB	5I	10M
Test																	
FC	100	135	23	3058	114 *	27.30	2	14	39	-	19399	9826	346	28.39	8-24	18	1
ODI	1	0	0	0	0		-	-	-	-	54	46	1	46.00	1-46	-	
List A	101	52	17	517	58	14.77	-	1	25	-	4965	3802	113	33.64	4-32	-	
20/20 Int	2	1	0	0	0	-	-	-	-	-	45	41	4	10.25	3-18	-	
20/20	16	10	2	77	19	9.62	-	-	3	-	328	386	23	16.78	3-18	-	

NORTH, M. J. — Hampshire

Name: Marcus James North

Role: Left-hand bat, right-arm off-spin bowler

Born: 28 July 1979, Pakenham, Melbourne, Australia

Height: 6ft 1in **Weight:** 12st 10lbs

County debut: 2004 (Durham), 2005 (Lancashire), 2006 (Derbyshire), 2007 (Gloucestershire)

County cap: 2007 (Gloucestershire)

1st-Class 200s: 3

Place in batting averages: 25th av. 50.00 (2007 19th av. 56.50)

Place in bowling averages: 137th av. 45.00

Wife: Joanne

Overseas tours: Australia U19 to Pakistan 1996-97, to South Africa (U19 World Cup) 1997-98; Commonwealth Bank [Australian] Cricket Academy to Zimbabwe 1998-99; Australia A to Pakistan 2005-06; Australia to South Africa 2008-09

Overseas teams played for: Western Australia 1999-2000 –
Extras: Commonwealth Bank [Australian] Cricket Academy 1998. Won President's Silver Trophy (season's best individual performance for Western Australia) for his 200* v Victoria at Melbourne in the Pura Cup 2001-02. Scored 200* and 132 in the second 'Test' v Pakistan U19 at Sheikhupura 1996-97, winning Man of the Match award (also Australia's Man of the 'Test' Series). Other awards include Man of the Match for Australia A v Zimbabweans at Adelaide 2003-04 (115). An overseas player with Durham 2004; a temporary overseas player with Lancashire during the 2005 season; a temporary overseas player with Derbyshire during the 2006 season; was a temporary overseas player with Gloucestershire during the 2007 season and returned as overseas player for 2008. Won the Walter Lawrence Trophy 2007 for the season's fastest first-class century for his 73-ball hundred (finishing with 106) v Leicestershire at Bristol. Captain of Western Australia. Joined Hampshire as overseas player for the first six weeks of 2009 in the place of Imran Tahir
Best batting: 239* Western Australia v Victoria, Perth 2006-07
Best bowling: 4-16 Durham v DUCCE, Riverside 2004

2008 Season

	M	Inn	NO	Runs	HS	Avg	100	50	Ct	St	Balls	Runs	Wkts	Avg	BB	5I	10M
Test																	
FC	12	20	2	900	104	50.00	1	8	13	-	1146	585	13	45.00	3-57	-	-
ODI																	
List A	10	9	3	195	85	32.50	-	2	3	-	324	307	6	51.16	3-32	-	
20/20 Int																	
20/20	7	7	2	194	45	38.80	-	-	2	-	107	132	1	132.00	1-39	-	

Career Performances

	M	Inn	NO	Runs	HS	Avg	100	50	Ct	St	Balls	Runs	Wkts	Avg	BB	5I	10M
Test																	
FC	118	207	20	8272	239 *	44.23	20	47	86	-	7113	3726	82	45.43	4-16	-	-
ODI																	
List A	120	113	14	3286	134 *	33.19	5	23	36	-	1909	1656	55	30.10	4-26	-	
20/20 Int																	
20/20	24	23	3	471	59	23.55	-	1	8	-	251	293	5	58.60	2-19	-	

NORTHEAST, S. A. Kent

Name: Sam Alexander Northeast
Role Right-hand top-order bat, off-spin bowler
Born: 16 October 1989, Ashford, Kent
Height: 5ft 11in **Weight:** 11st
Nickname: North, Bam, Nick Knight
County debut: 2007
Parents: Allan and Diane
Marital status: Single
Family links with cricket: 'My brother played Kent age-group as a kid'
Education: Harrow School
Qualifications: 10 GCSEs
Overseas tours: Harrow School to Sri Lanka 2004; England U16 to South Africa; England U19 to Malaysia 2006-07, to Sri Lanka 2007-08, Under 19 World Cup in Malaysia 2007-08, to South Africa 2008-09

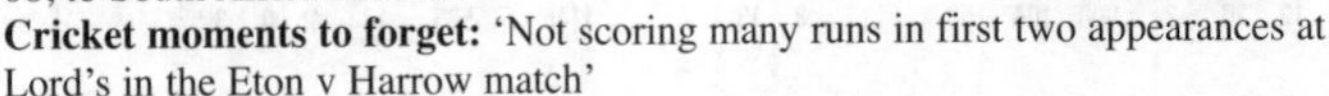

Cricket moments to forget: 'Not scoring many runs in first two appearances at Lord's in the Eton v Harrow match'
Cricket superstitions: 'Right pad on first'
Cricketers particularly admired: Graham Thorpe, Steve Waugh
Young players to look out for: Alex Blake, Paul Dixey, Glen Querl
Other sports played: Rackets, squash, cross-country running, football and rugby
Other sports followed: Football (Spurs), rugby (Bath)
Favourite band: Starsailor, Snow Patrol
Relaxations: 'Fishing, gardening; playing rackets releases stress'
Extras: Broke Graham Cowdrey's run record at Wellesley House (prep school). Captained England U15. *Daily Telegraph* Bunbury Scholarship 2005. BBC *Test Match Special* Young Cricketer of the Year 2005. Sir John Hobbs Silver Jubilee Memorial Prize for the outstanding U16 schoolboy cricketer 2005. Scored 96 on debut for Kent 2nd XI v Derbyshire 2nd XI at Beckenham 2005. Scored 62* for Sir JP Getty's XI v Sri Lankans in a 50-over game at Wormsley 2006. Top ten nominee for BBC Young Sports Personality of the Year 2006. Scored a century for Harrow v Eton at Lord's in July 2007. Attended Kent Academy
Opinions on cricket: 'Young players are getting more of a chance to shine in the game. Hopefully that will help me.'
Best batting: 5 Kent v Durham, Canterbury 2007

2008 Season

	M	Inn	NO	Runs	HS	Avg	100	50	Ct	St	Balls	Runs	Wkts	Avg	BB	5I	10M
Test																	
FC																	
ODI																	
List A																	
20/20 Int																	
20/20																	

Career Perfomances

	M	Inn	NO	Runs	HS	Avg	100	50	Ct	St	Balls	Runs	Wkts	Avg	BB	5I	10M
Test																	
FC	1	2	0	5	5	2.50	-	-	-	-	0	0	0		-	-	-
ODI																	
List A	1	0	0	0	0	-	-	-	-	0	0	0		-	-		
20/20 Int																	
20/20																	

O'BRIEN, N. J. P. Northamptonshire

Name: Niall John Peter O'Brien
Role: Left-hand bat, slow bowler, wicket-keeper
Born: 8 November 1981, Dublin
Height: 5ft 9in **Weight:** 12st
Nickname: Nobby, Hornswoggle
County debut: 2004 (Kent), 2007 (Northamptonshire)
ODI debut: 2006
50 dismissals in a season: 1
Place in batting averages: 43rd av. 45.85 (2007 196th av. 22.63)
Parents: Brendan and Camilla
Marital status: Single
Family links with cricket: 'Dad ex-captain of Ireland. My brother Kevin is a current Irish international. All the family played good club cricket.'
Education: Marian College, Ballsbridge, Dublin
Qualifications: 6 Leaving Certificates, Level 2 coaching
Career outside cricket: 'Property developer or footballer'

Off-season: 'Touring with Ireland, and relaxing'
Overseas tours: Ireland U19 to Sri Lanka (U19 World Cup) 1999-2000; Ireland to Namibia (ICC Inter-Continental Cup) 2005, to Scotland (European Championship) 2006, to Kenya (ICC World Cricket League) 2006-07, to West Indies (World Cup) 2006-07, plus Ireland age-group and A tours; Kent to Spain, France and Guernsey
Overseas teams played for: Railway Union CC, Dublin; Mosman DCC, Sydney 2000-02; University of Port Elizabeth Academy, South Africa 2002; North Sydney DCC 2003-05
Career highlights to date: 'Playing in the Cricket World Cup. Getting Man of the Match v Pakistan in World Cup [2006-07]'
Cricket moments to forget: 'Getting stumped v Pakistan in World Cup, needing 20 to win and having hit the previous ball for 6!!'
Cricket superstitions: 'None'
Cricketers particularly admired: Steve Waugh, Adam Gilchrist
Young players to look out for: Paul Stirling
Other sports played: Hockey (Railway Union, Dublin), football, golf
Other sports followed: Football (Everton), rugby (Ireland)
Favourite band: Oasis
Relaxations: 'Music; walking my dog; socialising'
Extras: Made Ireland senior debut v Denmark 2002 and has played first-class and one-day cricket for Ireland, including ODI (debut v Scotland at Ayr 2006) and C&G. Ireland Cricketer of the Year 2002. Scored 58* as Ireland defeated West Indians in 50-over game in Belfast 2004, winning Man of the Match award. Man of the Match v Pakistan in Kingston in the World Cup 2006-07 (72 plus two catches).
Best batting: 176 Ireland v United Arab Emirates, Windhoek 2005-06
Best bowling: 1-4 Kent v CUCCE, Fenner's 2006

2008 Season

	M	Inn	NO	Runs	HS	Avg	100	50	Ct	St	Balls	Runs	Wkts	Avg	BB	5I	10M
Test																	
FC	14	21	1	917	168	45.85	2	5	44	3	0	0	0		-	-	-
ODI																	
List A	11	11	0	314	95	28.54	-	2	9	5	0	0	0		-	-	
20/20 Int																	
20/20	11	11	1	217	69	21.70	-	1	5	2	0	0	0		-	-	

Career Performances

	M	Inn	NO	Runs	HS	Avg	100	50	Ct	St	Balls	Runs	Wkts	Avg	BB	5I	10M
Test																	
FC	66	96	13	2924	176	35.22	6	13	183	24	3	4	1	4.00	1-4	-	-
ODI	27	27	1	684	72	26.30	-	7	21	5	0	0	0		-	-	
List A	83	62	5	1326	95	23.26	-	9	64	24	0	0	0		-	-	
20/20 Int	4	3	0	38	22	12.66	-	-	3	1	0	0	0		-	-	
20/20	35	25	7	314	69	17.44	-	1	13	8	0	0	0		-	-	

ONIONS, G. Durham

Name: Graham Onions
Role: Right-hand bat, right-arm fast-medium bowler
Born: 9 September 1982, Gateshead
Height: 6ft 2in **Weight:** 11st 7lbs
Nickname: Wills
County debut: 2004
50 wickets in a season: 1
Place in batting averages: 241st av. 13.22 (2007 232nd av. 17.75)
Place in bowling averages: 47th av. 26.84 (2007 80th av. 33.11)
Parents: Maureen and Richard
Marital status: Single
Education: St Thomas More RC Comprehensive School, Blaydon
Qualifications: 10 GCSEs, GNVQ Advanced Science (Distinction), Level 2 coach
Career outside cricket: 'Newcastle United manager'
Off-season: 'Relax, take a holiday, hopefully get picked for the England Performance Programme'
Overseas tours: Durham to Dubai 2005, 2006; England A to Bangladesh 2006-07; England Performance Programme to India 2007-08; England Lions to India 2007-08
Overseas teams played for: South Perth CC 2004
Career highlights to date: 'Being selected in squad for England's NatWest Series against Pakistan [2006]. National Academy'
Cricket moments to forget: 'Getting out to my dad in a charity game!'
Cricket superstitions: 'Lick my fingers before I run in to bowl'
Cricketers particularly admired: Darren Gough, Paul Collingwood
Young players to look out for: Ben Harmison, Mark Turner
Other sports played: Badminton (England U17; plays for Durham County)
Other sports followed: Football (Newcastle United)
Favourite band: 'No favourite – prefer R&B'
Relaxations: 'Sleep, music, the pub with mates'
Extras: Attended UPE International Cricket Academy, Port Elizabeth 2005. Durham Young Player of the Year and Bowler of the Year 2006. ECB National Academy 2006-07. Represented England Lions 2007
Best batting: 41 Durham v Yorkshire, Headingley 2007
Best bowling: 8-101 Durham v Warwickshire, Edgbaston 2007

2008 Season

	M	Inn	NO	Runs	HS	Avg	100	50	Ct	St	Balls	Runs	Wkts	Avg	BB	5I	10M
Test																	
FC	9	11	2	119	36	13.22	-	-	3	-	1177	671	25	26.84	5-75	1	-
ODI																	
List A	13	7	2	56	19	11.20	-	-	2	-	569	479	19	25.21	3-56	-	
20/20 Int																	
20/20																	

Career Performances

	M	Inn	NO	Runs	HS	Avg	100	50	Ct	St	Balls	Runs	Wkts	Avg	BB	5I	10M
Test																	
FC	55	74	21	695	41	13.11	-	-	12	-	8296	5180	153	33.85	8-101	4	-
ODI																	
List A	47	19	5	102	19	7.28	-	-	6	-	1903	1651	53	31.15	3-39	-	
20/20 Int																	
20/20	13	4	0	37	31	9.25	-	-	4	-	282	291	11	26.45	3-25	-	

ORMOND, J. Surrey

Name: James (Jimmy) Ormond
Role: Right-hand bat, right-arm fast'ish' bowler, can also bowl off-spin
Born: 20 August 1977, Walsgrave, Coventry
Height: 6ft 3in **Weight:** 15st
Nickname: Jimmy, Horse
County debut: 1995 (Leicestershire), 2002 (Surrey)
County cap: 1999 (Leicestershire), 2003 (Surrey)
Test debut: 2001
50 wickets in a season: 4
Place in batting averages: 235th av. 14.00 (2007 276th av. 10.37)
Place in bowling averages: 134th av. 43.15 (2007 139th av. 53.33)
Parents: Richard and Margaret
Marital status: Married
Family links with cricket: 'Dad played years of cricket in Warwickshire'
Education: St Thomas More, Nuneaton; North Warwickshire College of Further Education

Qualifications: 6 GCSEs
Overseas tours: England U19 to Zimbabwe 1995-96; England A to Kenya and Sri Lanka 1997-98; England to India and New Zealand 2001-02
Overseas teams played for: Sydney University CC 1996, 1998, 1999
Cricketers particularly admired: Curtly Ambrose, Courtney Walsh, Allan Donald, Sachin Tendulkar, Brian Lara, Steve Griffin
Other sports played: Football, mountain biking, 'anything'
Other sports followed: Football (Coventry City)
Relaxations: Spending time with friends and family
Extras: Played for the Development of Excellence side and England U19. NBC Denis Compton Award for the most promising young Leicestershire player 1998, 1999, 2000. Made his Test debut against Australia at The Oval in 2001. Took 5-26 v Middlesex at The Oval in the Twenty20 2003 and was Man of the Match (4-11) at Trent Bridge in the inaugural final. Took four wickets in an over, all left-handers and including hat-trick (Hutton, Joyce, Weekes), in the Championship v Middlesex at Guildford 2003
Best batting: 64* Surrey v Hampshire, Rose Bowl 2008
Best bowling: 7-63 Surrey v Glamorgan, Cardiff 2005

2008 Season

	M	Inn	NO	Runs	HS	Avg	100	50	Ct	St	Balls	Runs	Wkts	Avg	BB	5I	10M
Test																	
FC	7	7	1	84	64 *	14.00	-	1	4	-	950	561	13	43.15	4-90	-	-
ODI																	
List A	2	1	0	3	3	3.00	-	-	-	-	78	75	2	37.50	2-41	-	
20/20 Int																	
20/20	3	1	1	12	12*	-	-	1	-	72	100	2	50.00	1-38	-		

Career Perfomances

	M	Inn	NO	Runs	HS	Avg	100	50	Ct	St	Balls	Runs	Wkts	Avg	BB	5I	10M
Test	2	4	1	38	18	12.66	-	-	-	-	372	185	2	92.50	1-70	-	-
FC	137	165	39	1911	64 *	15.16	-	3	31	-	25040	13479	448	30.08	7-63	20	1
ODI																	
List A	119	72	32	359	32	8.97	-	-	23	-	5370	3987	146	27.30	4-12	-	
20/20 Int																	
20/20	15	6	4	29	12 *	14.50	-	-	3	-	336	359	18	19.94	5-26	1	

68. Who topped the batting averages in the 2005 Ashes series?

O'SHEA, M. P. Glamorgan

Name: Michael Peter O'Shea
Role: Right-hand top-order bat, 'part-time' off-spin bowler
Born: 4 September 1987, Cardiff
Height: 5ft 11in **Weight:** 12st
Nickname: Chewey
County debut: 2005
Parents: Paul and June
Marital status: Single
Education: Barry Comprehensive School; Millfield School
Qualifications: 13 GCSEs
Overseas tours: England U19 to India 2004-05, to Bangladesh 2005-06; Glamorgan to India 2007-08
Career highlights to date: 'Championship debut v Kent'
Cricket moments to forget: 'Getting 0 on Championship debut'
Cricket superstitions: 'Put left pad on first'
Cricketers particularly admired: Damien Martyn, Andrew Flintoff
Young players to look out for: Chris Thompson, Rory Hamilton-Brown, Karl Brown, Andy Miller, Ben Wright, Greg Wood
Other sports played: Rugby (Millfield 1st XV – won national XVs competition)
Other sports followed: Rugby (Cardiff Blues, Wales)
Favourite band: Oasis, Westlife
Extras: Has represented England U15, U16, U17, U19. Played for Wales Minor Counties in the C&G 2005 and in Minor Counties competitions 2005-07
Best batting: 24 Glamorgan v Kent, Canterbury 2005

2008 Season (did not make any first-class or one-day appearances for his county)

Career Performances

	M	Inn	NO	Runs	HS	Avg	100	50	Ct	St	Balls	Runs	Wkts	Avg	BB	5I	10M
Test																	
FC	5	7	0	62	24	8.85	-	-	1	-	0	0	0		-	-	-
ODI																	
List A	7	7	1	90	49	15.00	-	-	3	-	180	194	3	64.66	2-37	-	
20/20 Int																	
20/20																	

OWEN, W. T. — Glamorgan

Name: William (Will) Thomas Owen
Role: Right-hand bat, right-arm fast-medium bowler
Born: 2 September 1988, St Asaph, North Wales
Height: 6ft **Weight:** 13st
Nickname: Willo
County debut: 2007
Parents: Haydn and Stephanie
Marital status: Single
Education: Prestatyn High School; UWIC
Qualifications: GCSEs and A-levels
Career outside cricket: Student (Sports Coaching course)
Career highlights to date: 'My first-class debut for Glamorgan against Gloucestershire 2007'
Cricketers particularly admired: Simon Jones
Young players to look out for: David Lloyd (Glamorgan Academy)
Other sports played: Rugby (represented North Wales at U12-U15)
Other sports followed: Football (Blackburn Rovers), rugby (Llanelli Scarlets)
Favourite band: Oasis
Relaxations: 'Going out with friends, playing Pro Evo and training'
Extras: Played for Wales Minor Counties in Minor Counties competitions 2007
Opinions on cricket: 'Cricket is changing rapidly, with the different formats of the game encouraging players to improvise new techniques and strategies, making the game more exciting for the spectators.'

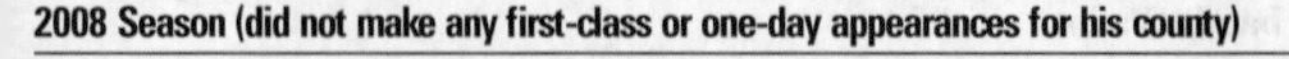

2008 Season (did not make any first-class or one-day appearances for his county)

Career Performances

	M	Inn	NO	Runs	HS	Avg	100	50	Ct	St	Balls	Runs	Wkts	Avg	BB	5I	10M
Test																	
FC	1	0	0	0	0		-	-	-	-	48	37	0		-	-	-
ODI																	
List A																	
20/20 Int																	
20/20																	

PALLADINO, A. P. Essex

Name: Antonio (Tony) Paul Palladino
Role: Right-hand bat, right-arm fast-medium bowler; all-rounder
Born: 29 June 1983, Whitechapel, London
Height: 6ft **Weight:** 12st 8lbs
Nickname: Dino, TP, Freddie, Italian Stallion
County debut: 2003
Place in batting averages: 234th av. 14.14
Place in bowling averages: 24th av. 22.88 (2007 57th av. 29.16)
Parents: Antonio and Kathleen
Marital status: 'Attached'
Family links with cricket: 'Dad played cricket in the Kent League'
Education: Cardinal Pole Secondary School; Anglia Polytechnic University
Qualifications: 9 GCSEs, Advanced GNVQ Leisure and Tourism
Overseas teams played for: Mount Lawley CC, Perth 2005-06
Career highlights to date: '6-41 v Kent 2003; 6-68 v Leics 2006; 111 v Hampshire 2nd XI 2006'
Cricket moments to forget: 'Losing to Sussex 2006 in the C&G Trophy when defending nearly 300 and they were 30-4. Felt sick for about a week' (*Just for the record, the fourth Sussex wicket fell at 56 at Chelmsford 2006, but … – Ed*)
Cricket superstitions: 'Try and get a corner spot in changing room'
Cricketers particularly admired: Ian Botham, Andy and Grant Flower, Kevin Brooks
Other sports played: Football, golf, snooker
Other sports followed: Football (Chelsea), baseball (Boston Red Sox)
Favourite band: 'Various artists'
Relaxations: 'Computer games, cinema, going out with the lads'
Extras: Represented England U17. Represented ECB U19 2000 and 2001. Played for Cambridge UCCE 2003, 2004, 2005. Recorded maiden first-class five-wicket return (6-41) v Kent at Canterbury 2003 in only his second Championship match. Represented British Universities 2005. His 6-68 v Leicestershire at Chelmsford 2006 included a spell of 5-9 in seven overs
Best batting: 41 Essex v Nottinghamshire, Trent Bridge 2004
Best bowling: 6-41 Essex v Kent, Canterbury 2003

2008 Season

	M	Inn	NO	Runs	HS	Avg	100	50	Ct	St	Balls	Runs	Wkts	Avg	BB	5I	10M
Test																	
FC	6	11	4	99	30*	14.14	-	-	7	-	953	412	18	22.88	4-29	-	-
ODI																	
List A	1	0	0	0	0	-		-	-	-	24	35	0	-	-		
20/20 Int																	
20/20																	

Career Performances

	M	Inn	NO	Runs	HS	Avg	100	50	Ct	St	Balls	Runs	Wkts	Avg	BB	5I	10M
Test																	
FC	36	43	16	328	41	12.14	-	-	18	-	4904	2754	70	39.34	6-41	2	-
ODI																	
List A	21	10	1	43	16	4.77	-	-	2	-	780	674	22	30.63	3-32	-	
20/20 Int																	
20/20	9	1	1	1	1*	-		-	-	-	162	202	10	20.20	2-3	-	

PANESAR, M. S. Northamptonshire

Name: Mudhsuden (Monty) Singh Panesar
Role: Left-hand bat, slow left-arm bowler
Born: 25 April 1982, Luton
Height: 6ft 1in **Weight:** 12st 7lbs
Nickname: Monty
County debut: 2001
County cap: 2006
Test debut: 2005-06
ODI debut: 2006-07
Twenty20 Int debut: 2006-07
50 wickets in a season: 3
Place in bowling averages: 119th av. 38.12 (2007 43rd av. 26.66)
Parents: Paramjit and Gursharan
Marital status: Single
Family links with cricket: 'Father used to play cricket'
Education: Stopsley High School, Luton; Bedford Modern School; Loughborough University
Qualifications: 10 GCSEs, 3 A-levels, Computer Science degree

Overseas tours: Bedford Modern School to Barbados 1999; England U19 to India 2000-01; Northamptonshire to Grenada 2001-02; British Universities to South Africa 2002; ECB National Academy to Australia and Sri Lanka 2002-03; England to India 2005-06, to Australia 2006-07, to West Indies (World Cup) 2006-07, to Sri Lanka 2007-08, to New Zealand 2007-08, to India 2008-09, to West Indies 2008-09; England Lions to India 2007-08
Career highlights to date: 'Playing for England'
Cricketers particularly admired: Sachin Tendulkar
Other sports followed: Football (Luton, Arsenal)
Relaxations: 'Reading'
Player website: www.monty-panesar.com
Extras: Represented England U19. Had match figures of 8-131 on first-class debut v Leicestershire at Northampton 2001, including 4-11 in the second innings. NBC Denis Compton Award for the most promising young Northamptonshire player 2001. Played for Loughborough UCCE 2002, 2004. Represented British Universities 2002, 2004, 2005. Winner of the Beard Liberation Front's 'Beard of the Year' award 2006. Had first innings figures of 5-92 in the third Test v Australia 2006-07, becoming the first England spinner to record a five-wicket innings return in a Test at Perth. One of *Wisden*'s Five Cricketers of the Year 2007. Had match figures of 10-187 (4-50/6-137) in the third Test v West Indies at Old Trafford 2007, winning Man of the Match award. England's Man of the [Test] Series v West Indies 2007. His 6-126 in the third Test in Napier was a key contribution to England's 2-1 series win over New Zealand in 2008
Best batting: 39* Northamptonshire v Worcestershire, Northampton 2005
Best bowling: 7-181 Northamptonshire v Essex, Chelmsford 2005

2008 Season

	M	Inn	NO	Runs	HS	Avg	100	50	Ct	St	Balls	Runs	Wkts	Avg	BB	5I	10M
Test	7	8	1	12	10	1.71	-	-	-	-	1561	657	22	29.86	6-37	1	-
FC	14	16	5	84	30 *	7.63	-	-	2	-	3185	1525	40	38.12	6-37	2	-
ODI																	
List A	6	3	2	22	17 *	22.00	-	-	-	-	246	169	6	28.16	3-36	-	
20/20 Int																	
20/20	3	1	1	3	3 *		-	-	1	-	36	59	1	59.00	1-21	-	

Career Performances

	M	Inn	NO	Runs	HS	Avg	100	50	Ct	St	Balls	Runs	Wkts	Avg	BB	5I	10M
Test	33	45	15	165	26	5.50	-	-	6	-	7699	3643	114	31.95	6-37	8	1
FC	89	115	41	585	39 *	7.90	-	-	22	-	20531	9872	319	30.94	7-181	19	3
ODI	26	8	3	26	13	5.20	-	-	3	-	1308	980	24	40.83	3-25	-	
List A	44	18	9	98	17 *	10.88	-	-	7	-	2088	1518	43	35.30	5-20	1	
20/20 Int	1	1	0	1	1	1.00	-	-	-	-	24	40	2	20.00	2-40	-	
20/20	10	3	1	6	3 *	3.00	-	-	1	-	204	294	11	26.72	2-22	-	

PARK, G. T. Derbyshire

Name: Garry Terence Park
Role: Right-hand bat, right-arm medium bowler, wicket-keeper
Born: 19 April 1983, Empangeni, South Africa
Height: 5ft 7in **Weight:** 10st 4lbs
Nickname: Parkie, Whippet
County debut: 2005 (one-day), 2006 (first-class) (both Durham)
Place in batting averages: 176th av. 25.28
Parents: Mike Park and Christine Reeves
Marital status: Single
Family links with cricket: 'Sean Park - Cambridgeshire, Craig Park - Huntingdonshire'
Education: Eshowe High School, South Africa; Anglia Ruskin University, Cambridge
Qualifications: Matric Exemption (South Africa), ECB Levels 1 and 2 coaching
Overseas tours: Cambridge UCCE to Grenada 2003
Overseas teams played for: Crusaders CC, Durban 2005; Zululand 2006-07
Career highlights to date: 'Hitting Tino Best for 20 off the over. Maiden century at Headingley to help Durham avoid dropping to Div 2'
Cricket moments to forget: 'Being peppered by Tino Best at the Riverside, Durham v West Indies A'
Cricket superstitions: 'None'
Cricketers particularly admired: Jonty Rhodes, Dale Benkenstein, ShivnarIne Chanderpaul
Young players to look out for: Scott Borthwick
Other sports played: Hockey (KwaZulu-Natal U15, U19), rugby (Natal U14), golf, tennis, squash
Other sports followed: Rugby (Natal Sharks)
Favourite band: Matchbox 20
Relaxations: 'Golf, music, travelling'
Extras: Played for Cambridge UCCE 2003-05. Durham 2nd XI Player of the Year 2006. Durham 2nd XI Batsman of the Year 2007. Signed for Derbyshire in October 2008
Best batting: 100* Durham v Yorkshire, Headingley 2006
Best bowling: 2-20 Durham v Lancashire, Old Trafford 2008

2008 Season

	M	Inn	NO	Runs	HS	Avg	100	50	Ct	St	Balls	Runs	Wkts	Avg	BB	5I	10M
Test																	
FC	1	2	0	21	19	10.50	-	-	1	-	48	20	2	10.00	2-20	-	-
ODI																	
List A	6	6	2	73	42 *	18.25	-	-	2	-	24	15	0		-	-	
20/20 Int																	
20/20	3	1	1	9	9 *		-	-	1	-	0	0	0		-	-	

Career Performances

	M	Inn	NO	Runs	HS	Avg	100	50	Ct	St	Balls	Runs	Wkts	Avg	BB	5I	10M
Test																	
FC	18	30	6	845	100 *	35.20	1	4	21	-	390	320	2	160.00	2-20	-	-
ODI																	
List A	16	14	3	198	42 *	18.00	-	-	7	-	24	15	0		-	-	
20/20 Int																	
20/20	9	5	2	72	25 *	24.00	-	-	2	-	6	7	0		-	-	

PARKER, L. C. — Warwickshire

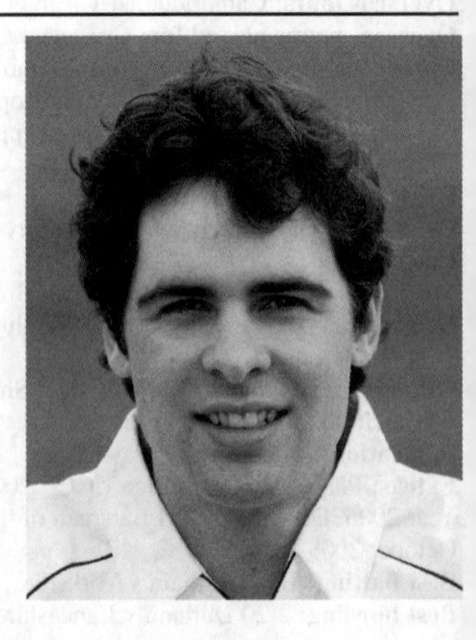

Name: Luke Charles Parker
Role: Right-hand bat, right-arm medium bowler
Born: 27 September 1983, Coventry
Height: 6ft **Weight:** 13st
Nickname: Parks
County debut: 2005
Place in batting averages: (2007 254th av. 13.50) (2006 154th av. 28.73)
Parents: Linda and Neil
Marital status: Single
Family links with cricket: 'Dad played for Lincolnshire'
Education: Finham Park; Oxford Brookes University
Qualifications: 8 GCSEs, 3 A-levels, ECB Level 1 coach
Overseas teams played for: United, Cape Town 2002-03
Cricket moments to forget: 'Dropping Matt Windows three times in an innings of 200-plus'

Cricket superstitions: 'Not really'
Cricketers particularly admired: Nick Knight, Damien Martyn
Other sports played: Football (Coventry City Academy U10-15)
Other sports followed: Football (Coventry City)
Favourite band: Mylo
Extras: Played for Warwickshire Board XI in the 2002 C&G. Played for Oxford UCCE 2004-06 (captain 2005). Represented British Universities 2005 and as captain v Sri Lankans at Fenner's 2006. Released at the end of September 2008
Best batting: 140 OUCCE v Durham, The Parks 2006
Best bowling: 2-37 OUCCE v Gloucestershire, The Parks 2005

2008 Season

	M	Inn	NO	Runs	HS	Avg	100	50	Ct	St	Balls	Runs	Wkts	Avg	BB	5I	10M
Test																	
FC	3	4	0	119	61	29.75	-	1	2	-	0	0	0		-	-	-
ODI																	
List A	4	4	0	42	19	10.50	-	-	2	-	0	0	0		-	-	
20/20 Int																	
20/20	3	2	0	27	18	13.50	-	-	-	-	0	0	0		-	-	

Career Performances

	M	Inn	NO	Runs	HS	Avg	100	50	Ct	St	Balls	Runs	Wkts	Avg	BB	5I	10M
Test																	
FC	28	43	3	1103	140	27.57	1	5	15	-	436	274	6	45.66	2-37	-	-
ODI																	
List A	8	8	1	82	19	11.71	-	-	4	-	12	11	0		-	-	
20/20 Int																	
20/20	6	4	1	32	18	10.66	-	-	-	-	0	0	0		-	-	

69. Who topped the bowling averages in the 2005 Ashes series?

PARRY, S. — Lancashire

Name: Stephen David Parry
Role: Right-hand bat, slow left-arm bowler
Born: 12 January 1986, Manchester
Height: 6ft **Weight:** 11st 7lbs
Nickname: Pazza
County debut: 2007
Parents: David and Ann-Marie
Marital status: Single
Education: Audenshaw High School, Greater Manchester
Qualifications: 9 GCSEs, 4 A-levels
Off-season: 'Playing cricket in Australia'
Overseas teams played for: Eastern Suburbs, Sydney 2005; Bundalaguah, Melbourne 2006, 2007; Gosnells, Perth 2008
Career highlights to date: 'Getting first full-time contract with Lancashire'
Cricket superstitions: 'None'
Cricketers particularly admired: Shane Warne
Other sports played: Football, table tennis
Other sports followed: Football (Man City), Australian Rules (St Kilda)
Favourite band: The Kooks
Extras: Lancashire Young Player of the Year. Played for Cumberland in Minor Counties competitions 2005, 2006. Recorded maiden first-class five-wicket return (5-23) on debut v DUCCE at Durham 2007
Best bowling: 5-23 Lancashire v DUCCE, Durham 2007

2008 Season (Did not make any first-class or one-day appearances)

Career Performances

	M	Inn	NO	Runs	HS	Avg	100	50	Ct	St	Balls	Runs	Wkts	Avg	BB	5I	10M
Test																	
FC	1	0	0	0	0		-	-	-	-	115	46	5	9.20	5-23	1	-
ODI																	
List A																	
20/20 Int																	
20/20																	

PARSONS, T. W. Hampshire

Name: Thomas (Tom) William Parsons
Role: Right-hand lower-order bat, right-arm fast-medium bowler
Born: 2 May 1987, Melbourne, Australia
Height: 6ft 3in **Weight:** 13st 5lbs
Nickname: Teeps, TP, Jonny Teepson
County debut: 2007 (one-day, Kent), 2008 (first-class, Kent)
Parents: Richard and Christine
Marital status: Single
Family links with cricket: 'Dad played Middlesex 2nd XI. Grandfathers, uncles and cousins have all played or play'
Education: Maidstone Grammar School; Loughborough University
Qualifications: 11 GCSEs, 3 A-levels, Level 2 cricket coach
Career highlights to date: 'First-class debut for Loughborough UCCE against Worcestershire. First-team debut for Kent v Sri Lanka A. Getting Vikram Solanki out for my first first-class wicket. Taking two wickets on debut for Kent – two players who have played Test match cricket for Sri Lanka'
Cricket moments to forget: 'Getting hit on the head without a helmet in a school game, meaning I missed all my A-levels and was hospitalised for a while. Getting out needing two to win off the last ball for Loughborough UCCE against Yorkshire'
Cricket superstitions: 'Sliding my bat over the crease after every boundary'
Cricketers particularly admired: Glenn McGrath, Matthew Hoggard, Nick Knight, Ian Bell
Young players to look out for: Johan Malcolm, Arun Harinath, Jigar Naik, James Day, John Bowden, Dom O'Connell, Jonty Parsons, Robert Hulme
Other sports played: Hockey (Loughborough Town), rugby (Rutherford Hall 1st XV), squash, golf
Other sports followed: Football (Arsenal, Gillingham), rugby (Harlequins)
Favourite band: Bloc Party
Relaxations: 'Films, going out with friends, watching sport'
Extras: Kent Academy 2005. Played for Loughborough UCCE 2007. Awarded a development contract at Hampshire for 2009.
Opinions on cricket: 'Enjoy every minute of it!'
Best batting: 12 LUCCE v Worcestershire, Kidderminster 2008
Best bowling: 3-70 LUCCE v Worcestershire, Worcester 2007

2008 Season

	M	Inn	NO	Runs	HS	Avg	100	50	Ct	St	Balls	Runs	Wkts	Avg	BB	5I	10M
Test																	
FC	3	2	1	14	12	14.00	-	-	-	-	353	196	4	49.00	2-28	-	-
ODI																	
List A																	
20/20 Int																	
20/20																	

Career Performances

	M	Inn	NO	Runs	HS	Avg	100	50	Ct	St	Balls	Runs	Wkts	Avg	BB	5I	10M
Test																	
FC	5	5	1	24	12	6.00	-	-	-	-	599	312	8	39.00	3-70	-	-
ODI																	
List A	1	0	0	0	0		-	-	-	-	36	41	2	20.50	2-41	-	
20/20 Int																	
20/20																	

PATEL, S. R. — Nottinghamshire

Name: Samit Rohit Patel
Role: Right-hand bat, left-arm orthodox spin bowler; all-rounder
Born: 30 November 1984, Leicester
Height: 5ft 8in **Weight:** 12st
Nickname: Pilchy
County debut: 2002
County cap: 2008
ODI debut: 2008
Place in batting averages: 20th av. 51.42 (2007 32nd av. 50.68)
Place in bowling averages: 118th av. 37.91 (2007 19th av. 23.50)
Parents: Rohit and Sejal
Marital status: Single
Family links with cricket: Father local league cricketer and brother Akhil is with Derbyshire
Education: Worksop College
Qualifications: 7 GCSEs, 2 A-levels
Career outside cricket: 'Want to be a coach'

Overseas tours: England U17 to Australia 2001; England U19 to Australia and (U19 World Cup) New Zealand 2001-02, to Australia 2002-03, to Bangladesh (U19 World Cup) 2003-04; England to India (one-day series) 2008, to West Indies (one-day series) 2008-09; England Lions to New Zealand 2008-09
Cricket moments to forget: 'Playing at Headingley in the Twenty20 Cup against Yorkshire, where I got hit for 28 in an over by Michael Lumb'
Cricket superstitions: 'Put my right pad on first'
Cricketers particularly admired: Sachin Tendulkar, Brian Lara
Young players to look out for: Akhil Patel
Other sports played: Rugby, hockey (both for Worksop College)
Other sports followed: Football (Nottingham Forest)
Favourite band: G-Unit
Relaxations: 'Listening to music; playing snooker; just generally relaxing'
Extras: Made Nottinghamshire 2nd XI debut in 1999, aged 14. Winner of inaugural BBC *Test Match Special* U15 Young Cricketer of the Year Award 2000. Represented England U19 2002, 2003 (captain in one-day series 2003) and 2004. Scored maiden Championship hundred (156) v Middlesex at Lord's 2006, progressing from century to 150 in 17 balls. Named in England's provisional squad for the Champions Trophy 2008. Part of England's ODI squad against South Africa 2008. In January 2009, Nottinghamshire gave him the go-ahead to sign up with the IPL
Best batting: 176 Nottinghamshire v Gloucestershire, Bristol 2007
Best bowling: 4-68 Nottinghamshire v DUCCE, Durham 2007

2008 Season

	M	Inn	NO	Runs	HS	Avg	100	50	Ct	St	Balls	Runs	Wkts	Avg	BB	5I	10M
Test																	
FC	14	22	3	977	135	51.42	2	7	7	-	1029	455	12	37.91	2-26	-	-
ODI	5	1	0	31	31	31.00	-	-	2	-	160	117	7	16.71	5-41	1	
List A	21	16	1	528	114	35.20	1	4	8	-	724	560	33	16.96	5-41	1	
20/20 Int																	
20/20	9	9	1	161	56	20.12	-	1	3	-	174	187	10	18.70	3-22	-	

Career Performances

	M	Inn	NO	Runs	HS	Avg	100	50	Ct	St	Balls	Runs	Wkts	Avg	BB	5I	10M
Test																	
FC	41	61	6	2678	176	48.69	8	15	19	-	2459	1170	34	34.41	4-68	-	-
ODI	6	1	0	31	31	31.00	-	-	3	-	202	139	8	17.37	5-41	1	
List A	78	63	12	1670	114	32.74	1	9	18	-	1806	1469	63	23.31	5-41	1	
20/20 Int																	
20/20	40	39	8	770	84 *	24.83	-	5	17	-	499	620	28	22.14	3-11	-	

PATTERSON, S. A. Yorkshire

Name: Steven Andrew Patterson
Role: Right-hand bat, right-arm fast-medium bowler
Born: 3 October 1983, Hull
Height: 6ft 4in **Weight:** 14st
Nickname: Dead
County debut: 2005
Place in bowling averages: 35th av. 25.36
Parents: Sue and Alan
Marital status: Single
Education: Malet Lambert School; St Mary's Sixth Form College; Leeds University
Qualifications: 11 GCSEs, 3 A-levels, BSc Maths, Level 2 cricket coach
Overseas tours: MCC A to UAE and Oman 2004
Overseas teams played for: Suburbs New Lynn CC, Auckland 2005-06
Career highlights to date: 'Making my first-class debut for Yorkshire'
Cricket moments to forget: 'Going in as nightwatchman and getting a first-ball duck!'
Cricket superstitions: 'Not really'
Cricketers particularly admired: Glenn McGrath, Allan Donald
Young players to look out for: Adam Lyth, James Lee
Other sports played: Football, golf, badminton, skiing, scuba diving
Favourite band: Coldplay
Relaxations: 'Playing guitar, travelling, reading'
Extras: Played for Yorkshire Board XI in the 2003 C&G. 2nd XI cap 2006. Signed a new two-year contract in October 2008
Best batting: 46 Yorkshire v Lancashire, Old Trafford 2006
Best bowling: 3-19 Yorkshire v Somerset, Taunton 2008

2008 Season

	M	Inn	NO	Runs	HS	Avg	100	50	Ct	St	Balls	Runs	Wkts	Avg	BB	5I	10M
Test																	
FC	4	5	2	36	17	12.00	-	-	1	-	583	279	11	25.36	3-19	-	-
ODI																	
List A	1	0	0	0	0		-	-	-	-	48	18	2	9.00	2-18	-	
20/20 Int																	
20/20																	

Career Performances

	M	Inn	NO	Runs	HS	Avg	100	50	Ct	St	Balls	Runs	Wkts	Avg	BB	5I	10M
Test																	
FC	11	12	3	121	46	13.44	-	-	3	-	1145	574	15	38.26	3-19	-	-
ODI																	
List A	18	11	10	69	25 *	69.00	-	-	3	-	808	688	16	43.00	3-11	-	
20/20 Int																	
20/20																	

PATTINSON, D. J. Nottinghamshire

Name: Darren John Pattinson
Role: Right-hand bat, right-arm fast-medium bowler
Born: 2 August 1979, Grimsby, Lincolnshire
County debut: 2008
County cap: 2008
Test debut: 2008
Place in bowling averages: 36th av. 25.61
Family links with cricket: Brother James was part of Australia's U19 World Cup squad in 2008
Career outside cricket: Former roofer
Overseas teams played for: Dandenong, Melbourne, Australia; Victoria 2006-07 –
Extras: Born in Grimsby, but raised in Australia. Holds a British passport and is not considered an overseas player. Surprise selection for England's second Test match against South Africa, 2008. Brother made debut for Victoria 2008-09
Best batting: 33 Nottinghamshire v Kent, Canterbury 2008
Best bowling: 6-30 Nottinghamshire v Lancashire, Trent Bridge 2008

2008 Season

	M	Inn	NO	Runs	HS	Avg	100	50	Ct	St	Balls	Runs	Wkts	Avg	BB	5I	10M
Test	1	2	0	21	13	10.50	-	-	-	-	181	96	2	48.00	2-95	-	
FC	13	14	0	139	33	9.92	-	-	1	-	2318	1255	49	25.61	6-30	4	
ODI																	
List A	12	5	1	33	13 *	8.25	-	-	2	-	528	469	21	22.33	4-29	-	
20/20 Int																	
20/20	7	1	0	4	4	4.00	-	-	1	-	120	136	8	17.00	3-18	-	

Career Performances

	M	Inn	NO	Runs	HS	Avg	100	50	Ct	St	Balls	Runs	Wkts	Avg	BB	5I	10M
Test	1	2	0	21	13	10.50	-	-	-	-	181	96	2	48.00	2-95	-	-
FC	18	22	2	154	33	7.70	-	-	2	-	3121	1702	60	28.36	6-30	4	-
ODI																	
List A	24	10	3	47	13 *	6.71	-	-	9	-	1007	826	34	24.29	4-29	-	
20/20 Int																	
20/20	9	2	1	8	4 *	8.00	-	-	1	-	153	189	8	23.62	3-18	-	

PEPLOE, C. T. Middlesex

Name: Christopher (Chris) Thomas Peploe
Role: Left-hand lower-order bat, slow left-arm bowler
Born: 26 April 1981, Hammersmith, London
Height: 6ft 4in **Weight:** 13st 7lbs
Nickname: Peps, Pepsy
County debut: 2003
Parents: Trevor and Margaret
Marital status: Single
Education: Twyford C of E High School; University of Surrey, Roehampton
Qualifications: 9 GCSEs, 3 A-levels, Sports Science degree, ECB Level 2 coach, YMCA gym instructor
Career outside cricket: Cricket coach
Overseas tours: MCC Young Cricketers to South Africa 2002, to Sri Lanka 2003; Middlesex to India 2004
Overseas teams played for: Northern Districts CC, Sydney
Cricket moments to forget: 'Bowling at Nick Knight and Craig Spearman when they both scored 300-plus in 2004'
Cricket superstitions: 'None'
Cricketers particularly admired: Daniel Vettori, Andrew Strauss, Phil Tufnell
Other sports played: Golf
Other sports followed: English rugby
Favourite band: Linkin Park
Relaxations: 'Music, movies, golf'
Extras: MCC Young Cricketer 2002-03. Released at the end of the 2008 season
Best batting: 46 Middlesex v Lancashire, Lord's 2006
Best bowling: 4-31 Middlesex v Yorkshire, Southgate 2006

2008 Season

	M	Inn	NO	Runs	HS	Avg	100	50	Ct	St	Balls	Runs	Wkts	Avg	BB	5I	10M
Test																	
FC	1	1	1	6	6 *		-	-	-	-	53	15	2	7.50	2-15	-	-
ODI																	
List A																	
20/20 Int																	
20/20																	

Career Performances

	M	Inn	NO	Runs	HS	Avg	100	50	Ct	St	Balls	Runs	Wkts	Avg	BB	5I	10M
Test																	
FC	30	41	7	530	46	15.58	-	-	11	-	5283	2839	56	50.69	4-31	-	-
ODI																	
List A	18	10	3	36	14 *	5.14	-	-	7	-	816	596	26	22.92	4-38	-	
20/20 Int																	
20/20	15	6	4	12	7	6.00	-	-	4	-	221	378	10	37.80	3-35	-	

PETERS, S. D. Northamptonshire

Name: Stephen David Peters
Role: Right-hand bat, leg-break bowler
Born: 10 December 1978, Harold Wood, Essex
Height: 5ft 11in **Weight:** 12st
Nickname: Pedro, Geezer
County debut: 1996 (Essex), 2002 (Worcestershire), 2006 (Northamptonshire)
County cap: 2002 (Worcestershire colours), 2007 (Northamptonshire)
1000 runs in a season: 2
Place in batting averages: 59th av. 41.26 (2007 105th av. 34.50)
Parents: Lesley and Brian
Marital status: Single
Family links with cricket: 'All family is linked with Upminster CC'
Education: Coopers Company and Coborn School
Qualifications: 9 GCSEs, Level 2 coaching
Off-season: 'Living in Queenstown, New Zealand!'

Overseas tours: Essex U14 to Barbados; Essex U15 to Hong Kong; England U19 to Pakistan 1996-97, to South Africa (including U19 World Cup) 1997-98
Overseas teams played for: Cornwall CC, Auckland 2001-02; Willetton CC, Perth 2002-03
Career highlights to date: 'Winning B&H Cup in 1998 with Essex. Northants cap 2007'
Cricket moments to forget: 'Running myself out for a pair against Durham in 2003'
Cricket superstitions: 'Binned them all!'
Cricketers particularly admired: 'Anyone who has played at the top level'
Young players to look out for: Oscar Hibbert
Other sports played: Golf, football
Other sports followed: Football (West Ham United)
Favourite band: Rooster
Relaxations: 'Enjoying Queenstown to the full this winter'
Extras: Sir John Hobbs Silver Jubilee Memorial Prize 1994. Represented England at U14, U15, U17 and U19. Scored century (110) on Essex first-class debut v Cambridge University at Fenner's 1996, aged 17 years 194 days. Essex Young Player of the Year 1996. Man of the Match in the U19 World Cup final in South Africa 1997-98 (107)
Opinions on cricket: 'Too many for my own good, probably!'
Best batting: 178 Northamptonshire v Essex, Northampton 2006
Best bowling: 1-19 Essex v Oxford University, Chelmsford 1999

2008 Season

	M	Inn	NO	Runs	HS	Avg	100	50	Ct	St	Balls	Runs	Wkts	Avg	BB	5I	10M
Test																	
FC	16	26	3	949	130 *	41.26	3	5	14	-	0	0	0		-	-	-
ODI																	
List A	11	11	2	374	103 *	41.55	1	3	3	-	0	0	0		-	-	
20/20 Int																	
20/20	1	0	0	0	0		-	-	-	-	0	0	0		-	-	

Career Performances

	M	Inn	NO	Runs	HS	Avg	100	50	Ct	St	Balls	Runs	Wkts	Avg	BB	5I	10M
Test																	
FC	164	279	24	8315	178	32.60	18	41	125	-	35	31	1	31.00	1-19	-	-
ODI																	
List A	143	131	8	2684	107	21.82	2	15	40	-	0	0	0		-	-	
20/20 Int																	
20/20	13	10	1	82	26 *	9.11	-	-	3	-	0	0	0		-	-	

PETTINI, M. L. Essex

Name: Mark Lewis Pettini
Role: Right-hand bat, occasional wicket-keeper, county captain
Born: 7 August 1983, Brighton
Height: 5ft 10in **Weight:** 11st 6lbs
Nickname: Swampy, the Carp
County debut: 2001
County cap: 2006
1000 runs in a season: 1
1st-Class 200s: 1
Place in batting averages: 78th av. 37.21 (2007 191st av. 23.23)
Parents: Pauline and Max
Marital status: Single
Family links with cricket: 'Brother plays'
Education: Comberton Village College and Hills Road Sixth Form College, Cambridge; Cardiff University
Qualifications: 10 GCSEs, 3 A-levels, Level 1 cricket coaching award
Overseas tours: England U19 to Australia and (U19 World Cup) New Zealand 2001-02; MCC to Sierra Leone and Nigeria; Essex to Cape Town
Overseas teams played for: Rockingham-Mandurah CC, Perth 2005-07; Northern Jets, Adelaide
Career highlights to date: 'Winning two Pro40 titles with Essex. Being made Essex captain [2007]. Winning the Friends Provident Trophy 2008'
Cricket moments to forget: 'Relegation to division two of Pro40 2007'
Cricket superstitions: 'Hundreds'
Cricketers particularly admired: Graham Gooch, Andy Flower, Ronnie Irani
Young players to look out for: Tom Westley, Adam Wheater
Other sports played: Darts
Other sports followed: Football (Liverpool)
Favourite band: White Stripes, Foo Fighters, Editors
Relaxations: 'Fishing, surfing, travelling, music'
Extras: Captained Cambridgeshire U11-U16. Played for Development of Excellence XI (South) 2001. Represented England U19 2002. Essex 2nd XI Player of the Year 2002. Represented British Universities 2003 and 2004. Took over as captain of Essex during the 2007 season following the retirement of Ronnie Irani. Included in initial England squad of 30 for the Twenty20 World Championship 2007-08. Now committed to Essex until 2010
Opinions on cricket: 'Great game but too much cricket in the season – 12 Championship games instead of 16. Twenty20 is great.'
Best batting: 208* Essex v Derbyshire, Chelmsford 2006

2008 Season

	M	Inn	NO	Runs	HS	Avg	100	50	Ct	St	Balls	Runs	Wkts	Avg	BB	5I	10M
Test																	
FC	18	28	5	856	153 *	37.21	1	6	9	-	72	129	0		-	-	-
ODI																	
List A	16	16	0	553	144	34.56	2	3	5	-	0	0	0		-	-	
20/20 Int																	
20/20	9	9	0	234	66	26.00	-	2	6	-	0	0	0				

Career Performances

	M	Inn	NO	Runs	HS	Avg	100	50	Ct	St	Balls	Runs	Wkts	Avg	BB	5I	10M
Test																	
FC	63	103	11	3194	208 *	34.71	4	20	50	-	72	129	0		-	-	-
ODI																	
List A	84	76	5	1888	144	26.59	3	13	29	-	0	0	0		-	-	
20/20 Int																	
20/20	39	36	3	777	66	23.54	-	4	14	-	0	0	0			-	

PHILANDER, V. D. — Middlesex

Name: Vernon Darryl Philander
Role: Right-hand bat, right-arm fast-medium bowler ; all-rounder
Born: 24 June 1985, Bellville, Cape Province, South Africa
Nickname: Pro
County debut: 2008
ODI debut: 2007
Twenty20 Int debut: 2007
Place in bowling averages: 57th av. 27.70
Overseas tours: South African Academy to Pakistan 2005; South Africa A to Zimbabwe 2006-07, to India 2007-08; South Africa to Ireland 2007-08, to Zimbabwe 2007-08, to England 2008 (one-day series)
Overseas teams played for: Western Province 2003-04 – 2005-06; Western Province Boland 2004-05; Cape Cobras 2005-06 –
Extras: Had a short spell with Devon in 2004, playing in two C&G Trophy matches and helping the side to a famous victory over Leicestershire. Has played for South

Africa U19s and South Africa A. Was selected for the South African one-day series against Bangladesh in 2008, but withdrew through injury. Joined Middlesex as overseas player for the first part of the 2008 season, replacing Ashley Noffke.
Best batting: 168 Western Province v Griqualand West, Kimberley 2004
Best bowling: 7-64 Cape Cobras v Lions, Potchefstroom 2008

2008 Season

	M	Inn	NO	Runs	HS	Avg	100	50	Ct	St	Balls	Runs	Wkts	Avg	BB	5I	10M
Test																	
FC	3	6	1	77	30	15.40	-	-	1	-	653	277	10	27.70	3-45	-	-
ODI	2	2	0	33	23	16.50	-	-	1	-	78	80	0				
List A	9	8	4	163	32 *	40.75	-	-	1	-	450	364	7	52.00	2-31	-	
20/20 Int																	
20/20																	

Career Performances

	M	Inn	NO	Runs	HS	Avg	100	50	Ct	St	Balls	Runs	Wkts	Avg	BB	5I	10M
Test																	
FC	35	55	5	1305	168	26.10	1	6	12	-	5985	2539	114	22.27	7-64	3	-
ODI	7	5	2	73	23	24.33	-	-	2	-	275	209	6	34.83	4-12	-	
List A	54	42	14	806	76 *	28.78	-	3	5	-	2313	1820	48	37.91	4-12		
20/20 Int	7	4	0	14	6	3.50	-	-	1	-	83	114	4	28.50	2-23	-	
20/20	29	21	8	302	56 *	23.23	-	1	10	-	335	472	14	33.71	2-15	-	

70. Name the Australian bowler who took sixteen wickets on his Test debut at Lord's in 1972.

PHILLIPS, B. J. — Somerset

Name: Ben James Phillips
Role: Right-hand bat, right-arm fast-medium bowler
Born: 30 September 1975, Lewisham, London
Height: 6ft 6in **Weight:** 15st
Nickname: Bennyphil, Bus
County debut: 1996 (Kent), 2002 (Northamptonshire), 2008 (Somerset)
County cap: 2005 (Northamptonshire)
Place in batting averages: 179th av. 22.55
Place in bowling averages: 83rd av. 31.66
Parents: Glynis and Trevor
Wife and date of marriage: Sarah Jane, 20 January 2003
Family links with cricket: Father and brother both keen club cricketers for Hayes CC (Kent)
Education: Langley Park School for Boys, Beckenham
Qualifications: 9 GCSEs, 3 A-levels
Overseas tours: Northamptonshire to Grenada 2002
Overseas teams played for: University of Queensland, Australia 1993-94; Cape Technikon Green Point, Cape Town 1994-95, 1996-98; University of Western Australia, Perth 1998-99; Valley, Brisbane 2001-02
Cricket superstitions: 'Arrive at the ground early – hate rushing!'
Cricketers particularly admired: Glenn McGrath, Jason Gillespie
Other sports followed: Football (West Ham United), rugby (Northampton Saints)
Relaxations: 'Enjoy swimming, watching a good movie, and just generally like spending time with family and friends'
Extras: Set Langley Park School record for the fastest half-century, off 11 balls. Represented England U19 Schools 1993-94
Best batting: 100* Kent v Lancashire, Old Trafford 1997
Best bowling: 6-29 Northamptonshire v CUCCE, Fenner's 2006

2008 Season

	M	Inn	NO	Runs	HS	Avg	100	50	Ct	St	Balls	Runs	Wkts	Avg	BB	5I	10M
Test																	
FC	10	13	4	203	53 *	22.55	-	1	3	-	1297	665	21	31.66	3-34	-	-
ODI																	
List A	5	2	0	31	17	15.50	-	-	3	-	258	237	9	26.33	3-47	-	
20/20 Int																	
20/20	5	5	1	59	26	14.75	-	-	-	-	66	96	0		-	-	

Career Performances

	M	Inn	NO	Runs	HS	Avg	100	50	Ct	St	Balls	Runs	Wkts	Avg	BB	5I	10M
Test																	
FC	90	127	21	2212	100 *	20.86	1	12	22	-	12211	6004	197	30.47	6-29	4	-
ODI																	
List A	97	64	19	833	44 *	18.51	-	-	26	-	4032	3245	108	30.04	4-25	-	
20/20 Int																	
20/20	30	25	8	394	41 *	23.17	-	-	10	-	606	823	30	27.43	4-18	-	

PHILLIPS, T. J. — Essex

Name: Timothy (Tim) James Phillips
Role: Left-hand bat, slow left-arm bowler
Born: 13 March 1981, Cambridge
Height: 6ft 1in **Weight:** 13st
Nickname: Pips
County debut: 1999
County cap: 2006
Place in batting averages: (2007 252nd av. 13.78)
Parents: Carolyn and Martin (deceased)
Marital status: Single
Family links with cricket: 'Father played in Lancashire League then village cricket in Essex. Brother Nick plays for local village, Lindsell'
Education: Felsted School; Durham University
Qualifications: 10 GCSEs, 3 A-levels, BA (Hons) Sport in the Community
Overseas tours: Felsted School to Australia 1995-96; England U19 to Malaysia and (U19 World Cup) Sri Lanka 1999-2000
Cricket moments to forget: '2003 season' (*Out for the whole of the season with cartilage and ligament damage to a knee*)
Cricketers particularly admired: Phil Tufnell
Other sports played: Golf, hockey (Essex Schools U14, U15; East of England U21 trials)
Other sports followed: Rugby union
Favourite band: The Libertines, Coldplay, The White Stripes
Relaxations: 'Music, gigs, socialising, fishing'

Extras: Holmwoods School Cricketer of the Year runner-up 1997 and 1998. Broke Nick Knight's and Elliott Wilson's record for runs in a season for Felsted School, scoring 1213 in 1999. NBC Denis Compton Award 1999. Played for Durham UCCE 2001 and 2002. Lost much of the 2008 season to injury
Best batting: 89 Essex v Worcestershire, Worcester 2005
Best bowling: 5-41 Essex v Derbyshire, Chelmsford 2006

2008 Season

	M	Inn	NO	Runs	HS	Avg	100	50	Ct	St	Balls	Runs	Wkts	Avg	BB	5I	10M
Test																	
FC	3	4	1	41	16	13.66	-	-	3	-	84	50	1	50.00	1-18	-	-
ODI																	
List A	3	2	1	28	22 *	28.00	-	-	-	-	52	49	3	16.33	2-4	-	
20/20 Int																	
20/20	1	1	0	7	7	7.00	-	-	1	-	18	19	0		-	-	

Career Performances

	M	Inn	NO	Runs	HS	Avg	100	50	Ct	St	Balls	Runs	Wkts	Avg	BB	5I	10M
Test																	
FC	47	64	8	1074	89	19.17	-	3	30	-	6153	3937	82	48.01	5-41	1	-
ODI																	
List A	34	21	9	196	24 *	16.33	-	-	10	-	956	754	34	22.17	5-34	1	
20/20 Int																	
20/20	16	8	2	65	31	10.83	-	-	5	-	177	211	7	30.14	2-11	-	

71. Who dismissed Australian Simon O'Donnell first ball, on his Test debut in 1985?

PIETERSEN, K. P. Hampshire

Name: Kevin Peter Pietersen
Role: Right-hand bat, right-arm off-spin bowler
Born: 27 June 1980, Pietermaritzburg, South Africa
Height: 6ft 4in **Weight:** 14st 9lbs
Nickname: KP, Kelv, Kapes
County debut: 2001 (Nottinghamshire), 2005 (Hampshire)
County cap: 2002 (Nottinghamshire), 2005 (Hampshire)
Test debut: 2005
ODI debut: 2004-05
Twenty20 Int debut: 2005
1000 runs in a season: 3
1st-Class 200s: 4
Place in batting averages: 9th av. 58.91 (2007 9th av. 62.38)
Parents: Jannie and Penny
Wife and date of marriage: Jessica, 29 December 2007
Education: Maritzburg College; University of South Africa
Qualifications: 3 A-levels
Overseas tours: Natal to Zimbabwe 1999-2000, to Australia 2000-01; Nottinghamshire to South Africa 2001, 2002; England A to Malaysia and India 2003-04; England to Zimbabwe (one-day series) 2004-05, to South Africa 2004-05 (one-day series), to Pakistan 2005-06, to India 2005-06, to India (ICC Champions Trophy) 2006-07, to Australia 2006-07, to West Indies (World Cup) 2006-07, to South Africa (World 20/20) 2007-08, to Sri Lanka 2007-08, to New Zealand 2007-08, to India 2008-09 (c), to West Indies 2008-09; ICC World XI to Australia (Super Series) 2005-06
Overseas teams played for: Berea Rovers, Durban 1997 – 2001-02; KwaZulu-Natal 1997-98 – 2000-01; Sydney University 2002-03
Career highlights to date: 'Scoring the three centuries in South Africa for England 2005'
Cricket moments to forget: 'Breaking my leg against Glamorgan in August 2002 in an NUL game'
Cricket superstitions: 'Left pad first'
Cricketers particularly admired: Shaun Pollock, Errol Stewart
Other sports played: Golf, swimming ('represented my state in 1992-93'), running
Other sports followed: Formula One (Ferrari), rugby (Natal Sharks)
Player website: www.kevinpietersen.com
Extras: Played for South Africa Schools B 1997. Scored 61* and had figures of 4-141 from 56 overs for KwaZulu-Natal v England XI 1999-2000. Scored 1275 first-

class runs in first season of county cricket 2001. Player of the [ODI] Series v South Africa 2004-05 (454 runs at 151.33, including the fastest hundred for England in ODIs, from 69 balls). Scored maiden Test century (158, including an Ashes record seven sixes) in the fifth Test v Australia at The Oval 2005, winning Man of the Match award. Scored maiden Test double century (226) in the second Test v West Indies at Headingley 2007, winning Man of the Match award. His other international awards include Man of the Match v Australia at Bristol in the NatWest Series 2005 (65-ball 91*), England's Man of the [Test] Series v Sri Lanka 2006, and Man of the Match in the first Test v India at Lord's 2007 (134). Scored 158 in the second Test v Australia at Adelaide 2006-07, in the process sharing with Paul Collingwood (206) in a record fourth-wicket partnership for England in Tests v Australia (310). ECB National Academy 2003-04, 2004-05. ICC Emerging Player of the Year and ICC ODI Player of the Year awards 2005. Appointed MBE in 2006 New Year Honours as part of 2005 Ashes-winning England team. One of *Wisden*'s Five Cricketers of the Year 2006. Autobiography *Crossing the Boundary: The Early Years in My Cricketing Life* published 2006. Succeeded Michael Vaughan as England captain in August 2008 - relinquished the post in January 2009. Is married to Liberty X singer Jessica Taylor
Best batting: 254* Nottinghamshire v Middlesex, Trent Bridge 2002
Best bowling: 4-31 Nottinghamshire v DUCCE, Trent Bridge 2003
Stop press: Signed to play in IPL 2009 when Bangalore Royal Challengers bid $1.55m in auction

2008 Season

	M	Inn	NO	Runs	HS	Avg	100	50	Ct	St	Balls	Runs	Wkts	Avg	BB	5I	10M
Test	7	11	0	607	152	55.18	3	1	5	-	129	73	1	73.00	1-0	-	-
FC	8	12	0	707	152	58.91	4	1	5	-	153	89	1	89.00	1-0	-	-
ODI	10	8	2	268	110 *	44.66	1	1	2	-	30	22	2	11.00	2-22	-	
List A	12	10	2	353	110 *	44.12	1	2	2	-	60	56	2	28.00	2-22	-	
20/20 Int	1	1	1	42	42 *		-	-	-	-	0	0	0		-	-	
20/20	2	2	1	85	43	85.00	-	-	1	-	18	33	3	11.00	3-33	-	

Career Performances

	M	Inn	NO	Runs	HS	Avg	100	50	Ct	St	Balls	Runs	Wkts	Avg	BB	5I	10M
Test	43	80	3	3890	226	50.51	14	11	29	-	609	431	4	107.75	1-0	-	-
FC	127	213	15	10172	254 *	51.37	36	39	109	-	5377	3104	60	51.73	4-31	-	-
ODI	82	73	14	2822	116	47.83	6	19	31	-	143	134	4	33.50	2-22	-	
List A	190	172	31	6257	147	44.37	11	40	73	-	2103	1853	38	48.76	3-14	-	
20/20 Int	14	14	1	363	79	27.92	-	1	6	-	0	0	0		-	-	
20/20	25	25	1	662	79	27.58	-	3	7	-	126	169	9	18.77	3-33	-	

PIOLET, S. A. — Warwickshire

Name: Steffan Andreas Piolet
Role: Right-hand bat, right-arm medium bowler
Born: 8 August 1988, Redhill
County debut: No first-team appearances
Education: Millfield School; Oxford Brookes University
Cricketers particularly admired: Jacques Kallis
Extras: Has played for Worcestershire 2nd XI (debut v Gloucestershire 2nd XI, Bristol, May 2006) and Sussex 2nd XI (debut v Yorkshire 2nd XI, Hove, June 2006). Made debut for Warwickshire 2nd XI v Middlesex 2nd XI, Northwood, June 2008

PIPE, D. J. — Derbyshire

Name: David James Pipe
Role: Right-hand bat, wicket-keeper
Born: 16 December 1977, Bradford
Height: 5ft 11in **Weight:** 13st
Nickname: Pipey
County debut: 1998 (Worcestershire), 2006 (Derbyshire)
County cap: 2002 (Worcestershire colours), 2007 (Derbyshire)
50 dismissals in a season: 1
Place in batting averages: 54th av. 42.00 (2007 98th av. 36.06)
Parents: David and Dorothy
Marital status: Single
Family links with cricket: 'My dad and uncle played in the local league'
Education: Queensbury Upper School; BICC

Qualifications: 8 GCSEs, BTEC National in Business and Finance, HND Leisure Management, senior coaching award, Diploma in Personal Training, Diploma in Sports Therapy
Overseas teams played for: Leeming Spartans CC/South Metropolitan Cricket Association, Perth 1998-99; Manly CC, Australia 1999-2004
Career highlights to date: 'Getting first hundred'
Cricket moments to forget: 'Any game we lose'
Cricket superstitions: 'None'
Cricketers particularly admired: Adam Gilchrist, Ian Healy
Young players to look out for: Brett D'Oliveira (Worcestershire Academy), Gary Ballance, Dan Redfern
Other sports followed: Rugby league (Bradford Bulls, Manly Sea Eagles), boxing ('all British fighters'), AFL (West Coast Eagles)
Relaxations: Training
Extras: MCC School of Merit Wilf Slack Memorial Trophy winner 1995. Took eight catches v Hertfordshire at Hertford in the C&G 2001 to set a new NatWest/C&G record for most dismissals in a match by a wicket-keeper. Dick Lygon Award 2002 (Worcestershire Club Man of the Year). Derbyshire Club Man of the Year 2006
Best batting: 133* Derbyshire v Essex, Chelmsford 2007

2008 Season

	M	Inn	NO	Runs	HS	Avg	100	50	Ct	St	Balls	Runs	Wkts	Avg	BB	5I	10M
Test																	
FC	9	15	3	504	133	42.00	1	3	23	1	0	0	0		-	-	-
ODI																	
List A	6	5	2	47	20	15.66	-	-	11	1	0	0	0		-	-	
20/20 Int																	
20/20	10	9	1	162	45	20.25	-	-	3	2	0	0	0		-		

Career Performances

	M	Inn	NO	Runs	HS	Avg	100	50	Ct	St	Balls	Runs	Wkts	Avg	BB	5I	10M
Test																	
FC	68	103	17	2377	133 *	27.63	4	9	189	19	0	0	0		-	-	-
ODI																	
List A	64	52	12	730	83	18.25	-	3	58	17	0	0	0		-	-	
20/20 Int																	
20/20	35	29	5	316	45	13.16	-	-	15	11	0	0	0		-		

PLUNKETT, L. E. — Durham

Name: Liam Edward Plunkett
Role: Right-hand bat, right-arm fast bowler
Born: 6 April 1985, Middlesbrough
Height: 6ft 4in **Weight:** 13st
Nickname: Pudsey
County debut: 2003
Test debut: 2005-06
ODI debut: 2005-06
Twenty20 Int debut: 2006
50 wickets in a season: 2
Place in batting averages: 146th av. 27.28 (2007 215th av. 20.38)
Place in bowling averages: 91st av. 32.50 (2007 68th av. 30.60)
Parents: Alan and Marie
Family links with cricket: 'Father played a good standard of local cricket'
Education: Nunthorpe Comprehensive, Teesside Tertiary College
Qualifications: 9 GCSEs, volleyball coaching badge
Overseas tours: England U19 to Australia 2002-03, to Bangladesh (U19 World Cup) 2003-04; England to Pakistan 2005-06, to India 2005-06, to Australia 2006-07, to West Indies (World Cup) 2006-07; England Lions to India 2007-08. England Performance Programme to India 2008-09. England Lions to New Zealand 2008-09
Overseas teams played for: Adelaide University 2005; Durban Dolphins, South Africa 2007-08
Career highlights to date: 'England debut'
Cricket moments to forget: 'Injury (oblique)' (*Out from July to September 2006 with a damaged oblique muscle*)
Cricket superstitions: 'None'
Cricketers particularly admired: Glenn McGrath
Young players to look out for: Ben Harmison
Other sports played: Golf, swimming
Other sports followed: Football (Middlesbrough, Arsenal)
Favourite band: 'R&B'
Extras: Became only the second bowler to record a five-wicket innings return on Championship debut for Durham, 5-53 v Yorkshire at Headingley 2003. Represented England U19 2003. NBC Denis Compton Award for the most promising young Durham player 2003, 2005. ECB National Academy 2004-05 (part-time), 2005-06. Friends Provident Man of the Match award in the semi-final v Essex at Riverside 2007 (4-15/30*). Joint top wicket-taker in Twenty20 for Durham in 2008
Opinions on cricket: 'Twenty20 game loaded towards batsmen.'

Best batting: 74* Durham v Somerset, Stockton 2005
Best bowling: 6-74 Durham v Hampshire, Riverside 2004

2008 Season

	M	Inn	NO	Runs	HS	Avg	100	50	Ct	St	Balls	Runs	Wkts	Avg	BB	5I	10M
Test																	
FC	7	9	2	191	68 *	27.28	-	2	5	-	775	520	16	32.50	3-49	-	
ODI																	
List A	9	6	2	146	72	36.50	-	1	3	-	343	299	6	49.83	2-54	-	
20/20 Int																	
20/20	11	6	3	35	13 *	11.66	-	-	3	-	220	228	13	17.53	3-16	-	

Career Performances

	M	Inn	NO	Runs	HS	Avg	100	50	Ct	St	Balls	Runs	Wkts	Avg	BB	5I	10M
Test	9	13	2	126	44 *	11.45	-	-	3	-	1538	916	23	39.82	3-17	-	
FC	68	102	21	1591	74 *	19.64	-	6	37	-	10432	6423	202	31.79	6-74	5	-
ODI	27	24	10	295	56	21.07	-	1	7	-	1291	1260	37	34.05	3-24	-	
List A	77	51	21	715	72	23.83	-	2	16	-	3490	3061	99	30.91	4-15	-	
20/20 Int	1	0	0	0	0		-	-	-	-	24	37	1	37.00	1-37	-	
20/20	22	12	7	64	13 *	12.80	-	-	7	-	428	505	21	24.04	3-16	-	

POLLOCK, S. M. — Durham

Name: Shaun Maclean Pollock
Role: Right-hand bat, right-arm fast-medium bowler
Born: 16 July 1973, Port Elizabeth, South Africa
Height: 6ft 3in
Nickname: Polly
County debut: 1996 (Warwickshire), 2008 (Durham)
County cap: 1996 (Warwickshire)
Test debut: 1995
ODI debut: 1996
Parents: Peter and Inez
Wife: Patricia ('Trish')
Children: Jemma, August 2003, Georgia, July 2006
Family links with cricket: Father played for Eastern Province and South Africa (1959-71)

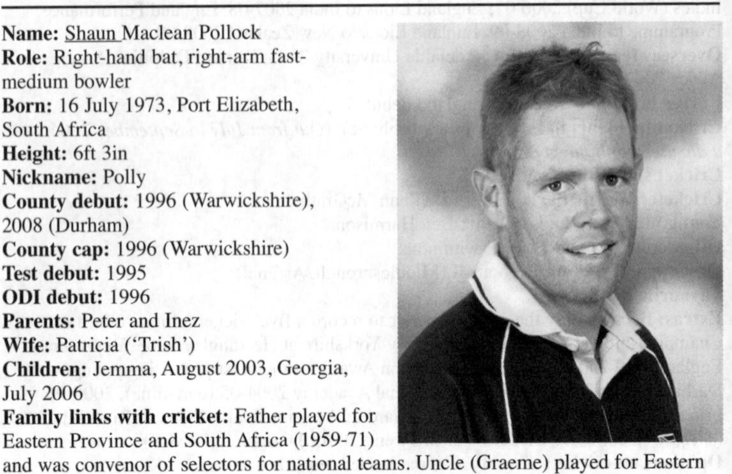

and was convenor of selectors for national teams. Uncle (Graeme) played for Eastern

Province, Transvaal and South Africa (1960-86) and is a national selector
Education: Northlands Primary School, Durban, Natal; Northwood, Durban, Natal; Natal University
Qualifications: B Comm
Overseas tours: South Africa Tertiary Team to Kenya and Zimbabwe 1994-95; South Africa U24 to Sri Lanka 1995-96; South Africa VI to Hong Kong Sixes 1995; South Africa to India and Pakistan (World Cup) 1995-96, to Pakistan 1997-98, to Australia 1997-98, to England 1998, to New Zealand 1998-99, to UK, Ireland and Holland (World Cup) 1999, to Zimbabwe 1999-2000, to India 1999-2000, to Sri Lanka 2000 (captain), to Australia (Super Challenge) 2000-01 (captain), to Kenya (ICC Knockout) 2000-01 (captain), to West Indies 2000-01 (captain), to Zimbabwe 2001-02 (captain), to Australia 2001-02 (captain), to Morocco (Morocco Cup) 2002 (captain), to Sri Lanka 2002-03 (ICC Champions Trophy) (captain), to Bangladesh 2003, to England 2003, to Pakistan 2003-04, to New Zealand 2003-04, to Sri Lanka 2004, to England 2004 (ICC Champions Trophy), to India 2004-05, to West Indies 2004-05, to Australia 2005-06, to India 2005-06, to Sri Lanka 2006, to India 2006-07 (ICC Champions Trophy), to West Indies 2006-07 (World Cup), to Pakistan 2007-08
Overseas teams played for: Natal/KwaZulu-Natal 1991-92 – 2003-04 Dolphins 2003-04 – 2007-08; Mumbai Indians (IPL) 2007-08
Other sports followed: Golf, hockey, tennis, rugby and soccer
Relaxations: Watching sport, spending time with friends and listening to music
Extras: Played for Natal Nuffield team and then selected for South Africa Schools in 1991. Made first-class debut for Natal B v Western Province B at Pietermaritzburg 1991-92. Was voted Player of the Series in the South Africa v England one-day series 1995-96. Won B&H Gold Award on Warwickshire debut v Leicestershire at Edgbaston 1996, during which game he became the first bowler to take four wickets (Macmillan, Whitaker, Robinson, Maddy) in four balls in the competition, ending up with 6-21. One of South Africa's five Players of the Year 1996, 1998 and 2001. Took 7-87 from 41 overs in Australia's first innings of the third Test at Adelaide 1997-98. Appointed captain of South Africa in April 2000. Was Man of the Series v Sri Lanka 2000-01, during which he became the second South African bowler to pass 200 Test wickets (at Durban) and scored a 95-ball maiden Test century (111 at Centurion, batting at No. 9). Topped batting averages (302 runs av. 75.50) and was second in bowling averages (20 wickets av. 23.20) in Test series in West Indies 2000-01, in the process scoring his second Test century batting at No. 9 (106*) in the third Test at Bridgetown and picking up Man of the Series award for Test and one-day matches. Recorded maiden Test ten-wicket match return (10-147) in the first Test v India at Bloemfontein 2001-02, winning Man of the Match award. Scored 113* in the unofficial 'Test' v India at Centurion 2001-02, winning Man of the Match award. Rejoined Warwickshire as overseas player for 2002. B&H Gold Award for his 64 and 4-12 v Glamorgan at Cardiff 2002. C&G Man of the Match award for his 47 plus 0-9 from eight overs v Staffordshire at Stone 2002. Scored maiden one-day century (111*) v Worcestershire at Worcester in the NUL 2002. Left Warwickshire at the end of the 2002 season. Announced his retirement from international cricket in January 2008. One of only six players to have scored over 3000 runs and taken over 300 wickets in Test matches.

Signed by Durham as an overseas player for the 2008 season. Joint top Twenty20 wicket-taker for his county in 2008

Best batting: 150* Warwickshire v Glamorgan, Edgbaston 1996

Best bowling: 7-33 Natal v Border, East London 1995

2008 Season

	M	Inn	NO	Runs	HS	Avg	100	50	Ct	St	Balls	Runs	Wkts	Avg	BB	5I	10M
Test																	
FC																	
ODI																	
List A	1	1	0	18	18	18.00	-	-	-	-	60	51	0		-	-	
20/20 Int																	
20/20	11	8	3	91	20	18.20	-	-	3	-	232	210	13	16.15	2-15	-	

Career Performances

	M	Inn	NO	Runs	HS	Avg	100	50	Ct	St	Balls	Runs	Wkts	Avg	BB	5I	10M
Test	108	156	39	3781	111	32.31	2	16	72	-	24353	9733	421	23.11	7-87	16	1
FC	186	267	55	7021	150 *	33.11	6	35	132	-	39067	15508	667	23.25	7-33	22	2
ODI	303	205	72	3519	130	26.45	1	14	108	-	15712	9631	393	24.50	6-35	5	
List A	435	297	91	5494	134 *	26.66	3	24	153	-	21588	13141	573	22.93	6-21	7	
20/20 Int	12	9	2	86	36 *	12.28	-	-	2	-	243	309	15	20.60	3-28	-	
20/20	46	34	7	569	59	21.07	-	1	9	-	937	996	45	22.13	3-12	-	

POONIA, N. S. — Warwickshire

Name: Navdeep (Navi) Singh Poonia

Role: Right-hand bat, right-arm medium bowler

Born: 11 May 1986, Glasgow

Height: 6ft 3in **Weight:** 14st

Nickname: Nav, Sat Nav

County debut: 2006

ODI debut: 2006

Twenty20 Int debut: 2007-08

Place in batting averages: 148th av. 27.15

Parents: Jaipal and Bindy Poonia

Marital status: Single

Family links with cricket: 'Dad played club cricket at Walsall CC'

Education: Moseley Park School; Wolverhampton University

Qualifications: 10 GCSEs, 2 A-levels, Levels 1 and 2 coaching

Overseas tours: Warwickshire Academy to South Africa 2005; Scotland to Bangladesh (one-day series) 2006-07, to Kenya (including ICC World Cricket League) 2006-07, to West Indies (World Cup) 2006-07, to Ireland (Quadrangular Series) 2007, to South Africa (World 20/20) 2007-08
Cricket superstitions: 'None'
Cricketers particularly admired: Sachin Tendulkar, Brian Lara, Allan Donald
Other sports played: Football, badminton
Other sports followed: Football (Man Utd and Glasgow Rangers)
Relaxations: 'Playing snooker with mates and cousins'
Extras: Played for Warwickshire Board XI in the 2003 C&G. Cyril Goodway (Warwickshire Old County Cricketers' Association) Trophy U17. Top-scored with 59 on county one-day debut v Nottinghamshire at Edgbaston in the C&G 2006. Has played one-day (including ODI and Twenty20 Int) cricket for Scotland
Best batting: 111 Warwickshire v Cambridge UCCE, Fenner's 2008

2008 Season

	M	Inn	NO	Runs	HS	Avg	100	50	Ct	St	Balls	Runs	Wkts	Avg	BB	5I	10M
Test																	
FC	12	19	0	516	111	27.15	1	2	5	-	0	0	0		-	-	-
ODI																	
List A	5	4	0	128	75	32.00	-	1	-	-	0	0	0		-	-	
20/20 Int																	
20/20	1	1	0	0	0	0.00	-	-	-	-	0	0	0		-	-	

Career Performances

	M	Inn	NO	Runs	HS	Avg	100	50	Ct	St	Balls	Runs	Wkts	Avg	BB	5I	10M
Test																	
FC	13	20	0	551	111	27.55	1	2	5	-	0	0	0		-	-	-
ODI	16	16	0	199	67	12.43	-	1	4	-	0	0	0		-	-	
List A	31	30	0	578	75	19.26	-	3	5	-	0	0	0		-	-	
20/20 Int	5	4	2	68	38 *	34.00	-	-	2	-	0	0	0		-	-	
20/20	9	8	2	100	38 *	16.66	-	-	2	-	0	0	0		-	-	

POPE, J. I. — Leicestershire

Name: Joel Ian Pope
Role: Right-hand bat, wicket-keeper
Born: 23 October 1988, Ashford, Middlesex
Height: 5ft 7in **Weight:** 10st 2lbs
Nickname: Popey
County debut: 2008 (one-day)
Parents: Tania and Ian
Marital status: Single
Family links with cricket: 'Uncle (Ben Scott) is wicket-keeper for Middlesex. Dad and Grandad played at club level for Wycombe House'
Education: Whitton Sports College
Qualifications: 9 GCSEs, Level 1 coach
Overseas tours: MCC Young Cricketers to St Kitts and Nevis 2007
Overseas teams played for: Melville CC, Perth 2007-08
Career highlights to date: 'Fielding for England as thirteenth man at Lord's against the West Indies'
Cricket superstitions: 'Put left pad on first'
Cricketers particularly admired: Jack Russell, Alec Stewart, Mike Hussey
Other sports played: Golf, football
Other sports followed: Football (Manchester United)
Favourite band: Oasis
Relaxations: 'Art, music'
Extras: MCC Young Cricketers 2007. Played for Middlesex U10-19, Middlesex Academy and 2nd XI. Plays for Sunbury CC.
Opinions on cricket: 'Quick and entertaining – good for the crowds.'

2008 Season

	M	Inn	NO	Runs	HS	Avg	100	50	Ct	St	Balls	Runs	Wkts	Avg	BB	5I	10M
Test																	
FC																	
ODI																	
List A	1	1	0	9	9	9.00	-	-	2	1	0	0	0		-	-	
20/20 Int																	
20/20																	

Career Performances

	M	Inn	NO	Runs	HS	Avg	100	50	Ct	St	Balls	Runs	Wkts	Avg	BB	5I	10M
Test																	
FC																	
ODI																	
List A	1	1	0	9	9	9.00	-	-	2	1	0	0	0		-	-	
20/20 Int																	
20/20																	

PORTERFIELD, W. T. S. Gloucestershire

Name: William Thomas Stuart Porterfield
Role: Left-hand bat, occasional right-arm off-break bowler
Born: 6 September 1984, Londonderry, Northern Ireland
Height: 5ft 11in **Weight:** 12st
Nickname: Purdy, Porty, Porters
County debut: 2008
ODI debut: 2006
Place in batting averages: 110th av. 31.79
Parents: William and Alison
Marital status: Single
Family links with cricket: Father played for Killyclooney CC
Education: Strabane Grammar School; Leeds Metropolitan University
Qualifications: BA (Hons) Physical Education (2.1)
Off-season: 'Training in Bristol and World Cup qualifiers with Ireland'
Overseas tours: Ireland U19 to Bangladesh (U19 World Cup) 2003-04; Ireland to Scotland (European Championship) 2006, to Kenya (ICC World Cricket League) 2006-07, to West Indies (World Cup) 2006-07, to South Africa 2008 (v Namibia), plus various Ireland age-group and A tours
Overseas teams played for: Rush CC, Dublin
Career highlights to date: '2006-07 World Cup in West Indies with Ireland'
Cricket moments to forget: 'Not qualifying for the Twenty20 World Championship in South Africa (2007)'
Cricketers particularly admired: Brian Lara
Young players to look out for: Paul Stirling
Other sports played: 'Rugby at school; bit of football'
Other sports followed: Football (Manchester United and Northern Ireland)

Relaxations: 'Socialising'
Extras: Played for Bradford/Leeds UCCE in 2004 and 2006. Played for MCC YC 2004-06. Attended ICC Winter Training Camp in South Africa 2006-07. Has represented Ireland in first-class and one-day cricket, including ODIs and C&G/Friends Provident. Man of the Match v Bermuda in Nairobi in the ICC World Cricket League 2006-07 (112*) and v Bangladesh in Bridgetown in the World Cup 2006-07 (85). Played for MCC in 2007. NBC Denis Compton Award for the most promising young Gloucestershire player 2008
Best batting: 166 Ireland v Bermuda, Dublin 2007
Best bowling: 1-57 Gloucestershire v Loughborough UCCE, Bristol 2008

2008 Season

	M	Inn	NO	Runs	HS	Avg	100	50	Ct	St	Balls	Runs	Wkts	Avg	BB	5I	10M
Test																	
FC	13	24	0	763	93	31.79	-	7	7	-	36	57	1	57.00	1-57	-	-
ODI																	
List A	8	7	0	225	69	32.14	-	2	1	-	0	0	0		-	-	
20/20 Int																	
20/20	3	3	0	73	62	24.33	-	1	2	-	0	0	0		-	-	

Career Performances

	M	Inn	NO	Runs	HS	Avg	100	50	Ct	St	Balls	Runs	Wkts	Avg	BB	5I	10M
Test																	
FC	21	35	1	1199	166	35.26	1	8	12	-	36	57	1	57.00	1-57	-	-
ODI	27	27	2	685	112 *	27.40	2	2	12	-	0	0	0		-	-	
List A	47	46	2	1261	112 *	28.65	2	7	15	-	0	0	0		-	-	
20/20 Int	4	3	0	11	7	3.66	-	-	1	-	0	0	0		-	-	
20/20	7	6	0	84	62	14.00	-	1	3	-	0	0	0		-	-	

72. While Ian Botham was scoring 149 not out in the Ashes Test at Headingley in 1981, who helped him out by scoring 56?

POTHAS, N. Hampshire

Name: Nicolas (Nic) Pothas
Role: Right-hand bat, wicket-keeper
Born: 18 November 1973, Johannesburg, South Africa
Height: 6ft 1in **Weight:** 13st 7lbs
Nickname: Skeg
County debut: 2002
County cap: 2003
ODI debut: 2000
50 dismissals in a season: 3
Place in batting averages: 18th av. 53.50 (2007 42nd av. 46.87)
Parents: Emmanuel and Penelope
Marital status: Single
Family links with cricket: 'Greek by nationality, therefore clearly none'
Education: King Edward VII High School; Rand Afrikaans University
Overseas tours: South Africa A to England 1996, to Sri Lanka 1998-99, to West Indies 2000-01; Gauteng to Australia 1997; South Africa to Singapore (Singapore Challenge) 2000-01
Overseas teams played for: Transvaal/Gauteng 1993-94 – 2001-02; Delhi Giants (ICL) 2008-09
Career highlights to date: 'First tour for South Africa A. Playing for South Africa'
Cricket superstitions: 'Too many to mention'
Cricketers particularly admired: Ray Jennings, Jimmy Cook, Robin Smith
Other sports played: Hockey (South Africa U21, Transvaal)
Other sports followed: Football (Manchester United)
Favourite band: Counting Crows, Gin Blossoms, Just Jinjer
Relaxations: 'Shopping; designing clothes; sleeping; gym'
Extras: Scored maiden first-class century (147) for South African Students v England tourists at Pietermaritzburg 1995-96. Benson and Hedges Young Player of the Year 1996. Transvaal Player of the Year 1996, 1998. C&G Man of the Match award v Glamorgan at Cardiff 2005 (114*). Scored 139 v Gloucestershire at Cheltenham 2005, in the process sharing with Andy Bichel (138) in a new Hampshire record partnership for the eighth wicket (257). Took seven catches in an innings v Lancashire at Old Trafford 2006, becoming the first Hampshire wicket-keeper to achieve the feat in a first-class match. Made 51 dismissals and scored 973 runs in first-class cricket 2005; 58 dismissals and 973 runs in first-class cricket 2006. Finished top of the Hampshire first-class run makers in 2008. Will captain Hampshire in the early-season absence of Dimitri Mascarenhas. Is not considered an overseas player

Best batting: 165 Gauteng v KwaZulu-Natal, Johannesburg 1998-99
Best bowling: 1-16 Hampshire v Middlesex, Lord's 2006

2008 Season

	M	Inn	NO	Runs	HS	Avg	100	50	Ct	St	Balls	Runs	Wkts	Avg	BB	5I	10M
Test																	
FC	14	23	5	963	137 *	53.50	3	3	45	1	0	0	0	-	-	-	-
ODI																	
List A	10	7	4	122	55	40.66	-	1	5	2	0	0	0	-	-	-	
20/20 Int																	
20/20	10	8	2	69	19	11.50	-	-	1	3	0	0	0	-	-	-	

Career Performances

	M	Inn	NO	Runs	HS	Avg	100	50	Ct	St	Balls	Runs	Wkts	Avg	BB	5I	10M
Test																	
FC	190	295	55	9788	165	40.78	23	48	535	45	120	63	1	63.00	1-16	-	-
ODI	3	1	0	24	24	24.00	-	-	4	1	0	0	0	-	-	-	
List A	218	183	65	4236	114 *	35.89	3	23	199	49	0	0	0	-	-	-	
20/20 Int																	
20/20	43	32	12	385	59	19.25	-	2	17	7	0	0	0	-	-	-	

POWELL, M. J. Warwickshire

Name: Michael James Powell
Role: Right-hand opening/middle-order bat, right-arm medium bowler
Born: 5 April 1975, Bolton
Height: 5ft 10in **Weight:** 12st 2lbs
Nickname: Arthur, Powelly
County debut: 1996
County cap: 1999
Benefit: 2008
1000 runs in a season: 1
1st-Class 200s: 1
Place in batting averages: 163rd av. 24.86 (2007 163rd av. 27.50)
Parents: Terry and Pat
Marital status: Single
Family links with cricket: 'Father loves the game. Brother John played for Warwickshire youth teams'
Education: Lawrence Sheriff Grammar School, Rugby

Qualifications: 6 GCSEs, 2 A-levels, Levels I-III ECB coaching awards
Career outside cricket: Coaching
Overseas tours: England U18 to South Africa 1992-93 (c), to Denmark 1993 (c); England U19 to Sri Lanka 1993-94; England A to West Indies 2000-01
Overseas teams played for: Avendale CC, Cape Town 1994-95, 1996-97, 2000-01; Griqualand West, South Africa 2001-02
Career highlights to date: 'B&H Cup winners 2002. Frizzell County Champions 2004'
Cricket superstitions: 'None'
Cricketers particularly admired: Dermot Reeve, Shaun Pollock, Allan Donald
Young players to look out for: Moeen Ali
Other sports played: Golf, rugby (Warwickshire U16-U18)
Other sports followed: Football
Extras: Captained Warwickshire U14-U19 and England U17 and U18. Became first uncapped Warwickshire player for 49 years to carry his bat, for 70* out of 130 v Nottinghamshire at Edgbaston 1998. Captain of Warwickshire 2001-03. Released at the end of September 2008
Best batting: 236 Warwickshire v OUCCE, The Parks 2001
Best bowling: 2-16 Warwickshire v Oxford University, The Parks 1998

2008 Season

	M	Inn	NO	Runs	HS	Avg	100	50	Ct	St	Balls	Runs	Wkts	Avg	BB	5I	10M
Test																	
FC	11	16	1	373	68 *	24.86	-	2	6	-	6	1	0		-	-	-
ODI																	
List A	6	6	2	151	47 *	37.75	-	-	3	-	0	0	0		-	-	
20/20 Int																	
20/20	9	5	2	64	25 *	21.33	-	-	3	-	0	0	0		-	-	

Career Performances

	M	Inn	NO	Runs	HS	Avg	100	50	Ct	St	Balls	Runs	Wkts	Avg	BB	5I	10M
Test																	
FC	149	246	12	7395	236	31.60	12	40	105	-	1320	745	11	67.72	2-16	-	-
ODI																	
List A	118	99	17	2118	101 *	25.82	1	5	56	-	824	727	25	29.08	5-40	1	
20/20 Int																	
20/20	24	18	6	264	44*	22.00	-	-	10	-	0	0	0		-	-	

73. Name the ground which is due to host an Ashes Test for the first time in 2009.

POWELL, M. J. — Glamorgan

Name: Michael John Powell
Role: Right-hand bat, right-arm off-break bowler
Born: 3 February 1977, Abergavenny
Height: 6ft 1in **Weight:** 14st 8lbs
Nickname: Powelly
County debut: 1997
County cap: 2000
1000 runs in a season: 5
1st-Class 200s: 3
Place in batting averages: 113th av. 31.52 (2007 30th av. 50.87)
Parents: Linda and John
Marital status: Single
Family links with cricket: 'Dad and Uncle Mike both played for Abergavenny'
Education: Crickhowell Secondary School; Pontypool College
Qualifications: 5 GCSEs, BTEC National Diploma in Sports Science, Level 1 coaching award
Overseas tours: Glamorgan to Cape Town 1999, 2002; England A to Sri Lanka 2004-05
Overseas teams played for: Wests, Brisbane 1996-97; Cornwall CC, Auckland 1998-99, 2000-01
Cricket moments to forget: 'You wouldn't want to forget any of it'
Cricket superstitions: 'None'
Other sports played: Rugby (Crickhowell RFC)
Other sports followed: Rugby (Cardiff)
Relaxations: Eating and sleeping
Extras: Scored 200* on first-class debut v Oxford University at The Parks 1997. Second XI Championship Player of the Year 1997 (1210 runs at 75.63). NBC Denis Compton Award for the most promising young Glamorgan player 2000. Acted as 12th man in the third Test v Sri Lanka at Old Trafford 2002, taking the catch that ended Sri Lanka's second innings. Included in England one-day squad for NatWest Series 2004. ECB National Academy 2004-05. Glamorgan Player of the Year 2006. Had a serious operation to remove a rib in 2007
Best batting: 299 Glamorgan v Gloucestershire, Cheltenham 2006
Best bowling: 2-39 Glamorgan v Oxford University, The Parks 1999

2008 Season

	M	Inn	NO	Runs	HS	Avg	100	50	Ct	St	Balls	Runs	Wkts	Avg	BB	5I	10M
Test																	
FC	16	26	3	725	120	31.52	1	3	15	-	0	0	0		-	-	-
ODI																	
List A	15	15	1	338	114 *	24.14	1	1	5	-	0	0	0		-	-	
20/20 Int																	
20/20	9	7	0	134	36	19.14	-	-	3	-	0	0	0		-	-	

Career Performances

	M	Inn	NO	Runs	HS	Avg	100	50	Ct	St	Balls	Runs	Wkts	Avg	BB	5I	10M
Test																	
FC	176	298	28	10577	299	39.17	23	51	113	-	164	132	2	66.00	2-39	-	-
ODI																	
List A	195	184	20	4550	114 *	27.74	1	25	78	-	24	26	1	26.00	1-26	-	
20/20 Int																	
20/20	34	31	2	668	68 *	23.03	-	5	12	-	0	0	0		-	-	

POYNTON, T. J. — Derbyshire

Name: Thomas (Tom) James Poynton
Role: Right-hand bat, wicket-keeper
Born: 25 November 1989, Burton-on-Trent, Staffordshire
Height: 5ft 10in **Weight:** 11st
Nickname: TP, Poynts
County debut: 2007
Parents: Keith and Sheena
Marital status: 'Long-term relationship – Megan Jacobs'
Family links with cricket: 'Brother plays at same club – Lullington Park CC. Both parents involved in club cricket and keen county supporters'
Education: John Taylor High School; Repton School (Sixth Form)
Qualifications: 11 GCSEs, 3 A-levels, Level 1 ECB coach
Career outside cricket: Part-time coach
Off-season: 'Winter training programme with Derbyshire; tour to South Africa with England U19s; ECB National Skill Sets, completing level 2 coaching badge, part-time

coaching with Derbyshire Cricket Board'
Overseas tours: Derbyshire Academy to South Africa 2006; Repton School to Grenada 2007; England U19 to South Africa 2008-09
Career highlights to date: 'Making first-class debut for Derbyshire v Middlesex in 2007, and being selected for England U19s to tour South Africa (*see above*)'
Cricket moments to forget: 'Pair on debut and Ant Botha dislocating my jaw during first first-class innings'
Cricket superstitions: 'None'
Cricketers particularly admired: Ian Healy, Adam Gilchrist, Jack Russell
Young players to look out for: Dan Redfern, Adam Poynton, Paul Borrington
Other sports played: Football (Repton 1st XI), golf ('recreational')
Other sports followed: Football (Manchester Utd)
Favourite band: Usher, Ne-Yo ('Like all music')
Relaxations: 'Music, FIFA or PES, spending time with my girlfriend'
Extras: Played for Derbyshire U10-U17 and for Midlands U14, U15, U17. Derbyshire Academy since 2004. Played in Bunbury Festival 2005. Derbyshire County Board Young Player of the Year 2006. Represented England U17 2006, 2007. Attended ECB National Skill Sets (wicket-keeping) 2006, 2007. Selected to tour South Africa with England U19s 2008-09. Youngest wicket-keeper to play first-class cricket for Derbyshire
Opinions on cricket: 'Grateful that a number of first-class counties are giving young players an opportunity to play at the highest level possible, reflecting the success of the county academy set-ups.'
Best batting: 14 Derbyshire v Bangladesh A, Derby 2008

2008 Season

	M	Inn	NO	Runs	HS	Avg	100	50	Ct	St	Balls	Runs	Wkts	Avg	BB	5I	10M
Test																	
FC	1	2	0	15	14	7.50	-	-	4	2	0	0	0		-	-	-
ODI																	
List A																	
20/20 Int																	
20/20																	

Career Performances

	M	Inn	NO	Runs	HS	Avg	100	50	Ct	St	Balls	Runs	Wkts	Avg	BB	5I	10M
Test																	
FC	3	5	0	17	14	3.40	-	-	7	2	0	0	0		-	-	-
ODI																	
List A	1	0	0	0	0		-	-	2	-	0	0	0		-	-	
20/20 Int																	
20/20	2	1	0	3	3	3.00	-	-	-	2	0	0	0		-	-	

PRINCE, A. G. — Lancashire

Name: Ashwell Gavin Prince
Role: Left-hand bat
Born: 28 May 1977, Port Elizabeth, Cape Province, South Africa
County debut: 2008 (Nottinghamshire)
Test debut: 2002
ODI debut: 2002
Place in batting averages: 17th av. 54.08
Overseas tours: South Africa to West Indies 2004-05, to Australia 2005-06, to Sri Lanka 2006, to Pakistan 2007-08, to Bangladesh 2007-08, to India 2007-08, to England 2008, to Australia 2008-09
Overseas teams played for: Eastern Province B 1995-96 – 1997-98; Eastern Province 1995-96 – 1996-97; Western Province 1997-98 – 2003-04; Western Province Boland 2004-05; Cape Cobras 2006-07 – 2007-08; Warriors 2008-09
Extras: Joined Nottinghamshire as overseas player in August 2008, after the signing of Adam Voges as a replacement for Mike Hussey fell through. Smashed 162* against Bangladesh in the second Test at Centurion in November 2008. Signed by Lancashire as temporary replacement for VVS Laxman during the early part of 2009 season
Best batting: 184 Western Province Boland v Lions, Paarl 2005
Best bowling: 2-11 South Africans v Middlesex, Uxbridge 2008

2008 Season

	M	Inn	NO	Runs	HS	Avg	100	50	Ct	St	Balls	Runs	Wkts	Avg	BB	5I	10M
Test	4	7	1	328	149	54.66	2	-	1	-	0	0	0		-	-	-
FC	10	14	2	649	149	54.08	3	2	4	-	66	49	2	24.50	2-11	-	-
ODI																	
List A	4	4	0	63	33	15.75	-	-	3	-	0	0	0		-	-	
20/20 Int																	
20/20																	

Career Performances

	M	Inn	NO	Runs	HS	Avg	100	50	Ct	St	Balls	Runs	Wkts	Avg	BB	5I	10M
Test	45	74	10	2703	149	42.23	9	7	25	-	96	47	1	47.00	1-2	-	-
FC	148	232	30	8498	184	42.06	21	40	90	-	276	166	4	41.50	2-11	-	-
ODI	52	41	12	1018	89 *	35.10	-	3	26	-	12	3	0		-	-	
List A	186	161	34	3942	89 *	31.03	-	21	88	-	91	86	0		-	-	
20/20 Int	1	1	0	5	5	5.00	-	-	-	-	0	0	0		-	-	
20/20	7	6	0	81	37	13.50	-	-	2	-	4	5	0		-	-	

PRIOR, M. J. Sussex

Name: Matthew (Matt) James Prior
Role: Right-hand bat, wicket-keeper
Born: 26 February 1982, Johannesburg, South Africa
Height: 5ft 11in **Weight:** 13st
Nickname: MP, Cheese
County debut: 2001
County cap: 2003
Test debut: 2007
ODI debut: 2004-05
Twenty20 Int debut: 2007
1000 runs in a season: 2
1st-Class 200s: 1
Place in batting averages: 32nd av. 47.27 (2007 119th av. 32.64)
Parents: Michael and Teresa
Marital status: Engaged
Education: Brighton College, East Sussex
Qualifications: 9 GCSEs, 3 A-levels, Level 1 coaching certificate

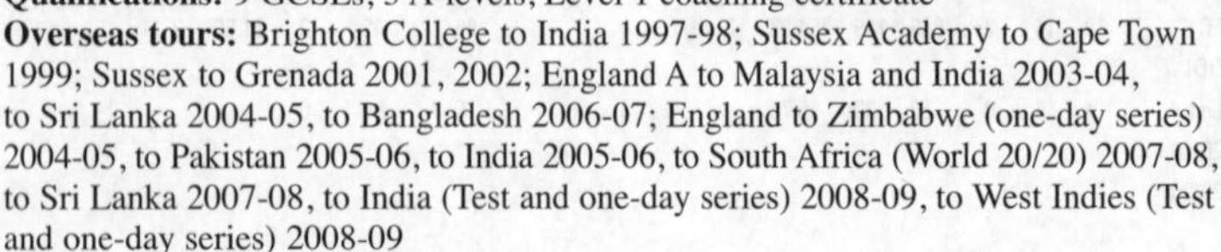

Overseas tours: Brighton College to India 1997-98; Sussex Academy to Cape Town 1999; Sussex to Grenada 2001, 2002; England A to Malaysia and India 2003-04, to Sri Lanka 2004-05, to Bangladesh 2006-07; England to Zimbabwe (one-day series) 2004-05, to Pakistan 2005-06, to India 2005-06, to South Africa (World 20/20) 2007-08, to Sri Lanka 2007-08, to India (Test and one-day series) 2008-09, to West Indies (Test and one-day series) 2008-09
Cricket moments to forget: 'Falling on to the stumps at The Rose Bowl on Sky TV!'
Cricket superstitions: 'Too many to name all of them'
Cricketers particularly admired: Steve Waugh, Alec Stewart, Mushtaq Ahmed, Murray Goodwin
Other sports played: Golf
Other sports followed: Football (Arsenal), golf, rugby

Favourite band: Red Hot Chili Peppers
Relaxations: 'Gym, listening to music'
Extras: Has played for Sussex since U12. Represented England U14-U19, captaining England U17. NBC Denis Compton Award for the most promising young Sussex player 2001, 2002, 2003. Umer Rashid Award for Most Improved [Sussex] Player 2003. ECB National Academy 2003-04, 2004-05, 2006-07. Became first England wicket-keeper to score a century (126*) on Test debut in the first Test v West Indies at Lord's 2007
Best batting: 201* Sussex v LUCCE, Hove 2004

2008 Season

	M	Inn	NO	Runs	HS	Avg	100	50	Ct	St	Balls	Runs	Wkts	Avg	BB	5I	10M
Test																	
FC	15	23	1	1040	133 *	47.27	3	7	37	1	0	0	0		-	-	-
ODI	5	4	1	120	45 *	40.00	-	-	13	1	0	0	0		-	-	
List A	16	14	1	600	137	46.15	1	3	25	3	0	0	0		-	-	
20/20 Int																	
20/20	10	9	0	155	56	17.22	-	1	2	-	0	0	0		-	-	

Career Performances

	M	Inn	NO	Runs	HS	Avg	100	50	Ct	St	Balls	Runs	Wkts	Avg	BB	5I	10M
Test	10	17	3	562	126 *	40.14	1	4	28	-	0	0	0		-	-	-
FC	134	212	20	7563	201 *	39.39	18	41	312	22	0	0	0		-	-	-
ODI	28	27	2	590	52	23.60	-	1	37	3	0	0	0		-	-	
List A	164	151	9	3862	144	27.19	4	21	144	25	0	0	0		-	-	
20/20 Int	5	5	0	116	32	23.20	-	-	4	1	0	0	0		-	-	
20/20	39	36	2	818	73	24.05	-	5	28	2	0	0	0		-	-	

74. Who took Mike Atherton's wicket seven times in the 1997 Ashes series?

PYRAH, R. M. — Yorkshire

Name: Richard (Rich) Michael Pyrah
Role: Right-hand bat, right-arm fast-medium bowler; all-rounder
Born: 1 November 1982, Dewsbury
Height: 6ft **Weight:** 12st 9lbs
Nickname: RP, Pyro
County debut: 2004
Place in batting averages: 228th av. 16.00
Parents: Mick and Lesley
Marital status: Single
Family links with cricket: 'Dad played local cricket in the Central Yorkshire League for Ossett'
Education: Ossett High School; Wakefield College
Qualifications: 10 GCSEs, Level 2 coach
Overseas tours: Yorkshire to Mumbai 2005
Overseas teams played for: Kaponga CC, New Zealand 2000-01, 2001-02; Taranaki District, New Zealand 2002-03; Campbelltown-Camden Ghosts, Sydney 2004-05
Career highlights to date: 'First first-class hundred. Four wickets in four balls [for Driffield] in 2007. Knocking 12 runs off the final over v Middlesex to win game [in Pro40 2007]'
Cricket moments to forget: 'Dropping a dolly of a catch in front of full crowd at Old Trafford and live on Sky Sports'
Cricket superstitions: 'None'
Cricketers particularly admired: Michael Vaughan, Darren Lehmann, Anthony McGrath
Young players to look out for: Oliver Hannon-Dalby, Adil Rashid
Other sports played: Golf, squash, football (had trials with Bradford City and Sheffield Wednesday)
Other sports followed: Football (Leeds United), rugby league (Leeds Rhinos)
Favourite band: Take That, Girls Aloud
Extras: C&G Man of the Match award for his 5-50 (plus 26 runs) for Yorkshire Board XI v Somerset at Scarborough in the third round 2002. His Bradford League awards include the all-rounders' and bowling averages trophies 2006. Yorkshire Fielder of the Year 2007. Has acted as 12th man for England
Opinions on cricket: 'Second XI cricket should mirror first-team competitions and rules to feed young players into county cricket. There should be a minimum number of English cricketers in each side who are eligible to play Test cricket, e.g. seven or eight.'

Best batting: 106 Yorkshire v LUCCE, Headingley 2007
Best bowling: 1-3 Yorkshire v LUCCE, Headingley 2007

2008 Season

	M	Inn	NO	Runs	HS	Avg	100	50	Ct	St	Balls	Runs	Wkts	Avg	BB	5I	10M
Test																	
FC	5	6	0	96	51	16.00	-	1	5	-	336	201	1	201.00	1-14	-	-
ODI																	
List A	18	9	4	83	26 *	16.60	-	-	10	-	632	585	24	24.37	4-35	-	
20/20 Int																	
20/20	9	5	2	16	8	5.33	-	-	6	-	180	209	14	14.92	4-20	-	

Career Performances

	M	Inn	NO	Runs	HS	Avg	100	50	Ct	St	Balls	Runs	Wkts	Avg	BB	5I	10M
Test																	
FC	12	17	1	438	106	27.37	1	2	6	-	504	278	5	55.60	1-3	-	
ODI																	
List A	54	38	8	509	42	16.96	-	-	22	-	1564	1437	58	24.77	5-50	1	
20/20 Int																	
20/20	25	16	5	126	33 *	11.45	-	-	11	-	252	300	20	15.00	4-20	-	

RAMPRAKASH, M. R. Surrey

Name: Mark Ravindra Ramprakash
Role: Right-hand bat, right-arm off-spin bowler
Born: 5 September 1969, Bushey, Herts
Height: 5ft 10in **Weight:** 12st 4lbs
Nickname: Ramps, Bloodaxe
County debut: 1987 (Middlesex), 2001 (Surrey)
County cap: 1990 (Middlesex), 2002 (Surrey)
Benefit: 2000 (Middlesex), 2008 (testimonial, Surrey)
Test debut: 1991
ODI debut: 1991
1000 runs in a season: 17
1st-Class 200s: 13
1st-Class 300s: 1
Place in batting averages: 6th av. 61.75 (2007 1st av. 101.30)

Parents: Deonarine and Jennifer
Wife and date of marriage: Van, 24 September 1993
Children: Cara, 1997; Anya, 2002
Family links with cricket: Father played club cricket in Guyana
Education: Gayton High School; Harrow Weald Sixth Form College
Qualifications: 6 O-levels, 2 A-levels, Level 3 cricket coach, Level 2 FA football coach
Overseas tours: England YC to Sri Lanka 1986-87, to Australia (U19 World Cup) 1987-88; England A to Pakistan 1990-91, to West Indies 1991-92, to India 1994-95 (vc); Lion Cubs to Barbados 1993; England to New Zealand 1991-92, to West Indies 1993-94, to Australia 1994-95, to South Africa 1995-96, to West Indies 1997-98, to Australia 1998-99, to South Africa 1999-2000, to Zimbabwe (one-day series) 2001-02, to India and New Zealand 2001-02
Overseas teams played for: Nairobi Jafferys, Kenya 1988; North Melbourne 1989; University of Perth 1996-97; Clico-Preysal, Trinidad 2004
Career highlights to date: 'My two Test hundreds, v West Indies and Australia'
Cricket moments to forget: 'Going up to receive an award I hadn't won!'
Cricket superstitions: 'Same piece of chewing gum in innings'
Cricketers particularly admired: 'All the great all-rounders'; Alec Stewart
Young players to look out for: Arun Harinath
Other sports played: Football (Corinthian Casuals FC, Arsenal Pro-Celeb XI)
Other sports followed: Football (Arsenal FC)
Extras: Voted Best U15 Schoolboy of 1985 by Cricket Society (Sir John Hobbs Silver Jubilee Memorial Prize) and Cricket Society's Most Promising Young Cricketer of the Year 1988. Man of the Match for his 56 in Middlesex's NatWest Trophy final win in 1988, on his debut in the competition. Represented England YC. Cricket Writers' Young Cricketer of the Year 1991. Middlesex captain May 1997 to the end of the 1999 season. Man of the Match in the fifth Test v West Indies at Bridgetown 1997-98 (154). Leading run-scorer in the single-division four-day era of the County Championship with 8392 runs (av. 56.32) 1993-99. Became first player to score a Championship century against all 18 first-class counties with his 110 v Middlesex at Lord's 2003. Surrey Players' Player of the Year 2003, 2004, 2005, 2006, 2007; Surrey Supporters' Player of the Year 2003, 2004. Vice-captain of Surrey 2004-05. In 2006 became the first English batsman to score 2000 first-class runs in a season since the start of the two-division Championship in 2000, reaching the landmark in a record 20 innings and finishing the season with 2278 runs at an average of 103.54. PCA Player of the Year 2006. Winner, with Karen Hardy, of *Strictly Come Dancing*, December 2006. One of *Wisden*'s Five Cricketers of the Year 2007. Scored century in each innings (196/130*) for the sixth time, v Lancashire at The Oval 2007 to become the first batsman to average more than 100 in consecutive English seasons, finishing with 2026 runs at an average of 101.30. In August 2008, he joined the select group of players who have completed one hundred first-class centuries when he scored a 'ton' against Yorkshire at Headingley on his way to topping the Surrey batting averages for the season
Best batting: 301* Surrey v Northamptonshire, The Oval 2006
Best bowling: 3-32 Middlesex v Glamorgan, Lord's 1998

2008 Season

	M	Inn	NO	Runs	HS	Avg	100	50	Ct	St	Balls	Runs	Wkts	Avg	BB	5I	10M
Test																	
FC	14	23	3	1235	200 *	61.75	6	1	4	-	0	0	0		-	-	-
ODI																	
List A	11	11	2	355	98	39.44	-	4	2	-	0	0	0		-	-	-
20/20 Int																	
20/20	10	10	0	186	60	18.60	-	1	6	-	0	0	0		-	-	-

Career Performances

	M	Inn	NO	Runs	HS	Avg	100	50	Ct	St	Balls	Runs	Wkts	Avg	BB	5I	10M
Test	52	92	6	2350	154	27.32	2	12	39	-	895	477	4	119.25	1-2	-	-
FC	415	684	87	31894	301 *	53.42	103	135	239	-	4171	2196	34	64.58	3-32	-	-
ODI	18	18	4	376	51	26.85	-	1	8	-	132	108	4	27.00	3-28	-	-
List A	390	378	61	12550	147 *	39.58	14	83	129	-	1734	1354	46	29.43	5-38	1	-
20/20 Int																	
20/20	44	44	7	1163	85 *	31.43	-	8	17	-	0	0	0		-	-	-

RANKIN, W. B. — Warwickshire

Name: William Boyd Rankin
Role: Left-hand lower-order bat, right-arm fast-medium bowler
Born: 5 July 1984, Londonderry
Height: 6ft 8in **Weight:** 16st 7lbs
Nickname: Boydo, Stankin
County debut: 2006 (one-day, Derbyshire), 2007 (first-class, Derbyshire), 2008 (Warwickshire)
ODI debut: 2006-07
Place in bowling averages: 72nd av. 30.16 (2007 58th av. 29.20)
Parents: Robert and Dawn
Marital status: Single
Family links with cricket: Both brothers (Robert and David) have played in Ireland age-group teams
Education: Strabane Grammar School; Harper Adams University College
Qualifications: 10 GCSEs, 3 A-levels, Level 1 cricket coaching
Career outside cricket: 'Student and work on home farm'

Overseas tours: Ireland U19 to Bangladesh (U19 World Cup) 2003-04; Ireland to Scotland (European Championship) 2006, to Kenya (ICC World Cricket League) 2006-07, to West Indies (World Cup) 2006-07, to South Africa (Intercontinental Cup) 2008, plus various Ireland age-group and A tours
Career highlights to date: 'Playing in 2006-07 Cricket World Cup, beating Pakistan and Bangladesh and tying with Zimbabwe'
Cricket moments to forget: 'U19 World Cup match against West Indies (2004)' (*Ireland U19 lost by just six runs*)
Cricket superstitions: 'None'
Cricketers particularly admired: Glenn McGrath, Curtly Ambrose
Young players to look out for: Gary Ballance, Daniel Redfern, Eoin Morgan
Other sports played: Rugby, football, badminton, snooker
Other sports followed: Football (Liverpool FC), rugby (Ulster)
Favourite band: Coldplay, Oasis
Relaxations: 'Shooting'
Extras: Attended European Cricket Academy in Spain. Formerly with Middlesex but made no first-team appearances. Has represented Ireland in first-class and ODI cricket. Left Derbyshire at the end of the 2007 season and joined Warwickshire for 2008. Part of the Ireland squad that faced Kenya in summer 2008. Took 4 wickets in Namibia's second innings during the Intercontinental Cup Final, which Ireland went on to win
Opinions on cricket: 'Twenty20 cricket brings good crowds to games, which is good for cricket and clubs. I feel all 2nd XI cricket one-day matches should be coloured clothing and white ball, as this will help get young players used to playing in these conditions; otherwise it's completely new to them when they play first-team cricket.'
Best batting: 12* Warwickshire v Glamorgan, Edgbaston 2008
Best bowling: 4-41 Derbyshire v Middlesex, Derby 2007

2008 Season

	M	Inn	NO	Runs	HS	Avg	100	50	Ct	St	Balls	Runs	Wkts	Avg	BB	5I	10M
Test																	
FC	5	6	3	31	12 *	10.33	-	-	2	-	519	362	12	30.16	4-80	-	-
ODI																	
List A																	
20/20 Int																	
20/20																	

Career Performances

	M	Inn	NO	Runs	HS	Avg	100	50	Ct	St	Balls	Runs	Wkts	Avg	BB	5I	10M
Test																	
FC	9	10	4	36	12 *	6.00	-	-	5	-	1134	744	27	27.55	4-41	-	-
ODI	12	5	3	16	7 *	8.00	-	-	2	-	428	375	14	26.78	3-32	-	
List A	19	9	5	25	7 *	6.25	-	-	2	-	665	629	19	33.10	3-32	-	
20/20 Int																	
20/20																	

RASHID, A. U. — Yorkshire

Name: Adil Usman Rashid
Role: Right-hand bat, right-arm leg-break bowler; all-rounder
Born: 17 February 1988, Bradford
Nickname: Dilly
County debut: 2006
Place in batting averages: 171st av. 23.48 (2007 50th av. 44.05)
Place in bowling averages: 86th av. 31.83 (2007 121st av. 42.16)
Family links with cricket: Brothers Amar and Haroon have both played for Bradford/Leeds UCCE
Overseas tours: England A to Bangladesh 2006-07; England Performance Programme to India 2007-08, 2008-09; England Lions to India 2007-08, 2008-09; England to India 2008-09; to West Indies 2008-09
Extras: Has attended Terry Jenner spin-bowling courses in Australia. Played for Yorkshire Academy 2005. Recorded maiden first-class five-wicket return (6-67 from 28 successive overs) on debut v Warwickshire at Scarborough 2006. Scored 114 then took 8-157 in India U19's first innings in the second 'Test' at Taunton 2006 to become the first England player to score a century and record a five-wicket innings return in an U19 international. 2nd XI cap 2006. Represented England Lions 2007. Cricket Writers' Club Young Cricketer of the Year 2007. NatWest PCA Young Player of the Year 2007. Topped the Yorkshire first-class bowling averages in 2008, with a 65-wicket haul
Best batting: 111 Yorkshire v Sussex, Hove 2008
Best bowling: 7-107 Yorkshire v Hampshire, The Rose Bowl 2008

2008 Season

	M	Inn	NO	Runs	HS	Avg	100	50	Ct	St	Balls	Runs	Wkts	Avg	BB	5I	10M
Test																	
FC	18	27	2	587	111	23.48	1	2	6	-	3829	2069	65	31.83	7-107	4	-
ODI																	
List A	17	8	3	101	41 *	20.20	-	-	7	-	465	384	12	32.00	3-37	-	
20/20 Int																	
20/20	8	6	2	18	10	4.50	-	-	3	-	126	162	7	23.14	4-24	-	

Career Performances

	M	Inn	NO	Runs	HS	Avg	100	50	Ct	St	Balls	Runs	Wkts	Avg	BB	5I	10M
Test																	
FC	43	61	9	1660	111	31.92	2	10	17	-	7988	4691	140	33.50	7-107	8	-
ODI																	
List A	23	13	3	151	41 *	15.10	-	-	10	-	735	639	17	37.58	3-37	-	
20/20 Int																	
20/20	8	6	2	18	10	4.50	-	-	3	-	126	162	7	23.14	4-24	-	

RAYNER, O. P. Sussex

Name: Oliver (Ollie) Philip Rayner
Role: Right-hand bat, right-arm off-spin bowler
Born: 1 November 1985, Walsrode, Germany
Height: 6ft 5¼in **Weight:** 16st
Nickname: Mervin, Rocket, Rain-cakes, KP ('Kelvin Pietersen, not Kevin!')
County debut: 2006
Place in batting averages: 214th av. 22.17
Place in bowling averages: 97th av. 33.61 (2007 61st av. 29.57)
Parents: Mark and Penny
Marital status: Single
Education: St Bede's, The Dicker, Hailsham, East Sussex
Qualifications: 7 GCSEs, 2 A-levels, Level 1 coaching
Overseas tours: Sussex Academy to Sri Lanka 2001, to South Africa 2003; England Performance Programme to India 2008-09
Overseas teams played for: University of Cape Town; Western Province
Cricket moments to forget: 'Chirping at Somerset, then getting a pair!'
Cricketers particularly admired: Andrew Flintoff, Shane Warne, Chris Gayle
Young players to look out for: Tom Smith, Krishna Singh
Other sports played: Football (Eastbourne Town Reserves; Eastbourne United 1st XI)
Other sports followed: Football (Brighton & Hove Albion)
Favourite band: Kanye West, Common, Talib Kwali
Relaxations: 'Bodyboarding, skiing, chilling with mates'
Extras: South of England U15. England Development Squad U19. Sussex 2nd XI Player of the Year 2005. Scored century (101) on first-class debut v Sri Lankans at Hove 2006, batting at No. 8
Best batting: 101 Sussex v Sri Lankans, Hove 2006
Best bowling: 5-49 Sussex v Hampshire, Arundel 2008

2008 Season

	M	Inn	NO	Runs	HS	Avg	100	50	Ct	St	Balls	Runs	Wkts	Avg	BB	5I	10M
Test																	
FC	11	13	4	159	22	17.66	-	-	8	-	2085	1042	31	33.61	5-49	2	-
ODI																	
List A	3	3	2	29	14 *	29.00	-	-	1	-	132	128	4	32.00	2-31	-	
20/20 Int																	
20/20																	

Career Performances

	M	Inn	NO	Runs	HS	Avg	100	50	Ct	St	Balls	Runs	Wkts	Avg	BB	5I	10M
Test																	
FC	20	24	6	353	101	19.61	1	-	17	-	3377	1804	51	35.37	5-49	3	-
ODI																	
List A	15	13	6	151	61	21.57	-	1	4	-	486	506	10	50.60	2-31	-	
20/20 Int																	
20/20	7	3	0	16	11	5.33	-	-	-	-	49	93	1	93.00	1-20	-	

READ, C. M. W. Nottinghamshire

Name: Christopher (Chris) Mark Wells Read
Role: Right-hand bat, wicket-keeper, county captain
Born: 10 August 1978, Paignton, Devon
Height: 5ft 8in **Weight:** 11st
Nickname: Readie, Reados
County debut: 1997 (one-day, Glos), 1998 (Notts)
County cap: 1999 (Notts)
Benefit: 2009
Test debut: 1999
ODI debut: 1999-2000
Twenty20 Int debut: 2006
1000 runs in a season: 1
50 dismissals in a season: 3
1st-Class 200s: 1
Place in batting averages: 44th av. 45.37 (2007 27th av. 52.68)
Parents: Geoffrey and Carolyn
Wife and date of marriage: Louise, 2 October 2004
Education: Torquay Boys' Grammar School; University of Bath; Loughborough University

Qualifications: 9 GCSEs, 4 A-levels, senior coaching award
Off-season: 'Preparing for my benefit year, 2009. Finishing my Level 3 coaching qualification, and setting up the Chris Read Academy.'
Overseas tours: West of England U13 to Netherlands 1991; West of England U15 to West Indies 1992-93; England U17 to Netherlands (International Youth Tournament) 1995; England U19 to Pakistan 1996-97; England A to Kenya and Sri Lanka 1997-98, to Zimbabwe and South Africa 1998-99, to West Indies 2000-01, 2005-06; England to South Africa and Zimbabwe 1999-2000, to Australia 2002-03 (VB Series), to Bangladesh and Sri Lanka 2003-04, to West Indies 2003-04, to South Africa 2004-05, to India (ICC Champions Trophy) 2006-07, to Australia 2006-07; British Universities to South Africa 2002; ECB National Academy to Australia and Sri Lanka 2002-03; England VI to Hong Kong 2005
Career highlights to date: 'Winning Test series v West Indies 2004'
Cricket moments to forget: 'Ducking a slower ball from Chris Cairns in second Test v New Zealand at Lord's 1999'
Cricketers particularly admired: Adam Gilchrist, Bruce French, Alan Knott, Bob Taylor, Jack Russell, Ian Healy
Young players to look out for: James Hildreth
Other sports played: Hockey (Devon U18, U21; West of England U17; South Nottingham)
Other sports followed: Football (Torquay United)
Favourite band: Stereophonics
Relaxations: 'Reading, listening to music, keeping fit and going out with friends'
Player website: www.thechrisreadcricketacademy.com
Extras: Played for Devon 1995-97. Represented England U18 1996 and England U19 1997. NBC Denis Compton Award for most promising young Gloucestershire player 1997. Was selected for the England A tour to Kenya and Sri Lanka 1997-98 aged 18 and without having played a first-class game. Recorded eight dismissals on Test debut in the first Test v New Zealand at Edgbaston 1999. Man of the Match in the first ODI v West Indies at Georgetown 2003-04 after striking a match-winning 15-ball 27 including three sixes and a four. ECB National Academy 2005-06. Scored 165* v Essex at Trent Bridge 2007, in the process sharing with David Hussey (275) in a new record fifth-wicket partnership for Nottinghamshire (359). Scored 240 v Essex at Chelmsford 2007, becoming the first Nottinghamshire wicket-keeper to score a double century. Appointed captain of Nottinghamshire in 2008
Opinions on cricket: 'Whilst new money being invested into the game in the short term is most welcome, administrators need to ensure that the longer-term future of the game is safeguarded. The balls we use in Championship cricket are not up to scratch. Choosing a ball can resemble a lottery, and many don't make it past 40 overs before they are changed.'
Best batting: 240 Nottinghamshire v Essex, Chelmsford 2007

2008 Season

	M	Inn	NO	Runs	HS	Avg	100	50	Ct	St	Balls	Runs	Wkts	Avg	BB	5I	10M
Test																	
FC	16	21	5	726	142	45.37	1	5	53	2	24	20	0		-	-	-
ODI																	
List A	14	13	4	249	53 *	27.66	-	1	16	5	0	0	0		-	-	
20/20 Int																	
20/20	9	8	2	115	31	19.16	-	-	4	4	0	0	0		-	-	

Career Performances

	M	Inn	NO	Runs	HS	Avg	100	50	Ct	St	Balls	Runs	Wkts	Avg	BB	5I	10M
Test	15	23	4	360	55	18.94	-	1	48	6	0	0	0		-	-	-
FC	206	306	50	8552	240	33.40	12	46	601	32	90	88	0		-	-	-
ODI	36	24	7	300	30 *	17.64	-	-	41	2	0	0	0		-	-	
List A	236	188	48	3951	135	28.22	2	12	240	53	0	0	0		-	-	
20/20 Int	1	1	0	13	13	13.00	-	-	1	-	0	0	0		-	-	
20/20	37	35	9	655	48 *	25.19	-	-	24	7	0	0	0		-	-	

REDFERN, D. J. — Derbyshire

Name: Daniel (Dan) James Redfern
Role: Left-hand bat, occasional right-arm off-spin bowler
Born: 18 April 1990, Shrewsbury, Shropshire
Height: 5ft 10in **Weight:** 11st
Nickname: Panda, Redders, Redskin
County debut: 2006 (one-day), 2007 (first-class)
Place in batting averages: (2007 143rd av. 30.00)
Parents: Michael and Shirley
Marital status: Single
Family links with cricket: 'Grandfathers, father and brother all played for Leycett CC, Staffs. Brother also plays Shropshire U21'
Education: Adams' Grammar School, Newport, Shropshire
Qualifications: 10 GCSEs, 'A-levels'
Off-season: 'Tour to South Africa with England U19 in January'
Overseas tours: England U16 to South Africa 2005-06; Derbyshire Academy to Port Elizabeth 2006-07; England U19 to Malaysia (U19 World Cup) 2007-08, to South Africa 2008-09

Career highlights to date: 'Playing for Derbyshire 1st XI and for England U19 v Pakistan. Winning Man of the Match in a televised game against Yorkshire in which I made 57 not out'
Cricket moments to forget: 'Run out by Lou Vincent on Sky [on county one-day debut]'
Cricket superstitions: 'None'
Cricketers particularly admired: Graham Thorpe
Young players to look out for: Liam Dawson, Tom Poynton, Jake Needham
Other sports played: 'A bit of golf'
Other sports followed: Football (Stoke City), rugby (Sale Sharks)
Favourite band: The Kooks
Relaxations: 'Watching telly, music, friends'
Extras: Has represented England U15, U16, U17 and U19. Neil Lloyd Memorial Trophy for Best Batsman at Bunbury Festival 2005. Made one-day debut for Derbyshire v Worcestershire at Worcester in Pro40 2006, aged 16. Made Minor Counties Trophy debut for Shropshire v Northumberland at Oswestry 2007, scoring 107
Opinions on cricket: 'Keep Pro40 - it's more exciting than 50-overs.'
Best batting: 69* Derbyshire v Glamorgan, Derby 2008
Best bowling: 1-7 Derbyshire v Somerset, Derby 2007
1-7 Derbyshire v Warwickshire, Edgbaston 2008

2008 Season

	M	Inn	NO	Runs	HS	Avg	100	50	Ct	St	Balls	Runs	Wkts	Avg	BB	5I	10M
Test																	
FC	4	6	1	159	69 *	31.80	-	1	1	-	108	54	1	54.00	1-7	-	-
ODI																	
List A	5	4	1	125	57 *	41.66	-	1	1	-	72	64	0		-	-	
20/20 Int																	
20/20	1	1	0	9	9	9.00	-	-	-	-	0	0	0		-	-	

Career Performances

	M	Inn	NO	Runs	HS	Avg	100	50	Ct	St	Balls	Runs	Wkts	Avg	BB	5I	10M
Test																	
FC	9	13	2	339	69 *	30.81	-	2	6	-	222	124	3	41.33	1-7	-	-
ODI																	
List A	11	9	1	185	57 *	23.12	-	1	1	-	72	64	0		-	-	
20/20 Int																	
20/20	1	1	0	9	9	9.00	-	-	-	-	0	0	0		-	-	

REES, G. P. Glamorgan

Name: Gareth Peter Rees
Role: Left-hand opening bat, right-arm fast-medium 'utility bowler'
Born: 8 April 1985, Swansea
Height: 6ft 1in **Weight:** 15st
Nickname: Gums, Max Headroom, Lionheart, Leg, Lego-hair, Worm
County debut: 2006
1000 runs in a season: 1
Place in batting averages: 62nd av. 40.29 (2007 189th av. 23.83)
Parents: Peter and Diane
Marital status: Single
Education: Coedcae Comprehensive, Llanelli; Coleg Sir Gar; Bath University
Qualifications: 10 GCSEs, 3 A-levels, Maths and Physics degree (First)
Off-season: 'Working (hopefully investment banking), and a two month research project at CERN, in Geneva, looking to find the "God" particle'
Overseas tours: Glamorgan to Guernsey 2006-07 ('and Mark Wallace's stag do, Galway 2007!')
Career highlights to date: 'Getting my first first-class century against Essex, and fielding short leg for Dean Cosker'
Cricket moments to forget: 'Getting run out by Ryan Watkins. Rooming with Adam Shantry'
Cricket superstitions: 'There's no such thing as luck!'
Cricketers particularly admired: Brian Lara, David Hemp
Other sports played: Golf, rugby (Wales U17, Llanelli Scarlets U21, Bath University)
Other sports followed: Rugby (Llanelli Scarlets, Felinfoel RFC)
Favourite band: Oasis
Relaxations: 'Facebook, researching using the compact muon solenoid at CERN searching for the "God" particle'
Extras: Played for Wales Minor Counties in the 2004 and 2005 C&G and in Minor Counties competitions 2002-07. Topped the Glamorgan batting averages for 2008
Opinions on cricket: 'Grounds should provide more activities for supporters and players for when it rains - for example, CHEERLEADERS!'
Best batting: 140 Glamorgan v Leicestershire, Cardiff 2008

2008 Season

	M	Inn	NO	Runs	HS	Avg	100	50	Ct	St	Balls	Runs	Wkts	Avg	BB	5I	10M
Test																	
FC	16	28	1	1088	140	40.29	3	6	20	-	0	0	0	-	-	-	-
ODI																	
List A																	
20/20 Int																	
20/20																	

Career Performances

	M	Inn	NO	Runs	HS	Avg	100	50	Ct	St	Balls	Runs	Wkts	Avg	BB	5I	10M
Test																	
FC	29	51	2	1601	140	32.67	5	9	29	-	0	0	0	-	-	-	-
ODI																	
List A	6	6	0	163	63	27.16	-	1	2	-	0	0	0	-	-	-	-
20/20 Int																	
20/20																	

RIAZUDDIN, H. Hampshire

Name: Hamza Riazuddin
Role: Right-hand bat, right-arm fast-medium bowler
Born: 19 December 1989, Hendon, Middlesex
County debut: 2008
Education: Bradfield College, Reading
Overseas tours: England U19 to South Africa 2009
Extras: Hampshire Cricket Academy player. Has also played for Hampshire 2nd XI. Awarded a development contract for 2009
Best batting: 4 Hampshire v Somerset, Taunton 2008
Best bowling: 1-21 Hampshire v Somerset, Taunton 2008

2008 Season

	M	Inn	NO	Runs	HS	Avg	100	50	Ct	St	Balls	Runs	Wkts	Avg	BB	5I	10M
Test																	
FC	1	1	0	4	4	4.00	-	-	-	-	174	99	1	99.00	1-21	-	-
ODI																	
List A	3	0	0	0	0		-	-	-	-	144	87	2	43.50	1-15	-	
20/20 Int																	
20/20	5	2	1	0	0 *	0.00	-	-	2	-	96	148	2	74.00	1-23	-	

Career Performances

	M	Inn	NO	Runs	HS	Avg	100	50	Ct	St	Balls	Runs	Wkts	Avg	BB	5I	10M
Test																	
FC	1	1	0	4	4	4.00	-	-	-	-	174	99	1	99.00	1-21	-	-
ODI																	
List A	3	0	0	0	0		-	-	-	-	144	87	2	43.50	1-15	-	
20/20 Int																	
20/20	5	2	1	0	0 *	0.00	-	-	2	-	96	148	2	74.00	1-23	-	

RICHARDSON, A. Middlesex

Name: Alan Richardson
Role: Right-hand bat, right-arm medium bowler
Born: 6 May 1975, Newcastle-under-Lyme, Staffs
Height: 6ft 2in **Weight:** 13st
Nickname: Richo
County debut: 1995 (Derbyshire), 1999 (Warwickshire), 2005 (Middlesex)
County cap: 2002 (Warwickshire), 2005 (Middlesex)
50 wickets in a season: 1
Place in batting averages: 243rd av. 13.16 (2007 261st av. 13.00)
Place in bowling averages: 25th av. 23.00 (2007 24th av. 24.21)
Parents: Roy and Sandra
Marital status: Single
Family links with cricket: 'Dad captained Little Stoke 3rd XI and now patrols the boundary with pint in hand at the Sid Jenkins Cricket Ground'
Education: Alleyne's High School, Stone; Stafford College of Further Education

Qualifications: 8 GCSEs, 2 A-levels, 2 AS-levels, Level 2 cricket coach
Career outside cricket: Landscape gardener
Overseas tours: Derbyshire to Malaga 1995; Warwickshire to Bloemfontein 2000, to Cape Town 2001, 2002, to Portugal 2003; England Lions to India 2007-08
Overseas teams played for: Northern Natal, South Africa 1994-96; Hawkesbury CC, Sydney 1997-99; Northern Districts, Sydney 1999-2000, 2001-03; Avendale, Cape Town 2000-01; Kyriang Mountains, Australia 2003-04
Career highlights to date: 'Getting capped by both Warwickshire and Middlesex. Doing well on my home debuts'
Cricket moments to forget: 'The whole 2006 season!' (*Out for four weeks with a broken thumb; for the rest of the season with a floating bone in the elbow*)
Cricket superstitions: 'None'
Other sports played: Football, golf, tennis ('all very badly')
Other sports followed: Football (Stoke City)
Favourite band: Josh Rouse, Jeff Buckley, The Housemartins
Extras: *Cricket World* award for best bowling performance in Oxford U19 Festival (8-60 v Devon). Topped Minor Counties bowling averages with Staffordshire 1998 and won Minor Counties bowling award. Most Improved 2nd XI Player 1999. Outstanding Performance of the Year 1999 for his 8-51 v Gloucestershire on home debut. Scored 91 v Hampshire at Edgbaston 2002, in the process sharing with Nick Knight (255*) in a Warwickshire record tenth-wicket stand of 214. Had first innings figures of 7-113 on first-class debut for Middlesex v Nottinghamshire at Lord's 2005
Opinions on cricket: 'Being a cricketer is almost fashionable now, and so attracting kids into the game shouldn't be a problem. Still think we need longer tea breaks.'
Best batting: 91 Warwickshire v Hampshire, Edgbaston 2002
Best bowling: 8-46 Warwickshire v Sussex, Edgbaston 2002

2008 Season

	M	Inn	NO	Runs	HS	Avg	100	50	Ct	St	Balls	Runs	Wkts	Avg	BB	5I	10M
Test																	
FC	9	8	2	79	26	13.16	-	-	3	-	1589	644	28	23.00	5-34	1	-
ODI																	
List A																	
20/20 Int																	
20/20																	

Career Performances

	M	Inn	NO	Runs	HS	Avg	100	50	Ct	St	Balls	Runs	Wkts	Avg	BB	5I	10M
Test																	
FC	102	102	38	721	91	11.26	-	1	28	-	18278	8739	303	28.84	8-46	9	1
ODI																	
List A	61	27	17	104	21 *	10.40	-	-	11	-	2680	2102	57	36.87	5-35	1	
20/20 Int																	
20/20	5	1	1	6	6 *		-	-	1	-	102	120	4	30.00	3-13	-	

ROBSON, S. D. — Middlesex

Name: Samuel (<u>Sam</u>) David Robson
Role: Right-hand bat, left-arm leg-break bowler
Born: 1 July 1989, Paddington, New South Wales, Australia
Nickname: Robbo
County debut: 2008 (one-day)
Cricketers particularly admired: Shane Warne, Andrew Flintoff
Other sports followed: Football (Arsenal)
Favourite band: Coldplay
Extras: Has represented Australia at U19 level, and New South Wales at both U17 and U19 level, as well as playing for New South Wales Colts. Played for Middlesex 2nd XI in 2008, and made his one-day debut for the county in Pro40 against Worcestershire at the end of the season

2008 Season

	M	Inn	NO	Runs	HS	Avg	100	50	Ct	St	Balls	Runs	Wkts	Avg	BB	5I	10M
Test																	
FC																	
ODI																	
List A	1	1	0	21	21	21.00	-	-	-	-	0	0	0		-	-	
20/20 Int																	
20/20																	

Career Performances

	M	Inn	NO	Runs	HS	Avg	100	50	Ct	St	Balls	Runs	Wkts	Avg	BB	5I	10M
Test																	
FC																	
ODI																	
List A	1	1	0	21	21	21.00	-	-	-	-	0	0	0		-	-	
20/20 Int																	
20/20																	

75. Which England wicketkeeper took six catches in an innings during the second Test of the 1990-91 series?

ROGERS, C. J. L. — Derbyshire

Name: Christopher (Chris) John Llewellyn Rogers
Role: Left-hand bat, leg-spin/right-arm medium bowler, county captain
Born: 31 August 1977, Sydney, Australia
Height: 5ft 11in **Weight:** 12st 8lbs
Nickname: Bucky
County debut: 2004 (Derbys), 2005 (Leics), 2006 (Northants)
Test debut: 2007-08
1000 runs in a season: 1
1st-Class 200s: 4
1st-Class 300s: 1
Place in batting averages: 12th av. 57.16 (2007 140th av. 30.92)
Family links with cricket: Father played for New South Wales and became cricket administrator
Overseas tours: Australia A to Pakistan 2007-08

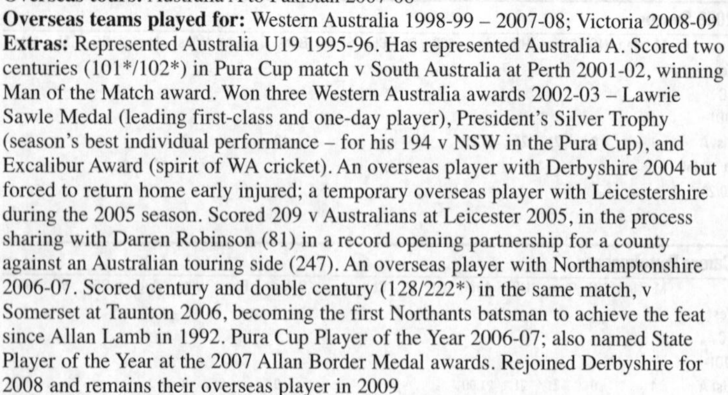

Overseas teams played for: Western Australia 1998-99 – 2007-08; Victoria 2008-09
Extras: Represented Australia U19 1995-96. Has represented Australia A. Scored two centuries (101*/102*) in Pura Cup match v South Australia at Perth 2001-02, winning Man of the Match award. Won three Western Australia awards 2002-03 – Lawrie Sawle Medal (leading first-class and one-day player), President's Silver Trophy (season's best individual performance – for his 194 v NSW in the Pura Cup), and Excalibur Award (spirit of WA cricket). An overseas player with Derbyshire 2004 but forced to return home early injured; a temporary overseas player with Leicestershire during the 2005 season. Scored 209 v Australians at Leicester 2005, in the process sharing with Darren Robinson (81) in a record opening partnership for a county against an Australian touring side (247). An overseas player with Northamptonshire 2006-07. Scored century and double century (128/222*) in the same match, v Somerset at Taunton 2006, becoming the first Northants batsman to achieve the feat since Allan Lamb in 1992. Pura Cup Player of the Year 2006-07; also named State Player of the Year at the 2007 Allan Border Medal awards. Rejoined Derbyshire for 2008 and remains their overseas player in 2009
Best batting: 319 Northamptonshire v Gloucestershire, Northampton 2006
Best bowling: 1-16 Northamptonshire v Leicestershire, Northampton 2006

2008 Season

	M	Inn	NO	Runs	HS	Avg	100	50	Ct	St	Balls	Runs	Wkts	Avg	BB	5I	10M
Test																	
FC	16	27	3	1372	248 *	57.16	4	8	15	-	22	13	0		-	-	-
ODI																	
List A	14	13	0	474	94	36.46	-	6	6	-	0	0	0		-	-	
20/20 Int																	
20/20																	

Career Performances

	M	Inn	NO	Runs	HS	Avg	100	50	Ct	St	Balls	Runs	Wkts	Avg	BB	5I	10M
Test	1	2	0	19	15	9.50	-	-	1	-	0	0	0		-	-	-
FC	125	223	13	10209	319	48.61	28	52	120	-	206	119	1	119.00	1-16	-	-
ODI																	
List A	90	86	6	2580	117 *	32.25	2	18	46	-	24	26	2	13.00	2-22	-	
20/20 Int																	
20/20	10	6	0	90	35	15.00	-	-	5	-	0	0	0		-	-	

ROWE, D. T. — Leicestershire

Name: Daniel Thomas Rowe
Role: Right-hand bat, right-arm fast-medium bowler
Born: 22 March 1984, Bridgend, South Wales
Height: 6ft **Weight:** 14st
Nickname: Dragon, Rowey, Rowster
County debut: 2006
Parents: Paul and Barbara
Marital status: Long-term girlfriend Emma
Family links with cricket: 'Brother played Mid-Glamorgan age groups'
Education: Archbishop McGrath Roman Catholic School; University of Glamorgan, Cardiff
Qualifications: 3 A-levels, BSc Sports and Health Science, Level 1 coaching
Career outside cricket: 'Coaching – nutrition in sport'
Overseas tours: Wales U16 to Jersey Festival 2000; Leicestershire CCC to Sri Lanka and India 2007

Overseas teams played for: Varsity Academy, Potchefstroom; International Pros, Potchefstroom 2007
Career highlights to date: '[Championship] debut against Essex CCC, scoring 85 and taking 2-27'
Cricketers particularly admired: Darren Gough, Chris Cairns, Allan Donald
Other sports played: Golf
Other sports followed: Rugby (Tondu, Ospreys), football (Manchester City)
Favourite band: Linkin Park
Relaxations: 'Golf, cinema, shopping, watching my brother play for Tondu RFC'
Extras: Represented Wales U12-U16, Mid-Glamorgan Schools and Glamorgan U17 and U19. Played for Cardiff UCCE 2004-06. Has also played for Somerset 2nd XI. Scored 85 on Championship debut v Essex at Leicester 2007, batting at No. 9
Best batting: 85 Leicestershire v Essex, Leicester 2007
Best bowling: 5-61 Leicestershire v OUCCE, The Parks 2007

2008 Season

	M	Inn	NO	Runs	HS	Avg	100	50	Ct	St	Balls	Runs	Wkts	Avg	BB	5I	10M
Test																	
FC	3	2	0	2	1	1.00	-	-	-	-	348	235	4	58.75	2-75	-	-
ODI																	
List A	3	2	1	18	17	18.00	-	-	-	-	66	92	1	92.00	1-49	-	
20/20 Int																	
20/20	2	1	1	11	11 *		-	-	1	-	24	42	1	42.00	1-26	-	

Career Performances

	M	Inn	NO	Runs	HS	Avg	100	50	Ct	St	Balls	Runs	Wkts	Avg	BB	5I	10M
Test																	
FC	9	9	1	139	85	17.37	-	1	1	-	936	684	18	38.00	5-61	1	-
ODI																	
List A	7	4	2	22	17	11.00	-	-	1	-	168	213	2	106.50	1-26	-	
20/20 Int																	
20/20	2	1	1	11	11 *		-	-	1	-	24	42	1	42.00	1-26	-	

76. Name the 6' 8" seam bowler who took thirteen England wickets for Australia at Melbourne in 1990.

ROY, J. J. — Surrey

Name: Jason Jonathan Roy
Role: Right-hand bat
Born: 21 July 1990, Reigate, Surrey
County debut: 2008 (one-day)
Education: Whitgift School
Qualifications: A Levels (Sports Science and Business Studies)
Off-season: 'At the Darren Lehmann Academy, and playing cricket in Adelaide.'
Overseas teams played for: Port Adelaide CC 2008-09
Extras: Lived in South Africa until moving to England at the age of 10. Represented Surrey at U16, U17 and U19 level, as well as playing for Surrey 2nd XI 2007-08. Scored 48 off 33 balls in his 2nd XI debut against Hampshire to help Surrey win by 3 runs. Represented the South at U17 level in the ECB Regional Festival in Loughborough in July 2007. Appeared as a substitute fielder for England's Test team against South Africa in the final Test of the 2008 series at The Oval. Awarded the Easter Group scholarship at the end of the 2008 season, allowing him to attend the Darren Lehmann Academy during the 2008-09 off-season. Turned down the offer of a place at St Mary's University College to concentrate on cricket

2008 Season

	M	Inn	NO	Runs	HS	Avg	100	50	Ct	St	Balls	Runs	Wkts	Avg	BB	5I	10M
Test																	
FC																	
ODI																	
List A	2	2	0	6	6	3.00	-	-	1	-	6	12	0	-	-		
20/20 Int																	
20/20	1	1	0	4	4	4.00	-	-	-	-	0	0	0	-	-		

Career Performances

	M	Inn	NO	Runs	HS	Avg	100	50	Ct	St	Balls	Runs	Wkts	Avg	BB	5I	10M
Test																	
FC																	
ODI																	
List A	2	2	0	6	6	3.00	-	-	1	-	6	12	0	-	-		
20/20 Int																	
20/20	1	1	0	4	4	4.00	-	-	-	-	0	0	0	-	-		

RUDGE, W. D. Gloucestershire

Name: William (Will) Douglas Rudge
Role: Right-hand lower-order bat, right-arm fast-medium bowler
Born: 15 July 1983, Bristol
Height: 6ft 4in **Weight:** 14st 6lbs
Nickname: Rudgey, Glasseye, Sloth
County debut: 2005
County cap: 2005
Parents: Barry and Susan
Marital status: Single
Family links with cricket: 'Dad played club cricket for Timsbury'
Education: Clifton College
Qualifications: 10 GCSEs, 3 A-levels
Overseas tours: Clifton College to Australia 1997, to Barbados 1999
Overseas teams played for: Albion CC, Tauranga, New Zealand 2001-02; Greeton CC, Tauranga, New Zealand 2002-03; Central CC, Rotorua, New Zealand 2004-05

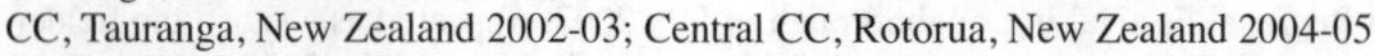

Career highlights to date: 'Debut v Sussex 2005 at Cheltenham'
Cricket moments to forget: 'Twenty20 v Somerset 2006. They set a new record 250 off their 20 overs'
Cricketers particularly admired: Glenn McGrath, Ian Botham, Curtly Ambrose
Other sports played: Rugby (at school), football (Bristol North West), golf
Other sports followed: Rugby (Bristol), football (Tottenham Hotspur)
Favourite band: The Stone Roses
Relaxations: 'Eating out, golf'
Extras: Played for Gloucestershire Board XI in the C&G 2002, 2003. NBC Denis Compton Award for the most promising young Gloucestershire player 2004. Released at the end of the 2008 season
Best batting: 19 Gloucestershire v Loughborough UCCE, Bristol 2008
Best bowling: 3-46 Gloucestershire v Bangladesh A, Bristol 2005

2008 Season

	M	Inn	NO	Runs	HS	Avg	100	50	Ct	St	Balls	Runs	Wkts	Avg	BB	5I	10M
Test																	
FC	2	2	2	26	19 *		-	-	-	-	312	190	4	47.50	3-76	-	-
ODI																	
List A	1	0	0	0	0		-	-	-	-	48	57	4	14.25	4-57	-	
20/20 Int																	
20/20	5	4	2	15	9 *	7.50	-	-	3	-	86	116	4	29.00	2-26	-	

Career Perfomances

	M	Inn	NO	Runs	HS	Avg	100	50	Ct	St	Balls	Runs	Wkts	Avg	BB	5I	10M
Test																	
FC	12	14	5	73	19 *	8.11	-	-	4	-	1399	1046	20	52.30	3-46	-	-
ODI																	
List A	6	4	1	9	4	3.00	-	-	-	-	215	206	9	22.88	4-57	-	
20/20 Int																	
20/20	8	5	2	16	9 *	5.33	-	-	3	-	144	221	8	27.62	3-37	-	

RUDOLPH, J. A. — Yorkshire

Name: Jacobus (Jacques) Andries Rudolph
Role: Left-hand bat, right-arm leg-spin bowler; county vice-captain
Born: 4 May 1981, Springs, South Africa
Height: 5ft 10in **Weight:** 12st 4lbs
Nickname: Jakes
County debut: 2007
County cap: 2007
Test debut: 2003
ODI debut: 2003
Twenty20 Int debut: 2005-06
1000 runs in a season: 2
1st-Class 200s: 2
Place in batting averages: 14th av. 56.17 (2007 18th av. 56.73)
Parents: Johan and Monica
Wife and date of marriage: Elna, 5 November 2003
Family links with cricket: 'Dad coaches the Namibian national side - my brother Gerhard plays for them.'
Education: Afrikaanse Hoer Seunskool ('Affies')
Off-season: 'Travelling in Africa'
Overseas tours: South Africa U19 to Pakistan 1998-99, to Sri Lanka (U19 World Cup) 1999-2000; South Africa A to Zimbabwe 2002-03, to Sri Lanka 2005-06; South Africa to Australia 2001-02, to Bangladesh 2003, to England 2003, to Pakistan 2003-04, to New Zealand 2003-04, to Sri Lanka 2004, to England (ICC Champions Trophy) 2004, to India 2004-05, to West Indies 2004-05, to Australia 2005-06, to Sri Lanka 2006
Overseas teams played for: Northerns B/Northerns 1997-98 – 2003-04; Titans 2003-04 – 2004-05; Eagles 2005-06 –
Career highlights to date: 'Making 222* on my Test debut.'

Cricketers particularly admired: Justin Langer
Young players to look out for: Adil Rashid
Other sports followed: Football (Manchester United)
Favourite band: U2, Dire Straits
Extras: Was twice on verge of Test debut – selected for the third Test v India at Centurion 2001-02, only for the match to be stripped of Test status due to the Denness Affair; chosen for the third Test v Australia in Sydney 2001-02, only for his selection to be overruled in favour of Justin Ontong. Man of the Match for his 222* on Test debut in the first Test v Bangladesh in Chittagong 2003; in the process shared with Boeta Dippenaar (177*) in the highest partnership for any wicket for South Africa in Tests (429*). One of *South African Cricket Annual*'s five Cricketers of the Year 2003. Scored second innings 102* to help save the first Test v Australia at Perth 2005-06. Was due to join Derbyshire as an overseas player in 2006 but withdrew with a shoulder problem. Joined Yorkshire in 2007; is no longer considered an overseas player. Man of the Match v Cape Cobras at Cape Town in the SuperSport Series 2007-08 (94/5-80)
Relaxations: 'Fly fishing and adventure motorbiking (travelling)'
Best batting: 222* South Africa v Bangladesh, Chittagong 2003
Best bowling: 5-80 Eagles v Cape Cobras, Cape Town, 2007

2008 Season

	M	Inn	NO	Runs	HS	Avg	100	50	Ct	St	Balls	Runs	Wkts	Avg	BB	5I	10M
Test																	
FC	16	24	1	1292	155	56.17	5	6	24	-	128	74	1	74.00	1-13	-	-
ODI																	
List A	18	16	2	675	120	48.21	1	5	9	-	18	19	0		-	-	
20/20 Int																	
20/20	9	8	1	191	56	27.28	-	1	1	-	0	0	0		-	-	

Career Performances

	M	Inn	NO	Runs	HS	Avg	100	50	Ct	St	Balls	Runs	Wkts	Avg	BB	5I	10M
Test	35	63	7	2028	222 *	36.21	5	8	22	-	664	432	4	108.00	1-1	-	-
FC	139	238	16	9710	222 *	43.73	28	44	128	-	4175	2324	58	40.06	5-80	3	-
ODI	45	39	6	1174	81	35.57	-	7	11	-	24	26	0		-	-	
List A	154	142	22	5237	134 *	43.64	7	33	51	-	377	341	10	34.10	4-40	-	
20/20 Int	1	1	1	6	6 *		-	-	-	-	0	0	0		-	-	
20/20	35	33	8	816	71	32.64	-	5	11	-	133	172	10	17.20	3-16	-	

77. Prior to the 2005 Ashes series, who said: 'I definitely believe that if any of our batsmen get out to Ashley Giles in the Tests they should go and hang themselves'?

SADLER, J. L. Derbyshire

Name: John Leonard Sadler
Role: Left-hand top-order bat, right-arm off-spin bowler
Born: 19 November 1981, Dewsbury, Yorkshire
Height: 5ft 11in **Weight:** 13st 5lbs
Nickname: Sads, Chrome, Super
County debut: 2002 (one-day, Yorkshire), 2003 (Leicestershire), 2008 (Derbyshire)
1000 runs in a season: 1
Place in batting averages: 189th av. 21.50 (2007 229th av. 17.88)
Parents: Sue and Mike ('Baz')
Marital status: Engaged
Family links with cricket: 'Dad played cricket for Ossett CC in the Yorkshire League for 30 years, fielding round the corner with his sun hat on; now coaches. Brothers Dave and Jamie represented Yorkshire Schools and now play local league in Yorkshire CYCL. Mum did the teas...'
Education: St Thomas à Becket RC Comprehensive School, Wakefield
Qualifications: 9 GCSEs, Levels I and II coaching awards
Off-season: 'Another nose operation, and three months in Perth, Western Australia'
Overseas tours: England U17 to Ireland; England U19 to Malaysia and (U19 World Cup) Sri Lanka 1999-2000, to India 2000-01; Yorkshire to Grenada 2002
Overseas teams played for: Tuart Hill, Perth 2001-02 – 2003-04
Career highlights to date: 'My first first-class century. Winning Twenty20 with Leicestershire 2004, 2006'
Cricket moments to forget: 'Being injured by Brett Lee (broken collarbone) in 2005'
Cricketers particularly admired: Robin Smith, Brian Lara, Sachin Tendulkar, Darren Lehmann
Other sports played: Five-a-side football, squash, golf - 'handicap 15'
Other sports followed: Football (Leeds United) - 'the Premier League in general'
Favourite band: Oasis
Extras: Played for Yorkshire Schools at all levels; attended Yorkshire Academy; awarded Yorkshire 2nd XI cap. Yorkshire Supporters' Club Young Player of the Year 1998. Represented England U14, U15, U17, U18 and U19. Left Leicestershire at the end of the 2007 season and joined Derbyshire for 2008
Relaxations: 'Walking the dog (Max)'
Opinions on cricket: 'The best game in the world... But still the hardest.'

Best batting: 145 Leicestershire v Surrey, Leicester 2003
145 Leicestershire v Sussex, Hove 2003
Best bowling: 1-5 Leicestershire v Middlesex, Southgate 2007

2008 Season

	M	Inn	NO	Runs	HS	Avg	100	50	Ct	St	Balls	Runs	Wkts	Avg	BB	5I	10M
Test																	
FC	8	14	0	301	50	21.50	-	1	2	-	60	57	1	57.00	1-57	-	
ODI																	
List A	10	9	1	209	46	26.12	-	-	-	-	0	0	0				
20/20 Int																	
20/20	6	5	0	38	25	7.60	-	-	2	-	24	34	0		-		

Career Performances

	M	Inn	NO	Runs	HS	Avg	100	50	Ct	St	Balls	Runs	Wkts	Avg	BB	5I	10M
Test																	
FC	60	103	12	2931	145	32.20	3	16	40	-	231	250	3	83.33	1-5	-	-
ODI																	
List A	83	77	12	1716	113 *	26.40	1	6	14		48	33	1	33.00	1-33	-	
20/20 Int																	
20/20	43	37	8	505	73	17.41	-	1	15		24	34	0		-		

78. By how many wickets did England lose the final Test of 2006-07 as the whitewash was completed?

SAGGERS, M. J. Kent

Name: Martin John Saggers
Role: Right-hand bat, right-arm fast-medium bowler
Born: 23 May 1972, King's Lynn
Height: 6ft 2in **Weight:** 14st
Nickname: Saggs, Jurgen
County debut: 1996 (Durham), 1999 (Kent) (*see* ***Extras***)
County cap: 2001 (Kent)
Test debut: 2003-04
Benefit: 2009
50 wickets in a season: 4
Place in batting averages: 253rd av. 11.22
Place in bowling averages: 110th av. 36.37 (2007 26th av. 24.37)
Parents: Brian and Edna
Wife and date of marriage: Samantha, 27 February 2004
Children: Ethan Patrick, 9 October 2005; Erin Savannah, 27 June 2008
Family links with cricket: Grandfather played in the Essex League
Education: Springwood High School; University of Huddersfield
Qualifications: BA (Hons) Architectural Studies International
Overseas tours: Kent to South Africa 2001; England VI to Hong Kong 2002; England to Bangladesh 2003-04
Overseas teams played for: Randburg CC, Johannesburg 1996-98, 2000-04; Southern Suburbs CC, Johannesburg 1998-99
Career highlights to date: 'Winning the Norwich Union League 2001. Making my Test debut in Bangladesh. Taking a wicket with my first delivery in Test cricket on English soil'
Cricket moments to forget: 'Any form of injury'
Cricket superstitions: 'Getting a corner spot in the changing room'
Cricketers particularly admired: Neil Foster, Allan Donald, Brad Robinson
Young players to look out for: Sam Northeast, Ethan Saggers
Other sports played: Golf (10 handicap)
Other sports followed: Football (Spurs), 'any form of motor sport'
Favourite band: Metallica, Prime Circle, Puddle of Mudd, Creed
Extras: Won Most Promising Uncapped Player Award 2000. Joint Kent Player of the Year 2000 (with David Masters). Underwood Award (Kent leading wicket-taker) 2001, 2002, 2003. *Kent Messenger* Group Readers' Player of the Season 2002. Shepherd Neame Award for Best Bowler 2002. Cowdrey Award (Kent Player of the Year) 2002. Scored career best 64 as nightwatchman as Kent scored a then county fourth-innings

record 429-5 to beat Worcestershire at Canterbury 2004. Took wicket (Mark Richardson) with his first delivery in Test cricket on English soil, in the second Test v New Zealand at Headingley 2004. Played two first-class, three List A and five Twenty20 matches for Essex on loan 2007

Opinions on cricket: 'Fantastic game! Twenty20 has brought a new lease of life to the game. Just hope we don't go on overkill for the one format of the game.'

Best batting: 64 Kent v Worcestershire, Canterbury 2004

Best bowling: 7-79 Kent v Durham, Riverside 2000

2008 Season

	M	Inn	NO	Runs	HS	Avg	100	50	Ct	St	Balls	Runs	Wkts	Avg	BB	5I	10M
Test																	
FC	11	16	7	101	33	11.22	-	-	1	-	1661	873	24	36.37	4-26	-	-
ODI																	
List A	1	1	1	3	3 *		-	-	-	-	36	43	0		-	-	
20/20 Int																	
20/20																	

Career Performances

	M	Inn	NO	Runs	HS	Avg	100	50	Ct	St	Balls	Runs	Wkts	Avg	BB	5I	10M
Test	3	3	0	1	1	.33	-	-	1	-	493	247	7	35.28	2-29	-	-
FC	115	143	41	1160	64	11.37	-	2	27	-	20023	10249	405	25.30	7-79	18	-
ODI																	
List A	123	67	34	302	34 *	9.15	-	-	23	-	5592	4197	166	25.28	5-22	2	
20/20 Int																	
20/20	10	1	0	5	5	5.00	-	-	2	-	186	256	6	42.66	2-14	-	

79. England were to win the Ashes in 2005, but by what margin did they lose the first Test at Lord's?

SAKER, N. C. Surrey

Name: Neil Clifford Saker
Role: Right-hand bat, right-arm fast bowler
Born: 20 September 1984, Tooting, London
Height: 6ft 4in **Weight:** 12st 7lbs
Nickname: Bulby, Sakes
County debut: 2003
Place in batting averages: (2007 265th av. 12.33)
Place in bowling averages: (2007 125th av. 43.26)
Parents: Pauline and Steve
Marital status: Single
Family links with cricket: 'Dad played league cricket in Surrey'
Education: Raynes Park High School; Nescot College, Ewell
Qualifications: ECB Level 1 coach, City & Guilds Carpentry

Overseas tours: Guildford CC to Trinidad and Tobago 2001; Surrey U19 to Sri Lanka 2002
Overseas teams played for: Randwick-Petersham, Sydney 2003-04; Blacktown CC, Sydney
Cricket superstitions: 'Bowling marker has to be lying on the grass, not pushed in'
Cricketers particularly admired: Brett Lee, Allan Donald
Young players to look out for: Jade Dernbach, Rory Hamilton-Brown, Danny Miller
Other sports played: Snooker, golf
Other sports followed: Football (Tottenham)
Favourite band: Queen
Relaxations: 'Music, sleeping and eating!'
Extras: First academy player at Surrey to sign full-time professional contract. Attended University of Port Elizabeth International Cricket Academy 2002-03. Released by Surrey at the end of the 2008 season.
Best batting: 58* Surrey v Essex, Colchester 2006
Best bowling: 5-76 Surrey v Lancashire, Old Trafford 2007

2008 Season

	M	Inn	NO	Runs	HS	Avg	100	50	Ct	St	Balls	Runs	Wkts	Avg	BB	5I	10M
Test																	
FC																	
ODI																	
List A	3	2	0	21	20	10.50	-	-	-	-	138	154	0		-	-	
20/20 Int																	
20/20																	

Career Performances

	M	Inn	NO	Runs	HS	Avg	100	50	Ct	St	Balls	Runs	Wkts	Avg	BB	5I	10M
Test																	
FC	18	23	4	272	58 *	14.31	-	1	5	-	2159	1578	31	50.90	5-76	1	-
ODI																	
List A	23	11	4	74	22	10.57	-	-	2	-	933	942	18	52.33	4-43	-	
20/20 Int																	
20/20	2	1	0	0	0	0.00	-	-	-	-	30	44	1	44.00	1-28	-	

SALES, D. J. G. — Northamptonshire

Name: David John Grimwood Sales
Role: Right-hand bat, right-arm medium bowler
Born: 3 December 1977, Carshalton, Surrey
Height: 6ft **Weight:** 14st 7lbs
Nickname: Jumble
County debut: 1994 (one-day), 1996 (first-class)
County cap: 1999
Benefit: 2007
1000 runs in a season: 5
1st-Class 200s: 6
1st-Class 300s: 1
Place in batting averages: 27th av. 49.43 (2007 22nd av. 55.36)
Parents: Daphne and John
Wife and date of marriage: Abigail, 22 September 2001
Children: James, 11 February 2003; Benjamin David, 3 March 2005; Charlie Matthew, 20 September 2006

Family links with cricket: Father played club cricket
Education: Caterham Boys' School, Surrey
Qualifications: 7 GCSEs, cricket coach
Overseas tours: England U15 to South Africa 1993; England U19 to West Indies 1994-95, to Zimbabwe 1995-96, to Pakistan 1996-97; England A to Kenya and Sri Lanka 1997-98, to Bangladesh and New Zealand 1999-2000, to West Indies 2000-01; Northamptonshire to Grenada 2000
Overseas teams played for: Wellington Firebirds, New Zealand 2001-02
Career highlights to date: '303 not out v Essex [1999]; 104 v Pakistan 2003'
Cricket moments to forget: 'Watching White and Powell for five hours, then getting 0' (*Rob White and Mark Powell shared in a new record Northamptonshire opening partnership of 375 v Gloucestershire at Northampton 2002*)
Cricket superstitions: 'None'
Cricketers particularly admired: Graham Gooch, Steve Waugh
Young players to look out for: Alex Wakely, Graeme White
Other sports followed: Rugby (Northampton Saints), golf, football (Crystal Palace)
Favourite band: Coldplay
Relaxations: Fishing and golf
Extras: Sir John Hobbs Silver Jubilee Memorial Prize 1993. Scored 56-ball 70* v Essex at Chelmsford in the Sunday League 1994, aged 16 years 289 days. Scored 210* on Championship debut v Worcs at Kidderminster 1996, aged 18 years 237 days. NBC Denis Compton Award for the most promising young Northamptonshire player 1996. Became the youngest Englishman to score a first-class triple century (303*) v Essex at Northampton 1999, aged 21 years 240 days. PCA/CGU Young Player of the Year 1999. Man of the Match for Wellington v Canterbury in the final of New Zealand's State Shield at Wellington 2001-02 (62). Captain of Northamptonshire 2004-07. Northamptonshire's top-scoring batsman in 2008
Best batting: 303* Northamptonshire v Essex, Northampton 1999
Best bowling: 4-25 Northamptonshire v Sri Lanka A, Northampton 1999

2008 Season

	M	Inn	NO	Runs	HS	Avg	100	50	Ct	St	Balls	Runs	Wkts	Avg	BB	5I	10M
Test																	
FC	17	27	4	1137	173	49.43	3	4	14	-	0	0	0		-	-	-
ODI																	
List A	12	12	2	333	96 *	33.30	-	3	3	-	0	0	0		-	-	
20/20 Int																	
20/20	11	10	2	253	71 *	31.62	-	2	7	-	0	0	0		-	-	

Career Performances

	M	Inn	NO	Runs	HS	Avg	100	50	Ct	St	Balls	Runs	Wkts	Avg	BB	5I	10M
Test																	
FC	188	299	28	11458	303 *	42.28	23	57	167	-	339	174	9	19.33	4-25	-	-
ODI																	
List A	229	217	30	6353	161	33.97	4	44	103	-	84	67	0		-	-	
20/20 Int																	
20/20	44	41	10	1074	78 *	34.64	-	10	25	-	12	23	1	23.00	1-10	-	

SALISBURY, I. D. K. Warwickshire

Name: Ian David Kenneth Salisbury
Role: Right-hand bat, leg-break bowler
Born: 21 January 1970, Moulton, Northampton
Height: 5ft 11in **Weight:** 12st 7lbs
Nickname: Solly, Dingle, Sals
County debut: 1989 (Sussex), 1997 (Surrey), 2008 (Warwickshire)
County cap: 1991 (Sussex), 1998 (Surrey), 2008 (Warwickshire)
Benefit: 2007 (Surrey)
Test debut: 1992
ODI debut: 1992-93
50 wickets in a season: 7
Place in batting averages: 103rd av. 32.75 (2007 219th av. 19.33)
Place in bowling averages: 58th av. 27.90 (2007 147th av. 67.72)
Parents: Dave and Margaret
Wife and date of marriage: Emma Louise, 25 September 1993
Children: Anya-Rose, 10 August 2002
Family links with cricket: 'Dad is vice-president of my first club, Brixworth. He also re-lays cricket squares (e.g. Lord's, Northampton, Leicester)'
Education: Moulton Comprehensive, Northampton
Qualifications: 7 O-levels, NCA coaching certificate
Overseas tours: England A to Pakistan 1990-91, to Bermuda and West Indies 1991-92, to India 1994-95, to Pakistan 1995-96; England to India and Sri Lanka 1992-93, to West Indies 1993-94, to Pakistan 2000-01; World Masters XI v Indian Masters XI November 1996 ('Masters aged 26?')
Overseas teams played for: University of New South Wales, Sydney 1997-2000

Cricketers particularly admired: 'Any that keep performing day in, day out, for both country and county'
Other sports played: 'Most sports'
Other sports followed: Football (Southampton FC, Northampton Town FC), rugby union (Northampton Saints), 'any England team'
Relaxations: 'Spending time with wife Emma; meeting friends and relaxing with them and eating out with good wine'
Extras: In 1992 was named Young Player of the Year by both the Wombwell Cricket Lovers and the Cricket Writers. One of *Wisden*'s Five Cricketers of the Year 1993. Won Bill O'Reilly Medal for Sydney first-grade player of the year 1999-2000. Took 800th first-class wicket (Tim Phillips) v Essex at Croydon 2006. Left Surrey at the end of the 2007 season and joined Warwickshire for 2008. His 6-100 against Essex in September 2008 was his fifth five-wicket haul of the season and helped to clinch promotion for his new county
Best batting: 103 Surrey v Hampshire, The Oval 2007
Best bowling: 8-60 Surrey v Somerset, The Oval 2000

2008 Season

	M	Inn	NO	Runs	HS	Avg	100	50	Ct	St	Balls	Runs	Wkts	Avg	BB	5I	10M
Test																	
FC	13	14	2	393	81	32.75	-	3	7	-	1612	865	31	27.90	6-100	5	-
ODI																	
List A	6	4	1	13	7 *	4.33	-	-	1	-	267	219	10	21.90	4-28	-	
20/20 Int																	
20/20	10	2	1	15	9	15.00	-	-	6	-	192	175	15	11.66	3-14	-	

Career Performances

	M	Inn	NO	Runs	HS	Avg	100	50	Ct	St	Balls	Runs	Wkts	Avg	BB	5I	10M
Test	15	25	3	368	50	16.72	-	1	5	-	2492	1539	20	76.95	4-163	-	-
FC	324	414	81	7012	103	21.05	3	26	206	-	56346	28865	884	32.65	8-60	40	6
ODI	4	2	1	7	5	7.00	-	-	1	-	186	177	5	35.40	3-41	-	
List A	255	166	47	1582	59 *	13.29	-	1	90	-	10841	8321	257	32.37	5-30	1	
20/20 Int																	
20/20	32	16	4	109	20	9.08	-	-	13	-	478	536	27	19.85	3-14	-	

80. Which Australian made his first Test century during the 1997 Ashes series?

SANDERSON, B. W. — Yorkshire

Name: Ben William Sanderson
Role: Right-hand bat, right-arm fast-medium bowler
Born: 3 January 1989, Sheffield
Height: 6ft **Weight:** 13st
Nickname: Sando
County debut: 2008
Parents: Roy and Lynne
Marital status: Single
Family links with cricket: 'Dad plays for Whitley Hall CC'
Education: Ecclesfield; Sheffield College
Qualifications: Plumber (trade)
Career highlights to date: 'Playing for Yorkshire 2nd XI. Winning U17 County Championship two years running'
Cricket moments to forget: 'Getting out on a hat-trick ball'

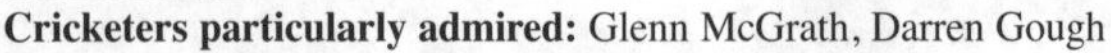

Cricketers particularly admired: Glenn McGrath, Darren Gough
Young players to look out for: Oliver Hannon-Dalby
Other sports played: Football (Hallam U19)
Other sports followed: Football (Sheffield Wednesday)
Favourite band: Milburn
Relaxations: 'Watching films'
Extras: Yorkshire Academy
Opinions on cricket: 'Glad to see the game moving forward and gaining interest with the public supporters.'
Best batting: 6 Yorkshire v Lancashire, Headingley 2008
Best bowling: 1-87 Yorkshire v Lancashire, Headingley 2008

2008 Season

	M	Inn	NO	Runs	HS	Avg	100	50	Ct	St	Balls	Runs	Wkts	Avg	BB	5I	10M
Test																	
FC	2	2	1	6	6	6.00	-	-	-	-	222	140	1	140.00	1-87	-	-
ODI																	
List A																	
20/20 Int																	
20/20																	

Career Performances

	M	Inn	NO	Runs	HS	Avg	100	50	Ct	St	Balls	Runs	Wkts	Avg	BB	5I	10M
Test																	
FC	2	2	1	6	6	6.00	-	-	-	-	222	140	1	140.00	1-87	-	-
ODI																	
List A																	
20/20 Int																	
20/20																	

SAQLAIN MUSHTAQ Surrey

Name: Saqlain Mushtaq
Role: Right-hand bat, off-spin bowler
Born: 29 December 1976, Lahore, Pakistan
Height: 5ft 9in
Nickname: Saqi, Baba
County debut: 1997 (Surrey), 2007 (Sussex)
County cap: 1998 (Surrey)
Test debut: 1995-96
ODI debut: 1995-96
50 wickets in a season: 5
Place in batting averages: 221st av. 17.16
Place in bowling averages: 87th av. 32.20 (2007 3rd av. 17.55)
Parents: Nasim Akhtar and Mushtaq Ahmed
Wife and date of marriage: Sana ('Sunny') Saqlain, 11 April 2000
Education: Lahore MAO College
Overseas tours: Pakistan U19 to New Zealand 1994-95; Pakistan to Australia 1995-96, to England 1996, to Australia 1996-97, to Sri Lanka 1996-97, to India 1996-97, to South Africa and Zimbabwe 1997-98, to India 1998-99, to Bangladesh (Wills International Cup) 1998-99, to UK, Ireland and Netherlands (World Cup) 1999, to Australia 1999-2000, to West Indies 1999-2000, to Kenya (ICC Knockout Trophy) 2000-01, to New Zealand 2000-01, to England 2001, to Bangladesh 2001-02, to Sharjah (v West Indies) 2001-02, to Sri Lanka and Sharjah (v Australia) 2002-03, to Zimbabwe and South Africa 2002-03, to Africa (World Cup) 2002-03, plus other one-day tournaments in Sri Lanka, Toronto, Sharjah, Kenya, Bangladesh, Singapore and Morocco
Overseas teams played for: PIA 1994-95 – 2003-04; Islamabad 1994-95 – 1997-98; Lahore 2003-04; Lahore Badshahs (ICL) 2008
Other sports played: Squash

Extras: Scored 79 in the first Test v Zimbabwe at Sheikhupura 1996-97, sharing with Wasim Akram (257*) in a world record eighth-wicket partnership in Tests (313). Took only the second hat-trick in World Cup cricket (Olonga, Huckle and Mbangwa), v Zimbabwe at The Oval 1999; it was his second hat-trick in ODIs v Zimbabwe. Topped the English first-class bowling averages in 1999, taking 58 wickets at 11.37 in seven games. One of *Wisden*'s Five Cricketers of the Year 2000. His series and match awards include Man of the [Test] Series v India 1998-99 (including 5-94/5-93 in Pakistan's victory in the first Test in Chennai) and v Zimbabwe 2002-03. Holds record for taking fewest matches to reach 100 ODI wickets (53 matches), 150 (78), 200 (104) and 250 (138), and also for the most ODI wickets in a calendar year (69 in 1997). An overseas player with Surrey 1997-2004 and in August-September 2005. Played for Ireland in the C&G 2006. Joined Sussex for 2007; left Sussex at the end of the 2007 season and rejoined Surrey for 2008. Is England-qualified
Best batting: 101* Pakistan v New Zealand, Christchurch 2000-01
Best bowling: 8-65 Surrey v Derbyshire, The Oval 1998

2008 Season

	M	Inn	NO	Runs	HS	Avg	100	50	Ct	St	Balls	Runs	Wkts	Avg	BB	5I	10M
Test																	
FC	14	16	4	206	50	17.16	-	1	2	-	2380	1288	40	32.20	6-50	3	-
ODI																	
List A	1	1	0	4	4	4.00	-	-	-	-	60	63	1	63.00	1-63	-	
20/20 Int																	
20/20	2	1	0	14	14	14.00	-	-	-	-	48	64	6	10.66	3-24	-	

Career Performances

	M	Inn	NO	Runs	HS	Avg	100	50	Ct	St	Balls	Runs	Wkts	Avg	BB	5I	10M
Test	49	78	14	927	101 *	14.48	1	2	15	-	14070	6206	208	29.83	8-164	13	3
FC	194	263	59	3407	101 *	16.70	1	14	67	-	44634	19630	833	23.56	8-65	60	15
ODI	169	98	38	711	37 *	11.85	-	-	40	-	8770	6275	288	21.78	5-20	6	
List A	323	182	67	1339	38 *	11.64	-	-	80	-	16062	11261	478	23.55	5-20	7	
20/20 Int																	
20/20	9	4	0	24	14	6.00	-	-	2	-	210	265	14	18.92	3-24	-	

81. In the 1997 Ashes series, whom did Ben Hollioake replace as the youngest ever England debutant?

SAXELBY, I. D. Gloucestershire

Name: Ian David Saxelby
Role: Right-hand bat, right-arm fast-medium bowler
Born: 22 May 1989, Nottingham
County debut: 2008
Family links with cricket: Uncle Kevin played for Nottinghamshire, and his late uncle Mark played for Derbyshire, Durham and Nottinghamshire.
Extras: Has represented England at U19 level, and played for Gloucestershire 2nd XI. Signed his first professional contract towards the end of the 2008 season
Best batting: 11* Gloucestershire v Middlesex, Bristol 2008
Best bowling: 1-64 Gloucestershire v Middlesex, Bristol 2008

2008 Season

	M	Inn	NO	Runs	HS	Avg	100	50	Ct	St	Balls	Runs	Wkts	Avg	BB	5I	10M
Test																	
FC	3	3	1	20	11 *	10.00	-	-	1	-	282	218	2	109.00	1-64	-	-
ODI																	
List A																	
20/20 Int																	
20/20																	

Career Performances

	M	Inn	NO	Runs	HS	Avg	100	50	Ct	St	Balls	Runs	Wkts	Avg	BB	5I	10M
Test																	
FC	3	3	1	20	11 *	10.00	-	-	1	-	282	218	2	109.00	1-64	-	-
ODI																	
List A																	
20/20 Int																	
20/20																	

SAYERS, J. J. Yorkshire

Name: Joseph (Joe) John Sayers
Role: Left-hand bat, right-arm off-spin bowler
Born: 5 November 1983, Leeds, Yorkshire
Height: 6ft **Weight:** 13st
Nickname: Mayor, Squiz
County debut: 2003 (one-day), 2004 (first-class)
County cap: 2007
Place in batting averages: (2007 110th av. 33.89)
Parents: Geraldine and Roger
Marital status: Single
Family links with cricket: 'Father played at school, but otherwise none'
Education: St Mary's RC Comprehensive School, Menston; Worcester College, Oxford University
Qualifications: 12 GCSEs, 4 A-levels, BA Physics (Oxon)
Overseas tours: Leeds Schools to South Africa 1998; Yorkshire U17 to South Africa 2001; England U17 to Australia 2001
Overseas teams played for: Manly-Warringah, Sydney 2004-05
Career highlights to date: 'Receiving my county cap for Yorkshire'
Cricket superstitions: 'None'
Cricketers particularly admired: Mark Ramprakash
Young players to look out for: Jonathan Bairstow
Other sports played: Football ('played as goalkeeper for Bradford City AFC for three years'), rowing (Worcester College)
Other sports followed: Rugby league (Leeds Rhinos), rugby union (Leeds Tykes), football
Favourite band: Coldplay
Relaxations: 'Drawing, painting, writing, watching movies'
Extras: Captained England U17 v Australia U17 at Adelaide 2001. Played for Oxford UCCE 2002, 2003, 2004 (captain 2003). Oxford Blue 2002, 2003, 2004. Represented England U19 2002, 2003 (captain in the third 'Test' 2003). Wrote weekly column 'View from the Balcony' for *Yorkshire Post* during the 2006 season. Carried bat for 122* v Middlesex at Scarborough 2006; carried bat again for a 553-minute 149* v Durham at Headingley 2007 and was on the field of play for the entire game
Opinions on cricket: 'County championship cricket has become extremely competitive, with any one side capable of beating any other and very few points separating the eventual champions from those placed below them in the table.'
Best batting: 187 Yorkshire v Kent, Tunbridge Wells 2007

2008 Season

	M	Inn	NO	Runs	HS	Avg	100	50	Ct	St	Balls	Runs	Wkts	Avg	BB	5I	10M
Test																	
FC	6	9	0	76	22	8.44	-	-	6	-	0	0	0		-	-	-
ODI																	
List A																	
20/20 Int																	
20/20																	

Career Performances

	M	Inn	NO	Runs	HS	Avg	100	50	Ct	St	Balls	Runs	Wkts	Avg	BB	5I	10M
Test																	
FC	59	96	8	2815	187	31.98	8	12	32	-	72	54	0		-	-	-
ODI																	
List A	13	13	2	249	62	22.63	-	2	-	-	54	71	1	71.00	1-31	-	
20/20 Int																	
20/20	3	1	0	12	12	12.00	-	-	2	-	0	0	0		-	-	

SCHOFIELD, C. P. Surrey

Name: Christopher (Chris) Paul Schofield
Role: Left-hand bat, right-arm leg-spin bowler; all-rounder
Born: 6 October 1978, Rochdale
Height: 6ft 2in **Weight:** 12st
Nickname: Schoey, Scho-boat
County debut: 1998 (Lancashire), 2006 (Surrey)
County cap: 2002 (Lancashire)
Test debut: 2000
Twenty20 Int debut: 2007-08
Place in batting averages: (2007 248th av. 14.33)
Place in bowling averages: (2007 117th av. 40.62)
Parents: David and Judith
Marital status: Single
Family links with cricket: Father played with local club team Whittles and brother with local team Littleborough
Education: Wardle High School, Rochdale
Qualifications: 4 GCSEs, NVQ Levels 2 and 3 in Information Technology

Off-season: 'Playing Grade cricket in Australia'
Overseas tours: England U17 to Bermuda 1997; England U19 to South Africa (including U19 World Cup) 1997-98; England A to Bangladesh and New Zealand 1999-2000, to West Indies 2000-01, to India 2007-08; ECB National Academy to Australia 2001-02; England to South Africa (World 20/20) 2007-08; England Performance Programme to India 2007-08
Career highlights to date: 'Two Tests and four Twenty20 games for England'
Cricket moments to forget: 'Tribunal against Lancashire'
Cricketers particularly admired: Shane Warne
Young players to look out for: Adil Rashid
Other sports played: Football, golf, snooker ('highest break 124')
Other sports followed: Football (Liverpool FC)
Favourite band: Matchbox 20
Relaxations: Listening to music, playing snooker, socialising, internet poker
Extras: Was part of England U19 World Cup winning squad 1997-98. Won double twice in two years with Littleborough CC (Wood Cup and Lancashire Cup 1997; League and Wood Cup 1998). Won Sir Ron Brierley/Crusaders Scholarship 1998. NBC Denis Compton Award for the most promising young Lancashire player 1998, 1999, 2000. Leading first-class wicket-taker on England A tour to West Indies 2000-01 (22 wickets; av. 26.27). Represented England Lions 2007
Best batting: 99 Lancashire v Warwickshire, Old Trafford 2004
Best bowling: 6-120 England A v Bangladesh, Chittagong 1999-2000

2008 Season

	M	Inn	NO	Runs	HS	Avg	100	50	Ct	St	Balls	Runs	Wkts	Avg	BB	5I	10M
Test																	
FC	2	4	0	36	20	9.00	-	-	-	-	238	143	1	143.00	1-69	-	
ODI																	
List A	6	5	1	66	58	16.50	-	1	2	-	262	232	3	77.33	1-26	-	
20/20 Int																	
20/20	6	5	2	39	16	13.00	-	-	1	-	120	167	7	23.85	2-29	-	

Career Performances

	M	Inn	NO	Runs	HS	Avg	100	50	Ct	St	Balls	Runs	Wkts	Avg	BB	5I	10M
Test	2	3	0	67	57	22.33	-	1	-	-	108	73	0	-	-	-	-
FC	78	109	15	2659	99	28.28	-	21	45	-	12415	6436	196	32.83	6-120	5	-
ODI																	
List A	113	83	21	1391	75 *	22.43	-	6	31	-	3400	2953	108	27.34	5-31	1	
20/20 Int	4	4	3	24	9 *	24.00	-	-	1	-	77	92	4	23.00	2-15	-	
20/20	29	20	8	154	27	12.83	-	-	6	-	401	458	32	14.31	4-12	-	

SCOTT, B. J. M. Middlesex

Name: Benjamin (Ben) James Matthew Scott
Role: Right-hand bat, wicket-keeper
Born: 4 August 1981, Isleworth
Height: 'Small' (5ft 9in) **Weight:** 11st 7lbs
Nickname: Scotty
County debut: 2002 (one-day, Surrey), 2003 (first-class, Surrey), 2004 (Middlesex)
County cap: 2007 (Middlesex)
50 dismissals in a season: 1
Place in batting averages: 101st av. 35.36 (2006 216th av. 19.07)
Parents: Terry and Edna
Marital status: Single
Family links with cricket: Father played for the Primitives; brother played local cricket. Nephew Joel Pope is with Leicestershire
Education: Whitton School, Richmond; Richmond College
Qualifications: 9 GCSEs, 3 A-levels studied, ECB Level 1 coach, YMCA Fitness Instructor's Award
Overseas tours: MCC YC to Cape Town 1999-2000; Middlesex to Mumbai, India 2005, 2006, to Antigua 2008-09 for Stanford Super Series; MCC to Uganda 2008; England Lions to New Zealand 2008-09
Overseas teams played for: Portland CC, Victoria 1999-2000; Mt Gambia, South Australia 2001-02; South Melbourne CC 2006
Career highlights to date: 'Scoring 101* at Lord's v Northants; just getting there with Nantie Hayward down the other end'
Cricket moments to forget: 'Being the hat-trick for Billy Taylor v Hampshire' (*At The Rose Bowl 2006*)
Cricket superstitions: 'None'
Cricketers particularly admired: Alec Stewart, Jack Russell, Nad Shahid
Young players to look out for: Eoin Morgan, Joel Pope
Other sports played: Golf
Favourite band: Michael Jackson, The Jacksons, Usher
Relaxations: Music, golf, TV
Extras: Middlesex YC cap. Represented ESCA U14 and U15. Played for Development of Excellence XI 1999. Finchley CC Player of the Season 2000
Best batting: 164* Middlesex v Northamptonshire, Uxbridge 2008

2008 Season

	M	Inn	NO	Runs	HS	Avg	100	50	Ct	St	Balls	Runs	Wkts	Avg	BB	5I	10M
Test																	
FC	15	22	3	754	164 *	39.68	1	7	50	3	3	1	0		-	-	-
ODI																	
List A	13	11	1	120	52	12.00	-	1	8	6	0	0	0		-	-	
20/20 Int																	
20/20	13	9	4	68	31 *	13.60	-	-	4	5	0	0	0		-	-	

Career Performances

	M	Inn	NO	Runs	HS	Avg	100	50	Ct	St	Balls	Runs	Wkts	Avg	BB	5I	10M
Test																	
FC	60	90	18	2148	164 *	29.83	3	13	159	19	3	1	0		-	-	-
ODI																	
List A	78	46	13	604	73 *	18.30	-	4	65	26	0	0	0		-	-	
20/20 Int																	
20/20	40	28	14	218	32 *	15.57	-	-	13	17	0	0	0		-	-	

SHAFAYAT, B. M. — Nottinghamshire

Name: Bilal Mustafa Shafayat
Role: Right-hand bat, right-arm fast-medium bowler, occasional wicket-keeper
Born: 10 July 1984, Nottingham
Height: 5ft 7in **Weight:** 10st 7lbs
Nickname: Billy, Muzzy, Our Kid
County debut: 2001 (Nottinghamshire), 2005 (Northamptonshire)
1000 runs in a season: 1
Place in batting averages: 56th av. 41.61 (2007 138th av. 31.11)
Parents: Mohammad Shafayat and Mahfooza Begum
Marital status: Single
Family links with cricket: 'Brother Rashid played for Notts up to 2nd XI and is now playing in Staffordshire Premier (took ten wickets in a game 2003). Uncle Nadeem played for PCC. Father just loves it!'
Education: Greenwood Dale; Nottingham Bluecoat School and Sixth Form College
Qualifications: 9 GCSEs, 2 A-levels, Level 1 coaching

Career outside cricket: 'Investing a little'
Off-season: 'Playing first-class cricket in Pakistan as an overseas player for Pakistan Customs, and then going to Cape Town.'
Overseas tours: ZRK to Pakistan 2000; Sparkhill ('Kadeer Ali's dad's academy') to Pakistan; England U17 to Australia 2000-01; England U19 to Australia and (U19 World Cup) New Zealand 2001-02, to Australia 2002-03 (c); Nottinghamshire to South Africa 2002, 2003; England A to Malaysia and India 2003-04; MCC to Uganda 2008
Overseas teams played for: National Bank of Pakistan 2004-05; Pakistan Customs 2008-09
Career highlights to date: 'Making my first-class debut for Notts v Middlesex (scoring 72). Scoring a hundred and double hundred v India in final U19 "Test" 2002. Scoring crucial hundred v Worcestershire for promotion in Championship. Beating Australia U19 in first "Test" 2002-03, scoring 66, 108 and taking six wickets'
Cricket moments to forget: 'Losing U19 "Test" series to Australia'
Cricketers particularly admired: Sachin Tendulkar, Carl Hooper, Mark Ramprakash
Young players to look out for: Owais Walait
Other sports played: Football, badminton, squash, pool
Other sports followed: Football (Liverpool), boxing, snooker
Favourite band: Khalil Hussary, Ahmad Bukhatir
Relaxations: 'Voluntary work for SAS Trust charity'
Extras: Scored 72 on Championship debut v Middlesex at Trent Bridge 2001, aged 16 years 360 days. NBC Denis Compton Award for the most promising young Nottinghamshire player 2001, 2002. Scored record-equalling four 'Test' centuries for England U19. BBC East Midlands Junior Sportsman of the Year 2003. ECB National Academy 2003-04. Left Northamptonshire at the end of the 2006 season and rejoined Nottinghamshire for 2007. Keeping wicket for Pakistan Customs during the 2008-09 off-season
Opinions on cricket: 'The game has moved rapidly forward due to Twenty20, which is good for the value of the players and the game.'
Best batting: 161 Northamptonshire v Derbyshire, Derby 2005
Best bowling: 2-25 Northamptonshire v Pakistanis, Northampton 2006

2008 Season

	M	Inn	NO	Runs	HS	Avg	100	50	Ct	St	Balls	Runs	Wkts	Avg	BB	5I	10M
Test																	
FC	10	15	2	541	118	41.61	2	2	7	-	102	59	0		-	-	-
ODI																	
List A	12	12	2	255	67 *	25.50	-	1	6	-	0	0	0		-	-	
20/20 Int																	
20/20	8	7	3	84	32	21.00	-	-	5	-	0	0	0				

Career Performances

	M	Inn	NO	Runs	HS	Avg	100	50	Ct	St	Balls	Runs	Wkts	Avg	BB	5I	10M
Test																	
FC	90	153	6	4732	161	32.19	8	27	78	6	728	498	4	124.50	2-25	-	-
ODI																	
List A	100	94	8	1981	104	23.03	1	7	36	2	790	730	24	30.41	4-33	-	
20/20 Int																	
20/20	37	29	5	409	40	17.04	-	-	11	1	120	191	4	47.75	2-13	-	

SHAH, O. A. Middlesex

Name: Owais Alam Shah
Role: Right-hand bat, off-spin bowler
Born: 22 October 1978, Karachi, Pakistan
Height: 6ft 1in **Weight:** 13st 7lbs
Nickname: Ace, The Mauler
County debut: 1995 (one-day), 1996 (first-class)
County cap: 1999
Benefit: 2008
Test debut: 2005-06
ODI debut: 2001
Twenty20 Int debut: 2007
1000 runs in a season: 7
1st-Class 200s: 1
Place in batting averages: 6th av. 70.93 (2006 96th av. 35.96)
Parents: Jamshed and Mehjabeen
Wife and date of marriage: Gemma, 25 September 2004
Family links with cricket: Father played for his college side
Education: Isleworth and Syon School; Lampton School, Hounslow; Westminster University, Harrow
Qualifications: 7 GCSEs, 2 A-levels
Overseas tours: England U19 to Zimbabwe 1995-96, to South Africa (including U19 World Cup) 1997-98 (c); England A to Australia 1996-97, to Kenya and Sri Lanka 1997-98, to Sri Lanka 2004-05, to West Indies 2005-06; ECB National Academy to Australia 2001-02; England to Zimbabwe (one-day series) 2001-02, to India and New Zealand 2001-02 (one-day series), to Sri Lanka (ICC Champions Trophy) 2002-03, to Australia 2002-03 (VB Series), to India 2005-06, to South Africa (World 20/20) 2007-08, to Sri Lanka 2007-08, to New Zealand 2007-08, to India 2008-09, to West Indies 2008-09

Overseas teams played for: University of Western Australia, Perth
Career highlights to date: '[Debut] Test match against India in Mumbai'
Cricket moments to forget: 'Getting a pair in first-class cricket'
Cricketers particularly admired: Viv Richards, Sachin Tendulkar, Mark Waugh
Young players to look out for: Graham Onions, Nick Compton, Eoin Morgan
Other sports played: Snooker
Other sports followed: Football ('like to watch Manchester United play')
Favourite band: 'Too many to mention'
Relaxations: 'Movies, eating out'
Extras: Man of the U17 'Test' series v India 1994. Captained England U19 to success in the 1997-98 U19 World Cup in South Africa, scoring 54* in the final; captain of England U19 v Pakistan U19 1998. Cricket Writers' Young Player of the Year 2001. Middlesex Player of the Year 2002. Vice-captain of Middlesex 2002 to June 2004. Leading run-scorer in English first-class cricket 2005 (1728 runs; av. 66.46). Made Test debut in the third Test v India at Mumbai 2005-06, scoring 88. Man of the Match in the second Twenty20 Int v West Indies at The Oval 2007 (55*). ECB National Academy 2004-05, 2005-06, 2006-07. Man of the Match in the second ODI v Sri Lanka in Dambulla 2007-08 (82)
Best batting: 203 Middlesex v Derbyshire, Southgate 2001
Best bowling: 3-33 Middlesex v Gloucestershire, Bristol 1999
Stop press: Signed by Delhi Daredevils for IPL 2009

2008 Season

	M	Inn	NO	Runs	HS	Avg	100	50	Ct	St	Balls	Runs	Wkts	Avg	BB	5I	10M
Test																	
FC	14	25	1	1012	144	42.16	3	6	14	-	124	89	1	89.00	1-7	-	-
ODI	10	8	1	278	69	39.71	-	2	4	-	18	30	0		-	-	
List A	21	19	3	669	96 *	41.81	-	6	7	-	48	67	0		-	-	
20/20 Int	1	0	0	0	0	-	-	1	-	0	0	0		-	-		
20/20	5	4	1	136	75	45.33	-	1	2	-	0	0	0		-	-	

Career Performances

	M	Inn	NO	Runs	HS	Avg	100	50	Ct	St	Balls	Runs	Wkts	Avg	BB	5I	10M
Test	2	4	0	136	88	34.00	-	1	1	-	0	0	0		-	-	
FC	196	333	31	12984	203	42.99	35	66	154	-	1938	1324	22	60.18	3-33	-	-
ODI	47	43	5	1052	107 *	27.68	1	6	13	-	114	126	3	42.00	1-18	-	
List A	277	261	33	7643	134	33.52	11	47	92	-	753	755	18	41.94	2-2	-	
20/20 Int	10	9	1	235	55 *	29.37	-	1	3	-	0	0	0		-	-	
20/20	38	37	7	1009	79	33.63	-	7	10	-	13	11	1	11.00	1-10	-	

SHAHZAD, A. Yorkshire

Name: Ajmal Shahzad
Role: Right-hand bat, right-arm fast bowler; all-rounder
Born: 27 July 1985, Bradford
Height: 6ft **Weight:** 13st 8lbs
Nickname: The Dark Destroyer, AJ
County debut: 2004 (one-day), 2006 (first-class)
Parents: Parveen and Mohammed
Marital status: Single
Family links with cricket: 'Father played in Bradford League'
Education: Bradford Grammar School, Woodhouse Grove School; Leeds Metropolitan University
Qualifications: 9 GCSEs, 4 A-levels
Overseas tours: Schools tours to Scotland and Grenada; England U18 to Netherlands 2003
Career highlights to date: 'Making my debut for Yorkshire and being the first British-born Asian to play for YCCC'
Cricket moments to forget: 'Playing against Ireland in Holland – enough said. Also ripping my side (getting a side strain) in Twenty20 quarter-final in Essex'
Cricket superstitions: 'Put right pad on before left'
Cricketers particularly admired: Wasim Akram, Waqar Younis, Craig White, Anthony McGrath
Young players to look out for: Adam Lyth, Moeen Ali
Other sports played: Badminton (Yorkshire U15-U17), rugby (school), squash (school)
Other sports followed: Rugby league (Bradford Bulls)
Favourite band: Danny Bond, DJ Veteran, Jamie Duggan, DJ Leverton
Relaxations: 'Socialising, gym, study and Islam'
Extras: First British-born Asian to play for Yorkshire first team. Man of the Match in first match representing England – century and 3-22
Best batting: 35 Yorkshire v Hampshire, Headingley 2008
Best bowling: 4-22 Yorkshire v Sussex, Headingley 2007

2008 Season

	M	Inn	NO	Runs	HS	Avg	100	50	Ct	St	Balls	Runs	Wkts	Avg	BB	5I	10M
Test																	
FC	1	1	0	35	35	35.00	-	-	-	-	144	64	3	21.33	2-43	-	-
ODI																	
List A	2	1	0	33	33	33.00	-	-	-	-	96	55	1	55.00	1-30	-	
20/20 Int																	
20/20																	

Career Performances

	M	Inn	NO	Runs	HS	Avg	100	50	Ct	St	Balls	Runs	Wkts	Avg	BB	5I	10M
Test																	
FC	8	9	3	102	35	17.00	-	-	-	-	772	452	12	37.66	4-22	-	-
ODI																	
List A	9	7	2	60	33	12.00	-	-	-	-	408	334	12	27.83	5-51	1	
20/20 Int																	
20/20	1	1	1	2	2*		-	-	-	-	18	22	2	11.00	2-22		

SHANKAR, A. A. — Lancashire

Name: Adrian Anton Shankar
Role: Right-hand bat, right-arm off-break bowler
Born: 7 May 1985, Ascot, Berkshire
County debut: No first-team appearance
Education: Bedford School; Queen's College, Cambridge
Qualifications: Law degree
Other sports played: Football (was with Arsenal Academy), tennis
Extras: Former member of Middlesex Academy. Played for MCC against UCCE and for MCC Young Cricketers 2007. Has also played for Cambridge UCCE , Cambridge University (2002-05) and Bedfordshire (2000-06). Spent the first half of the 2008 season playing for Kent 2nd XI, and the second half for Lancashire 2nd XI. Signed for Lancashire in November 2008
Best batting: 143 Cambridge University v Oxford University, The Parks 2002

2008 Season (did not make any first-class or one-day appearances)

Career Performances

	M	Inn	NO	Runs	HS	Avg	100	50	Ct	St	Balls	Runs	Wkts	Avg	BB	5I	10M
Test																	
FC	12	20	0	384	143	19.20	1	-	5	-	0	0	0		-	-	-
ODI																	
List A	1	1	0	27	27	27.00	-	-	-	-	0	0	0		-	-	
20/20 Int																	
20/20																	

SHANTRY, A. J. Glamorgan

Name: Adam John Shantry
Role: Left-hand bat, left-arm swing bowler
Born: 13 November 1982, Bristol
Height: 6ft 2in **Weight:** 14st 4lbs
Nickname: Shants, Cyril, Piece
County debut: 2003 (Northamptonshire), 2005 (one-day, Warwickshire), 2006 (first-class, Warwickshire), 2008 (Glamorgan)
Place in bowling averages: 4th av. 18.16
Parents: Brian and Josephine
Marital status: Single
Family links with cricket: 'Father Brian played for Gloucestershire. Brother Jack mistakenly thinks he's a better batsman than I am'
Education: The Priory School, Shrewsbury; Shrewsbury Sixth Form College
Qualifications: 11 GCSEs, 4 A-levels, Level 2 coaching
Off-season: 'Working for Dyke Yaxley, enhancing my table tennis skills, and installing CCTV to protect my garden from palm tree theft.'
Overseas tours: England U19 to India 2004-05; Warwickshire to Grenada 2007
Overseas teams played for: Balwyn, Melbourne 2001-02; Subiaco-Floreat, Perth 2004-05 – 2006-07
Career highlights to date: 'Five-fors against New Zealanders and West Indies A. Ten wickets against Warwickshire 2008.'
Cricket moments to forget: 'Giving Tino Best a send-off, forgetting that I still had to bat'

Cricket superstitions: 'Never wear underwear when fielding'
Cricketers particularly admired: Jason Gillespie, Wasim Akram
Young players to look out for: Jack Shantry, Tom Maynard
Other sports played: Football, table tennis
Other sports followed: Football (Bristol City)
Favourite band: Feeder, Escape The Fate, Beyond All Reason
Relaxations: 'Full contact Scrabble, Boggle, fishing, music, enjoying Gareth Rees's company.'
Extras: England U17 squad. Represented ESCA U18 2001. Radio Shropshire Young Player of the Year 2001. Took 3-8 (including spell of three wickets in five balls before conceding a run) on Championship debut v Somerset at Northampton 2003. Took 5-37 v New Zealanders in 50-over match at Northampton 2004, winning Carlsberg Man of the Match award. His 5-15 v Warwickshire 2nd XI at Kenilworth 2004 included four wickets in four balls (bowled, bowled, lbw, bowled). Took 5-49 on first-class debut for Warwickshire v West Indies A at Edgbaston 2006. Took four wickets in his first four overs on Championship debut for Warwickshire v Sussex at Hove 2007 for innings figures of 4-31. Left Warwickshire at the end of the 2007 season and joined Glamorgan for 2008
Opinions on cricket: 'Can we have more chocolate at tea, please?'
Best batting: 38* Northamptonshire v Somerset, Northampton 2003
Best bowling: 5-49 Warwickshire v West Indies A, Edgbaston 2006

2008 Season

	M	Inn	NO	Runs	HS	Avg	100	50	Ct	St	Balls	Runs	Wkts	Avg	BB	5I	10M
Test																	
FC	7	9	4	32	16	6.40	-	-	3	-	1100	545	30	18.16	5-52	2	1
ODI																	
List A																	
20/20 Int																	
20/20																	

Career Performances

	M	Inn	NO	Runs	HS	Avg	100	50	Ct	St	Balls	Runs	Wkts	Avg	BB	5I	10M
Test																	
FC	15	19	9	108	38 *	10.80	-	-	6	-	1932	984	51	19.29	5-49	3	1
ODI																	
List A	9	4	1	26	15	8.66	-	-	6	-	294	228	11	20.72	5-37	1	
20/20 Int																	
20/20	1	0	0	0	0		-	-	-	-	12	31	0		-	-	

SHOAIB AKHTAR Surrey

Name: Shoaib Akhtar
Role: Right-hand bat, right-arm fast bowler
Born: 13 August 1975, Rawalpindi, Pakistan
Height: 6ft
County debut: 2001 (Somerset; see ***Extras***), 2003 (Durham), 2005 (Worcestershire), 2008 (Surrey)
County colours: 2005 (Worcestershire)
Test debut: 1997-98
ODI debut: 1997-98
Twenty20 Int debut: 2006
ducation: Elliott High School, Rawalpindi; Asghar Mal Government College, Rawalpindi
Overseas tours: Pakistan A to England 1997; Pakistan to South Africa 1997-98, to Zimbabwe 1997-98, to Malaysia (Commonwealth Games) 1998-99, to India 1998-99, to UK, Ireland and Holland (World Cup) 1999, to Australia 1999-2000, to West Indies 1999-2000, to England 2001, to Bangladesh 2001-02, to Sharjah (v West Indies) 2001-02, to Sri Lanka (ICC Champions Trophy) 2002-03, to Sri Lanka and Sharjah (v Australia) 2002-03, to Zimbabwe 2002-03, to South Africa 2002-03, to Africa (World Cup) 2002-03, to England (NatWest Challenge) 2003, to New Zealand 2003-04, to England (ICC Champions Trophy) 2004, to Australia 2004-05, to England 2006,to South Africa 2006-07, to India 2007-08, plus other one-day series and tournaments in Bangladesh, India, Sharjah, New Zealand, Kenya, Australia, Holland and Sri Lanka; Asian Cricket Council XI to South Africa (Afro-Asia Cup) 2005-06; ICC World XI to Australia (Super Series) 2005-06
Overseas teams played for: Rawalpindi 1993-94 – 1998-99, 2003-04; Pakistan International Airlines 1994-95 – 1995-96; Agriculture Development Bank of Pakistan 1996-97 – 1997-98; Khan Research Labs 2001-02 – 2008-09; Kolkata Knight Riders (IPL) 2007-08
Extras: Nicknamed the Rawalpindi Express. Represented Pakistan U19. Played one first-class match for Somerset 2001, v Australians at Taunton. Took 6-11 from 8.2 overs as New Zealand were bowled out for 73 in their first innings of the first Test at Lahore 2001-02. Bowled the first official 100mph delivery (timed at 100.23mph) to Nick Knight v England at Cape Town in the World Cup 2002-03. An overseas player with Durham June to September 2003 and in 2004. Durham Bowler of the Year 2003. His Test awards include Man of the Match in the second Test v Bangladesh at Peshawar 2003-04 (6-50/4-30) and in the second Test v New Zealand at Wellington 2003-04 (5-48/6-30). His ODI awards include Man of the Series in the

Coca-Cola Sharjah Cup 1998-99 and in the Super Challenge II v Australia 2002. An overseas player with Worcestershire 2005. Took 6-16 v Gloucestershire at Worcester in the totesport League 2005, the best ever one-day league figures by a Worcestershire bowler

Best batting: 59* Khan Research Laboratories v PIA, Lahore (C) 2001-02

Best bowling: 6-11 Pakistan v New Zealand, Lahore 2002

2008 Season

	M	Inn	NO	Runs	HS	Avg	100	50	Ct	St	Balls	Runs	Wkts	Avg	BB	5I	10M
Test																	
FC	2	4	1	69	32	23.00	-	-	2	-	198	117	1	117.00	1-54	-	-
ODI																	
List A																	
20/20 Int																	
20/20																	

Career Performances

	M	Inn	NO	Runs	HS	Avg	100	50	Ct	St	Balls	Runs	Wkts	Avg	BB	5I	10M
Test	46	67	13	544	47	10.07	-	-	12	-	8143	4574	178	25.69	6-11	12	2
FC	130	182	50	1619	59 *	12.26	-	1	40	-	20043	12041	451	26.69	6-11	28	2
ODI	138	67	31	345	43	9.58	-	-	17	-	6558	5080	219	23.19	6-16	4	
List A	182	97	35	733	56	11.82	-	1	28	-	8688	6777	288	23.53	6-16	6	
20/20 Int	3	1	1	1	1 *		-	-	1	-	66	83	5	16.60	2-22	-	
20/20	15	9	2	40	14	5.71	-	-	3	-	306	369	20	18.45	5-23	1	

82. Which words did Cricket Australia (the country's governing body) decide would not be considered racist if used by spectators during the 2006-07 Ashes tour?

SHRECK, C. E. Nottinghamshire

Name: Charles (Charlie) Edward Shreck
Role: Right-hand bat, right-arm fast-medium bowler
Born: 6 January 1978, Truro
Height: 6ft 7in **Weight:** 15st 7lbs
Nickname: Shrecker, Ogre, Stoat, Chough
County debut: 2002 (one-day), 2003 (first-class)
County cap: 2006
50 wickets in a season: 1
Place in bowling averages: 68th av. 29.78 (2007 45th av. 27.10)
Parents: Peter and Sheila
Marital status: Single
Family links with cricket: 'Grandfather watched Southampton'
Education: Truro School
Qualifications: Level 1 coaching
Overseas tours: Cornwall U17 to South Africa 1997; England Lions to India 2007-08
Overseas teams played for: Merewether District CC, NSW 1997-98; Hutt District CC, New Zealand 2000-03; Wellington, New Zealand 2005-06
Cricket moments to forget: 'Being run out off the last ball of the game against Shropshire, walking off – we lost!'
Cricket superstitions: 'None'
Cricketers particularly admired: Viv Richards, Michael Holding, Ian Botham
Young players to look out for: Michael Munday, Carl Gazzard
Relaxations: 'Swimming, music'
Extras: C&G Man of the Match award for his 5-19 for Cornwall v Worcestershire at Truro 2002. Took wicket (Vikram Solanki) with his third ball in county cricket v Worcestershire at Trent Bridge in the NUL 2002, going on to record maiden one-day league five-wicket return (5-35). Took four wickets in six balls, including hat-trick (Smith, Morgan, Weekes), v Middlesex at Lord's 2006. Took 61 first-class wickets in 2006 (including 12-129 v Middlesex at Trent Bridge), having missed the entire 2005 season after undergoing back surgery. Nottinghamshire Player of the Year 2006, 2008. Called up to squad for England Lions tour of India 2007-08
Best batting: 19 Nottinghamshire v Essex, Chelmsford 2003
Best bowling: 8-31 Nottinghamshire v Middlesex, Trent Bridge 2006

2008 Season

	M	Inn	NO	Runs	HS	Avg	100	50	Ct	St	Balls	Runs	Wkts	Avg	BB	5I	10M
Test																	
FC	16	18	12	13	4 *	2.16	-	-	8	-	3687	1817	61	29.78	5-40	2	-
ODI																	
List A	13	6	4	4	2 *	2.00	-	-	3	-	578	392	12	32.66	2-33	-	
20/20 Int																	
20/20	5	3	2	3	2 *	3.00	-	-	1	-	90	103	6	17.16	4-22	-	

Career Performances

	M	Inn	NO	Runs	HS	Avg	100	50	Ct	St	Balls	Runs	Wkts	Avg	BB	5I	10M
Test																	
FC	69	78	46	116	19	3.62	-	-	26	-	13991	7532	268	28.10	8-31	18	2
ODI																	
List A	48	18	12	44	9 *	7.33	-	-	12	-	2219	1890	62	30.48	5-19	2	
20/20 Int																	
20/20	22	6	5	10	6 ß*	10.00	-	-	4	-	457	597	23	25.95	4-22	-	

SIDEBOTTOM, R. J. Nottinghamshire

Name: Ryan Jay Sidebottom
Role: Left-hand bat, left-arm fast bowler
Born: 15 January 1978, Huddersfield
Height: 6ft 4in **Weight:** 14st 7lbs
Nickname: Siddy, Sexual, Jazz
County debut: 1997 (Yorkshire), 2004 (Nottinghamshire)
County cap: 2000 (Yorkshire), 2004 (Nottinghamshire)
Test debut: 2001
ODI debut: 2001-02
Twenty20 Int debut: 2007
50 wickets in a season: 2
Place in batting averages: 255th av. 10.83 (2007 243rd av. 15.36)
Place in bowling averages: 21st av. 22.72 (2007 65th av. 29.89)
Parents: Arnie and Gillian
Marital status: Single
Family links with sport: Father played cricket for Yorkshire and England and football for Manchester United and Huddersfield Town

Education: King James Grammar School, Almondbury
Qualifications: 5 GCSEs
Overseas tours: England U17 to Netherlands 1995; MCC to Bangladesh 1999-2000; England A to West Indies 2000-01; England to Zimbabwe (one-day series) 2001-02, to Sri Lanka 2007-08, to New Zealand 2007-08, to India (one-day series) 2008-09, to West Indies (Test and one-day series) 2008-09; ECB National Academy to Australia 2001-02
Overseas teams played for: Ringwood, Melbourne 1998
Cricketers particularly admired: Darren Gough, Chris Silverwood, Glenn McGrath
Young players to look out for: Joe Sayers
Other sports played: Football (once with Sheffield United), 'all sports'
Other sports followed: 'Love rugby league (any team)', football (Man Utd)
Relaxations: 'Music (R&B), films, clubbing, going out with my team-mates'
Extras: NBC Denis Compton Award for the most promising young Yorkshire player 1999, 2000. Took 5-31 (8-65 in match) for England A v Jamaica at Kingston in the Busta Cup 2000-01, winning the Man of the Match award; topped tour first-class bowling averages (16 wickets; av. 16.81). Made Test debut in the first Test v Pakistan at Lord's 2001 (England's 100th Test at the ground), becoming the tenth player to follow his father into the England Test team. Recalled to Test side after six years for the second Test v West Indies at Headingley 2007, returning match figures of 8-86 (4-42/4-44). Man of the [ODI] Series v Sri Lanka 2007-08. Named as one of *Wisden*'s Five Cricketers of the Year 2008.
Best batting: 54 Yorkshire v Glamorgan, Cardiff 1998
Best bowling: 7-97 Yorkshire v Derbyshire, Headingley 2003

2008 Season

	M	Inn	NO	Runs	HS	Avg	100	50	Ct	St	Balls	Runs	Wkts	Avg	BB	5I	10M
Test	5	6	2	52	22	13.00	-	-	2	-	1284	542	23	23.56	6-67	1	-
FC	7	9	3	65	22	10.83	-	-	2	-	1806	750	33	22.72	6-67	2	-
ODI	3	2	2	18	10 *		-	-	1	-	168	150	2	75.00	2-55	-	
List A	4	3	3	26	10 *		-	-	1	-	216	173	3	57.66	2-55	-	
20/20 Int																	
20/20																	

Career Performances

	M	Inn	NO	Runs	HS	Avg	100	50	Ct	St	Balls	Runs	Wkts	Avg	BB	5I	10M
Test	18	27	10	266	31	15.64	-	-	5	-	4272	1952	76	25.68	7-47	5	1
FC	126	163	48	1361	54	11.83	-	1	45	-	22236	10371	410	25.29	7-97	17	2
ODI	16	10	5	51	15	10.20	-	-	3	-	865	661	24	27.54	3-19	-	
List A	154	69	32	404	32	10.91	-	-	33	-	6848	4886	162	30.16	6-40	2	
20/20 Int	4	1	1	5	5 *		-	-	2	-	92	102	8	12.75	3-16	-	
20/20	19	6	5	28	12 *	28.00	-	-	6	-	405	445	25	17.80	3-16	-	

SILVERWOOD, C. E. W. Middlesex

Name: Christopher (Chris) Eric Wilfred Silverwood
Role: Right-hand bat, right-arm fast bowler
Born: 5 March 1975, Pontefract
Height: 6ft 1in **Weight:** 12st 9lbs
Nickname: Spoons, Silvers, Chubby
County debut: 1993 (Yorkshire), 2006 (Middlesex)
County cap: 1996 (Yorkshire), 2006 (Middlesex)
Benefit: 2004 (Yorkshire)
Test debut: 1996-97
ODI debut: 1996-97
50 wickets in a season: 2
Place in batting averages: (2007 266th av. 12.22)
Place in bowling averages: (2007 51st av. 28.22)
Parents: Brenda
Wife and date of marriage: Victoria, 2006
Family links with cricket: 'Dad played a bit'
Education: Garforth Comprehensive
Qualifications: 8 GCSEs, City and Guilds in Leisure and Recreation
Overseas tours: England A to Kenya and Sri Lanka 1997-98, to Bangladesh and New Zealand 1999-2000, to West Indies 2000-01; England to Zimbabwe and New Zealand 1996-97, to West Indies 1997-98, to Bangladesh (Wills International Cup) 1998-99, to South Africa 1999-2000, to Zimbabwe (one-day series) 2001-02, to Australia 2002-03; England VI to Hong Kong 2002, 2003
Overseas teams played for: Wellington, Cape Town 1993-94, 1995-96
Career highlights to date: 'Making Test debut. Winning the Championship [2001]'
Cricketers particularly admired: Ian Botham, Allan Donald
Other sports played: Karate (black belt), rugby league, athletics (represented Yorkshire)
Other sports followed: Rugby league (Castleford)
Extras: NBC Denis Compton Award for the most promising young Yorkshire player 1996. Attended Yorkshire Academy. Represented England U19. C&G Man of the Match awards v Northamptonshire at Northampton 2002 (61/2-35) and v Dorset at Dean Park 2004 (4-18). Took 500th first-class wicket (Andrew Gale) against his old county, Yorkshire, at Southgate 2006, finishing with match figures of 8-64
Best batting: 80 Yorkshire v Durham, Riverside 2005
Best bowling: 7-93 Yorkshire v Kent, Headingley 1997

2008 Season

	M	Inn	NO	Runs	HS	Avg	100	50	Ct	St	Balls	Runs	Wkts	Avg	BB	5I	10M
Test																	
FC	3	3	2	70	33 *	70.00	-	-	1	-	364	160	6	26.66	2-11	-	-
ODI																	
List A																	
20/20 Int																	
20/20																	

Career Performances

	M	Inn	NO	Runs	HS	Avg	100	50	Ct	St	Balls	Runs	Wkts	Avg	BB	5I	10M
Test	6	7	3	29	10	7.25	-	-	2	-	828	444	11	40.36	5-91	1	-
FC	178	234	47	2962	80	15.83	-	9	41	-	29083	15394	570	27.00	7-93	25	1
ODI	7	4	0	17	12	4.25	-	-	-	-	306	244	6	40.66	3-43	-	
List A	192	110	37	1002	61	13.72	-	4	29	-	8626	6145	250	24.58	5-28	1	
20/20 Int																	
20/20	14	8	4	44	13 *	11.00	-	-	4	-	306	398	12	33.16	2-22	-	

SIMPSON, J. A. — Middlesex

Name: John Andrew Simpson
Role: Left-hand bat, wicket-keeper
Born: 13 July 1988, Ramsbottom, Bury, Lancashire
Height: 5ft 10in
Nickname: Simmo
County debut: 2008
Family links with cricket: Father, Jack, played in the Lancashire League.
Off-season: Darren Lehmann Academy, Adelaide
Overseas tours: England U19 to India 2004-05, to Bangladesh 2005-06, Sri Lanka (U19 World Cup) 2006
Cricketers particularly admired: Adam Gilchrist, Jack Russell, Ian Healy, Ricky Ponting, Brian Lara
Other sports followed: Golf, football (Newcastle United)
Relaxations: 'Gym, visiting family'
Extras: Represented Lancashire in every age group from U11 upwards. NBC Denis

Compton Award for the most promising young Lancashire player 2004. Lancashire Academy 2004-07. Joined Lancashire on a scholarship in 2007. Played for the 2nd XI at Lancashire, Durham and Nottinghamshire during the 2007 season. MCC Young Cricketer 2008. Signed a two-year contract with Middlesex in June 2008. Came on as substitute wicket-keeper when Ben Scott injured his ankle during the Middlesex v Northamptonshire match in September 2008, taking two catches (not his first-class debut). Received the Betfair Scholarship Award, which affords the recipient a place at the Darren Lehmann Academy, at the end of the 2008 season

SMITH, B. F. — Worcestershire

Name: Benjamin (Ben) Francis Smith
Role: Right-hand bat, right-arm medium bowler
Born: 3 April 1972, Corby
Height: 5ft 9in **Weight:** 11st
Nickname: Turnip, Sven
County debut: 1990 (Leicestershire), 2002 (Worcestershire)
County cap: 1995 (Leicestershire), 2002 (Worcestershire colours)
1000 runs in a season: 7
1st-Class 200s: 3
Benefit: 2009
Place in batting averages: 46th av. 44.79 (2007 155th av. 27.95)
Parents: Keith and Janet
Wife and date of marriage: Lisa, 10 October 1998
Children: Ruby, 6 November 2005
Family links with cricket: Father, grandfather and uncles all played club and representative cricket
Education: Kibworth High School; Robert Smyth, Market Harborough
Qualifications: 5 O-levels, 8 GCSEs, NCA coaching certificate
Overseas tours: England YC to New Zealand 1990-91; MCC to Bangladesh 1999-2000; 'numerous pre-season tours to South Africa, Caribbean and Sri Lanka'
Overseas teams played for: Alexandria, Zimbabwe 1990; Bankstown-Canterbury, Sydney 1993-96; Central Hawke's Bay CC, New Zealand 1997-98; Central Districts, New Zealand 2000-02
Career highlights to date: 'Winning 1996 County Championship'
Cricket moments to forget: 'Lord's finals'
Cricketers particularly admired: Viv Richards, David Gower, Steve Waugh
Young players to look out for: Steve Davies

Other sports played: Tennis (Leicestershire aged 12), golf, touch rugby
Other sports followed: Rugby union (Leicester Tigers)
Favourite band: Coldplay
Relaxations: 'Music, DIY, good wine'
Extras: Cricket Society Young Player of the Year 1991. Vice-captain of Leicestershire 2001. Scored century (137) on first-class debut for Worcestershire v OUCCE at The Parks and another (129) on Championship debut for the county v Gloucestershire at Worcester 2002 to become the first player to achieve this 'double' for Worcestershire. Worcestershire Supporters' Player of the Year 2002. Worcestershire Player of the Year 2003. Scored 187 v Gloucestershire at Worcester 2004, in the process sharing with Graeme Hick (262) in the highest first-class partnership ever made at New Road (417). Scored 203 v Somerset at Taunton 2006, in the process sharing with Graeme Hick (182) in a Worcestershire record partnership for the fourth wicket (330). Captain of Worcestershire 2003 until standing down in August 2004
Best batting: 204 Leicestershire v Surrey, The Oval 1998
Best bowling: 1-5 Leicestershire v Essex, Ilford 1991

2008 Season

	M	Inn	NO	Runs	HS	Avg	100	50	Ct	St	Balls	Runs	Wkts	Avg	BB	5I	10M
Test																	
FC	16	25	1	1075	99	44.79	-	11	12	-	0	0	0		-	-	-
ODI																	
List A	15	14	2	411	107	34.25	1	1	6	-	0	0	0		-	-	
20/20 Int																	
20/20	9	8	1	161	46	23.00	-	-	5	-	0	0	0		-	-	

Career Performances

	M	Inn	NO	Runs	HS	Avg	100	50	Ct	St	Balls	Runs	Wkts	Avg	BB	5I	10M
Test																	
FC	312	488	53	17869	204	41.07	40	94	196	-	653	488	4	122.00	1-5	-	-
ODI																	
List A	379	365	52	9581	115	30.61	3	59	135	-	127	121	2	60.50	1-2	-	
20/20 Int																	
20/20	41	39	3	695	105	19.30	1	1	20	-	0	0	0		-	-	

83. Who succeeded Don Bradman as captain of Australia?

SMITH, D. R. — Sussex

Name: Dwayne Romel Smith
Role: Right-hand bat, right-arm medium bowler, occasional wicket-keeper; all-rounder
Born: 12 April 1983, St Michael, Barbados
Height: 6ft 1in **Weight:** 13st 3lbs
Nickname: Agent Smith
County debut: 2008 (one-day)
Test debut: 2004
ODI debut: 2004
Twenty20 Int debut: 2006
Parents: Lorraine Smith and Wilbur Bruce
Marital status: Single
Family links with cricket: 'My dad'
Education: Garrison Secondary School, Barbados
Off-ssason: 'Training and working on my batting and bowling'
Overseas tours: West Indies to South Africa (Test and one-day series) 2003-04, to England 2004 (one-day series), to Sri Lanka (Indian Oil Cup) 2005, to New Zealand 2005-06 (one-day series), to Malaysia (DLF Cup) 2006-07, to India (one-day series) 2006-07, to Pakistan 2006-07 (one-day series), to England 2007 (one-day series), to Ireland (Quadrangular series) 2007

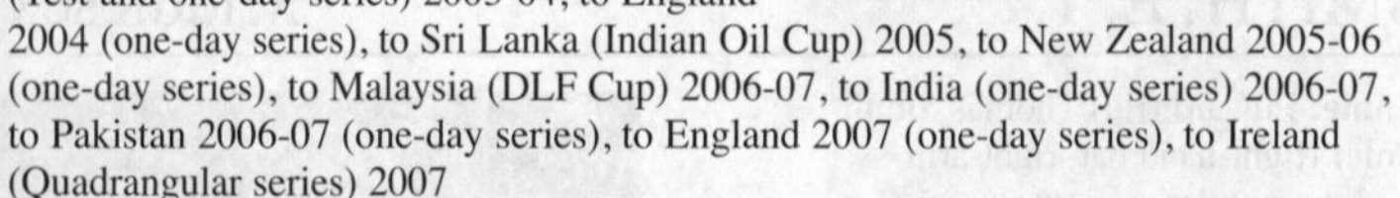

Overseas teams played for: Barbados 2001-02 – ; Mumbai Indians (IPL) 2007-08, 2008-09
Career highlights to date: 'Scoring a hundred on my Test debut against South Africa'
Cricket moments to forget: 'Losing to Australia in the 2006 Champions Trophy Final'
Cricketers particularly admired: Brian Lara, Jonty Rhodes
Young players to look out for: Jonathan Carter (Barbados)
Other sports played: 'None'
Other sports followed: Football (Manchester United)
Favourite band: Square One
Relaxations: 'Partying and the beach'
Extras: Scored 105* on his Test debut against South Africa in Cape Town in January 2004, his 93-ball century being the fastest ever by a debutant in Test cricket. Joined Sussex as a replacement for the injured Mushtaq Ahmed in June 2008. Has since signed a two-year contract with the county
Best batting: 105* West Indies v South Africa , Cape Town 2004
Best bowling: 4-22 Barbados v Trinidad & Tobago, Pointe-a-Pierre, 2007

2008 Season

	M	Inn	NO	Runs	HS	Avg	100	50	Ct	St	Balls	Runs	Wkts	Avg	BB	5I	10M
Test																	
FC																	
ODI																	
List A	7	6	1	73	25	14.60	-	-	6	-	108	76	1	76.00	1-25	-	
20/20 Int																	
20/20	10	9	1	185	72 *	23.12	-	1	2	-	210	297	12	24.75	3-14	-	

Career Performances

	M	Inn	NO	Runs	HS	Avg	100	50	Ct	St	Balls	Runs	Wkts	Avg	BB	5I	10M
Test	10	14	1	320	105 *	24.61	1	-	9	-	651	344	7	49.14	3-71	-	-
FC	60	99	6	2562	114	27.54	5	8	62	-	4933	2479	87	28.49	4-22	-	-
ODI	71	56	3	791	68	14.92	-	2	24	-	2264	1813	49	37.00	5-45	1	
List A	108	90	6	1610	96	19.16	-	7	38	-	3023	2434	64	38.03	5-45	1	
20/20 Int	5	5	0	49	29	9.80	-	-	-	-	80	108	5	21.60	3-24	-	
20/20	23	21	1	302	72 *	15.10	-	1	5	-	423	548	28	19.57	4-9	-	

SMITH, E. T. — Middlesex

Name: Edward (Ed) Thomas Smith
Role: Right-hand bat, right-arm medium bowler
Born: 19 July 1977, Pembury, Kent
Height: 6ft 2in **Weight:** 13st
Nickname: Smudge
County debut: 1996 (Kent), 2005 (Middlesex)
County cap: 2001 (Kent), 2005 (Middlesex)
Test debut: 2003
1000 runs in a season: 8
1st-Class 200s: 2
Place in batting averages: 67th av. 39.70 (2007 15th av. 58.04)
Parents: Jonathan and Gillie
Marital status: Single
Family links with cricket: 'Dad wrote *Good Enough?* with Chris Cowdrey'
Education: Tonbridge School; Peterhouse, Cambridge University
Qualifications: 11 GCSEs, 3 A-levels, degree in History
Career outside cricket: Journalism; broadcasting

Overseas tours: England A to Malaysia and India 2003-04
Overseas teams played for: University CC, Perth, Western Australia
Career highlights to date: 'My Test debut'
Cricket moments to forget: 'Getting a pair at Chelmsford 2003'
Cricket superstitions: 'Left pad on first'
Cricketers particularly admired: Steve Waugh, Rahul Dravid
Other sports played: Squash, golf
Other sports followed: Football (Arsenal FC), baseball (New York Mets)
Favourite band: Bob Dylan
Relaxations: 'Listening to music, reading, going to concerts'
Extras: Scored century (101) on first-class debut v Glamorgan 1996; was also the first person to score 50 or more in each of his first six first-class games. Cambridge Blue 1996. Represented England U19. Equalled Kent record of four consecutive first-class centuries with his 108 v Essex at Canterbury 2003. *Kent Messenger* Readers' Player of the Year 2003. Denness Award (Kent leading run-scorer) 2003. Cowdrey Award (Kent Player of the Season) 2003. Slazenger 'Sheer Instinct' award for 2003. Books *Playing Hard Ball* (about baseball) published 2001 and *On and Off the Field* published 2004; series *Peak Performance* (comparing sporting and musical performance) broadcast on Radio 3 2005. Captained Middlesex 2007 and 2008. Announced his retirement from first-class cricket in November 2008.
Best batting: 213 Kent v Warwickshire, Canterbury 2003
Best bowling: 1-60 Middlesex v Sussex, Southgate 2006

2008 Season

	M	Inn	NO	Runs	HS	Avg	100	50	Ct	St	Balls	Runs	Wkts	Avg	BB	5I	10M
Test																	
FC	6	10	0	397	88	39.70	-	4	3	-	0	0	0		-	-	-
ODI																	
List A	5	5	0	130	75	26.00	-	1	2	-	0	0	0		-	-	
20/20 Int																	
20/20	2	2	0	60	33	30.00	-	-	1	-	0	0	0		-	-	

Career Performances

	M	Inn	NO	Runs	HS	Avg	100	50	Ct	St	Balls	Runs	Wkts	Avg	BB	5I	10M
Test	3	5	0	87	64	17.40	-	1	5	-	0	0	0		-	-	-
FC	191	325	19	12789	213	41.79	34	54	85	-	108	119	1	119.00	1-60	-	-
ODI																	
List A	134	131	9	3798	122	31.13	2	26	29	-	0	0	0		-	-	
20/20 Int																	
20/20	25	25	0	573	85	22.92	-	3	6	-	0	0	0		-	-	

SMITH, G. M. — Derbyshire

Name: Gregory (Greg) Marc Smith
Role: Right-hand bat, right-arm medium/off-spin bowler; all-rounder
Born: 20 April 1983, Johannesburg, South Africa
Height: 5ft 8½in **Weight:** 11st 5lbs
Nickname: Smithy, Smudge
County debut: 2006
Place in batting averages: 100th av. 33.25 (2007 197th av. 22.61)
Place in bowling averages: 139th av. 45.63 (2007 95th av. 34.45)
Parents: Ian and Nadine
Wife and date of marriage: Bethany, 10 October 2008
Family links with cricket: 'Dad used to be financial adviser of the UCB [United Cricket Board of South Africa]'
Education: St Stithians College; UNISA (University of South Africa);
Qualifications: Matriculation, Level 2 coaching certificate
Overseas tours: South Africa U19 to New Zealand (U19 World Cup) 2001-02
Overseas teams played for: Old Edwardians, Johannesburg; Griqualand West 2003-04; Frankston (Melbourne) 2007-08
Career highlights to date: 'Scoring half-century in U19 World Cup final v Australia. Scoring a century in Twenty20 v Yorkshire in 2008'
Cricket moments to forget: 'Getting my first pair.'
Cricketers particularly admired: Ashley Smith, Nyan Doshi, Jon Lewis
Young players to look out for: Ed Jones, Dom Telo
Other sports played: Golf, tennis
Other sports followed: Football (Arsenal), rugby (Sharks)
Favourite band: Coldplay
Extras: Represented Gauteng U13, U15, U19. South Africa Academy 2003-04. Most Improved Derbyshire player 2007
Opinions on cricket: 'Too many flat wickets - not enough turning ones for me to turn it on! More Twenty20 - I really love it, because I'm good at it.'
Best batting: 113 Derbyshire v Middlesex, Derby 2008
Best bowling: 3-31 Derbyshire v Middlesex, Southgate 2007

2008 Season

	M	Inn	NO	Runs	HS	Avg	100	50	Ct	St	Balls	Runs	Wkts	Avg	BB	5I	10M
Test																	
FC	13	21	1	665	113	33.25	1	6	1	-	855	502	11	45.63	2-53	-	-
ODI																	
List A	8	8	1	116	35 *	16.57	-	-	2	-	108	117	2	58.50	1-14	-	
20/20 Int																	
20/20	10	10	1	275	100 *	30.55	1	1	3	-	0	0	0		-	-	

Career Performances

	M	Inn	NO	Runs	HS	Avg	100	50	Ct	St	Balls	Runs	Wkts	Avg	BB	5I	10M
Test																	
FC	39	68	5	1610	113	25.55	1	12	10	-	2865	1624	39	41.64	3-31	-	-
ODI																	
List A	38	38	2	821	88	22.80	-	4	14	-	781	777	21	37.00	3-19	-	
20/20 Int																	
20/20	15	15	1	399	100 *	28.50	1	2	3	-	24	37	0		-	-	

SMITH, G. P. — Leicestershire

Name: Greg Philip Smith
Role: Right-hand bat, slow left-arm orthodox bowler
Born: 16 November 1988, Leicester
County debut: 2008
Place in batting averages: 188th av. 21.50
Education: Durham University
Extras: Has played for England U19, Leicestershire 2nd XI and Kibworth CC (in the Leicestershire Premier League). Will not return to action in 2009 until his studies at Durham University end
Best batting: 54 Leicestershire v Derbyshire, Grace Road 2008
Best bowling: 1-64 Leicestershire v Gloucestershire, Grace Road 2008

2008 Season

	M	Inn	NO	Runs	HS	Avg	100	50	Ct	St	Balls	Runs	Wkts	Avg	BB	5I	10M
Test																	
FC	6	10	0	215	54	21.50	-	1	2	-	30	64	1	64.00	1-64	-	-
ODI																	
List A	2	2	0	71	58	35.50	-	1	-	-	0	0	0		-	-	
20/20 Int																	
20/20																	

Career Performances

	M	Inn	NO	Runs	HS	Avg	100	50	Ct	St	Balls	Runs	Wkts	Avg	BB	5I	10M
Test																	
FC	6	10	0	215	54	21.50	-	1	2	-	30	64	1	64.00	1-64	-	-
ODI																	
List A	2	2	0	71	58	35.50	-	1	-	-	0	0	0		-	-	
20/20 Int																	
20/20																	

SMITH, T. C. P. — Lancashire

Name: Thomas (Tom) Christopher Pascoe Smith
Role: Left-hand bat, right-arm fast-medium bowler; all-rounder
Born: 26 December 1985, Liverpool
Height: 6ft 3in **Weight:** 14st
Nickname: Smudger, Yeti
County debut: 2005
Place in batting averages: 102nd av. 32.77
Place in bowling averages: 77th av 31.12
Parents: Mark and Jacqui
Marital status: Single
Family links with cricket: Brother Lancashire U19. Father and stepfather play for local village teams
Education: Parklands High School; Runshaw College
Qualifications: 10 GCSEs, 4 A-levels
Overseas tours: England U19 to India 2004-05; England A to Bangladesh 2006-07
Career highlights to date: 'Contract with Lancs and being picked for National Academy 2005-06'

Cricket moments to forget: 'First-ball duck on my first-class debut'
Cricket superstitions: 'Right pad on first'
Cricketers particularly admired: Andrew Flintoff, Ricky Ponting
Young players to look out for: Karl Brown
Other sports played: Football, golf, swimming
Other sports followed: Football (Liverpool FC)
Favourite band: Oasis, Goo Goo Dolls, Kelly Clarkson
Relaxations: 'Watching films and socialising with friends'
Extras: NBC Denis Compton Award for the most promising young Lancashire player 2005, 2006, 2007. Represented England U19 2005. ECB National Academy 2005-06, 2006-07. On loan to Leicestershire for part of the 2008 season
Best batting: 63 Leicestershire v Warwickshire, Grace Road 2008
Best bowling: 4-57 Lancashire v Yorkshire, Headingley 2006

2008 Season

	M	Inn	NO	Runs	HS	Avg	100	50	Ct	St	Balls	Runs	Wkts	Avg	BB	5I	10M
Test																	
FC	10	12	3	295	63	32.77	-	1	7	-	1598	747	24	31.12	3-28	-	-
ODI																	
List A	8	7	3	92	52	23.00	-	1	1	-	355	263	13	20.23	3-14	-	
20/20 Int																	
20/20	3	1	1	5	5 *		-	-	2	-	40	51	1	51.00	1-21	-	

Career Performances

	M	Inn	NO	Runs	HS	Avg	100	50	Ct	St	Balls	Runs	Wkts	Avg	BB	5I	10M
Test																	
FC	33	38	10	660	63	23.57	-	1	29	-	4711	2256	69	32.69	4-57	-	-
ODI																	
List A	26	16	6	178	52	17.80	-	1	6	-	955	727	29	25.06	3-8	-	
20/20 Int																	
20/20	15	9	4	79	21	15.80	-	-	6	-	244	310	10	31.00	3-15	-	

84. Who took hat-tricks for Australia against England in both 1902 and 1904?

SMITH, T. M. J. Sussex

Name: Thomas Michael John Smith
Role: Right-hand bat, slow left-arm orthodox bowler
Born: 29 August 1987, Eastbourne, Sussex
Height: 5ft 9in **Weight:** 11st 7lbs
Nickname: Smudge
County debut: 2006 (one-day), 2007 (first-class)
Parents: Michael and Claudine
Marital status: Single
Education: Seaford Head Community College; Sussex Downs College
Qualifications: NVQ Level 2 in plumbing
Off-season: 'North Shore CC in Auckland'
Overseas tours: Sussex Academy to Cape Town 2003, 2005
Overseas teams played for: Police CC, Cape Town 2007-08; North Shore CC, Auckland, New Zealand 2008-09
Career highlights to date: 'Captaining Sussex 2nd XI to the 2nd XI Championship'

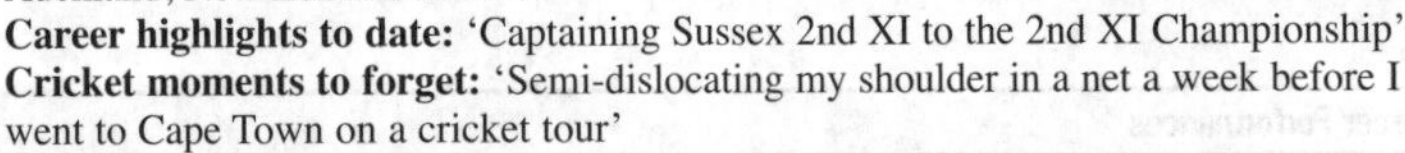

Cricket moments to forget: 'Semi-dislocating my shoulder in a net a week before I went to Cape Town on a cricket tour'
Cricket superstitions: 'None'
Cricketers particularly admired: Daniel Vettori, Monty Panesar, Mike Yardy
Young players to look out for: Matt Machan, Ben Brown, Will Beer
Other sports played: Football (Seaford Town FC), golf
Favourite band: The Subways
Relaxations: 'Watching *Lost*!'
Extras: Sussex 2nd XI Player of the Year 2006. Sussex League Young Player of the Year 2006
Opinions on cricket: 'Good that younger players are getting more opportunity and also Twenty20 great competition.'
Best batting: 2 Sussex v Sri Lanka A, Hove 2007
Best bowling: 1-52 Sussex v Sri Lanka A, Hove 2007

2008 Season

	M	Inn	NO	Runs	HS	Avg	100	50	Ct	St	Balls	Runs	Wkts	Avg	BB	5I	10M
Test																	
FC																	
ODI																	
List A	5	2	0	22	15	11.00	-	-	5	-	192	167	2	83.50	1-35	-	
20/20 Int																	
20/20	1	1	1	3	3*		-	-	-	-	12	14	0		-	-	

Career Performances

	M	Inn	NO	Runs	HS	Avg	100	50	Ct	St	Balls	Runs	Wkts	Avg	BB	5I	10M
Test																	
FC	1	1	0	2	2	2.00	-	-	-	-	78	79	1	79.00	1-52	-	-
ODI																	
List A	8	2	0	22	15	11.00	-	-	7	-	312	312	5	62.40	2-45	-	
20/20 Int																	
20/20	2	1	1	3	3*		-	-	-	-	12	14	0		-	-	

SMITH, W. R. — Durham

Name: William (Will) Rew Smith
Role: Right-hand top-order bat, right-arm off-break bowler, occasional wicket-keeper; county captain
Born: 28 September 1982, Luton, Bedfordshire
Height: 5ft 9in **Weight:** 12st
Nickname: Smudger, Jiggy
County debut: 2002 (Nottinghamshire), 2007 (Durham)
1st-Class 200s: 1
Place in batting averages: 21st av. 51.38 (2007 186th av. 23.95)
Parents: Jim and Barbara
Marital status: Single ('long-term partner – Claire')
Family links with cricket: 'Brother played county age-group; father a cricket "statto"'
Education: Bedford School; Durham University; Staffordshire University
Qualifications: 3 A-levels, BSc Molecular Biology and Biochemistry, Level 2 cricket coach

Career outside cricket: Media and journalism
Off-season: 'Gordon District CC in Sydney'
Overseas tours: British Universities to South Africa 2004; Nottinghamshire to Cape Town; Durham to Cape Town
Overseas teams played for: Gordon DCC, Sydney 2001-02, 2006-07, 2008-09
Career highlights to date: 'Being part of Durham's Friends Provident Trophy winning side 2007. Maiden Championship century against Surrey.' (*He went on to make 201**)
Cricket moments to forget: 'Any dropped catch – luckily not too many!'
Cricket superstitions: 'None'
Cricketers particularly admired: Michael Di Venuto, Dale Benkenstein
Young players to look out for: Scott Borthwick
Other sports played: 'Not much any more – used to play good level hockey and rugby; five-a-side football now!'
Other sports followed: Football (Rushden & Diamonds), rugby (Bedford), horse racing, golf
Favourite band: Glasvegas, Muse
Relaxations: 'Music, going to gigs, reading, socialising'
Extras: Represented England U16-U18. Played for Durham UCCE 2003-05 (captain 2004-05). Represented British Universities 2004, 2005 (captain 2005). Nottinghamshire 2nd XI Player of the Year 2005. Took over the county captaincy from Dale Benkenstein in November 2008
Opinions on cricket: 'Make sure umpires are source of authority and have final say.'
Best batting: 201* Durham v Surrey, Guildford 2008
Best bowling: 3-34 DUCCE v Leicestershire, Leicester 2005

2008 Season

	M	Inn	NO	Runs	HS	Avg	100	50	Ct	St	Balls	Runs	Wkts	Avg	BB	5I	10M
Test																	
FC	12	20	2	925	201 *	51.38	3	3	2	-	0	0	0		-	-	-
ODI																	
List A	11	10	0	247	56	24.70	-	2	8	-	5	6	1	6.00	1-6	-	
20/20 Int																	
20/20	11	11	1	245	51	24.50	-	1	6	-	0	0	0		-	-	

Career Performances

	M	Inn	NO	Runs	HS	Avg	100	50	Ct	St	Balls	Runs	Wkts	Avg	BB	5I	10M
Test																	
FC	53	87	5	2599	201 *	31.69	6	6	27	-	645	494	8	61.75	3-34	-	-
ODI																	
List A	49	44	3	1101	103	26.85	1	8	20	-	5	6	1	6.00	1-6	-	
20/20 Int																	
20/20	35	29	5	514	55	21.41	-	3	19	-	24	39	1	39.00	1-31	-	

SNAPE, J. N. Leicestershire

Name: Jeremy Nicholas Snape
Role: Right-hand bat, off-spin bowler; all-rounder
Born: 27 April 1973, Stoke-on-Trent
Height: 5ft 8in **Weight:** 12st
Nickname: Snapper
County debut: 1992 (Northamptonshire), 1999 (Gloucestershire), 2003 (Leicestershire)
County cap: 1999 (Gloucestershire), 2003 (Leicestershire)
Testimonial: 2008 (Leicestershire)
ODI debut: 2001-02
Twenty20 Int debut: 2007-08
Parents: Keith and Barbara
Wife and date of marriage: Joanne, 4 October 2003
Children: Tamsin, 26 September 2005
Family links with cricket: 'Brother Jonathan plays at Rode Park in Cheshire'
Education: Denstone College, Staffordshire; Durham University; Loughborough University
Qualifications: 8 GCSEs, 3 A-levels, BSc Natural Science, MSc Sport Psychology
Career outside cricket: Director of Sporting Edge – performance coaching company (www.thesportingedge.co.uk)
Overseas tours: England U18 to Canada (International Youth Tournament) 1991 (c); England U19 to Pakistan 1991-92; Durham University to South Africa 1993, to Vienna (European Indoor Championships) 1994; Northamptonshire to Cape Town 1993; Christians in Sport to Zimbabwe 1994-95; Troubadours to South Africa 1997; Gloucestershire to South Africa 1999; England to Zimbabwe (one-day series) 2001-02, to India and New Zealand 2001-02 (one-day series), to Sri Lanka (ICC Champions Trophy) 2002-03, to Australia 2002-03 (VB Series), to South Africa (World 20/20) 2007-08
Overseas teams played for: Petone, Wellington, New Zealand 1994-95; Wainuiamata, Wellington, New Zealand 1995-96; Techs CC, Cape Town 1996-99
Career highlights to date: 'England debut. England ODI in Calcutta – 120,000 people. Twenty20 Cup wins'
Cricket moments to forget: 'Breaking my thumb in Australia 2003 and being ruled out of World Cup'
Cricketers particularly admired: Allan Lamb, Jack Russell
Other sports followed: Rugby (Leicester Tigers)
Relaxations: Travelling, music, cooking, good food and wine

Player website: www.jeremysnape2008.co.uk
Extras: Sir John Hobbs Silver Jubilee Memorial Prize 1988. B&H Gold Award for his 3-34 for Combined Universities v Worcestershire at The Parks 1992. Player of the Tournament at European Indoor 6-a-side Championships 1994. Made ODI debut in the first ODI v Zimbabwe at Harare 2001-02, winning Man of the Match award for his 2-39 and brilliant catch. BBC West Country Sports Cricketer of the Year for 2001. Struck 16-ball 34*, including winning runs, in the Twenty20 Cup final at Edgbaston 2004. Captain of Leicestershire 2006 to the end of August 2007. Retired at the end of the 2008 season
Opinions on cricket: 'The game seems to be in a fairly healthy state, with divisional cricket working well. Twenty20 has been hugely refreshing, and following a very successful World Cup in South Africa, it has become a global brand. Cricket has never been more widespread internationally, which opens many opportunities. England must now strive for consistently elite performance on the international stage, which will also fuel a more successful domestic competition.'
Best batting: 131 Gloucestershire v Sussex, Cheltenham 2001
Best bowling: 5-65 Northamptonshire v Durham, Northampton 1995

2008 Season

	M	Inn	NO	Runs	HS	Avg	100	50	Ct	St	Balls	Runs	Wkts	Avg	BB	5I	10M
Test																	
FC																	
ODI																	
List A	1	1	0	21	21	21.00	-	-	-	-	12	23	0		-	-	
20/20 Int																	
20/20	5	4	1	21	11 *	7.00	-	-	1	-	72	93	3	31.00	2-18	-	

Career Performances

	M	Inn	NO	Runs	HS	Avg	100	50	Ct	St	Balls	Runs	Wkts	Avg	BB	5I	10M
Test																	
FC	121	180	31	4194	131	28.14	3	23	74	-	10728	5583	113	49.40	5-65	1	-
ODI	10	7	3	118	38	29.50	-	-	5	-	529	403	13	31.00	3-43	-	
List A	272	219	58	3737	104 *	23.21	1	13	95	-	8393	6505	222	29.30	5-32	1	
20/20 Int	1	1	0	7	7	7.00	-	-	1	-	6	12	0		-	-	
20/20	46	40	15	577	47 *	23.08	-	-	16	-	706	790	39	20.25	4-22	-	

SNELL, S. D. Gloucestershire

Name: Steven David Snell
Role: Right-hand bat, wicket-keeper
Born: 27 February 1983, Winchester
Height: 6ft **Weight:** 11st 7lbs
Nickname: Snelly, Glove Monkey, Gonzo, Jaws
County debut: 2005
County cap: 2005
Place in batting averages: 34th av. 47.20
Parents: Jonathan and Sandra
Marital status: Single
Family links with cricket: 'Grandad and Dad both keen amateur cricketers. Brothers Rob and Peter both play at Ventnor Cricket Club (the real home of cricket!) on the Isle of Wight'
Education: Sandown High School, Isle of Wight
Qualifications: 10 GCSEs, 2 A-levels, ECB Level 2 cricket coach, FA Level 1 football coach, EBA basketball coach, YMCA fitness instructor
Overseas tours: MCC Young Cricketers to Cape Town 2002, to Lanzarote 2003, to Sri Lanka 2004; MCC B to USA 2004
Overseas teams played for: Hermanus, Cape Town 2001-02; Brighton, Melbourne 2003-05
Career highlights to date: '83* on first-class debut against Bangladesh A'
Cricket moments to forget: 'Breaking my jaw in three places during nets at Lord's'
Cricket superstitions: 'Always have to ask somebody if I have the right shirt on. Bordering on obsessive-compulsive…'
Cricketers particularly admired: Jack Russell, Ian Healy, Jonty Rhodes
Young players to look out for: Will Rudge, Tom Stayt, Ben Woodhouse, Peter Snell
Other sports played: Football, squash ('thought I was half-decent till I played Matt Windows')
Other sports followed: Football (Portsmouth FC)
Favourite band: John Mayer, The Killers
Relaxations: 'Enjoy writing about the game; meals out; lying on Sandown beach on the Isle of Wight'
Extras: Played for Hampshire Board XI in the 2002 C&G. Attended World Cricket Academy, Mumbai 2003; International Cricket Academy, Port Elizabeth 2005. NBC Denis Compton Award for most promising young Gloucestershire player 2005
Best batting: 127 Gloucestershire v Worcestershire, New Road (Worcester) 2008

2008 Season

	M	Inn	NO	Runs	HS	Avg	100	50	Ct	St	Balls	Runs	Wkts	Avg	BB	5I	10M
Test																	
FC	16	24	4	944	127	47.20	1	9	38	1	18	15	0		-	-	-
ODI																	
List A	2	1	0	11	11	11.00	-	-	2	-	0	0	0		-	-	
20/20 Int																	
20/20																	

Career Performances

	M	Inn	NO	Runs	HS	Avg	100	50	Ct	St	Balls	Runs	Wkts	Avg	BB	5I	10M
Test																	
FC	22	36	5	1142	127	36.83	1	10	50	1	18	15	0		-	-	-
ODI																	
List A	12	9	0	42	17	4.66	-	-	18	-	0	0	0		-	-	
20/20 Int																	
20/20																	

SOLANKI, V. S. — Worcestershire

Name: Vikram Singh Solanki
Role: Right-hand bat, right-arm off-spin bowler, county captain
Born: 1 April 1976, Udaipur, India
Height: 6ft **Weight:** 12st
Nickname: Vik
County debut: 1993 (one-day), 1995 (first-class)
County cap: 1998; colours, 2002
Benefit: 2007
ODI debut: 1999-2000
Twenty20 Int debut: 2005
1000 runs in a season: 3
1st-Class 200s: 3
Place in batting averages: 37th av. 46.95 (2007 131st av. 31.42)
Parents: Mr Vijay Singh and Mrs Florabel Solanki
Marital status: Single
Family links with cricket: 'Father played in India. Brother Vishal is a keen cricketer'
Education: Regis School, Wolverhampton; Open University

Qualifications: 9 GCSEs, 3 A-levels
Overseas tours: England U18 to South Africa 1992-93, to Denmark (ICC Youth Tournament) 1994; England U19 to West Indies 1994-95; Worcestershire CCC to Barbados 1996, to Zimbabwe 1997; England A to Zimbabwe and South Africa 1998-99, to Bangladesh and New Zealand 1999-2000, to West Indies 2000-01, to Sri Lanka 2004-05, to West Indies 2005-06 (c); England to South Africa and Zimbabwe 1999-2000 (one-day series), to Kenya (ICC Knockout Trophy) 2000-01, to Pakistan 2000-01 (one-day series), to Bangladesh and Sri Lanka 2003-04 (one-day series), to Zimbabwe (one-day series) 2004-05, to South Africa 2004-05 (one-day series), to Pakistan 2005-06 (one-day series), to India 2005-06 (one-day series), to South Africa (World 20/20) 2007-08
Overseas teams played for: Midland-Guildford, Perth, Western Australia; Rajasthan, India 2006-07; Mumbai Champs (ICL) 2007-08
Career highlights to date: 'Playing for England'
Cricket moments to forget: 'Losing to Scotland (NatWest 1998)'
Cricketers particularly admired: Sachin Tendulkar, Graeme Hick
Other sports played: 'Enjoy most sports'
Relaxations: 'Reading; spending time with family and friends'
Extras: NBC Denis Compton Award for most promising young Worcestershire player 1995. Scored more first-class runs (1339) in 1999 season than any other English player. Scored 106 v South Africa at The Oval in the NatWest Series 2003, winning the Man of the Match award and sharing with Marcus Trescothick (114*) in a record England opening partnership in ODIs (200). Man of the Match in the third ODI v Zimbabwe at Bulawayo 2004-05 (100*). C&G Man of the Match awards for his 127 (plus three catches and a run-out) in the semi-final v Warwickshire at Edgbaston 2004 and for his 115 in the final v Gloucestershire at Lord's 2004. Captain of Worcestershire since 2005. His 270 v Gloucestershire in July 2008 was the season's highest individual score in Division 2
Best batting: 270 Worcestershire v Gloucestershire, Cheltenham 2008
Best bowling: 5-40 Worcestershire v Middlesex, Lord's 2004

2008 Season

	M	Inn	NO	Runs	HS	Avg	100	50	Ct	St	Balls	Runs	Wkts	Avg	BB	5I	10M
Test																	
FC	15	25	1	1127	270	46.95	4	5	7	-	42	11	0	-	-	-	
ODI																	
List A	16	16	1	717	94	47.80	-	8	6	-	48	51	0	-	-		
20/20 Int																	
20/20	9	9	0	175	51	19.44	-	2	5	-	48	64	2	32.00	1-9	-	

Career Performances

	M	Inn	NO	Runs	HS	Avg	100	50	Ct	St	Balls	Runs	Wkts	Avg	BB	5I	10M
Test																	
FC	235	387	24	13306	270	36.65	25	71	244	-	6829	3956	84	47.09	5-40	4	1
ODI	51	46	5	1097	106	26.75	2	5	16	-	111	105	1	105.00	1-17	-	
List A	334	307	25	8953	164 *	31.74	13	51	126	-	1043	925	26	35.57	4-14	-	
20/20 Int	3	3	0	76	43	25.33	-	-	3	-	0	0	0		-	-	
20/20	31	30	0	841	92	28.03	-	6	20	-	66	100	3	33.33	1-9	-	

SPEARMAN, C. M. Gloucestershire

Name: Craig Murray Spearman
Role: Right-hand opening bat
Born: 4 July 1972, Auckland, New Zealand
Height: 6ft **Weight:** 13st 7lbs
Nickname: Spears
County debut: 2002
County cap: 2002
Benefit: 2008
Test debut: 1995-96
ODI debut: 1995-96
1000 runs in a season: 3
1st-Class 200s: 2
1st-Class 300s: 1
Place in batting averages: 186th av. 21.62 (2007 69th av. 40.47)
Parents: Murray and Sandra
Wife and date of marriage: Maree, 4 March 2004
Education: Kelston Boys High School, Auckland; Massey University, Palmerston North, New Zealand
Qualifications: Bachelor of Business Studies (BBS; Finance major)
Overseas tours: New Zealand to India and Pakistan (World Cup) 1995-96, to West Indies 1995-96, to Sharjah (Singer Champions Trophy) 1996-97, to Pakistan 1996-97, to Zimbabwe 1997-98, to Australia 1997-98 (CUB Series), to Sri Lanka 1998, to India 1999-2000, to Zimbabwe 2000-01, to Kenya (ICC Knockout Trophy) 2000-01, to South Africa 2000-01; FICA World XI to New Zealand 2004-05
Overseas teams played for: Auckland 1993-96; Central Districts 1996-97 – 2000-01, 2002-03 – 2004-05
Career highlights to date: 'Playing international cricket; Test century; winning ICC Knockout Trophy with New Zealand; winning two C&G finals with Gloucestershire; scoring 341 for Gloucestershire v Middlesex (highest score for Gloucestershire)'

Cricket moments to forget: 'Misfielding on the boundary at the SCG in the fifth over and hearing about it for the next 45 overs'
Cricket superstitions: 'None'
Cricketers particularly admired: Gordon Greenidge
Other sports played: Golf, tennis
Other sports followed: Rugby, golf, football
Favourite band: U2
Relaxations: 'Sleeping'
Extras: Gloucestershire Players' Player of the Year 2002. Scored 123-ball 153 v Warwickshire at Gloucester in the NCL 2003 to set a new individual record score for Gloucestershire in the one-day league. Vice-captain of Gloucestershire 2003. Scored 341, the highest individual score for Gloucestershire in first-class cricket, v Middlesex at Gloucester 2004. C&G Man of the Match award for his 122-ball 143* in the semi-final v Yorkshire at Bristol 2004. Struck century (100) before lunch on first day v Surrey at Bristol 2006. Is England-qualified
Best batting: 341 Gloucestershire v Middlesex, Gloucester 2004
Best bowling: 1-37 Central Districts v Wellington, New Plymouth 1999-2000

2008 Season

	M	Inn	NO	Runs	HS	Avg	100	50	Ct	St	Balls	Runs	Wkts	Avg	BB	5I	10M
Test																	
FC	5	9	1	173	95	21.62	-	1	2	-	0	0	0		-	-	-
ODI																	
List A	9	8	2	393	140 *	65.50	1	3	1	-	0	0	0		-	-	
20/20 Int																	
20/20	4	4	1	43	20	14.33	-	-	1	-	0	0	0		-	-	

Career Performances

	M	Inn	NO	Runs	HS	Avg	100	50	Ct	St	Balls	Runs	Wkts	Avg	BB	5I	10M
Test	19	37	2	922	112	26.34	1	3	21	-	0	0	0		-	-	-
FC	195	351	16	12815	341	38.25	30	55	188	-	78	55	1	55.00	1-37	-	-
ODI	51	50	0	936	86	18.72	-	5	15	-	3	6	0		-	-	
List A	276	273	9	7719	153	29.23	8	48	101	-	33	43	0		-	-	
20/20 Int																	
20/20	42	38	3	697	88	19.91	-	4	13	-	0	0	0		-	-	

85. Which England batsman scored his 5,000th Test run in the first match of the 1997 Ashes series?

SPRIEGEL, M. N. W. Surrey

Name: Matthew Neil William Spriegel
Role: Left-hand bat, right-arm off-spin bowler; all-rounder
Born: 4 March 1987, Epsom, Surrey
Height: 6ft 3in **Weight:** 13st 8lbs
Nickname: Spriegs
County debut: 2008
Place in batting averages: 172nd av. 23.22
Parents: Geoff and Julie
Marital status: Single
Education: Whitgift School, South Croydon; Loughborough University
Qualifications: 11 GCSEs, 1 AS-level, 3 A-levels, Level 1 ECB coach
Career outside cricket: Student
Off-season: 'In my final year of studying Sports and Exercise Science at Loughborough'

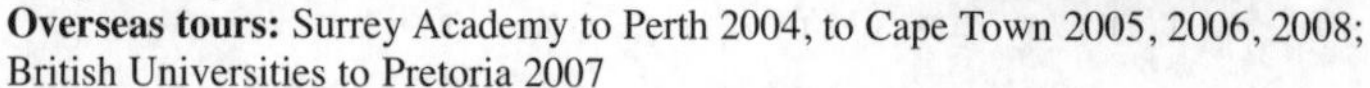

Overseas tours: Surrey Academy to Perth 2004, to Cape Town 2005, 2006, 2008; British Universities to Pretoria 2007
Overseas teams played for: Subiaco Marist CC, Perth 2005-06
Career highlights to date: 'Taking 7-85 and scoring 96 in the same game for Surrey against Kent in the 2nd XI Championship 2006. Making my Championship debut for Surrey'
Cricket moments to forget: 'Scoring three ducks in six innings on tour in Perth in 2004'
Cricketers particularly admired: Steve Waugh
Young players to look out for: Tom Danby, Brian Williams
Other sports played: Golf, football
Favourite band: The Wombats
Relaxations: 'Golf'
Extras: Captained Loughborough UCCE 2007
Opinions on cricket: 'Preparation is the most important thing'
Best batting: 51 Surrey v Nottinghamshire, Trent Bridge 2008
Best bowling: 2-28 Surrey v Hampshire, The Oval 2008

2008 Season

	M	Inn	NO	Runs	HS	Avg	100	50	Ct	St	Balls	Runs	Wkts	Avg	BB	5I	10M
Test																	
FC	12	19	1	418	51	23.22	-	1	2	-	396	249	7	35.57	2-28	-	-
ODI																	
List A	10	9	6	189	54	63.00	-	1	5	-	342	266	5	53.20	1-17	-	
20/20 Int																	
20/20	9	8	7	52	12	52.00	-	-	1	-	162	192	6	32.00	2-16	-	

Career Performances

	M	Inn	NO	Runs	HS	Avg	100	50	Ct	St	Balls	Runs	Wkts	Avg	BB	5I	10M
Test																	
FC	15	25	2	518	51	22.52	-	1	6	-	594	355	10	35.50	2-28	-	-
ODI																	
List A	10	9	6	189	54	63.00	-	1	5	-	342	266	5	53.20	1-17	-	
20/20 Int																	
20/20	9	8	7	52	12	52.00	-	-	1	-	162	192	6	32.00	2-16	-	

STAYT, T. P. Gloucestershire

Name: Thomas (Tom) Patrick Stayt
Role: Right-hand bat, right-arm fast-medium bowler
Born: 20 January 1986, Salisbury
Height: 6ft 2in **Weight:** 11st
Nickname: Staytie, Stick
County debut: 2007
County cap: 2007
Parents: Patrick and Jane
Marital status: Single
Family links with cricket: 'Dad plays occasionally for Erlestoke and Coulston Cricket Club and is part-time groundsman'
Education: Lavington School, Market Lavington; St Augustine's Catholic College, Trowbridge; University of Exeter
Qualifications: 1 AS-Level, 3 A-Levels, BA (Hons) Accounting and Finance
Career highlights to date: 'Making first-class debut at Lord's, August 2007'
Cricket moments to forget: 'Being run out by Chris Taylor without facing a ball on first-class debut at Lord's'

Cricket superstitions: 'Get to the ground early'
Cricketers particularly admired: Jon Lewis, Allan Donald, Courtney Walsh
Young players to look out for: James Campbell, Paul James, James Brown, Andy Fairbairn
Other sports played: 'Will try anything'
Other sports followed: Rugby union (Gloucester)
Favourite band: John Legend
Relaxations: 'Spending time with mates and girlfriend; watching sport'
Best batting: 6 Gloucestershire v Middlesex, Bristol 2007
Best bowling: 3-51 Gloucestershire v Middlesex, Lord's 2007

2008 Season

	M	Inn	NO	Runs	HS	Avg	100	50	Ct	St	Balls	Runs	Wkts	Avg	BB	5I	10M
Test																	
FC																	
ODI																	
List A	1	0	0	0	0		-	-	-	-	29	34	0		-	-	
20/20 Int																	
20/20																	

Career Performances

	M	Inn	NO	Runs	HS	Avg	100	50	Ct	St	Balls	Runs	Wkts	Avg	BB	5I	10M
Test																	
FC	3	3	1	9	6	4.50	-	-	2	-	354	218	4	54.50	3-51	-	-
ODI																	
List A	1	0	0	0	0		-	-	-	-	29	34	0		-	-	
20/20 Int																	
20/20																	

STEVENS, D. I. Kent

Name: Darren Ian Stevens
Role: Right-hand top-order bat, right-arm medium bowler
Born: 30 April 1976, Leicester
Height: 5ft 11in **Weight:** 13st 7lbs
Nickname: Stevo
County debut: 1997 (Leicestershire), 2005 (Kent)
County cap: 2002 (Leicestershire), 2005 (Kent)
1000 runs in a season: 1
1st-Class 200s: 1
Place in batting averages: 174th av. 23.15 (2007 92nd av. 36.94)
Place in bowling averages: 88th av. 32.20 (2007 37th av. 25.41)
Parents: Maddy and Bob
Marital status: Single
Family links with cricket: Father and grandfather played league cricket in Leicestershire
Education: Mount Grace High School; John Cleveland College, Hinckley; Hinckley Tech; Charles Klein College
Qualifications: 5 GCSEs, BTEC National in Sports Studies
Overseas tours: Leicestershire U19 to South Africa 1994-95; Leicestershire to Barbados 1998, to Sri Lanka 1999, to Potchefstroom 2001; ECB National Academy to Australia and Sri Lanka 2002-03; London CCC to West Indies 2007-08
Overseas teams played for: Wanderers CC, Johannesburg, South Africa 1996-97; Rhodes University, Grahamstown, South Africa 1997-98; Fairfield CC, Sydney 1998-99; Hawthorn-Waverley, Melbourne 1999-2000; Taita CC, Wellington, New Zealand 2000-01; Ringwood CC, Melbourne 2001-02
Career highlights to date: 'Winning the 2007 Twenty20'
Cricket moments to forget: 'Losing in my first final in the C&G against Somerset 2001'
Cricket superstitions: 'Left pad first'
Cricketers particularly admired: Ricky Ponting
Young players to look out for: Joe Denly, Sam Northeast
Other sports played: Golf, squash
Other sports followed: Rugby union (Leicester Tigers), football (Dover FC)
Favourite band: Snow Patrol
Relaxations: 'Spending time with friends'

Extras: Received painting from Sir Colin Cowdrey on day of maiden first-class 100 (130 in fourth Championship match), v Sussex at Arundel 1999. Won Sir Ron Brierley/Crusaders Scholarship 1999. Included in provisional England squad of 30 for the 2002-03 World Cup. Kent Player of the Year 2005.
Best batting: 208 Kent v Glamorgan, Canterbury 2005
Best bowling: 4-36 Kent v Yorkshire, Canterbury 2006

2008 Season

	M	Inn	NO	Runs	HS	Avg	100	50	Ct	St	Balls	Runs	Wkts	Avg	BB	5I	10M
Test																	
FC	14	21	1	463	127	23.15	1	1	9	-	738	322	10	32.20	4-70	-	
ODI																	
List A	15	13	3	336	119 *	33.60	1	1	7	-	354	286	5	57.20	2-27	-	
20/20 Int																	
20/20	13	13	5	267	69	33.37	-	1	5	-	96	140	5	28.00	2-29	-	

Career Performances

	M	Inn	NO	Runs	HS	Avg	100	50	Ct	St	Balls	Runs	Wkts	Avg	BB	5I	10M
Test																	
FC	138	226	14	6807	208	32.10	13	38	111	-	4697	2383	64	37.23	4-36	-	
ODI																	
List A	192	180	17	4717	133	28.93	4	30	76	-	1829	1472	44	33.45	5-32	1	
20/20 Int																	
20/20	54	49	8	919	69	22.41	-	2	17	-	252	317	14	22.64	4-14	-	

STONEMAN, M. D. Durham

Name: Mark Daniel Stoneman
Role: Left-hand top-order bat,
'right-arm variations'
Born: 26 June 1987, Newcastle upon Tyne
Height: 5ft 11in **Weight:** 12st 7lbs
Nickname: Rocky, Doug
County debut: 2007
Place in batting averages: 198th av. 20.42 (2007 184th av. 24.60)
Parents: Ian and Pauline
Marital status: 'On the lookout'
Family links with cricket: 'Father played. Grandfather played and was also an umpire'
Education: Whickham Comprehensive School, Gateshead,
Whickham 6th Form
Qualifications: 11 GCSEs, 3 A-levels

Career outside cricket: 'Socialite!'
Off-season: 'Going to Australia'
Overseas tours: Durham Development Squad to Mumbai 2004-05; England U19 to Malaysia and Sri Lanka (U19 World Cup) 2005-06; Durham pre-season tours to Dubai, Cape Town and Johannesburg
Overseas teams played for: St George DCC, Sydney; Mulgrave CC, Melbourne
Cricket moments to forget: 'Numerous run-outs with Michael DiVenuto'
Cricket superstitions: 'Right pad on first'
Cricketers particularly admired: Michael DiVenuto, Neil McKenzie, Shiv Chanderpaul, Marcus Trescothick
Young players to look out for: Mark Turner, Ben Harmison, Karl Turner
Other sports played: Golf, fishing, shooting, darts, pool, bingo
Other sports followed: Football (Newcastle United FC), rugby
Favourite band: Supertramp
Relaxations: 'Music and films'
Extras: Has represented England at U17 and U19 level. Attended Darren Lehmann Talent Squad, Adelaide, January-March 2006
Best batting: 101 Durham v Sussex, Riverside 2007

2008 Season

	M	Inn	NO	Runs	HS	Avg	100	50	Ct	St	Balls	Runs	Wkts	Avg	BB	5I	10M
Test																	
FC	13	22	1	429	60 *	20.42	-	3	4	-	0	0	0		-	-	-
ODI																	
List A	1	1	0	21	21	21.00	-	-	-	-	0	0	0		-	-	
20/20 Int																	
20/20																	

Career Performances

	M	Inn	NO	Runs	HS	Avg	100	50	Ct	St	Balls	Runs	Wkts	Avg	BB	5I	10M
Test																	
FC	21	37	1	798	101	22.16	1	4	9	-	0	0	0		-	-	-
ODI																	
List A	1	1	0	21	21	21.00	-	-	-	-	0	0	0		-	-	
20/20 Int																	
20/20																	

STRAUSS, A. J. Middlesex

Name: Andrew John Strauss
Role: Left-hand bat, left-arm medium bowler
Born: 2 March 1977, Johannesburg, South Africa
Height: 5ft 11in **Weight:** 13st
Nickname: Straussy, Johann, Levi, Mareman, Muppet, Lord Brocket
County debut: 1997 (one-day), 1998 (first-class)
County cap: 2001
Test debut: 2004
ODI debut: 2003
Twenty20 Int debut: 2005
1000 runs in a season: 3
Place in batting averages: 35th av 47.03 (2007 118th av. 32.81)
Parents: David and Dawn
Wife and date of marriage: Ruth, 18 October 2003
Children: Samuel David, December 2005; Luca, July 2008
Education: Radley College; Durham University
Qualifications: 4 A-levels, BA (Hons) Economics
Overseas tours: Durham University to Zimbabwe 1997-98; Middlesex to South Africa 2000; ECB National Academy to Australia 2001-02; England to Bangladesh and Sri Lanka 2003-04 (one-day series), to West Indies 2003-04, to Zimbabwe (one-day series) 2004-05, to South Africa 2004-05, to Pakistan 2005-06, to India 2005-06, to India (ICC Champions Trophy) 2006-07, to Australia 2006-07, to West Indies (World Cup) 2006-07, to New Zealand 2007-08, to India 2008-09, to West Indies 2009 (Captain for Tests, ODIs and Twenty20s)
Overseas teams played for: Sydney University 1998-99; Mosman, Sydney 1999-2001; Northern Districts, New Zealand 2007-08
Cricketers particularly admired: Allan Donald, Brian Lara, Saqlain Mushtaq
Other sports played: Golf (Durham University 1998), rugby (Durham University 1996-97)
Other sports followed: 'Anything with a ball'
Extras: Middlesex Player of the Year 2001. Scored century (112) plus 83 in second innings on Test debut in the first Test v New Zealand at Lord's (his home ground) 2004, winning Man of the Match award. Scored century (100) v West Indies, also at Lord's, in the NatWest Series 2004, in the process sharing with Andrew Flintoff (123) in a new record partnership for England in ODIs (226). Wombwell Cricket Lovers' Society George Spofforth Cricketer of the Year 2004. Captain of Middlesex 2002-04. Scored 126 in the first Test v South Africa at Port Elizabeth 2004-05, achieving feat

of scoring a Test century on home and away debuts and becoming first player to score a Test century in his first innings against each of first three opponents. His other series and match awards include Man of the [Test] Series v South Africa 2004-05 (656 runs at 72.88) and England's Man of the [Test] Series v Pakistan 2006. Vodafone England Cricketer of the Year 2004-05. One of *Wisden*'s Five Cricketers of the Year 2005. Appointed MBE in 2006 New Year Honours as part of 2005 Ashes-winning England team. Man of the Series v New Zealand, summer 2008. First England batsman to score two centuries in a Test v India in that country, 2008-09

Best batting: 177 England v New Zealand, Napier 2007-08

Best bowling: 1-16 Middlesex v Nottinghamshire, Lord's 2007

2008 Season

	M	Inn	NO	Runs	HS	Avg	100	50	Ct	St	Balls	Runs	Wkts	Avg	BB	5I	10M
Test	7	11	0	446	106	40.54	1	3	9	-	0	0	0		-	-	-
FC	16	27	1	1223	172	47.03	3	6	18	-	6	5	0		-	-	-
ODI																	
List A	8	8	0	323	163	40.37	1	1	2	-	0	0	0		-	-	
20/20 Int																	
20/20	6	6	0	88	27	14.66	-	-	2	-	0	0	0		-	-	

Career Performances

	M	Inn	NO	Runs	HS	Avg	100	50	Ct	St	Balls	Runs	Wkts	Avg	BB	5I	10M
Test	53	98	2	3943	177	41.07	12	14	66	-	0	0	0		-	-	-
FC	162	288	13	11283	177	41.02	28	50	135	-	90	79	2	39.50	1-16	-	-
ODI	78	77	7	2239	152	31.98	2	14	28	-	6	3	0		-	-	
List A	199	192	13	5461	163	30.50	6	34	60	-	6	3	0		-	-	
20/20 Int	3	3	0	51	33	17.00	-	-	1	-	0	0	0		-	-	
20/20	24	24	0	455	60	18.95	-	2	11	-	0	0	0		-	-	

86. Who took 7-66 and 4-27 to help England to success in an Ashes Test at The Oval in 1997?

STUBBINGS, S.D. Derbyshire

Name: Stephen David Stubbings
Role: Left-hand bat, right-arm bowler 'all disciplines', occasional wicket-keeper
Born: 31 March 1978, Huddersfield
Height: 6ft 4in **Weight:** 15st 5lbs
Nickname: Stubbo, Hollywood, Wilton Shagpile, The Plank
County debut: 1997
County cap: 2001
Benefit: 2008
1000 runs in a season: 4
Place in batting averages: 112th av. 31.62 (2007 136th av. 31.28)
Parents: Marie and David
Marital status: Single
Family links with cricket: 'Father and brother both played, as I did, for Delacombe Park Cricket Club in Melbourne, Australia'
Education: Frankston High School; Swinburne University – both Melbourne, Australia
Qualifications: Victorian Certificate of Education (VCE), Level 2 coaching
Career outside cricket: Coach, journalist
Off-season: 'Coaching and being coached'
Overseas tours: Derbyshire to Portugal 2000
Overseas teams played for: Delacombe Park CC, Melbourne 1989-90 – 1993-94; Frankston Peninsula CC, Victoria 1994-95 – 1999-2000, 2002-03 – 2005-06; Kingborough CC, Tasmania 2000-01 – 2001-02
Career highlights to date: '2006 Championship season at Derbyshire'
Cricket moments to forget: '2005 Championship season at Derbyshire'
Cricket superstitions: 'No shaving on first day of a game'
Cricketers particularly admired: Michael DiVenuto
Other sports played: Golf, Aussie Rules, football
Other sports followed: AFL (Essendon Bombers), football (Cambridge United FC)
Favourite band: Powderfinger
Extras: Represented Victoria at all junior levels. Spent two years on the cricket programme at the Victorian Institute of Sport. Scored 135* v Kent at Canterbury 2000, taking part in an unbroken opening partnership of 293 with Steve Titchard (141*); it was the first occasion on which Derbyshire had batted all day without losing a wicket. Derbyshire Player of the Year 2001 and 2006
Best batting: 151 Derbyshire v Somerset, Taunton 2005

2008 Season

	M	Inn	NO	Runs	HS	Avg	100	50	Ct	St	Balls	Runs	Wkts	Avg	BB	5I	10M
Test																	
FC	10	18	2	506	62 *	31.62	-	2	5	-	36	42	0		-	-	-
ODI																	
List A	6	5	1	207	95 *	51.75	-	2	3	-	0	0	0		-	-	
20/20 Int																	
20/20																	

Career Performances

	M	Inn	NO	Runs	HS	Avg	100	50	Ct	St	Balls	Runs	Wkts	Avg	BB	5I	10M
Test																	
FC	132	240	13	7261	151	31.98	12	37	60	-	96	121	0		-	-	-
ODI																	
List A	114	106	6	2624	110	26.24	1	15	20	-	0	0	0		-	-	
20/20 Int																	
20/20	9	9	1	186	57	23.25	-	2	4	-	0	0	0		-	-	

SUPPIAH, A. V. — Somerset

Name: Arul Vivasvan Suppiah
Role: Right-hand bat, left-arm orthodox spin bowler
Born: 30 August 1983, Kuala Lumpur, Malaysia
Height: 6ft **Weight:** 12st 7lbs
Nickname: Ruley, Ja Rule
County debut: 2002
Parents: Suppiah and Baanumathi
Marital status: Single
Family links with cricket: Brother Rohan Vishnu Suppiah has played cricket for Malaysia
Education: Millfield School; Exeter University
Qualifications: 9 GCSEs, 4 A-levels, BA (Hons) in Accounting and Finance, Level 1 coaching qualification
Overseas tours: Millfield School to South Africa 1997, to Sri Lanka 1999; West of England U15 to West Indies 1998; Malaysia to Sharjah (Asian Cricket Council Trophy) 2000-01, to Nepal (ACC Fast Track Countries Tournament) 2005

Overseas teams played for: Doubleview Carine CC, Perth 2005-06; Old Edwardians, Johannesburg 2006-07
Career highlights to date: 'Making my first-class debut v West Indies A for Somerset 2002; making my debut in the NUL for Somerset v Durham 2002; being the youngest ever cricketer to play for Malaysia; playing for England through the age groups; maiden first-class hundred for Somerset against Derbyshire 2005'
Cricket moments to forget: 'Being bowled out for a golden duck off the seventh ball of the over'
Cricket superstitions: 'Right pad first'
Cricketers particularly admired: Sachin Tendulkar, Wasim Akram, Marcus Trescothick
Young players to look out for: Jos Buttler
Other sports played: Hockey (Somerset U16), badminton (Millfield School 1st team)
Other sports followed: Football (Manchester United)
Favourite band: Red Hot Chili Peppers
Relaxations: 'Starbucks'
Extras: Made debut for Malaysia aged 15. Represented England U14, U15, U17 and U18. Somerset U15 Player of the Year 1998. West of England U15 Player of the Year 1998. Most Promising Sportsman for Malaysia 2000. NBC Denis Compton Award for the most promising young Somerset player 2002
Best batting: 123 Somerset v Derbyshire, Derby 2005
Best bowling: 3-46 Somerset v West Indies A, Taunton 2002

2008 Season

	M	Inn	NO	Runs	HS	Avg	100	50	Ct	St	Balls	Runs	Wkts	Avg	BB	5I	10M
Test																	
FC	3	5	0	163	61	32.60	-	1	-	-	276	165	2	82.50	2-54	-	-
ODI																	
List A	7	7	1	119	33	19.83	-	-	5	-	156	188	4	47.00	2-35	-	
20/20 Int																	
20/20	6	6	3	75	32 *	25.00	-	-	1	-	84	110	4	27.50	3-36	-	

Career Performances

	M	Inn	NO	Runs	HS	Avg	100	50	Ct	St	Balls	Runs	Wkts	Avg	BB	5I	10M
Test																	
FC	28	47	1	1324	123	28.78	1	8	11	-	1405	950	14	67.85	3-46	-	-
ODI																	
List A	42	41	3	940	79	24.73	-	5	18	-	1035	968	29	33.37	4-39	-	
20/20 Int																	
20/20	23	15	5	149	32 *	14.90	-	-	8	-	216	292	13	22.46	3-36	-	

SUTCLIFFE, I. J. Lancashire

Name: Iain John Sutcliffe
Role: Left-hand bat, leg-spin bowler
Born: 20 December 1974, Leeds
Height: 6ft 2in **Weight:** 13st
Nickname: Sutty
County debut: 1995 (Leicestershire), 2003 (Lancashire) (*see* ***Extras***)
County cap: 1997 (Leicestershire), 2003 (Lancashire)
1000 runs in a season: 3
1st-Class 200s: 1
Place in batting averages: 230th av. 14.90 (2007 149th av. 29.00)
Parents: John and Valerie
Marital status: Single
Education: Leeds Grammar School; Oxford University
Qualifications: 10 GCSEs, 4 A-levels, 2.1 PPE degree
Overseas tours: Leeds GS to Kenya; Leicestershire to South Africa, to West Indies, to Sri Lanka
Career highlights to date: 'Championship winner's medal 1998'
Cricketers particularly admired: Brian Lara, David Gower
Other sports played: Boxing (Oxford Blue 1994, 1995; British Universities Light-middleweight Champion 1993)
Other sports followed: Football (Liverpool)
Relaxations: Socialising, cinema
Extras: NBC Denis Compton Award for most promising young Leicestershire player 1996. Played NCA England U14 and NCA Development Team U18/U19. Scored 55 of Leicestershire's first innings total of 96 v Pakistanis at Leicester 2001. Leicestershire vice-captain 2002. Leicestershire Player of the Year 2002. Scored century (102*) v Surrey at Whitgift School in the totesport League 2004, in the process sharing with Mark Chilton (115) in a new Lancashire record opening stand in one-day cricket (223). Played one first-class match for Northamptonshire on loan 2007. Retired before the end of the 2008 season
Best batting: 203 Leicestershire v Glamorgan, Cardiff 2001
Best bowling: 2-21 Oxford University v Cambridge University, Lord's 1996

2008 Season

	M	Inn	NO	Runs	HS	Avg	100	50	Ct	St	Balls	Runs	Wkts	Avg	BB	5I	10M
Test																	
FC	7	11	0	164	50	14.90	-	1	3	-	0	0	0		-	-	-
ODI																	
List A	1	1	0	16	16	16.00	-	-	-	-	0	0	0		-	-	
20/20 Int																	
20/20																	

Career Performances

	M	Inn	NO	Runs	HS	Avg	100	50	Ct	St	Balls	Runs	Wkts	Avg	BB	5I	10M
Test																	
FC	191	305	28	9464	203	34.16	16	51	110	-	447	330	9	36.66	2-21	-	-
ODI																	
List A	124	122	11	3238	105 *	29.17	4	20	27	-	0	0	0		-	-	
20/20 Int																	
20/20	4	3	0	4	4	1.33	-	-	-	-	0	0	0		-	-	

SUTTON, L. D. Lancashire

Name: Luke David Sutton
Role: Right-hand bat, wicket-keeper, 'right-arm rubbish'
Born: 4 October 1976, Keynsham
Height: 5ft 11in **Weight:** 12st 13lbs
Nickname: Sutts
County debut: 1997 (Somerset), 2000 (Derbyshire), 2006 (Lancashire)
County cap: 2002 (Derbyshire), 2007 (Lancashire)
50 dismissals in a season: 1
Place in batting averages: 149th av. 27.11 (2007 96th av. 36.68)
Parents: David and Molly
Wife and date of marriage: Jude, 7 October 2006
Education: Millfield School; Durham University
Qualifications: 9 GCSEs, 4 A-levels, 2.1 degree in Economics, CeMAP 1, 2 and 3, Level 1 coaching
Career outside cricket: 'Running Activate Sport camps'

Overseas tours: Various Somerset Schools tours to Netherlands; West of England U15 to West Indies 1991; Millfield School to Zimbabwe 1993, to Sri Lanka 1994; Durham University to Zimbabwe 1997
Overseas teams played for: UNSW, Sydney 1998-99; Northville, Port Elizabeth, South Africa 1999-2000; Subiaco Marist, Perth 2000-01
Career highlights to date: 'Scoring my highest first-class score to date of 151* in the Roses match at Old Trafford in 2006'
Cricket moments to forget: 'Losing the C&G final and the Championship to Sussex in 2006'
Cricket superstitions: 'Plenty!'
Cricketers particularly admired: Ian Healy, Jack Russell, Alec Stewart, Steve Waugh
Young players to look out for: Tom Smith, Karl Brown, Steven Croft
Other sports followed: Football (Derby County), rugby (Bath)
Relaxations: 'Quality time with family and friends'
Extras: Captained England U15 and also represented England U18 and U19. Won Sir John Hobbs Silver Jubilee Memorial Prize for the U16 Cricketer of the Year in 1992 and the Gray-Nicolls Award for the English Schools Cricketer of the Year in 1995. Voted Derbyshire 2nd XI Player of the Year 2000. NBC Denis Compton Award for the most promising young Derbyshire player 2000, 2001, 2002. Captain of Derbyshire 2004-05. Scored 151* v Yorkshire at Old Trafford 2006, setting a new record for the highest Championship score by a Lancashire wicket-keeper. 'Set up a charity with my brother Noel called Freddie Fight, which raises money for CAH research; CAH (congenital adrenal hyperplasia) is a condition suffered by my nephew Freddie'
Best batting: 151* Lancashire v Yorkshire, Old Trafford 2006

2008 Season

	M	Inn	NO	Runs	HS	Avg	100	50	Ct	St	Balls	Runs	Wkts	Avg	BB	5I	10M
Test																	
FC	15	21	4	461	55	27.11	-	1	54	2	0	0	0		-	-	-
ODI																	
List A	7	5	0	55	24	11.00	-	-	10	-	0	0	0		-	-	
20/20 Int																	
20/20																	

Career Performances

	M	Inn	NO	Runs	HS	Avg	100	50	Ct	St	Balls	Runs	Wkts	Avg	BB	5I	10M
Test																	
FC	130	210	30	5812	151 *	32.28	9	18	315	14	0	0	0		-		-
ODI																	
List A	139	119	23	1796	83	18.70	-	6	155	19	0	0	0		-	-	
20/20 Int																	
20/20	16	14	4	306	61 *	30.60	-	1	9	7	0	0	0		-	-	

SWANN, G. P. Nottinghamshire

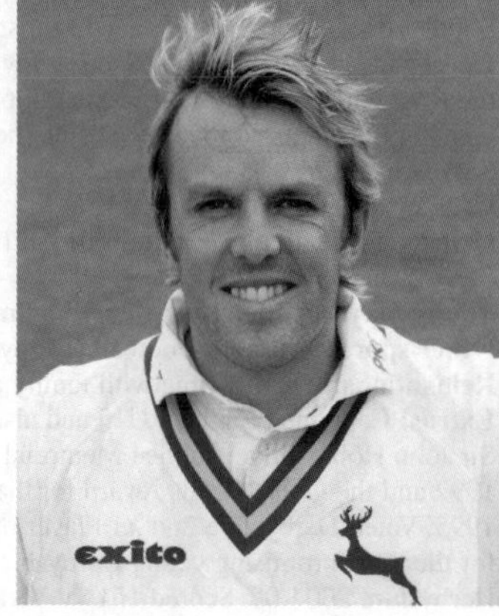

Name: Graeme Peter Swann
Role: Right-hand bat, right-arm off-spin bowler
Born: 24 March 1979, Northampton
Height: 6ft **Weight:** 13st
Nickname: G-spot, Besty
County debut: 1997 (one-day, Northants), 1998 (first-class, Northants), 2005 (Notts)
County cap: 1999 (Northants)
ODI debut: 1999-2000
Twety20 Int debut: 2007-08
50 wickets in a season: 1
Place in batting averages: 84th av. 36.62 (2007 124th av. 32.25)
Place in bowling averages: 70th av. 29.96 (2007 83rd av. 33.40)
Parents: Ray and Mavis
Marital status: Single
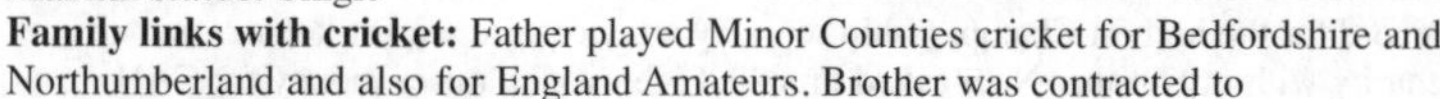
Family links with cricket: Father played Minor Counties cricket for Bedfordshire and Northumberland and also for England Amateurs. Brother was contracted to Northamptonshire and Lancashire. 'Cat is named after Gus Logie'
Education: Sponne School, Towcester
Qualifications: 10 GCSEs, 4 A-levels, Levels 1 and 2 coaching awards, 'London Marathon sub 2hr 45min certificate'
Career outside cricket: 'After-dinner speaking, journalism'
Overseas tours: England U19 to South Africa (including U19 World Cup) 1997-98; England A to Zimbabwe and South Africa 1998-99, to West Indies 2000-01, to Sri Lanka 2004-05; England to South Africa 1999-2000, to Sri Lanka 2007-08, to New Zealand 2007-08, to India (Test and one-day series) 2008-09, to West Indies (Test and one-day series) 2008-09; ECB National Academy to Australia 2001-02
Overseas teams played for: Old Colts, Christchurch 2002-03
Career highlights to date: 'Winning County Championship [2005]'
Cricket moments to forget: 'Being hit for an enormous six by Peter Such'
Cricketers particularly admired: Neil Foster, Devon Malcolm
Other sports played: Golf, rugby (Northants U14, U15, U16), football (Old Northamptonians Chenecks FC)
Other sports followed: Football (Newcastle United)
Favourite band: Oasis, The Fratellis, The Stone Roses, The Charlatans
Extras: Played for England U14, U15, U17 and U19. Gray-Nicolls Len Newbery Schools Cricketer of the Year 1996. Took 8-118 for England U19 in second 'Test' v Pakistan U19 1998, the best ever figures for England in an U19 'Test'. Cricket

Society's Leading Young All-rounder award 1999, 2002. Man of the Match for England A v Windward Islands in St Lucia in the Busta Cup 2000-01. ECB National Academy 2004-05. Scored 33-ball 59, then took 5-17 v Gloucestershire at Trent Bridge in the Pro40 2007. Man of the Match in the third ODI v Sri Lanka in Dambulla 2007-08 (4-34/25)

Best batting: 183 Northamptonshire v Gloucestershire, Bristol 2002

Best bowling: 7-33 Northamptonshire v Derbyshire, Northampton 2003

2008 Season

	M	Inn	NO	Runs	HS	Avg	100	50	Ct	St	Balls	Runs	Wkts	Avg	BB	5I	10M
Test																	
FC	14	18	2	586	82	36.62	-	5	16	-	2165	959	32	29.96	4-25	-	-
ODI	5	4	0	45	29	11.25	-	-	3	-	234	163	7	23.28	2-33	-	
List A	18	16	0	281	61	17.56	-	1	10	-	843	555	26	21.34	4-35	-	
20/20 Int	1	0	0	0	0		-	-	-	-	24	21	2	10.50	2-21	-	
20/20	1	0	0	0	0		-	-	-	-	24	21	2	10.50	2-21	-	

Career Performances

	M	Inn	NO	Runs	HS	Avg	100	50	Ct	St	Balls	Runs	Wkts	Avg	BB	5I	10M
Test																	
FC	171	240	17	6034	183	27.05	4	31	125	-	28449	14213	432	32.90	7-33	15	3
ODI	12	9	0	136	34	15.11	-	-	7	-	534	387	14	27.64	4-34	-	
List A	196	156	15	2786	83	19.75	-	14	65	-	7622	5588	205	27.25	5-17	2	
20/20 Int	3	2	2	18	15 *		-	-	-	-	60	67	5	13.40	2-21	-	
20/20	37	35	5	594	62	19.80	-	2	10	-	810	899	45	19.97	3-16	-	

87. Who scored England's winning runs in the 2005 Trent Bridge Test which England won by three wickets?

TAHIR, N. Warwickshire

Name: Naqaash Tahir
Role: Right-hand bat, right-arm fast bowler
Born: 14 November 1983, Birmingham
Height: 5ft 10in **Weight:** 11st
Nickname: Naq, Naqy
County debut: 2004
Place in bowling averages: (2007 50th av. 27.76)
Parents: Mohammed Amin and Ishrat Nasreen
Marital status: Single
Family links with cricket: 'Dad played club cricket and brother played for Worcestershire and Warwickshire'
Education: Moseley School; Spring Hill College
Qualifications: 3 GCSEs, Level 1 coaching
Overseas tours: Warwickshire U15 to South Africa 1999
Overseas teams played for: Mirpur, Pakistan; Subiaco-Floreat, Perth
Cricket superstitions: 'Putting my pads on in a certain way'
Cricketers particularly admired: Waqar Younis, Wasim Akram, Brett Lee, Darren Gough
Young players to look out for: Moeen Ali
Other sports played: Football
Other sports followed: Football (Man Utd)
Relaxations: 'Watching TV; PlayStation 2'
Extras: Has been Moseley Ashfield U15 Player of the Year, Warwickshire U15 Youth Player of the Year, Warwickshire U19 Players' Player of the Year and Warwickshire U19 Player of the Year (Coney Edmonds Trophy). Had match figures of 8-90 (4-47/4-43) on Championship debut v Worcestershire at Edgbaston 2004
Best batting: 49 Warwickshire v Worcestershire, Worcester 2004
Best bowling: 7-107 Warwickshire v Lancashire, Blackpool 2006

2008 Season

	M	Inn	NO	Runs	HS	Avg	100	50	Ct	St	Balls	Runs	Wkts	Avg	BB	5I	10M
Test																	
FC	6	6	2	69	37	17.25	-	-	1	-	1055	561	8	70.12	3-49	-	-
ODI																	
List A	4	2	1	17	13 *	17.00	-	-	-	-	168	111	2	55.50	2-47	-	
20/20 Int																	
20/20																	

Career Performances

	M	Inn	NO	Runs	HS	Avg	100	50	Ct	St	Balls	Runs	Wkts	Avg	BB	5I	10M
Test																	
FC	37	39	12	437	49	16.18	-	-	3	-	4819	2734	85	32.16	7-107	1	-
ODI																	
List A	13	5	3	19	13 *	9.50	-	-	1	-	444	338	5	67.60	2-47	-	
20/20 Int																	
20/20																	

TAYLOR, B. V. — Hampshire

Name: Billy Victor Taylor
Role: Left-hand bat, right-arm fast-medium bowler
Born: 11 January 1977, Southampton
Height: 6ft 3in **Weight:** 13st 4lbs
Nickname: Tav, Crusty
County debut: 1999 (Sussex), 2004 (Hampshire)
County cap: 2006 (Hampshire)
Parents: Jackie and Victor
Marital status: Single
Family links with cricket: 'Learnt from and played cricket with both my brothers, Martin and James'
Education: Bitterne Park; Southampton Tech College; Sparsholt Agricultural College, Hampshire
Qualifications: 10 GCSEs, NVQ Level 2 Carpentry and Joinery, NTPC Tree Surgery, Level 2 coaching
Career outside cricket: 'Hopefully falconry'
Off-season: 'Training and flying birds of prey'
Overseas tours: Sussex/Hampshire to Cyprus 1999; Sussex to Grenada 2002

Overseas teams played for: Central Hawke's Bay, New Zealand 1996-97; Manawatu Foxton CC and Horowhenua rep team, New Zealand 1998-99, 2000-01; Te Puke 2002
Career highlights to date: 'Winning the County Championship in 2003 [with Sussex]. Being capped for Hampshire. All my three hat-tricks'
Cricket moments to forget: 'Don't want to forget any moments as it's such a great career and too short a one'
Cricket superstitions: 'Have a towel hanging out of back of trousers, and wearing sweat band and wristwatch'
Cricketers particularly admired: Malcolm Marshall, Robin Smith, Mushtaq Ahmed
Young players to look out for: Liam Dawson
Other sports played: Golf and falconry
Other sports followed: Football (Havant & Waterlooville) - 'follow my brother playing football for Totton FC'
Favourite band: Dido, Black Eyed Peas
Relaxations: Falconry
Extras: Took 98 wickets in New Zealand club cricket in 1998-99. Sussex 2nd XI Player of the Year 1999, 2000. Took hat-trick (Ormond, Sampson, Giddins) v Surrey at Hove in the B&H and another (G. Flower, Maddy, Malcolm) v Leicestershire at Leicester in the C&G, both in 2002. Took Championship hat-trick (Compton, Weekes, Scott) v Middlesex at The Rose Bowl 2006, finishing with 6-32. Has appeared only in limited-over competitions since his last first-class game for the county in 2006. Is an ambassador for the charity Honeypot, which provides respite holidays and support to young carers and vulnerable children
Opinions on cricket: 'Should play more Twenty20 and one-day matches.'
Best batting: 40 Hampshire v Essex, Rose Bowl 2004
Best bowling: 6-32 Hampshire v Middlesex, Rose Bowl 2006

2008 Season

	M	Inn	NO	Runs	HS	Avg	100	50	Ct	St	Balls	Runs	Wkts	Avg	BB	5I	10M
Test																	
FC																	
ODI																	
List A	14	3	2	4	4 *	4.00	-	-	4	-	612	515	16	32.18	4-26	-	
20/20 Int																	
20/20	9	2	2	3	3 *		-	-	-	-	198	256	6	42.66	2-18	-	

Career Perfomances

	M	Inn	NO	Runs	HS	Avg	100	50	Ct	St	Balls	Runs	Wkts	Avg	BB	5I	10M
Test																	
FC	53	68	26	431	40	10.26	-	-	6	-	8286	4483	135	33.20	6-32	4	-
ODI																	
List A	132	56	27	186	21 *	6.41	-	-	25	-	5811	4285	164	26.12	5-28	1	
20/20 Int																	
20/20	30	8	7	20	12 *	20.00	-	-	3	-	570	700	23	30.43	2-9	-	

TAYLOR, C. G. Gloucestershire

Name: Christopher (Chris) Glyn Taylor
Role: Right-hand bat, right-arm off-spin bowler
Born: 27 September 1976, Bristol
Height: 5ft 8in **Weight:** 10st
Nickname: Tales, Tootsie
County debut: 2000
County cap: 2001
1000 runs in a season: 1
Place in batting averages: 52nd av. 42.34 (2007 79th av. 38.57)
Place in bowling averages: (2007 79th av. 33.10)
Parents: Chris and Maggie
Wife and date of marriage: Sarah, 8 December 2001
Children: Harriet, 2003; Alexandra, 2004, Jonty 2007
Family links with cricket: Father and grandfather both played local club cricket
Education: Colston's Collegiate School, Bristol
Qualifications: GCSEs and A-levels
Overseas teams played for: Harbord CC, Manly, Australia 2000
Cricket moments to forget: 'B&H loss to Surrey at Lord's [2001]'
Cricketers particularly admired: Jonty Rhodes, Mark Waugh
Other sports played: Rugby, hockey (both county level); squash, tennis
Other sports followed: Rugby
Relaxations: Fishing
Extras: Represented England Schools U18. In 1995 won the Cricket Society's A. A. Thomson Fielding Prize and Wetherell Award for Leading All-rounder in English Schools Cricket. Scored maiden first-class century (104) v Middlesex 2000, becoming the first player to score a century at Lord's on Championship debut; also the first player to score a century for Gloucestershire in match that was both first-class and Championship debut. NBC Denis Compton Award for the most promising young Gloucestershire player 2000. Four-day captain of Gloucestershire 2004-05. Became a member of the English Academy coaching staff in 2008
Best batting: 196 Gloucestershire v Nottinghamshire, Trent Bridge 2001
Best bowling: 4-52 Gloucestershire v Northamptonshire, Northampton 2007

2008 Season

	M	Inn	NO	Runs	HS	Avg	100	50	Ct	St	Balls	Runs	Wkts	Avg	BB	5I	10M
Test																	
FC	17	30	4	1101	137	42.34	2	8	6	-	288	175	2	87.50	1-14	-	-
ODI																	
List A	12	9	1	290	79	36.25	-	4	8	-	18	31	0		-	-	
20/20 Int																	
20/20	7	7	1	169	66	28.16	-	1	1	-	0	0	0		-	-	

Career Performances

	M	Inn	NO	Runs	HS	Avg	100	50	Ct	St	Balls	Runs	Wkts	Avg	BB	5I	10M
Test																	
FC	114	201	15	6436	196	34.60	16	26	74	-	1665	1038	18	57.66	4-52	-	-
ODI																	
List A	139	125	17	2521	93	23.34	-	15	57	1	278	258	8	32.25	2-5	-	
20/20 Int																	
20/20	43	39	10	851	83	29.34	-	4	16	-	6	11	0		-	-	

TAYLOR, C. R. Yorkshire

Name: Christopher (Chris) Robert Taylor
Role: Right-hand top-order bat, right-arm fast-medium 'bouncer' bowler
Born: 21 February 1981, Leeds
Height: 6ft 4in **Weight:** 15st
Nickname: CT
County debut: 2001 (Yorkshire), 2006 (Derbyshire)
Place in batting averages: 196th av. 20.50 (2007 153rd av. 28.00)
Parents: Phil and Elaine
Wife and date of marriage: Charlotte, 10 February 2007
Family links with cricket: 'Dad slogged a few in the Dales Council League, Mum gave good throw-downs and brother (Moo) is captain of Morley CC in Bradford League'
Education: Benton Park High School, Rawdon
Qualifications: 9 GCSEs, 4 A-levels, qualified cricket coach
Career outside cricket: 'Own my own cricket coaching busness in Yorkshire and Derbyshire (www.procricketcoachingacademy.com), and a cricket bat business

(www.playinthevcricketbats.com)'
Overseas tours: Yorkshire to Grenada 2002
Overseas teams played for: Western Suburbs Magpies, Sydney 1999-2002; Fairfield-Liverpool Lions, Sydney 2003-05
Career highlights to date: 'Winning County Championship with Yorkshire 2001. Becoming first Derbyshire player to score a century on both my four-day and one-day debut for the club'
Cricket moments to forget: 'Pair on Sky in the Roses match 2002!'
Cricketers particularly admired: Geoffrey Boycott, Anthony McGrath, Stephen Stubbings
Young players to look out for: Oliver Hannon-Dalby, Jonny Bairstow
Other sports played: Football (goalkeeper; played for Farsley Celtic FC)
Other sports followed: Football ('mighty Everton'), rugby league (Leeds Rhinos)
Relaxations: 'Swilling, cricket coaching, listening to Steve Patterson'
Extras: Represented Yorkshire U10-U17. Neil Lloyd Trophy for top run-scorer at Bunbury Festival 1996. Represented England U15, U17 and U19. Yorkshire CCC Supporters' Club Young Player of the Year 1999. Became first Derbyshire player to score a hundred on both first-class debut (102 v Oxford UCCE at The Parks 2006) and one-day debut (100 v Yorkshire at Headingley in the C&G 2006) for the county. Scored 564 List A runs at 62.66 in 2006 and was named Derbyshire One-Day Player of the Season. Derbyshire Supporters' Player of the Year 2006. Left Derbyshire at the end of the 2007 season and rejoined Yorkshire for 2008
Opinions on cricket: 'Think we play far too much cricket. Never have chance to refresh and work on key aspects of the game. Still far too many Kolpaks and non-English-qualified players in our game – give our young players a chance first!'
Best batting: 121 Derbyshire v Glamorgan, Cardiff 2006

2008 Season

	M	Inn	NO	Runs	HS	Avg	100	50	Ct	St	Balls	Runs	Wkts	Avg	BB	5I	10M
Test																	
FC	4	6	0	123	48	20.50	-	-	1	-	0	0	0		-	-	-
ODI																	
List A	2	2	0	45	23	22.50	-	-	-	-	0	0	0		-	-	
20/20 Int																	
20/20	2	2	1	10	10 *	10.00	-	-	-	-	0	0	0		-	-	

Career Performances

	M	Inn	NO	Runs	HS	Avg	100	50	Ct	St	Balls	Runs	Wkts	Avg	BB	5I	10M
Test																	
FC	39	65	3	1615	121	26.04	3	8	23	-	0	0	0		-	-	-
ODI																	
List A	22	21	5	738	111 *	46.12	2	2	7	-	0	0	0		-	-	
20/20 Int																	
20/20	16	14	7	157	28 *	22.42	-	-	4	-	0	0	0		-	-	

TAYLOR, J. W. A. — Leicestershire

Name: James William Arthur Taylor
Role: Right-hand bat, leg-spin bowler
Born: 6 January 1990, Nottingham
Height: 5ft 7in **Weight:** 10st 7lbs
Nickname: Jimmy, Titch
County debut: 2008
Education: Shrewsbury School
Qualifications: 9 GCSEs, 4 AS-Levels, 3 A-Levels
Overseas tours: England U19 to Malaysia (U19 World Cup) 2007-08, to South Africa 2008-09
Extras: Played for Worcestershire 2nd XI 2006, 2007. Played one match for Shropshire in the Minor Counties Championship 2007. Played for Midlands U17 at ECB U17 Regional Festival at Loughborough 2007. Included in the England U19 squad to South Africa 2008-09; scored 85 in the third ODI, helping England to their first win of the series
Best batting: 51 Leicestershire v Bangladesh A, Grace Road 2008

2008 Season

	M	Inn	NO	Runs	HS	Avg	100	50	Ct	St	Balls	Runs	Wkts	Avg	BB	5I	10M
Test																	
FC	4	5	0	64	51	12.80	-	1	4	-	0	0	0		-	-	-
ODI																	
List A	4	2	1	80	43 *	80.00	-	-	-	-	0	0	0		-	-	
20/20 Int																	
20/20	3	2	0	32	22	16.00	-	-	-	-	0	0	0		-	-	

Career Performances

	M	Inn	NO	Runs	HS	Avg	100	50	Ct	St	Balls	Runs	Wkts	Avg	BB	5I	10M
Test																	
FC	4	5	0	64	51	12.80	-	1	4	-	0	0	0		-	-	-
ODI																	
List A	4	2	1	80	43 *	80.00	-	-	-	-	0	0	0		-	-	
20/20 Int																	
20/20	3	2	0	32	22	16.00	-	-	-	-	0	0	0		-	-	

TELO, F. D Derbyshire

Name: Filipe Dominic Telo
Role: Right-hand bat, right-arm fast-medium bowler
Born: 4 March 1986, Cape Town, South Africa
County debut: 2008
Place in batting averages: 213th av. 18.13
Overseas teams played for: Western Province 2005-06 – 2007-08, Cape Cobras 2005-06 – 2007-08
Extras: Signed for Derbyshire in April 2008
Best batting: 134* Western Province v Boland, Paarl 2007
Best bowling: 1-36 Derbyshire v Essex, Derby 2008

2008 Season

	M	Inn	NO	Runs	HS	Avg	100	50	Ct	St	Balls	Runs	Wkts	Avg	BB	5I	10M
Test																	
FC	8	15	0	272	69	18.13	-	2	3	-	30	36	1	36.00	1-36	-	
ODI																	
List A	5	5	2	70	39	23.33	-	-	-	-	0	0	0		-	-	
20/20 Int																	
20/20	8	8	0	134	33	16.75	-	-	2	-	0	0	0		-	-	

Career Performances

	M	Inn	NO	Runs	HS	Avg	100	50	Ct	St	Balls	Runs	Wkts	Avg	BB	5I	10M
Test																	
FC	25	45	3	1401	134 *	33.35	3	6	8	-	47	48	1	48.00	1-36	-	
ODI																	
List A	22	20	2	476	90	26.44	-	4	3	-	0	0	0		-	-	
20/20 Int																	
20/20	16	13	0	256	48	19.69	-	-	4	-	0	0	0		-	-	

TEN DOESCHATE, R. N. Essex

Name: Ryan Neil ten Doeschate
Role: Right-hand bat, right-arm fast-medium bowler; all-rounder
Born: 30 June 1980, Port Elizabeth, South Africa
Height: 5ft 11in **Weight:** 13st 5lbs
Nickname: Tendo
County debut: 2003
County cap: 2006
ODI debut: 2006
Twenty20 Int debut: 2008
1st-Class 200s: 1
Place in batting averages: 69th av. 39.09 (2007 70th av. 40.42)
Place in bowling averages: 26th av. 23.06
Parents: Boudewyn and Ingrid
Marital status: Single
Education: Fairbairn College; University of Cape Town
Qualifications: Business science degree
Overseas tours: Netherlands to Ireland (ICC Trophy) 2005, to Scotland (European Championship) 2006, to South Africa (ICC Associates Tri-Series) 2006-07, to Kenya (ICC World Cricket League) 2006-07, to West Indies (World Cup) 2006-07, to Ireland (Quadrangular Series) 2007
Overseas teams played for: Western Province, South Africa; Bloemendaal, Netherlands; Rockingham-Mandurah, Australia
Career highlights to date: 'Winning totesport in 2005. Getting county cap'
Cricket moments to forget: 'My county debut at Chelmsford'
Cricketers particularly admired: Jacques Kallis, Kepler Wessels
Young players to look out for: Tom Westley, Mervyn Westfield
Other sports played: Rugby
Other sports followed: Football (Arsenal), rugby (Stormers)
Favourite band: Phil Collins
Relaxations: Golf, tennis, reading
Extras: Has played first-class and one-day cricket (including ODIs and Twenty20 Internationals) for Netherlands. Scored 686 runs (av. 228.66) in the ICC Inter-Continental Cup 2006, recording four consecutive centuries, including twin hundreds (138/100) v Bermuda and a competition record 259* (plus match figures of 6-20/3-92) v Canada, both in Pretoria. His match awards include Man of the Match v Bermuda in Nairobi in the ICC World Cricket League 2006-07 (3-37/109*). Shortlisted for the ICC Associate ODI Player of the Year 2007; ICC Associate Player of the Year 2008. Leading first-class wicket-taker for Essex 2008. Is not considered an overseas player

Best batting: 259* Netherlands v Canada, Pretoria (SCC) 2006
Best bowling: 6-20 Netherlands v Canada, Pretoria (SCC) 2006

2008 Season

	M	Inn	NO	Runs	HS	Avg	100	50	Ct	St	Balls	Runs	Wkts	Avg	BB	5I	10M
Test																	
FC	17	24	2	860	146	39.09	2	4	10	-	1686	992	43	23.06	6-57	2	-
ODI																	
List A	17	14	3	467	99 *	42.45	-	4	5	-	470	464	15	30.93	3-30	-	
20/20 Int																	
20/20	12	10	1	138	35	15.33	-	-	1	-	215	243	13	18.69	4-24	-	

Career Performances

	M	Inn	NO	Runs	HS	Avg	100	50	Ct	St	Balls	Runs	Wkts	Avg	BB	5I	10M
Test																	
FC	55	75	8	3309	259 *	49.38	13	10	30	-	5063	3398	102	33.31	6-20	4	-
ODI	19	18	5	662	109 *	50.92	1	4	7	-	873	713	35	20.37	4-31	-	
List A	89	71	20	2085	109 *	40.88	1	12	31	-	2136	1913	90	21.25	5-50	1	
20/20 Int	3	3	1	84	56	42.00	-	1	1	-	72	67	6	11.16	3-23	-	
20/20	44	36	11	585	56	23.40	-	1	14	-	420	492	24	20.50	4-24	-	

THOMAS, A. C. — Somerset

Name: Alfonso Clive Thomas
Role: Right-hand bat, right-arm fast-medium bowler
Born: 9 February 1977, Cape Town, South Africa
County debut: 2007 (Warwickshire), 2008 (Somerset)
Twenty20 Int debut: 2006-07
Place in batting averages: 209th av. 19.25 (2007 204th av. 21.66)
Place in bowling averages: 51st av. 27.23 (2007 103rd av. 36.70)
Overseas tours: South Africa VI to Hong Kong 2001; South Africa A to Zimbabwe 2004, 2006-07; South Africa to India 2004-05; South Africa Emerging Players to Australia (Cricket Australia Emerging Players Tournament) 2006

Overseas teams played for: Western Province B 1998-99; North West 2000-01 – 2002-03; Northerns 2003-04 – 2005-06; Titans 2003-04 – 2006-07; Dolphins 2003-04 –
Extras: Played for South African Board President's XI v India A 2001-02, for South Africa A v India A 2001-02 and v England XI 2004-05, and for Rest of South Africa v Indians 2006-07. His match awards include Man of the Match v Dolphins at Pietermaritzburg in the SuperSport Series 2006-07 (5-55/2-46) and v Lions at Potchefstroom in the SuperSport Series 2006-07 (4-43/3-67 plus 54). Played for Staffordshire in the C&G 2005. Was a temporary overseas player with Warwickshire during August and September 2007. Signed for Somerset in February 2008
Best batting: 119* North West v Northerns, Centurion 2002-03
Best bowling: 7-54 Titans v Cape Cobras, Cape Town 2005-06

2008 Season

	M	Inn	NO	Runs	HS	Avg	100	50	Ct	St	Balls	Runs	Wkts	Avg	BB	5I	10M
Test																	
FC	11	15	3	231	43	19.25	-	-	4	-	1520	817	30	27.23	5-46	2	-
ODI																	
List A	12	9	6	46	16	15.33	-	-	1	-	540	497	15	33.13	2-23	-	
20/20 Int																	
20/20	8	2	1	1	1 *	1.00	-	-	3	-	158	170	11	15.45	4-27	-	

Career Performances

	M	Inn	NO	Runs	HS	Avg	100	50	Ct	St	Balls	Runs	Wkts	Avg	BB	5I	10M
Test																	
FC	83	123	26	2492	119 *	25.69	2	8	29	-	15514	7136	269	26.52	7-54	13	1
ODI																	
List A	92	54	25	425	27 *	14.65	-	-	15	-	4148	3337	107	31.18	4-31	-	
20/20 Int	1	0	0	0	0		-	-	-	-	24	25	3	8.33	3-25	-	
20/20	36	9	4	61	27	12.20	-	-	9	-	656	824	31	26.58	4-27	-	

88. In 2005, who said: "I was a gibbering wreck when I went out. But once I got out there with Pietersen he was absolutely brilliant ….. I'll love him forever." ?

THOMPSON, J. G. — Gloucestershire

Name: Jackson Gladwin Thompson
Role: Left-hand bat, right-arm off-spin bowler, occasional wicket-keeper
Born: 7 February 1986, Ozar Township, India
Height: 6ft 4in **Weight:** 16st
Nickname: Jacko, 'will also answer to "Zino"'
County debut: 2007
County cap: 2007
Parents: Gladwin and Balarojamma
Marital status: Single
Family links with cricket: 'Cousin plays for Mumbai'
Education: St Benedict's Sports College; University of Gloucestershire (studying for BSc in Computer Science)
Qualifications: 12 GCSEs, 3 A-levels
Overseas tours: Oman U17 to Bangladesh (Asia Cricket Council U17 Asia Cup) 2000-01
Cricket moments to forget: 'Misfield on first-class debut for Gloucestershire that went for a boundary'
Cricket superstitions: 'None'
Cricketers particularly admired: Matthew Hayden
Young players to look out for: Isaac Reid, James Campbell
Other sports played: Football ('occasional')
Other sports followed: Football (Arsenal)
Relaxations: 'Internet surfing'
Extras: Played for Gloucestershire Board XI in the 2003 C&G. Gloucestershire CCC Academy Player of the Year 2006
Opinions on cricket: 'Fast, demanding and commercial.'
Best batting: 21 Gloucestershire v Middlesex, Bristol 2007

2008 Season

	M	Inn	NO	Runs	HS	Avg	100	50	Ct	St	Balls	Runs	Wkts	Avg	BB	5I	10M
Test																	
FC																	
ODI																	
List A																	
20/20 Int																	
20/20	4	4	0	22	22	5.50	-	-	3	-	0	0	0		-	-	

Career Performances

	M	Inn	NO	Runs	HS	Avg	100	50	Ct	St	Balls	Runs	Wkts	Avg	BB	5I	10M
Test																	
FC	1	2	0	32	21	16.00	-	-	-	-	0	0	0		-	-	
ODI																	
List A	2	2	0	8	7	4.00	-	-	-	-	0	0	0		-	-	
20/20 Int																	
20/20	4	4	0	22	22	5.50	-	-	3	-	0	0	0		-	-	

THORNELY, M. A. Sussex

Name: Michael Alistair Thornely
Role: Right-hand top-order bat, right-arm fast-medium bowler
Born: 19 October 1987, London
Height: 6ft 1in **Weight:** 13st
Nickname: T-Bone, A-Bomb, Chubs, Thorners
County debut: 2007
1st-Class 200s: 1
Parents: Richard and Jan
Marital status: Single
Family links with cricket: 'Uncle played for Cambridgeshire'
Education: Brighton College
Qualifications: 8 GCSEs, 3 A-levels
Overseas tours: Brighton College to Sri Lanka; Sussex Academy to Cape Town 2003, 2005; Sussex to Mumbai 2004
Overseas teams played for: Subiaco Marist CC, Perth 2007-08
Career highlights to date: '150 v Essex 2nd XI for Sussex 2nd XI 2007'
Cricket moments to forget: 'Forgetting my whites for my first county game (U11) and getting a first-ball duck'
Cricket superstitions: 'Not superstitious'
Cricketers particularly admired: Mark Waugh, Michael Vaughan, Kevin Pietersen
Young players to look out for: Matt Machan, Ben Brown, Will Beer
Other sports played: Rugby (Sussex)
Other sports followed: Football (Man United), rugby (Harlequins)
Favourite band: Red Hot Chili Peppers, Razorlight, Justin Timberlake
Relaxations: 'Listening to music, watching movies, seeing friends'
Extras: Scored 1350 runs for Brighton College 2005, including six centuries. Scored more than 800 runs for Sussex 2nd XI in 2007

Opinions on cricket: 'I like the way the Twenty20 format has affected the longer forms of the game, with players inventing new shots and increasing scoring rates resulting in a more appealing game.'
Best batting: 11 Sussex v Indians, Hove 2007

2008 Season

	M	Inn	NO	Runs	HS	Avg	100	50	Ct	St	Balls	Runs	Wkts	Avg	BB	5I	10M
Test																	
FC	2	4	1	13	6 *	4.33	-	-	2	-	24	25	0		-	-	-
ODI																	
List A																	
20/20 Int																	
20/20																	

Career Performances

	M	Inn	NO	Runs	HS	Avg	100	50	Ct	St	Balls	Runs	Wkts	Avg	BB	5I	10M
Test																	
FC	4	7	1	28	11	4.66	-	-	6	-	24	25	0		-	-	-
ODI																	
List A	1	0	0	0	0		-	-	-	-	0	0	0		-	-	
20/20 Int																	
20/20																	

89. How old was Colin Cowdrey when he faced up to the pace of Lillee and Thomson at Perth in 1974?

THORP, C. D. Durham

Name: Callum David Thorp
Role: Right-hand bat, right-arm fast-medium bowler
Born: 11 January 1975, Perth, Western Australia
Height: 6ft 3in **Weight:** 13st 5lbs
County debut: 2005
Place in batting averages: 242nd av. 13.18
Place in bowling averages: 10th av. 19.62
Parents: Annette and David
Marital status: Single
Education: Servite College, Western Australia
Overseas teams played for: Western Warriors 2002-03 – 2003-04; Wanneroo DCC
Cricket superstitions: 'Left shoe on first'
Cricketers particularly admired: Mike Hussey
Young players to look out for: Graham Onions, Luke Evans
Other sports followed: AFL (West Coast Eagles), football (West Ham United)
Relaxations: 'Golf'
Extras: Took 4-58 for Western Australia v England XI in two-day match at Perth 2002-03. Attended Commonwealth Bank [Australian] Cricket Academy 2003. Took 6-17 v Scotland at The Grange in the C&G 2006, the best one-day figures for Durham since the county gained first-class status, following up with 100 runs (75/28) and ten wickets (6-55/5-42) in the Championship match v Hampshire at The Rose Bowl later that week. His second-innings figures of 7-88 v Kent in September 2008 made a major contribution to the win that confirmed Durham as 2008 County Champions. Has British parents and is not considered an overseas player
Best batting: 75 Durham v Hampshire, Rose Bowl 2006
Best bowling: 7-88 Durham v Kent , Canterbury 2008

2008 Season

	M	Inn	NO	Runs	HS	Avg	100	50	Ct	St	Balls	Runs	Wkts	Avg	BB	5I	10M
Test																	
FC	12	15	4	145	29 *	13.18	-	-	6	-	1928	981	50	19.62	7-88	3	-
ODI																	
List A	6	4	1	28	13	9.33	-	-	2	-	298	166	8	20.75	2-16	-	
20/20 Int																	
20/20																	

Career Performances

	M	Inn	NO	Runs	HS	Avg	100	50	Ct	St	Balls	Runs	Wkts	Avg	BB	5I	10M
Test																	
FC	37	54	7	626	75	13.31	-	2	15	-	5541	2870	109	26.33	7-88	5	1
ODI																	
List A	35	22	7	261	52	17.40	-	1	6	-	1633	1176	45	26.13	6-17	1	
20/20 Int																	
20/20	9	6	0	63	13	10.50	-	-	1	-	162	266	3	88.66	2-32	-	

TOMLINSON, J. A. Hampshire

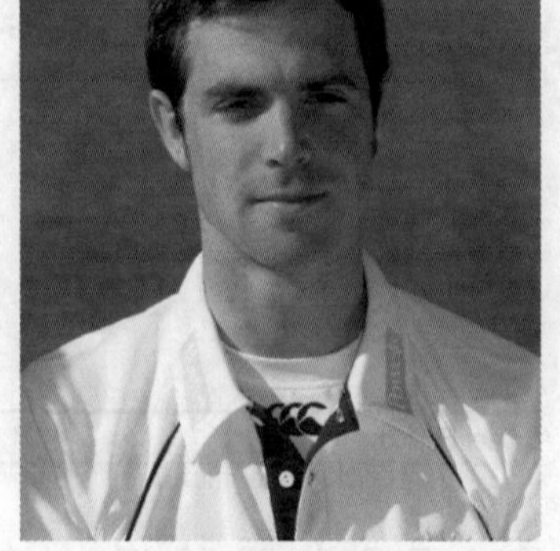

Name: James Andrew Tomlinson
Role: Left-hand lower-order bat, left-arm fast-medium bowler
Born: 12 June 1982, Winchester
Height: 6ft 1in **Weight:** 12st 7lbs
Nickname: Tommo, T-Bird, Mr T, Dangerous Dave
County debut: 2002
Place in batting averages: 233rd av. 14.50
Place in bowling averages: 33rd av. 24.76 (2007 116th av. 40.61)
Parents: Ian and Janet
Marital status: Single
Family links with cricket: 'Both grandads played at a high level in Yorkshire leagues. Brothers Ralph (Dulwich CC) and Hugh (Winterslow CC) both play, and have given me great support throughout my career'
Education: Harrow Way Community School, Andover; Cricklade College, Andover; Cardiff University
Qualifications: 3 A-levels, 2.1 degree in Education and Psychology
Career outside cricket: 'Patient!'
Off-season: 'Another operation on my ankle. Golf, fitness work'
Overseas teams played for: South Perth 2004-05, 2006-07
Career highlights to date: '35* v Lancashire 2008; 8-46 v Somerset 2008. Being leading wicket-taker with 67 championship victims in 2008. The last two months of the 2008 season were an amazing experience.'
Cricket moments to forget: 'Tearing a rib muscle on the first day of the 2005 season. Any dropped catch'
Cricket superstitions: 'None'

Cricketers particularly admired: Wasim Akram, Shane Warne, Darren Gough, Dimitri Mascarenhas, Malcolm Marshall, Robin Smith, Ryan Sidebottom
Young players to look out for: Chris Wood, James Vince
Other sports played: Golf, darts
Other sports followed: Football (West Ham United)
Favourite band: U2
Relaxations: 'Ornithology, wildlife in general'
Extras: Played for Development of Excellence XI (South) 2001. Played for Cardiff UCCE 2002-03. Represented British Universities 2002-03. NBC Denis Compton Award for the most promising young Hampshire player 2003. Cardiff University Sportsperson of the Year award 2003. Leading first-class wicket-taker for his county in 2008. Hampshire Player of the Season 2008
Opinions on cricket: 'Keep limiting Kolpak and non-English qualified players. Encourage home-grown talent. 2nd XI cricket should be four-day and Twenty20, not three-day.'
Best batting: 35* Hampshire v Lancashire, Rose Bowl 2008
Best bowling: 8-46 Hampshire v Somerset, Taunton 2008

2008 Season

	M	Inn	NO	Runs	HS	Avg	100	50	Ct	St	Balls	Runs	Wkts	Avg	BB	5I	10M
Test																	
FC	16	20	10	145	35 *	14.50	-	-	4	-	2786	1659	67	24.76	8-46	4	1
ODI																	
List A	2	1	0	3	3	3.00	-	-	-	-	54	64	2	32.00	2-24	-	
20/20 Int																	
20/20																	

Career Performances

	M	Inn	NO	Runs	HS	Avg	100	50	Ct	St	Balls	Runs	Wkts	Avg	BB	5I	10M
Test																	
FC	38	50	23	240	35 *	8.88	-	-	10	-	6110	3918	114	34.36	8-46	6	1
ODI																	
List A	22	12	4	18	6	2.25	-	-	3	-	887	715	20	35.75	4-47	-	
20/20 Int																	
20/20	2	1	0	5	5	5.00	-	-	-	-	42	48	1	48.00	1-20	-	

TOOR, K. S. Middlesex

Name: Kabir Singh Toor
Role: Right-hand bat, leg-spin bowler
Born: 30 April 1990, Watford, Hertfordshire
County debut: No first-team appearance
Education: John Lyon School, Harrow
Extras: Made 2nd XI Championship debut 2006. Played for Middlesex U17. Played for South U17 in ECB U17 Regional Festival at Loughborough 2007. Plays for Radlett CC

TREDWELL, J. C. Kent

Name: James Cullum Tredwell
Role: Left-hand bat, right-arm off-spin bowler
Born: 27 February 1982, Ashford, Kent
Height: 5ft 11in **Weight:** 14st 2lbs
Nickname: Tredders, Pingu, Chad
County debut: 2001
County cap: 2007
Place in batting averages: 178th av. 22.57 (2007 166th av. 26.70)
Place in bowling averages: 142nd av. 49.14 (2007 100th av. 35.69)
Parents: John and Rosemary
Marital status: Single
Family links with cricket: Father played for Ashford and Folkestone in Kent League
Education: Southlands Community Comprehensive
Qualifications: 10 GCSEs, 2 A-levels, ECB Level 1 coach

Overseas tours: Kent U17 to Sri Lanka 1998-99; Kent to Port Elizabeth 2002; England A to Malaysia and India 2003-04; England Performance Programme to India 2007-08; England to New Zealand 2007-08 (one-day series)
Overseas teams played for: Redlands Tigers, Brisbane 2000-02
Cricket moments to forget: 'Being hit for six in a crucial B&H Cup match v Essex, which probably cost Kent's qualification to next stage'
Cricketers particularly admired: 'All the great spinners'
Extras: Represented England U19 2001 (captain in second 'Test'). Kent Most Improved Player Award 2003. NBC Denis Compton Award for the most promising young Kent player 2003. ECB National Academy 2003-04. Took over captaincy of England A in India 2003-04 after Alex Gidman was forced to return home with a hand injury. Chosen for the MCC team that played champions Sussex in the opening fixture of the 2008 season.
Best batting: 123* Kent v New Zealand, Canterbury 2008
Best bowling: 6-47 Kent v Surrey, Canterbury 2007

2008 Season

	M	Inn	NO	Runs	HS	Avg	100	50	Ct	St	Balls	Runs	Wkts	Avg	BB	5I	10M
Test																	
FC	18	29	3	587	123*	22.57	1	3	20	-	2378	1327	27	49.14	3-19	-	-
ODI																	
List A	18	11	7	57	20*	14.25	-	-	6	-	568	500	15	33.33	4-32	-	
20/20 Int																	
20/20	13	5	4	6	2*	6.00-	-	7	-	246	264	16	16.50	3-9	-		

Career Performances

	M	Inn	NO	Runs	HS	Avg	100	50	Ct	St	Balls	Runs	Wkts	Avg	BB	5I	10M
Test																	
FC	71	103	12	1994	123*	21.91	2	8	72	-	11290	6364	154	41.32	6-47	3	1
ODI																	
List A	122	90	33	1108	88	19.43	-	4	56	-	4788	3771	116	32.50	4-16	-	
20/20 Int																	
20/20	50	27	6	252	34	12.00	-	-	19	-	852	1046	44	23.77	4-21	-	

TREGO, P. D. Somerset

Name: Peter David Trego
Role: Right-hand bat, right-arm fast-medium/occasional leg-break bowler; all-rounder
Born: 12 June 1981, Weston-super-Mare
Height: 6ft **Weight:** 13st 7lbs
Nickname: Tregs, Steve the Pirate, Pikey, Ying
County debut: 2000 (Somerset), 2003 (Kent), 2005 (Middlesex)
County cap: 2007 (Somerset)
Place in batting averages: 51st av. 42.45 (2007 28th av. 52.25)
Place in bowling averages: 34th av. 24.78 (2007 94th av. 34.27)
Parents: Carol and Paul
Wife and date of marriage: Claire, 8 May 2000
Children: Amelia Ann, 9 July 2001; Davis Paul, 8 February 2005; Dexter Gerard, 15 November 2007
Family links with cricket: 'Brother on staff at Somerset 1997; unlucky not to get a better go – batter and off-spin bowler'
Education: Wyvern Comprehensive, Weston-super-Mare
Qualifications: 'School of Life'
Career outside cricket: 'Being a dad, and thinking about life after cricket'
Off-season: 'Training, and just trying to improve everything about my game.'
Overseas tours: Somerset to Cape Town 2000, 2001, 2006, to India 2007, to Abu Dhabi 2008
Career highlights to date: 'County cap 10 June 2007'
Cricket moments to forget: 'All of 2003'
Cricket superstitions: 'None'
Cricketers particularly admired: Ian Botham, Graham Rose, Justin Langer, Andrew Caddick, Marcus Trescothick, Ian Blackwell
Young players to look out for: James Hildreth, 'my sons'
Other sports played: Football (semi-professional with Weston-super-Mare and Margate FC), golf (Weston-super-Mare first team; 2 handicap)
Other sports followed: Football (Man Utd), golf (Tiger Woods)
Favourite band: Kings of Leon, Metallica, Elvis
Relaxations: 'Trampolining with the kids'
Extras: Represented England U19. NBC Denis Compton Award for the most promising young Somerset player 2000. Scored 140 at Taunton 2002 as Somerset,

chasing 454 to win, tied with West Indies A. 'I'm very proud of being the first player ever to incur a five-run penalty for replacing Jamie Cox and nobody thinking to tell Mr Dudleston.' 'Played football in the FA Cup on *Match of the Day* – that was cool up until the part where I was 'megged to let in the goal to send us out; but still got Star Man in the paper.' Left Middlesex at the end of the 2005 season and rejoined Somerset for 2006. Scored 63-ball 78 and took 4-61 v Middlesex at Lord's in the Friends Provident 2007. Wetherall All-rounder of the Year 2007

Opinions on cricket: 'Just hope that the long form of the game is looked after as much as the short. I will personally be as proud, if not more proud, of my first-class record when I hang my boots up. It's the true test of your skill...'

Best batting: 140 Somerset v West Indies A, Taunton 2002

Best bowling: 6-59 Middlesex v Nottinghamshire, Trent Bridge 2005

2008 Season

	M	Inn	NO	Runs	HS	Avg	100	50	Ct	St	Balls	Runs	Wkts	Avg	BB	5I	10M
Test																	
FC	16	23	3	849	86	42.45	-	7	3	-	1160	694	28	24.78	4-52	-	-
ODI																	
List A	11	8	1	194	56 *	27.71	-	1	5	-	493	467	12	38.91	3-37	-	
20/20 Int																	
20/20	8	8	0	225	79	28.12	-	1	3	-	0	0	0		-	-	

Career Performances

	M	Inn	NO	Runs	HS	Avg	100	50	Ct	St	Balls	Runs	Wkts	Avg	BB	5I	10M
Test																	
FC	67	97	13	3049	140	36.29	6	17	20	-	6917	4638	125	37.10	6-59	1	-
ODI																	
List A	70	58	10	758	78	15.79	-	2	18	-	2304	2198	69	31.85	5-44	1	
20/20 Int																	
20/20	23	22	3	423	79	22.26	-	1	5	-	206	302	13	23.23	2-17	-	

90. Prior to Mike Atherton captaining England for the 42nd time during the 1997 Ashes series, who held the record for the greatest number of Test sides captained?

TREMLETT, C. T. Hampshire

Name: Christopher (Chris) Timothy Tremlett
Role: Right-hand bat, right-arm fast-medium bowler
Born: 2 September 1981, Southampton
Height: 6ft 7in **Weight:** 16st 1lb
Nickname: Twiggy, Goober
County debut: 2000
County cap: 2004
Test debut: 2007
ODI debut: 2005
Twenty20 Int debut: 2007-08
Place in batting averages: 215th av. 17.58 (2007 147th av. 29.00)
Place in bowling averages: 103rd av. 34.54 (2007 90th av. 33.96)
Parents: Timothy and Carolyn
Marital status: Single
Family links with cricket: Grandfather [Maurice] played for Somerset and in three Tests for England. Father played for Hampshire and is now director of cricket at the county
Education: Thornden School, Chandlers Ford; Taunton's College, Southampton
Qualifications: 5 GCSEs, BTEC National Diploma in Sports Science, Level 2 coach
Overseas tours: West of England U15 to West Indies 1997; Hampshire U16 to Jersey; England U17 to Northern Ireland (ECC Colts Festival) 1999; England U19 to India 2000-01; ECB National Academy to Australia 2001-02, to Australia and Sri Lanka 2002-03; England VI to Hong Kong 2004; England to Australia 2006-07 (C'wealth Bank Series), to South Africa (World 20/20) 2007-08, to Sri Lanka 2007-08 (one-day series), to New Zealand 2007-08 (one-day series); England Performance Programme to India 2007-08
Cricketers particularly admired: Glenn McGrath, Mark Waugh, Shane Warne
Other sports played: Basketball, volleyball
Other sports followed: Football (Arsenal)
Relaxations: 'Socialising with friends; cinema'
Extras: Took wicket (Mark Richardson) with first ball in first-class cricket v New Zealand A at Portsmouth 2000; finished with debut match figures of 6-91. Represented England U19. NBC Denis Compton Award for the most promising young Hampshire player 2000, 2001. Hampshire Young Player of the Year 2001. Took Championship hat-trick (Ealham, Swann, G. Smith) v Nottinghamshire at Trent Bridge 2005. ECB National Academy 2006-07. Played against New Zealand in the 2008 ODI series
Best batting: 64 Hampshire v Gloucestershire, Rose Bowl 2005
Best bowling: 6-44 Hampshire v Sussex, Hove 2005

2008 Season

	M	Inn	NO	Runs	HS	Avg	100	50	Ct	St	Balls	Runs	Wkts	Avg	BB	5I	10M
Test																	
FC	13	19	2	299	60	17.58	-	3	6	-	2300	1071	31	34.54	5-67	1	-
ODI	1	1	0	3	3	3.00	-	-	1	-	60	24	1	24.00	1-24	-	
List A	9	4	0	16	9	4.00	-	-	2	-	440	376	10	37.60	3-54	-	
20/20 Int																	
20/20	4	2	1	10	8	10.00	-	-	-	-	94	106	7	15.14	4-25	-	

Career Performances

	M	Inn	NO	Runs	HS	Avg	100	50	Ct	St	Balls	Runs	Wkts	Avg	BB	5I	10M
Test	3	5	1	50	25 *	12.50	-	-	1	-	859	386	13	29.69	3-12	-	-
FC	85	114	31	1563	64	18.83	-	6	25	-	14343	7719	275	28.06	6-44	7	-
ODI	9	6	2	38	19 *	9.50	-	-	2	-	479	419	9	46.55	4-32	-	
List A	104	61	17	389	38 *	8.84	-	-	21	-	4825	3744	147	25.46	4-25	-	
20/20 Int	1	0	0	0	0		-	-	-	-	24	45	2	22.50	2-45	-	
20/20	21	11	4	58	13	8.28	-	-	4	-	436	525	28	18.75	4-25	-	

TRESCOTHICK, M. E. Somerset

Name: Marcus Edward Trescothick
Role: Left-hand bat, right-arm swing bowler, reserve wicket-keeper; county vice-captain
Born: 25 December 1975, Keynsham, Bristol
Height: 6ft 3in **Weight:** 14st 7lbs
Nickname: Banger, Tres
County debut: 1993
County cap: 1999
Benefit: 2008
Test debut: 2000
ODI debut: 2000
Twenty20 Int debut: 2005
1000 runs in a season: 1
1st-Class 200s: 2
Place in batting averages: 38th av. 46.59 (2007 10th av. 61.04)
Parents: Martyn and Lin
Wife and date of marriage: Hayley, 24 January 2004
Children: Ellie, April 2005
Family links with cricket: Father played for Somerset 2nd XI; uncle played club cricket

Education: Sir Bernard Lovell School, Bristol
Qualifications: 7 GCSEs
Overseas tours: England U18 to South Africa 1992-93; England U19 to Sri Lanka 1993-94, to West Indies 1994-95 (c); England A to Bangladesh and New Zealand 1999-2000; England to Kenya (ICC Knockout Trophy) 2000-01, to Pakistan and Sri Lanka 2000-01, to Zimbabwe (one-day series) 2001-02, to India and New Zealand 2001-02, to Sri Lanka (ICC Champions Trophy) 2002-03, to Australia 2002-03, to Africa (World Cup) 2002-03, to Bangladesh and Sri Lanka 2003-04, to West Indies 2003-04, to South Africa 2004-05, to Pakistan 2005-06, to India 2005-06, to Australia 2006-07
Overseas teams played for: Melville CC, Perth 1997-99
Cricketers particularly admired: Adam Gilchrist, Andy Caddick
Other sports followed: Golf, football (Bristol City FC)
Relaxations: 'Spending time at home, playing golf'
Extras: Scored more than 1000 runs for England U19. Took hat-trick (Gilchrist, Angel, McIntyre) for Somerset v Young Australia at Taunton 1995. NBC Denis Compton Award for the most promising young Somerset player 1996, 1997. PCA Player of the Year 2000. Sports.com Cricketer of the Year 2001. BBC West Country Sports Sportsman of the Year 2001. One of *Indian Cricket*'s five Cricketers of the Year 2002. Scored 114* v South Africa at The Oval in the NatWest Series 2003, sharing with Vikram Solanki (106) in a record England opening partnership in ODIs (200). Scored century in each innings (105/107) in the second Test v West Indies at Edgbaston 2004. Man of the Match in his 100th ODI v Bangladesh at The Oval in the NatWest Series 2005 (100*). His Test awards include England's Man of the Series v Bangladesh 2005 and Man of the Match in the fifth Test v South Africa at The Oval 2003 (219/69*). His other ODI awards include Man of the Series v West Indies 2003-04 and Man of the Match v Australia at Headingley in the NatWest Challenge 2005 (104*). One of *Wisden*'s Five Cricketers of the Year 2005. Appointed MBE in 2006 New Year Honours as part of 2005 Ashes-winning England team. Announced his retirement from international cricket in March 2008. Topped the Somerset batting averages in all forms of cricket in 2008. His autobiography, *Coming Back To Me*, won the William Hill Sports Book of the Year Award in November 2008
Best batting: 284 Somerset v Northamptonshire, Northampton 2007
Best bowling: 4-36 Somerset v Young Australia, Taunton 1995

2008 Season

	M	Inn	NO	Runs	HS	Avg	100	50	Ct	St	Balls	Runs	Wkts	Avg	BB	5I	10M
Test																	
FC	16	28	1	1258	158	46.59	3	8	19	-	0	0	0		-	-	-
ODI																	
List A	15	14	0	603	184	43.07	2	2	1	-	0	0	0		-	-	
20/20 Int																	
20/20	8	8	0	306	107	38.25	1	1	6	-	0	0	0		-	-	

Career Performances

	M	Inn	NO	Runs	HS	Avg	100	50	Ct	St	Balls	Runs	Wkts	Avg	BB	5I	10M
Test	76	143	10	5825	219	43.79	14	29	95	-	300	155	1	155.00	1-34	-	-
FC	239	412	21	14828	284	37.92	31	76	293	-	2674	1541	36	42.80	4-36	-	-
ODI	123	122	6	4335	137	37.37	12	21	49	-	232	219	4	54.75	2-7	-	
List A	303	290	23	9976	184	37.36	26	46	112	-	2004	1636	57	28.70	4-50	-	
20/20 Int	3	3	0	166	72	55.33	-	2	2	-	0	0	0		-	-	
20/20	18	18	0	701	107	38.94	1	5	11	-	0	0	0		-	-	

TROTT, I. J. L. Warwickshire

Name: Ian Jonathan Leonard Trott
Role: Right-hand bat, right-arm medium bowler; all-rounder
Born: 22 April 1981, Cape Town, South Africa
Height: 6ft **Weight:** 13st 5lbs
Nickname: Booger
County debut: 2003
County cap: 2005
Twenty20 Int debut: 2007
1000 runs in a season: 3
1st-Class 200s: 1
Place in batting averages: 5th av. 62.00 (2007 199th av. 22.52)
Place in bowlng averages: 140th av. 46.30
Parents: Ian and Donna
Marital status: Single
Family links with cricket: Father a professional cricket coach. Brother (Kenny Jackson) played for Western Province and Boland. Is related to the late-19th-century Test cricketers Albert (Australia and England) and Harry Trott (Australia)
Education: Rondebosch Boys' High School; Stellenbosch University
Qualifications: Level 2 coaching
Overseas tours: South Africa U15 to England (U15 World Cup) 1996; South Africa U19 to Pakistan 1998-99, to Sri Lanka (U19 World Cup) 1999-2000; England Performance Programme to India 2007-08; England Lions to India 2007-08, to New Zealand 2008-09
Overseas teams played for: Boland 1999-2000 – 2000-01; Western Province 2001-02; Otago 2005-06
Cricket superstitions: 'Personal'
Cricketers particularly admired: Sachin Tendulkar, Adam Hollioake, Steve Waugh

Other sports played: Hockey (Western Province U16, U18, U21), golf
Other sports followed: Football (Tottenham Hotspur)
Favourite band: Roxette, Robbie Williams
Relaxations: 'Music, watching sport'
Extras: Represented South Africa A. Struck 245 on debut for Warwickshire 2nd XI v Somerset 2nd XI at Knowle & Dorridge 2002. Scored century (134) on Championship debut for Warwickshire v Sussex at Edgbaston 2003. Became the first player to bat for the full 20 overs in the Twenty20, for a 54-ball 65* v Gloucestershire at Edgbaston 2003. Represented England Lions 2007. Called up to England's ODI squad, June 2007. Scored over 2000 runs in all competitions during the 2008 season
Best batting: 210 Warwickshire v Sussex, Edgbaston 2005
Best bowling: 7-39 Warwickshire v Kent, Canterbury 2003

2008 Season

	M	Inn	NO	Runs	HS	Avg	100	50	Ct	St	Balls	Runs	Wkts	Avg	BB	5I	10M
Test																	
FC	16	25	5	1240	181	62.00	3	6	16	-	917	463	10	46.30	3-44	-	-
ODI																	
List A	14	14	3	546	120*	49.63	2	3	6	-	132	130	6	21.66	2-17	-	
20/20 Int																	
20/20	11	10	3	268	61*	38.28	-	2	3	-	0	0	0		-	-	

Career Performances

	M	Inn	NO	Runs	HS	Avg	100	50	Ct	St	Balls	Runs	Wkts	Avg	BB	5I	10M
Test																	
FC	116	196	21	7102	210	40.58	14	37	116	-	3396	1904	44	43.27	7-39	1	-
ODI																	
List A	131	122	26	4019	125*	41.86	8	24	43	-	1123	1064	42	25.33	4-55	-	
20/20 Int	2	2	0	11	9	5.50-	-	-	-	0	0	0		-	-		
20/20	45	40	10	1086	75*	36.20	-	5	13	-	132	200	7	28.57	2-19	-	

91. Who wrote a television play entitled *The Final Test*? It was later made into a film, starring Jack Warner.

TROUGHTON, J. O. — Warwickshire

Name: Jamie (Jim) Oliver Troughton
Role: Left-hand bat, slow left-arm bowler
Born: 2 March 1979, London
Height: 5ft 11in **Weight:** 13st
Nickname: Troughts
County debut: 2001
County cap: 2002
ODI debut: 2003
1000 runs in a season: 1
Place in batting averages: 26th av. 49.80 (2007 59th av. 42.83)
Parents: Ali and David
Wife and date of marriage: Naomi, 28 September 2002
Children: Eva, February 2007
Family links with cricket: Father was a Middlesex Colt. Great-grandfather Henry Crichton played for Warwickshire. 'Younger brother is a Stratford Panther'
Education: Trinity School, Leamington Spa; Birmingham University
Qualifications: 3 A-levels, BSc Sport & Exercise Psychology, Level 1 coaching
Career outside cricket: 'Work in progress'
Overseas tours: Warwickshire Development of Excellence squad to Cape Town; MCC to Australia and Singapore 2001; ECB National Academy to Australia and Sri Lanka 2002-03
Overseas teams played for: Harvinia CC, Bloemfontein, South Africa 2000; Avendale CC, Cape Town 2001-02; Belville CC, Cape Town 2003-04; Claremont-Nedlands CC, Perth 2004-05
Career highlights to date: 'B&H final 2002, England call-up 2003, county champions 2004, highest first-class score 2007'
Cricket superstitions: 'Don't leave straight ones'
Cricketers particularly admired: Brian Lara, Graham Thorpe, Nick Knight, Ashley Giles
Young players to look out for: Chris Woakes
Other sports played: Football (Stoke City youth player)
Other sports followed: 'Hooked on Manchester United since going to their soccer school aged five'
Favourite band: Stone Roses, Beatles, Red Hot Chili Peppers
Relaxations: 'Movies, music, going abroad'
Extras: Is grandson of *Dr Who* actor Patrick Troughton; father also an actor. County colours U12-U19. Has represented England U15, U16 and U17. Represented ECB

Midlands U19 1998. Has won the Alec Hastilow Trophy and the Coney Edmonds Trophy (Warwickshire awards). Warwickshire 2nd XI Player of the Year 2001. Scored 1067 first-class runs in his first full season 2002. NBC Denis Compton Award for the most promising young Warwickshire player 2002. Warwickshire Young Player and Most Improved Player of the Year 2002
Opinions on cricket: '[Should have] three main competitions – 50-over, Twenty20, four-day. Fewer games, therefore more intensity in those games.'
Best batting: 162 Warwickshire v Worcestershire, Worcester 2007
Best bowling: 3-1 Warwickshire v CUCCE, Fenner's 2004

2008 Season

	M	Inn	NO	Runs	HS	Avg	100	50	Ct	St	Balls	Runs	Wkts	Avg	BB	5I	10M
Test																	
FC	14	20	5	747	138 *	49.80	1	6	13	-	36	25	0		-	-	-
ODI																	
List A	9	9	1	214	87	26.75	-	1	2	-	0	0	0		-	-	
20/20 Int																	
20/20	11	10	1	254	57	28.22	-	1	5	-	6	3	0		-	-	

Career Performances

	M	Inn	NO	Runs	HS	Avg	100	50	Ct	St	Balls	Runs	Wkts	Avg	BB	5I	10M
Test																	
FC	93	143	14	5085	162	39.41	14	27	43	-	2359	1416	22	64.36	3-1	-	-
ODI	6	5	1	36	20	9.00	-	-	1	-	0	0	0		-	-	
List A	107	96	9	2411	115 *	27.71	2	11	38	-	736	644	25	25.76	4-23	-	
20/20 Int																	
20/20	40	35	2	646	57	19.57	-	2	16	-	96	127	6	21.16	2-10	-	

92. Sid Barnes made 234 against England in 1946.
Which other Australian batsman made exactly the same score in the same innings?

TUDOR, A. J. Surrey

Name: Alexander (Alex) Jeremy Tudor
Role: Right-hand bat, right-arm fast bowler
Born: 23 October 1977, West Brompton, London
Height: 6ft 4in **Weight:** 13st 7lbs
Nickname: Big Al, Bambi, Tudes
County debut: 1995 (Surrey), 2005 (Essex)
County cap: 1999 (Surrey)
Test debut: 1998-99
ODI debut: 2002
Place in batting averages: 206th av. 19.71 (2007 271st av. 11.20)
Place in bowling averages: 143rd av. 52.57 (99th av. 35.41)
Parents: Daryll and Jennifer
Marital status: Engaged to Francesca
Children: Sienna
Family links with cricket: Brother was on the staff at The Oval
Education: St Mark's C of E, Fulham; City of Westminster College
Overseas tours: England U15 to South Africa 1992-93; England U19 to Zimbabwe 1995-96, to Pakistan 1996-97; England to Australia 1998-99, to South Africa 1999-2000, to Pakistan 2000-01, to Australia 2002-03; England A to West Indies 2000-01; ECB National Academy to Australia 2001-02, 2002-03
Cricketers particularly admired: Curtly Ambrose, Brian Lara
Other sports followed: Basketball, football (QPR)
Relaxations: Listening to music
Extras: Played for London Schools at all ages from U8. Represented England U17. MCC Young Cricketer. Took 4-89 in Australia's first innings on Test debut at Perth 1998-99; his victims included both Waugh twins. Scored 99* in second innings of the first Test v New Zealand at Edgbaston 1999, bettering the highest score by a nightwatchman for England (Harold Larwood's 98 v Australia at Sydney 1932-33) and winning Man of the Match award. Cricket Writers' Club Young Cricketer of the Year 1999. Recorded match figures of 7-109 in the third Test v Sri Lanka at Old Trafford 2002, winning Man of the Match award. Rejoined Surrey from Essex in October 2008
Best batting: 144 Essex v Derbyshire, Chelmsford 2006
Best bowling: 7-48 Surrey v Lancashire, The Oval 2000

2008 Season

	M	Inn	NO	Runs	HS	Avg	100	50	Ct	St	Balls	Runs	Wkts	Avg	BB	5I	10M
Test																	
FC	9	15	1	276	68	19.71	-	1	1	-	1206	736	14	52.57	3-46	-	-
ODI																	
List A	5	3	2	22	16 *	22.00	-	-	-	-	150	162	4	40.50	2-38	-	
20/20 Int																	
20/20																	

Career Performances

	M	Inn	NO	Runs	HS	Avg	100	50	Ct	St	Balls	Runs	Wkts	Avg	BB	5I	10M
Test	10	16	4	229	99 *	19.08	-	1	3	-	1512	963	28	34.39	5-44	1	-
FC	125	163	32	2877	144	21.96	2	9	35	-	17591	10606	347	30.56	7-48	14	-
ODI	3	2	1	9	6	9.00	-	-	1	-	127	136	4	34.00	2-30	-	
List A	79	53	16	464	56	12.54	-	1	21	-	3337	2663	109	24.43	4-26	-	
20/20 Int																	
20/20																	

TURNER, K. Durham

Name: Karl Turner
Role: Left-hand bat, right-arm medium bowler
Born: 29 November 1987, Dryburn, Durham
County debut: No first-team appearance
Overseas tours: Durham Academy to Sri Lanka 2008-09
Extras: Played for Stockton CC in the North East Premier League 2008. Awarded a development contract with Durham 2009.

TURNER, M. L. Somerset

Name: Mark Leif Turner
Role: Right-hand lower-order bat, right-arm fast-medium bowler
Born: 23 October 1984, Sunderland
Height: 6ft **Weight:** 12st 12lbs
Nickname: Tina, Racing Pigeon, Gimp
County debut: 2005 (Durham), 2007 (Somerset)
Parents: Kenny and Eileen
Marital status: 'Living with partner'
Family links with cricket: 'Brother Ian played county juniors and was a well-respected local player'
Education: Thornhill Comprehensive School
Qualifications: 7 GCSEs, Level 2 coaching
Overseas tours: England U19 to Bangladesh (U19 World Cup) 2003-04; Durham to India 2004, to South Africa 2005, to Dubai 2005
Career highlights to date: 'Being part of the Somerset team that achieved double promotion'
Cricket moments to forget: 'Dropping a dolly on Sky for England U19'
Cricketers particularly admired: Allan Donald, Andrew Caddick, Marcus Trescothick, Sachin Tendulkar, Dale Benkenstein, Keith Parsons
Young players to look out for: James Hildreth, Ben Harmison, Mark Stoneman
Other sports played: Football (junior with Manchester Utd and Sunderland), golf, fishing
Other sports followed: Football (Sunderland AFC)
Favourite band: 'Anything that is neo-soul, old school R&B (Maxwell, Keith Sweat etc.)'
Extras: Represented England U19 2003 and 2004, returning match figures of 9-104 (5-57/4-47) in the second 'Test' v Bangladesh U19 at Taunton 2004. ECB Elite Fast Bowler Development Programme to Florida, 2008-09
Opinions on cricket: 'Two-division format is good and the difference between the two divisions is becoming stronger.'
Best batting: 57 Somerset v Derbyshire, Taunton 2007
Best bowling: 4-30 Somerset v LUCCE, Taunton 2007

2008 Season

	M	Inn	NO	Runs	HS	Avg	100	50	Ct	St	Balls	Runs	Wkts	Avg	BB	5I	10M
Test																	
FC	2	3	0	7	4	2.33	-	-	1	-	246	178	3	59.33	3-53	-	-
ODI																	
List A	3	1	1	8	8 *	-	-	-	-	-	133	139	6	23.16	3-39	-	
20/20 Int																	
20/20	8	3	0	9	7	3.00	-	-	-	-	156	231	9	25.66	2-22	-	

Career Performances

	M	Inn	NO	Runs	HS	Avg	100	50	Ct	St	Balls	Runs	Wkts	Avg	BB	5I	10M
Test																	
FC	8	8	2	89	57	14.83	-	1	2	-	1143	742	15	49.46	4-30	-	-
ODI																	
List A	9	5	3	23	11 *	11.50	-	-	-	-	375	359	11	32.63	3-39	-	
20/20 Int																	
20/20	13	6	2	12	7	3.00	-	-	1	-	222	337	10	33.70	2-22	-	

UDAL, S. D. — Middlesex

Name: Shaun David Udal
Role: Right-hand bat, off-spin bowler; county captain
Born: 18 March 1969, Farnborough, Hampshire
Height: 6ft 2in **Weight:** 14st
Nickname: Shaggy
County debut: 1989 (Hampshire)
County cap: 1992 (Hampshire)
Benefit: 2002 (Hampshire)
Test debut: 2005-06
ODI debut: 1994
50 wickets in a season: 7
Place in batting averages: 66th av. 39.71
Place in bowling averages: 96th av. 33.00 (2007 84th av. 33.50)
Parents: Robin and Mary
Wife and date of marriage: Emma, 5 October 1991
Children: Katherine Mary, 26 August 1992; Rebecca Jane, 17 November 1995; Jack David, 23 August 2004

Family links with cricket: 'Great-grandfather – MCC; grandfather [G. F. Udal] – Middlesex and Leicestershire; father – Camberley CC for 40 years; brother – captain Camberley CC'
Education: Cove Comprehensive, Farnborough
Qualifications: 8 CSEs, print finisher, company director
Off-season: 'Twenty20 Stanford Series, Champions League in India, speaking and working for Masuri.'
Career outside cricket: 'Media – printing company; Masuri helmets; clothing – graphics and embroidery'
Overseas tours: England to Australia 1994-95, to Pakistan 2005-06, to India 2005-06; England A to Pakistan 1995-96; England XI to New Zealand (Cricket Max) 1997; Hampshire to Anguilla 1998, to Cape Town 2001; Middlesex to Antigua for Stanford Super Series 2008-09
Overseas teams played for: Hamilton Wickham, Newcastle, NSW 1989-90
Career highlights to date: 'Captain of Hants in C&G final 2005. Being picked for England again aged 36. Twenty20 win, 2008.'
Cricket moments to forget: 'Getting out twice as nightwatchman, hooking'
Cricket superstitions: 'Left everything on first'
Cricketers particularly admired: Sir Ian Botham, Shane Warne, Robin Smith, Tim Murtagh
Young players to look out for: David Malan, Billy Godleman, Steve Finn, Danny Evans
Other sports played: Golf (14 handicap), football
Other sports followed: Football (West Ham Utd, Aldershot Town, Eastleigh FC)
Favourite band: Take That
Relaxations: 'My children, eating out, the odd beer!'
Extras: Scored double hundred for Camberley CC in 40-over game. Man of the Match on NatWest debut against Berkshire 1991. Hampshire Cricket Association Player of the Year 1993. Vice-captain of Hampshire 1998-2000. Hampshire Players' Player of the Year 2001, 2002. Skipper of Hampshire in C&G final at Lord's 2005, becoming the first Hampshire-born captain to lift silverware for the county. Had second innings figures of 4-14 as England defeated India in the third Test at Mumbai 2005-06. Leading wicket-taker for Hampshire in one-day cricket; all-time sixth-highest wicket-taker for Hampshire. President of Camberley CC. Retired at the end of the 2007 season but later accepted an invitation to join Middlesex for 2008. Captained Middlesex in the Stanford Series 2008; appointed county captain in September 2008.
Opinions on cricket: 'It's still a great game. Some of the younger players seem more interested in cars, phones, etc. than in performing on the pitch...'
Best batting: 117* Hampshire v Warwickshire, Southampton 1997
Best bowling: 8-50 Hampshire v Sussex, Southampton 1992

2008 Season

	M	Inn	NO	Runs	HS	Avg	100	50	Ct	St	Balls	Runs	Wkts	Avg	BB	5I	10M
Test																	
FC	14	20	6	556	91	39.71	-	4	1	-	2210	1122	34	33.00	5-36	1	-
ODI																	
List A	13	9	2	146	45	20.85	-	-	3	-	594	498	14	35.57	3-21	-	
20/20 Int																	
20/20	13	7	4	99	40 *	33.00	-	-	3	-	288	299	12	24.91	3-19	-	

Career Performances

	M	Inn	NO	Runs	HS	Avg	100	50	Ct	St	Balls	Runs	Wkts	Avg	BB	5I	10M
Test	4	7	1	109	33 *	18.16	-	-	1	-	596	344	8	43.00	4-14	-	-
FC	274	387	74	7317	117 *	23.37	1	32	117	-	50001	24771	758	32.67	8-50	34	4
ODI	11	7	4	35	11 *	11.66	-	-	1	-	612	400	9	44.44	2-37	-	
List A	384	247	77	2702	78	15.89	-	8	124	-	17677	13028	432	30.15	5-43	1	
20/20 Int																	
20/20	38	25	11	287	40 *	20.50	-	-	10	-	753	856	37	23.13	3-19	-	

VAN DER WATH, J. J. Northamptonshire

Name: Johannes Jacobus van der Wath
Role: Right-hand bat, right-arm fast-medium bowler; all-rounder
Born: 10 January 1978, Newcastle, Natal, South Africa
County debut: 2005 (Sussex), 2007 (Northamptonshire)
ODI debut: 2005-06
Twenty20 Int debut: 2005-06
Place in batting averages: 190th av. 21.14 (2007 150th av. 28.83)
Place in bowling averages: 13th av. 20.30 (2007 21st av. 23.67)
Education: Ermelo High School
Overseas tours: South Africa A to Sri Lanka 2005-06, to Zimbabwe 2006-07; South Africa to Australia 2005-06 (VB Series), to Sri Lanka 2006, to Zimbabwe (one-day series) 2007-08

Overseas teams played for: Easterns 1995-96 – 1996-97; Free State 1997-98 – 2003-04; Eagles 2004-05 – 2006-07; Mumbai Champs (ICL) 2007-08, 2008-09
Extras: Represented South Africa U19 1996-97. Scored century (100) and recorded five-wicket innings return (5-30) v Titans at Bloemfontein in the SuperSport Series 2004-05, winning the Man of the Match award. His other match awards include Man of the Match v Dolphins at Durban in the Standard Bank Cup 2004-05 (2-38/91) and v Titans at Centurion in the final of the Standard Bank Cup 2005-06 (3-25/20). Represented South Africa in the Twenty20 World Championship 2007-08. Was an overseas player with Sussex for the first half of the 2005 season; an overseas player with Northamptonshire since 2007. Northamptonshire's top first-class wicket-taker in 2008 with 43; 12 of these came in one match against Middlesex in June
Best batting: 113* Free State v KwaZulu-Natal, Bloemfontein 2001-02
Best bowling: 7-60 Northamptonshire v Middlesex, Uxbridge 2008

2008 Season

	M	Inn	NO	Runs	HS	Avg	100	50	Ct	St	Balls	Runs	Wkts	Avg	BB	5I	10M
Test																	
FC	11	10	3	148	75 *	21.14	-	1	-	-	1648	869	43	20.20	7-60	3	1
ODI																	
List A	8	6	2	104	29 *	26.00	-	-	1	-	389	309	10	30.90	2-21	-	
20/20 Int																	
20/20	10	6	2	31	14	7.75	-	-	2	-	216	255	7	36.42	1-14	-	

Career Performances

	M	Inn	NO	Runs	HS	Avg	100	50	Ct	St	Balls	Runs	Wkts	Avg	BB	5I	10M
Test																	
FC	81	120	22	2376	113 *	24.24	2	14	25	-	13585	6700	260	25.76	7-60	14	1
ODI	10	8	2	89	37 *	14.83	-	-	3	-	526	551	13	42.38	2-21	-	
List A	125	99	30	1909	91	27.66	-	11	30	-	5451	4389	158	27.77	4-31	-	
20/20 Int	8	4	1	46	21	15.33	-	-	-	-	186	231	8	28.87	2-31	-	
20/20	48	32	9	318	48 *	13.82	-	-	3	-	947	1168	43	27.16	2-8	-	

VAN JAARSVELD, M. Kent

Name: Martin van Jaarsveld
Role: Right-hand top-order bat, right-arm off-spin bowler
Born: 18 June 1974, Klerksdorp, South Africa
Height: 6ft 2in **Weight:** 12st 12lbs
Nickname: Jarre
County debut: 2004 (Northamptonshire), 2005 (Kent)
County cap: 2005 (Kent)
Test debut: 2002-03
ODI debut: 2002-03
1000 runs in a season: 4
1st-Class 200s: 3
Place in batting averages: 31st av. 47.91 (2007 46th av. 45.95)
Place in bowling averages: 12th av. 20.00
Parents: Leon and Isobel
Wife and date of marriage: Jill, 6 May 2005
Education: Warmbads High School; University of Pretoria
Qualifications: BComm (Financial Management)
Overseas tours: South Africa A to Sri Lanka 1998, to Zimbabwe 2002-03, to Australia 2002-03; South Africa Academy to Zimbabwe 1998-99; South Africa to England 2003, to New Zealand 2003-04, to Sri Lanka 2004, to England (ICC Champions Trophy) 2004, to India 2004-05
Overseas teams played for: Northern Transvaal/Northerns Titans 1994-95 – 2003-04; Titans 2004-05 –
Career highlights to date: 'Playing for South Africa. Being chosen as one of the five Cricketers of the Year in South Africa 2002'
Cricket moments to forget: 'Losing the NatWest Series final [playing for South Africa] at Lord's, July 2003'
Cricket superstitions: 'Left pad first when padding up'
Cricketers particularly admired: Gary Kirsten, Michael Atherton
Young players to look out for: Neil Dexter, Joe Denly
Other sports played: Golf, tennis
Other sports followed: Rugby (Blue Bulls), football (Blackburn Rovers)
Favourite band: Snow Patrol
Relaxations: 'Spending time with friends and family'
Extras: Scored 182* and 158* v Griqualand West at Centurion 2001-02, becoming only the second batsman to record two 150s in the same match in South Africa. Player of the SuperSport Series 2001-02 (934 runs at 84.90); also topped South African first-

class averages 2001-02 (1268 runs at 74.58). One of *South African Cricket Annual*'s five Cricketers of the Year 2002. Was an overseas player with Northamptonshire 2004. Scored a century in each innings (118/111) on first-class debut for Kent, v Warwickshire at Canterbury 2005, becoming the first Kent debutant to achieve the feat. Scored 168 v Surrey at Tunbridge Wells 2005, in the process sharing with Robert Key (189) in a new Kent record third-wicket partnership (323). Retired from international cricket in February 2005. Leading run-scorer in the SuperSport Series 2006-07 with 828 runs (av. 55.20). Finished top of the Kent first-class batting averages for 2008 with 1150 runs. PCA Player of the Year 2008. Is no longer considered an overseas player.
Opinions on cricket: 'I think the standard of county cricket, with the inclusion of overseas players and the odd Kolpak player is very strong and although there is a lot of resistance I do think the English game has benefited from it.'
Best batting: 262* Kent v Glamorgan, Cardiff 2005
Best bowling: 5-33 Kent v Surrey, The Oval, 2008

2008 Season

	M	Inn	NO	Runs	HS	Avg	100	50	Ct	St	Balls	Runs	Wkts	Avg	BB	5I	10M
Test																	
FC	16	27	3	1150	133	47.91	4	7	28	-	462	220	11	20.00	5-33	1	-
ODI																	
List A	16	16	4	907	124	75.58	4	5	5	-	72	81	2	40.50	1-26	-	
20/20 Int																	
20/20	12	11	0	140	32	12.72	-	-	8	-	6	13	0		-	-	

Career Performances

	M	Inn	NO	Runs	HS	Avg	100	50	Ct	St	Balls	Runs	Wkts	Avg	BB	5I	10M
Test	9	15	2	397	73	30.53	-	3	11	-	42	28	0		-	-	-
FC	201	340	31	13904	262 *	44.99	41	67	284	-	2321	1178	37	31.83	5-33	1	-
ODI	11	7	1	124	45	20.66	-	-	4	-	31	18	2	9.00	1-0	-	
List A	235	217	33	7433	124	40.39	12	48	132	-	1100	968	24	40.33	3-43	-	
20/20 Int																	
20/20	64	59	9	1229	76 *	24.58	-	8	43	-	72	105	4	26.25	2-19	-	

VAUGHAN, M. P. Yorkshire

Name: Michael Paul Vaughan
Role: Right-hand bat, off-spin bowler
Born: 29 October 1974, Eccles, Manchester
Height: 6ft 2in **Weight:** 11st 7lbs
Nickname: Frankie, Virgil
County debut: 1993
County cap: 1995
Benefit: 2005
Test debut: 1999-2000
ODI debut: 2000-01
Twenty20 Int debut: 2005
1000 runs in a season: 4
Place in batting averages: 161st av. 25.00 (2007 48th av. 44.58)
Parents: Graham John and Dee
Wife and date of marriage: Nichola, September 2003
Children: Tallulah Grace, 4 June 2004; Archie, December 2005

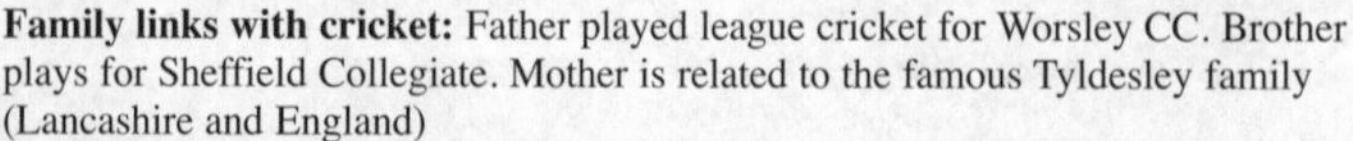

Family links with cricket: Father played league cricket for Worsley CC. Brother plays for Sheffield Collegiate. Mother is related to the famous Tyldesley family (Lancashire and England)
Education: Silverdale Comprehensive, Sheffield
Qualifications: 7 GCSEs
Overseas tours: Yorkshire to West Indies 1994, to South Africa 1995, to Zimbabwe 1996; England U19 to India 1992-93, to Sri Lanka 1993-94 (c); England A to India 1994-95, to Australia 1996-97, to Zimbabwe and South Africa 1998-99 (c); England to South Africa 1999-2000, to Pakistan and Sri Lanka 2000-01, to India and New Zealand 2001-02, to Australia 2002-03, to Africa (World Cup) 2002-03, to Bangladesh and Sri Lanka 2003-04 (c), to West Indies 2003-04 (c), to Zimbabwe (one-day series) 2004-05 (c), to South Africa 2004-05 (c), to Pakistan 2005-06 (c), to India 2005-06 (c), to Australia 2006-07 (C'wealth Bank Series; c), to West Indies (World Cup) 2006-07 (c), to Sri Lanka 2007-08 (Test c), to New Zealand 2007-08 (Test c)
Cricketers particularly admired: Darren Lehmann, 'all the Yorkshire and England squads'
Other sports played: Football (Baslow FC), golf (10 handicap)
Other sports followed: Football (Sheffield Wednesday), all golf
Relaxations: Most sports. 'Enjoy a good meal with friends'
Extras: Maurice Leyland Batting Award 1990; Cricket Society's Most Promising Young Cricketer 1993; A. A. Thompson Memorial Trophy 1993. Scored 1066 runs in first full season of first-class cricket 1994. Captained England U19. PCA Player of the

Year 2002. Highest-scoring batsman in Test cricket for the calendar year 2002 (1481 runs). One of *Wisden*'s Five Cricketers of the Year 2003. Topped Pricewaterhouse Coopers rankings for Test batsmen in early summer 2003. Vodafone Cricketer of the Year 2002-03. Scored century in each innings (103/101*) in the first Test v West Indies at Lord's 2004. His international awards include England's Man of the [Test] Series v India 2002 (615 runs at 102.50) and Man of the [Test] Series v Australia 2002-03 (633 runs at 63.30), as well as Man of the Match v Australia at Edgbaston in the ICC Champions Trophy 2004 (86/2-42 plus run-out). England one-day captain from May 2003 to June 2007 and England Test captain from July 2003; led England to a Test series win over Australia in 2005, their first Ashes success for 18 years, and was appointed OBE in 2006 New Year Honours. Book *A Year in the Sun* published 2003. Scored century (103) in the second Test v West Indies at his home ground of Headingley 2007 on his return to Test cricket after 18 months out through injury. England 12-month central contract 2007-08. Resigned England captaincy before the final Test v South Africa in 2008, England having already lost the series
Best batting: 197 England v India, Trent Bridge 2002
Best bowling: 4-39 Yorkshire v Oxford University, The Parks 1994

2008 Season

	M	Inn	NO	Runs	HS	Avg	100	50	Ct	St	Balls	Runs	Wkts	Avg	BB	5I	10M
Test	6	9	0	240	106	26.66	1	-	1	-	0	0	0		-	-	-
FC	12	18	0	450	106	25.00	1	1	4	-	36	47	0		-	-	-
ODI																	
List A	2	2	0	38	22	19.00	-	-	-	-	0	0	0		-	-	
20/20 Int																	
20/20	7	7	0	104	34	14.85	-	-	1	-	48	72	1	72.00	1-21	-	

Career Performances

	M	Inn	NO	Runs	HS	Avg	100	50	Ct	St	Balls	Runs	Wkts	Avg	BB	5I	10M
Test	82	147	9	5719	197	41.44	18	18	44	-	978	561	6	93.50	2-71	-	-
FC	262	460	27	16136	197	37.26	42	68	117	-	9342	5245	114	46.00	4-39	-	-
ODI	86	83	10	1982	90 *	27.15	-	16	25	-	796	649	16	40.56	4-22	-	
List A	276	267	25	6958	125 *	28.75	3	43	87	-	3303	2538	78	32.53	4-22	-	
20/20 Int	2	2	0	27	27	13.50	-	-	-	-	0	0	0		-	-	
20/20	9	9	0	131	34	14.55	-	-	1	-	48	72	1	72.00	1-21	-	

VINCE, J. M. Hampshire

Name: <u>James</u> Michael Vince
Role: Right-hand bat, right-arm medium/ off-spin bowler
Born: 14 March 1991, Cuckfield, Sussex
County debut: No first-team appearance
Education: St Mary's CE Primary School, Warminster Secondary School
Off-season: 'Grade cricket in Australia'
Overseas teams played for: Melville CC, Australia 2008-09
Other sports played: Football (former Reading FC Academy player)
Extras: Has played for Chippenham CC and Wiltshire CCC; has represented Wiltshire at U15 and U17 level, as well as representing West of England U17s. Scored a century for Hampshire Academy v Portsmouth aged 14. First century for Hampshire 2nd XI 2007. Scored a career-best 210, including 33 boundaries, for Melville v Midland Guildford in October 2008. Awarded a development contract at Hampshire for 2009

93. Who co-wrote a novel which featured an Australian cricketer being murdered while playing against England at Lord's?

VINCENT, L. — Lancashire

Name: Lou Vincent
Role: Right-hand bat, right-arm medium bowler, wicket-keeper
Born: 11 November 1978, Warkworth, Auckland, New Zealand
Height: 5ft 10in **Weight:** 12st 7lbs
Nickname: Flusher
County debut: 2006 (Worcestershire), 2008 (Lancashire)
Test debut: 2001
ODI debut: 2001
Twenty20 Int debut: 2005-06
1st-Class 200s: 1
Place in batting averages: 164th av. 24.72
Parents: Mike and Kathy
Wife and date of marriage: Elly, August 2006
Children: Molly, April 2006
Family links with cricket: 'Great-Grandma used to make cookies for the great Eddie Paynter'
Qualifications: Level III lawn bowls coach

Overseas tours: New Zealand U19 to South Africa (U19 World Cup) 1997-98; New Zealand Academy to Australia 1999-2000; New Zealand A to South Africa 2004-05; New Zealand to Sharjah (ARY Gold Cup) 2000-01, to Australia 2001-02, to Pakistan 2002, to West Indies 2002, to Sri Lanka (ICC Champions Trophy) 2002-03, to Africa (World Cup) 2002-03, to India 2003-04, to Zimbabwe 2005-06, to South Africa 2005-06 (one-day series), to India (ICC Champions Trophy) 2006-07, to Australia (Commonwealth Bank Series) 2006-07, plus other one-day tournaments in Sri Lanka and India
Overseas teams played for: Auckland 1997-98 – 2007-08; Chin Hill CC, Kaukapakapa, New Zealand 2004 – ; Chandigarh Lions (ICL) 2007-08, 2008-09
Career highlights to date: 'Places cricket takes me around the world'
Cricket moments to forget: 'Pair on debut for Worcestershire'
Extras: Played for Suffolk in the C&G 2005. Scored century (104) on Test debut in the third Test v Australia at Perth 2001-02. Scored 120-ball 172 v Zimbabwe at Harare 2005-06, breaking Glenn Turner's 30-year-old record for the highest individual innings for New Zealand in an ODI and winning the Man of the Match award. Signed as an overseas player for Worcestershire in 2006, scoring 83 from 91 balls on his county debut v Yorkshire in the C&G Trophy. Scored 114 v Essex at Worcester 2006, becoming the first Worcestershire player to score a century before lunch since Glenn Turner in 1982. Called up to the New Zealand squad for the Commonwealth Bank

Series in Australia 2006-07 on the retirement of Nathan Astle, winning Man of the Match v England at Perth (76). Announced his retirement from international cricket in February 2008 after his New Zealand contract was cancelled due to his involvement in the ICL. Signed as an overseas player by Lancashire in June 2008 to replace Mohammad Yousuf.
Best batting: 224 New Zealand v Sri Lanka, Wellington, 2005
Best bowling: 2-37 Auckland v Wellington, Auckland 2000

2008 Season

	M	Inn	NO	Runs	HS	Avg	100	50	Ct	St	Balls	Runs	Wkts	Avg	BB	5I	10M
Test																	
FC	6	12	1	272	83	24.72	-	2	6	-	0	0	0		-	-	-
ODI																	
List A	5	5	0	65	50	13.00	-	1	1	-	0	0	0		-	-	
20/20 Int																	
20/20	10	10	2	268	102 *	33.50	1	2	8	-	0	0	0		-	-	

Career Performances

	M	Inn	NO	Runs	HS	Avg	100	50	Ct	St	Balls	Runs	Wkts	Avg	BB	5I	10M
Test	23	40	1	1332	224	34.15	3	9	19	-	6	2	0		-	-	-
FC	92	151	11	4922	224	35.15	10	29	108	-	1003	527	10	52.70	2-37	-	-
ODI	102	99	10	2413	172	27.11	3	11	41	-	20	25	1	25.00	1-0	-	
List A	194	188	13	5036	172	28.77	7	27	109	3	213	217	4	54.25	2-25	-	
20/20 Int	9	9	0	174	42	19.33	-	-	1	-	0	0	0		-	-	
20/20	35	35	2	865	102 *	26.21	1	4	15	-	50	73	4	18.25	3-28	-	

94. What was the nickname given to Ray Illingworth's England side, which re-gained the Ashes in Australia in 1970-71?

VOGES, A. C. Nottinghamshire

Name: Adam Charles Voges
Role: Right-hand bat, left-arm wrist-spin bowler
Born: 4 October 1979, Subiaco, Perth, Australia
Height: 6ft 1in
Nickname: Kenny
County debut: 2007 (one-day, Hampshire), 2008 (first-class, Nottinghamshire)
ODI debut: 2006-07
Twenty20 Int debut: 2007-08
Place in batting averages: 82nd av. 36.88
Overseas tours: Australia U19 to England 1999; Australian Cricket Academy to Bangladesh 2000-01, to South Africa 2006-07, to Zimbabwe 2006-07 (c); University of Western Australia to India 2006-07; Australia to New Zealand (one-day series) 2006-07; Australia A to Pakistan 2007-08, to India 2008-09
Overseas teams played for: Western Australia 2002-03 –
Extras: Played for the Prime Minister's XI v West Indians 2005-06 and v England XI 2006-07. Represented Australia Centre of Excellence in Cricket Australia Emerging Players Tournament 2006. Scored 62-ball 100* v New South Wales at Sydney in the ING Cup 2004-05, the then fastest century in the competition's history, winning Man of the Match award. His other match awards include Man of the Match v Victoria at Perth in the ING Cup 2006-07 (82). Was a temporary overseas player with Hampshire during the 2007 season as a replacement for Stuart Clark. Made Twenty20 Int debut v New Zealand at Perth 2007-08. Overseas player with Nottinghamshire 2008
Best batting: 178 Western Australia v Queensland, Perth 2005-06
Best bowling: 4-92 Western Australia v South Australia, Adelaide 2006-07

2008 Season

	M	Inn	NO	Runs	HS	Avg	100	50	Ct	St	Balls	Runs	Wkts	Avg	BB	5I	10M
Test																	
FC	12	20	3	627	77	36.88	-	4	11	-	90	37	3	12.33	3-21	-	-
ODI																	
List A	11	11	3	467	85	58.37	-	5	5	-	12	14	1	14.00	1-14	-	
20/20 Int																	
20/20	9	9	1	302	59	37.75	-	3	5	-	14	27	0		-	-	

Career Performances

	M	Inn	NO	Runs	HS	Avg	100	50	Ct	St	Balls	Runs	Wkts	Avg	BB	5I	10M
Test																	
FC	54	91	13	2986	180	38.28	7	12	62	-	1578	883	22	40.13	4-92	-	-
ODI	1	1	1	16	16 *	-	-	-	1	-	18	33	0	-	-	-	
List A	57	54	12	1955	100 *	46.54	1	18	19	-	810	711	13	54.69	3-33	-	
20/20 Int	2	1	0	26	26	26.00	-	-	1	-	12	5	2	2.50	2-5	-	
20/20	30	29	4	807	74 *	32.28	-	6	12	-	149	226	10	22.60	2-4	-	

WAGG, G. G. Derbyshire

Name: Graham Grant Wagg
Role: Right-hand bat, left-arm fast-medium bowler
Born: 28 April 1983, Rugby
Height: 6ft **Weight:** 13st
Nickname: Waggy, GG
County debut: 2002 (Warwickshire), 2006 (Derbyshire)
County cap: 2007 (Derbyshire)
50 wickets in a season: 2
Place in batting averages: 152 av. 26.90 (2007 137th av. 31.17)
Place in bowling averages: 48th av. 26.98 (2007 87th av. 33.67)
Parents: John and Dawn
Marital status: Single, 'but getting close to the special day'
Children: Brayden Grant, 28 September 2008
Family links with cricket: 'Dad played for Warwickshire Seconds, and coached in local leagues in Rugby'
Education: Ashlawn School, Rugby; Warwickshire College ('Sports Science - struggling')
Qualifications: Level 1 cricket coach ('coached in South Africa and Holland')
Off-season: 'Spend as much time as possible with my little boy and my girlfriend Jade'
Overseas tours: Warwickshire Development tour to South Africa 1998, to West Indies 2000; England A to Malaysia and India 2003-04; England Sixes to Hong Kong 2008
Overseas teams played for: Hams Tech, East London, South Africa 1999; HBS, Netherlands

Career highlights to date: 'Winning our first match for Derby at Derby for four years. Getting 6-38 against Somerset [at Taunton 2006] to win us the game. My first first-class century in 2008. Taking ten wickets and scoring 100 runs in the same game.'
Cricket moments to forget: 'Bowling at Cameron White at Derby when he made 260 in no time, Ravi Bopara getting dropped on 0, then smacking me all around the ground afterwards (thanks, Birchy!)'
Cricketers particularly admired: Brett Lee, Ravi Bopara
Young players to look out for: Dan Redfern
Other sports played: Snooker, fishing, football, rugby
Other sports followed: Football (Man United), snooker (Ronnie O'Sullivan)
Relaxations: 'Casino, snooker, partying'
Extras: Represented England U16, U17, U18, U19 as well as Development of Excellence (Midlands) XI. Scored 42* from 50 balls, 51 from 57 balls and took 4-43 on first-class debut v Somerset at Edgbaston 2002. NBC Denis Compton Award for the most promising young Warwickshire player 2003. ECB National Academy 2003-04. Took over 50 wickets in 2008 for the second season in succession.
Best batting: 108 Derbyshire v Northamptonshire, Northampton 2008
Best bowling: 6-38 Derbyshire v Somerset, Taunton 2006

2008 Season

	M	Inn	NO	Runs	HS	Avg	100	50	Ct	St	Balls	Runs	Wkts	Avg	BB	5I	10M
Test																	
FC	16	23	3	538	108	26.90	1	2	6	-	2730	1590	59	26.94	6-56	2	1
ODI																	
List A	12	10	0	77	15	7.70	-	-	5	-	528	439	17	25.82	4-35	-	
20/20 Int																	
20/20	10	8	4	96	27 *	24.00	-	-	3	-	192	254	8	31.75	3-23	-	

Career Performances

	M	Inn	NO	Runs	HS	Avg	100	50	Ct	St	Balls	Runs	Wkts	Avg	BB	5I	10M
Test																	
FC	50	73	10	1669	108	26.49	1	9	18	-	8011	5005	159	31.47	6-38	5	1
ODI																	
List A	62	47	3	623	45	14.15	-	-	17	-	2279	2141	69	31.02	4-35	-	
20/20 Int																	
20/20	35	29	7	361	27 *	16.40	-	-	10	-	520	707	26	27.19	3-23	-	

WAGH, M. A. Nottinghamshire

Name: Mark Anant Wagh
Role: Right-hand bat, off-spin bowler
Born: 20 October 1976, Birmingham
Height: 6ft 2in **Weight:** 13st
Nickname: Waggy
County debut: 1997 (Warwickshire), 2007 (Nottinghamshire)
County cap: 2000 (Warwickshire)
1000 runs in a season: 4
1st-Class 200s: 1
1st-Class 300s: 1
Place in batting averages: 36th av. 46.95 (2007 25th av. 54.58)
Parents: Mohan and Rita
Marital status: Single
Education: King Edward's School, Birmingham; Keble College, Oxford
Qualifications: BA degree, Level 2 coaching award
Overseas tours: Warwickshire U19 to South Africa 1992; ECB National Academy to Australia 2001-02; MCC to Uganda 2007-08.
Career highlights to date:
'315 at Lord's 2001'
Cricket moments to forget:
'Too many to mention'
Cricketers particularly admired:
Andy Flower
Young players to look out for: Moeen Ali
Favourite band: Dido
Extras: Oxford Blue 1996-98; Oxford University captain 1997. Scored maiden first-class century (116) for Oxford University v Glamorgan at The Parks 1997, following up with another hundred (101) in the second innings. His 315 v Middlesex at Lord's 2001 is the equal second highest individual Championship score made at Lord's behind Jack Hobbs's 316* in 1926 (although Percy Holmes's 315 in 1925 was unbeaten). C&G Man of the Match award for his 102* v Kent at Edgbaston 2004. Included in preliminary England one-day squad of 30 for ICC Champions Trophy 2004
Best batting: 315 Warwickshire v Middlesex, Lord's 2001
Best bowling: 7-222 Warwickshire v Lancashire, Edgbaston 2003

2008 Season

	M	Inn	NO	Runs	HS	Avg	100	50	Ct	St	Balls	Runs	Wkts	Avg	BB	5I	10M
Test																	
FC	15	24	2	1033	141	46.95	2	8	3	-	54	11	0		-	-	-
ODI																	
List A	15	15	1	244	50 *	17.42	-	1	1	-	0	0	0		-	-	
20/20 Int																	
20/20																	

Career Performances

	M	Inn	NO	Runs	HS	Avg	100	50	Ct	St	Balls	Runs	Wkts	Avg	BB	5I	10M
Test																	
FC	172	284	24	10420	315	40.07	25	53	76	-	8697	4611	100	46.11	7-222	2	-
ODI																	
List A	98	94	8	2343	102 *	27.24	1	17	19	-	1096	862	25	34.48	4-35	-	
20/20 Int																	
20/20	18	15	0	288	56	19.20	-	1	5	-	75	106	5	21.20	2-16	-	

WAINWRIGHT, D. J. Yorkshire

Name: David John Wainwright
Role: Left-hand bat, left-arm orthodox spin bowler
Born: 21 March 1985, Pontefract
Height: 5ft 9in **Weight:** 9st 6lbs
Nickname: Wainers
County debut: 2004
Parents: Paul and Debbie
Marital status: Single
Family links with cricket: 'Grandfather (Harry Heritage) represented Yorkshire Schoolboys 1950-51'
Education: Hemsworth High School; Hemsworth Arts and Community College; Loughborough University
Qualifications: 10 GCSEs, 3 A-levels, Sports Science and Physics degree, Level 2 coaching
Overseas tours: Yorkshire U15 to South Africa 2000
Overseas teams played for: Grovedale CC, Geelong, Melbourne 2006-07
Career highlights to date: 'Winning at Lord's in BUSA final for Loughborough'

Cricketers particularly admired: Brian Lara, Daniel Vettori
Young players to look out for: Chris Murtagh, Richard Morris
Other sports played: Football, golf
Other sports followed: Football (Liverpool FC)
Favourite band: Will Smith, Leona Lewis
Relaxations: Listening to music
Extras: Best bowling award at Bunbury Festival for North of England U15. Played for Loughborough UCCE 2005-06. Represented British Universities 2005-06
Opinions on cricket: 'One overseas player (only) is good for younger players to be given an opportunity to play first-class cricket.'
Best batting: 104* Yorkshire v Sussex, Hove 2008
Best bowling: 4-48 LUCCE v Worcestershire, Kidderminster 2005

2008 Season

	M	Inn	NO	Runs	HS	Avg	100	50	Ct	St	Balls	Runs	Wkts	Avg	BB	5I	10M
Test																	
FC	4	6	1	165	104 *	33.00	1	-	2	-	511	246	8	30.75	3-9	-	-
ODI																	
List A	7	3	3	29	13 *		-	-	-	-	192	166	3	55.33	2-33	-	
20/20 Int																	
20/20	2	1	1	3	3 *		-	-	-	-	23	45	0		-	-	

Career Performances

	M	Inn	NO	Runs	HS	Avg	100	50	Ct	St	Balls	Runs	Wkts	Avg	BB	5I	10M
Test																	
FC	14	18	4	439	104 *	31.35	1	1	9	-	1890	1012	30	33.73	4-48	-	-
ODI																	
List A	19	7	4	62	26	20.66	-	-	1	-	546	459	12	38.25	2-30	-	
20/20 Int																	
20/20	9	3	1	6	3 *	3.00	-	-	2	-	161	173	8	21.62	3-6	-	

WAKELY, A. G. Northamptonshire

Name: Alexander (Alex) George Wakely
Role: Right-hand bat, right-arm off-spin bowler; batting all-rounder
Born: 3 November 1988, Hammersmith, London
Height: 6ft 2in **Weight:** 14st 1lbs
Nickname: Baby Seal, Wakers
County debut: 2007
Place in batting averages: 223rd av. 16.85 (2007 205th av. 21.12)
Parents: Jan and John
Marital status: Single
Family links with cricket: 'Father played club and representative cricket. Uncle umpired first-class cricket for ten years'
Education: Bedford School
Qualifications: 11 GCSEs, 3 A-levels
Career outside cricket: 'Golf'
Off-season: 'Training until Christmas, then India and South Africa for a month'
Overseas tours: Bedford School to Australia 2003, 2005-06; England U16 to South Africa 2004; England U19 to Malaysia 2006-07, to Malaysia (U19 World Cup) 2007-08 (c), to Sri Lanka 2007-08
Career highlights to date: '108 for England U19 to beat Sri Lanka 2007' (*HSBC Invitational 1st Tri-Series 2006-07, Kuala Lumpur*); 63 on my debut for Somerset in 2007. Marcus Trescothick as my first wicket.'
Cricket moments to forget: 'Diving for a ball on Championship debut and losing my trousers (still get letters about it). First-ball duck on my TV debut v Sussex.'
Cricketers particularly admired: Ricky Ponting, David Sales
Young players to look out for: James Kettleborough
Other sports played: Golf (5 handicap), hockey (regional and GB trials), football (Meppershall FC), rugby (school 1st XV), tennis (LTA junior competitions)
Other sports followed: Rugby (Northampton Saints), football (Luton Town), golf, tennis
Favourite band: Elvis
Relaxations: 'Golf, and time with my girlfriend'
Extras: Bunbury Scholarship for Batting 2004. Played for Bedfordshire in the 2005 C&G. Northamptonshire Young Player of the Year 2006. Represented England U19 2007. Scored 66 on first-class debut v Somerset at Taunton, following up with 55 in second match v Nottinghamshire at Northampton 2007. NBC Denis Compton Award for the most promising young Northamptonshire player 2008
Opinions on cricket: 'More Twenty20 to be played, but more time to practise as the season is so packed.'

Best batting: 66 Northamptonshire v Somerset, Taunton 2007
Best bowling: 2-62 Northamptonshire v Somerset, Taunton 2007

2008 Season

	M	Inn	NO	Runs	HS	Avg	100	50	Ct	St	Balls	Runs	Wkts	Avg	BB	5I	10M
Test																	
FC	5	8	1	118	53	16.85	-	1	4	-	6	4	0		-	-	-
ODI																	
List A	1	1	0	1	1	1.00	-	-	-	-	0	0	0		-	-	
20/20 Int																	
20/20																	

Career Performances

	M	Inn	NO	Runs	HS	Avg	100	50	Ct	St	Balls	Runs	Wkts	Avg	BB	5I	10M
Test																	
FC	9	16	1	287	66	19.13	-	3	5	-	180	131	3	43.66	2-62	-	-
ODI																	
List A	4	4	0	18	14	4.50	-	-	1	-	18	14	2	7.00	2-14	-	
20/20 Int																	
20/20																	

WALKER, M. J. — Essex

Name: Matthew (Matt) Jonathan Walker
Role: Left-hand bat
Born: 2 January 1974, Gravesend
Height: 5ft 6in **Weight:** 13st
Nickname: Walks, Pumba
County debut: 1992-93 (Kent)
County cap: 2000 (Kent)
Benefit: 2008 (Kent)
1000 runs in a season: 3
1st-Class 200s: 1
Place in batting averages: 257th av. 10.44 (2007 67th av. 40.72)
Parents: Richard and June
Wife and date of marriage: Claudia, 25 September 1999
Children: Charlie Jack, 20 November 2002; Lexie, 19 January 2007

Family links with cricket: 'Dad played Kent and Middlesex 2nd XIs and was on Lord's groundstaff. Grandfather kept wicket for Kent. Mum was women's cricket coach'
Education: King's School, Rochester
Qualifications: 9 GCSEs, 2 A-levels, advanced cricket coaching certificate
Career outside cricket: PE teacher
Overseas tours: Kent U17 to New Zealand 1990-91; England U19 to Pakistan 1991-92, to India 1992-93 (c); Kent to Zimbabwe 1993
Career highlights to date: 'Captaining England U19. Winning Norwich Union League 2001'
Cricket moments to forget: 'Losing Lord's B&H final v Surrey 1997'
Cricket superstitions: 'None'
Cricketers particularly admired: Darren Lehmann, Nick Knight, Mark Ramprakash
Young players to look out for: Alex Blake, Neil Dexter
Other sports played: Hockey (England U14-U21 [captain U15-U17]), rugby (Kent U18)
Other sports followed: Football (Charlton Athletic), hockey (Gore Court HC)
Favourite band: Razorlight, Arctic Monkeys, Jeff Buckley
Relaxations: 'Music and films'
Extras: Captained England U16 cricket and hockey teams in same year. Sir John Hobbs Silver Jubilee Memorial Prize for outstanding U16 cricketer 1989. Captained England U19 1993. Woolwich Kent League's Young Cricketer of the Year 1994. Scored 275* against Somerset in 1996 – the highest ever individual score by a Kent batsman at Canterbury. Ealham Award for Fielding Excellence 2003, 2004, 2005. Cowdrey Award (Kent Player of the Year) 2004, 2006. Vice-captain of Kent 2005. Denness Award (Kent leading run-scorer) 2006. Scored century in each innings (142/157) v Lancashire at Canterbury 2007. Signed for Essex for the 2009 season. Became an Eminent Roffensian 1995
Opinions on cricket: 'The game is in great shape and domestic cricket is as competitive as ever.'
Best batting: 275* Kent v Somerset, Canterbury 1996
Best bowling: 2-21 Kent v Middlesex, Canterbury 2004

2008 Season

	M	Inn	NO	Runs	HS	Avg	100	50	Ct	St	Balls	Runs	Wkts	Avg	BB	5I	10M
Test																	
FC	6	10	1	94	23	10.44	-	-	-	-	54	40	1	40.00	1-34	-	-
ODI																	
List A	7	7	0	168	43	24.00	-	-	1	-	0	0	0		-	-	
20/20 Int																	
20/20	3	3	0	20	12	6.66	-	-	1	-	0	0	0		-	-	

Career Performances

	M	Inn	NO	Runs	HS	Avg	100	50	Ct	St	Balls	Runs	Wkts	Avg	BB	5I	10M
Test																	
FC	183	301	32	9768	275 *	36.31	25	40	121	-	1876	1121	22	50.95	2-21	-	-
ODI																	
List A	257	234	34	5665	117	28.32	3	34	70	-	886	740	30	24.66	4-24	-	
20/20 Int																	
20/20	40	38	6	765	58 *	23.90	-	1	4	-	0	0	0		-	-	

WALLACE, M. A. Glamorgan

Name: Mark Alexander Wallace
Role: Left-hand bat, wicket-keeper
Born: 19 November 1981, Abergavenny
Height: 5ft 10in **Weight:** 11st 9lbs
Nickname: Wally, Wash, Grom, Screech, Kyle, Marcellus
County debut: 1999
County cap: 2003
50 dismissals in a season: 2
Place in batting averages: 140th av. 27.83 (2007 181st av. 24.77)
Parents: Ryland and Alvine
Wife and date of marriage: Lucy, 28 October 2007
Family links with cricket: 'Father plays for Wales Over 50'
Education: Crickhowell High School; Staffordshire University
Qualifications: 10 GCSEs, 2 A-levels, Level 2 coach, BA (Hons) Journalism
Career outside cricket: 'Hopefully journalism'
Overseas tours: England U19 to New Zealand 1998-99, to Malaysia and (U19 World Cup) Sri Lanka 1999-2000, to India 2000-01; ECB National Academy to Australia 2001-02, to Australia and Sri Lanka 2002-03; MCC to New Zealand and Papua New Guinea 2007
Overseas teams played for: Port Adelaide, South Australia 2001-02; Redlands Tigers, Brisbane 2004-06
Career highlights to date: 'Academy tours. Winning one-day league 2002 and 2004'
Cricket moments to forget: 'Summer 2007'
Cricketers particularly admired: Ian Healy, Adam Gilchrist, Chris Read, Matt Elliott, Keith Piper

Young players to look out for: James Harris, Imran Hassan, Chris Woakes, Gareth Rees
Other sports played: Golf, touch rugby ('playmaker')
Other sports followed: Football (Merthyr Tydfil FC), rugby (Cardiff Blues)
Favourite band: Stereophonics, Shania Twain
Relaxations: 'Golf, TV'
Extras: Represented England U17. Represented England U19 1998, 1999 and 2000 (captain for second 'Test' 2000). Made first-class debut v Somerset at Taunton 1999 aged 17 years 287 days – youngest ever Glamorgan wicket-keeper. NBC Denis Compton Award 1999. Captained ECB National Academy to innings victory over Commonwealth Bank [Australian] Cricket Academy at Adelaide 2001-02. Glamorgan Young Player of the Year 2002. Byron Denning Glamorgan Clubman of the Year Award 2003. Captained Glamorgan v Somerset at Taunton 2007 in the absence of David Hemp
Opinions on cricket: 'The impact of Twenty20 on the world game may have an irretrievably negative impact on Test and first-class cricket. It may soon be so financially rewarding to play Twenty20 that many players will play it exclusively and not bother playing the traditional forms.'
Best batting: 128 Glamorgan v Gloucestershire, Bristol 2007

2008 Season

	M	Inn	NO	Runs	HS	Avg	100	50	Ct	St	Balls	Runs	Wkts	Avg	BB	5I	10M
Test																	
FC	16	24	0	668	72	27.83	-	4	31	5	0	0	0		-	-	-
ODI																	
List A	15	13	5	311	85	38.87	-	2	13	3	0	0	0		-	-	
20/20 Int																	
20/20	9	7	3	115	28 *	28.75	-	-	2	2	0	0	0		-	-	

Career Performances

	M	Inn	NO	Runs	HS	Avg	100	50	Ct	St	Balls	Runs	Wkts	Avg	BB	5I	10M
Test																	
FC	134	219	16	5577	128	27.47	6	28	344	27	0	0	0		-	-	-
ODI																	
List A	128	101	23	1516	85	19.43	-	2	128	29	0	0	0		-	-	
20/20 Int																	
20/20	42	32	12	491	35 *	24.55	-	-	14	7	0	0	0		-	-	

WALTERS, S. J. — Surrey

Name: Stewart Jonathan Walters
Role: Right-hand bat, right-arm slow-medium/leg-spin bowler
Born: 25 June 1983, Mornington, Victoria, Australia
Height: 6ft **Weight:** 12st 13lbs
Nickname: Roadie
County debut: 2005 (one-day), 2006 (first-class)
Place in batting averages: 229th av. 15.87 (2007 209th av. 20.72)
Parents: Stewart and Sue
Wife and date of marriage: Jacki, 25 February 2006
Children: Maddison, 19 February 2008
Family links with cricket: 'Father played'
Education: Guildford Grammar School, Perth, Western Australia
Career outside cricket: Fitness trainer
Off-season: 'Grade cricket in Perth'
Overseas teams played for: Midland-Guildford CC, Perth; Perth CC 2007-08 –
Career highlights to date: 'Scoring 91 v Northamptonshire in Pro40, 2008'
Cricket moments to forget: 'Mushtaq Ahmed!!'
Cricket superstitions: 'Right pad first'
Cricketers particularly admired: Justin Langer
Young players to look out for: Chris Jordan
Other sports played: Australian Rules football (AFL)
Other sports followed: Australian Rules (Collingwood)
Relaxations: 'Running, keeping fit'
Extras: Captain of Western Australia U17 for two years
Opinions on cricket: 'Still a great game, moving forwards and getting faster all the time.'
Best batting: 70 Surrey v Durham, The Oval 2007
Best bowling: 1-4 Surrey v Durham, Riverside 2007

2008 Season

	M	Inn	NO	Runs	HS	Avg	100	50	Ct	St	Balls	Runs	Wkts	Avg	BB	5I	10M
Test																	
FC	6	8	0	127	40	15.87	-	-	3	-	90	52	0		-	-	-
ODI																	
List A	6	6	0	168	91	28.00	-	1	7	-	6	8	0		-	-	
20/20 Int																	
20/20	1	1	1	10	10 *	-	-	-	-	-	0	0	0		-	-	

Career Performances

	M	Inn	NO	Runs	HS	Avg	100	50	Ct	St	Balls	Runs	Wkts	Avg	BB	5I	10M
Test																	
FC	17	26	1	521	70	20.84	-	2	15	-	294	149	3	49.66	1-4	-	-
ODI																	
List A	25	23	4	383	91	20.15	-	1	13	-	141	143	2	71.50	1-12	-	
20/20 Int																	
20/20	11	6	2	49	18	12.25	-	-	7	-	12	17	0		-	-	

WATERS, H. T. Glamorgan

Name: Huw Thomas Waters
Role: Right-hand bat, right-arm medium-fast bowler
Born: 26 September 1986, Cardiff
Height: 6ft 2in **Weight:** 14st
Nickname: Muddy
County debut: 2005
Place in batting averages: (2007 274th av. 10.87)
Place in bowling averages: (2007 137th av. 49.40)
Parents: Valerie and Donald
Marital status: Single
Family links with cricket: 'Long line of club cricketers, most notably Big Don, a stalwart of the old 3 Counties League'
Education: Llantarnam CS; Monmouth School
Qualifications: 8 GCSEs, 'a couple of A-levels – somehow!', Level 2 cricket coach
Overseas tours: West Region to West Indies 2002; Wales U16 to Jersey 2002;

Monmouth School to St Lucia 2003; England U19 to Bangladesh 2005-06, to Sri Lanka (U19 World Cup) 2005-06
Overseas teams played for: Westmeadows CC, Melbourne 2007-08
Career highlights to date: 'Making debut. Taking my first five-for'
Cricket moments to forget: 'Running Matt Elliott out on 96 when I was batting with him!'
Cricketers particularly admired: Glenn McGrath
Young players to look out for: 'Our academy boys'
Other sports played: Football ('mainly during warm-ups')
Other sports followed: Football (Manchester United)
Favourite band: Coldplay, 'any indie rock'
Relaxations: 'Listening to music, watching Manchester United'
Extras: Played for Wales Minor Counties in the C&G 2005 and in Minor Counties competitions 2004-07
Opinions on cricket: 'Gaining more interest due to Twenty20. Should just have one one-day competition. Glad only one overseas – means youngsters get more of a chance.'
Best batting: 34 Glamorgan v Kent, Canterbury 2005
Best bowling: 5-86 Glamorgan v Somerset, Taunton 2006

2008 Season

	M	Inn	NO	Runs	HS	Avg	100	50	Ct	St	Balls	Runs	Wkts	Avg	BB	5I	10M
Test																	
FC	1	1	1	10	10 *		-	-	1	-	54	26	1	26.00	1-9	-	-
ODI																	
List A	1	0	0	0	0		-	-	-	-	60	53	0		-	-	
20/20 Int																	
20/20																	

Career Performances

	M	Inn	NO	Runs	HS	Avg	100	50	Ct	St	Balls	Runs	Wkts	Avg	BB	5I	10M
Test																	
FC	23	37	18	145	34	7.63	-	-	6	-	2532	1479	39	37.92	5-86	1	-
ODI																	
List A	12	7	3	22	8	5.50	-	-	-	-	516	530	8	66.25	3-47	-	
20/20 Int																	
20/20																	

WATKINS, R. E. Glamorgan

Name: Ryan Edward Watkins
Role: Left-hand bat, right-arm medium-fast bowler, occasional wicket-keeper; all-rounder
Born: 9 June 1983, Abergavenny, Monmouthshire
Height: 6ft **Weight:** 13st 12lbs
Nickname: Tets, Maverick, Big Red, Commando, Roider
County debut: 2003 (one-day), 2005 (first-class)
Place in batting averages: 239th av. 13.42 (2007 259th av. 13.23)
Place in bowling averages: (2007 119th av. 41.10)
Parents: Huw and Gaynor
Wife and date of marriage: Lisa, 16 October 2005
Family links with cricket: 'Father was captain of Abergavenny 4ths; brother all-rounder for Blackwood CC'
Education: Pontllanfraith Comprehensive School; Crosskeys College
Qualifications: Numerous academic qualifications; Level 2 coach, qualified tyre and exhaust fitter, 'Working Safely' Level 1 qualified
Career outside cricket: 'Police officer'
Off-season: 'In Adelaide, playing for the Buffalos'
Overseas tours: Glamorgan to Guernsey 2006, 2007, Mumbai 2008; Commandos tour to Egypt 2007
Overseas teams played for: North Balwyn CC, Victoria, Australia 2003
Career highlights to date: 'Being voted Man of the Match in the Glamorgan v Nottinghamshire end-of-season football victory. Glamorgan Young Player of the Year 2006. Every time I play for Glamorgan'
Cricket moments to forget: None. 'I thoroughly enjoy every moment I play cricket'
Cricket superstitions: 'Right pad on first'
Cricketers particularly admired: Brian Lara, Matt Hayden, Jason Gillespie, Gareth Rees
Young players to look out for: Tom Baker BTCC
Other sports played: Football (Clydach Wasps AFC - Gwent County Div 1)
Other sports followed: Football (Tottenham Hotspur), rugby (Cardiff Blues), 'Markham Tigers'
Favourite band: Westlife
Relaxations: 'Playing golf; walking my dog, Missy'

Extras: Played for Wales Minor Counties in Minor Counties competitions 2003-07. Took five catches in an innings v Gloucestershire at Cheltenham 2006, equalling Glamorgan record. Glamorgan Young Player of the Year 2006. Glamorgan's leading wicket-taker in the 2008 season
Opinions on cricket: 'Love it!!!'
Best batting: 87 Glamorgan v Essex, Cardiff 2006
Best bowling: 4-40 Glamorgan v Worcestershire, Worcester 2006

2008 Season

	M	Inn	NO	Runs	HS	Avg	100	50	Ct	St	Balls	Runs	Wkts	Avg	BB	5I	10M
Test																	
FC	6	9	2	94	33	13.42	-	-	3	-	728	469	7	67.00	3-76	-	-
ODI																	
List A	2	1	0	0	0	0.00	-	-	-	-	92	79	3	26.33	2-41	-	
20/20 Int																	
20/20	8	2	1	4	4 *	4.00	-	-	-	-	138	195	11	17.72	2-20	-	

Career Performances

	M	Inn	NO	Runs	HS	Avg	100	50	Ct	St	Balls	Runs	Wkts	Avg	BB	5I	10M
Test																	
FC	33	56	4	951	87	18.28	-	2	18	-	2932	1927	39	49.41	4-40	-	-
ODI																	
List A	20	16	3	215	39	16.53	-	-	1	-	610	650	16	40.62	2-25	-	
20/20 Int																	
20/20	17	4	3	11	6 *	11.00	-	-	5	-	276	389	20	19.45	3-33	-	

95. Who is the only fast bowler to have captained England in an Ashes series since before World War Two?

WESSELS, M.H. Northamptonshire

Name: Mattheus Hendrik (Riki) Wessels
Role: Right-hand bat, wicket-keeper
Born: 12 November 1985, Nambour, Australia
Height: 5ft 10½in **Weight:** 11st 7lbs
Nickname: Weasel
County debut: 2005
Place in batting averages: 109th av. 32.00 (2007 134th av. 31.35)
Parents: Kepler and Sally
Marital status: Engaged
Family links with cricket: 'Dad' (*Kepler Wessels played Test and ODI cricket for Australia and South Africa between 1982-83 and 1994-95*)
Education: Woodridge College, Port Elizabeth
Overseas teams played for: Pirates CC, Port Elizabeth
Cricket moments to forget: 'Getting my first and last pair; tearing my hamstring going for a run'
Cricket superstitions: 'None'
Cricketers particularly admired: Justin Langer
Young players to look out for: Alex Wakely
Other sports played: Hockey, archery
Other sports followed: Football (Spurs)
Favourite band: Linkin Park
Extras: Northamptonshire Academy Players' Player of the Year 2004. Northamptonshire Young Player of the Year (Frank Rudd Trophy) 2004. Made first-class debut for MCC v West Indians at Arundel 2004. Scored maiden first-class century (102) v Somerset at Northampton 2005 after coming to the wicket on a hat-trick ball
Best batting: 107 Northamptonshire v Durham, Riverside 2005

2008 Season

	M	Inn	NO	Runs	HS	Avg	100	50	Ct	St	Balls	Runs	Wkts	Avg	BB	5I	10M
Test																	
FC	13	19	1	576	95	32.00	-	6	13	2	12	13	0		-	-	-
ODI																	
List A	10	10	0	336	100	33.60	1	2	4	-	0	0	0		-	-	
20/20 Int																	
20/20	11	10	2	143	43 *	17.87	-	-	1	-	0	0	0		-	-	

Career Performances

	M	Inn	NO	Runs	HS	Avg	100	50	Ct	St	Balls	Runs	Wkts	Avg	BB	5I	10M
Test																	
FC	51	83	7	2150	107	28.28	3	13	100	10	12	13	0		-	-	-
ODI																	
List A	57	53	6	1299	100	27.63	1	7	44	-	0	0	0		-	-	
20/20 Int																	
20/20	34	26	6	407	49 *	20.35	-	-	9	9	0	0	0		-	-	

WESTFIELD, M. S. — Essex

Name: Mervyn (Merv) Simon Westfield
Role: Right-hand bat, right-arm fast bowler
Born: 5 May 1988, Romford
Height: 6ft 1in **Weight:** 12st
Nickname: Swerve
County debut: 2005
Parents: Pamela and Mervyn
Marital status: Single
Family links with cricket: 'Dad used to play cricket and my older brother played for Essex for a couple of years'
Education: The Chafford School, Rainham; Havering College
Qualifications: 8 GCSEs, Level 1 coaching
Overseas tours: England U16 to South Africa 2004-05; England U19 to Malaysia 2006-07
Career highlights to date: 'Taking four wickets against Somerset and scoring 32 runs as well in 2006'
Cricketers particularly admired: Andy Flower, Andy Bichel
Young players to look out for: Maurice Chambers, Tom Westley, Adil Rashid

Other sports followed: Football (Manchester United)
Favourite band: TOK
Relaxations: 'Socialising with friends, listening to music'
Extras: Wanstead U11 Young Player of the Year 1997. Wanstead U11 All-Rounder of 1998. Havering District U13 Best Innings 2000. MCC Cricketer of the Year 2003, 2004. *Daily Telegraph* Bunbury Scholar 2003 (Best Fast Bowler; scholarship entailed a week's training with England A)
Best batting: 32 Essex v Somerset, Southend 2006
Best bowling: 4-72 Essex v Somerset, Southend 2006

2008 Seasonn (Did not make any first-class or one-day appearances)

Career Performances

	M	Inn	NO	Runs	HS	Avg	100	50	Ct	St	Balls	Runs	Wkts	Avg	BB	5I	10M
Test																	
FC	5	7	3	45	32	11.25	-	-	1	-	444	334	7	47.71	4-72	-	-
ODI																	
List A	2	2	2	6	4 *		-	-	1	-	36	38	0			-	-
20/20 Int																	
20/20																	

WESTLEY, T. Essex

Name: Thomas (Tom) Westley
Role: Right-hand top-order bat, right-arm off-spin bowler
Born: 13 March 1989, Cambridge
Height: 6ft 2in
Nickname: Spongebob, Pup
County debut: 2006 (one-day), 2007 (first-class)
Place in batting averages: 183rd av. 21.92 (2007 129th av. 31.85)
Parents: Ade and Mags
Family links with cricket: 'Dad has played village club cricket in Cambridgeshire, along with uncle and brother'
Education: Linton Village College; Hills Road Sixth Form College (both Cambridge)
Overseas tours: England U16 to South Africa 2004-05; England U19 to Malaysia (U19 World Cup) 2007-08

Cricket moments to forget: 'King pair against Surrey 2nd XI 2005'
Cricket superstitions: 'Mark my crease three times before every over and after every boundary'
Cricketers particularly admired: Steve Waugh, Sachin Tendulkar, Andy Flower, Alastair Cook
Young players to look out for: Mervyn Westfield, Adam Wheater
Other sports followed: Football (Newcastle United)
Extras: Played for MCC 2007. Represented England U19 2007 and 2008 (captain). NBC Denis Compton Award for most promising young Essex Player 2008
Best batting: 93* Essex v Derbyshire, Derby 2008
Best bowling: 1-19 Essex v New Zealanders, Chelmsford 2008

2008 Season

	M	Inn	NO	Runs	HS	Avg	100	50	Ct	St	Balls	Runs	Wkts	Avg	BB	5I	10M
Test																	
FC	9	17	3	307	93*	21.92	-	2	5	-	90	58	1	58.00	1-19	-	-
ODI																	
List A																	
20/20 Int																	
20/20																	

Career Performances

	M	Inn	NO	Runs	HS	Avg	100	50	Ct	St	Balls	Runs	Wkts	Avg	BB	5I	10M
Test																	
FC	15	26	5	530	93*	25.23	-	3	8	-	120	82	2	41.00	1-19	-	-
ODI																	
List A	3	2	0	37	36	18.50	-	-	-	-	0	0	0		-	-	
20/20 Int																	
20/20																	

96. Who took forty-one English wickets in the 1978-79 Ashes series?

WESTWOOD, I. J. — Warwickshire

Name: Ian James Westwood
Role: Left-hand opening bat, right-arm off-spin bowler; club captain
Born: 13 July 1982, Birmingham
Height: 5ft 8in **Weight:** 11st
Nickname: Westy, Wezzo
County debut: 2003
Place in batting averages: 127th av. 29.76 (2007 80th av. 38.55)
Parents: Ann and Dave
Marital status: Single
Family links with cricket: 'Brother played Warwickshire Youth cricket'
Education: Wheelers Lane, Kings Heath; Solihull Sixth Form College
Qualifications: 10 GCSEs, BTEC Sports Science, Level 2 cricket coaching
Off-season: 'Working'
Overseas tours: Warwickshire Development squad to Cape Town 1998
Overseas teams played for: Hawkesbury CC, Sydney 2001-02; University CC, Perth 2004-05, 2005-06
Career highlights to date: 'First Championship century for Warwickshire'
Cricket moments to forget: 'Too many to mention'
Cricket superstitions: 'None'
Cricketers particularly admired: Brian Lara
Young players to look out for: Chris Woakes
Other sports played: Football (Coleshill Town FC)
Other sports followed: Football (Birmingham City)
Favourite band: Fleetwood Mac
Relaxations: 'Music, poker, TV'
Extras: Scored 250* v Worcestershire 2nd XI at Barnt Green 2003, sharing with Jonathan Trott (248) in an opening partnership of 429; also took 6-104 in Worcestershire 2nd XI's only innings. NBC Denis Compton Award for most promising young Warwickshire player 2007. Named as county captain November 2008.
Opinions on cricket: 'Too many Kolpaks'
Best batting: 178 Warwickshire v West Indies A, Edgbaston 2006
Best bowling: 2-46 Warwickshire v Kent, Edgbaston 2006

2008 Season

	M	Inn	NO	Runs	HS	Avg	100	50	Ct	St	Balls	Runs	Wkts	Avg	BB	5I	10M
Test																	
FC	11	17	0	506	176	29.76	1	2	5	-	12	2	0		-	-	-
ODI																	
List A	9	8	0	203	65	25.37	-	2	-	-	6	2	0		-	-	
20/20 Int																	
20/20	7	5	3	63	35 *	31.50	-	-	1	-	6	13	0		-	-	

Career Performances

	M	Inn	NO	Runs	HS	Avg	100	50	Ct	St	Balls	Runs	Wkts	Avg	BB	5I	10M
Test																	
FC	51	87	9	2811	178	36.03	6	14	24	-	257	173	4	43.25	2-46	-	-
ODI																	
List A	34	30	4	637	65	24.50	-	3	4	-	192	150	2	75.00	1-28	-	
20/20 Int																	
20/20	17	10	8	96	35 *	48.00	-	-	3	-	54	91	5	18.20	3-29	-	

WHARF, A. G. B. Glamorgan

Name: Alexander (Alex) George Busfield Wharf
Role: Right-hand bat, right-arm fast-medium bowler; all-rounder
Born: 4 June 1975, Bradford
Height: 6ft 4in **Weight:** 15st
Nickname: Gangster
County debut: 1994 (Yorks), 1998 (Notts), 2000 (Glamorgan)
County cap: 2000 (Glamorgan)
ODI debut: 2004
50 wickets in a season: 1
Place in batting averages: 187th av. 21.54 (2007 116th av. 33.00)
Place in bowling averages: 133rd av. 42.66 (2007 98th av. 35.05)
Parents: Jane and Derek
Wife and date of marriage: Shelley Jane, 1 December 2001
Children: Tristan Jack Busfield Wharf, 15 November 1997; Alf Alexander Busfield Wharf, 30 June 2001

Family links with cricket: Father played local cricket and brother Simon plays local cricket
Education: Buttershaw Upper School, Bradford; Thomas Danby College, Leeds
Qualifications: 6 GCSEs, City & Guilds in Sports Management, NCA coaching award, junior football coaching award
Overseas tours: England to Zimbabwe (one-day series) 2004-05, to South Africa 2004-05 (one-day series); England VI to Hong Kong 2005; England A to West Indies 2005-06; various pre-season tours with Yorkshire, Nottinghamshire and Glamorgan; MCC to Uganda 2007-08
Overseas teams played for: Somerset West, Cape Town 1993-95; Johnsonville CC, Wellington, New Zealand 1996-97; Universities, Wellington 1998-99
Cricket moments to forget: 'Too many to mention'
Cricket superstitions: 'None'
Cricketers particularly admired: Ian Botham
Other sports played: Football
Other sports followed: Football (Manchester United, Bradford City)
Relaxations: 'Spending time with family and friends, movies, PlayStation 2, eating (too much), TV, gym, football'
Extras: Took hat-trick (Wagg, Knight, Pretorius) v Warwickshire at Edgbaston in the totesport League 2004. Had figures of 6-5 v Kent at Cardiff in the totesport League 2004 (match reduced to 25 overs a side). Made ODI debut v India at Trent Bridge in the NatWest Challenge 2004, taking a wicket in each of his first three overs, finishing with 3-30 and winning Man of the Match award
Best batting: 128* Glamorgan v Gloucestershire, Bristol 2007
Best bowling: 6-59 Glamorgan v Gloucestershire, Bristol 2005

2008 Season

	M	Inn	NO	Runs	HS	Avg	100	50	Ct	St	Balls	Runs	Wkts	Avg	BB	5I	10M
Test																	
FC	10	14	3	237	51 *	21.54	-	1	3	-	1154	896	21	42.66	3-10	-	-
ODI																	
List A	13	10	3	88	27 *	12.57	-	-	-	-	491	424	22	19.27	4-50	-	
20/20 Int																	
20/20	6	2	1	11	11	11.00	-	-	2	-	108	214	5	42.80	2-46	-	

Career Performances

	M	Inn	NO	Runs	HS	Avg	100	50	Ct	St	Balls	Runs	Wkts	Avg	BB	5I	10M
Test																	
FC	121	184	29	3570	128 *	23.03	6	14	63	-	16825	10941	293	37.34	6-59	5	1
ODI	13	5	3	19	9	9.50	-	-	1	-	584	428	18	23.77	4-24	-	
List A	154	109	22	1411	72	16.21	-	1	42	-	6497	5552	192	28.91	6-5	1	
20/20 Int																	
20/20	29	16	7	137	19	15.22	-	-	5	-	567	930	36	25.83	4-39	-	

WHEATER, A. J. — Essex

Name: Adam Jack Wheater
Role: Right-hand bat, wicket-keeper
Born: 13 February 1990, Whipps Cross, London
County debut: 2008
Overseas tours: England U19 to South Africa 2008-09
Extras: Played for Essex U17. Made 2nd XI Championship debut 2006. Played for South U17 in ECB U17 Regional Festival at Loughborough 2007. Has played for England U19. Plays for Saffron Walden CC
Best batting: 22 Essex v Derbyshire, Derby 2008

2008 Season

	M	Inn	NO	Runs	HS	Avg	100	50	Ct	St	Balls	Runs	Wkts	Avg	BB	5I	10M
Test																	
FC	2	1	0	22	22	22.00	-	-	3	-	0	0	0		-	-	-
ODI																	
List A																	
20/20 Int																	
20/20																	

Career Performances

	M	Inn	NO	Runs	HS	Avg	100	50	Ct	St	Balls	Runs	Wkts	Avg	BB	5I	10M
Test																	
FC	2	1	0	22	22	22.00	-	-	3	-	0	0	0		-	-	-
ODI																	
List A																	
20/20 Int																	
20/20																	

WHEELDON, D. A. Worcestershire

Name: David Antony Wheeldon
Role: Left-hand bat, leg-spin bowler
Born: 12 April 1989, Staffordshire
Height: 5ft 8in **Weight:** 11st 8lbs
Nickname: Wheels
County debut: No first-team appearance
Education: Painsley Catholic High School; Moorlands 6th Form; Worcester University
Qualifications: 12 GCSEs, 3 A-levels
Overseas tours: England U16 to South Africa 2005
Other sports followed: Football (Stoke City)
Extras: Made 2nd XI Championship debut 2006. Played for Staffordshire in the Minor Counties Championship 2006

WHELAN, C. D. Worcestershire

Name: Christopher (Chris) David Whelan
Role: Right-hand bat, right-arm fast bowler
Born: 8 May 1986, Liverpool
Height: 6ft 2in **Weight:** 12st 8lbs
Nickname: R-Kid, Wheelo, Scouse, Juan
County debut: 2004 (one-day, Middlesex), 2005 (first-class, Middlesex)
Place in bowling averages: 123rd av. 40.10
Parents: Sue and Dave
Marital status: Single
Family links with cricket: 'Dad was an accomplished left-hand opening bat'
Education: St Margaret's High School, Liverpool; St Margaret's 6th Form
Qualifications: 11 GCSEs, 3 A-levels, Level 1 coaching
Career outside cricket: 'Property'
Off-season: 'In Worcester, lifting the Gym'
Overseas tours: Middlesex to Mumbai 2004-05, 2005-06, to Perth, WA 2007-08
Overseas teams played for: Randwick-Petersham, Sydney 2005-06; Fairfield Liverpool CC, Sydney 2007-08
Career highlights to date: 'Playing at Lord's – Pro40 debut'
Cricket superstitions: 'Clean socks every session'
Cricketers particularly admired: Brett Lee

Young players to look out for: Alexi Kervezee
Other sports played: Football, golf
Other sports followed: Football (Everton)
Favourite band: Fall-out Boy
Relaxations: 'Internet poker; DVDs'
Extras: Merseyside Young Sports Personality of the Year 2004-05. Left Middlesex at the end of the 2007 season and joined Worcestershire for 2008
Opinions on cricket: 'Cricket is moving in the right direction with emphasis on four-day cricket and Twenty20. Reduce the number of Kolpaks to help English players gain more experience at the top level. '
Best batting: 58 Worcestershire v Middlesex, Kidderminster 2008
Best bowling: 4-66 Worcestershire v Warwickshire, New Road 2008

2008 Season

	M	Inn	NO	Runs	HS	Avg	100	50	Ct	St	Balls	Runs	Wkts	Avg	BB	5I	10M
Test																	
FC	6	5	2	82	58	27.33	-	1	1	-	485	401	10	40.10	4-66	-	-
ODI																	
List A	6	2	0	4	4	2.00	-	-	1	-	162	189	8	23.62	4-78	-	
20/20 Int																	
20/20	6	2	1	2	2	2.00	-	-	1	-	102	165	7	23.57	2-24	-	

Career Performances

	M	Inn	NO	Runs	HS	Avg	100	50	Ct	St	Balls	Runs	Wkts	Avg	BB	5I	10M
Test																	
FC	9	8	3	92	58	18.40	-	1	1	-	790	614	21	29.23	4-66	-	-
ODI																	
List A	11	6	0	15	6	2.50	-	-	1	-	312	361	9	40.11	4-78	-	
20/20 Int																	
20/20	6	2	1	2	2	2.00	-	-	1	-	102	165	7	23.57	2-24	-	

WHITE, C. Yorkshire

Name: Craig White
Role: Right-hand bat, right-arm fast-medium bowler
Born: 16 December 1969, Morley, Yorkshire
Height: 6ft 1in **Weight:** 11st 11lbs
Nickname: Chalky, Bassey
County debut: 1990
County cap: 1993
Benefit: 2002
Test debut: 1994
ODI debut: 1994-95
Place in batting averages: (2007 182nd av. 24.77)
Parents: Fred Emsley and Cynthia Anne
Wife and date of marriage: Elizabeth Anne, 19 September 1992
Family links with cricket: Father played for Pudsey St Lawrence
Education: Flora Hill High School; Bendigo Senior High School (both Victoria, Australia)
Overseas tours: Australia YC to West Indies 1989-90; England A to Pakistan 1995-96, to Australia 1996-97; England to Australia 1994-95, to India and Pakistan (World Cup) 1995-96, to Zimbabwe and New Zealand 1996-97, to South Africa and Zimbabwe 1999-2000 (one-day series), to Kenya (ICC Knockout Trophy) 2000-01, to Pakistan and Sri Lanka 2000-01, to India and New Zealand 2001-02, to Australia 2002-03, to Africa (World Cup) 2002-03
Overseas teams played for: Victoria, Australia 1990-91; Central Districts, New Zealand 1999-2000
Cricketers particularly admired: Graeme Hick, Mark Waugh, Brian Lara
Other sports followed: Leeds RFC, motocross, golf, tennis
Relaxations: Playing guitar, reading, gardening and socialising
Extras: Man of the Match in the second ODI v Zimbabwe at Bulawayo 1999-2000 (5-21/26). Took National League hat-trick (Fleming, Patel, Masters) v Kent at Headingley 2000. Scored 93 in the first Test at Lahore 2000-01, in the process sharing with Graham Thorpe (118) in a new record sixth-wicket partnership for England in Tests v Pakistan (166). Scored maiden Test century (121) in the second Test v India at Ahmedabad 2001-02, winning Man of the Match award. C&G Man of the Match award for his 4-35 and 78-ball 100* in the semi-final v Surrey at Headingley 2002. Captain of Yorkshire 2004-06. Has not played a first-class game for the county since August 2007.
Best batting: 186 Yorkshire v Lancashire, Old Trafford 2001
Best bowling: 8-55 Yorkshire v Gloucestershire, Gloucester 1998

2008 Season

	M	Inn	NO	Runs	HS	Avg	100	50	Ct	St	Balls	Runs	Wkts	Avg	BB	5I	10M
Test																	
FC																	
ODI																	
List A	7	7	3	195	69 *	48.75	-	2	2	-	0	0	0		-	-	
20/20 Int																	
20/20	2	2	0	26	26	13.00	-	-	-	-	1	0	1	0.00	1-0	-	

Career Perfomances

	M	Inn	NO	Runs	HS	Avg	100	50	Ct	St	Balls	Runs	Wkts	Avg	BB	5I	10M
Test	30	50	7	1052	121	24.46	1	5	14	-	3959	2220	59	37.62	5-32	3	-
FC	276	438	57	12395	186	32.53	21	62	167	-	21286	11260	395	28.50	8-55	11	-
ODI	51	41	5	568	57 *	15.77	-	1	12	-	2364	1726	65	26.55	5-21	1	
List A	362	323	47	7317	148	26.51	5	30	101	-	11575	8462	337	25.10	5-19	3	
20/20 Int																	
20/20	33	31	0	570	55	18.38	-	2	8	-	71	132	2	66.00	1-0	-	

WHITE, G. G. — Northamptonshire

Name: Graeme Geoffrey White
Role: Right-hand bat, slow left-arm bowler; all-rounder
Born: 18 April 1987, Milton Keynes
Height: 5ft 11in **Weight:** 10st
Nickname: Whitey, Chalky, Pony
County debut: 2006
Parents: David and Sophie
Marital status: Single
Family links with cricket: Sister Rachel played England Women U17. Father played good standard club cricket and is also a Level 2 coach. Brother Russell played county U11
Education: Stowe School, Buckingham
Qualifications: 9 GCSEs, 1 AS-level, 3 A-levels, coaching Level 2
Overseas tours: Stowe School to India 2004; England U19 to Sri Lanka (U19 World Cup) 2005-06
Career highlights to date: 'Representing my country at the U19 World Cup in Sri Lanka in 2006 and reaching the semi-finals'

Cricket moments to forget: 'Getting hit for five sixes in one over playing for Stowe School (they kept going further!)'
Cricket superstitions: 'Putting pads on from the top down'
Cricketers particularly admired: Bishan Bedi, Phil Tufnell, Daniel Vettori
Young players to look out for: Russell White, Moeen Ali, Andy Miller
Other sports played: Badminton, hockey, football
Other sports followed: Football ('big Manchester United fan')
Favourite band: Kings of Leon, Bloc Party
Relaxations: 'Like listening to music. Playing PS2'
Extras: Represented England U15, U17 and U19. Dorothy Radd Shield (Northamptonshire) 2003. Colin Shillington Award (Stowe School) 2005. NBC Denis Compton Award for the most promising young Northamptonshire player 2004, 2005, 2007
Best batting: 65 Northamptonshire v Glamorgan, Colwyn Bay 2007
Best bowling: 2-35 Northamptonshire v CUCCE, Fenner's 2007

2008 Season

	M	Inn	NO	Runs	HS	Avg	100	50	Ct	St	Balls	Runs	Wkts	Avg	BB	5I	10M
Test																	
FC	1	1	0	0	0	0.00	-	-	-	-	114	63	0		-	-	-
ODI																	
List A	1	0	0	0	0		-	-	-	-	36	29	0		-	-	
20/20 Int																	
20/20																	

Career Performances

	M	Inn	NO	Runs	HS	Avg	100	50	Ct	St	Balls	Runs	Wkts	Avg	BB	5I	10M
Test																	
FC	6	6	0	108	65	18.00	-	1	1	-	642	284	3	94.66	2-35	-	-
ODI																	
List A	6	3	0	16	14	5.33	-	-	3	-	210	174	4	43.50	2-44	-	
20/20 Int																	
20/20	4	0	0	0	0		-	-	1	-	30	70	1	70.00	1-10	-	

97. Who scored 179 not out in the Ashes Test at Headingly in 2001?

WHITE, R. A. Northamptonshire

Name: Robert (Rob) Allan White
Role: Right-hand bat, leg-spin bowler
Born: 15 October 1979, Chelmsford, Essex
Height: 5ft 11in **Weight:** 13st 7lbs
Nickname: Whitey
County debut: 2000
1st-Class 200s: 1
1000 runs in a season: 1
Place in batting averages: 28th av. 49.38 (2007 91st av. 37.31)
Parents: Dennis and Ann
Wife and date of marriage: Emma, 20 December 2008
Family links with cricket: 'Grandfather on Essex committee for many years. Dad flailed the willow and brother travels the local leagues high and low'
Education: Stowe School, Buckingham; St John's College, Durham University; Loughborough University
Qualifications: 9 GCSEs, 3 A-levels, Degree in Politics
Off-season: 'Having an operation on my knee. Getting married just before Christmas'
Overseas tours: British Universities to South Africa 2001
Overseas teams played for: Mount Lawley, Perth, WA 2002-03
Career highlights to date: 'Scoring 277 v Gloucestershire in 2002, the highest maiden century by an Englishman.'
Cricket moments to forget: 'Franklyn Rose telling me my mates had bet £10 that he couldn't injure me, as I walked out to play Lashings. Brother-in-law Ryan Cummings getting me out last year'
Cricketers particularly admired: Viv Richards
Young players to look out for: Alex Wakeley
Other sports played: Badminton, squash, golf, kabaddi
Other sports followed: Football (West Ham), rugby (Northampton Saints)
Extras: Northamptonshire League Young Player of the Year and Youth Cricketer of the Year 1999. Northamptonshire Young Player of the Year (Frank Rudd Trophy) 2001. Played for Loughborough UCCE 2001, 2002 and 2003. Recorded the highest maiden century in the history of English first-class cricket (277, including a hundred before lunch on the first day), v Gloucestershire at Northampton 2002 in his fifth first-class match. NBC Denis Compton Award for the most promising young Northamptonshire player 2002. Represented British Universities 2003
Opinions on cricket: 'The structure of cricket has been moving in the right direction over the last five years'

Best batting: 277 Northamptonshire v Gloucestershire, Northampton 2002
Best bowling: 2-30 Northamptonshire v Gloucestershire, Northampton 2002

2008 Season

	M	Inn	NO	Runs	HS	Avg	100	50	Ct	St	Balls	Runs	Wkts	Avg	BB	5I	10M
Test																	
FC	15	25	4	1037	132 *	49.38	3	6	11	-	0	0	0		-	-	-
ODI																	
List A	11	10	0	213	111	21.30	1	1	2	-	0	0	0		-	-	
20/20 Int																	
20/20	11	11	2	288	94 *	32.00	-	1	3	-	0	0	0		-	-	

Career Performances

	M	Inn	NO	Runs	HS	Avg	100	50	Ct	St	Balls	Runs	Wkts	Avg	BB	5I	10M
Test																	
FC	70	119	11	3690	277	34.16	6	17	44	-	1120	800	14	57.14	2-30	-	-
ODI																	
List A	64	61	2	1197	111	20.28	2	5	12	-	54	55	2	27.50	2-18	-	
20/20 Int																	
20/20	31	28	3	605	94 *	24.20	-	3	6	-	0	0	0		-	-	

WHITE, W. A. — Derbyshire

Name: Wayne Andrew White
Role: Right-hand bat, right-arm fast-medium bowler; all-rounder
Born: 22 April 1985, Derby
Height: 6ft 2in **Weight:** 13st
Nickname: Chalky, Stix, Philip Schofield
County debut: 2005
Place in batting averages: (2007 277th av. 10.16)
Place in bowling averages: (2007 104th av. 38.58)
Parents: John and Sharon
Marital status: Single
Family links with cricket: 'Brother U13 Midlands/Derbyshire'
Education: John Port School, Etwall; Nottingham University

Qualifications: 11 GCSEs, 4 A-levels, BA Politics
Career outside cricket: 'Semi-professional footballer; internet business – www.darts-store.com'
Career highlights to date: 'First wicket for Derbyshire – Anthony McGrath; and 5-87 v Northamptonshire [2007]'
Cricket moments to forget: '0-107 in the first innings of my debut against Yorkshire'
Cricketers particularly admired: Mike Hendrick, Graeme Welch, Andy Caddick
Young players to look out for: Jake Needham
Other sports played: Football (Gresley Rovers, Burton Albion, Mickleover Sports, Derby County), golf
Other sports followed: Football (Derby County, LA Galaxy)
Favourite band: Arctic Monkeys, Stone Roses
Relaxations: 'Internet, Xbox 360, spread betting'
Extras: Scored 76 and took 7-18 on club cricket debut for Swarkestone. NBC Denis Compton Award for the most promising young Derbyshire player 2006. Released at the end of the 2008 season
Opinions on cricket: 'Scrap Pro40. One hour for lunch.'
Best batting: 19* Derbyshire v Surrey, Derby 2006
Best bowling: 5-87 Derbyshire v Northamptonshire, Northampton 2007

2008 Season

	M	Inn	NO	Runs	HS	Avg	100	50	Ct	St	Balls	Runs	Wkts	Avg	BB	5I	10M
Test																	
FC	4	6	1	40	18	8.00	-	-	2	-	588	374	8	46.75	2-33	-	-
ODI																	
List A	3	3	1	18	10	9.00	-	-	-	-	90	101	3	33.66	3-47	-	
20/20 Int																	
20/20																	

Career Performances

	M	Inn	NO	Runs	HS	Avg	100	50	Ct	St	Balls	Runs	Wkts	Avg	BB	5I	10M
Test																	
FC	11	16	3	146	19 *	11.23	-	-	5	-	1745	1200	31	38.70	5-87	1	
ODI																	
List A	14	10	4	79	25	13.16	-	-	4	-	545	538	10	53.80	3-47	-	
20/20 Int																	
20/20																	

WHITELEY, R. A. Derbyshire

Name: Ross Andrew Whiteley
Role: Left-hand bat, left-arm medium-fast bowler, wicket-keeper; all-rounder
Born: 13 September 1988, Sheffield, Yorkshire
Height: 6ft 2in **Weight:** 13st 5lbs
Nickname: Rossco
County debut: 2008
Parents: Sue and Steve
Marital status: Single
Family links with cricket: 'Brother, Adam, played Derbyshire age-groups and some Derbyshire 2nd XI games.'
Education: Westfield School, Sheffield; Repton School 6th form; Leeds Metropolitan University
Qualifications: 10 GCSEs, 3 A-levels
Career outside cricket: 'Student'

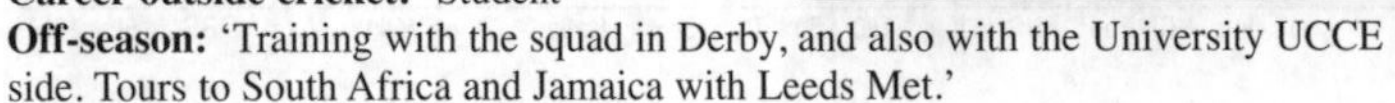

Off-season: 'Training with the squad in Derby, and also with the University UCCE side. Tours to South Africa and Jamaica with Leeds Met.'
Overseas tours: Repton to Sri Lanka 2005; Derbyshire Academy to South Africa 2006
Career highlights to date: 'Making my first-team debut against Glamorgan at Cardiff in a floodlit Pro40 game on Sky.'
Cricket moments to forget: 'Breaking my nose and getting knocked unconscious in winter nets 2005, attempting to pull the triallists'
Cricket superstitions: 'When batting, scrape the mark three times when I come on strike.'
Cricketers particularly admired: Michael Bevan, Ryan Sidebottom
Young players to look out for: Dan Redfern, Edward Jones
Other sports played: Football (Repton 1st XI), rugby (Repton 1st XV)
Other sports followed: Football (Sheffield United)
Favourite band: Oasis - 'but more into funky electro house'
Relaxations: Gym, socialising with friends, DJ-ing, sleep
Extras: Played for Chesterfield CC. Made Derbyshire 2nd XI debut in 2006.
Opinions on cricket: 'The introduction of Twenty20 cricket has had an effect on the way teams go about structuring an innings in all the other forms of cricket, resulting in higher-scoring games and much more interesting run chases.'
Best batting: 27 Derbyshire v Leicestershire, Grace Road 2008

2008 Season

	M	Inn	NO	Runs	HS	Avg	100	50	Ct	St	Balls	Runs	Wkts	Avg	BB	5I	10M
Test																	
FC	1	2	0	45	27	22.50	-	-	-	-	66	38	0		-	-	-
ODI																	
List A	1	1	0	24	24	24.00	-	-	1	-	12	12	0		-	-	
20/20 Int																	
20/20																	

Career Performances

	M	Inn	NO	Runs	HS	Avg	100	50	Ct	St	Balls	Runs	Wkts	Avg	BB	5I	10M
Test																	
FC	1	2	0	45	27	22.50	-	-	-	-	66	38	0		-	-	-
ODI																	
List A	1	1	0	24	24	24.00	-	-	1	-	12	12	0		-	-	
20/20 Int																	
20/20																	

WIGLEY, D. H. — Northamptonshire

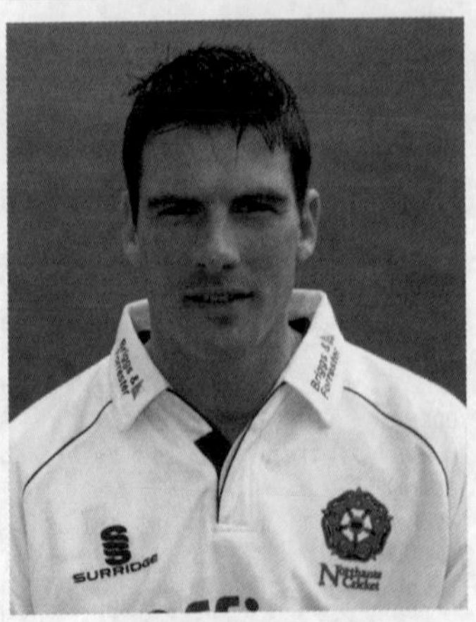

Name: David Harry Wigley
Role: Right-hand bat, right-arm fast-medium bowler
Born: 26 October 1981, Bradford, Yorkshire
Height: 6ft 3in **Weight:** 14st
Nickname: Wiggy, Wiggers, Wigs
County debut: 2002 (Yorkshire), 2003 (Worcestershire), 2006 (Northamptonshire)
County colours: 2003 (Worcestershire)
Place in batting averages: (2007 200th av. 22.30)
Place in bowling averages: 106th av. 35.16 (2007 47th av. 27.52)
Parents: Max and Judith
Marital status: Single
Family links with cricket: Father played league cricket in Liverpool Competition, Bradford League and Durham Senior League
Education: St Mary's RC Comprehensive, Menston; Loughborough University
Qualifications: 9 GCSEs, 3 A-levels, degree in Sport and Exercise Science, ECB Level I coaching

Overseas tours: British Universities to Cape Town 2004
Overseas teams played for: Gormandale CC, Victoria 2001; Mount Lawley CC, Perth 2004-05
Career highlights to date: 'Taking my first five-for in first-class cricket against Pakistan'
Cricket moments to forget: 'Losing Uni final at Lord's 2004 in last over'
Cricket superstitions: 'Must turn to left to run in and bowl'
Cricketers particularly admired: Darren Gough, Andrew Flintoff
Young players to look out for: Moeen Ali
Other sports played: Golf, rugby ('used to play to decent standard; gave up at 16')
Other sports followed: Football (Leeds United), rugby (Llanelli Scarlets)
Relaxations: 'Music, films, golf'
Extras: Played for ECB Schools v Sri Lanka U19 2000. Yorkshire U19 Bowling Award 2000. Played for Loughborough UCCE 2002-04 (captain 2004), taking 5-52 v Oxford in the UCCE One-Day Challenge at Lord's and 5-71 v Hampshire at The Rose Bowl 2002. Represented British Universities 2003 and (as captain) 2004
Opinions on cricket: 'Probably play too much county cricket, not allowing enough time for recovery and practice.'
Best batting: 70 Northamptonshire v Middlesex, Northampton 2007
Best bowling: 5-77 Northamptonshire v Pakistanis, Northampton 2006

2008 Season

	M	Inn	NO	Runs	HS	Avg	100	50	Ct	St	Balls	Runs	Wkts	Avg	BB	5I	10M
Test																	
FC	9	11	4	60	18 *	8.57	-	-	2	-	1248	844	24	35.16	5-78	1	-
ODI																	
List A	2	1	0	0	0	0.00	-	-	-	-	78	80	0		-	-	
20/20 Int																	
20/20																	

Career Performances

	M	Inn	NO	Runs	HS	Avg	100	50	Ct	St	Balls	Runs	Wkts	Avg	BB	5I	10M
Test																	
FC	38	47	14	458	70	13.87	-	2	17	-	5364	3702	104	35.59	5-77	2	-
ODI																	
List A	23	11	0	32	10	2.90	-	-	4	-	792	832	15	55.46	4-37	-	
20/20 Int																	
20/20	2	1	0	1	1	1.00	-	-	-	-	30	33	1	33.00	1-8	-	

WILLIAMS, R. E. M. — Middlesex

Name: Robert (Robbie) Edward Morgan Williams
Role: Right-hand bat, right-arm fast-medium bowler
Born: 19 January 1987, Pembury, Kent
Height: 6ft **Weight:** 13st 2lbs
County debut: 2007
Parents: Gail and Tim
Marital status: Single
Education: Marlborough College; Durham University
Qualifications: 3 A-levels
Overseas tours: Marlborough College to South Africa 2003
Overseas teams played for: Corrimal, Wollongong 2005-06
Career highlights to date: 'Taking five wickets on Championship debut'
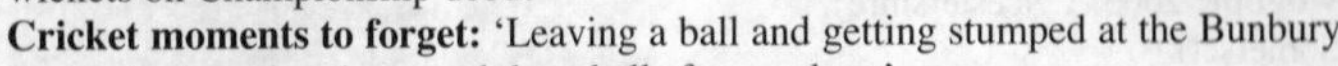
Cricket moments to forget: 'Leaving a ball and getting stumped at the Bunbury Festival when nine down and three balls from a draw'
Cricket superstitions: 'Batsmen can be jinxed'
Cricketers particularly admired: Brett Lee
Young players to look out for: Laurie Evans, Steven Finn
Other sports played: Rugby (Marlborough College 1st XV), hockey (Marlborough College 1st XI)
Other sports followed: Rugby union (Leicester Tigers)
Favourite band: Pendulum
Relaxations: 'Sudoku, yoga, table tennis'
Extras: Played for Durham UCCE 2007, taking 5-70 v Lancashire at Durham. Played for MCC 2007. Took 5-112 on Championship debut v Essex at Chelmsford 2007. Played for Durham UCCE in 2008
Best batting: 15 Middlesex v Essex, Chelmsford 2007
Best bowling: 5-70 DUCCE v Lancashire, Durham 2007

2008 Season

	M	Inn	NO	Runs	HS	Avg	100	50	Ct	St	Balls	Runs	Wkts	Avg	BB	5I	10M
Test																	
FC	1	1	0	4	4	4.00	-	-	-	-	78	39	4	9.75	4-39	-	-
ODI																	
List A																	
20/20 Int																	
20/20																	

Career Performances

	M	Inn	NO	Runs	HS	Avg	100	50	Ct	St	Balls	Runs	Wkts	Avg	BB	5I	10M
Test																	
FC	6	9	4	34	15	6.80	-	-	2	-	874	563	17	33.11	5-70	2	-
ODI																	
List A	1	0	0	0	0		-	-	-	-	36	49	0		-	-	
20/20 Int																	
20/20																	

WILLOUGHBY, C. M. Somerset

Name: Charl Myles Willoughby
Role: Left-hand bat, left-arm fast-medium bowler
Born: 3 December 1974, Cape Town, South Africa
Height: 6ft 3in **Weight:** 12st 12lbs
Nickname: Puppy, Harry
County debut: 2005 (Leicestershire), 2006 (Somerset)
County cap: 2005 (Leicestershire), 2007 (Somerset)
Test debut: 2003
ODI debut: 1999-2000
50 wickets in a season: 2
Place in batting averages: 252nd av. 11.66
Place in bowling averages: 38th av. 25.90 (2007 31st av. 24.67)
Parents: David and Belinda
Wife and date of marriage: Nicky, 17 April 2004
Children: Cole, 18 October 2006

Family links with cricket: 'Father played club cricket'
Education: Wynberg Boys' High School; Stellenbosch University and UNISA
Overseas tours: South Africa Academy to Zimbabwe 1998-99; South Africa A to West Indies 2000, to Zimbabwe 2004; South Africa to Sharjah (Coca-Cola Sharjah Cup) 1999-2000, to Bangladesh 2003, to England 2003
Overseas teams played for: Boland 1994-95 – 1999-2000; Western Province 2000-01 – 2003-04; Western Province Boland 2003-04 – 2004-05; Cape Cobras 2005-06 – 2006-07
Career highlights to date: 'Test and ODI debuts. Four wickets in four balls in first-class match v Dolphins'

Cricket moments to forget: 'Dislocating my shoulder diving on boundary'
Cricketers particularly admired: Graeme Smith, Andrew Flintoff, Wasim Akram
Young players to look out for: JP Duminy, Stuart Broad
Other sports followed: Rugby (Stormers)
Favourite band: Coldplay
Relaxations: 'Movies and time with my wife'
Extras: Played for Berkshire in the NatWest 2000. Took four wickets in four balls v Dolphins at Durban in the Supersport Series 2005-06; the feat was spread over two innings and consisted of a hat-trick (Mhlongo, Gobind, Hayward) plus the wicket of Watson with his first ball of the second innings. Has won several match awards, including Man of the Match for South Africa A v Barbados at Bridgetown 2000 (6-24) and for Leicestershire v Somerset at Leicester in the C&G 2005 (6-16; the best one-day return by a Leicestershire bowler). An overseas player with Leicestershire 2005. Joined Somerset in 2006. Is no longer considered an overseas player
Best batting: 47 Somerset v Worcestershire, Taunton 2006
Best bowling: 7-44 Somerset v Gloucestershire, Taunton 2006

2008 Season

	M	Inn	NO	Runs	HS	Avg	100	50	Ct	St	Balls	Runs	Wkts	Avg	BB	5I	10M
Test																	
FC	17	17	11	70	18	11.66	-	-	1	-	3066	1399	54	25.90	4-65	-	-
ODI																	
List A	15	4	4	9	5 *	-	-	-	2	-	768	512	17	30.11	4-33	-	
20/20 Int																	
20/20	5	1	1	2	2 *	-	-	-	2	-	102	136	4	34.00	2-28	-	

Career Performances

	M	Inn	NO	Runs	HS	Avg	100	50	Ct	St	Balls	Runs	Wkts	Avg	BB	5I	10M
Test	2	0	0	0	0		-	-	-	-	300	125	1	125.00	1-47	-	-
FC	177	202	92	676	47	6.14	-	-	37	-	35526	16443	662	24.83	7-44	27	3
ODI	3	2	0	0	0	0.00	-	-	-	-	168	148	2	74.00	2-39	-	
List A	193	57	32	132	12 *	5.28	-	-	26	-	9440	6499	240	27.07	6-16	5	
20/20 Int																	
20/20	50	11	9	22	11	11.00	-	-	9	-	1097	1250	54	23.14	4-9	-	

98. By what margin did England beat Australia in the second Test at Edgbaston in 2005?

WILSON, G. C. Surrey

Name: Gary Craig Wilson
Role: Right-hand bat, wicket-keeper, very occasional right-arm medium bowler
Born: 5 February 1986, Dundonald, Co Roscommon, Ireland
Height: 5ft 10in **Weight:** 13st 2lbs
Nickname: Gaz, Wils
County debut: 2008 (one-day)
ODI debut: 2007
Twenty20 Int debut: 2008
Parents: George and Iris
Marital status: 'Unmarried'
Family links with cricket: 'Dad played league cricket in Ireland'
Education: Methodist College, Belfast
Qualifications: 10 GCSEs, 3 A-levels, gym instructor Level 2, FA Level 1
Career outside cricket: 'Bit of coaching'

Overseas tours: Ireland U19 to Bangladesh (U19 World Cup) 2003-04, to Sri Lanka (U19 World Cup) 2005-06; Ireland A to UAE (EurAsia Series) 2006, plus various Ireland age-group and Ireland A tours
Overseas teams played for: Portland Colts CC, Melbourne 2004-05; Durbanville CC, Cape Town 2006-07
Career highlights to date: 'Playing first game of U19 World Cup in Bangladesh; beating Scotland in the Inter-Continental Cup by three runs; being signed by Surrey'
Cricket moments to forget: 'Being beaten by three wickets by New Zealand in U19 World Cup 2005-06 after scoring 304; being beaten by four runs by England in the same World Cup; pair on debut for Surrey 2nd XI'
Cricket superstitions: 'Left pad first'
Cricketers particularly admired: Alec Stewart, Brian Lara, Mark Boucher
Young players to look out for: Gary Kidd, William Porterfield, Paul Stirling
Other sports played: Rugby, football, golf ('badly')
Other sports followed: Football (Man United), rugby (Ireland)
Favourite band: 'Any really'
Extras: Player of the Tournament at European U19 Championship 2003 and 2004. MCC Young Cricketer 2005-06. Has represented Ireland in first-class and one-day cricket, including an ODI and the 2006 C&G and 2007 Friends Provident; has also represented Ireland A in one-day (List A) cricket
Opinions on cricket: 'A lot of cricket being played in England – good for the advertising of the game; wouldn't fancy being a quick bowler, though.'
Best batting: 27 Ireland v Netherlands Rotterdam, 2008

2008 Season

	M	Inn	NO	Runs	HS	Avg	100	50	Ct	St	Balls	Runs	Wkts	Avg	BB	5I	10M
Test																	
FC																	
ODI																	
List A	7	6	1	128	58	25.60	-	1	3	2	0	0	0		-	-	
20/20 Int																	
20/20	2	2	0	1	1	.50	-	-	3	-	0	0	0		-	-	

Career Performances

	M	Inn	NO	Runs	HS	Avg	100	50	Ct	St	Balls	Runs	Wkts	Avg	BB	5I	10M
Test																	
FC	5	6	1	51	27	10.20	-	-	9	-	0	0	0		-	-	-
ODI	7	7	0	132	51	18.85	-	1	4	1	0	0	0		-	-	
List A	25	23	1	476	58	21.63	-	5	20	4	0	0	0		-	-	
20/20 Int	4	3	0	21	14	7.00	-	-	-	-	0	0	0		-	-	
20/20	6	5	0	22	14	4.40	-	-	3	-	0	0	0		-	-	

WISEMAN, P. J. — Durham

Name: Paul John Wiseman
Role: Right-hand bat, right-arm off-spin bowler
Born: 4 May 1970, Auckland, New Zealand
Nickname: Whiz
County debut: 2006
Test debut: 1998
ODI debut: 1997-98
Place in batting averages: 167th av. 23.95 (2007 212th av. 20.57)
Place in bowling averages: 107th av. 36.11 (2007 64th av. 29.84)
Overseas tours: New Zealand Academy to South Africa 1997; New Zealand A to India 2001-02, to South Africa 2004-05, to Sri Lanka 2005-06; New Zealand to Zimbabwe 1997-98, to Sri Lanka 1998, to Malaysia (Commonwealth Games) 1998-99, to Bangladesh (Wills International Cup) 1998-99, to India 1999-2000, to Zimbabwe 2000-01, to Kenya (ICC Knockout Trophy) 2000-01, to South Africa 2000-01, to Australia 2001-02, to Sri Lanka 2003, to India 2003-04, to Bangladesh 2004-05, to

Australia 2004-05, plus other one-day tournaments and series in Sharjah, Singapore and Namibia
Overseas teams played for: Auckland 1991-92 – 1993-94; Otago 1994-95 – 2000-01; Canterbury 2001-02 – 2005-06
Extras: Has played cricket in the Lancashire Leagues for Rishton (1999), Haslingden (2005) and Milnrow (2005); and for Walkden in the Bolton League (2006). Man of the Match in the first Test v Zimbabwe at Bulawayo 2000-01 (5-90/3-54). His 9-13 (16.4-9-13-9) for Canterbury v Central Districts in the State Championship at Christchurch 2004-05 is the second best innings return in New Zealand first-class cricket history. Joined Durham towards the end of the 2006 season. Holds a British passport and is not considered an overseas player
Best batting: 130 Canterbury v Northern Districts, Hamilton 2005-06
Best bowling: 9-13 Canterbury v Central Districts, Christchurch (VG) 2004-05

2008 Season

	M	Inn	NO	Runs	HS	Avg	100	50	Ct	St	Balls	Runs	Wkts	Avg	BB	5I	10M
Test																	
FC	16	22	2	479	65	23.95	-	3	1	-	1182	614	17	36.11	4-87	-	-
ODI																	
List A	1	0	0	0	0		-	-	-	-	48	27	2	13.50	2-27	-	
20/20 Int																	
20/20	3	0	0	0	0		-	-	1	-	24	39	1	39.00	1-31	-	

Career Performances

	M	Inn	NO	Runs	HS	Avg	100	50	Ct	St	Balls	Runs	Wkts	Avg	BB	5I	10M
Test	25	34	8	366	36	14.07	-	-	11	-	5660	2903	61	47.59	5-82	2	-
FC	186	254	51	4254	130	20.95	2	16	79	-	34292	15727	466	33.74	9-13	18	4
ODI	15	7	5	45	16	22.50	-	-	2	-	450	368	12	30.66	4-45	-	
List A	120	82	19	967	65 *	15.34	-	2	28	-	4789	3414	84	40.64	4-45	-	
20/20 Int																	
20/20	10	1	0	0	0	0.00	-	-	3	-	120	152	9	16.88	2-20	-	

99. Upon completion of the 2005 Ashes Tests, who said: 'It's been my best ever series, but unfortunately it's not been good enough'?

WOAKES, C. R. Warwickshire

Name: Christopher (Chris) Roger Woakes
Role: Right-hand bat, right-arm fast-medium bowler
Born: 2 March 1989, Birmingham
Height: 6ft 2in **Weight:** 13st
Nickname: Woakesy, Jokes, Cheetah
County debut: 2006
Place in batting averages: 144th av. 27.44
Place in bowling averages: 14th av. 20.48
Parents: Roger and Elaine
Marital status: Single
Family links with cricket: 'Stepbrothers played club cricket'
Education: Barr Beacon Language School, Walsall
Qualifications: 7 GCSEs, 3 A-levels, Level 1 cricket coaching
Off-season: 'Staying fit and going to South Africa - Bloemfontein - January to March 2009'
Career outside cricket: 'Have not got a clue'
Overseas tours: Warwickshire Academy to Cape Town 2005; England U19 to Malaysia (U19 World Cup) 2007-08, to Sri Lanka 2007-08
Career highlights to date: 'Making Championship debut and representing England U19 v Pakistan 2007. Maiden 5-wicket haul v Glamorgan at Cardiff in the County Championship.'
Cricket superstitions: 'Always turn to my left at end of bowling run-up'
Cricketers particularly admired: Allan Donald, Glenn McGrath
Young players to look out for: Liam Dawson, Tom Lewis, James Harris
Other sports played: Football, golf, snooker
Other sports followed: Football (Aston Villa)
Favourite band: Feeder, Snow Patrol
Relaxations: 'Snooker, golf, music'
Extras: Played for Herefordshire in Minor Counties competitions 2006-07. England U17 squad 2006. Represented England U19 2007. Achieved a ten-wicket match haul (6-68, 4-94) in the final Championship game of the season v Glamorgan at Edgbaston in September 2008. NBC Denis Compton Award for the most promising young Warwickshire player 2008
Opinions on cricket: 'Twenty20 is a good game and is improving the sport and its popularity, but Test cricket and four-day cricket should always play the major role in the cricket arena.'
Best batting: 64* Warwickshire v Cambridge UCCE, Fenner's 2008
Best bowling: 6-68 Warwickshire v Glamorgan, Edgbaston 2008

2008 Season

	M	Inn	NO	Runs	HS	Avg	100	50	Ct	St	Balls	Runs	Wkts	Avg	BB	5I	10M
Test																	
FC	11	12	3	247	64 *	27.44	-	1	7	-	1848	922	45	20.48	6-68	3	1
ODI																	
List A	9	6	2	68	31 *	17.00	-	-	-	-	252	232	3	77.33	1-21	-	
20/20 Int																	
20/20	11	3	3	4	2 *		-	-	2	-	170	267	7	38.14	4-21	-	

Career Performances

	M	Inn	NO	Runs	HS	Avg	100	50	Ct	St	Balls	Runs	Wkts	Avg	BB	5I	10M
Test																	
FC	13	15	4	274	64 *	24.90	-	1	11	-	2104	1114	49	22.73	6-68	3	1
ODI																	
List A	10	6	2	68	31 *	17.00	-	-	-	-	252	232	3	77.33	1-21	-	
20/20 Int																	
20/20	11	3	3	4	2 *		-	-	2	-	170	267	7	38.14	4-21	-	

WOOD, M. J. Glamorgan

Name: Matthew James Wood
Role: Right-hand opening bat, off-spin bowler
Born: 6 April 1977, Huddersfield
Height: 5ft 9in **Weight:** 12st
Nickname: Ronnie, Chuddy
County debut: 1997 (Yorkshire), 2008 (Glamorgan)
County cap: 2001 (Yorkshire)
1000 runs in a season: 4
1st-Class 200s: 3
Place in batting averages: 208th av. 19.27
Parents: Roger and Kathryn
Marital status: Single
Family links with cricket: 'Father played for local team Emley. Mum made the teas and sister Caroline scored'
Education: Shelley High School and Sixth Form Centre
Qualifications: 9 GCSEs, 2 A-levels, NCA coaching award

Overseas tours: England U19 to Zimbabwe 1995-96; Yorkshire CCC to West Indies 1996-97, to Cape Town 1997, 1998; MCC to Kenya 1999, to Bangladesh 1999-2000; ECB National Academy to Australia 2001-02
Overseas teams played for: Somerset West CC, Cape Town 1994-95; Upper Hutt United CC, New Zealand 1997-98; Mosman Park, Western Australia 2000-01; Mosman CC, Sydney 2004-05
Career highlights to date: 'Being on the pitch as fielding 12th man for England series win v South Africa at Headingley [1998]. Winning the Championship in 2001 and winning the C&G 2002 at Lord's'
Cricket moments to forget: 'Most of the 2002 season'
Cricket superstitions: 'Not any more'
Cricketers particularly admired: Darren Lehmann, Matthew Maynard, Stephen Fleming, Michael Vaughan
Other sports played: Football (Kirkburton FC)
Other sports followed: Football (Liverpool FC)
Favourite band: Atomic Kitten
Relaxations: 'Socialising, eating out, golf, DIY'
Extras: Represented England U17. Attended Yorkshire Academy. Scored 1000 first-class runs in first full season 1998. Yorkshire Coach's Player of the Year, Yorkshire Club Player of the Year and Yorkshire Players' Player of the Year 2003. Set a new Yorkshire record individual score in the NatWest/C&G (160 from 124 balls) v Devon at Exmouth 2004, winning Man of the Match award. Vice-captain of Yorkshire 2003-04. Left Yorkshire during the 2007 season and has joined Glamorgan for 2008
Best batting: 207 Yorkshire v Somerset, Taunton 2003
Best bowling: 1-4 Yorkshire v Somerset, Headingley 2003
Stop press: Announced his retirement in February 2009.

2008 Season

	M	Inn	NO	Runs	HS	Avg	100	50	Ct	St	Balls	Runs	Wkts	Avg	BB	5I	10M
Test																	
FC	7	12	1	212	83 *	19.27	-	1	5	-	6	0	0		-	-	-
ODI																	
List A	6	6	1	193	91 *	38.60	-	2	3	-	25	22	0		-	-	
20/20 Int																	
20/20																	

Career Performances

	M	Inn	NO	Runs	HS	Avg	100	50	Ct	St	Balls	Runs	Wkts	Avg	BB	5I	10M
Test																	
FC	136	236	21	7032	207	32.70	16	31	118	-	84	43	2	21.50	1-4	-	-
ODI																	
List A	152	141	15	3464	160	27.49	5	16	60	-	91	98	3	32.66	3-45	-	
20/20 Int																	
20/20	15	15	3	328	96 *	27.33	-	2	11	-	18	32	2	16.00	1-11	-	

WOOD, M. J. Nottinghamshire

Name: Matthew James Wood
Role: Right-hand bat, right-arm off-spin bowler
Born: 30 September 1980, Exeter
Height: 5ft 11in **Weight:** 12st 6lbs
Nickname: Woody, Gran, Moo
County debut: 2001 (Somerset), 2008 (Nottinghamshire)
County cap: 2005 (Somerset)
1000 runs in a season: 1
1st-Class 200s: 1
Place in batting averages: 151st av. 26.95
Parents: James and Trina
Marital status: Single
Family links with cricket: Father is chairman of Devon Cricket Board
Education: Exmouth College; Exeter University
Qualifications: 10 GCSEs, 2 A-levels, ECB Level 3 coach
Career outside cricket: Coach
Overseas tours: West of England U15 to West Indies 1995
Overseas teams played for: Doubleview CC, Perth 2001, 2002
Career highlights to date: 'Winning the Twenty20 Cup and scoring 297 v Yorkshire'
Cricket moments to forget: 'Getting a pair v Essex 2005'
Cricket superstitions: 'None'
Cricketers particularly admired: Marcus Trescothick
Other sports followed: Football (Liverpool FC), horse racing
Relaxations: Golf
Extras: NBC Denis Compton Award for the most promising young Somerset player 2001. Scored century in each innings (106/131) v Surrey at Taunton 2002. Somerset Player of the Year 2002. Scored 297 v Yorkshire at Taunton 2005, the fifth highest individual score in Somerset's history. Vice-captain of Somerset July 2005-2006. Left Somerset at the end of the 2007 season and joined Nottinghamshire for 2008
Best batting: 297 Somerset v Yorkshire, Taunton 2005

2008 Season

	M	Inn	NO	Runs	HS	Avg	100	50	Ct	St	Balls	Runs	Wkts	Avg	BB	5I	10M
Test																	
FC	14	21	1	539	98	26.95	-	4	4	-	0	0	0		-	-	-
ODI																	
List A	8	8	0	124	50	15.50	-	1	-	-	0	0	0		-	-	
20/20 Int																	
20/20	1	1	0	10	10	10.00	-	-	-	-	0	0	0		-	-	

Career Performances

	M	Inn	NO	Runs	HS	Avg	100	50	Ct	St	Balls	Runs	Wkts	Avg	BB	5I	10M
Test																	
FC	90	153	7	4914	297	33.65	9	31	30	-	85	68	0		-	-	-
ODI																	
List A	83	79	4	2072	129	27.62	2	14	12	-	0	0	0		-	-	
20/20 Int																	
20/20	30	30	0	869	94	28.96	-	5	5	-	0	0	0		-	-	

WOODMAN, R. J. Gloucestershire

Name: Robert James Woodman
Role: Left-hand bat, left-arm medium-fast bowler
Born: 12 October 1986, Taunton, Somerset
Height: 5ft 11in
Nickname: Woody
County debut: 2005 (Somerset), 2008 (Gloucestershire)
Education: The Castle School, Taunton; Richard Huish College
Overseas tours: West of England U15 to West Indies; England U19 to Bangladesh 2005-06, to Sri Lanka (U19 World Cup) 2005-06
Overseas teams played for: Valley DCC, Brisbane, Australia 2008-09
Other sports played: Football (Bristol City Academy), basketball (Taunton Tigers Basketball Academy), tennis (South West Tennis Academy)
Other sports followed: Football (Tottenham Hotspur)

Extras: Played for Somerset in 2005; Somerset 2nd XI 2005-07; Devon 2007; MCC Young Cricketers 2008, as well as club cricket in the West of England. Played for MCC v Bangladesh A at Durham in a 50-over match in 2008. Has represented England at U15 and U17 level. Signed for Gloucestershire in September 2008, a week after scoring a century for MMC Young Cricketers v Gloucestershire 2nd XI
Best batting: 46* Somerset v Worcestershire, Worcester 2005
Best bowling: 4-65 Gloucestershire v Essex, Bristol 2008

2008 Season

	M	Inn	NO	Runs	HS	Avg	100	50	Ct	St	Balls	Runs	Wkts	Avg	BB	5I	10M
Test																	
FC	1	2	0	15	13	7.50	-	-	-	-	69	65	4	16.25	4-65	-	-
ODI																	
List A	1	1	0	14	14	14.00	-	-	-	-	18	27	0		-	-	
20/20 Int																	
20/20																	

Career Performances

	M	Inn	NO	Runs	HS	Avg	100	50	Ct	St	Balls	Runs	Wkts	Avg	BB	5I	10M
Test																	
FC	4	6	1	69	46*	13.80	-	-	-	-	465	333	6	55.50	4-65	-	-
ODI																	
List A	5	1	0	14	14	14.00	-	-	2	-	150	163	1	163.00	1-38	-	
20/20 Int																	
20/20	2	2	2	1	1*		-	-	-	-	42	63	2	31.50	2-37	-	

WRIGHT, B. J. Glamorgan

Name: Ben James Wright
Role: Right-hand bat, right-arm medium bowler
Born: 5 December 1987, Fulwood, Preston
Height: 5ft 8in **Weight:** 11st
Nickname: Kevin, Space, Bej
County debut: 2006
Place in batting averages: (2007 213th av. 20.56)
Parents: Julia and Peter
Marital status: Single
Education: Cowbridge Comprehensive
Qualifications: 11 GCSEs
Overseas tours: West of England U15 to West Indies 2003; England U16 to South Africa 2004; England U19 to Bangladesh 2005-06, to Sri Lanka (U19 World Cup) 2005-06, to Malaysia 2006-07

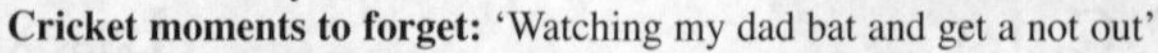

Cricket moments to forget: 'Watching my dad bat and get a not out'
Cricket superstitions: 'All left kit goes on before right'
Cricketers particularly admired: Matthew Maynard
Young players to look out for: 'All the Glamorgan youngsters'
Other sports played: Rugby (Wales U16)
Other sports followed: Football (Man Utd), rugby (Leicester Tigers)
Favourite band: 'All R&B'
Relaxations: 'Spending time with girlfriend and watching TV'
Extras: Sir John Hobbs Memorial Prize 2003. A.A. Thomson Fielding Prize 2003. BBC *Test Match Special* U15 Young Cricketer of the Year Award 2003. Played for Wales Minor Counties in Minor Counties competitions 2005-06. Represented England U19 2006, 2007. NBC Denis Compton Award for the most promising young Glamorgan player 2006. Scored maiden first-class century (108) v Leicestershire at Leicester 2007 aged 19, becoming the youngest Glamorgan centurion since Matthew Maynard in 1985
Best batting: 108 Glamorgan v Leicestershire, Leicester 2007
Best bowling: 1-14 Glamorgan v Essex, Chelmsford 2007

2008 Season

	M	Inn	NO	Runs	HS	Avg	100	50	Ct	St	Balls	Runs	Wkts	Avg	BB	5I	10M
Test																	
FC																	
ODI																	
List A	14	14	2	283	60	23.58	-	2	5	-	24	16	0		-	-	
20/20 Int																	
20/20	6	5	2	32	9 *	10.66	-	-	4	-	0	0	0		-	-	

Career Performances

	M	Inn	NO	Runs	HS	Avg	100	50	Ct	St	Balls	Runs	Wkts	Avg	BB	5I	10M
Test																	
FC	12	19	2	401	108	23.58	1	2	15	-	132	89	2	44.50	1-14	-	-
ODI																	
List A	28	27	2	547	61	21.88	-	3	7	-	72	69	0		-	-	
20/20 Int																	
20/20	12	10	6	132	35 *	33.00	-	-	5	-	0	0	0		-	-	

WRIGHT, C. J. C. Essex

Name: Christopher (Chris) Julian Clement Wright
Role: Right-hand bat, right-arm fast-medium bowler
Born: 14 July 1985, Chipping Norton, Oxfordshire
Height: 6ft 3in **Weight:** 12st
Nickname: Wrighty, Baron, Jesus, Gypsy
County debut: 2004 (Middlesex), 2008 (Essex)
Place in batting averages: 203rd av. 20.11
Place in bowling averages: 53rd av. 27.31
Parents: Alan and Nikki
Marital status: Single
Family links with cricket: 'Dad plays for Hampshire Over 50s'
Education: Eggars School, Alton; Alton College; Anglia Polytechnic University
Qualifications: 11 GCSEs, 4 A-levels, HND in Sports Science
Career outside cricket: 'Family business – Hygienics Limited'
Off-season: 'Perth'

Overseas tours: Cambridge UCCE to Grenada 2004; Essex to Dubai 2008
Overseas teams played for: Tamil Union C&AC, Colombo 2005-06
Career highlights to date: 'Middlesex debut v Yorkshire. First match at Lord's. 70-odd not out v Middlesex (*71* at Chelmsford, April 2008*). Friends Provident Trophy win 2008. 6-22 v Leicestershire.'
Cricket moments to forget: 'Relegation for Middlesex. Any dropped catch.'
Cricket superstitions: 'Not really; they make people crazy'
Cricketers particularly admired: Jason Gillespie, Courtney Walsh
Young players to look out for: Jaik Mickleburgh. Adam Wheater, Varun Chopra, Merv Westfield, Tom Westley, Maurice Chambers
Other sports played: Basketball, table football, poker
Other sports followed: Football (Arsenal), basketball (Dallas Mavericks)
Favourite band: Rage Against The Machine - 'closely followed by Linkin Park'
Relaxations: 'Poker, cinema, restaurants'
Extras: Played for Cambridge UCCE 2004-05. Represented British Universities 2005. Left Middlesex at the end of the 2007 season and joined Essex for 2008
Opinions on cricket: 'Don't tamper with it too much! Would like to play teams from the Midlands and the North more in one-day cricket'
Best batting: 76 CUCCE v Essex, Fenner's 2005
Best bowling: 6-22 Essex v Leicestershire, Grace Road 2008

2008 Season

	M	Inn	NO	Runs	HS	Avg	100	50	Ct	St	Balls	Runs	Wkts	Avg	BB	5I	10M
Test																	
FC	11	12	3	181	71 *	20.11	-	1	4	-	1439	792	29	27.31	6-22	1	-
ODI																	
List A	12	5	0	33	23	6.60	-	-	4	-	396	335	9	37.22	3-3	-	
20/20 Int																	
20/20																	

Career Perfomances

	M	Inn	NO	Runs	HS	Avg	100	50	Ct	St	Balls	Runs	Wkts	Avg	BB	5I	10M
Test																	
FC	29	37	6	625	76	20.16	-	3	9	-	3663	2416	52	46.46	6-22	1	-
ODI																	
List A	33	18	7	102	23	9.27	-	-	7	-	1242	1089	24	45.37	3-3	-	
20/20 Int																	
20/20	4	1	1	1	1 *	-	-	2	-		78	109	3	36.33	2-24	-	

100. Which marvellous dancer took England's only hat-trick in an Ashes Test during the twentieth century?

WRIGHT, L. J. Sussex

Name: Luke James Wright
Role: Right-hand bat, right-arm medium-fast bowler; all-rounder
Born: 7 March 1985, Grantham
Height: 6ft **Weight:** 13st
Nickname: Wrighty
County debut: 2003 (Leicestershire), 2004 (Sussex)
County cap: 2007 (Sussex)
ODI debut: 2007
Twenty20 Int debut: 2007-08
Place in batting averages: 85th av. 36.52 (2007 34th av. 49.57)
Place in bowling averages: 147th av. 61.66 (2007 129th av. 44.21)
Parents: Keith and Anna
Marital status: Single
Family links with cricket: 'Father very keen cricketer (Level 2 coach).' Brother Ashley played for Leicestershire
Education: Belvoir High School, Bottesford; Ratcliffe College, Leicester; Loughborough University
Qualifications: 8 GCSEs, National Diploma in Sports Science and Sports Massage, ECB Level 1 coaching
Overseas tours: Leicestershire U13 to South Africa; Leicestershire U15 to South Africa; England U19 to Australia 2002-03, to Bangladesh (U19 World Cup) 2003-04; England A to West Indies 2005-06; England to South Africa (World 20/20) 2007-08, to Sri Lanka 2007-08 (one-day series), to New Zealand 2007-08 (one-day series), to India (one-day series) 2008-09; England Performance Programme to India 2007-08 (*see Extras*); England Lions to New Zealand 2008-09
Cricket superstitions: 'Too many to name'
Cricketers particularly admired: Andrew Flintoff, Jacques Kallis
Other sports played: Football, hockey, squash, tennis
Other sports followed: Football (Newcastle United)
Relaxations: Music, cinema, going out
Extras: NBC Denis Compton Award for the most promising young Leicestershire player 2002. Took the first ever hat-trick for England U19 in one-day cricket, v South Africa U19 at Hove 2003. Scored maiden first-class century (100) on Sussex debut v Loughborough UCCE at Hove 2004. ECB National Academy 2004-05 (part-time), 2005-06. Leading run-scorer in the Twenty20 2007 with 346 runs (av. 43.25), including 45-ball 103 v Kent at Canterbury and 48-ball 98 v Hampshire at Hove. ODI debut in the sixth ODI v India at The Oval 2007, scoring 50. Was forced to return home from England Performance Programme in India 2007-08 with a foot injury.

Best batting: 155* Sussex v MCC, Lord's 2008
Best bowling: 3-33 Sussex v Surrey, Hove 2005

2008 Season

	M	Inn	NO	Runs	HS	Avg	100	50	Ct	St	Balls	Runs	Wkts	Avg	BB	5I	10M
Test																	
FC	13	20	3	621	155 *	36.52	2	1	8	-	1143	740	12	61.66	2-46	-	
ODI	10	7	1	108	52	18.00	-	1	5	-	138	115	3	38.33	2-34	-	
List A	20	16	3	268	52	20.61	-	1	5	-	526	466	18	25.88	4-56	-	
20/20 Int	1	1	0	24	24	24.00	-	-	-	-	24	32	1	32.00	1-32	-	
20/20	2	2	0	25	24	12.50	-	-	-	-	42	46	1	46.00	1-32	-	

Career Performances

	M	Inn	NO	Runs	HS	Avg	100	50	Ct	St	Balls	Runs	Wkts	Avg	BB	5I	10M
Test																	
FC	45	63	12	1536	155 *	30.11	3	7	24	-	4205	2469	55	44.89	3-33	-	-
ODI	16	11	1	229	52	22.90	-	2	6	-	186	157	3	52.33	2-34	-	
List A	95	69	12	1153	125	20.22	1	3	25	-	2922	2551	70	36.44	4-12	-	
20/20 Int	8	8	0	98	30	12.25	-	-	3	-	30	45	1	45.00	1-32	-	
20/20	38	29	3	532	103	20.46	1	1	16	-	486	643	28	22.96	3-17	-	

WYATT, A. C. F. — Leicestershire

Name: Alex C. F. Wyatt
Role: Right-hand bat, right-arm fast bowler
Born: 23 July 1990, Roehampton, London
Education: Oakham School, Rutland
County debut: No first-team appearance
Extras: Former Leicestershire Academy player. Leicestershire Second XI 2007. Played for Leicestershire & Rutland U17s 2007. Followed in Stuart Broad's footsteps at Oakham School, the educational establishment whose Director of Cricket, Frank Hayes, is a former England batsman. Taking a gap year to allow him to accept a twelve-month contract with Leicestershire for 2009. Spent winter in Potchesfroom in South Africa, working with former Leicestershire player Gordon Parsons, who now works as a perfomance coach

YARDY, M. H. — Sussex

Name: Michael (Mike) Howard Yardy
Role: Left-hand bat, left-arm medium/spin bowler, county captain
Born: 27 November 1980, Pembury, Kent
Height: 6ft **Weight:** 14st 2lbs
Nickname: Yards, Paolo
County debut: 1999 (one-day), 2000 (first-class)
County cap: 2005
ODI debut: 2006
Twenty20 Int debut: 2006
1000 runs in a season: 1
1st-Class 200s: 1
Place in batting averages: 83rd av. 36.69 (2007 81st av. 38.52)
Parents: Beverly and Howard
Wife and date of marriage: Karin, October 2005
Children: Syenna Lucienne, 24 December 2006
Family links with cricket: 'Brother plays for local team'
Education: William Parker School, Hastings
Qualifications: 5 GCSEs, 2 A-levels, ECB Level 1 coach, Sports Psychology diploma
Overseas tours: Sussex Academy to Barbados 1997; Sussex to Grenada 2001, 2002; England A to West Indies 2005-06, to Bangladesh 2006-07 (c); England to India (ICC Champions Trophy) 2006-07; England Lions to India 2007-08 (c)
Overseas teams played for: Cape Town CC 1999
Cricket superstitions: 'Loads – all secret'
Cricketers particularly admired: 'All those who have reached the pinnacle of their careers'
Other sports followed: Football (West Ham)
Favourite band: Bluetones
Relaxations: 'Watching West Ham; relaxing with my wife'
Extras: Played for Sussex U15, U16 and U19. Represented England U17. Attended Sussex Academy. Sussex Most Improved Player 2001. His 257 v Bangladeshis at Hove 2005 is the highest individual score for Sussex against a touring side; also took 5-83 in Bangladeshis' second innings. Scored 159* v Warwickshire at Hove 2006, in the process sharing with Murray Goodwin (214*) in a new Sussex record partnership for the third wicket (385*). ECB National Academy 2005-06, 2006-07. Vice-captain of Sussex 2007; took over from Chris Adams as county captain in September 2008
Best batting: 257 Sussex v Bangladeshis, Hove 2005
Best bowling: 5-83 Sussex v Bangladeshis, Hove 2005

2008 Season

	M	Inn	NO	Runs	HS	Avg	100	50	Ct	St	Balls	Runs	Wkts	Avg	BB	5I	10M
Test																	
FC	16	27	1	954	93	36.69	-	7	8	-	676	367	2	183.50	1-32	-	-
ODI																	
List A	10	9	0	294	54	32.66	-	3	5	-	468	421	9	46.77	3-54	-	
20/20 Int																	
20/20	10	9	3	129	43	21.50	-	-	2	-	228	273	10	27.30	3-24	-	

Career Performances

	M	Inn	NO	Runs	HS	Avg	100	50	Ct	St	Balls	Runs	Wkts	Avg	BB	5I	10M
Test																	
FC	103	175	16	6165	257	38.77	12	31	74	-	3028	1683	22	76.50	5-83	1	-
ODI	6	5	1	49	19	12.25	-	-	1	-	252	135	4	33.75	3-24	-	
List A	128	114	15	2041	98 *	20.61	-	11	54	-	3403	2743	77	35.62	6-27	1	
20/20 Int	3	2	2	47	24 *		-	-	2	-	60	85	2	42.50	1-20	-	
20/20	33	27	11	449	68 *	28.06	-	1	11	-	498	601	19	31.63	3-24	-	

YASIR ARAFAT — Sussex

Name: Yasir Arafat Satti
Role: Right-hand bat, right-arm fast bowler
Born: 12 March 1982, Rawalpindi, Punjab, Pakistan
Height: 5ft 9½in **Weight:** 11st 11lbs
Nickname: Yas
County debut: 2006 (Sussex), 2007 (Kent)
County cap: 2006 (Sussex), 2007 (Kent)
Test debut: 2007-08
ODI debut: 1999-2000
Twenty20 Int debut: 2007-08
Place in batting averages: 136th av. 28.21 (2007 141st av. 30.75)
Place in bowling averages: 66th av. 29.07 (2007 76th av. 32.66)
Parents: M. Idrees (father)
Marital status: Single
Family links with cricket: 'Father plays club cricket'
Education: Gordon College, Rawalpindi

Overseas tours: Pakistan U15 to England (U15 World Cup) 1996; Pakistan U19 to Australia 1997-98, to Sri Lanka (U19 World Cup) 1999-2000; Pakistan A to UAE (UAE National Day Tournament) 1999-2000, to Kenya 2000, to Sri Lanka 2001, 2004-05, to UAE (EurAsia Cricket Series) 2006; Pakistan to Sharjah (ARY Gold Cup) 2000-01, to India (ICC Champions Trophy) 2006-07, to West Indies (World Cup) 2006-07, to South Africa (World 20/20) 2007-08, to India 2007-08
Overseas teams played for: Rawalpindi 1997-98, 2000-01 – 2001-02, 2003-04 – 2005-06; Pakistan Reserves 1999-2000; Khan Research Laboratories 1999-2000 – 2004-05, 2006-07 – ; REDCO 1999-2000; National Bank of Pakistan 2005-06; Federal Areas 2008-09
Career highlights to date: 'Playing for Pakistan'
Cricket moments to forget: 'Nil'
Cricket superstitions: 'Nil'
Other sports played: Football
Other sports followed: Football (Real Madrid)
Relaxations: 'Watching movies and music'
Extras: Pakistan domestic Player of the Year 2003-04. Played for Clydesdale CC, Scotland 2001-06 and for Scotland in the totesport and C&G 2004-05. Became fourth bowler in history of first-class cricket to take five wickets in six balls, for Rawalpindi v Faisalabad at Rawalpindi in the Quaid-e-Azam Trophy 2004-05; his feat, spread across two innings, included a hat-trick. Was an overseas player with Sussex from June to September 2006; was an overseas player with Kent 2007 and 2008; signed at the end of the 2008 season to return to Sussex as overseas player for 2009. Made Test debut in the third Test v India at Bangalore 2007-08
Best batting: 122 Kent v Sussex, Canterbury 2007
Best bowling: 7-102 Rawalpindi v Sialkot, Sialkot 2001-02

2008 Season

	M	Inn	NO	Runs	HS	Avg	100	50	Ct	St	Balls	Runs	Wkts	Avg	BB	5I	10M
Test																	
FC	12	19	5	395	90 *	28.21	-	2	1	-	1906	1105	38	29.07	6-86	1	-
ODI																	
List A	12	5	2	81	27	27.00	-	-	2	-	610	479	27	17.74	4-29	-	
20/20 Int																	
20/20	13	8	2	130	42	21.66	-	-	2	-	264	341	23	14.82	4-17	-	

Career Performances

	M	Inn	NO	Runs	HS	Avg	100	50	Ct	St	Balls	Runs	Wkts	Avg	BB	5I	10M
Test	1	2	0	44	44	22.00	-	-	-	-	315	210	7	30.00	5-161	1	-
FC	142	217	33	5095	122	27.69	4	28	44	-	23547	13497	573	23.55	7-102	32	3
ODI	8	6	2	48	27	12.00	-	-	1	-	294	274	4	68.50	1-28	-	
List A	175	127	33	1979	87	21.05	-	7	35	-	8454	6731	289	23.29	6-24	5	
20/20 Int	4	4	2	46	17	23.00	-	-	1	-	78	103	2	51.50	1-31	-	
20/20	44	31	9	406	49	18.45	-	-	5	-	871	1184	59	20.06	4-17	-	

ZONDEKI, M. Warwickshire

Name: Monde Zondeki
Role: Right-hand bat, right-arm fast bowler
Born: 25 July 1982, King William's Town, South Africa
County debut: 2008
Test debut: 2003
ODI debut: 2002-03
Twenty20 Int debut: 2005-06
Place in bowling averages: 128th av. 41.60
Education: Dale College, South Africa
Overseas tours: South Africa U19 to New Zealand 2000-01; South Africa A to Sri Lanka 2005-06; South Africa to England 2003, to West Indies 2004-05, to Australia 2005-06 (VB Series), to England 2008, to Australia 2008-09
Overseas teams played for: Border 2000-01 – 2004-05; Warriors 2004-05; Cape Cobras 2005-06 – ; has also played for Western Province and Eastern Cape

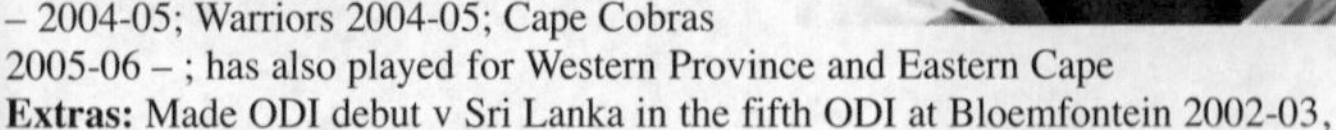

Extras: Made ODI debut v Sri Lanka in the fifth ODI at Bloemfontein 2002-03, taking a wicket (Marvan Atapattu) with his first ball in international cricket. Represented South Africa in the 2002-03 World Cup. Made Test debut in the fourth Test v England at Headingley 2003, scoring 59 and sharing with Gary Kirsten in a record-equalling eighth-wicket partnership for South Africa in Tests (150). His match awards include Man of the Match in the second Test v Zimbabwe at Centurion 2004-05 (3-66/6-39). Represented African XI v Asian Cricket Council XI in the Afro-Asia Cup 2005-06. Man of the Match for South Africa A v West Indians at East London 2007-08 (5-39/3-61). Is nephew of the late South African government minister Steve Tshwete
Best batting: 59 South Africa v England, Headingley 2003
Best bowling: 6-39 South Africa v Zimbabwe, Centurion 2004-05

2008 Season

	M	Inn	NO	Runs	HS	Avg	100	50	Ct	St	Balls	Runs	Wkts	Avg	BB	5I	10M
Test																	
FC	5	5	3	21	9	10.50	-	-	-	-	662	416	10	41.60	4-125	-	-
ODI																	
List A	4	2	1	2	2	2.00	-	-	-	-	172	158	1	158.00	1-56	-	
20/20 Int																	
20/20																	

Career Performances

	M	Inn	NO	Runs	HS	Avg	100	50	Ct	St	Balls	Runs	Wkts	Avg	BB	5I	10M
Test	5	4	0	82	59	20.50	-	1	1	-	692	438	16	27.37	6-39	1	-
FC	71	98	31	626	59	9.34	-	1	22	-	11900	6372	221	28.83	6-39	9	1
ODI	11	3	2	4	3*	4.00	-	-	3	-	456	414	8	51.75	2-46	-	
List A	75	29	12	125	23	.35	-	-	12	-	3252	2657	85	31.25	6-37	2	
20/20 Int	1	1	0	0	0	0.00	-	-	-	-	18	41	1	41.00	1-41	-	
20/20	7	2	1	1	1*	1.00	-	-	1	-	118	172	4	43.00	2-19	-	

THE UMPIRES

BAILEY, R. J.

Name: Robert (Rob) John Bailey
Born: 28 October 1963, Biddulph, Stoke-on-Trent
Height: 6ft 3in
Nickname: Bailers
Wife and date of marriage: Rachel, 11 April 1987
Children: Harry, 7 March 1991; Alexandra, 13 November 1993
Family links with cricket: 'Son Harry plays for Northampton Saints CC'
Education: Biddulph High School
Career outside cricket: Rob Bailey Ceramics ('promotional mugs etc.')
Other sports played: Badminton (county schools)
Other sports followed: 'All football clubs that I supply mugs to!'
Appointed to 1st-Class list: 2006
Umpiring honours: Stood at Twenty20 finals day 2008
Counties as player: Northamptonshire, Derbyshire
Role: Right-hand bat, off-spin bowler
County debut: 1982 (Northamptonshire), 2000 (Derbyshire)
County cap: 1985 (Northamptonshire), 2000 (Derbyshire)
Benefit: 1993 (Northamptonshire)
Test debut: 1988
ODI debut (matches): 1984-85 (4)
1000 runs in a season: 13
1st-Class 200s: 4
One-Day 100s: 9
One-Day 5 w. in innings: 1
Overseas tours: England to Sharjah 1984-85, 1986-87, to India 1988-89 (cancelled), to West Indies 1989-90
Overseas teams played for: Rhodes University, Grahamstown, South Africa 1982-83; Uitenhage CC, South Africa 1983-85; Fitzroy CC, Melbourne 1985-86; Gosnells CC, Perth 1987-88
Highlights of playing career: 'Loved all of it'
Extras: Won three consecutive NatWest Man of the Match awards 1995 and three consecutive B&H Gold Awards 1996. Northamptonshire captain 1996-97. In 1999 became sixth player to pass 20,000 first-class runs for Northamptonshire
Best batting: 224* Northamptonshire v Glamorgan, Swansea 1986
Best bowling: 5-54 Northamptonshire v Nottinghamshire, Northampton 1993

First-Class Career Performances

	M	Inn	NO	Runs	HS	Avg	100	Ct	St	Runs	Wkts	Avg	BB	5I	10M
Test	4	8	0	119	43	14.87	-	-	-						
FC	374	628	89	21844	224*	40.52	47	272	-	5144	121	42.51	5-54	2	-

BAINTON, N. L.

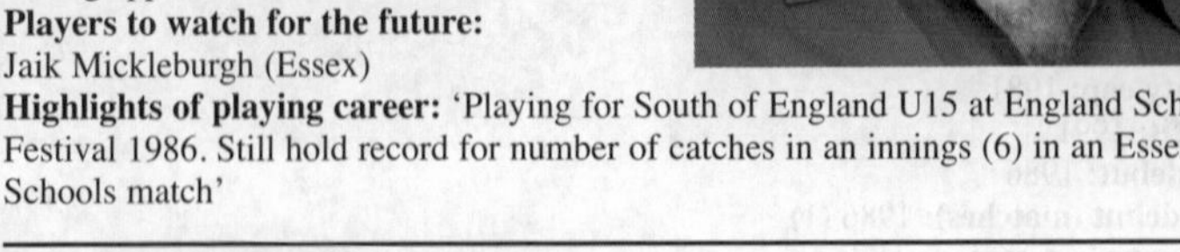

Name: Neil Laurence Bainton
Born: 2 October 1970, Romford, Essex
Height: 5ft 8in
Wife and date of marriage: Kay, 25 October 1997
Family links with cricket: Father played and umpired club cricket
Education: Ilford County High School
Career outside cricket: 'Postman'
Off-season: 'Postman in Braintree, Essex'
Other sports followed: Football (West Ham 'and whichever local team my mate plays for!')
Appointed to 1st-Class list: 2006
Highlights of umpiring career: 'Being appointed to first-class list'
Players to watch for the future: Jaik Mickleburgh (Essex)
Highlights of playing career: 'Playing for South of England U15 at England Schools Festival 1986. Still hold record for number of catches in an innings (6) in an Essex Schools match'

Did not play first-class cricket

BENSON, M. R.

Name: Mark Richard Benson
Born: 6 July 1958, Shoreham, Sussex
Height: 5ft 10in
Nickname: Benny
Wife and date of marriage: Sarah Patricia, 20 September 1986
Children: Laurence, 16 October 1987; Edward, 23 June 1990
Education: Sutton Valence School
Other sports played: Bridge, golf, swimming, cycling
Relaxations: Bridge, golf
Appointed to 1st-Class list: 2000
International panel: 2004-2006
Elite panel: 2006 –
Tests umpired: 26 (plus 8 as TV umpire)
ODIs umpired: 72 (plus 25 as TV umpire)
Twenty20 Ints umpired: 16 (plus 3 as TV umpire)
Other umpiring honours: Stood in the C&G Trophy final 2003. Umpired in the 2006-07 World Cup and the Twenty20 World Championship 2007-08

County as player: Kent
Role: Left-hand bat
County debut: 1980
County cap: 1981
Benefit: 1991
Test debut: 1986
ODI debut (matches): 1986 (1)
1000 runs in a season: 11
1st-Class 200s: 1
One-Day 100s: 5
Overseas tours: None
Highlights of playing career: '257 v Hampshire. Winning Sunday League as captain of Kent. Two 90s to win a game against Hampshire with Malcolm Marshall bowling. One of only four cricketers in the history of Kent to have scored more than 10,000 runs and have an average in excess of 40 [in a completed career]'
Extras: Scored 1000 runs in first full season. Kent captain 1991-95
Best batting: 257 Kent v Hampshire, Southampton 1991
Best bowling: 2-55 Kent v Surrey, Dartford 1986

First-Class Career Performances

	M	Inn	NO	Runs	HS	Avg	100	Ct	St	Runs	Wkts	Avg	BB	5I	10M
Test	1	2	0	51	30	25.50	-	-	-						
FC	292	491	34	18387	257	40.23	48	140	-	493	5	98.60	2-55	-	-

BODENHAM, M. J. D.

Name: Martin John Dale Bodenham
Born: 23 April 1950, Brighton
Height: 6 ft 1 in
Marital status: Single
Family links with cricket: 'Father was a qualified cricket umpire'
Education: Goring Hall School
Career outside cricket: Football Association referee coach: '12 designated referees assigned to me for the whole of the football season'
Other sports played: Golf
Other sports followed: Horse racing
Relaxations: Veteran car enthusiast – 'owner of a car which is over 100 years old'
Appointed to 1st-Class list: 2009
Umpiring honours: Umpired 2 Sussex League Cup Finals
Highlights of umpiring career: 'Initially being appointed to the ECB Reserve List (3 seasons) and then on to the Full List for season 2009'
Players to watch for the future: Joe Denly, Luke Wright, Ben Brown
County as player: 'Played for Sussex in a number of 2nd XI Championship matches'
Role: Batsman, wicket-keeper
Cricket moments to forget: 'Being out to the first ball of a Sussex League match'
Extras: Ex-FIFA International Football Referee. Football League Referee 1978-1992 and FA Premier League Referee 1992-1998; refereed the 1997 League Cup Final and three FA Cup semi-finals. Reserve Referee European Cup Final AC Milan v Barcelona 1994. Took up umpiring following retirement as football referee in 1998; Sussex League; in 2006 added by ECB to its reserve list; first first-class game Essex v Loughborough UCCE, Chelmsford, 15-17 April 2006
Opinions on cricket: 'Competitive but must always be played in the right spirit. Attendance at all types of matches (particularly one-day games) on the increase so the game must be in a healthy state'

Did not play first-class cricket

COOK, N.G.B.

Name: Nicholas (Nick) Grant Billson Cook
Born: 17 June 1956, Leicester
Height: 6ft
Nickname: Beast, Rag'ead
Wife and date of marriage: Shan, 20 September 1991
Children: None
Education: Lutterworth High
Career outside cricket: Cricket pro at Rugby School
Other sports followed: Football (Leicester City), rugby (Leicester Tigers), National Hunt racing
Relaxations: See above
Appointed to 1st-Class list: 2009
Highlights of umpiring career: 'Being appointed to the first-class panel'
Players to watch for the future: Josh Cobb
Counties as player: Leicestershire, Northamptonshire
Role: Right-hand bat, slow left-arm leg-spin bowler
Overseas tours: England to New Zealand (1984), to Pakistan (1984), to Pakistan (1987)
Cricket moments to forget: 'When David Boon swept me in 1989 to win the Ashes back for Australia'
Extras: Played 15 Tests and 3 ODIs for England
Best batting: 75 Leicestershire v Somerset, Taunton 1980
Best bowling: 7-34 Northamptonshire v Essex, Chelmsford 1992
Opinions on cricket: 'Cricketers are very athletic sportsmen these days, but some of the subtleties, such as field placings for, and the use of, spin bowlers, are perhaps being overlooked. The game is in a pretty healthy state, both internationally and countywise. Perhaps we have one one-day competition too many, but I disagree entirely with the bandwagon that says we play too much cricket.'

First-Class Career Performances

	M	Inn	NO	Runs	HS	Avg	100	Ct	St	Runs	Wkts	Avg	BB	5I	10M
Test	15	25	4	179	31	8.52	-	5		1689	52	32.48	6-65	4	1
FC	356	365	96	3138	75	11.67	-	197		25507	879	29.02	7-34	31	4

COWLEY, N. G. C.

Name: Nigel Geoffrey Charles Cowley
Born: 1 March 1953, Shaftesbury, Dorset
Height: 5ft 6½in
Marital status: Divorced
Children: Mark Antony, 14 June 1973; Darren James, 30 October 1976
Family links with cricket: Darren played Hampshire Schools U11, U12, U13; Natal Schools 1993, 1994, 1995; and toured India with South Africa U19 1996
Education: Duchy Manor, Mere, Wiltshire
Other sports played: Golf (8 handicap)
Other sports followed: Football (Liverpool FC)
Appointed to 1st-Class list: 2000
Counties as player: Hampshire, Glamorgan
Role: Right-hand bat, off-spin bowler
County debut: 1974 (Hampshire), 1990 (Glamorgan)
County cap: 1978 (Hampshire)
Benefit: 1988 (Hampshire)
1000 runs in a season: 1
50 wickets in a season: 2
One-Day 5 w. in innings: 1
Overseas tours: Hampshire to Barbados 1985, 1986, 1987, to Dubai 1989
Overseas teams played for: Paarl CC 1982-83; Amanzimtoti 1984-96 (both South Africa)
Extras: Played for Dorset 1972. NatWest Man of the Match award
Best batting: 109* Hampshire v Somerset, Taunton 1977
Best bowling: 6-48 Hampshire v Leicestershire, Southampton 1982

First-Class Career Performances

	M	Inn	NO	Runs	HS	Avg	100	Ct	St	Runs	Wkts	Avg	BB	5I	10M
Test															
FC	271	375	62	7309	109*	23.35	2	105	-	14879	437	34.04	6-48	5	

DUDLESTON, B.

Name: Barry Dudleston
Born: 16 July 1945, Bebington, Cheshire
Height: 5ft 9in
Nickname: Danny
Wife and date of marriage: Louise Wendy, 19 October 1994
Children: Sharon Louise, 29 October 1968; Matthew Barry, 12 September 1988; Jack Nicholas, 29 April 1998
Family links with cricket: 'Dad was a league cricketer'
Education: Stockport School
Career outside cricket: Managing director of Sunsport Ltd
Other sports played: Golf
Other sports followed: All sports
Relaxations: Bridge, red wine
Appointed to 1st-Class list: 1984
First appointed to Test panel: 1991
Tests umpired: 2 (plus 4 as TV umpire)
ODIs umpired: 4 (plus 6 as TV umpire)

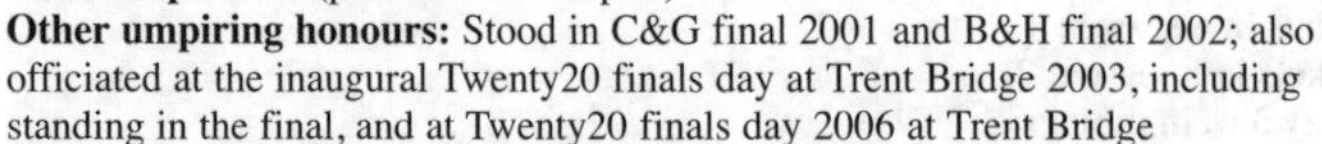

Other umpiring honours: Stood in C&G final 2001 and B&H final 2002; also officiated at the inaugural Twenty20 finals day at Trent Bridge 2003, including standing in the final, and at Twenty20 finals day 2006 at Trent Bridge
Highlight of umpiring career: 'A Lord's Test match'
Players to watch for the future: Chris Woakes
Counties as player: Leicestershire, Gloucestershire
Role: Right-hand opening bat, slow left-arm bowler, occasional wicket-keeper
County debut: 1966 (Leicestershire), 1981 (Gloucestershire)
County cap: 1969 (Leicestershire)
Benefit: 1980 (Leicestershire)
1000 runs in a season: 8
1st-Class 200s: 1
One-Day 100s: 4
Overseas tours: Kent (as guest player) to West Indies 1972; D.H. Robins' XI to West Indies 1973; Wisden XI to West Indies 1984; MCC to Kenya 1993
Overseas teams played for: Rhodesia/Zimbabwe-Rhodesia 1976-80
Highlights of playing career: 'Winning County Championship [with Leicestershire]'
Extras: Played for England U25. Holder with John Steele of the highest first-wicket partnership for Leicestershire, 390 v Derbyshire at Leicester in 1979. Fastest player in Rhodesian cricket history to 1000 first-class runs in Currie Cup; second fastest ever in Currie Cup

Best batting: 202 Leicestershire v Derbyshire, Leicester 1979
Best bowling: 4-6 Leicestershire v Surrey, Leicester 1972

First-Class Career Performances

	M	Inn	NO	Runs	HS	Avg	100	Ct	St	Runs	Wkts	Avg	BB	5I	10M
Test															
FC	295	501	47	14747	202	32.48	32	234	7	1365	47	29.04	4-6	-	-

EVANS, J. H.

Name: Jeffrey (Jeff) Howard Evans
Born: 7 August 1954, Llanelli
Height: 5ft 8in
Children: Rhian; Siân
Education: Llanelli Boys Grammar School; Dudley College of Education
Career outside cricket: Supply teaching
Off-season: 'Supply teaching. Umpiring in Indian Cricket League'
Other sports followed: 'Most sports, rugby in particular'
Relaxations: 'Walking, keeping fit'
Appointed to 1st-Class list: 2001
Other umpiring honours: Toured Namibia and Uganda 2004-05 with MCC (as umpire)
Highlights of umpiring career: 'First Championship match – Yorkshire v Somerset at Headingley 2001'
Players to watch for the future: Ravi Bopara
Cricket moments to forget: 'Any error of judgement!'
County as player: Did not play first-class cricket. Played league cricket in South Wales as a right-hand bat
Extras: Coach to Welsh Schools Cricket Association team on tour to Australia 1993. Taught in the Gwendraeth Grammar School – 'the old "outside-half factory"'
Opinions on cricket: 'Would like to see more honesty throughout the game!'

Did not play first-class cricket

GARRATT, S. A.

Name: Stephen (Steve) Arthur Garratt
Born: 5 July 1953, Nottingham
Height: 6ft 2in
Nickname: Trigger
Wife and date of marriage: Marion, 1975
Children: Mark, 26; Chris, 24;
Farris (grandson), 4
Family links with cricket: 'Father Arthur played local club cricket in Nottingham'
Education: Arnold County High School, Nottingham
Career outside cricket: Retired police officer
Off-season: 'Taking holidays with my wife'
Other sports played: Rugby union, football
Other sports followed: 'All sports'
Relaxations: 'Walk on the beach at Whitby'
Appointed to 1st-Class list: 2008
Highlights of umpiring career: 'MCC tour to Argentina, 2008'
Players to watch for the future: Adam Lyth, Chris Woakes, Liam Dawson
County as player: Did not play first-class cricket

Did not play first-class cricket

GOUGH, M. A.

Name: Michael Andrew Gough
Born: 18 December 1979, Hartlepool
Height: 6ft 5in
Nickname: Goughy
Wife and date of marriage: Charlotte Rae.
3 February 2006
Children: None
Education: English Martyrs School and Sixth Form College, Hartlepool
Family links with cricket: 'Father Michael played minor counties for Durham'
Other sports played: Football
Other sports followed: Football (Hartlepool United), rugby, golf
Off-season: 'Keeping fit - jogging, walking, swimming, gym'
Relaxations: 'Eating out, sport on TV, reading, sudoku'

Umpiring career: Started 2005 after retirement from first-class game; appointed to ECB reserve list 2006. Believed to be the youngest first-class umpire in the history of the game, a year younger than either David Constant or the legendary interwar umpire Frank Chester.
Appointed to 1st-Class list: 2009
Counties as player: Durham
Role: Right-hand bat; right-arm off-spin bowler
County debut: 1998
1st-Class 50s: 15
1st-Class 100s: 2
1st-Class 5 w. in innings: 1
1st-Class catches: 57
One-Day 100s: 1
Place in batting averages: 202nd av. 23.36 (2002 31st av. 51.33)
Strike rate: 57.33 (career 82.86)
Overseas tours: England U17 to Bermuda (international youth tournament winners) 1997; England U19 to South Africa (1997), to New Zealand (1998-99); England A to Bangladesh (1999), to New Zealand (1999-2000)
Overseas teams played for: Claremont Nedlands, Perth, Australia 2001 – 2003
Highlights of playing career: U19 World Cup final win v New Zealand 1997-98; captaining England U19s and A tour to Bangladesh and New Zealand; promotion to Division 1 with Durham, 1999; fielding 12th man for England v Australia, Perth, 2003
Extras: Captained North of England and England U15. Part of winning England U17 team at the International Youth Tournament in Bermuda 1997. Durham CCC Young Player of the Year 1997. Scored 62 on first-class debut, v Essex at Riverside 1998. Became youngest player to score a first-class century for Durham, 123 against Cambridge University at Fenner's 1998, aged 18 years 151 days. Captained England U19 v Australia U19 1999. C&G Man of the Match award for his 132 (his maiden one-day century) v Wales at Cardiff 2002. Carried his bat for 75* v Essex at Riverside 2002
Best batting: 123 Durham v Cambridge University, Fenner's 1998
Best bowling: 5-66 Durham v Middlesex, Riverside 2001

First-Class Career Performances

	M	Inn	NO	Runs	HS	Avg	100	Ct	St	Runs	Wkts	Avg	BB	5I	10M
Test															
FC	67	119	3	2952	123	25.44	2	58		1350	30	45.00	5-66	1	-

GOULD, I. J.

Name: Ian James Gould
Born: 19 August 1957, Taplow, Bucks
Height: 5ft 7in
Nickname: Gunner
Wife and date of marriage: Joanne, 27 September 1986
Children: Gemma; Michael; George
Education: Westgate Secondary Modern, Slough
Other sports played: Golf
Other sports followed: Football (Arsenal), racing
Appointed to 1st-Class list: 2002
International panel: 2006 –
Tests umpired: 2 (plus 6 as TV umpire)
ODIs umpired: 31 (plus 8 as TV umpire)
Twenty20 Ints umpired: 3 (plus 2 as TV umpire)

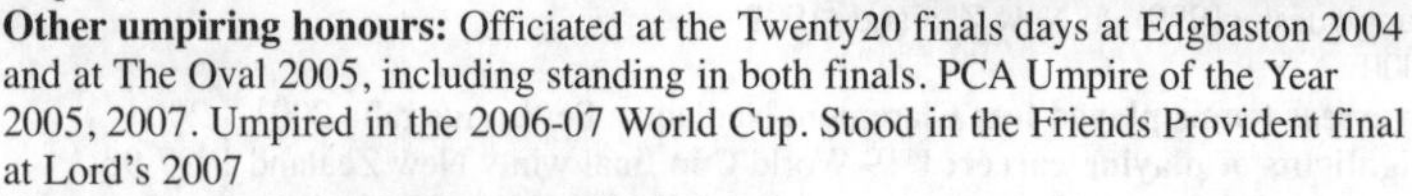

Other umpiring honours: Officiated at the Twenty20 finals days at Edgbaston 2004 and at The Oval 2005, including standing in both finals. PCA Umpire of the Year 2005, 2007. Umpired in the 2006-07 World Cup. Stood in the Friends Provident final at Lord's 2007
Players to watch for the future: Ollie Rayner
Counties as player: Middlesex, Sussex
Role: Left-hand bat, wicket-keeper
County debut: 1975 (Middlesex), 1981 (Sussex)
County cap: 1977 (Middlesex), 1981 (Sussex)
Benefit: 1990 (Sussex)
ODI debut (matches): 1982-83 (18)
Overseas tours: England YC to West Indies 1976; D.H. Robins' XI to Canada 1978-79; International XI to Pakistan 1980-81; England to Australia and New Zealand 1982-83; MCC to Namibia
Overseas teams played for: Auckland 1979-80
Highlights of playing career: 'Playing in the World Cup'
Extras: Represented England in the 1983 World Cup. Retired from county cricket in 1991
Best batting: 128 Middlesex v Worcestershire, Worcester 1978
Best bowling: 3-10 Sussex v Surrey, The Oval 1989

irst-Class Career Performances

	M	Inn	NO	Runs	HS	Avg	100	Ct	St	Runs	Wkts	Avg	Best	5I	10M
Test															
FC	297	399	63	8756	128	26.06	4	536	67	365	7	52.14	3-10	-	-

HARRIS, M. J.

Name: Michael John Harris
Born: 25 May 1944, St Just-in-Roseland, Cornwall
Height: 6ft 1in
Nickname: Pasty
Wife and date of marriage: Danielle Ruth, 10 September 1969
Children: Jodie; Richard
Education: Gerrans Comprehensive
Career outside cricket: Sports teacher
Other sports followed: Squash, golf
Appointed to 1st-Class list: 1998
Counties as player: Middlesex, Nottinghamshire
Role: Right-hand bat, leg-break bowler, wicket-keeper
County debut: 1964 (Middlesex), 1969 (Nottinghamshire)
County cap: 1967 (Middlesex), 1970 (Nottinghamshire)
1000 runs in a season: 11
1st-Class 200s: 1
One-Day 100s: 3
Overseas teams played for: Eastern Province 1971-72; Wellington 1975-76
Extras: Shared Middlesex then record first-wicket partnership of 312 with Eric Russell v Pakistanis at Lord's 1967. Scored nine centuries in 1971 to equal Nottinghamshire county record for a season, scoring two centuries in a match twice and totalling 2238 runs at an average of 50.86
Best batting: 201* Nottinghamshire v Glamorgan, Trent Bridge 1973
Best bowling: 4-16 Nottinghamshire v Warwickshire, Trent Bridge 1969

First-Class Career Performances

	M	Inn	NO	Runs	HS	Avg	100	Ct	St	Runs	Wkts	Avg	BB	5I	10M
Test															
FC	344	581	58	19196	201*	36.70	41	288	14	3459	79	43.78	4-16	-	-

HARTLEY, P. J.

Name: Peter John (Jack) Hartley
Born: 18 April 1960, Keighley, Yorkshire
Height: 6ft
Nickname: Jack
Wife and date of marriage: Sharon, 12 March 1988
Children: Megan, 25 April 1993; Courtney, 25 July 1995
Family links with cricket: Father and brother played local league cricket
Education: Greenhead Grammar School, Keighley; Bradford College
Off-season: 'Playing golf and skiing as often as possible'
Other sports played: Golf (2 handicap)
Other sports followed: Football (Chelsea)
Relaxations: 'Walking'
Appointed to 1st-Class list: 2003
International panel: 2006 – (as TV umpire)
Tests umpired: 5 as TV umpire
ODIs umpired: 4 (plus 8 as TV umpire)
Twenty20 Ints umpired: 3 (plus 2 as TV umpire)
Other umpiring honours: Officiated at Twenty20 finals day 2006 at Trent Bridge, including standing in the final. Umpired his first ODI in 2007 – England v India, The Oval. Umpired U19 World Cup final 2008 in Malaysia
Highlights of umpiring career: 'Above [ODI], and umpired Friends Provident final 2007, plus the U19 World Cup final'
Counties as player: Warwickshire, Yorkshire, Hampshire
Role: Right-hand bat, right-arm fast-medium bowler
County debut: 1982 (Warwickshire), 1985 (Yorkshire), 1998 (Hampshire)
County cap: 1987 (Yorkshire), 1998 (Hampshire)
Benefit: 1996 (Yorkshire)
50 wickets in a season: 7
One-Day 5 w. in innings: 5
Overseas tours: Yorkshire pre-season tours to Barbados 1986-87, to South Africa 1991-92, 1992-93, to Zimbabwe
Overseas teams played for: Melville, New Zealand 1983-84; Adelaide, Australia 1985-86; Harmony and Orange Free State, South Africa 1988-89
Highlights of playing career: 'Hat-trick and taking 9-41 in same game'
Extras: His 9-41 v Derbyshire at Chesterfield 1995 contained a spell of five wickets in nine balls, including a hat-trick (DeFreitas, Harrison, Cork). Returned 8-65, his best

figures for Hampshire, against Yorkshire, his former county, at Basingstoke 1999. Recorded his highest B&H score (32*) and best one-day analysis (5-20) v Sussex at Hove 2000. Retired from county cricket at the end of the 2000 season
Opinions on cricket: 'Game in good shape; let's not let four-day cricket decline. Twenty20 has some yards to go yet.'
Best batting: 127* Yorkshire v Lancashire, Old Trafford 1988
Best bowling: 9-41 Yorkshire v Derbyshire, Chesterfield 1995

First-Class Career Performances

	M	Inn	NO	Runs	HS	Avg	100	Ct	St	Runs	Wkts	Avg	BB	5I	10M
Test															
FC	232	283	66	4321	127*	19.91	2	68	-	20635	683	30.21	9-41	23	3

HOLDER, J. W.

Name: John Wakefield Holder
Born: 19 March 1945, Barbados
Height: 5ft 11in
Nickname: Benson
Wife's name: Glenda
Children: Christopher, 1968; Nigel, 1970
Education: Combermere High School, Barbados; Rochdale College
Other sports followed: Football (Manchester United)
Relaxations: 'Regular visits to the gym trying to keep fit. Love watching wildlife programmes on TV and travel'
Appointed to 1st-Class list: 1983
First appointed to Test panel: 1988
Tests umpired: 11 (plus 5 as TV umpire)
ODIs umpired: 19 (plus 3 as TV umpire)
Other umpiring honours: Umpired in Nehru Cup in India and in Pakistan v India Test series 1989-90. Umpired in Pepsi Champions Trophy, Sharjah 1993-94 and Masters Cup, Sharjah 1995-96. MCC tours to Kenya 1999, 2002 and to Greece 2003 (as umpire). Has stood in Refuge Assurance Cup, B&H Cup and NatWest Trophy finals and in C&G Trophy final 2002. Officiated at the inaugural Twenty20 finals day at Trent Bridge 2003, including standing in the final, and at finals day at The Oval 2005. Has been appointed as a Regional Umpires Performance Manager by the ICC, with responsibility for Europe, the Caribbean and the Americas
Highlights of umpiring career: 'First and last Test matches at Lord's'
Players to watch for the future: Chris Woakes, James Harris, Liam Dawson

County as player: Hampshire
Role: Right-hand bat, right-arm fast bowler
County debut: 1968
50 wickets in a season: 1
Cricket moments to forget: 'My second Test match at Headingley when I made three poor decisions
Opinions on cricket: 'The proliferation of Kolpak players in country cricket will, in the long term, adversely affect the national team. Fewer British-born youngsters will get the chance to develop'
Extras: Championship hat-trick v Kent at Southampton 1972. Retired from county cricket in 1972
Best batting: 33 Hampshire v Sussex, Hove 1971
Best bowling: 7-79 Hampshire v Gloucestershire, Gloucester 1972

First-Class Career Performances

	M	Inn	NO	Runs	HS	Avg	100	Ct	St	Runs	Wkts	Avg	BB	5I	10M
Test															
FC	47	49	14	374	33	10.68	-	12	-	3415	139	24.56	7-79	5	1

HOLDER, V. A.

Name: Vanburn Alonza Holder
Born: 8 October 1945, St Michael, Barbados
Height: 6ft 3in
Nickname: Vanny
Wife and date of marriage: Chris, 19 July 1980
Children: James, 2 September 1981
Education: St Leonard's Secondary Modern; Community High
Off-season: 'Relaxing'
Other sports followed: Football (Liverpool)
Relaxations: Music, doing crosswords
Appointed to 1st-Class list: 1992
ODIs umpired: 2 as TV umpire
County as player: Worcestershire
Role: Right-hand bat, right-arm fast-medium bowler
County debut: 1968
County cap: 1970
Benefit: 1979
Test debut: 1969
ODI debut (matches): 1973 (12)

50 wickets in a season: 9
One-Day 5 w. in innings: 3
Overseas tours: West Indies to England 1969, 1973, 1975 (World Cup), 1976, to India, Sri Lanka and Pakistan 1974-75, to Australia 1975-76, to India and Sri Lanka 1978-79 (vc); Rest of the World to Pakistan 1973-74
Overseas teams played for: Barbados 1966-78
Extras: Made his debut for Barbados in the Shell Shield competition in 1966-67. Won John Player League 1973 and County Championship 1974 with Worcestershire. Played in West Indies 1975 World Cup winning side
Best batting: 122 Barbados v Trinidad, Bridgetown 1973-74
Best bowling: 7-40 Worcestershire v Glamorgan, Cardiff 1974

First-Class Career Performances

	M	Inn	NO	Runs	HS	Avg	100	Ct	St	Runs	Wkts	Avg	BB	5I	10M
Test	40	59	11	682	42	14.20	-	16	-	3627	109	33.27	6-28	3	-
FC	311	354	81	3559	122	13.03	1	98	-	23183	948	24.45	7-40	38	3

ILLINGWORTH, R. K.

Name: Richard Keith Illingworth
Born: 23 August 1963, Greengates, near Bradford, Yorkshire
Height: 5ft 11in
Nickname: Harry, Lucy, 'H'
Wife and date of marriage: Anne Louise, 20 September 1985
Children: Miles, 28 August 1987; Thomas, 20 April 1989
Family links with cricket: Father and mother involved around Bradford League
Education: Salts GS
Off-season: 'Coaching'
Other sports played: Golf, cycling, running
Other sports followed: Football (Leeds), rugby league (Bradford Bulls), rugby union (Worcester)
Relaxations: 'Watching my two sons playing sport; cooking; wine tasting'
Appointed to 1st-Class list: 2006
Highlights of umpiring career: Twenty20 finals 2008
Players to watch for the future: Dan Redfern, John Clare
Counties as player: Worcestershire, Derbyshire
Role: Right-hand bat, left-arm orthodox spin bowler

County debut: 1982 (Worcestershire), 2001 (Derbyshire)
County cap: 1986 (Worcestershire)
Benefit: 1997 (Worcestershire)
Test debut: 1991
ODI debut (matches): 1991 (25)
50 wickets in a season: 5
One-Day 5 w. in innings: 2
Overseas tours: England A to Kenya and Zimbabwe 1989-90, to Pakistan and Sri Lanka 1990-91; England to New Zealand and Australia (World Cup) 1991-92, to South Africa 1995-96, to India and Pakistan (World Cup) 1995-96
Overseas teams played for: Brisbane Colts 1982-83; Zingari, Pietermaritzburg, South Africa 1984-85, 1988-89; University/St Heliers, New Zealand 1986-88; Natal 1988-89; Abahani, Bangladesh 1994
Highlights of playing career: 'Playing for England. Being part of many Worcestershire trophy wins. Wicket [Phil Simmons of West Indies] with first ball in Test cricket'
Cricket moments to forget: 'None, apart from getting out for nought or dropping catches (of which there were a few)'
Extras: Scored three centuries batting as a nightwatchman. First Worcestershire bowler to take a one-day hat-trick, v Sussex at Hove in the Sunday League 1993. Retired from county cricket at the end of the 2001 season
Best batting: 120* Worcestershire v Warwickshire, Worcester 1987
Best bowling: 7-50 Worcestershire v Oxford University, The Parks 1985

First-Class Career Performances

	M	Inn	NO	Runs	HS	Avg	100	Ct	St	Runs	Wkts	Avg	BB	5I	10M
Test	9	14	7	128	28	18.28	-	5	-	615	19	32.36	4-96	-	-
FC	376	435	122	7027	120*	22.45	4	161	-	26213	831	31.54	7-50	27	6

JESTY, T. E.

Name: Trevor Edward Jesty
Born: 2 June 1948, Gosport, Hampshire
Height: 5ft 9in
Nickname: Jets
Wife and date of marriage: Jacqueline, 12 September 1970
Children: Graeme Barry, 27 September 1972; Lorna Samantha, 7 November 1976
Family links with cricket: Daughter played for England XI 2000
Education: Privett County Secondary Modern, Gosport
Other sports followed: Football (Arsenal)
Relaxations: Gardening, reading
Appointed to 1st-Class list: 1994
ODIs umpired: 3 as TV umpire
Counties as player: Hampshire, Surrey, Lancashire
Role: Right-hand bat, right-arm medium bowler
County debut: 1966 (Hampshire), 1985 (Surrey), 1988 (Lancashire)
County cap: 1971 (Hampshire), 1985 (Surrey), 1990 (Lancashire)
Benefit: 1982 (Hampshire)
ODI debut (matches): 1982-83 (10)
1000 runs in a season: 10
50 wickets in a season: 2
1st-Class 200s: 2
One-Day 100s: 7
Overseas tours: International XI to West Indies 1982; joined England tour to Australia 1982-83; Lancashire to Zimbabwe 1989
Overseas teams played for: Border, South Africa 1973-74; Griqualand West 1974-76, 1980-81; Canterbury, New Zealand 1979-80
Highlights of playing career: 'Winning Championship with Hampshire in 1973. Playing against Australia for England in one-day match on 1982-83 tour'
Extras: One of *Wisden*'s Five Cricketers of the Year 1983
Best batting: 248 Hampshire v Cambridge University, Fenner's 1984
Best bowling: 7-75 Hampshire v Worcestershire, Southampton 1976

First-Class Career Performances

	M	Inn	NO	Runs	HS	Avg	100	Ct	St	Runs	Wkts	Avg	BB	5I	10M
Test															
FC	490	777	107	21916	248	32.71	35	265	1	16075	585	27.47	7-75	19	-

KETTLEBOROUGH, R. A.

Name: Richard Allan Kettleborough
Born: 15 March 1973, Sheffield
Height: 5ft 10in
Nickname: Ketts
Wife and date of marriage: Lucy, 6 October 2007
Children: Millie Hannah, 16 October 2008
Family links with cricket: 'Dad played league cricket'
Education: Worksop College; Airedale and Wharfdale College
Career outside cricket: Groundsman
Other sports played: Football, golf
Other sports followed: Football (Sheffield Wednesday FC)
Relaxations: 'Socialising with friends'
Appointed to 1st-Class list: 2006
International panel: 2008 – (as TV umpire)
Tests umpired: 1 as TV umpire
ODIs umpired: 3 as TV umpire
Twenty20 Ints umpired: 2 as TV umpire
Other umpiring honours: Stood in the International 20:20 Club Championship 2005
Highlights of umpiring career: 'Any major match appointment'
Players to watch for the future: Adil Rashid, Liam Dawson
Counties as player: Yorkshire, Middlesex
Role: Left-hand bat
County debut: 1994 (Yorkshire), 1998 (Middlesex)
Overseas tours: England U18 to Canada 1991; Yorkshire to South Africa 1994, to Zimbabwe 1995, to West Indies 1996; MCC to Hong Kong 2000, to Kenya 2001, to Australia 2002-03, to UAE 2004, to Namibia and Uganda 2005, to India 2006
Overseas teams played for: Somerset West, Cape Town 1993-94; Constantia, Cape Town 2003
Highlights of playing career: 'Yorkshire debut 1994. Maiden first-class hundred v Essex 1996. Winning National Club Knockout with Sheffield Collegiate 2000'
Cricket moments to forget: '1998 and 1999 in London'
Extras: MCC Young Cricketer of the Year 1988. Yorkshire Young Player of the Year 1996
Opinions on cricket: 'Reduce the number of non-English-qualified players in county cricket.'
Best batting: 108 Yorkshire v Essex, Headingley 1996
Best bowling: 2-26 Yorkshire v Nottinghamshire, Scarborough 1996

First-Class Career Performances

	M	Inn	NO	Runs	HS	Avg	100	Ct	St	Runs	Wkts	Avg	BB	5I	10M
Test															
FC	33	56	6	1258	108	25.16	1	20	-	243	3	81.00	2-26	-	-

LLONG, N. J.

Name: Nigel James Llong
Born: 11 February 1969, Ashford, Kent
Height: 6ft
Nickname: Nidge
Wife and date of marriage: Melissa, 20 February 1999
Children: Andrew Stuart, 30 August 2002; Matthew James, 14 December 2004
Family links with cricket: Father and brother played local club cricket
Education: North School for Boys, Ashford
Off-season: Coaching – Duke of York School, Dover
Other sports followed: Football (Arsenal), 'generally most sports'
Relaxations: Fishing
Appointed to 1st-Class list: 2002
International panel: 2004-2006 as TV umpire; 2006 –
Tests umpired: 4 (plus 11 as TV umpire)
ODIs umpired: 24 (plus 18 as TV umpire)
Twenty20 Ints umpired: 10 (plus 3 as TV umpire)
Other umpiring honours: Officiated at Twenty20 finals days at Edgbaston 2004, including standing in the final, and 2007. Stood in his first Test match in January 2008 – the first Test between New Zealand and Bangladesh at Dunedin
Highlights of umpiring career: 'Umpired at Twenty20 World Championship, South Africa 2007-08'
County as player: Kent
Role: Left-hand bat, right-arm off-spin bowler
County debut: 1991
County cap: 1993
One-Day 100s: 2
Overseas tours: Kent to Zimbabwe 1993
Overseas teams played for: Ashburton, Melbourne 1988-90, 1996-97; Green Point, Cape Town 1990-95

Highlights of playing career: 'B&H final 1997. Sunday League winners 1995. First Championship hundred, Lord's 1993'
Cricket moments to forget: 'Sunday League [1993], last match against Glamorgan at Canterbury – lost the match and were runners-up. Plus not making the most of my ability'
Extras: Kent Young Player of the Year 1992. Man of the Match in 2nd XI Trophy semi-final and final 1999. Retired from county cricket in September 1999 and played for Norfolk in 2000
Opinions on cricket: 'Umpires watch every ball of a game. It's amazing how little their opinions are valued!'
Best batting: 130 Kent v Hampshire, Canterbury 1996
Best bowling: 5-21 Kent v Middlesex, Canterbury 1996

First-Class Career Performances

	M	Inn	NO	Runs	HS	Avg	100	Ct	St	Runs	Wkts	Avg	BB	5I	10M
Test															
FC	68	108	11	3024	130	31.17	6	59	-	1259	35	35.97	5-21	2	-

LLOYDS, J. W.

Name: Jeremy William Lloyds
Born: 17 November 1954, Penang, Malaya
Height: 5ft 11in
Nickname: Jerry
Wife and date of marriage: Janine, 16 September 1997
Children: Kaeli, 16 November 1991
Family links with cricket: Father played cricket in Malaya. Brother Chris played for Somerset 2nd XI
Education: Blundell's School, Tiverton
Career outside cricket: Coaching and setting up Western Province Youth Programme 1992-95 in South Africa
Off-season: 'Getting a job'
Other sports played: Golf (6 handicap)
Other sports followed: Golf, football (Tottenham Hotspur), American football (San Francisco 49ers), Formula One and saloon car racing, rugby (Gloucester)
Relaxations: 'Reading, music and spending time at home with my family'
Appointed to 1st-Class list: 1998
International panel: 2002-2004 as TV umpire; 2004-2006
Tests umpired: 5 (plus 10 as TV umpire)

ODIs umpired: 18 (plus 22 as TV umpire)
Twenty20 Ints umpired: 1
Other umpiring honours: Stood in the C&G final 2006. Officiated at Twenty20 finals day 2007 and 2008
Counties as player: Somerset, Gloucestershire
Role: Left-hand bat, off-spin bowler
County debut: 1979 (Somerset), 1985 (Gloucestershire)
County cap: 1982 (Somerset), 1985 (Gloucestershire)
1000 runs in a season: 3
Overseas tours: Somerset to Antigua 1982; Gloucestershire to Barbados 1985, to Sri Lanka 1987
Overseas teams played for: St Stithian's Old Boys, Johannesburg 1978-79; Toombull DCC, Brisbane 1980-82; North Sydney District 1982-83; Alberton, Johannesburg 1984; Preston CC, Melbourne 1986; Orange Free State 1987; Fish Hoek CC, Cape Town 1988-92
Highlights of playing career: 'Winning 1983 NatWest final'
Extras: Highest score in Brisbane Premier League 1980-81 (165). Britannic Player of the Month July 1987. Gloucestershire Player of the Year 1987. Leading run-scorer in Western Province Cricket League 1988, 1989
Opinions on cricket: 'Would take too long. I would suggest that by having central contracts we are creating elitism. Batsmen must be allowed to bat and bowlers to bowl whenever possible. Net bowling/batting is never quite the same.'
Best batting: 132* Somerset v Northamptonshire, Northampton 1982
Best bowling: 7-88 Somerset v Essex, Chelmsford 1982

First-Class Career Performances

	M	Inn	NO	Runs	HS	Avg	100	Ct	St	Runs	Wkts	Avg	BB	5I	10M
Test															
FC	267	408	64	10679	132*	31.04	10	229	-	12943	333	38.86	7-88	13	1

MALLENDER, N. A.

Name: Neil Alan Mallender
Born: 13 August 1961, Kirk Sandall, Doncaster
Height: 6ft
Nickname: Ghostie
Marital status: Divorced
Children: Kirstie, 20; Dominic, 17; Jacob, 12
Education: Beverley Grammar School
Off-season: Training
Other sports played: Golf (2 handicap)
Other sports followed: 'Most sports'
Relaxations: 'Watching sport; music'
Appointed to 1st-Class list: 1999
International panel: 2002-2004
Tests umpired: 3 (plus 5 as TV umpire)
ODIs umpired: 22 (plus 10 as TV umpire)
Other umpiring honours: Went with MCC to umpire in Namibia March/April 2001. PCA Umpire of the Year 2001, 2002, 2003, 2004, 2006, 2008. Stood in the 2002-03 World Cup. Umpired the 2004, 2005 and 2006 C&G Trophy finals. Officiated at Twenty20 finals day at Edgbaston 2007, including standing in the final; and in 2008
Highlights of umpiring career: 'First ODI at Lord's, Twenty20 finals day 2007 and 2008'
Players to watch for the future: James Tomlinson, Adil Rashid, Chris Jordan, Chris Woakes, Liam Dawson
Counties as player: Northamptonshire, Somerset
Role: Right-hand bat, right-arm fast-medium bowler
County debut: 1980 (Northamptonshire), 1987 (Somerset)
County cap: 1984 (Northamptonshire), 1987 (Somerset)
Benefit: 1994 (Somerset)
Test debut: 1992
50 wickets in a season: 6
One-Day 5 w. in innings: 3
Overseas tours: England YC to West Indies 1979-80
Overseas teams played for: Kaikorai, Dunedin, New Zealand; University, Wellington, New Zealand; Otago, New Zealand 1983-84 – 1992-93
Highlights of playing career: 'Test debut at Headingley'
Extras: Represented England YC 1980-81. Took 5-50 on Test debut v Pakistan at Headingley in 1992. Retired from county cricket in 1996
Best batting: 100* Otago v Central Districts, Palmerston North 1991-92
Best bowling: 7-27 Otago v Auckland, Auckland 1984-85

First-Class Career Performances

	M	Inn	NO	Runs	HS	Avg	100	Ct	St	Runs	Wkts	Avg	BB	5I	10M
Test	2	3	0	8	4	2.66	-	-	-	215	10	21.50	5-50	1	-
FC	345	396	122	4709	100*	17.18	1	111	-	24654	937	26.31	7-27	36	5

MILLNS, D. J.

Name: David James Millns
Born: 27 February 1965, Mansfield
Height: 6ft 3in
Nickname: Rocket Man
Marital status: Divorced
Children: Dylan, 17 April 1998; Lucas, 10 October 2000; Jessica, 16 October 2001
Education: Samuel Barlow Junior; Garibaldi Comprehensive; North Notts College of Further Education; Nottingham Trent Polytechnic
Off-season: 'Work for Redbox Marketing Ltd'
Other sports played: Golf
Other sports followed: 'Football (Manchester City), American football (New England Patriots), baseball (Boston Redsocks)
Relaxations: Gym, cinema, reading
Umpiring career: First first-class match Glamorgan v Oxford UCCE, the Parks 2007; ECB reserve list 2007
Appointed to 1st-Class list: 2009
Players to watch for the future: Eoin Morgan, Ben Sanderson, Richard Jones
Counties as player: Nottinghamshire 1988-89, Leicestershire 1990-1999, Nottinghamshire 2000
Role: Left-hand bat; right-arm fast-medium bowler
County debut: 1988 (Nottinghamshire), 1990 (Leicestershire)
County cap: 1991 (Leicestershire), 2000 (Nottinghamshire – *see Extras*)
Benefit: 1999 (Leicestershire)
50 wickets in a season: 4
1st-Class 50s: 8
1st-Class 100s: 3
1st-Class 5 w. in innings: 23
1st-Class 10 w. in match: 4
1st-Class catches: 76

Overseas tours: Leicestershire to South Africa 1994, 1995, to Holland 1994, 1996, to Barbados 1998
Overseas teams played for: Uitenhage, Port Elizabeth, South Africa 1988-89; Birkenhead, Auckland 1989-91; Tasmania, Australia 1994-95; Boland, South Africa 1996-97
Highlights of playing career: 'Last player in Championship cricket to score a century (103) and take 10 wickets in match (10 for 128), Leicestershire versus Essex 1996'
Cricket moments to forget: 'Batting at the other end to Phil Whitticase when he lost 13 teeth after being hit by Neil Williams.'
Extras: Harold Larwood Bowling Award 1984. Asked to be released by Nottinghamshire at the end of the 1989 season and joined Leicestershire in 1990. Finished third in national bowling averages in 1990. Britannic Assurance Player of the Month in August 1991 after taking 9-37 v Derbyshire, the best Leicestershire figures since George Geary's 10-18 v Glamorgan in 1929. Was players' representative on Cricketers' Association Executive for Leicestershire. Leicestershire Cricketer of the Year 1992. Leicestershire Bowling Award 1990, 1991, 1992 and 1994. Left Leicestershire at the end of the 1999 season and rejoined Nottinghamshire for 2000, taking 5-58 v Northamptonshire at Trent Bridge in his first match. Retired during the 2001 season
Opinions on cricket: 'As every old pro will tell you, "We were better in our day!" It's still a great game.'
Best batting: 121 Leicestershire v Northamptonshire, Northampton 1997
Best bowling: 9-37 Leicestershire v Derbyshire, Derby 1991

First-Class Career Performances

	M	Inn	NO	Runs	HS	Avg	100	Ct	St	Runs	Wkts	Avg	BB	5I	10M
Test															
FC	171	203	63	3082	121	22.01	3	76	-	15129	553	27.36	9-37	23	4

ROBINSON, R. T.

Name: Robert Timothy (Tim) Robinson
Born: 21 November 1958, Sutton-in-Ashfield, Nottinghamshire
Height: 6ft
Nickname: Robbo
Marital status: Divorced
Children: Philip; Alex
Family links with cricket: 'Father, uncles all played local cricket'
Education: Dunstable GS; High Pavement GS; Sheffield University
Career outside cricket: 'Accountancy. Sports promotions'
Off-season: 'Working for sports retail/promotions company'
Other sports played: Golf, squash
Other sports followed: Golf, rugby, football

Appointed to 1st-Class list: 2007
Players to watch for the future: Eoin Morgan, Will Smith
County as player: Nottinghamshire
Role: Right-hand opening bat
County debut: 1978
County cap: 1983
Benefit: 1992
Test debut: 1984-85
ODI debut (matches): 1984-85 (26)
1000 runs in a season: 14
1st-Class 200s: 3
One-Day 100s: 9
Overseas tours: England to India and Sri Lanka 1984-85, to West Indies 1985-86, to India and Pakistan (World Cup) 1987-88, to Pakistan 1987-88, to New Zealand and Australia 1987-88, plus two one-day tournaments in Sharjah; unofficial England XI to South Africa 1989-90
Highlights of playing career: '175 v Aussies, home Test debut 1985' (*In the first Test at Headingley*)
Cricket moments to forget: 'Retiring from first-class cricket'
Extras: One of *Wisden*'s Five Cricketers of the Year 1986. Second in the list of Nottinghamshire first-class run-scorers behind George Gunn. Captain of Nottinghamshire 1988-95. Retired from county cricket at the end of the 1999 season
Opinions on cricket: 'Do not let money spoil it!'
Best batting: 220* Nottinghamshire v Yorkshire, Trent Bridge 1990
Best bowling: 1-22 Nottinghamshire v Northamptonshire, Northampton 1982

First-Class Career Performances

	M	Inn	NO	Runs	HS	Avg	100	Ct	St	Runs	Wkts	Avg	BB	5I	10M
Test	29	49	5	1601	175	36.38	4	8	-	0	0		-	-	-
FC	425	739	85	27571	220*	42.15	63	257	-	289	4	72.25	1-22	-	-

SHARP, G.

Name: George Sharp
Born: 12 March 1950, West Hartlepool, County Durham
Height: 5ft 11in
Nickname: Sharpy
Wife and date of marriage: Audrey, 14 September 1974
Children: Gareth James, 27 June 1984
Education: Elwick Road Secondary Modern, Hartlepool
Career outside cricket: Watching all sports
Off-season: Working as joint director of GSB Loams Ltd for soils and top dressing
Other sports played: Golf (8 handicap)
Other sports followed: Football (Newcastle Utd and Middlesbrough), rugby (Northampton Saints)
Relaxations: Golf; 'spend a lot of time in the gym during the off-season'
Appointed to 1st-Class list: 1992
International panel: 1996-2002
Tests umpired: 15 (plus 1 as TV umpire)
ODIs umpired: 31 (plus 13 as TV umpire)
Other umpiring honours: Has umpired three B&H finals and one NatWest final and stood in the inaugural C&G final 2001 and the 2002 final; also officiated at the inaugural Twenty20 finals day at Trent Bridge 2003, at finals day 2005 at The Oval and at finals day 2006 at Trent Bridge. Has stood in four overseas tournaments, including the Singer Cup (India, Sri Lanka, Pakistan) in Singapore 1995-96 and the Singer Champions Trophy (Pakistan, Sri Lanka, New Zealand) in Sharjah 1996-97
County as player: Northamptonshire
Role: Right-hand bat, wicket-keeper
County debut: 1967
County cap: 1973
Benefit: 1982
Overseas tours: England Counties XI to Barbados and Trinidad 1975
Best batting: 98 Northamptonshire v Yorkshire, Northampton 1983
Best bowling: 1-47 Northamptonshire v Yorkshire, Northampton 1980

First-Class Career Performances

	M	Inn	NO	Runs	HS	Avg	100	Ct	St	Runs	Wkts	Avg	BB	5I	10M
Test															
FC	306	396	81	6254	98	19.85	-	565	90	70	1	70.00	1-47	-	-

STEELE, J. F.

Name: John Frederick Steele
Born: 23 July 1946, Stafford
Height: 5ft 10in
Nickname: Steely
Wife and date of marriage: Susan, 17 April 1977
Children: Sarah Jane, 2 April 1982; Robert Alfred, 10 April 1985
Family links with cricket: Uncle Stan played for Staffordshire. Brother David played for Northamptonshire, Derbyshire and England. Cousin Brian Crump played for Northamptonshire and Staffordshire
Education: Endon School, Stoke-on-Trent; Stafford College
Other sports followed: Football (Stoke City, Port Vale), golf
Relaxations: Music and walking
Appointed to 1st-Class list: 1997
Counties as player: Leicestershire, Glamorgan
Role: Right-hand bat, slow left-arm bowler
County debut: 1970 (Leicestershire), 1984 (Glamorgan)
County cap: 1971 (Leicestershire), 1984 (Glamorgan)
Benefit: 1983 (Leicestershire)
1000 runs in a season: 6
One-Day 100s: 1
One-Day 5 w. in innings: 4
Overseas teams played for: Springs HSOB, Northern Transvaal 1971-73; Pine Town CC, Natal 1973-74, 1982-83; Natal 1975-76, 1978-79
Extras: Played for England U25. Was voted Natal's Best Bowler in 1975-76. First-wicket record partnership for Leicestershire of 390 with Barry Dudleston v Derbyshire at Leicester 1979. Won two Man of the Match Awards in the Gillette Cup and four in the Benson and Hedges Cup. Won the award for the most catches in a season in 1984
Best batting: 195 Leicestershire v Derbyshire, Leicester 1971
Best bowling: 7-29 Natal B v Griqualand West, Umzinto 1973-74
7-29 Leicestershire v Gloucestershire, Leicester 1980

First-Class Career Performances

	M	Inn	NO	Runs	HS	Avg	100	Ct	St	Runs	Wkts	Avg	BB	5I	10M
Test															
FC	379	605	85	15053	195	28.94	21	414	-	15793	584	27.04	7-29	16	-

WILLEY, P.

Name: Peter Willey
Born: 6 December 1949, Sedgefield, County Durham
Height: 6ft 1in
Nickname: Will, 'many unprintable'
Wife and date of marriage: Charmaine, 23 September 1971
Children: Heather Jane, 11 September 1985; David, 28 February 1990
Family links with cricket: Father played local club cricket in County Durham
Education: Seaham Secondary School, County Durham
Other sports followed: All sports
Relaxations: 'Dog-walking, keeping fit (??), fishing'
Appointed to 1st-Class list: 1993
International panel: 1996-2003
Tests umpired: 25 (plus 7 as TV umpire)
ODIs umpired: 34 (plus 16 as TV umpire)
Other umpiring honours: Stood in the 1999 and 2002-03 World Cups, in the 1999 Benson and Hedges Super Cup final and in the 2004 C&G Trophy final. Officiated at Twenty20 finals days at The Oval 2005 and Edgbaston 2007, including standing in both finals. Chairman of the First-Class Umpires' Association
Counties as player: Northamptonshire, Leicestershire
Role: Right-hand bat, off-break bowler
County debut: 1966 (Northamptonshire), 1984 (Leicestershire)
County cap: 1971 (Northamptonshire), 1984 (Leicestershire)
Benefit: 1981 (Northamptonshire)
Test debut: 1976
ODI debut (matches): 1977 (26)
1000 runs in a season: 10
50 wickets in a season: 2
1st-Class 200s: 1
One-Day 100s: 9
Overseas tours: England to Australia and India 1979-80, to West Indies 1980-81, 1985-86; unofficial England XI to South Africa 1981-82
Overseas teams played for: Eastern Province, South Africa 1982-85
Cricket moments to forget: 'First ball in first-class cricket (v Cambridge University), bowled – thought it can only get better'

Extras: Became youngest player ever to play for Northamptonshire, at 16 years 180 days, v Cambridge University in 1966. Leicestershire captain 1987. Played for Northumberland in 1992. Offered membership of the ICC Elite Panel of umpires in 2002 but declined because of the amount of time the appointment would require away from his family

Opinions on cricket: 'Too much "robot" coaching from nine-year-olds to county standard. Players don't seem to be allowed individual batting styles or bowling actions. Bowling actions changed in case of injury. Too much time spent looking at video analysis and training instead of more time spent in nets. Seems bowling length and line (Pollock, McGrath) is a thing of the past.'

Best batting: 227 Northamptonshire v Somerset, Northampton 1976

Best bowling: 7-37 Northamptonshire v Oxford University, The Parks 1975

First-Class Career Performances

	M	Inn	NO	Runs	HS	Avg	100	Ct	St	Runs	Wkts	Avg	BB	5I	10M
Test	26	50	6	1184	102*	26.90	2	3	-	456	7	65.14	2-73	-	-
FC	559	918	121	24361	227	30.56	44	235	-	23400	756	30.95	7-37	26	3

APPENDICES

Roll of Honour 2008
First-class Averages 2008
Index of Players by County

ROLL OF HONOUR 2008

LV COUNTY CHAMPIONSHIP

Division One

		P	W	L	D	T	Bt	Bl	Pts
1	Durham (I/2)	16	6	3	7	0	37	41	190
2	Nottinghamshire (II/2)	16	5	3	8	0	37	43	182
3	Hampshire (I/5)	16	5	4	7	0	33	47	178
4	Somerset (II/1)	16	3	2	11	0	44	44	174
5	Lancashire (I/3)	16	5	2	9	0	24	40	170
6	Sussex (I/1)	16	2	2	12	0	45	38	159
7	Yorkshire (I/6)	16	2	5	9	0	50	45	159
8	Kent (I/7)	16	4	6	6	0	30	44	154
9	Surrey (I/4)	16	0	5	11	0	45	36	124

The bottom two counties were relegated to Division Two for the 2009 season. Positions in 2007 in brackets.

Division Two

		P	W	L	D	T	Bt	Bl	Pts
1	Warwickshire (I/8)	16	5	0	11	0	53	46	213
2	Worcestershire (I/9)	16	6	2	8	0	40	45	196
3	Middlesex (II/3)	16	4	5	7	0	46	45	175
4	Northamptonshire (II/5)	16	3	3	10	0	52	35	169
5	Essex (II/4)	16	5	6	5	0	36	45	168
6	Derbyshire (II/6)	16	4	3	9	0	33	46	167
7	Leicestershire (II/8)	16	3	4	9	0	29	43	150
8	Glamorgan (II/9)	16	3	5	8	0	26	36	136
9	Gloucestershire (II/7)	16	0	5	11	0	42	38	122

The top two counties were promoted to Division One for the 2009 season. Positions in 2007 in brackets.

The following sides incurred points deductions for slow over rates in 2008:
Surrey 1, Derbyshire 4, Essex 3, Gloucestershire 2, Worcestershire 5.

NATWEST PRO40 LEAGUE

Division One

		P	W	L	NR	T	Pts
1	Sussex (I/5)	8	5	1	0	2	12
2	Hampshire (I/4)	8	4	2	0	2	10
3	Durham (II/1)	8	4	3	0	1	9
4	Nottinghamshire (I/2)	8	4	4	0	0	8
5	Gloucestershire (I/6)	8	3	3	0	2	8
6	Somerset (II/2)	8	3	4	1	2	7
7	Worcestershire (I/1)	8	2	3	1	2	7
8	Lancashire (I/3)	8	1	3	0	4	6
9	Middlesex (II/3)	8	2	5	0	1	5

Sussex were champions and the bottom two counties were relegated to Division Two for the 2009 season, Worcestershire (I/7) stayed up after a play-off with Glamorgan (II/3). Positions in 2007 in brackets.

Division Two

		P	W	L	NR	T	Pts
1	Essex (I/9)	8	6	0	1	1	14
2	Yorkshire (II/6)	8	5	1	1	1	12
3	Glamorgan (II/9)	8	5	3	0	0	10
4	Kent (II/5)	8	4	2	0	2	10
5	Surrey (II/4)	8	4	4	0	0	8
6	Warwickshire (I/8)	8	3	3	0	2	8
7	Leicestershire (II/7)	8	1	4	1	2	5
8	Derbyshire (II/8)	8	1	6	0	0	3
9	Northamptonshire (I/7)	8	0	6	0	2	2

The top two counties (see note above) were promoted to Division One for the 2008 season. Positions in 2007 in brackets.

FRIENDS PROVIDENT TROPHY

Winners: Essex

Runners-up: Kent

TWENTY20 CUP

Winners: Middlesex

Runners-up: Kent

Semi-finalists: Durham, Essex

2008 AVERAGES (all first-class matches)

BATTING AVERAGES

Qualifying requirements: 6 completed innings and an average of over 10.00

	Name	M	Inn	NO	Runs	HS	Avg	SR	100	50
1	T Frost	13	18	6	1003	242*	83.58	46.13	2	4
2	HM Amla	7	10	1	663	172	73.66	61.61	3	2
3	AB de Vills	7	10	2	588	174	73.50	52.59	2	1
4	L Klusener	14	20	5	1095	202*	73.00	64.14	2	9
5	IJL Trott	16	25	5	1240	181	62.00	52.12	3	6
6	MR Ramprakash	14	23	3	1235	200*	61.75	48.69	6	1
7	GC Smith	6	10	2	491	154*	61.37	58.59	2	1
8	JJ Cobb	8	10	3	419	148*	59.85	40.67	1	2
9	KP Pietersen	8	12	0	707	152	58.91	64.86	4	1
10	MW Goodwin	16	25	2	1343	184	58.39	52.52	6	5
11	MA Butcher	6	10	1	521	205	57.88	50.33	2	1
12	CJL Rogers	16	27	3	1372	248*	57.16	60.25	4	8
13	HD Ackerman	16	26	3	1302	199	56.60	62.68	6	3
14	JA Rudolph	16	24	1	1292	155	56.17	54.35	5	6
15	SC Moore	16	30	4	1451	156	55.80	64.69	6	6
16	RS Bopara	15	26	3	1256	150	54.60	68.14	4	7
17	AG Prince	10	14	2	649	149	54.08	51.26	3	2
18	N Pothas	14	23	5	963	137*	53.50	49.53	3	3
19	PA Nixon	16	24	6	954	106*	53.00	51.53	1	6
20	SR Patel	14	22	3	977	135	51.42	71.36	2	7
21	WR Smith	2	20	2	925	201*	51.38	45.79	3	3
22	A Mahmood	6	8	2	306	116	51.00	73.20	1	1
23	IR Bell	11	17	1	813	215	50.81	59.86	2	2
24	MJ Nicholson	9	12	3	453	133	50.33	62.74	1	1
25	MJ North	12	20	2	900	104	50.00	63.06	1	8
26	JO Troughton	14	20	5	747	138*	49.80	44.86	1	6
27	DJG Sales	17	27	4	1137	173	49.43	65.23	3	4
28	RA White	15	25	4	1037	132*	49.38	82.30	3	6
29	EJG Morgan	17	29	7	1085	137*	49.31	46.86	3	5
30	JH Kallis	7	11	3	391	160*	48.87	58.44	1	3
31	M van Jaarsveld	16	27	3	1150	133	47.91	60.46	4	7
32	MJ Prior	15	23	1	1040	133*	47.27	67.97	3	7
33	PJ Horton	16	26	3	1087	152	47.26	53.70	3	7
34	SD Snell	16	24	4	944	127	47.20	47.27	1	9
35	AJ Strauss	16	27	1	1223	172	47.03	53.73	3	6
36	VS Solanki	15	25	1	1127	270	46.95	66.13	4	5

	Name	M	Inn	NO	Runs	HS	Avg	SR	100	50
37	MA Wagh	15	24	2	1033	141	46.95	56.01	2	8
38	ME Trescothick	16	28	1	1258	158	46.59	59.06	3	8
39	ID Blackwell	17	25	1	1115	158	46.45	67.33	4	7
40	MJ di Venuto	16	28	4	1115	184	46.45	56.94	2	8
41	U Afzaal	16	26	5	975	134*	46.42	50.38	2	7
42	GA Hick	11	18	3	689	149	45.93	68.28	2	2
43	NJ O'Brien	14	21	1	917	168	45.85	63.63	2	5
44	CMW Read	16	21	5	726	142	45.37	60.85	1	5
45	Z de Bruyn	16	25	3	997	120	45.31	53.68	3	5
46	BF Smith	16	25	1	1075	99	44.79	52.72	0	11
47	JS Foster	17	25	4	926	132*	44.09	52.22	3	4
48	JL Langer	15	26	1	1083	188	43.32	69.91	3	7
49	DM Benkenstein	15	23	4	817	110	43.00	51.64	1	7
50	JL Clare	13	18	5	555	129*	42.69	67.51	1	5
51	PD Trego	16	23	3	849	86	42.45	73.76	0	7
52	CG Taylor	17	30	4	1101	137	42.34	67.67	2	8
53	OA Shah	14	25	1	1012	144	42.16	49.85	3	6
54	DJ Pipe	9	15	3	504	133	42.00	72.62	1	3
55	SA Newman	15	25	0	1044	129	41.76	62.51	2	8
56	BM Shafayat	10	15	2	541	118	41.61	49.49	2	2
57	SM Davies	16	24	6	748	99*	41.55	63.93	0	5
58	R Malcolm-Hansen	5	7	1	248	93	41.33	67.94	0	2
59	SD Peters	16	26	3	949	130*	41.26	51.38	3	5
60	DL Maddy	14	22	3	778	138	40.94	53.69	3	3
61	MJ Brown	14	26	3	940	104*	40.86	46.28	1	6
62	GP Rees	16	28	1	1088	140	40.29	56.99	3	6
63	N Boje	13	17	1	644	226*	40.25	62.52	2	1
64	DKH Mitchell	16	29	6	922	102	40.08	45.87	1	4
65	SD Udal	14	20	6	556	91	39.71	61.23	0	4
66	DJ Malan	10	16	2	556	132*	39.71	44.33	1	4
67	ET Smith	6	10	0	397	88	39.70	53.79	0	4
68	BJM Scott	15	22	3	754	164*	39.68	51.36	1	7
69	RN ten Doeschate	17	24	2	860	146	39.09	68.58	2	4
70	AW Gale	15	23	0	899	150	39.08	53.35	3	3
71	LRPL Taylor	6	12	1	429	154*	39.00	74.22	2	0
72	BB McCullum	6	12	1	426	97	38.72	73.32	0	3
73	AN Cook	11	19	0	732	95	38.52	52.32	0	7
74	MA Hardinges	6	9	2	268	82	38.28	74.44	0	2
75	RWT Key	16	27	3	918	178*	38.25	55.06	2	4
76	CD Nash	17	30	4	980	108	37.69	51.60	2	5
77	S Chanderpaul	8	12	1	411	138	37.36	46.23	1	2
78	ML Pettini	18	28	5	856	153*	37.21	58.87	1	6
79	JM How	6	11	1	372	74	37.20	50.54	0	4
80	SP Crook	4	6	0	223	63	37.16	69.90	0	2

	Name	M	Inn	NO	Runs	HS	Avg	SR	100	50
81	SG Law	13	21	2	704	158*	37.05	49.78	1	4
82	AC Voges	12	20	3	627	77	36.88	52.60	0	4
83	MH Yardy	16	27	1	954	93	36.69	45.06	0	7
84	GP Swann	14	18	2	586	82	36.62	72.43	0	5
85	LJ Wright	13	20	3	621	155*	36.52	61.54	2	1
86	AJ Redmond	7	13	0	473	146	36.38	42.08	2	1
87	AD Brown	7	9	2	252	76*	36.00	61.76	0	2
88	Kadeer Ali	12	22	0	791	161	35.95	47.16	3	2
89	EC Joyce	17	28	1	966	101	35.77	52.72	1	7
90	Tamim Iqbal	4	7	0	250	78	35.71	61.72	0	3
91	SCJ Broad	10	11	1	357	76	35.70	51.73	0	4
92	R Martin-Jenkins	17	23	5	642	73*	35.66	56.66	0	6
93	DO Brown	9	15	4	385	83	35.00	53.62	0	3
94	JDP Oram	5	9	1	279	101	34.87	57.52	1	1
95	DL Hemp	15	25	3	763	104	34.68	53.13	2	5
96	A McGrath	14	21	0	728	144	34.66	48.72	2	3
97	DJ Birch	12	20	1	652	77	34.31	51.82	0	3
98	TT Bresnan	14	20	5	506	84*	33.73	45.95	0	2
99	PM Borrington	12	20	4	537	102*	33.56	35.99	1	3
100	GM Smith	13	21	1	665	113	33.25	52.48	1	6
101	CD Hopkinson	17	27	3	789	106	32.87	42.01	1	4
102	TC Smith	12	3	2	95	63	32.77	37.29	0	1
103	IDK Salisbury	13	14	2	393	81	32.75	72.91	0	3
104	MJ Lumb	16	27	2	818	107	32.72	42.47	1	6
105	SJ Croft	13	19	1	585	122	32.50	42.82	1	3
106	AJ Hall	10	9	1	257	58	32.12	50.79	0	2
107	ND McKenzie	10	19	2	546	138	32.11	41.61	1	2
108	JC Hildreth	18	32	2	962	158	32.06	56.15	1	6
109	MH Wessels	13	19	1	576	95	32.00	57.14	0	6
110	WTS Porterfield	13	24	0	763	93	31.79	38.88	0	7
111	PD Collingwood	8	13	3	317	135	31.70	52.74	1	1
112	SD Stubbings	10	18	2	506	62*	31.62	44.11	0	2
113	MJ Powell	16	26	3	725	120	31.52	52.27	1	3
114	MA Carberry	16	29	3	815	108	31.34	43.23	1	4
115	WW Hinds	9	13	0	407	76	31.30	60.83	0	3
116	TR Ambrose	14	19	3	500	156*	31.25	51.28	1	2
117	A Lyth	14	21	0	645	132	30.71	51.43	1	5
118	NM Carter	13	14	0	430	84	30.71	72.75	0	4
119	AD Mascarenhas	15	24	2	673	99	30.59	53.66	0	3
120	GJ Kruis	10	14	8	183	50*	30.50	59.03	0	1
121	GO Jones	17	26	4	668	106	30.36	52.43	1	3
122	HJH Marshall	16	29	1	850	121	30.35	54.62	2	5
123	JL Denly	17	30	0	905	149	30.16	60.81	2	4
124	GJ Batty	15	20	6	422	66	30.14	51.97	0	3

	Name	M	Inn	NO	Runs	HS	Avg	SR	100	50
125	JWM Dalrymple	16	25	1	723	106	30.12	45.30	1	6
126	MM Ali	6	9	2	210	92	30.00	45.35	0	1
127	IJ Westwood	11	17	0	506	176	29.76	43.06	1	2
128	RDB Croft	15	20	4	474	89*	29.62	49.01	0	2
129	BA Godleman	15	25	0	736	106	29.44	40.32	1	3
130	JN Batty	16	25	4	616	136*	29.33	35.24	2	3
131	J Allenby	17	23	3	586	138*	29.30	48.42	1	3
132	V Chopra	11	18	1	497	155	29.23	45.76	1	2
133	NJ Dexter	10	13	1	350	105	29.16	41.81	1	2
134	C Kieswetter	17	26	4	635	67*	28.86	52.00	0	2
135	CC Benham	8	13	0	374	89	28.76	46.40	0	3
136	Yasir Arafat	12	19	5	395	90*	28.21	62.30	0	2
137	MV Boucher	7	8	2	169	45*	28.16	45.43	0	0
138	Nazimuddin	4	7	1	169	75	28.16	58.88	0	1
139	SM Ervine	13	22	1	587	94*	27.95	63.66	0	5
140	MA Wallace	16	24	0	668	72	27.83	52.97	0	4
141	JP Crawley	9	16	1	416	104	27.73	48.59	1	2
142	LA Dawson	5	8	1	193	100*	27.57	47.65	1	0
143	MJ Chilton	7	12	1	303	102	27.54	43.65	1	1
144	CR Woakes	11	12	3	247	64*	27.44	63.17	0	1
145	JER Gallian	17	31	0	848	171	27.35	48.45	1	5
146	LE Plunkett	7	9	2	191	68*	27.28	50.13	0	2
147	PJ Franks	8	11	2	245	52	27.22	52.46	0	1
148	NS Poonia	12	19	0	516	111	27.15	48.35	1	2
149	LD Sutton	15	21	4	461	55	27.11	34.27	0	1
150	MAG Boyce	17	26	1	674	106	26.96	39.46	1	4
151	MJ Wood	14	21	1	539	98	26.95	48.12	0	4
152	GG Wagg	16	23	3	538	108	26.90	67.08	1	2
153	G Chapple	11	13	2	288	52*	26.18	65.75	0	1
154	TJ New	16	25	3	573	109	26.04	44.38	1	1
155	R Clarke	13	20	0	518	81	25.90	51.18	0	3
156	JD Middlebrook	14	19	3	414	75	25.87	47.15	0	1
157	JM Kemp	10	17	1	412	102	25.75	56.20	1	3
158	HH Dippenaar	12	19	2	431	84*	25.35	50.23	0	3
159	F du Plessis	12	19	1	453	57	25.16	46.89	0	4
160	MP Vaughan	12	18	0	450	106	25.00	45.77	1	1
161	JAH Marshall	6	11	1	250	128	25.00	45.45	1	0
162	J du Toit	10	16	0	399	103	24.93	48.89	1	1
163	MJ Powell	11	16	1	373	68*	24.86	38.37	0	2
164	L Vincent	6	12	1	272	83	24.72	49.27	0	2
165	A Flintoff	8	14	4	245	62*	24.50	67.67	0	1
166	APR Gidman	13	23	3	481	73	24.05	54.47	0	2
167	PJ Wiseman	16	22	2	479	65	23.95	54.12	0	3
168	JAR Harris	5	9	2	167	46	23.85	33.80	0	0

	Name	M	Inn	NO	Runs	HS	Avg	SR	100	50
169	GL Brophy	16	24	1	546	70	23.73	51.95	0	4
170	CJ Adams	15	23	3	474	61	23.70	53.86	0	2
171	AU Rashid	18	27	2	587	111	23.48	42.72	1	2
172	MNW Spriegel	12	19	1	418	51	23.22	37.86	0	1
173	R McLaren	16	23	3	464	65*	23.20	47.63	0	2
174	DI Stevens	14	21	1	463	127	23.15	65.02	1	1
175	KD Mills	5	9	2	160	57	22.85	46.24	0	2
176	FA Klokker	4	8	1	160	103*	22.85	33.54	1	0
177	NJ Edwards	8	15	0	341	99	22.73	68.20	0	2
178	JC Tredwell	18	29	3	587	123*	22.57	38.46	1	3
179	BJ Phillips	10	13	4	203	53*	22.55	56.86	0	1
180	JN Gillespie	13	20	5	332	52	22.13	49.11	0	1
181	WI Jefferson	13	21	1	442	98	22.10	55.66	0	2
182	RKJ Dawson	5	7	1	132	40	22.00	55.69	0	0
183	T Westley	9	17	3	307	93*	21.92	46.51	0	2
184	AG Botha	13	16	3	283	62	21.76	39.85	0	3
185	RN Grant	6	11	0	239	75	21.72	42.90	0	2
186	CM Spearman	5	9	1	173	95	21.62	65.03	0	1
187	AG Wharf	10	14	3	237	51*	21.54	49.47	0	1
188	JL Sadler	8	14	0	301	50	21.50	34.83	0	1
189	GP Smith	6	10	0	215	54	21.50	38.18	0	1
190	JJ van der Wath	11	10	3	148	75*	21.14	53.81	0	1
191	P Mustard	16	24	1	483	92	21.00	48.93	0	4
192	J Needham	8	14	6	168	36	21.00	37.50	0	0
193	GA Lamb	9	15	2	272	54*	20.92	35.97	0	1
194	MA Ealham	14	17	1	329	130*	20.56	52.47	1	0
195	CW Henderson	16	21	4	349	66	20.52	50.07	0	4
196	GR Napier	7	8	0	164	76	20.50	87.70	0	1
197	CR Taylor	4	6	0	123	48	20.50	38.31	0	0
198	MD Stoneman	13	22	1	429	60*	20.42	37.27	0	3
199	DR Flynn	7	11	3	163	49	20.37	34.38	0	0
200	DS Harrison	14	18	2	325	64*	20.31	93.65	0	2
201	Junaid Siddique	4	7	0	141	50	20.14	42.98	0	1
202	M Kartik	7	10	2	161	44	20.12	53.31	0	0
203	CJC Wright	11	12	3	181	71*	20.11	58.38	0	1
204	PS Jones	9	12	2	199	27*	19.90	58.70	0	0
205	JGE Benning	6	8	0	159	69	19.87	56.18	0	1
206	AJ Tudor	9	15	1	276	68	19.71	56.21	0	1
207	RT Timms	4	7	0	137	55	19.57	37.22	0	1
208	MJ Wood	7	12	1	212	83*	19.27	50.23	0	1
209	AC Thomas	11	15	3	231	43	19.25	44.00	0	0
210	SJ Harmison	14	15	6	172	49*	19.11	66.92	0	0
211	TJ Murtagh	17	25	3	402	49	18.27	57.84	0	0
212	Kabir Ali	11	15	2	236	46	18.15	51.30	0	0

	Name	M	Inn	NO	Runs	HS	Avg	SR	100	50
213	FD Telo	8	15	0	272	69	18.13	49.27	0	2
214	OP Rayner	11	13	4	159	22	17.66	36.05	0	0
215	CT Tremlett	13	19	2	299	60	17.58	52.09	0	3
216	CJ Jordan	8	9	2	123	57	17.57	43.92	0	1
217	AR Caddick	10	12	4	140	35*	17.50	41.29	0	0
218	G Keedy	13	18	4	243	64	17.35	32.31	0	1
219	CK Langeveldt	12	15	3	208	40	17.33	113.66	0	0
220	Saqlain Mushtaq	14	16	4	206	50	17.16	44.49	0	1
221	JHK Adams	7	12	0	206	50	17.16	35.21	0	1
222	J Lewis	14	20	5	253	51	16.86	65.37	0	1
223	AG Wakely	5	8	1	118	53	16.85	31.72	0	1
224	GM Andrew	12	15	3	199	38*	16.58	37.26	0	0
225	BW Harmison	12	18	1	281	39	16.52	34.95	0	0
226	Naved-ul-Hasan	7	10	3	114	22	16.28	91.20	0	0
227	DG Cork	9	11	1	162	43	16.20	63.28	0	0
228	RM Pyrah	5	6	0	96	51	16.00	38.55	0	1
229	SJ Walters	6	8	0	127	40	15.87	43.34	0	0
230	IJ Sutcliffe	7	11	0	164	50	14.90	41.20	0	1
231	D Gough	8	11	1	148	34	14.80	61.15	0	0
232	DA Cosker	8	13	2	160	42	14.54	45.58	0	0
233	JA Tomlinson	16	20	10	145	35*	14.50	40.27	0	0
234	AP Palladino	6	11	4	99	30*	14.14	32.89	0	0
235	J Ormond	7	7	1	84	64*	14.00	35.14	0	1
236	SP Jones	9	11	4	97	25	13.85	62.17	0	0
237	DL Vettori	4	7	1	83	48	13.83	47.42	0	0
238	MB Loye	10	16	1	203	61	13.53	40.92	0	1
239	RE Watkins	6	9	2	94	33	13.42	33.57	0	0
240	AR Adams	8	11	1	133	58	13.30	73.48	0	1
241	G Onions	9	11	2	119	36	13.22	50.85	0	0
242	CD Thorp	12	15	4	145	29*	13.18	63.31	0	0
243	A Richardson	9	8	2	79	26	13.16	51.29	0	0
244	JM Anderson	10	11	4	92	34	13.14	34.20	0	0
245	MJ Hoggard	14	18	6	154	28*	12.83	37.65	0	0
246	GW Flower	5	7	0	87	39	12.42	39.54	0	0
247	D du Preez	10	13	3	122	22	12.20	55.45	0	0
248	SJ Magoffin	7	9	2	85	33	12.14	57.82	0	0
249	DJ Balcombe	6	10	3	85	20*	12.14	36.63	0	0
250	MN Malik	15	20	5	178	41	11.86	38.61	0	0
251	TL Maynard	5	7	0	82	26	11.71	40.59	0	0
252	CM Willoughby	17	17	11	70	18	11.66	79.54	0	0
253	MJ Saggers	11	16	7	101	33	11.22	34.23	0	0
254	Danish Kaneria	9	14	3	123	22	11.18	72.35	0	0
255	RJ Sidebottom	7	9	3	65	22	10.83	28.50	0	0
256	DD Masters	14	17	3	147	27	10.50	43.88	0	0

	Name	M	Inn	NO	Runs	HS	Avg	SR	100	50
257	MJ Walker	6	10	1	94	23	10.44	40.00	0	0
258	SI Mahmood	12	15	4	113	33	10.27	70.62	0	0

BOWLING AVERAGES
Qualifying requirement: 10 wickets taken

	Name	M	Balls	Runs	Wkts	Avg	RPO	BB	5I
1	M Davies	12	1526	600	41	14.63	2.35	8-24	4
2	Imran Tahir	7	1550	734	44	16.68	2.84	7-66	3
3	SP Jones	9	1266	757	42	18.02	3.58	5-30	4
4	AJ Shantry	7	1100	545	30	18.16	2.97	5-52	2
5	KJ Dean	4	537	262	14	18.71	2.92	6-46	1
6	Kabir Ali	11	1869	1106	59	18.74	3.55	6-58	4
7	AR Adams	8	1384	594	31	19.16	2.57	4-39	0
8	SE Bond	4	595	365	19	19.21	3.68	7-66	2
9	Azhar Mahmood	6	882	404	21	19.23	2.74	6-55	2
10	CD Thorp	12	1928	981	50	19.62	3.05	7-88	3
11	DP Nannes	5	646	393	20	19.65	3.65	6-32	1
12	M van Jaarsveld	16	462	220	11	20.00	2.85	5-33	1
13	JJ van der Wath	11	1648	869	43	20.20	3.16	7-60	3
14	CR Woakes	11	1848	922	45	20.48	2.99	6-68	3
15	G Chapple	11	1997	861	42	20.50	2.58	6-40	2
16	Amjad Khan	6	871	433	21	20.61	2.98	3-10	0
17	JM Anderson	10	2086	1031	49	21.04	2.96	7-43	2
18	Danish Kaneria	9	1892	852	40	21.30	2.70	7-157	4
19	AJ Hall	10	1042	535	24	22.29	3.08	5-81	1
20	CK Langeveldt	12	2509	1238	55	22.50	2.96	5-40	3
21	RJ Sidebottom	7	1806	750	33	22.72	2.49	6-67	2
22	D du Preez	10	1635	730	32	22.81	2.67	5-48	1
23	SJ Harmison	14	2833	1486	65	22.86	3.14	6-122	2
24	AP Palladino	6	953	412	18	22.88	2.59	4-29	0
25	A Richardson	9	1589	644	28	23.00	2.43	5-34	1
26	RN ten Doeschate	17	1686	992	43	23.06	3.53	6-57	2
27	DD Masters	14	2655	980	42	23.33	2.21	6-24	2
28	R McLaren	16	2400	1179	50	23.58	2.94	6-75	2
29	DA Mascarenhas	15	2368	977	41	23.82	2.47	6-67	2
30	SJ Cliff	3	446	241	10	24.10	3.24	4-42	0
31	EJ Morse	4	599	315	13	24.23	3.15	6-102	2
32	MJ Hoggard	14	2237	1096	45	24.35	2.93	6-57	1
33	JA Tomlinson	16	2786	1659	67	24.76	3.57	8-46	4
34	PD Trego	16	1160	694	28	24.78	3.58	4-52	0
35	SA Patterson	4	583	279	11	25.36	2.87	3-19	0
36	DJ Pattinson	13	2318	1255	49	25.61	3.24	6-30	4
37	GR Napier	7	1037	567	22	25.77	3.28	6-103	1

	Name	M	Balls	Runs	Wkts	Avg	RPO	BB	5I
38	CM Willoughby	17	3066	1399	54	25.90	2.73	4-65	0
39	DL Maddy	14	924	442	17	26.00	2.87	4-25	0
40	RH Joseph	15	2515	1433	55	26.05	3.41	6-32	2
41	WW Hinds	9	528	261	10	26.10	2.96	3-22	0
42	Imran Arif	6	953	575	22	26.13	3.62	5-50	1
43	J Needham	8	973	503	19	26.47	3.10	6-49	1
44	KD Mills	5	763	345	13	26.53	2.71	3-41	0
45	DL Vettori	4	770	346	13	26.61	2.69	5-66	2
46	IE O'Brien	5	841	402	15	26.80	2.86	4-74	0
47	G Onions	9	1177	671	25	26.84	3.42	5-75	1
48	GG Wagg	16	2730	1590	59	26.94	3.49	6-56	2
49	DO Brown	9	693	432	16	27.00	3.74	5-38	1
50	TJ Murtagh	17	3035	1734	64	27.09	3.42	7-95	3
51	AC Thomas	11	1520	817	30	27.23	3.22	5-46	2
52	CJC Wright	11	1439	792	29	27.31	3.30	6-22	1
53	BW Harmison	12	681	437	16	27.31	3.85	4-27	0
54	TG Southee	4	567	329	12	27.41	3.48	5-42	1
55	TD Groenwald	3	552	303	11	27.54	3.29	5-24	1
56	DG Cork	9	1218	552	20	27.60	2.71	3-33	0
57	VD Philander	3	653	277	10	27.70	2.54	3-45	0
58	IDK Salisbury	13	1612	865	31	27.90	3.21	6-100	5
59	CD Collymore	9	1610	727	26	27.96	2.70	4-47	0
60	RDB Croft	15	3062	1262	45	28.04	2.47	6-45	2
61	JL Clare	13	1546	871	31	28.09	3.38	7-74	1
62	J Allenby	17	1624	736	26	28.30	2.71	4-40	0
63	TT Bresnan	14	2526	1278	45	28.40	3.03	5-94	1
64	SP Kirby	13	2317	1149	40	28.72	2.97	5-60	1
65	J Lewis	14	2357	1009	35	28.82	2.56	5-64	1
66	Yasir Arafat	12	1906	1105	38	29.07	3.47	6-86	1
67	MA Ealham	14	2176	887	30	29.56	2.44	7-59	1
68	CE Shreck	16	3687	1817	61	29.78	2.95	5-40	2
69	MS Mason	7	862	329	11	29.90	2.29	2-26	0
70	GP Swann	14	2165	959	32	29.96	2.65	4-25	0
71	JD Lewry	15	2327	1234	41	30.09	3.18	4-56	0
72	WB Rankin	5	519	362	12	30.16	4.18	4-80	0
73	A Flintoff	8	1579	664	22	30.18	2.52	4-21	0
74	GJP Kruger	10	1801	970	32	30.31	3.23	5-47	2
75	JH Kallis	7	654	335	11	30.45	3.07	3-31	0
76	GJ Batty	15	2325	1042	34	30.64	2.68	5-33	2
77	TC Smith	10	1598	747	24	31.12	2.80	3-28	0
78	NM Carter	13	2242	1278	41	31.17	3.42	6-100	2
79	LM Daggett	5	1014	593	19	31.21	3.50	4-41	0
80	PS Jones	9	1364	848	27	31.40	3.73	5-53	2
81	CW Henderson	16	3273	1294	41	31.56	2.37	5-39	1

	Name	M	Balls	Runs	Wkts	Avg	RPO	BB	5I
82	M Morkel	7	1096	664	21	31.61	3.63	4-52	0
83	BJ Phillips	10	1297	665	21	31.66	3.07	3-34	0
84	OJ Newby	10	1163	793	25	31.72	4.09	5-69	1
85	D Evans	10	1446	954	30	31.80	3.95	6-35	2
86	AU Rashid	18	3829	2069	65	31.83	3.24	7-107	4
87	Saqlain Mushtaq	14	2380	1288	40	32.20	3.24	6-50	3
88	DI Stevens	14	738	322	10	32.20	2.61	4-70	0
89	JE Anyon	7	1370	844	26	32.46	3.69	6-82	1
90	LE Plunkett	7	775	520	16	32.50	4.02	3-49	0
91	SI Mahmood	12	1937	1147	35	32.77	3.55	5-76	1
92	SJ Magoffin	7	1212	755	23	32.82	3.73	4-49	0
93	A Nel	7	1328	624	19	32.84	2.81	3-25	0
94	R Martin-Jenkins	17	2325	1052	32	32.87	2.71	3-36	0
95	JAR Harris	5	656	362	11	32.90	3.31	3-40	0
96	SD Udal	14	2210	1122	34	33.00	3.04	5-36	1
97	OP Rayner	11	2085	1042	31	33.61	2.99	5-49	2
98	M Ntini	7	1104	681	20	34.05	3.70	5-94	1
99	M Kartik	7	1344	545	16	34.06	2.43	4-101	0
100	SCJ Broad	10	1924	1091	32	34.09	3.40	4-39	0
101	RS Bopara	15	1619	959	28	34.25	3.55	4-33	0
102	DA Cosker	8	1118	656	19	34.52	3.52	5-81	1
103	CT Tremlett	13	2300	1071	31	34.54	2.79	5-67	1
104	JD Middlebrook	14	2066	1086	31	35.03	3.15	5-69	1
105	MN Malik	15	2801	1475	42	35.11	3.15	6-46	3
106	DH Wigley	9	1248	844	24	35.16	4.05	5-78	1
107	PJ Wiseman	16	1182	614	17	36.11	3.11	4-87	0
108	N Boje	13	2405	1194	33	36.18	2.97	4-26	0
109	J Louw	7	1074	545	15	36.33	3.04	3-42	0
110	MJ Saggers	11	1661	873	24	36.37	3.15	4-26	0
111	MA Hardinges	6	597	366	10	36.60	3.67	2-13	0
112	SJ Croft	13	966	586	16	36.62	3.63	4-51	0
113	JW Dernbach	10	1296	844	23	36.69	3.90	6-72	1
114	AJ Ireland	9	1309	846	23	36.78	3.87	3-33	0
115	JN Gillespie	13	2093	902	24	37.58	2.58	4-32	0
116	GM Andrew	12	1433	1018	27	37.70	4.26	5-58	1
117	Naved-ul-Hasan	7	919	606	16	37.87	3.95	4-86	0
118	SR Patel	14	1029	455	12	37.91	2.65	2-26	0
119	MS Panesar	14	3185	1525	40	38.12	2.87	6-37	2
120	DS Harrison	14	2188	1150	30	38.33	3.15	4-49	0
121	CS Martin	11	1759	1002	26	38.53	3.41	5-84	1
122	ST Finn	13	1790	1086	28	38.78	3.64	4-80	0
123	CD Whelan	6	485	401	10	40.10	4.96	4-66	0
124	Mushtaq Ahmed	6	1357	777	19	40.89	3.43	5-83	1
125	MK Munday	5	608	410	10	41.00	4.04	3-18	0

	Name	M	Balls	Runs	Wkts	Avg	RPO	BB	5I
126	GJ Kruis	10	1773	903	22	41.04	3.05	5-47	1
127	G Keedy	13	2529	1157	28	41.32	2.74	5-56	1
128	PT Collins	12	1851	1121	27	41.51	3.63	4-111	0
129	M Zondeki	5	662	416	10	41.60	3.77	4-125	0
130	AR Caddick	10	1694	1047	25	41.88	3.70	5-118	1
131	R Clarke	13	974	630	15	42.00	3.88	4-87	0
132	DS Lucas	16	2542	1533	36	42.58	3.61	5-30	1
133	AG Wharf	10	1154	896	21	42.66	4.65	3-10	0
134	J Ormond	7	950	561	13	43.15	3.54	4-90	0
135	PL Harris	7	1133	609	14	43.50	3.22	3-129	0
136	ID Blackwell	17	2406	978	22	44.45	2.43	4-74	0
137	MJ North	12	1146	585	13	45.00	3.06	3-57	0
138	AG Botha	13	1476	677	15	45.13	2.75	4-77	0
139	GM Smith	13	855	502	11	45.63	3.52	2-53	0
140	IJL Trott	16	917	463	10	46.30	3.02	3-44	0
141	CJ Jordan	8	954	570	12	47.50	3.58	3-32	0
142	JC Tredwell	18	2378	1327	27	49.14	3.34	3-19	0
143	AJ Tudor	9	1206	736	14	52.57	3.66	3-46	0
144	PJ Franks	8	1032	632	12	52.66	3.67	2-25	0
145	MJ Nicholson	9	1134	625	11	56.81	3.30	3-44	0
146	TL Hemingway	4	958	570	10	57.00	3.56	2-32	0
147	LJ Wright	13	1143	740	12	61.66	3.88	2-46	0
148	ND Doshi	9	1548	825	13	63.46	3.19	3-84	0
149	JF Brown	10	1690	825	10	82.50	2.92	2-33	0

INDEX OF PLAYERS BY COUNTY

*denotes not registered for the 2009 season. Where a player is known to have moved in the off-season he is listed under his new county.

DERBYSHIRE

DURHAM

ESSEX

GLAMORGAN

INDEX OF PLAYERS BY COUNTY

GLOUCESTERSHIRE

HAMPSHIRE

KENT

LANCASHIRE

INDEX OF PLAYERS BY COUNTY

LEICESTERSHIRE

MIDDLESEX

NORTHAMPTONSHIRE

INDEX OF PLAYERS BY COUNTY

NOTTINGHAMSHIRE

ADAMS, A.R.*
BROAD, S.C.J.
BROWN, A.D.
BROWN, J.F.
CAIRNS, C.L.
CLOUGH, G.D.
EALHAM, M.A.
FLETCHER, L.J.
FRANKS, P.J.
HALES, A.D.
HARRIS, A.J.
JEFFERSON, W.I.
PATEL, S.R.
PATTINSON, D.J.
READ, C.M.W.
SHAFAYAT, B.M.
SHRECK, C.E.
SIDEBOTTOM, R.J.
SWANN, G.P.
VOGES, A.C.
WAGH, M.A.
WOOD, M.J.

SOMERSET

BANKS, O.A.C.
BLACKWELL, I.D.
BURKE, J.
BUTTLER, J.
CADDICK, A.R.
DE BRUYN, Z.
DIBBLE, A.
DURSTON, W.J.
EDWARDS, N.J.
FRANCIS, J.D.
GAZZARD, C.M.
HILDRETH, J.C.
JONES, C.
JONES, P.S.
KIESWETTER, C.
LANGER, J.L.
LETT, R.J.H.
MUNDAY, M.K.
PHILLIPS, B.J.
SPURWAY, S.H.P.*
SUPPIAH, A.V.
THOMAS, A.C.
TREGO, P.D.
TRESCOTHICK, M.E.
TURNER, M.L.
WALLER, M.
WILLOUGHBY, C.M.

SURREY

ABDUL RAZZAQ*
AFZAAL, U.
BATTY, J.N.
BENNING, J.G.E.
BROWN, M.J.
BUTCHER, M.A.
CLINTON, R.S.*
COLLINS, P.T.
DERNBACH, J.
FRYLINK, R.*
HODGSON, L.J.*
JEWELL, T.M.
JORDAN, C.J.
LEWIS, C.C.
MEAKER, S.C.
MURTAZA HUSSAIN
NEWMAN, S.A.
NICHOLSON, M.J.*
ORMOND, J.
RAMPRAKASH, M.R.
ROY, J.J.
SAKER, N.C.*
SAQLAIN MUSHTAQ*
SCHOFIELD, C.P.
SHOAIB AKHTAR*
SPRIEGEL, M.N.W.
TUDOR, A.J.
WILSON, G.C.

SUSSEX

ADAMS, C.J.*
AGA, R.G.
BEER, W.A.T.*
BROWN, B.C.*
COLLYMORE, C.C.
GOODWIN, M.W.
HAMILTON-BROWN, R.J.*
HARRIS, R.J.*
HODD, A.J.
HOPKINSON, C.D.
JOYCE, E.C.
KIRTLEY, R.J.
LEWRY, J.D.
LIDDLE, C.J.
MARTIN-JENKINS, R.S.C.
MOHAMMAD SAMI*
MUSHTAQ AHMED*
NASH, C.D.
PRIOR, M.J.
RAYNER, O.P.
SMITH, T.M.J.
THORNELY, M.A.
WRIGHT, L.J.
YARDY, M.H.
YASIR ARAFAT

INDEX OF PLAYERS BY COUNTY

QUIZ ANSWERS

1. 1882
2. Kevin Pietersen
3. Paul Collingwood (206)
4. Fred Spofforth
5. 'Chuck' Fleetwood-Smith
6. Three
7. Wally Hammond and Don Bradman
8. Allan Border
9. Geoff Boycott
10. 309 not out
11. Tony Lock
12. Len Hutton
13. 28
14. 31
15. George 'Gubby' Allen
16. Bob Woolmer
17. Richie Benaud
18. Steve Waugh
19. Mark Waugh
20. Mark
21. Melbourne
22. 1920s (1928)
23. John Morris
24. 167
25. Once (1934)
26. 1998-99
27. Frank Tyson
28. Fred Trueman
29. Warwick Armstrong
30. 1920-21
31. Fred Grace
32. Rod Marsh
33. Rod Marsh and Dennis Lillee
34. Allan Border
35. Simon Jones
36. Mark Taylor
37. Phil Tufnell
38. 1900s (1902)
39. Shane Warne (6-122 and 6-124)
40. Headingley
41. Godfrey Evans
42. Billy Murdoch (Aus)
43. Billy Murdoch
44. 138
45. Harold Larwood
46. Seven
47. 92
48. 50
49. 4-0
50. Ray Illingworth
51. Graham Gooch
52. Graham Thorpe
53. 445
54. Ray Lindwall
55. The Nawab of Pataudi (Senior)
56. None
57. Alan Knott
58. Mike Gatting
59. David 'Bumble' Lloyd
60. Bill O'Reilly
61. Eric Hollies
62. In 2006-07
63. Archie MacLaren and Joe Darling
64. David Steele
65. Geoff Boycott
66. 1989
67. David Gower
68. Kevin Petersen (52.55)
69. Shane Warne (19.92)
70. Bob Massie
71. Ian Botham
72. Graham Dilley
73. Sophia Gardens, Cardiff
74. Glenn McGrath
75. Jack Russell
76. Bruce Reid
77. Terry Alderman
78. 10
79. 239 runs
80. Ricky Ponting
81. Brian Close (1949)
82. Poms/Pommies
83. Lindsay Hassett
84. Hugh Trumble
85. Mike Atherton
86. Phil Tufnell
87. Ashley Giles
88. Ashley Giles
89. 42
90. Peter May
91. Terence Rattigan
92. Don Bradman
93. Ted Dexter
94. Dad's Army
95. Bob Willis (1982-83)
96. Rodney Hogg
97. Mark Butcher
98. Two runs.
99. Shane Warne
100. Darren Gough